Readings in Global Marketing

Edited by

Michael R. Czinkota and Ilkka A. Ronkainen

The Dryden Press
Harcourt Brace & Company Limited
London   Fort Worth   New York   Orlando
Philadelphia   San Diego   Toronto   Sydney   Tokyo

The Dryden Press
24/28 Oval Road,
London NW1 7DX

A catalogue record for this book is available from the British Library
ISBN 003–099008–4

Typeset by Fakenham Photosetting
Printed in Great Britain at WBC Book Manufacturers, Bridgend, Mid Glamorgan

Contents

Introduction and overview   ix
M. R. Czinkota and I. A. Ronkainen

PART I: STRATEGIC GLOBAL MARKETING ISSUES   1

1. Global marketing 2000: a marketing survival guide.   3
   M. R. Czinkota and I. A. Ronkainen
   Marketing Management, **1**(Winter), 37–45 (1992)

2. Trading blocs: opportunity or demise for trade?   14
   I. A. Ronkainen
   Multinational Business Review, **1**(Spring), 1–9 (1993)

3. The EC '92 and Eastern Europe: effects of integration vs. disintegration.   25
   M. R. Czinkota
   Columbia Journal of World Business, **26**(Spring), 20–27 (1991)

4. Global neighbours: poor relations.   36
   M. R. Czinkota
   Marketing Management, **2**(4), 46–52 (1994)

5. A national export assistance policy for new and growing businesses.   44
   M. R. Czinkota
   Journal of International Marketing, **2**(1), 91–101 (1994)

6. Evolution of global marketing strategy: scale, scope and synergy.   53
   S. P. Douglas and C. S. Craig
   Columbia Journal of World Business, **24**(Fall), 47–59 (1989)

7. Global strategy and multinationals' entry mode choice.   73
   W. C. Kim and P. Hwang
   Journal of International Business Studies, **23**(1), 29–53 (1992)

8. Successful export marketing management: some empirical evidence.   96
   T. K. Madsen
   International Marketing Review, **6**(4), 41–57 (1989)

9. Strategic alliances in the triad: an exploratory study.   111
   V. Terpstra and B. L. Simonin
   Journal of International Marketing, **1**(1), 4–25 (1993)

PART II: THE GLOBAL MARKETING MIX   133

10. Identification of global consumer segments: a behavioural framework.   135
    S. S. Hassan and L. P. Katsanis
    Journal of International Consumer Marketing, **3**(2), 11–28 (1991)

11. Decentralized R&D for global product development: strategic implications
    for the multinational corporation.   145
    A. O. Ogbuehi and R. A. Bellas, Jr.
    International Marketing Review, **9**(5), 60–70 (1992)

12. Product development the Japanese way.   156
    M. R. Czinkota and M. Kotabe
    Journal of Business Strategy, **11**(November/December), 31–36 (1990)

13. Matching product category and country image perceptions: a framework for
    managing country-of-origin effects.   162
    M. S. Roth and J. B. Romeo
    Journal of International Business Studies, **23**(3), 477–497 (1992)

14. International counterfeiters: marketing success without the cost and the risk.   181
    M. G. Harvey and I. A. Ronkainen
    Columbia Journal of World Business, **20**(Fall), 37–45 (1985)

15. Product and promotion transfers in consumer goods multinationals.   195
    J. S. Hill and W. L. James
    International Marketing Review, **8**(2), 6–17 (1991)

16. International advertising strategies of multinational corporations.   206
    R. E. Hite and C. Fraser
    Journal of Advertising Research, **28**(August/September), 9–17 (1988)

17. Managing the multinational sales force.   219
    J. S. Hill, R. R. Still and Ü. O. Boya
    International Marketing Review, **8**(1), 19–31 (1991)

18. International market entry and expansion via independent or integrated
    channels of distribution.   232
    E. Anderson and A. T. Coughlan
    Journal of Marketing, **51**(January), 71–82 (1987)

19. The developing internationalization of retailing.   249
    A. D. Treadgold
    International Journal of Retail & Distribution Management, **18**(2), 4–11 (1990)

PART III: GLOBAL MARKETING PERFORMANCE AND IMPLEMENTATION   261

20. The influence of global marketing standardization on performance.   263
    S. Samiee and K. Roth
    Journal of Marketing, **56**(April), 1–17 (1992)

21. Innovation orientation, environment and performance: a comparison of US
    and European markets.   288
    F. A. Manu
    Journal of International Business Studies, **23**(2), 333–359 (1992)

22. A performance comparison of continental and national businesses in Europe.   312
    G. S. Yip
    International Marketing Review, **8**(2), 31–39 (1991)

23. Bridging national and global marketing strategies through regional
    operations.   322
    J. D. Daniels
    International Marketing Review, **4**(Autumn), 29–44 (1987)

24. Implementing a pan-European marketing strategy.   340
    G. Guido
    Long Range Planning, **24**(5), 23–33 (1991)

25. Competition in global markets: a case study of American and Japanese
    competition in the British market.   356
    P. Doyle, J. Saunders and V. Wong
    Journal of International Business Studies, **23**(3), 419–442 (1992)

26. Creating European organizations that work.   376
    N. Blackwell, J.-P. Bizet, P. Child and D. Hensley
    The McKinsey Quarterly, **24**(2), 31–43 (1991)

27. The new country managers.   386
    J. A. Quelch
    The McKinsey Quarterly, **25**(4), 155–165 (1992)

    Index   394

Introduction and Overview

Michael R. Czinkota and Ilkka A. Ronkainen

'Think globally, act locally' has become the battlecry of marketers around the world. But being involved in global sales, having global brands or operations in different countries may not be enough in today's marketplace to maintain a sustainable long-term competitive advantage. Marketers need to exert leverage on corporate capabilities around the world so that the company as a whole is greater than the sum of its parts (Maruca, 1994). Capabilities, regardless of their origin, will have to be levered in all of the operations worldwide.

Globalization is a business initiative based on the premise that the world is becoming more homogeneous and that distinctions between national markets are not only fading but, for some products, will eventually disappear. As a result, marketers need to globalize their strategy by formulating it across markets or segments within those markets to take advantage of underlying market, cost, environmental, and competitive factors.

Globalization has been debated for the last 30 years starting with the existence of a global consumer (Dichter, 1962) and the merits of extending marketing programmes to international markets (Ryans, 1969). With environmental changes, it was suggested that inexpensive air travel and new technologies led consumers the world over to think and shop increasingly alike (Levitt, 1983). Furthermore, growing similarities in educational backgrounds, income levels, and lifestyles were also to have caused consumers in the main markets of the world, namely North America, Western Europe, and the developed economies of the Asia-Pacific to convergence in consumption patterns (Ohmae, 1985).

Much of the debate focused on the standardization vs. localization challenge with proponents and opponents occasionally using the same company examples to claim that their views were correct (*Advertising Age*, 1984). While most agree on the direction of the forces shaping the world markets, strategic responses to these forces still cause considerable disagreement. Successful global marketers have accepted a studied belief that process and product technologies are the same the world over. By concentrating on fewer basic solutions, marketers can cater to a universal need for quality at the lowest possible cost. At the same time, marketers have to remain responsive to differences between national and regional markets. Respecting differences is critical not only in terms of customer preferences but also internally within the company itself. Globalization calls for geocentric thinking in levering the human resources of the company on a worldwide basis. Using resources more efficiently worldwide also means empowering country organizations to participate in decision making beyond their own borders and beyond mere execution of plans. It is often on the implementation side of globalization that the most significant changes in organizations become evident.

Globalization has often been associated only with large-scale multinational marketers. However, sheer size is no longer a buffer against competition in markets where customers are demanding specialized and customized products. With the advent of electronic process technology, these so-called mini-nationals are able to compete on price and quality—often with greater flexibility. By taking advantage of today's more open trading regions, they can serve the world from a handful of manufacturing bases, sparing them from the necessity of building a plant in every country. Developments in information technology have enabled mininationals to both access data throughout most of the world and to run inexpensive and responsive sales and service operations across languages and time zones. The smaller bureaucracies of the mini-nationals allow them to move swiftly in seizing new markets and developing new products, typically in focused markets. In many cases, these new markets have been developed by the mininationals themselves (*Business Week*, 1993).

With these issues in mind, this collection of 27 articles has been compiled to cover the essential issues related to global marketing efforts: the environmental drivers, the globalization process within firms, the global marketing mix, and the implementation and level of success of global marketing programmes.

1. STRATEGIC GLOBAL MARKETING ISSUES

The first section can be divided into two sets of articles: the first group of articles relates to the environment of globalization and the second focuses on the firms internationalization and globalization strategies.

The first article by Czinkota and Ronkainen (Reading 1) elaborates on the 13 most prominent trends and issues that will shape marketing in the 1990s and into the next century according to a panel of experts in business, government, and academia. New issues have moved into the forefront of international marketing: environmental concerns, globalization, and trading blocs. The shift from a view ten years earlier, which considered the international trade framework and the international debt problem key concerns (Czinkota, 1986), is a reflection of a major turnabout in the international perspective, driven by both political and economic developments as well as society's new views. Given the advances in information and communications technology, these trends become diffused far more quickly than before. Another implication of the shift is the increasing role of corporations in shaping the world environment. While trading blocs are being formed around the world, as shown in the article by Ronkainen (Reading 2), regionalism will not degenerate into protectionism, mainly because of global trade flows and international direct investment by corporations. As a matter of fact, the appropriate interpretation is that these blocs are actually the building elements for global free trade and as such will enhance the opportunity for global marketers.

Geographically, the major developments for global marketers will be in Central and Eastern Europe, Latin America, and the Asia–Pacific. As trading blocs expands, there will be two different types of challenges: those within the bloc and those between blocs. The decision to increase the membership in a trading bloc (such as the European Union) cannot only be a political one as argued by Michael Czinkota (Reading 3). The lowering of government entry barriers is insufficient by itself in incorporating new members who often may be less endowed. What is needed is an effort to bring the new or potential members' companies up to the level of competitiveness required through funding, training, investment, and technology sharing often through strategic alliances. Reading 4 by Czinkota focuses on one of the world's most important trading relationships between the United States and Japan. Relationships between countries have to be broadened for global trade's benefit to include increased information flow, collaboration between corporate entities, and increased understanding by improvements in the human resources of firms to better understand global realities.

Michael Czinkota provides in Reading 5 a bridge to the second segment of Part I. To be ready for the new realities of the global market place, marketers need to assess their own strategies of penetrating new geographic markets or expanding their presence in existing ones. The proper role of the government is often debated, especially as to its effects. Government support can be appropriate if it improves the functioning of markets and helps overcome the short-term and risk-averse orientation of (domestic) firms (Kotabe and Czinkota, 1992).

Douglas and Craig (Reading 6) offer an excellent review of the development of effective global marketing strategy. This development is assessed across the different stages of a company's internationalization, from initial entry, through market expansion, and finally to global rationalization of operations. Included in this analysis are some of the challenges faced in reaching the final stage of globalization: e.g., how to lever experience gained in one market to other markets and how to exploit local market knowledge and expertise to be seen as a local in each of the individual markets of operation. These points are further highlighted in the contribution by Chan and Whang (Reading 7). The major conclusion drawn is that entry decisions are no longer made with only the targeted market in mind but that global strategic considerations are incorporated into the choice of entry mode from the beginning. Increasingly, global marketers are including three factors in determining their country selection: the traditional criterion of stand-alone attractiveness of a market, global strategic importance (such as excellence in design), and possible synergies due to market similarity or competitive need (Yip, 1992).

The two last articles of Part I are dedicated to marketing issues in firms at different stages of their globalization process. Tage Madsen's article (Reading 8) outlines correlates with high-performance export activities. The success of these new-generation global players can be related to their focus and concentration on being a leader in their niche, by giving decision-making power to people with market knowledge, and by solving customers' problems by involving them rather than by pushing standardized solutions upon them (Rennie, 1993). The most prominent manifestation of globalization can be seen in the dramatic increase in intra-firm cooperation. The world is too large and the competition too keen for even the largest multinational marketers to do everything independently. Technologies are converging and markets becoming integrated, thus making the costs and risks of both product and market development even greater. Partly as a reaction and partly to exploit these developments, the formation of strategic alliances with suppliers, customers, government entities, companies in other industries,

and even competitors has increased to achieve goals such as market entry, rationalization of production, and cost savings (Coopers & Lybrand, 1984). The concluding
article by Terpstra and Simonin (Reading 9) examines these alliances in terms of
patterns, similarities, and differences between cooperative efforts formed in the major
markets of the world.

2. THE GLOBAL MARKETING MIX

The identification of global markets and the development of the marketing mix to cater
to the markets' needs is covered in Part II. Most of the literature in international/global
marketing has focused on the elements of the marketing mix, especially production and
promotion, are either standardized or localized. The articles chosen for this section
expand on the discussion to include market segmentation as well as other elements of the
marketing programme.

Effective segmentation, i.e., recognition that groups within markets differ sufficiently
to warrant individual marketing mixes, allows global marketers to take advantage of the
benefits of standardization (such as consistency in positioning) while addressing the
unique needs and expectations of a specific target group. This approach means ignoring
political boundaries that define markets in many cases. Hassan and Katsanis (Reading
10) suggest that the emergence of segments that span across country-markets is already
evident, e.g., the teenager segment.

Product development is at the heart of the global marketing process. New products
should be developed and old ones modified to cater to new or changing customer needs
on a global or regional basis. It is no longer prudent nor feasible for marketers to develop
products in one location (typically at domestic R&D centres) and introduce products
first in the home market and then sequentially in others. The response has been to
decentralize R&D for global product development as shown in Reading 11 by Ogbuehi
and Bellas. Investments in R&D facilities abroad are being made for very valid reasons
including the following: to aid technology transfer to local subsidiaries, to generate
goodwill with local governments, to develop new products expressly for the market/
region in which the facility is located, to develop new products and processes for
application in the company's worldwide markets, and to generate new technology of a
long-term exploratory nature (Ronstadt, 1978). Some companies have assigned some of
their R&D units responsibility to operate as centres of excellence for a particular
product or industry (Schlender, 1994). A significant benefit of having R&D units abroad
to also to learn from the differences that exist in other markets or cultures. These types of
differences are highlighted by Czinkota and Kotabe (Reading 12) with respect to Japan
where the emphasis is on continual technological improvement aimed at making an
already successful product even better for customers.

As much as global marketers benefit from having multiple production bases around
the world, some challenges may also emerge. Customers have been shown to perceive
products differently based on their country of origin (Bilkey and Nes, 1982). Reading 13
by Roth and Romeo shows that such perceptions will vary depending on how well the
country's perceived production and marketing strengths are related to the product
category. Another challenge for global marketers is intellectual property violation which
has spread from high-visibility, strong-brand-name goods to high-technology goods and

services. Especially hard hit are the most innovative, fastest-growing industries such as computer software, pharmaceuticals, and entertainment (Rice, 1991). Harvey and Ronkainen (Reading 14) outline the extent of the problem as well as both the public sector and private sector response and remedies.

Product and promotion transfers are the essence of global marketing. The objective of the article by Hill and James (Reading 15) is to present the extent to which marketers of consumer nondurables globalize their product lines and brand images in promoting these lines. The overall conclusion is that marketers should circulate their global product portfolios and promotions among subsidiaries and encourage communications among affiliates given that affiliates are often good sources of new product ideas. The following article by Hite and Fraser (Reading 16) addresses the transferability of advertising campaigns. Marketers who use standardized advertising strategy are likely to be involved in capital goods industries but are a minority among firms that engage in campaigns in marketing around the world. Most agree to the need to localize advertising elements such as language, models, and scenic backgrounds for better impact. The localization of global ideas can be achieved by various tactics, such as adopting a modular approach, localizing international symbols, and using advertising agencies that have global reach (*Business International*, 1988).

Sales efforts are typically considered more local than most of the other marketing efforts in that parent organizations should not interfere with affiliate sales administration and personal selling practices. However, as shown by Hill, Still, and Boya (Reading 17), some marketers may opt for standardized sales strategies throughout a region. However, for this to work, personal selling has to be the most significant promotional effort used and the marketer's efforts should be organized by product on a global basis, facilitating the worldwide flows of products and marketing information.

Channel of distribution choice is one of the most fundamental decisions in the internationalization of the firm. Given that marketers are looking for the most effective way of penetrating markets, global or regional approaches may either not be available or be the best alternative available. Especially in earlier stages of international operations, marketers rely on independent local entities for their local market expertise. The fact that marketers favour using independent intermediaries (as opposed to their own sales efforts) in markets that differ culturally from their experiences further complicates the ability of the company to globalize or regionalize their efforts, as shown in Reading 18 by Anderson and Coughlan. In some cases, marketers may not have to function as the change agent themselves; that role may be taken by intermediaries who are undertaking the internationalization effort themselves. For example, retailers are extending their operations by entering new markets or by forming cross-border alliances with other retailers thereby opening possibilities in new markets for companies whose products they carry. The last article in this section by Treadgold (Reading 19) suggests that as retailers seek growth opportunities, one of the most attractive alternatives may indeed be the global one.

3. GLOBAL MARKETING PERFORMANCE AND IMPLEMENTATION

The final selection of articles includes contributions on the performance and implementation of global marketing strategies. The bottom-line issue is whether globalization efforts bring benefits beyond the glamour of novelty to the firms that employ them in terms of profitability, competitiveness, and efficiency.

While the authors of the first article of this section (Samiee and Roth, Reading 20) found no difference in performance levels between companies standardizing as much of their operations globally and those who do not, they also suggest that the reason may be more on the improper definition and identification of intermarket segments than anything else. Furthermore, global standardization may not be an optimal approach in all markets or for all products of the firm or all elements of the marketing mix. As a matter of fact, adaptation is significant in the operations of some of the world's most global marketers (Quelch and Hoff, 1986).

The next set of articles (Readings 21 and 22) address the challenges in the implementation of global strategies. The first of these articles by Manu suggests that differences in market environments of different countries may influence the type of strategies developed by companies as well as the impact of those strategies. Even though companies may pursue similar generic strategies (e.g., to be a pioneer) in new markets, care should be taken in understanding their implications. The following article by Yip argues that single-market benefits may not be available in the short term and that investment in globalization be treated as an investment with a longer-term payback. The reason for this is that integrating markets may long display their differences of culture, language, and consumption.

Articles 23 and 24 acknowledge the fact that movement towards implementing global strategies may have to move incrementally through regional operations. Daniels (Reading 23) sees as the most significant barrier not only national differences but also internal challenges in managerial autonomy that has to be bridged. An example of such a bridging effort is provided in the following article by Guido (Reading 24) which provides a marketing-mix specific discussion on how to implement a regional marketing programme.

Organizational features often distinguish successful global marketers from those who profess to be global but fall short in the implementation of their strategies. In the comparison between US and Japanese global marketers in the British market (Doyle, Saunders, and Wong, Reading 25), the Japanese marketers are shown to exhibit certain behaviours associated with global success: commitment to the market, flexibility in organization to facilitate innovation, team work and mutual problem solving. US companies, on the other hand, were seen to take too broad an approach by too many controls and rigid implementation of a regional strategy excluding market-specific flexibility. The following article by Blackwell, Bizet, Child and Hensley (Reading 26) is dedicated to this very question: how to overcome the internal problems of global/regional strategy implementation. Globalization is a change process that may go against the grain of existing power structures, the needed skill levels or infrastructures, or may be threatening to those in present structures. Furthermore, the not-invented-here syndrome may emerge if strategy formulation has not included implementor input during the planning process. In general, successful marketers coordinate their decision making globally, with more central direction than less successful competitors. But at the same time it is done in a way that maintains the integrity of the affiliates involved (Theuerkauf et al., 1993). Changes are nevertheless inevitable as globalization programmes are put into effect. One such change is highlighted in the last entry of this volume (Quelch, Reading 27). The role of the country manager is changing from great authority and autonomy to corporate representative in the local environment. Many of the previously local decisions are now subordinated to global strategic moves.

4. SUMMARY

Include

Many marketing managers have to face the increasing globalization of markets and competition. In many industries, the major players have decided to compete in all of the major markets of the world. The challenges in this process are considerable. Marketers will have to assess their core businesses, formulate global strategy in terms of target market choice and competitive strategy, develop appropriate marketing mixes to match the needs of the markets, and make sure their organizations are ready for these new programmes (Czinkota and Ronkainen, 1996).

REFERENCES

Advertising Age (1984) 'Colleague (Philip Kotler) Says Levitt Wrong'. June 25: 50.

Bilkey, W. J. and Nes, E. (1982) 'Country-of-Origin Effects on Product Evaluations'. *Journal of International Business Studies*, **13**(Spring/Summer): 88–99.

Business International (1988) 'Global Marketing Campaigns with a Local Touch'. July 4: 205–210.

Business Week (1993) 'Mininationals are Making Maximum Impact'. September 6: 66–69.

Coopers & Lybrand (1984) *Collaborative Ventures: An Emerging Phenomenon in the Information Industry.* Coopers & Lybrand, New York, p. 3.

Czinkota, M. R. (1986) 'International Trade and Business in the Late 1980s: An Integrated U.S. Policy Perspective'. *Journal of International Business Studies*, **17**(Spring): 127–134.

Czinkota, M. R. and Ronkainen, I. A. (1996) *Global Marketing*, The Dryden Press, Ft. Worth, TX, figure 7.2.

Dichter, E. (1962) 'The World Customer'. *Harvard Business Review*, **40**(July–August): 113–122.

Kotabe, M. and Czinkota, M. R. (1992) 'State Government Promotion of Manufacturing Exports: A Gap Analysis'. *Journal of International Business Studies*, **23**(Winter): 637–658.

Levitt, T. (1983) *The Marketing Imagination*. The Free Press, New York, pp. 20–49.

Maruca, R. F. (1994) 'The Right Way to Go Global: An Interview with Whirlpool CEO David Whitwam'. *The Harvard Business Review*, **72**(March–April): 134–145.

Ohmae, K. (1985) *Triad Power—The Coming Shape of Global Competition*. The Free Press, New York, pp. 22–27.

Quelch, J. A. and Hoff, E. J. (1986) 'Customizing Global Marketing'. *Harvard Business Review*, **64**(May/June): 59–68.

Rennie, M. W. (1993) 'Born Global'. *The McKinsey Quarterly*, **30**(4): 45–52.

Rice, F. (1991) 'How Copycats Steal Billions'. *Fortune* (April 22): 157–64.

Ronstadt, R. (1978) 'International R&D: The Establishment and Evolution of Research and Development Abroad by U.S. Multinationals'. *Journal of International Business Studies*, **9**(Spring/Summer: 7–24.

Ryans, J. K. (1969) 'Is It Too Soon to Put a Tiger in Every Tank'. *Columbia Journal of World Business*, **4**(March/April): 69–75.

Schlender, B. R. (1994) 'Matsushita Shows How to Go Global'. *Fortune* (July 11): 88–92.

Theuerkauf, I., Ernst, D. and Mahini, A. (1993) 'Think Local, Organize ...?' *The McKinsey Quarterly*, **30**(1): 107–114.

Yip, G. S. (1992) *Total Global Strategy*, The Free Press, New York.

Part I

Strategic Global Marketing Issues

CONTENTS

1 Global marketing 2000: a marketing survival guide   3

MICHAEL R. CZINKOTA and ILKKA A. RONKAINEN, *Marketing Management*
(1992), **1**(Winter), 37–45

2 Trading blocs: opportunity or demise for trade?   14

ILKKA A. RONKAINEN, *Multinational Business Review* (1993), **1**(Spring), 1–9

3 The EC '92 and Eastern Europe: effects of integration vs.
   disintegration   25

MICHAEL R. CZINKOTA, *Columbia Journal of World Business* (1991),
26(Spring), 20–27

4 Global neighbours: poor relations   36

MICHAEL R. CZINKOTA, *Marketing Management* (1994), **2**(4), 46–52

5 A national export assistance policy for new and growing
   businesses   44

MICHAEL R. CZINKOTA *Journal of International Marketing* (1994), **2**(1), 91–
101

6 Evolution of global marketing strategy: scale, scope and
   synergy   53

SUSAN P. DOUGLAS and C. SAMUEL CRAIG, *Columbia Journal of World
Business* (1989), **24**(Fall), 47–59

7 Global strategy and multinationals' entry mode choice   73

W. CHAN KIM and PETER HWANG, *Journal of International Business Studies*
(1992), **23**(1), 29–53

8 Successful export marketing management: Some empirical
   evidence   96

TAGE KOED MADSEN, *International Marketing Review* (1989), **6**(4), 41–57

9 Strategic alliances in the triad: an exploratory study   111

VERN TERPSTRA and BERNARD L. SIMONIN, *Journal of International
Marketing* (1993), **1**(1), 4–25

1

Global Marketing 2000: a Marketing Survival Guide

Michael R. Czinkota and Ilkka A. Ronkainen

There are 13 trends and issues that define the shape of international marketing in the 1990s and beyond, according to 29 business, government, and academic experts in the United States, Japan, and Western and Central Europe. The environment is their main concern; how can marketers make products environmentally friendly without compromising product performance or consumer values?

Global corporate operations, then emerging trading blocs and regionalism, ranked second and third as critical issues. The experts, participating in a worldwide Delphi study, also cite technological change as a major issue, particularly in communications and information applications. Additionally, they anticipate major developments in services marketing and human capital development.

Geographically, Eastern and Central Europe, and the Pacific Rim emerge as critical marketing arenas, while aiding the Third World becomes an even greater challenge to developed nations.

Financial and human capital trends will have significant impact, the experts predict. And they foresee extensive social debate over energy policies.

Rarely has a decade started with so many new opportunities. Beyond the short-term problems of economic recession, global revolutions are under way in all aspects of life: management, politics, communications, and technology. The word 'global' itself has assumed a new meaning, referring to a boundless mobility and competition in social, business, and intellectual arenas.

No longer just an alternative, global marketing has become an imperative for business. Customer and supplier networks operate worldwide, blurring geographic and political barriers and making them increasingly irrelevant to business decisions and locations.

Over the past two decades, world trade has climbed from $200 billion to $4 trillion, and increases in foreign direct investment have begun to rival trade growth. Countries and companies that had never been considered major participants in international marketing are now important players, some of them displaying remarkable economic prowess.

Reprinted with permission from *Marketing Management*, Vol. 1, Winter, pp. 37–45

Being a marketing winner means relishing the pace of change rather than fearing it. As product development costs rise, product life cycles shorten, and technological diffusion speeds up worldwide, marketers face unprecedented challenges to their customary ways of practising their craft.

QUESTIONS FOR THE EXPERTS

Our study draws a road map to the future of global marketing, to guide business planners, policy makers, researchers, and those who teach tomorrow's marketing executives. We asked 29 experts in business, government, and academia in the United States, Japan, and Western and Central Europe, to ponder three broad questions:

1. What are the major global trends and issues affecting marketing in the 1990s and beyond?
2. How severely will they affect international marketers?
3. How should marketers respond strategically?

Conducting the study with American Marketing Association sponsorship, we employed a Delphi approach, using rounds of assessment, argument, and reargument to create agreement or define areas of dissent among panelists. They addressed our three questions, and ranked their choice of key issues on a three-point scale for 'high', 'medium', or 'low' importance and impact.

Once we organized their replies, panelists swapped comments, endorsing or disputing the views comprising this report. See the Appendix, 'Debate in a Global Village', for details about the research.

ISSUES THAT MATTER MOST

Table 1 lists the 13 most prominent trends and issues that will shape international marketing in this decade and into the next century, according to our panel. We ranked them based on the panel's estimation of their overall importance to the world economy, and in terms of their specific impact on international marketing management.

Comparing the results to an earlier study we conducted shows some interesting differences. In the mid-1980s, the international trade framework, international debt, and US trade policy ranked as the most important issues. For the 1990s, those have dropped to the lowest cluster. And issues either in the lowest cluster (trading blocs) or not mentioned at all (environment) in the mid-1980s have now moved to the forefront. Even though the earlier Delphi study focused only on the United States, the shifts reflect a major turnabout in the international perspective, driven both by recent political and geographic developments and society's new priorities.

We also asked participants to elaborate on the issues and peer into the future. Here is a summary of their comments.

Table 1. Critical international marketing trends and issues

Cluster 1
   Environment (2.64)
   Globalization (2.53)
   Trading blocs/regionalism (2.44)
Cluster 2
   Technology (2.38)
   Services (2.30)
   Human capital (2.29)
   Central Europe (2.27)
   Pacific Rim (2.26)
Cluster 3
   Third World (2.20)
   World finance (2.02)
   Foreign direct investment (1.90)
   International trade framework (1.90)
   Energy (1.72)

Note: Scale value combining importance and impact:
   3 = High;   2 = Medium;   1 = Low.

THE ENVIRONMENT

No other issue rated higher among participants than the environment. Growing public concern about the rapid deterioration of the natural environment, environmental pollution, and global warming will provide major new-product opportunities.

Consumers will demand more environmentally friendly products that don't require too much compromise on performance and value. Technological advances, economic expansion, and the natural environment will compete in the 'quality of life' arena worldwide. Global television will put the differences between the haves and have-nots into sharp relief.

Corporations will have to find solutions to environmental challenges through marketing strategies, products, and services in order to remain competitive. Management will resist the additional business costs and taxes required for environmental protection, at least until investors and other constituent groups assure executives that environmental concern is acceptable even if it cuts into profit.

New technologies for handling waste, sewage, and air pollution will proliferate, creating a new environmental order to keep cities livable. Product standardization will become one method of ensuring environmentally safe products. And interest in truly 'natural' products will grow, even if some are less convenient to use. Construction will emphasize heat, sound, indoor air, and moisture control—for resource conservation and greater occupant health. All trends will produce major new business opportunities.

GLOBALIZATION

Although some respondents consider market globalization a *fait accompli,* the 1990s will produce refined global strategies. The winners will be the companies that standardize global manufacturing, regularly offer innovative solutions to the market and tailor products and services to meet local preferences.

Political integration will create new regional and global consumer segments. Competing anywhere in them will require a global outlook as trade barriers decline, as we expect they will in the long run.

Country-specific organizations will decline while 'stateless' corporations emerge, dispersing their headquarters operations and production facilities. They will seek creative collaborations with other firms to merge complementary skills and gain access to new markets. Corporate hierarchies will continue to flatten in response to the worldwide integration of markets.

Locally tailored products based on global production strategies will proliferate. Consumption patterns across cultures will homogenize, producing more market share for global brands. Yet the challenge of maintaining local-market initiative with global products will increase the need for local marketing and production that adapts brands to regional and local tastes—a different tasting Coca-Cola in different regions, for example. Production standardization, combined with customization at the point of purchase designed to fulfil customer needs precisely, will become a key strategic option.

TRADING BLOCS

While Delphi participants agreed that trading blocs are important, they voiced different opinions about their effect. Panelists do not expect regionalism to degenerate into protectionism, mainly because of global trade and direct investment by multinational corporations. Yet some believe intra-bloc trade growth will parallel global trade. Others consider regionalism as a step to more global marketing. On balance, they see emerging trade blocs in Europe, North America, and elsewhere as having medium- to long-term impact, with little short-run effect on international marketing.

TECHNOLOGY

The pace of technology development will continue to accelerate, transforming traditional industries, the panelists say. More products will contain microchips, becoming more user friendly and achieving faster market adoption. Technological development that is too rapid, however, may lead to technology monopolization. And too fast a diffusion may discourage corporate investment in new, risky technologies, the panelists caution.

Production labour will be displaced by automation, but corporations will create more product development jobs. The transition will be slow and patchy, however, without increased training. Those new jobs will benefit from corporate research and development spending that becomes a larger portion of total product cost. Firms will integrate management and R&D to commercialize new technology faster and better.

'Techno-nationalism' will create government-supported R&D centres in major industrial markets, but it will not seriously inhibit active international R&D collaboration between firms in industrialized nations. Meanwhile, the high costs of the R&D game will price it beyond the reach of most of the world, widening the gap between developed and developing countries. Governments will have less money for R&D; innovation will rely on individuals and corporations as governments are forced to spend more on social services.

Information and communications

Information and communications technology advances will transform all aspects of international marketing. Suppliers in the field will compete fiercely for one of the biggest business opportunities of the decade.

Computers, television, and telecommunications will merge into instantaneous world communications systems. Individuals will carry their communications media with them, perhaps in a wristwatch-size device. Distance and place will become far less important in business.

Even with their greater service, telecommunications will become cheaper; advances in multiplexing, fibre optics, and other technologies will cut costs. Innovations will displace much of today's hardware, making the ability to use new technologies more critical to business success.

Greater dependence on technology also means more vulnerability to acts of God, sabotage, terrorism, and other forces *majeure*. But more capacity and capability in communications systems compensates for the extra risk and prompts greater use of redundancy in systems design to ensure reliability.

Effects on consumers

Individuals will grow more sophisticated about their needs, they will exercise more influence on corporations, and will expect rapid response to their requests. Offering customization, immediate availability, and a wide array of choice will be marketing essentials.

Computers will become easier to use, allowing more home shopping. Yet many consumers will still rely on traditional outlets for most purchases.

Effects on marketers

Technology will shorten the life span of products, requiring more efficient, faster, and better targeted marketing. Interactive marketing will expand.

Marketers will become less isolated from other parts of their companies. They will depend fully on communication systems. Armed with data bases offering almost unlimited market and customer detail, marketers will combine disparate data sources to create profiles as precise as that of the individual consumer, in order to respond to market requirements and exceed the service competitors offer.

Technology will change distribution patterns. For example, various middlemen in the distribution chain will disappear, made redundant by direct, paperless communications between stores and producers. New types of business organizations will link manufacturers, retailers, and consumers in private telecommunications networks, each vying for market leadership. While marketing promotions are likely to decline, the new marketing networks will compete on the basis of user-friendly computer and communications power.

On the downside, with all the instantaneous data they will have on hand, marketers will be more susceptible to short-term pressures.

SERVICES

Service industries will compete worldwide in all markets. Heated international competition fuelled by worldwide data exchange will generate a 24-hour service attitude. Success in service industries will depend on a sophisticated knowledge of different market segments' needs and fast, customized response to them.

HUMAN CAPITAL

Managers will need to acquire new skills to work with personnel in corporations without boundaries or borders. We may see the resurgence of the Renaissance person supplanting the era of the specialist. Companies will better combine the respective strengths of different cultures into productive teamwork.

Rising cost and immigration restrictions will retard labour mobility, however, particularly in Europe and Japan. Automation and shifting plant locations will be preferable to depending on restricted labour migration. At the same time, however, more common information shared among cultures worldwide will mitigate differences in national and regional labour capabilities.

Corporations facing shortages in both skilled labour and multicultural management talent will demand more from training and education programmes. Continuous investment in human resources will become one of the most compelling competitive factors in a borderless world for corporations and governments alike. Companies will have to stress training unskilled workers. Governments need to prevent large underclasses of unemployed from developing. In the United States, attitudes toward the importance of a college education will change, giving more recognition to highly skilled vocational workers.

CENTRAL AND EASTERN EUROPE

Political and economic change in Eastern and Central Europe will continue to be uneven. Czechoslovakia, Hungary, and Poland, for example, will continue to outdistance the Balkan states in economic development and political stability. Chaos in the former Soviet Union will continue for some time, as those nations wrestle with the overhang of 70 years of a command economy. Western firms hoping to find another Taiwan, Hong Kong, or Malaysia in the Soviet states will be deeply disappointed.

Unmet expectations about free-market economies, however unrealistic they may be, will disappoint consumers deeply. Shrinking domestic markets, labour unrest, and a policy climate that will opt for stricter government controls will reveal how little experience the public and private sectors have in dealing with new realities.

Instability in Eastern Europe will create high uncertainty in Western Europe. Western firms will invest in non-inflation sensitive East European assets such as real estate, and the raw material sector.

Increasingly, however, Eastern Europe will become a significant source of products and services. New trading and financing techniques will emerge for Westerners dealing with central governments or directly with firms. Privatization will be a key issue, transforming state-owned enterprises into joint stock companies or joint ventures. Trade and business associations will grow as marketing techniques take root and middle management ranks strengthen.

The shortage of hard currency will make development of an Eastern European regional monetary system a must for the emerging democracies, which will also need a regional cooperative system to replace COMECON.

Considering the major risk those developments pose, only patient Western capital will enter those markets until economies and political systems stabilize, our panelists expect. It is likely that only major corporations will make long-term commitments. The considerable potential of Eastern Europe will justify the risk, and large companies will be able to weather the short-term difficulties. Smaller enterprises, however, will concentrate on 'take the money and run' ventures.

Finally, Western analysts will invest more effort in Central and Eastern European country risk evaluation.

PACIFIC RIM

Japan's role as the economic leader of the Pacific Rim will solidify. More Japanese-foreign joint ventures will emerge. But that relentless Japanese economic drive will not lead to a commensurate political leadership role. Regional development will not require a Japanese-led trading bloc, and Japan herself will continue efforts to reap the benefits of the current free trade system.

Competition within the Rim will not be so pacific. Malaysia, Indonesia, and Thailand will join the Four Tigers—Korea, Taiwan, Singapore and Hong Kong—as the region's economic powerhouses. Although rates of growth in those economies will be extraordinary over the coming few years, their overall global impact will be limited. China looms as the region's economic giant, certainly in potential if not yet in actual trade activity. In terms of international marketing effort imports, exports, and foreign direct investment, however, the Four and soon Seven Tigers may rival or supplant even the Japanese.

The United States will remain the Pacific region's largest market. Japan's role will wane in the long-term because of weak political desire and international political skill within Japan, and a lack of political acceptance outside Japan, our Delphi panelists predict. The Pacific region will welcome Japanese economic assistance until it is no longer needed. Japan's financial aid will not buy it much long-term political gain.

THIRD WORLD

The long-term picture in the Third World is not encouraging. Disparities between developed and developing countries will widen, and differences among social groups within countries will also increase. Debt crises will endure in the poorest countries, where societies will also continue to suffer extreme political uncertainty. The result will be greater polarization and conflict between the haves and have-nots.

Differences among developing countries will also expand, with rewards going to those instituting political and economic change. The concept of a third world poised between rival superpowers will disappear, to be replaced by a north–south distinction.

Economic collapse in developing countries will eventually harm industrialized nations. Their problems are our problems too. The industrialized North will support international solutions to the South's problems, but we do not see that as a likelihood within the next five years.

From a business standpoint, worker shortages in some developed countries will drive labour-intensive manufacturing operations to developing countries. To that extent, global management strategies will mitigate north–south economic disparities to some degree. So too will government aid and investment credits from developed countries to friendly regimes—including those in China and the former USSR—strengthening them against forces hostile to the industrialized West. Economic and political stability now should pay off in maturing markets later.

Hence the governments of wealthy countries, supported by private sector financing and investment, will invest in the have-nots to create business opportunities for the future.

WORLD FINANCE

Relatively low savings rates, growing government obligations, and increasing global competition for capital will lead to relatively high real interest rates worldwide, we expect. Global capitalization requirements will force banks to become more conservative in their lending, for example. Industrialized countries will attempt to narrow the gap between savings and investment, but many country-specific programmes will be thwarted by international financial and economic linkages.

Easier access to financing sources will become critical to corporate survival in the capital-intensive manufacturing sector. Worldwide financial markets, growing increasingly integrated, will provide that access by liberalizing investment policies and keeping capital readily available for fiscally sound, politically stable investment anywhere on the globe. But that will not help risky investment in developing nations, notwithstanding Western governments' guarantees and inducements. The insurance sector will play a growing role where risky investments are made.

FOREIGN DIRECT INVESTMENT

The key factor is that foreign direct investment will increasingly become more liquid, responding tactically rather than strategically to changing economic opportunities worldwide. For example, the traditional approach saw foreign direct investment as a long-term strategic decision to, say, 'penetrate Europe' or 'develop a presence in Asia'. A company entering the European market, for instance, would site a plant in Germany as the centre of its long-term operations.

In years to come, foreign investment decisions increasingly will be driven by short-term advantages and be less of a long-term commitment. For example, a company might decide to open a plant in Spain to take advantage of current low-cost production factors, recognizing that within five years or so, it might move the plant to Hungary.

Initially, the United States will be the prime target for foreign direct investment. However, foreign capital is unlikely to expand during the decade to the point where it can directly or indirectly dominate many US corporations. Foreign firms instead will continue to try to position themselves as 'locals' to avoid governmental restrictions.

However, as other areas of the world such as the European Community, establish themselves as safe havens, foreign investment growth in the United States will slow.

INTERNATIONAL TRADE FRAMEWORK

Global trade imbalances seem to have passed their peak, thanks to multilateral trade negotiations. But in the future, strengthening regional trading blocs will alter the purpose and importance of trade's key forum, the General Agreement on Tariffs and Trade (GATT). Huge regional blocs in Europe and North America, for example, will become the trade regulators by balancing each others' influence. GATT will weaken only in the sense that its original job, tariff reduction, is close to completion. However, trading nations and blocs will not want to abolish GATT; they recognize the overall importance of free trade and an impartial, supranational regulatory organization, particularly for developing countries.

ENERGY

Prices are likely to remain low for the next five years and beyond, in part because oil increasingly will be devoted to transportation purposes only. National debates over energy sources will become increasingly difficult to resolve, pitting nuclear power critics against those concerned with the fossil fuel contribution to global warming.

Nevertheless, energy for home and industry will eventually rely on nuclear sources, our Delphi panel predicts.

Alternative energy sources, such as wind, geothermal, and the like, will be neither abundant nor efficient enough to fulfil the need. Active and passive solar energy systems, however, will produce remarkable energy savings and protect the environment. Solar energy conservation will become a greater priority in building architecture.

A SURVIVAL GUIDE

Some of the issues of concern to our international Delphi panel are already beginning to earn public recognition. But others seem to have escaped wide attention so far, particularly on a regional basis.

Also, we were surprised by some of the group's predictions. For instance, we did not expect such emphasis on the environment, a concern uniformly shared by the panel's business executives, policy makers, and academics in all participating geographic regions. Similarly, their confidence in the survival of the multilateral world trade framework counters the short-term pessimism now widely expressed about GATT and its stalled Uruguay Round.

For the marketer, change is a key driver of success. But just waiting for change to happen and then reacting to it is not the best way to plan.

If marketing as a discipline is to stay at the forefront of business strategy, it must anticipate change and provide early warnings to other business functions about what is ahead. Marketing must maintain a role as a key change agent in society, contributing to its betterment.

Marketing management must produce integrated solutions that resolve society's conflicting demands with better ways of achieving social and economic goals.

APPENDIX. DEBATE IN A GLOBAL VILLAGE

This article reports the results of a Delphi study conducted under American Marketing Association auspices among 29 business, government, and academic decision makers. They reside in the United States, Japan, Western Europe, and Central Europe. We overcame geographical dispersion by using various rounds of contact to refine the panel's collective judgments.

Forecasting trends in an era of rapid change is difficult, even more so if the researcher attempts to survey mass opinion. It is better to seek depth over breadth in such circumstances, and ask a select group of experts rather than apply quantitative analysis to hordes of the rank and file. Our choice of study design also continues the qualitative thrust of an earlier, domestic issues-oriented AMA project, 'Marketing 2000 and Beyond'.

To examine global trends, we could have perused current literature, conducting the kind of content analysis that researcher David R. Wheeler calls a 'valuable predictor of the characteristics and behavior of target markets'. But the delays we expected collecting literature from around the world, and the potential bias a US-based analyst might apply to writing aimed at other cultures, argued against that approach.

A second method would have convened experts at one location, but that was impossible. So we used the Delphi technique which has proven effective capturing the collective thinking of groups that cannot meet in one place. Delphi employs rounds of assessment, argument, and counterargument among participants until they reach a consensus or clearly defined disagreement. Typically, no more than 30 people participate, lest a larger number inhibit expression. It is important, therefore, to pick participants carefully.

We recruited presidents or vice presidents in charge of international operations. At the policy-maker level, we drew participants from legislative and administrative echelons, and current or former senior staff members of national or supranational organizations. In academics, we invited chaired professors of international marketing or heads of international research institutes.

The profile of participants (see Table 2) indicates the number and type and locations

Table 2. Profile of participants in the Delphi study

Business participants (14)

  Marketing (10)

    Multinational (5)

- US (2)
- EC + EFTA (1)
- Japan (1)
- Central Europe (1)

    Exporter/Importer (5)

- US (2)
- EC + EFTA (1)
- Japan (1)
- Central Europe (1)

  Finance (4)

- US (1)
- EC + EFTA (1)
- Japan (2)

Range of positions: chief executive officer, president/international operations, vice president (international, governmental affairs), director of treasury operations.

Government policy participants (12)

  Legislative (3)

- US (1)
- EC + EFTA (1)
- Central Europe (1)

  Administrative (9)

- US (5) (Export Import Bank of the US, Office of the US Trade Representative, Department of the Treasury, Department of Commerce, White House.)
- Japan (1)
- Central Europe (1)
- Supranational (2) (GATT, OECD)

Range of positions: advisor, ambassador, assistant secretary, counsel to, general counsel, member of parliament, staff director.

Academic participants (3)

- US (1)
- EC + EFTA (1)
- Central Europe (1)

Range of positions: chaired professor, head of international research institute.

---

of panelists contributing to the study. Given the dominant role of the 'Triad', we selected most participants from the United States, Western Europe, and Japan. We also chose some from Central Europe because of the major changes occurring there.

Each Delphi round requires considerable effort; not everyone accepted our invitations. As is typical in forming Delphi groups, we selected and screened three candidates for each individual who eventually participated. We hit some obstacles in balancing the panel. For various reasons we could not secure legislative and academic representatives from Japan. And because there is so little private sector activity in Central Europe, we could not get a representative from a private bank there to join us.

2

Trading Blocs: Opportunity or Demise for Trade?

Ilkka A. Ronkainen

INTRODUCTION

Of the major trends and issues that define the shape of international marketing in the 1990s and beyond, trading blocs are one of the most significant (Czinkota and Ronkainen, 1992). The drivers of regional economic integration around the world are political will, market forces, and the fact that GATT negotiations seem to have been going nowhere for a considerable period of time. While the role of politics has been acknowledged as the major driver of regionalization in the past, market forces and corporate moves may indeed be making as significant of a contribution to the phenomenon today. The debate is raging over the impact of regionalization on trade and consequent welfare of nations, and whether trading blocs are nothing but a new version of protectionism or an intermediate step necessary to achieve worldwide free trade.

This paper is divided into three parts. The first part will define trading blocs, their basic characteristics, and projected future developments. The second part will focus on the arguments presented for and against them as factors impacting on world trade. The final part will focus more on the role of the private sector in regionalization as well as corporate adjustment to the phenomenon.

TRADING BLOCS

Trading blocs defined

A trading bloc is a preferential economic arrangement between a group of countries that reduces intra-regional barriers to trade in goods. Some have included freedom of movement in services, investment and capital as well. The total number of such arrangements has been estimated presently at 32 (Brand, 1991) while a total of 50 have been reviewed by the GATT (Schott, 1989). Included in this definition are preferential trade agreements (e.g., the Caribbean Basin Initiative), free trade areas (e.g., the United States–

Reprinted with permission from *Multinational Business Review*, Vol. 1, No. 1, pp. 1–9
© 1993 Multinational Business Review

Canada Free Trade Agreement), customs unions (e.g., the South African Customs Union), common markets (e.g., the Central American Common Market), and economic unions (e.g., the European Community).

Historically, successful trading blocs have consisted of member countries with similar levels of per capita GNP, geographic proximity, compatible trading regimes, and political commitment to regional organization (Schott, 1991). While the European Community (EC), especially in its early stages with six members, displayed all of these characteristics, recent developments have shown that political will to cooperate does overcome consequences of dissimilarity in the first three characteristics. The addition of Greece, Spain and Portugal into the EC, and the trilateral negotiations to create the North American Free Trade Agreement (NAFTA) indicate that disparities can be overcome. The gains and losses of the members have to be sorted out so that on balance every member does come out ahead. Furthermore, with wide discrepancies, a basic mistrust of the powerful member(s) may be a hindrance, especially on the political front.

The reasons why trading blocs emerge have evolved over the years. While the political rationale is still predominant, the globalization of world economy may be emerging as a significant driver in the process that may finally lead to worldwide free trade. Fear has been proposed as a significant factor in convincing countries to overcome differences; e.g., European unity initially was seen as an antidote to war, and the 1992 phenomenon driven by fear of American and Japanese industrial dominance. In Asia, however, fear (of Japan's dominance) has kept countries from forging any formal new trade regime. Nevertheless, the economies of every nation in the region are pulling closer than ever before with a *de-facto* trading bloc in place by the end of the century. The driver: intra-Asian trade and investment.

BLOCS NOW AND IN THE FUTURE

Figure 1 presents a hypothetical scenario as to how trading blocs may emerge in the long term. The three acknowledged trading blocs will serve as the main elements. Present outsiders will cooperate, and eventually join, the three main systems. Proposed and possible linkages are also indicated. For example, world trade powers with interests in more than one region may have to be involved beyond their 'own' bloc; for example, the United States will have to become more involved in the Asia-Pacific should it want to maintain its status (Tanzer, 1990).

The European Community is the only one of the proposed blocs that already acts as a superstate. The 12 members of the Community have ceded substantial sovereignty to the Community and will do even more as per the Maastricht Treaty. Even with the euphoria of the 1992 phenomenon there is substantial disagreement among present members of the future (e.g., Denmark refusing to ratify the Maastricht Treaty) and the future course of the Community, especially in terms of its expansion. The EC's first expansion will be through the European Free Trade Association (EFTA) in the formation of the European Economic Area (EEA), and eventually (within the 1990s) through the membership of most of the EFTA members in the Community. Further expansion is under debate. For example, Turkey, Cyprus, and Malta have long had their applications in Brussels. The emerging democracies of Central Europe (NEDs) as well as

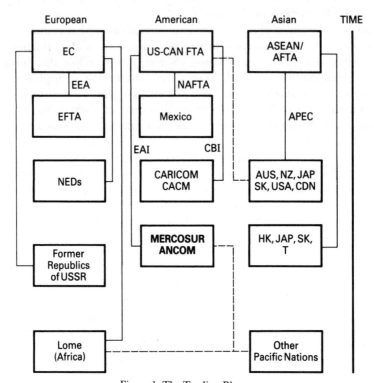

Figure 1. The Trading Blocs.
Solid lines = existing or proposed arrangements within a bloc
Broken lines = existing or proposed arrangements involving members in two separate blocs

EC	European Community
EFTA	European Free Trade Association
EEA	European Economic Area
NED	Newly-emerging democracy
NAFTA	North American Free Trade Agreement
CARICOM	Caribbean Common Market
CACM	Central American Common Market
CBI	Caribbean Basin Initiative
EAI	Enterprise for the Americas Initiative
MERCOSUR	Southern Common Market
ANCOM	Andean Common Market
ASEAN	Association of Southeast Asian Nations
AFTA	ASEAN Free Trade Area
APEC	Asia Pacific Economic Cooperation
EAEG	East Asian Economic Group
AUS	Australia
NZ	New Zealand
JAP	Japan
SK	South Korea
HK	Hong Kong
T	Taiwan

some of the republics of the former Soviet Union have indicated urgency in becoming members. Present members are divided whether to grant special concessions to the NEDs in helping them both in modernization and democratization. Much will depend on the NEDs' ability to change their economies to operate in free markets; in this sense Hungary is emerging as the best candidate.

Another major European trading arrangement is the Lome Convention. Lome is a preferential trading agreement between the former European empires and their former African, Caribbean, and Pacific (ACP) colonies, which today constitute 69 separate countries. Some believe that if economic unity succeeds in Africa, an African Common Market may eventually join into the European trading bloc. In 1991, the member states of the Organization of African Unity signed a treaty to establish the African Common Market by year 2020. The major dilemma of African economic unity is the lack of a leader to this effort. The African bridge to the European Community may come from Morocco which has applied for membership.

Lome will also provide the European Community with connection to the other two trading blocs (as indicated by Figure 1); however, the members through which these ties are maintained are not the key players. Furthermore, some of the nations (such as those in the Pacific) may not necessarily be part of any arrangement.

After three failed tries this century, the United States and Canada signed a free trade agreement that went into effect on January 1, 1989. North American free trade is likely to expand in the near future with the inclusion of Mexico into NAFTA. While the pact is facing challenges both in Canada and in the United States (due to political changes), it will be ratified given the interlinkages of the three economies (*Business Week*, 1992a). The Bush Administration set as one of their main trade-policy goals the formation of a hemispheric free trade area under the Enterprise for the Americas Initiative (EAI). This initiative is already taking form. The aim of the members of the Southern Common Market, MERCOSUR, is to eliminate tariff barriers altogether by the end of 1994 and prepare the economies for a possible hemispheric trade bloc with NAFTA (*Business Week*, 1992b). The CBI beneficiaries (most of the Caribbean and Central American countries) will lose many of their benefits under NAFTA. This means that they will cooperate more closely among each other through the Caribbean Common Market (CARICOM) and the Central American Common Market (CACM) arrangements. Mexico and the CACM have already started planning for a free trade arrangement.

The development in Asia has been quite different from that in Europe and in the Americas. While European and North American arrangements have been driven by political will, market forces may force more formal integration on the politicians in Asia. While Japan is the dominant force in the area to take leadership in such an endeavour, neither the Japanese themselves nor the other nations want Japan to do it. The concept of a 'Co-Prosperity Sphere' of 50 years ago has made nations wary of Japan's influence (Thornton, 1992). Also, in terms of economic and political distance, the potential member countries are far from each other, especially if comparisons are made with the EC. However, increasing regional integration around the world may be driving Asian interest in it for pragmatic reasons. First, European and American markets are significant for the Asian producers and some type of organization or bloc may be needed to maintain leverage and balance against the two other blocs. Secondly, given that much of the growth in trade for the nations in the region is from intra-Asian trade, having a common understanding and policy will become necessary. A future arrangement will most likely be using the frame of the most established arrangement in the region, the Association of Southeast Asian Nations (ASEAN). Before late 1991, ASEAN had no real structures and consensus was reached through informal consultations. In October 1991, ASEAN members (Brunei, Indonesia, Malaysia, Philippines, Singapore, and Thailand) announced the formation of a customs union called Asean Free Trade Area (AFTA). The Malaysians have pushed for the formation of the East Asia Economic Group (EAEG) which add Hong Kong, Japan, South Korea, and Taiwan to the list. This proposal makes sense since without Japan and the rapidly-industrializing countries of the region, such as South Korea and Taiwan, the effect of the arrangement would be nominal. Japan's reaction has been generally negative towards all types of regionalization efforts mainly because it has had the most to gain from free-trade efforts. However, part of what has been driving regionalization has been Japan's reluctance to foster some of the elements that promote free trade; for example, reciprocity (Krugman, 1992). Should the other trading blocs turn against Japan, her only resort may be to work towards a more formal trade arrangement in the Asia-Pacific.

Another formal proposal for cooperation would start building bridges between two emerging trade blocs. Some individuals have publicly called for a US–Japan common market. Given the differences on all fronts between the two, the proposal may be quite unrealistic at this time. Negotiated trade liberalization will not open Japanese markets due to major institutional differences as seen in many rounds of successful negotiations but totally unsatisfactory results. The only solution, especially for the US government, is to forge better cooperation between the government and the private sector to improve competitiveness (Czinkota and Kotabe, 1992).

In 1988, Australia proposed the Asia Pacific Economic Cooperation (APEC) as an annual forum to maintain a balance in negotiations. The proposal calls for ASEAN members to be joined by Australia, New Zealand, Japan, South Korea, Canada, and the United States. The model for APEC would not be the EC with its Brussels bureaucracy but the Organization for Economic Cooperation and Development (OECD), which is a centre for research and high-level discussion. However, the future actions of the other two blocs will determine how quickly and in what manner the Asian bloc (whatever it is!) will respond. Also, the stakes are the highest for the Asian nations in the present round of GATT negotiations since their traditional export markets have been in Europe and in North America and, in this sense, very dependent on free access.

WHAT ABOUT GATT?

Trading blocs discriminate explicitly and implicitly against outsiders by granting preferences only to member countries. This in itself is not a violation of GATT as long as barriers are not raised to third countries. However, even if the rule has been violated, as it is in many cases, the issue has not been contested for various reasons. First, some regional efforts have had a political agenda, such as promoting democracy in a given region. Secondly, countries have not raised the red flag in fear that their own arrangements fall under scrutiny. This does not mean that GATT is incapable of handling regional trading blocs; what it does mean, however, is that new rules have to be agreed upon as to what is and what is not permissible in managing bloc trade (Thurow, 1990).

The bigger question is naturally the future of GATT itself. Despite assurances of break-throughs in negotiations all throughout 1992, the Uruguay-round of negotiations seems to be hopelessly bogged down due to differences even between members of the same bloc; e.g., French resistance to any concessions in agriculture. If the present round is an indication of the length of time it takes to reach agreement on multilateralism, many may want to give up. As a matter of fact, many have argued that political will has been directed at forming blocs rather than preserving GATT.

If GATT fails to provide comprehensive answers in the reasonable future, like-minded nations, most likely members of regional blocs, will negotiate an open-ended supplement to GATT principles and achieve their goals within blocs and to maintain progress in the process toward multilateralism. One such proposal would involve the OECD nations which would establish their own Free Trade and Investment Area (Hufbauer, 1989). Proposers of such plans all want to have their ideas added to the GATT principles rather than having them replaced altogether. However, the rules are changed. To make regionalism eventually turn into multilateralism requires that agreed-upon rules be enfored rather than overlooked for one reason or another. Japan has requested that a mechanism be set up under GATT which would supervise regional integration to ensure that she would get a fair hearing if protectionist trade barriers increase along with growing economic regionalism (*Far Eastern Economic Review*, 1992).

BUILDING BLOCKS VS. STUMBLING BLOCKS

The role of the trading blocs is seen very differently by its protagonists and its antagonists. Some see trading blocs only as a version of protectionism and government intervention in trade, and that the inevitable result will be a return to protectionism similar to that of the 1930s with trade wars draining world welfare. Some, however, feel that blocs are an inevitable stage in an evolutionary process toward free trade worldwide and argue that the globalization of trade and foreign direct investment by multinational corporations will make protectionist tendencies difficult (*Business Week*, 1990). The question boils down to which forces will win: political or economic.

THE CONSTRUCTIVE ROLE OF BLOCS

Blocs are seen as building blocks towards multilateralism: once the commitment to market forces has been made at the regional level, it will be easier to move on. Furthermore, if GATT in its present format has outlived its usefulness, blocs may be able to effect new rules quicker than can 108 countries. Some, especially in the United States and Europe, see blocs as a way to reduce barriers to international trade and investment more efficiently than multilateral negotiations. Markets that have heretofore remained closed to individual countries may now be open by the force and leverage of a bloc. (Naturally, the effect can also be a trade war!) This argument has been used specifically with reference to Japan. The context here also includes non-tariff barriers to trade, something the GATT has been unable to deal with, but an issue that trading blocs, mainly the EC, have dealt with internally quite well.

Statistics also indicate substantial increases in trade among members belonging to blocs. This is not uniform, however, and will depend largely on what existed before the arrangement took place. In most cases, trading blocs are formed among regional neighbours who already have significant trade among each other, and trade-creating effects (both quantitatively and qualitatively) will be greater than trade diverting effects. In 1991, for example, a total of 71% of EC and EFTA members were within the European Economic Area. The share of the United States in Mexico's exports is 80% (*The Wall Street Journal Reports*, 1992). The effects of trading blocs on trade diversion and trade creation will vary on a case-by-case basis. As a rule, the bigger the initial trade flows between partners, the higher tariffs were before the arrangement and the lower they are after, the more likely is that the bottom-line effect would be positive (*The Economist*, 1992a). In the latter part of the 1980s, intra-bloc trade was growing at rates double compared to bloc members trade with outsiders (Finn, 1989).

THE DESTRUCTIVE ROLE OF BLOCS

Trading blocs are being used in policy discussion as one of the biggest threats to free trade (Lee, 1991). Large powerful blocs are seen protecting their markets against outsiders with restrictions on imports and investments. As a result country-specific inefficiencies will be transferred to the regional level to the detriment of global efficiency. Nations outside blocs, especially those reliant on markets such as the United States, might be seriously hurt in that their accounts may have been lost to Mexico, for example. Trading blocs are putting pressure on the GATT system itself to the degree that the system may collapse. Should that happen, the world could be without any all-encompassing structure to govern trade and investment flows.

The strongest argument for free trade, and therefore against any arrangements, is efficiency (Krugman, 1991). Even if regionalization is not accompanied by barriers against extra-bloc imports, the result may be suboptimal decisions. A bloc's industrial policy may promote and support investment in a sector which could not survive in a world without trade barriers (Weiss, 1992). The Lome Convention has allowed products special free entry into the European market from former colonies. This has created an inefficiency in that relatively expensive bananas from Africa get in duty free, while relatively inexpensive bananas from Central America are priced out of the market due to tariffs.

Trade flows will change if blocs gather strength during the 1990s. While European intra-bloc is vigorous, the same cannot be said for the Americas and Asia where intra-bloc exports account only for 42% and 31% respectively. However, NAFTA and the discussions on EAI have allowed nations of Latin America to take bold steps in liberalizing trade (Lord, 1992). This will most certainly mean increased hemispheric trade flows. Overall intra-Asian trade, both exports and imports, is expected to grow to 55% of the total by the year 2000, exporting more to itself than to its biggest trading partner, North America.

The status of present non-members is threatened; therefore, they are making moves to join blocs to ensure continued access to their main markets (for example, Latin American nations for the US market). The impact will not be positive for developing countries whose exports mainly go to the developed industrialized countries (for example, 95% for Africa). They will be the big losers should the GATT effort fail. In that case, they have to seek access to the blocs as a member or through some other method of gaining preferential treatment. Naturally, the ideal situation would be that for both groups the GATT's round success would guarantee them that access. Outsiders will be hurt even if there is no overt attempt to do so. Even those developing countries that are members of a trading arrangement (e.g., Economic Community of West African States), will suffer because intra-bloc trade is relatively small; typically no more than 15% of total exports.

One of the doomsday scenarios of the near future is a trade war. What makes this scenario possible is that trading blocs might feel a need to flex their muscles and match any retaliatory measure by another bloc blow for blow (Silas, 1992). Worst still, each bloc may feel that such a war can be won. Each has solid resources of capital and technology as well as considerable natural resources (or at least access to them). Furthermore, each has abundant labour readily available. The problem is that if such a process of protectionism is started, it is quite difficult to stop and reverse. An excellent example of this scenario is a trade dispute between the United States and Europe which has its roots in a 30-year agreement that the Europeans have not followed despite GATT findings for the United States. EC subsidies deprived US farmers of the benefits of negotiations in the 1960s in which the United States made concessions to get Europe to cut tariffs on oilseed imports to zero (*The Washington Post*, 1992). This example is alarming on two accounts: first, it shows the lack of authority of the GATT, and secondly, it indicates the willingness of the two big traders to start a trade war if necessary.

The economic effects of trade liberalization have been studied and modelled extensively. In one such attempt different results were obtained for scenarios varying from global liberalization to intra-bloc liberalization as well as to inter-bloc protectionism (Petersen, 1992). With a worldwide reduction of barriers, worldwide GDP would increase by 1% and world trade grow by 6%. If liberalization only occurred within the three main blocs, GDP would grow by 0.4%, trade by 3%. Should the blocs raise barriers between each other, gains would be negligible: 0.1% increase in GDP and 1% in world trade. GATT negotiators estimate $200 billion in world trade if the Uruguay Round is successfully completed (*The Economist*, 1992b). For the United States and Europe the failure of the GATT talks may not be a disaster: they can fall back on their substantial home markets. This fact may have hindered the political will to get the present round of negotiations completed. However, trade is one-fifth of the gross world product which means that major new barriers, be they protectionist blocs or attempts to manage trade, will have a negative impact on world welfare.

The proposed solution will not only strengthen GATT's resolve and authority but start acknowledging the potential challenge of the blocs to freer trade. For example, regional arrangements, such as a free trade area, could be allowed to set a common external tariff only at a level equivalent to that of the lowest level of any member state. This would minimize the trade-diversionary aspect of the new arrangement. Similarly, procedures used in managed trade, such as anti-dumping duties and orderly marketing arrangements, must be closely scrutinized and rules governing them strengthened. Bilateral deals typically have protectionist overtones, and what was supposed to have been a short-term solution turns into a long-term status quo (Waldmann, 1986). Without GATT, or with the present situation of GATT's rules being ignored, regional blocs may too often involve bilateral arrangements for political (especially domestic) expe-diency rather than concern for the bigger picture. But given that the present dead-lock situation is caused by the violation and ignoring of GATT rules, namely the EC's common agricultural policy, finding solutions may be difficult.

CORPORATE ROLE AND RESPONSE

The proliferation of blocs means that businesses will be facing ever-intensifying compe-tition and trading difficulties for sales to companies inside a bloc (*Business International*, 1992). Adjusting to these competitive pressures may mean adjusting to the emerging blocs but global corporations will also mould the shape of these blocs and how they eventually deal with non-members. Since it is the business firms that engages in inter-national commerce and investment, globalization of business may indeed be a signifi-cant determinant in how the world shapes up.

Corporations' investments are an important consideration in regionalization. On the one hand, investments are made in the various blocs to ensure continued access to the markets should protectionist barriers be erected. In a sense this necessity to be present in all of the three main trading blocs may foster inefficiency since investments are not made with objective optimization in mind (Stix, 1991). However, if trading blocs attract nations with similar consumer/customer profiles (and especially if the inter-bloc differ-ences are substantial), these investments do make sense from an overall business-development and customer-service point of view. Regional strategies may then, in turn, accelerate the convergence of the different markets that form the trading bloc.

Japan's potential leadership of an Asian trading bloc is determined more by corporate investment than it is by political decision. Japanese production investment in the ASEAN is increasingly integrated and complementary across borders. In electronics, for example, high-precision and high-value-added components are produced in technologi-cally advanced Singapore and then shipped to areas of cheaper labour such as Malaysia for assembly (Tanzer, 1990). This investment, in turn, has helped advance the economic fortunes of the ASEAN countries resulting, for example, in a dramatic growth of a well-to-do middle class. This technology transfer has helped Japan as well. Not only has Japan been able to move on to higher technology in its own production but it has also ensured growing markets closer to home, especially if the Americans and Europeans start erecting trade barriers.

Many companies may not have the resources nor the time to invest in all of the emerging trading blocs. To ensure future competitive capability, strategic alliances have been forged across national and regional borders (Ostry, 1990). For example, IBM has alliances with both European and Japanese computer and telecommunications giants such as L. M. Ericsson and Fujitsu. These alliances involve arrangements ranging from contract manufacturing to joint research and development. Corporate mergers have occurred across regional borders to guarantee access to blocs as local entities. For example, the major reason stated for the merger between US SmithKline and British Beecham was that the company wants to be as much at home in Washington DC as it does in Brussels (*Business Week*, 1990).

What impact will these corporate investments and alliances have on blocs and the threat that blocs are indeed basically protectionist? The 'stateless' corporation may be able to move production and investment wherever it gets its best return without concern for a particular country or a region. Technology has made such transfers relatively swift and quite painless. First of all, corporations and their assets can no longer be held hostage by a dismayed or ill-willing government or even a supranational organization. Secondly, it is becoming increasingly difficult to establish a product's national/regional origin which would make protectionist moves correspondingly challenging. Finally, the interdependence that is being formed by companies may also spill over in a major way to the national and regional level as well. As has been shown recently, tariff barriers erected against Japanese and European imports into the United States have ended up hurting US businesses as well. In 1991, IBM urged the US government to remove an anti-dumping duty that it had imposed on certain computer display screens imported from Japan. The effect of this duty was that American-built computers using this component became uncompetitive against models built completely in Japan. IBM has emphasized its argument by saying that it might otherwise be forced to move some of its production offshore (Weidenbaum, 1992).

CONCLUSION

While no one is questioning the potential benefits of worldwide free trade, many are resolved to having intermediate steps to get to the point. Much will depend on the completion of the Uruguay Round of GATT negotiations which were, at least at the end of 1992, stalled. The only positive sign beyond the fact that the remaining problems are indeed solvable is that GATT negotiators are already preparing for the next round of negotiations which would include issues of competitive policy and the environment (Vihma, 1992).

In arguing for eventual free world trade, the analogy to dancing may be quite appropriate: two steps forward, one step back to move ahead. Regional trade blocs may indeed be the only way multilateralism can be forwarded, especially if the GATT loses its power as an institution to promote the concept. The proposed three trading blocs will gather more countries around them through various preferential arrangements with some members working within two groups. The future superpower summits are not going to be on arms as were the summits of the past, but rather on trade and investment issues with three blocs negotiating for liberalization rather than over a hundred countries of different minds and sizes. In one sense regionalism may result in a step backwards, especially if blocs erect external barriers. However, the long-term benefit of liberalization of trade among more countries may be the two steps forward.

While nations are dancing, however, they have to keep in mind the ever-increasing impact that global corporations will have on their decision making. Interdependence has been woven into trade and investment flows at fundamental levels, the effects of which cannot be ignored.

REFERENCES

Brand, J. L. (1991) 'The New World Order'. *Vital Speeches of the Day*, **58**(December): 155–160.
Business International (1992) 'The New World Order: Regional Trading Blocs'. January 13, 1.

Business Week (1990) 'The Stateless Corporation'. May 14, 98–106.

Business Week (1992a) 'Building Free Trade Bloc by Bloc'. May 25, 26–27.

Business Week (1992b) 'The World's Newest Trade Bloc'. May 4, 50–51.

Czinkota, M. R. and Ronkainen, I. A. (1992) 'Global Marketing 2000: A Marketing Survival Guide'. *Marketing Management,* **1**(Winter): 37–45.

Czinkota, M. R. and Kotabe, M. (1992) 'America's New World Trade Order'. *Marketing Management,* **1**(Summer): 49–56.

The Economist (1992a) 'Building Blocs or Stumbling Blocs?' October 31, 69.

The Economist (1992b) 'Blink for God's Sake'. October 31, 70.

Far Eastern Economic Review (1992) 'Round and Round'. May 7, 70.

Finn, E. A. (1989) 'Sons of Smoot-Hawley'. *Forbes,* February 16, 38–40.

Hufbauer, G. C. (1989) 'Beyond GATT'. *Foreign Policy,* **77**(Winter): 64–76.

Krugman, P. (1991) 'The Move Toward Free Trade Zones'. *Economic Review,* **76**(November/December): 5–25.

Krugman, P. (1992) 'A Global Economy Is Not the Wave of the Future'. *Financial Executive,* **8**(March/April): 10–13.

Lee, S. (1991) 'Are We Building New Berlin Walls?' *Forbes,* January 7, 86–89.

Lord, M. J. (1992) 'Latin American Exports Change with the Times'. *The IDB* (September/October): 4–5.

Ostry, S. (1990) 'The Implications of Developing Trends in Trade Policy'. *Business Economics,* **25**(January): 23–27.

Petersen, C. E. (1992) 'Trade Conflict and Resolution Methodologies'. *Conflict and Peace Economics,* **82**(2): 62–66.

Schott, J. J. (1989) *Free Trade Areas and U.S. Trade Policy.* Washington: Institute for International Economics, annex A.

Schott, J. J. (1991) 'Trading Blocs and the World Trading System'. *World Economy,* **14**(March): 2–17.

Silas, J. (1992) 'Free Trade or Competing Blocs?' *Vital Speeches of the Day,* **58**(March): 299–301.

Stix, D. (1991) 'History Lesson'. *Forbes,* January 7, 89.

Tanzer, A. (1990) 'What's Wrong with this Picture?' *Forbes,* November 26, 154–163.

Thornton, E. (1992) 'Will Japan Rule a New Trade Bloc?' *Fortune,* October 5, 131–132.

Thurow, L. C. (1990) 'GATT Is Dead'. *Journal of Accountancy,* **170**(September): 36–39.

Vihma, P. (1992) 'GATT Kituu, Kauppablokit Nousevat'. *Talouselama,* number 11, 42–43.

Walldmann, R. J. (1986) *Managed Trade: The New Competition Between Nations.* Ballinger Books, Cambridge, MA, p. 71.

The Wall Street Journal Reports (1992) 'One America'. September 24, R1–R28.

The Washington Post (1992) 'Behind the U.S.—European Trade Wars'. November 6, A22.

Weidenbaum, M. (1992) 'Regionalization Versus Globalization of World Trade'. *Executive Speeches,* **6**(March): 16–19.

Weiss, J. (1992) 'Who's Afraid of Industrial Policy?' *Europe* (June): 28–29.

3

The EC '92 and Eastern Europe: Effects of Integration vs. Disintegration

Michael R. Czinkota

By the end of the 1980s researchers, business executives and policymakers alike began to believe that economic integration of the EC was sufficiently well understood, and its impact reasonably predictable. However, the revolutions in Eastern Europe have cast an entirely new light on the future of Europe. EC market integration and expansion will directly affect, and will be directly affected by, the mega-changes in Eastern Europe. Only by analysing the EC's impact on Eastern Europe can one speculate on alternative scenarios for the decade of the 1990s.

THE EMERGENCE OF WESTERN EUROPEAN INTEGRATION

For years Western Europe's economies characteristically had low GNP growth rates and growing unemployment levels. GNP growth rates averaged only 1.6% from 1979 through 1985.[1] Labour costs were increasing on a comparative international basis, manufacturing productivity gains were low, and the trade momentum was shifting to Asia. As a result, many observers decided to attribute a fatal case of 'Eurosclerosis' to Western Europe and discount its future as a serious global competitor. Unwilling to be written off, Western European voters abandoned their socialist governments. The new leaders decided to change Europe's apparent destiny by pressing ahead on the full economic integration of the EC.

In 1985, a white paper of the European Community proposed radical reforms which were to be implemented through 279 legal and regulatory changes by the end of 1992. These reforms aimed to expand the internal European market, harmonize regulations and government intervention, and tear down the barriers of red tape. In a sharp turnabout from previous policies, the removal of physical, technical and fiscal barriers, combined with deregulation, was expected to revitalize the dynamism, efficiency and competitiveness of the Western European nations. To the surprise of many observers and even some of the participants, important and rapid progress towards an EC '92 was achieved during the late 1980s. For the first time since Homer had introduced the term

Reprinted with permission from *Columbia Journal of World Business*, Vol. 26, Spring, pp. 20–27
© 1991 Columbia Journal of World Business

'Europe' to the world, the emergence of an economic and political entity by that name seemed possible.[2]

CONTINUED CHANGE IN EUROPE

In spite of an apparently successful transition towards European integration, a new picture emerged in late 1989. Instead of experiencing a stabilizing integrative thrust, Europe finds itself today amidst historic political and economic shifts, which are likely to have a significant effect, economically and geopolitically. The fall of the Iron Curtain, which within less than a year converted the Communist empire into a socialist league, raises entirely new issues for the EC with its 320 million consumers and $4.6 trillion GNP. Within a short year, Eastern Europe and the Soviet Union, with their population of 400 million and a GNP of $4 trillion, have begun to shift their political and economic orientation towards a market economy, and are knocking on the EC's door.[3] Currently, officials in Brussels negate any major effect of these developments on the integration of the EC 12. Public policy states the need to consolidate the base of the existing European Community before making any hasty moves. Realistically, however, the political opportunity of the moment, accompanied by fervent Eurocentrism and the vision of great shifts in geopolitics, makes it unlikely that the EC will pass up these developments. In any case the countries of Eastern Europe will be exposed to the effects of European integration.

The impact of European integration on Eastern Europe has been analysed by Alan M. Rugman and Alain Verbeke (1990), using the model shown in Figure 1. They classify the possible effects of integration into government-imposed entry barriers and natural entry barriers.[4]

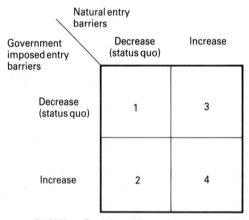

Figure 1. The Impact of '1992' on Outsiders. (*Source:* Rugman and Verbeke, 1990.[4])

Rugman and Verbeke developed their model in order to track the impact on individual corporations. Since Eastern Europe is only now beginning to familiarize itself with the concept of the privately-held firm, the analysis restricts itself to aggregate considerations of the Eastern European economies. Even though such aggregation runs the risk of blurring some important distinctions between the individual nations of Eastern Europe, it permits the better identification of major trends and directions which are likely to affect Eastern Europe. Secondly, Rugman and Verbeke confine themselves to the outward impact of the EC's integration. The Latin *actio reactio* is directly applicable to the relationship between an integrated Europe consisting of its current 12 member nations and the NEDs of Eastern Europe. Therefore, how changes in Eastern Europe are likely to affect the integration process within the EC itself must also fall under scrutiny.

GOVERNMENT-IMPOSED ENTRY BARRIERS

Looking at key alternatives, Eastern Europe and the EC clearly face two major scenarios. One consists of closer collaboration and, perhaps, integration; the other consists of separation, where the EC forms its own bloc and operates independently of Eastern Europe.

The individual Eastern European nations have made their intents clear. Hungary has already applied for associate status in the EC. Hungary has also put forward its candidacy for membership in other international organizations in order to demonstrate its commitment to working closely with the West. For example, at the May 1989 meeting of the European Conference of Ministers of Transport (ECMT), agreement in principle was reached to admit Hungary as an observer. Similarly, Poland has applied for membership to the same organization.[5] Romania began its reintegration with the West by subtly offering to assist the Western nations in the conflict with Iraq. Czechoslovakia and Poland have pronounced their desire for close collaboration with the European Community in order to develop market-based economies. In sum, the Eastern European nations have clearly and repeatedly indicated their preference and desire for close affiliation, if not integration, with the European Community of 12.

On the EC side, public enthusiasm for an integration of Eastern Europe with the EC appears less pronounced. Clearly, from an economic perspective, too many imponderables exist to allow sober economic planning for such integration at this time. However, the relationship between the two regions is only to a small degree driven by economic considerations alone. Taking the example of West German reunification with East Germany, political considerations were paramount. For example, carefully developed economic evidence pointed towards the unacceptability of translating the East German currency at a rate of one-to-one for the West German Mark. On July 2, 1990, the West German government decided to carry out such a conversion, due solely to political considerations.[6]

To some degree the European Community sees itself in the 1990s as a newly emerging world power, providing the balance to the already emerged trading blocs of North America and Asia. Yet it is unlikely that the EC will disregard the geopolitical dimensions of today. The threat of open conflict or social chaos in Eastern Europe, which is considered a possibility by some, and the effect of such upheavals on the stability of the European Community, will certainly be one important reason to encourage the route towards collaboration.[7]

The European Community realizes that the shouts and cries for democracy in Eastern Europe were not only driven by political, but also by economic factors. Freedom meant not only the right to free elections, but also subsumed the expectation of an increased standard of living in the form of colour televisions, cars, and the many benefits of a consumer society. To sustain this drive towards democracy, the fulfilment of the economic desires of individuals must at least appear to be attainable. Therefore, it is in the interest of the EC as a whole to contribute towards the democratization of the NEDs by searching for ways to bring about Western prosperity.

Of equal, if not greater, importance will be the drive by Germany to foster closer cooperation. Germany is the one country within the EC most deeply exposed to Eastern Europe. This exposure results not only from natural geographic conditions, but also from the historical responsibility towards Poland and Czechoslovakia still burdening Germany. Furthermore, the integration of Germany leaves the country with continued close ties to Eastern Europe through all those German individuals and firms which used to be in 'East Germany'. These ties not only result in the potential for collaboration, but also in an obligation to former Eastern European contracts which still need to be fulfilled. Germany's announcement that it will pay $8 billion to the Soviet Union in order to help relocate Soviet troops, combined with previous measures such as the extension of large credit lines to Eastern Europe, clearly indicates the country's willingness to bring Eastern Europe closer to the EC. Given Germany's major position within the EC, holding both political and economic weight, one is likely to encounter a major thrust for the lowering of EC government entry barriers for Eastern Europe.

NATURAL ENTRY BARRIERS

As stated earlier, the purpose of integration is to increase efficiency, productivity, and to confer specific benefits on firms operating within the European Community. Irritating delays at border crossings, multiple and time-consuming documentation procedures, differing safety requirements, and highly onerous transport authorization requirements were only some examples of the existing inhibitions to doing business within the EC. With transport activities alone representing more than 7% of the Community's GNP, an integrated market in which goods could flow freely will have considerable economic consequences for industry and trade.[8] On an overall basis, the gains from an integrated European Community have been estimated to amount to a total GNP increase ranging between 4.5 and 7%, or $230 billion in 1988 prices.[9] Clearly, such benefits may well increase barriers to outsiders, particularly Eastern Europeans.

In spite of the rationale developed earlier for governments, which indicates that governmental barriers are likely to be lowered towards Eastern Europe, the same cannot automatically be expected for the area of natural entry barriers. First of all, companies and individuals may not be in agreement with the governmental rationale. For example, a poll taken in May 1990 among West German managers found that 63% of the respondents considered the proposed European Community single market more important than German reunification.[10] Even more important, irrespective of the desire of individual firms or of the EC policymakers, is a growing system incompatibility between NED and EC countries that may develop a new dynamic. It is particularly this possible incompatibility among economic systems which raises the greatest concern. Therefore, differences between the EC and Eastern Europe need further analysis.

To stave off incompatibility, Eastern European countries are working extremely hard to introduce market forces into their economies. Repeated major austerity programmes have shaken Poland and significantly decreased the standard of living of its population. Yet support for the internal economic transformation remains. The Soviet Union has announced its 500-day plan, which calls for the privatization of 70% of all industrial enterprises and 90% of construction and retail trade by the end of 1991.[11] Major economic transformations and reforms are taking place in Eastern Europe, to involve these countries more in European and global economic relations.[12]

Yet, all the announced intentions for change do not automatically result in change itself. For example, the abolition of a centrally-planned economy does not create a market economy. Laws permitting the emergence of private sector entrepreneurs do not create entrepreneurship. The reduction of price controls does not automatically make goods available for purchase. It must be understood that there are deeply ingrained systemic differences in interests and values within Eastern Europe. Highly prized and fully accepted fundamentals of the market economy in the EC, such as the reliance on competition, the agreement with profit motivation, and the willingness to live with risk on a corporate and personal level, are not yet accepted or ingrained in Eastern Europe.

In order to carry out a systematic evaluation of the directionality of natural entry barriers, Michael Porter's model of determinants of national competitive advantage is helpful. He has identified four broad attributes of nations that shape the environment in which local firms compete and that promote or impede the creating of competitive advantage.[13] By analysing the different factors and their likely development in the short- and medium-term future, both within the EC and within Eastern Europe, it becomes possible to outline trends for natural barrier formation or deletion.

CHANGES IN COMPETITIVE ADVANTAGE

1. Local factor conditions

The first major determinant identified by Porter consists of local factor conditions. On the human resource side, the integration of the EC permits easier transfer of human resources. Clearly, this will assist the Community in employing those resources more efficiently. By comparison, the removal of the yoke of Communism is also likely to stimulate the human resources of the NEDs and encourage experimentation, specialization, and the individual's desire to improve his/her quality of life.

In regard to physical resources, the EC already benefits from a substantial existing base. Integration would bring them further potential for improvement. For example, physical resources were regionalized, but may now be available to the entire Community. The NED's physical resources, particularly in the areas of land and other natural resources, are widely available. However, these physical resources and their use must be seen in combination with their past abuse. For example, the major utilization of coal for energy generation, strip mining, and the disregard for environmental issues need to be taken together with the growing Eastern European awareness that there is more to quality of life than the financial standard of living alone. Therefore, it can be expected that in the immediate future, the use of physical resources will be reconsidered and that this reconsideration will lead to a decline in yield.

With regard to knowledge resources, the EC benefits from a significant stock of scientific, technical and market knowledge. Closer collaboration and concentration is likely to increase that stock. Eastern European knowledge resources are also substantial. For example, it is claimed that the USSR and Eastern Europe possess about 35–40% of all researchers and engineers working in the world.[14] At the same time, these knowledge resources are unequally distributed across the Eastern European countries. In many nations, worker elitism replaced intellectual elitism for more than four decades. Yet, given the increasing openness of these societies, it can be expected that the knowledge resources of the NEDs are likely to increase.

Capital resources, both physical and financial, are a major strength of the EC. The amount of existing investment, the capital available to finance industry and the new ability of capital to flow freely across the Community can be expected to vastly improve the competitiveness of EC firms. By contrast, capital forms one of the primary shortages within the NEDs. Even though major programmes are being designed to attract hidden personal savings into the economy, NEDs are relying to a large degree on attracting capital from abroad. Although NEDs are likely to suffer from a shortage of capital resources in the years to come, major inflows of investment capital and short-term financing are currently taking place.

The infrastructure of the EC, which includes the transportation and communications systems, health care systems, the housing stock and cultural institutions, is at a world-class level. The decrease of red tape is likely to improve infrastructural advantages even more. By contrast, the NEDs are suffering their greatest deficiencies in their infra-structure. Transportation systems, particularly those leading to the West, are either non-existent or in disrepair. The housing stock is in need of a total overhaul. Communi-cations systems will take years to improve. Market intermediaries often do not exist. Payments and funds transfer systems are inadequate. Major efforts are being gradually taken to improve the infrastructure in Eastern Europe. For example, the desire of the Soviet Union to obtain fibre optic telephone lines, or Hungary's attempt to upgrade its telephone network, are evidence of concrete improvements. However, infrastructural shortcomings will impede the NEDs for years to come.

2. Demand conditions

According to Porter, demand conditions are a second major determinant. He postulates that the existence of strong market segments with a high demand for products, together with sophisticated buyers, greatly contributes to international competitiveness.

Regarding segment structure, the integration is likely to further strengthen demand segments. The free flow of goods and collaboration among nations will enable EC firms to benefit from economies of scale and lead to a strengthening of industries which respond to large segment demands. In the NEDs, on the other hand, demand conditions are very heavy. Yet these demands are distributed over a wide array of industries and products and are unlikely in the short-term to confer major benefits on local industries. Furthermore, the extremely limited availability of accurate market information makes a correct and detailed assessment of short-term demand very unlikely.

The nature of buyers within the EC is very sophisticated. Customers are capable of making informed decisions, understanding market development, and exploiting the inherent dynamics of a competitive system. Buyers in the NEDs, in turn, suffer from great shortcomings. In many instances, they have never been exposed to the problem of decision-making, their preferences are ill-formed and they are therefore poorly trained to make market choices.[15] As a result, they are unlikely to pressure local firms, forcing them to offer high levels of quality or service. For the immediate future, the pent-up demand is much more likely to respond to product availability than to product sophistication.

3. Related and supporting industries

A third major determinant consists of the presence of related and supporting industries. Porter postulates that high-powered supplier industries or related industries will encourage innovation and competitiveness.

In the European Community, high-quality industries do exist. The integration is likely to bring about even more mutual reinforcement for excellence in quality than is already present. Therefore, this determinant is likely to strengthen in an integrated community. The NEDs, however, have not benefited from past developments of such support industries. Specialization demands of the COMECON system, together with the rigidity of the governmental plan, neglected to develop these interlinkages between industries. Even in an era of blossoming entrepreneurship, it is unlikely that such linkages will develop rapidly. Rather, individual industries and firms are likely to fend mainly for themselves, without the ability to grow systemic development of complementary ties with supplier and related industries.

4. Corporate conditions

Firm strategy, structure, and rivalry form the fourth determinant of Porter's competitiveness components. Management within the EC is already well-trained, and is likely to grow even more sophisticated with integration. The goals of companies are mostly well-defined, and in many instances will be more refined with increasing exposure to larger markets. Management is well-entrenched and has a thorough understanding of business operations. The NEDs are increasingly finding their shortage of management expertise to be a major drawback. In the past, management mainly consisted of skilful manoeuvring within the allocation process. The planned economies, for example, required that firms request tools seven years in advance. Ordering was done haphazardly, since requested quantities were always reduced, and surplus allocations could always be traded with other firms. The driving mechanism for management was therefore not a responsiveness to existing needs, but rather plan fulfilment achieved with a finely-honed allocation mentality.[16]

In addition, many of the former 'managers' in Eastern Europe have either left their posts or been forced to leave by the employees. As a result, there is a general management gap within Eastern Europe. Since most of these countries did not value, nor demand, market-related management for the past five decades, it will be difficult to fill this void. Even though major efforts are underway to obtain managerial training (for example, the Economic University of Budapest has formed an International Management Centre to train new managers), this gap, particularly at senior levels, is unlikely to be closed soon.[17] The changeover from a planned system to a market economy is therefore likely to make this gap much more apparent in the next years than it was in the past.

Commitment is a second major component of firm strategy. Firms in the EC have amply demonstrated in the past their willingness to put forth a sustained managerial commitment and are benefiting from a similar commitment from capital markets and employees. Few changes are evident in the degree of such commitment. By historical tradition, such commitment in the NEDs is virtually nonexistent.

In the past, plan fulfilment represented the commitment of the year. Capital markets never had to form or express any commitment, since capital was allocated. Employees are, to a large degree, still caught up in old work habits which consisted of never having to run a full shift. The notion of, 'They pretend to pay us and we pretend to work', is still very strong. The gradual dismantlement of the past policy of the 'Iron Rice Bowl' which made layoffs virtually impossible is reducing rather than increasing the commitment of employees. Since most firms also lack strategic orientation, it is difficult to build up commitment on the employees' side. As a result, even though there is a major drive towards the desire for the benefits of the market economy, its implementation is seen with great suspicion, rather than commitment.

Porter identifies that domestic rivalry is strongly associated with competitive advantage. Within the EC, this rivalry may be on the rise as borders fall. However, at the same time, large EC firms are increasingly aiming for a reduction of such vigorous rivalry by forming strategic alliances throughout the Community. Furthermore, the integration of the Community is unlikely to materially alter the regional activities of smaller firms. Therefore, domestic rivalry may be on the decrease in EC '92. Within NEDs, domestic rivalry among firms is only now beginning to blossom, since central planning never permitted such competition.

New business formations appear to be slowing down in the EC. Currently, the trend seems to be in the direction of consolidation rather than new formation. By contrast, in the NEDs business formations are the new lifeblood of the economies. Many individuals wish, at least for the time being, to try out their entrepreneurial skills. It appears, therefore, that new business formations will strongly increase within Eastern Europe.

5. Government

Finally, Porter ascribes that governments will influence the other four determinants. EC governments and their bureaucracies have lengthy experience in working with their economies and inducing change for key economic variables. By contrast, most governments in the NEDs, particularly their elected officials, are new to the task of governing and have either very limited or no experience at all. The litmus test applied for individual appointments or electability of representatives often consists of non-membership in the Communist party apparatus, or of 'Where were you?' during significant political events such as the 1968 invasion of Czechoslovakia or the 1956 revolution in Hungary. This lack of experience, together with all the other shortcomings listed above, indicates that the ability of Eastern European governments to successfully shape the key competitive determinants is much lower than in the EC.

Table 1 compares the determinants of national advantage between the EC and the

Table 1. Determinants of national advantage: a comparison

	EC	NEDs
Factor conditions		
Human resources	+	+
Physical resources	+	−
Knowledge resources	+	+
Capital resources	+	+
Infrastructure	+	−
Demand conditions		
Segment structure	+	−
Nature of buyers	+	−
Related and supporting industries		
Supplier industries	+	−
Related industries	+	−
Firm strategy, structure and rivalry		
Management	+	−
Commitment	+	−
Domestic rivalry	−	+
New business formation	−	+

newly emerging democracies. As can be seen, the preponderance of the evidence seems to indicate an overwhelming advantage for the EC. As a result, it is likely that natural entry barriers, particularly in the short- and medium-term, will be increasing for the NEDs. Coming back to the concept developed by Rugman and Verbeke it can be expected that Eastern Europe will fall in quadrant three, consisting of an environment with lower government barriers and higher natural entry barriers.

Such a scenario is disheartening for Eastern Europe. This is particularly the case since Eastern Europe firms will not have the alternative, sought by many other outsiders of the EC, to participate in the benefits of integration through direct investment in the EC. Their intrinsic economic shortcomings, particularly that of shallow capital resources, will prevent such a development. The only option to enable Eastern Europe to escape from quadrant three is foreign direct investment by outsiders into Eastern Europe. Such investment would be accompanied by factor conditions, particularly on their management and resource side, which could counteract some of the NED shortcomings. It appears that this benefit of foreign direct investment has been recognized, judging by the frequent appeals of Eastern Europeans to Western investors. However, existing legal uncertainties, combined with property rights difficulties and the existence of old bureaucracies whose members still have deeply ingrained training to be less than helpful, creative, or forthcoming, inhibit such efforts and have made many foreign investors cautious.

THE IMPACT OF EASTERN EUROPE ON THE EUROPEAN COMMUNITY

The formation of the EC '92 will not just effect Eastern Europe. The EC itself will also be affected by the political and economic changes which have occurred in the NEDs. Some of these effects are already visible. For example, one key attractiveness of joining the

Community, on the part of the poorer countries such as Spain, Portugal and Greece, was the fact that a large transfer of resources and investment could be expected from wealthier countries, such as Germany. A European sunbelt of new industries was envisioned.

Today, most German resources are likely to flow into rehabilitating the economy of 'East Germany' since budget planners predict a need for $48–85 billion for 1991 alone.[18] Funds will also be required for investment in other Eastern European countries and for major transfer payments, which will continue to be made either in forms of direct funding or government credit and guarantees, in order to facilitate the withdrawal of Soviet troops and some stability in the Soviet economy. Since even Germany's capital base is limited, this reorientation of funds will dry up, to a large degree, the flow of funds to those EC members which had expected such a flow. Clearly, such change is likely to create discord within the EC.

Furthermore, individual EC members will be affected in different fashions by Eastern European developments. For example, those countries whose firms are investing in Eastern Europe will be more exposed to the threat of social chaos or the disruption in foreign production. Some members of the EC are likely to be more concerned about Eastern European development. Simple geography will also affect the orientation of individual country members of the EC. Proximity to political danger zones does matter, as do established ties and relationships. Differences in concern and in desire for action are likely to lead to disharmony within the Community. The developments in Eastern Europe are therefore likely to contribute to instability within the EC rather than to its stability.

CONCLUSIONS

It must be remembered that for the individual citizens of the EC, the support of regional integration and the sound coalition for open markets is predicted on the expectation that the result will be economic growth and reduced unemployment. In exchange for that hope, individuals are willing to trade in their blue and green passports for uniform red documents and to support sometimes onerous harmonization directives. If these hopes are not fulfilled, however, the popular sentiment may be quick to shift. Just as governments were voted into office to overcome the threat of 'Eurosclerosis', they can be turned out of office by the electorate. If the high expectations placed in the integration of the EC are not met, it is possible that individual attitudes will shift radically and that coalitions which are currently strong will fall apart. For example, if all the deregulation and barrier removal within the EC results only in major increases in efficiency without the commensurate market expansion, problems are likely to develop. This is particularly the case if all the freed-up resources do not find new places of productivity.

As desirable as the Eastern European developments are politically for the EC, these very same developments have thrust a major new burden upon the Community. The EC has little experience dealing with such a burden, nor are there adequate forecasting tools to predict the ultimate outcome. In spite of major governmental goodwill towards Eastern Europe, the EC faces some tough choices in '92. Concentrating on internal affairs will only, due to the increase in natural entry barriers, over time result in major disappointment and disenchantment in Eastern Europe. Such a development, in turn, brings with it the distinct potential for social upheaval and chaos. The EC must recognize that economic borders are just as divisive and perhaps even more painful than political borders.

The EC must therefore undertake steps which will incorporate Eastern Europe within the common European home, and conveys to Eastern Europeans many of the economic benefits of the Western world. A simple lowering of government barriers will be insufficient to achieve such a goal. The Community must actively search for ways to bridge the growing gap between itself and the NEDs through a reduction of natural entry barriers. This will require major programmes designed to alter the determinants of national advantage of the Eastern European nations and involve funding, training, investment, and technology sharing. Not doing so would result in a major human failure of the West and a major threat to the continued viability of the EC. It must be understood that instability does not just result from tanks, but also from the knowledge that the next-door neighbour lives in poverty-driven volatility.

NOTES

1. International Financial Statistics, International Monetary Fund, Washington, D.C., 1988.
2. Homer (1970) *The Homeric Hymns: The Hymn to Pythian Apollo* (Trans. by Charles Boer). Swallow Press, Ohio University, Athens, Ohio.
3. This GNP estimate is derived from the *1988 World Factbook* of the Central Intelligence Agency. More recent insights into Eastern European economies indicate this estimate may well have been overstated.
4. Rugman, A. M. and Verbeke, A. 'Corporate Strategy After the Free Trade Agreement and Europe 1992', Ontario Centre for International Business, working paper 27, March 1990, p. 11.
5. 'US Mission to the Organization for Economic Cooperation and Development (OECD)', outgoing telegram, July 2, 1989, p. 5.
6. The one-to-one conversation applied only to a capped amount per person. It was carried out in spite of major initial opposition by the Bundesbank in order to fulfil a publicly perceived pledge made earlier by Chancellor Kohl.
7. Sweeney, R. J. 'Outlook for the European Monetary Union: The Message from Eastern Europe', Georgetown University Working Paper, September 1990.
8. *White Paper of the European Communities*, Brussels, 1985, p. 29.
9. Cecchini, P. *1992: The European Challenge*, Wildwood House, Aldershot, 1988.
10. Allensbach Demographic Institute, West Germany, May 22, 1990.
11. Remnick, D. 'Gorbachev Shifts on Economy', *The Washington Post*, Thursday, September 13, 1990: A1, A30–A31.
12. Simai, M. *East-West Cooperation at the End of the 1980s: Global Issues, Foreign Direct Investments, and Debts*, Hungarian Scientific Council for World Economy, Budapest, 1989, p. 23.
13. Porter, M. E. (1990) *The Competitive Advantage of Nations*, The Free Press, New York.
14. Simai, p. 21.
15. Johansson, J. K. *Marketing, Free Choice and the New International Order*, Georgetown University, March 2, 1990, p. 10.
16. Maruyama, M. (1990) 'Some Management Considerations in the Economic Reorganization of Eastern Europe', *Academy of Management Executive*, **4**(2), 90–91.
17. Batki M. (1989) 'East Bloc Meets Mysterious West'. *U.S. News and World Report*, July 31, 42.
18. Hoffman, W. (1990) 'Wechsel auf Deutschland' (Bill of Exchange for Germany), *Die Zeit*, No. 37, September 14, 9–10.

4

Global Neighbours: Poor Relations

Michael R. Czinkota

We are witnessing historic changes in global relations in the 1990s. The new greeting in Washington is Shalom-Salaam, the North American Free Trade accord is becoming a reality, and the disparate nations of Europe are uniting more strongly than under Charlemagne's reign.

However, as the rest of the world leans toward peace, cooperation, and market expansion, friction increasingly mars US–Japanese relations. Critics wallow in the alleged economic dangers that Japan poses to world trade and accuse it of striving for world dominance. Highly public accusations ricochet across the Pacific, many going beyond economic analysis and pandering to fear.

In opinion polls, more than two-thirds of Americans say that they regard Japan as more threatening than the former Soviet Union. *The Washington Post* reports that 63% of US consumers claim they make an effort to avoid buying Japanese products. Cities have cancelled contracts with Japanese firms, and baseball fans vehemently protested Nintendo's purchase of the Seattle Mariners.

This divisiveness cannot continue. Society is preoccupied with issues such as air and water pollution, global warming, ecosystem maintenance, new diseases, major local conflicts, increases in world armament, and sudden shifts in the world's energy supply. Even industrialized nations face problems such as stagnant demand and rising unemployment. We are coming to recognize that no country can successfully address and resolve these issues alone. We must, therefore, find ways to collaborate.

Improving the US–Japanese trade relationship is key to fostering such collaboration. As US Ambassador to Japan Walter Mondale stated during his confirmation hearings, 'Constant trade friction weakens public support in both the United States and Japan for our alliance, and it threatens our ability to cooperate on a broader agenda'.

With the demise of the Soviet empire, Japan and the United States have lost much of their former commonality of purpose. The dramatic changes sweeping through Eastern Europe and the former Soviet Union since 1988 have vanquished a major threat that previously tied the two countries closely together. Now that Japan and the United States aren't seeing red any more, both are trying to decide how much or whether they still need each other.

Close-up inspection without a mutual bond can be detrimental; it lets us discover the

Reprinted with permission from *Marketing Management*, Vol. 2, No. 4, pp. 46–52 warts and the flab without having the relationship. It's important that we find another common purpose that will build and develop the relationship on an elevated plane. And the former Soviet empire still can be the catalyst that moves us in that direction.

BILATERAL FOCUS

Some of the friction between the United States and Japan stems from the trade negotiations framing the US–Japanese relationship to date. Traditionally, negotiations have focused on foreign access to markets in Japan, a country which historically has tried to insulate itself from imports. Early on, the focus of General Agreement on Tariffs and Trade (GATT) negotiations was on lowering tariffs and reducing entry restrictions.

Although they were onerous and protracted, these negotiations did move a higher volume of imports into Japan. Because of simultaneous large increases in Japanese exports, however, trade imbalances have grown. As a result of the ever-widening US trade deficit with Japan, negotiations have gradually taken on a bilateral focus.

Sector-specific deals, self-imposed quotas, voluntary import expansions, and government-mandated imbalance adjustments now are emerging in these negotiations. Although some US companies and even some industries are boosting their exports to Japan, trade imbalances persist, and no matter what Japan-bashers say, even the most successful negotiations will not affect the domestic economy in any major way.

For example, the US government links $1 billion of US exports to about 19,000 jobs. The harshest among the realistic critics accuse Japan of 'rejecting' $10 billion of US trade annually. Therefore, even if the United States immediately increased exports to Japan by this unlikely amount, 190,000 jobs would be created at best. In the context of 8.8 million unemployed, the economic impact of such a trade shift on the United States would not be radical.

However, misleading demagoguery that continuously raises and shatters expectations produces broad-based resentment among the public that eventually may take on a political expression. The level of political discontent is rising in both nations, and the original road toward more liberalized trade may yet turn into a slippery slope leading toward managed trade.

A new, less traditional approach to trade negotiations seeks outcome-based changes in areas that historically have not been considered part of trade policy, such as distribution systems, business linkages, and savings rates. The key idea seems to be to make the market abroad more like the market at home. Even though Japan has asked for some changes in the US economy, these negotiations primarily smooth the way for US firms trying to do business in Japan. The Strategic Impediments Initiative, as put forth during the Bush administration, marked the beginning of such a direction; the current discussion of 'Structural Convergence Talks' may be even more wide-ranging.

Because of changes in Japan's domestic business environment and micro-managed, sector-specific trade performance criteria, policy makers expect to correct the trade imbalance at last. But, realistically, such an approach is likely to be limited to cosmetic gains, trying as it does to change deeply entrenched cultural values in Japan. A solution will continue to be elusive and the relationship will only become more troubled. And the approach could backfire if it triggers anti-US sentiment in Japan. This could imperil existing US sales to Japan and perhaps even motivate some Japanese firms to limit shipments of crucial components to the United States, thus leading to a direct confrontation.

REAL ALTERNATIVES

Some alternatives can lead to real improvement in US–Japanese trade relations. First, US measures should focus on information, collaboration, and human capital. For example, Americans do very little to learn about Japan and absorb widely available information. In 1991, only 1,180 US students attended school in Japan, whereas more than 30,000 Japanese students came to the United States. Unless we learn to observe and absorb Japanese knowledge and know-how to a greater extent, we will continue to be surprised by 'new' developments because we weren't paying attention.

In light of the knowledge explosion, the rising cost of research, and the increasing risk of investment, the need for corporate collaboration has never been greater. Contrary to current anti-trust legislation, such collaboration should be encouraged, particularly in areas of rapid technological change and substantial social need such as environmental safety, health care, new materials development, and biotechnology.

Companies should collaborate on both products and processes. For example, quality performance can become the focus of a cooperative effort throughout an entire industry and include manufacturers, suppliers, and customers at home and abroad.

US firms are trimming down, primarily by shedding personnel. But in many instances, this trend toward leanness means customers receive less and less service. With the demise of mass production and mass consumption, augmented service becomes imperative for global success. We need to instil a service ethic into our work force and managements that not only demands service, but also is prepared to provide it.

Japan's role

Members of the upper echelons of Japan's policy community recognize the need to increase Japan's involvement in world issues and in world imports. However, in shaping new trade relations, Japan's public sector can and must do more. As we have seen, rules and regulations that appeared to be immutable can change. As the vilification of the close business relations of the Japanese *keiretsu* gradually gives way to 'relationship marketing' in the United States, Japan is lifting the large-store law restrictions, agreeing to import large quantities of rice, and accepting the practice of discounting.

However, many obstacles to Japanese importation persist, such as closed supplier relationships, secret market sharing arrangements, and collusive bidding practices. It is incumbent on the government of Japan to address and resolve the inequities created by such practices aggressively. But reforms cannot be confined to the public sector; Japanese firms also need to overhaul their thinking.

For example, in Japan, it is considered a good thing for the individual firm to maximize its exports. yet, when the context is broadened to include political acceptability, repercussions by trading partners, and threats to international market access, such a narrow view of trade participation may be inappropriate. And the public as well as the private sector in Japan must understand that it is rationally and economically necessary to increase the inflow of products and services.

Some experts claim that *endaka*, the rising value of the yen, will resolve import problems in Japan by making exports dear and imports cheap. However, because intra-firm and intra-industry trade are rapidly becoming decisive determinants of trade flows, trade follows investment. US foreign direct investment in Japan amounts to roughly $23 billion. At the same time, Japanese cumulative investment in the United States is more than $87 billion. Unless direct foreign investment in Japan increases dramatically, trade frictions will continue. Making foreign investment growth possible must become a major priority for the Japanese government. It can provide information on and access to investment opportunities and offer an attractive financial and investment environment.

THE BIG PICTURE

The best way to resolve the conflicts between the United States and Japan is to emphasize multilateral trade relations within a new context. Take the science of astronomy as an analogy. More than two thousand years ago, Pythagoras and Aristotle, using the best available knowledge, came up with a geocentric view of our universe, where everything circled around the earth. It took until the 16th century before Copernicus and Galileo understood additional factors better and taught (with much inhibition) a heliocentric view, which recognized that the earth revolved around the sun. And only early in this century did Harlow Shapley again broaden our view by discovering that we are only one solar system rotating at the periphery of the Milky Way.

Today we are in a similar situation in our trade relations. During the 1950s, our economic view was strictly domestic-based. By the late 1970s, this perspective expanded to include a few key players one had to take into account. This view prevails today, most likely because the United States and Japan together account for nearly 40% of the world's GNP. But it's time to broaden this perspective. Companies and nations that adopt a 'galax-centric' view recognize that many other new, and not so new, players exist out there. And, like it or not, these players must be incorporated into our actions and considerations.

THE RUSSIAN CONNECTION

The entry of Eastern and Central Europe and the former Soviet Union into our world trade picture offers a new arena for US–Japanese collaboration—as a precursor to global improvement. The member countries of the former Soviet empire together have a GNP of about $3 trillion. Their traditional trade dependence was about $450 billion, with 60%–80% of trade carried out within the bloc. Today, trade within the bloc has shrunk to one-fifth of its former value.

Germany is a good benchmark for the region because its economic and political conditions provide the best possible scenario for adjustment. In 1992, capital transfers to the former East Germany amounted to $90 billion; in 1993, the amount transferred rose to $100 billion. Hans Tietmeyer, the new president of the Bundesbank, predicts transfers will amount to $1 trillion by the end of this decade.

Projecting these annual transfers of $6,000 per capita into the rest of Eastern Europe comes to $600 billion. For the former Soviet Union, the equivalent transfer amount would be $1.8 trillion per year. These numbers contrast sharply with actual government transfers which, on a worldwide basis, are less than $10 billion, and it is unlikely that public funds will ever exceed a very small percentage of the total funds required. The impetus will have to come from private investment and the retention of current funds (which, according to Yegor Gaidar, one of the economic architects of the new Russia, currently flow out from the Soviet Union at a rate of about $20 billion a year).

Private investors, however, will be interested only if they can expect an attractive return. The potential is there, but it can only be fulfilled through local production and trade. Given traditional trade dependence estimates, these new participants in world trade can unleash competition to the tune of $270 billion, or 5% of world trade. Although that may not seem like much, such competition is likely to be concentrated in the fields of light manufacturing, steel, agriculture, and textiles because of the competitive structure of the newly liberated economies. And these industries, of course, are the very ones already under heavy competitive pressure; they are the traditional sacred cows of industrial countries and developing nations alike.

Uninhibited trade flow of this magnitude with such a narrow concentration will bring about world production loss and unemployment that far exceeds anything considered in the current US–Japanese trade negotiations. It will have a major impact on employment and economic growth performance, particularly in light of the existing weaknesses in the global economy. But it is also here that major sources of future growth and market expansion lie.

Given these major inflows, nations will display their inherent tendency to erect barriers to these new trade streams. Yet, doing so will jeopardize world stability, because economic barriers are just as painful and divisive as political ones. Even if only a few countries erected barriers to free trade the onslaught of imports would force other countries to follow suit.

COLLABORATION AND COMPETITION

Multilateral collaboration can avert or at least reduce the threat of such market calamities. Such negotiations offer hope for new market opportunities and contribute to a better and more secure environment around the globe. Yet, collaboration is only part of the answer. Market access is a necessary but insufficient condition for competitive success. As Japan's Ambassador Kuriyama said recently in Washington, it is critical to combine collaboration with competition; after all, lack of competition brought about the collapse of the socialist system. But in order to pass on the competitive spirit, one first must foster competitive capability.

Both Japanese and US firms can make a difference in this area. Collaborative marketing is essential to build markets abroad and develop viable supply sources. The current political shifts in former Eastern Bloc countries signal the *beginning* of a process. The intent to change does not automatically result in change itself. Abolishing a centrally planned economy, for example, does not create a market economy; legislating to permit private sector entrepreneurship does not create entrepreneurship; lifting price controls does not immediately make goods available or affordable.

Deeply ingrained systemic differences between these restructuring economies and market values continue. Highly prized, fully accepted fundamentals of a market economy—such as the reliance on competition, support of the profit motive, and the willingness to live with risk on a corporate and personal level—are not yet accepted in these fledgling democracies. Managerial decision making is new and complicated, and because of the total lack of prior market orientation, even simple reforms require an almost unimaginable array of decisions about licenses, rules, and standards. Because knowledge of pricing, advertising, and research also is lacking, corporate responsiveness to demands is difficult.

Continuing pent-up demand, accompanied by lack of capital, means that product availability and financing matter much more in these countries than does product sophistication. Even buyers need education because they have never been exposed to the problem of decision making and their preferences are vague and undefined.

FILLING GAPS

All of these marketing shortcomings must be addressed, especially the gaps in logistics and distribution, which are key to successful competition. Both US and Japanese marketers excel in these areas, and their collaboration in transferring these capabilities to the new players can form the basis for a revised mutual relationship.

The total cost of distribution in both the United States and Japan is running close to 11% of GNP. By 1995, experts predict that 40% of shipments in US companies will be under a just-in-time/quick response regime. In contrast, eastern Europe and the former Soviet Union are just beginning to learn about the rhythm of demand and the need to bring supply in line with it.

These countries are battling space constraints, poor supply lines, nonexistent distribution and service centres, limited rolling stock, and insufficient transportation systems. Producers know nothing about benchmarking, inventory carrying cost, store assortment efficiencies, and replenishment techniques. Only poorly understood are the need for information development and exchange systems, for integrated supplier–distributor alliances, and for efficient communication systems such as electronic data interchange. Distribution costs in Eastern Europe and Russia are well above 30% of GNP, and it will take a long time to develop responsive, consumer-driven systems. The United States and Japan can take several steps immediately to assist in overcoming these weaknesses.

Information assistance

Japan and the United States should form a council for distribution and logistics assistance that includes members from the public and private sector. On the public sector side, the council could benefit from the rich resources of military logistics. On the private side, membership should be drawn from architects, transportation planners, warehousing experts, logisticians, and distribution channel authorities.

This council can present proposals for streamlining and setting priorities for the distribution of existing products and services, as well as assist in establishing requirements for the merging, market-oriented output. Concurrently, existing programmes that fund visiting professors, lecturers, student exchanges, and expert programmes, should focus on the distribution and logistics theme. Furthermore, foreign commercial service staff members should be trained in the field so they can recognize and report on situations where assistance would be useful.

Implementation support

Portions of existing funding programmes should be dedicated to distribution and logistics. This includes funding through development organizations and international institutions as well as commercial transactions. For example, it is of only limited use to allocate funds to provide grain unless the grain gets distributed efficiently. Those who make large investments in telecommunications need to consider the communication/distribution linkages and incorporate specific ties between suppliers and customers at home and abroad.

In general, investment in services designed to improve the logistics infrastructure should receive at least as much encouragement and support as does investment in production facilities. An improved retail structure is just as important as a new bottling plant.

We all must recognize that unless the new players of the former Soviet bloc are empowered by integrating these distribution and logistics dimensions into their market orientation, they will not become part of the competitive marketplace of the West. Without such integration, economic friction will soon lead to political heat and destruction that will affect us all.

INSEPARABLE DESTINIES

Trade negotiations that stress competition and collaboration—with a focus on Eastern Europe and the former Soviet Union—will help create a new paradigm for US–Japanese trade relations. The current narrow view of our relationship must be broadened quickly to achieve positive results. The existing friction can be overcome more easily if we recognize how much more is at stake, living as we do in an era when major fissures are appearing in the parchment of the future writers of history.

The United States and Japan must work together as partners, acknowledging and respecting our differences and striving for global improvement. This must become a decade of collaboration and competition, the era of a galax-centric perspective which provides us again with a commonality of purpose. We need to begin talking with, not at, each other in order to achieve that elusive new world order in a way that is acceptable, tolerable and beneficial to all participants.

As President Clinton has stated, 'There is no more important bilateral relationship in the world than that which exists between the United States and Japan. Our two nations now share a fundamental interdependence, and our destinies have become inseparable.'

This inseparability is the trigger that will propel us beyond our narrow confines to joint action and elevate any measure of success to a new plateau.

Bridging the geographic and economic distance between Japan and the United States will converge our interest, bring us closer together, and give marketers in both nations the opportunity to perform in their areas of greatest strength: serving as agents of change, fulfilling needs, improving the standard of living, and enhancing the quality of life.

ADDITIONAL READING

Bowersox, D. J., Daugherty, P. J., Droege, C. L., Germain, R. N., Rogers, D. S. (1992) *Logistical Excellence*. Digital Press, Burlington, Mass.

Czinkota, M. R. and Kotabe, M., eds. (1993) *The Japanese Distribution System*. Probus Publishers, Chicago.

Krugman, P. (ed.) (1991) *Trade Within Japan: Has the Door Opened Wider?* University of Chicago Press, Chicago.

Report on Unfair Trade Policies by Major Trading Partners (1993) Subcommittee on Unfair Trade Policies and Measures, Industrial Structure Council, Ministry of International Trade and Industry, Tokyo, May 11.

Tyson, L. D. (1992) *Who's Bashing Whom? Trade Conflict in High-Technology Industries*. Institute for International Economics, Washington, D.C.

United States International Trade Commission (1990) *Japan's Distribution System and Options for Improving U.S. Access*. U.S. ITC, Washington, D.C.

5

A National Export Assistance Policy for New and Growing Businesses

Michael R. Czinkota

Exporting is one of many market expansion activities of the firm. As such, exporting is similar to looking for new customers in the next town, the next state, or on the other coast; it differs only in that national borders are crossed, and international accounts and currencies are involved. Yet, these differences make exports special from a policy perspective.

From a macro perspective, exports are special because they can affect currency values and the fiscal and monetary policies of governments, shape public perception of competitiveness, and determine the level of imports a country can afford. Abroad, exports augment the availability and choice of goods and services for individuals, and improve the standard of living and quality of life. On the level of the firm, exports offer the opportunity for economies of scale. By broadening its market reach and serving customers abroad, a firm can produce more and do so more efficiently, which is particularly important if domestic sales are below break even levels. As a result, the firm may achieve lower costs and higher profits both at home and abroad. Through exporting the firm benefits from market diversification, taking advantage of different growth rates in different markets, and gaining stability by not being overly dependent on any particular market. Exporting also lets the firm learn from the competition, makes it sensitive to different demand structures and cultural dimensions, and proves its ability to survive in a less familiar environment in spite of higher transaction costs. All these lessons can make the firm a stronger competitor at home. Finally, since exporting is only one possible international marketing strategy, it may well lead to the employment of additional strategies such as direct foreign investment, joint ventures, franchising or licensing—all of which contribute to the growth and economic strength of the firm, and, on an aggregate level, to the economic security of a nation.

THE EXPORT COMPETITIVENESS OF NEW AND GROWING BUSINESSES

Many see the global market as the exclusive realm of large, multinational corporations. It is commonly explained that almost half of US exports are made by the 100 largest

Reprinted with permission from *Journal of International Marketing*, Vol. 2, No. 1, pp. 91–101 corporations, and that 80% of US exports are carried out by only 2,500 firms. Over-looked is the fact that thousands of smaller sized firms have been fuelling a US export boom, which has supported the economy in times of limited domestic growth. A large portion of export shipments from the United States are for less than $10,000 and there are more than 100,000 US firms that export at least occasionally.

The reason for this export success of smaller firms lies in the new determinants of competitiveness, as framed by the wishes and needs of the foreign buyers. Other than in the distant past, where price alone was at the forefront, buyers today also expect an excellent product fit, high levels of corporate responsiveness, a substantial service orientation, and high corporate commitment. New and growing firms stack up well on all these dimensions compared to their larger brethren and may even have a competitive advantage.

Take the issue of product fit. In today's era of niche marketing, where specialization rather than mass production is prized, the customization of operations is often crucial. In a large corporate system, changes are often subject to delays as various layers of management are consulted, cost recalculated, and multiple communication levels exercised. In a smaller operation, procedures can more easily be adopted to the special needs of the customer or to local requirements.

Smaller firms can offer clearer lines of accountability since the decision maker can be more visible and responsive to the customer. During negotiations, or later on, if something does not go according to plan, the customer knows who to contact to fix the problem. Smaller firms are better equipped to handle exceptions. Since international sales situations have high variability, either in terms of the time or the nature of the sale, a smaller firm can provide a more flexible framework for the decision process. Exceptions can be handled when they occur rather than after waiting for concurrence from other levels of the organization. Smaller firms offer their customers better inward and outward communication linkages, which are direct between the provider of a service or product and its user. The result is a short response time. If a special situation should arise, response can be immediate, direct, and predictable to the customer, providing precisely those competitive ingredients that reduce risk and costs.

Smaller firms also have the most to gain from the experience curve effects of exporting. Research by the Boston Consulting Group has shown that each time cumulative output of a firm doubles, the costs on value added decrease between 20 and 30%. Due to the small original base, it is much easier for a new or growing business to double cumulative output and reap the resulting benefits than it is for a large established firm. Most importantly, once a small firm goes international, it usually does so with the full commitment of the owner and top management. The foreign customer therefore knows that this is an activity which has management's heart and soul behind it. In today's times where we are moving, on a global level, away from the transaction marketing and toward relationship marketing, such a perception may be crucial in providing the winning edge.

COPING WITH OBSTACLES

All these advantages do not remove the existing obstacles to international market prosperity. Smaller firms in particular tend to encounter five types of export-related problem areas (Kotabe and Czinkota, 1992). One of these concerns logistics—arranging transportation, determining transport rates, handling documentation, obtaining financial information, coordinating distribution, packaging, and obtaining insurance. Another one consists of legal procedures and typically covers government red tape, product liability, licensing, and customs/duty issues. The servicing of exports is a third area, where the firm needs to provide parts availability, repair service, and technical advice. Sales promotion is a fourth area; firms need to cope with advertising, sales effort, and the obtaining of marketing information. The fifth problem area concerns foreign market intelligence, which covers information on the location of markets, trade restrictions, and competition overseas.

These obstacles, both real and perceived, often prevent firms from exporting. Many managers often see only the risks involved in exporting rather than the opportunities that the international market can present. As a result, the United States still under-exports when compared to other nations. US merchandise exports from only 7.5% of GNP, compared to 24.1% for Germany and 23% for Canada. On a per capita basis, the United Kingdom exported in 1992 $3,250 for every man, woman, and child. The figure for Japan is $2,660; for the United States, it is only $1,750. Given the plenitude of benefits to be derived from exporting, it therefore seems worthwhile and necessary to increase the export activities of US firms.

A PERSPECTIVE ON EXPORT PROMOTION

Even though exports are important, in times of tight budget constraints and competing public priorities, it is important to ask why firms should be enticed into exporting through the use of public funds. Given the motivation of business activity by profit, one could argue that the profit opportunities for exporters should be enough of an incentive to motivate firms to export.

The export development process

To explore this issue, it is helpful to understand the export development process within the firm. Typically, firms evolve along different stages to become experienced exporters (Czinkota and Ronkainen, 1993). These stages start out with a firm being uninterested in things international. Management frequently will not even fill an unsolicited export order. Should such orders or other international market stimuli continue over time, however, a firm may move to the stage of export awareness, or even export interest. Management will begin to accumulate information about foreign markets and may consider the feasibility of exporting. At the export trial stage, the firm is likely to fill selected export orders, serve few customers, and expand into countries that are geographically close or culturally similar to the home country. At the export evaluation stage, firms consider the impact of exporting on overall corporate activities. If expectations placed in exporting are not met, the firm is likely to discontinue its export efforts and either seek alternative international growth opportunities or restrict itself to the domestic market. If the evaluation is positive, the firm will, over time, move on to become an export adapter, make frequent shipments to many customers in more countries, and incorporate international considerations into its planning.

In each of these stages, firms have different concerns. For example, at the awareness level, firms worry mainly about information on foreign markets and customers. At the interest stage, firms become concerned about the mechanics of exporting. During the export tryout, communication, logistics, and the sales effort become key problems. At evaluation time, government regulations and financing take on greater importance. In the adaptation stage, service delivery and control are major issues. Figure 1 describes this export development process and summarizes these stages and concerns.

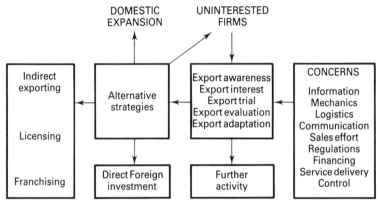

Figure 1. The Expert Development Process.

A divergence of profit and risk

As a firm moves through these stages, unusual things can happen to both risk and profit. In light of the gradual development of expertise, the many concerns, and a firm's uncertainty with the new environment it is about to enter, management's perception of risk exposure grows. In its previous domestic expansion, the firm has gradually learned about the market, and therefore managed to have its risk decline. In the course of international expansion, the firm now encounters new factors such as currency exchange rates and their vagaries, greater distances, new modes of transportation, new government regulations, new legal and financial systems, new languages, and cultural diversity. As a result, the firm is exposed to increased risk. At the same time, due to the investment needs of the exporting effort, in areas such as information acquisition, market research, and trade financing, the immediate profit performance may deteriorate. Even though international market familiarity and diversification effects are likely to reduce the risk below the previous 'domestic only' level, and increase profitability as well, in the short and medium term, managers may face an unusual and perhaps unacceptable situation—rising risk accompanied by decreasing profitability. In light of this reality, and not knowing whether there will be a pot of gold at the end of the rainbow, many executives either do not initiate export activities or discontinue them. A temporary gap in the working of market forces seems to exist. Government export assistance can help firms over this rough patch to the point where profits increase and risk heads downward. Bridging this short-term market gap may well be the key role of export assistance, and the major justification for the involvement of the public sector. Figure 2 illustrates this process.

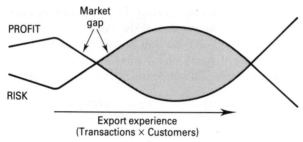

Figure 2. Profit and Risk During Export Initiation.

Linkages among assistance components

If export assistance and promotion are to be rendered, it becomes important to consider how budgets and efforts should be expended in order to be most effective. Figure 3 provides a structural perspective of the linkage between export assistance, the firm, the international market and, eventually, export performance. The firm is separated into its organizational and its managerial dimension. Organizational key determinants of business and export success are size, human and financial resources, technology, service and quality orientation, information system, research capabilities, market insights and connections, and the firm's capabilities to manage regulations. The managerial characteristics that research has most closely linked to export success are education, international exposure, expertise, international orientation, and commitment. These two corporate dimensions, subject to the opportunities and constraints of the international market environment, determine the degree of the firm's export involvement. This involvement in turn will result in export performance, which can be measured in three different ways. Efficiency refers to the relationship between corporate input employed and the resulting outputs achieved. Typically, efficiency is measured through the proxy of export profitability. Effectiveness refers to relative business success when compared to other competitors in the market, and is often measured in terms of market share and export sales growth. Competitive position addresses the overall strength of a firm arising from its distinct competencies, management style, and resource deployment. Typical indicators here are the overall quality and competence of a firm's export activities.

Export assistance can aim at the organizational characteristics and capabilities of the firm and try to improve those. It can also work with the managerial characteristics and contribute to their positive change. All this is subject to continued involvement on the part of providers of export assistance with the international market environment, both in terms of learning from as well as shaping the environment. Export assistance will be most effective when it either reduces the risk to the firm or increases its profitability from export operations, particularly when the stage-specific concerns of firms are taken into account. For example, providing information on market potential abroad is likely to decrease the risks (both real and perceived) to the firm. Offering low-cost credit is likely

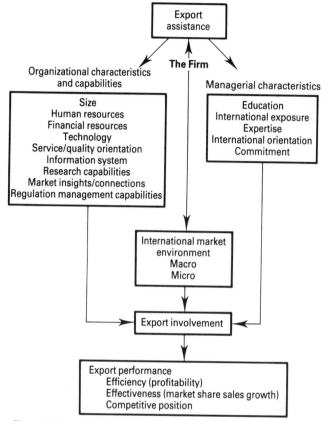

Figure 3. Export Assistance and Performance—A Structural Model.

to increase the profitability. Macro assistance in the foreign market environment can consist of international trade negotiations designed to break down foreign barriers to entry. Micro assistance consists of learning from the foreign market and its customers, and passing on that knowledge to enable domestic firms to adjust to that market.

An industry example

It is important to recognize the linkages between these efforts and the need for them to occur simultaneously. Otherwise there will be more results like the ones obtained from the US–Japan wood products initiative. In that particular case, which the author researched with the US General Accounting Office (US GAO, 1993), US trade negotiations with Japan were conducted for more than a decade, so that more US solid wood products could enter the Japanese market. High-level meetings, ongoing negotiations, government financial support, and industry demonstration projects were to achieve that goal. Japanese building codes and product certification procedures were changed and tariffs were lowered. The Foreign Agricultural Service spent more than $17 million to promote US wood-product sales to Japan. The result? Canadian lumber companies are the leading wood exporters to the Japanese market. There were only marginal increases in US exports and export-related jobs.

There are reasons for this outcome. US products were not tailored to the Japanese market. Japanese builders prefer post-and-beam construction, which requires 4 × 3 inch lumber and 3 × 6 foot modules to match the standard tatami mats that cover floors. But US companies were either unaware of those requirements or unwilling to meet them. Instead, the US producers focused on the standard 2 × 4 products used in the United States, even though only 7% of new homes in Japan use that standard. In effect, US negotiators and companies focused their energies on increasing the US presence in the smallest part of the market, rather than pursuing the biggest market. This focus was the result of trying to sell what is produced, rather than producing what foreign customers want to buy. In addition, some of the US firms that did enter the Japanese market did so with only limited enthusiasm and commitment. In contrast to the Canadian firms, many companies paid little attention to product quality and appearance and did not deliver after-sales service. Few firms translated their product information into Japanese or wrote manuals describing the new type of construction. Those US companies that did try to vigorously pursue the new market encountered major problems in obtaining information about specific market requirements. They also had trouble adjusting their production processes to meet Japanese product specifications and obtaining financing to pay for new equipment and larger export inventories. Without these resources, their efforts were severely handicapped.

In sum, a well-intended approach did not achieve its deserved success since the focus rested on the wrong opportunities, the needs of customers were not sufficiently taken into account, firms were unable or unwilling to adjust to market requirements, and the linkages between all these components were not taken into account.

SOME POLICY IMPLICATIONS AND ISSUES

Here then are some conclusions about the dimensions that should guide export assistance efforts, in particular where new and growing businesses are concerned. There are only six of them, but each one is equally crucial.

Clarity of purpose

Agreement needs to be reached on what export assistance is to achieve. Some of the objectives currently competing with each other are global fairness, the opening of world markets, and economic activity and jobs in the United States. Public funds are too scarce, as is our capacity to negotiate, and our capability to achieve negotiation success—to invest funds and government attention solely to right wrongs or for the sake of fairness. There needs to be explicit recognition of the fact that the times are over when the United States opened foreign markets simply for the well being of the world. Though it might be a delightful side effect to also see other nations' trade increase after the United States has broken down trade barriers, they key focus should rest on US employment.

Clarification is also needed for the time frame involved. Given a short-term orientation, emphasis on a temporary increase in the export sales of multinational corporations will be most desirable. A more long-term orientation will concentrate efforts on introducing more and new firms to the global market.

Tightness of focus

Export assistance needs to achieve either a specific reduction of risk or an increase of profits for firms. It should be concentrated primarily in those areas where profit and risk inconsistencies produce market gaps, and be linked directly to identifiable organizational or managerial characteristics that need improvement. Otherwise, assistance supports only exports that would have taken place anyway. Such a focus, of course, requires the implementation of evaluation criteria and measurement mechanisms, which determine the effectiveness of export assistance (Cavusgil, 1990; Seringhaus and Rosson, 1990). I believe that for policy purposes, such measurement should not be based on the firm's export performance, which is mainly controlled by the corporation. Rather, the measurement should be based on the export involvement of the firm, focusing on the number of customers, transactions, and countries served.

Coordination of approaches

Coordination must occur both within and outside the government. Within government, it will be crucial to set overall effectiveness priorities and to trade off export assistance programmes across agencies. Otherwise, an economic sector with relatively low employment effects could consume resources in an over proportionate fashion while priority industries would suffer from insufficient support. The fact that the agricultural sector spends about 74% of total federal export promotion outlays may serve as an example (US GAO, 1992). Externally, export assistance must be directly linked to domestic industries to ensure that the policy gains abroad can be taken advantage of by firms. Doing so must include collaboration for both product and process technologies, which now play a crucial role in attaining global competitiveness, similar to the much supported field of science. For example, the issue of quality performance can well become the focus of a cooperative effort throughout an entire industry, its suppliers and customers alike. Rather than concentrate only on the well entrenched industries, it is particularly important here to include a focus on sunrise industries.

Emphasis on strengths

Within government, export assistance should emphasize those areas where government can bring a particular strength to bear—such as contact, prowess in opening doors abroad, or information collection capabilities. Externally, programmes should aim at the large opportunities abroad. As far as firms are concerned, attention should not just concentrate on assisting or bailing out industries in trouble, but also on helping successful firms to do better.

Targeting of crucial factors

Export assistance is likely to have the greatest impact when it serves the needs of companies. Programmes therefore should start out by analysing the current level of international involvement of the firm and then deliver assistance appropriate to the firm's needs. For example, help with after-sales service delivery is most appropriate for firms at the adaptation stage; firms at the awareness stage worry much more about information and mechanics. Assistance must also take foreign market conditions and foreign buyer preferences into account, and communicate the resulting constraints and opportunities to domestic firms. It is easier to sell what is in demand.

Boldness of vision

In spite of the need to improve ongoing programmes, there should be a spark of boldness which goes beyond ensuring that things are done right, but checks whether one can do more right things. One could, for example, think about domestic and international efforts to set standards for technology and quality. One could go beyond products in such an effort and also include services and agriculture. One could even include the grading of enzymes, meats, hormones, and other products developed by biotechnology firms. There could be efforts to develop the domestic mentoring services of a senior executive corps to provide much needed international experience to new and growing firms. Or one could think about the development of a national forfeiting institution to be of major assistance in handling the financial and documentation aspects of exporting.

In a world of rapidly changing global realities, the future is shrouded in much uncertainty. Yet the likelihood of continued and closer global linkages and interdependence is high. Our firms need to be prepared for the global marketplace. If we can help them to grow and successfully meet the competition on foreign shores as well as on ours, we will have strengthened them and the nation.

REFERENCES

Cavusgil, S. T. (1990) 'Export Development Efforts in the United States: Experiences and Lessons Learned'. In *International Perspectives on Trade Promotion and Assistance*, eds S. T. Cavusgil and M. R. Czinkota, pp. 173–183. Quorum Books, New York.

Czinkota, M. R. and Ronkainen, I. A. (1993) *International Marketing*. 3rd edn. The Dryden Press, Fort Worth.

Kotabe, M. and Czinkota, M. R. (1992) 'State Government Promotion of Manufacturing Exports: A GAP Analysis'. *Journal of International Business Studies* 4: 637–658.

Seringhaus, R. F. H. and Rosson, P. J. (1990) *Government Export Promotion: A Global Perspective*. Routledge, London.

United States General Accounting Office (1992) *Export Promotion: U.S. Programs Lack Coherence*. Government Printing Office, Washington, D.C.

United States General Accounting Office (1993) *Agricultural Marketing: Export Opportunities for Wood Products in Japan Call for Customer Focus*. Government Printing Office, Washington, D.C.

6

Evolution of Global Marketing Strategy: Scale, Scope and Synergy

Susan P. Douglas and C. Samuel Craig

In recent years, issues relating to international marketing strategy have stirred increasing interest. To date, however, much of the discussion has focused on specific decisions rather than broader strategic issues. The inherent complexity and dynamic aspects of strategy formulation in international markets have frequently been ignored. Yet, a firm's strategic thrust and key decisions will change as it expands its operations overseas. The process of internationalization thus involves a firm moving through successive phases, each characterized by new strategic challenges and decision priorities.

Previous discussion of international marketing strategy has, however, tended to focus on the initial stage of entry into international markets. Often the perspective of a novice in international markets is adopted. Consequently, attention has centred on decisions such as the choice of countries to enter, the mode of operation to adopt, or the extent to which products or positioning can be standardized or must be adapted for different country markets (Cavusgil and Nevin, 1981; Keegan, 1969; Hill and Still, 1984). This latter issue in particular has attracted considerable attention and has been the source of much controversy in recent years (Levitt, 1983; Douglas and Craig, 1986; Douglas and Wind, 1987; Walters, 1986).

Emphasis on initial international market entry and issues of standardization were appropriate in the 1960s and early 1970s, when many companies, whether of US or other national origin, had only limited experience in international markets. Today, however, many companies already have operations in a number of countries. Consequently, the issues they face are infinitely more complex than those faced by companies contemplating initial foreign market entry. In determining the direction for future growth, the costs of expansion into new countries have to be weighted with those of expansion within the existing matrix of country operations. The extent to which operations are coordinated and integrated across countries and product divisions must also be determined in order to optimize the transfer of knowledge and experience, and take advantage of potential synergies arising from the multinational character of operations.

The key issues and strategic imperatives facing the firm will vary depending on the degree of experience and the future of operations in international markets. In the initial

Reprinted from *Columbia Journal of World Business*, Vol. 24, Fall, pp. 47–59
© 1989 Columbia Journal of World Business. Reprinted with permission

phase of entry into international markets, a key objective is the geographic expansion of operations to identify markets overseas for existing products and services and to lever potential economies of scale in production and marketing. Once an initial beachhead has been established, emphasis shifts to developing local markets and exploiting potential economies of scope, building upon the existing geographic base. In the third phase, attention shifts to consolidation of overseas expansion initiatives, and improved coordination and integration of operations to take advantage of potential synergies in multinational operations.

The purpose of this article is to examine each of these phases, together with their underlying dynamics, and the forces which trigger movement from one phase to another. The key issues and levers which characterize each phase are highlighted, and the implications for the formulation of global marketing strategy are discussed.

STRATEGY FORMULATION IN INTERNATIONAL MARKETS

An evolutionary perspective of internationalization of the firm has been adopted by a number of authors in the areas of international economics and international management. The theory of the international product life-cycle, propounded by Vernon and others (Vernon, 1966; Wells, 1972), identifies a number of phases in the internationalization process based on the location of production. In the initial phase, a firm exports to overseas markets from a domestic production base. As market potential builds up, overseas production facilities are established. Low cost local competition then enters the market, and ultimately exports to the home market of the initial entrant, thus challenging its international market position.

A number of empirical studies examining this theory have been conducted (Davidson, 1983; Hirst, 1967). These suggest that the theory provides an adequate explanation of US foreign direct investment in the 1960s and 1970s. More recent developments such as the emergence of global competition and integration of markets suggest, however, a considerably more complex pattern of internationalization.

In-depth studies of the internationalization process of several firms have also been conducted, focusing on their acquisition and use of knowledge about foreign markets and the growth of involvement overseas (Johanson and Vahlue, 1977; Johanson and Wiedersheim-Paul, 1975; Wiedersheim-Paul, Olson and Welch, 1978; Cavusgil, 1980). These studies suggest that the internationalization process is gradual, involving incremental commitments to overseas markets rather than major foreign production investments at a single point in time. These studies tend, however, to focus on the early stages of internationalization, and on the relation between information acquisition and market commitment, rather than issues related to strategy formulation.

The EPRG framework developed by Perlmutter (Perlmutter, 1969) also identifies four stages in the evolution of the multinational corporation, each characterized by different management attitudes and orientations. In the first stage, ethnocentrism, overseas operations are viewed as subordinate to domestic operations, and domestic performance standards are applied to overseas subsidiaries. The polycentric or host country orientation emphasizes local cultural differences, and evaluation and control procedures are established locally, with little communication between headquarters and subsidiaries. A regiocentric orientation focuses on regional organization of authority and communication flows, while a geocentric or global orientation aims for collaboration between headquarters and subsidiaries to identify standards and procedures which meet both worldwide and local goals and objectives. While this approach has been linked to different organizational structures and policies, it provides few explicit guidelines for strategy formulation and implementation.

Formulating strategy explicitly with regard to international markets is crucial for a number of reasons. Initial forays into international markets are often unsystematic and somewhat haphazard, resulting from an unsolicited export order from a foreign buyer, an order from a domestic customer for his overseas operations, or interest expressed by an importer or potential business partner in a foreign market. Consequently, it is important to establish objectives with regard to international market operations, especially in terms of the level of involvement and degree of risk as part of a systematic evaluation of opportunities worldwide. Otherwise, international activities will lack direction, resulting from creeping commitment and sporadic efforts, and will not necessarily be targeted to the most attractive opportunities for the firm in world markets.

Strategy formulation in international markets involves a number of key parameters whose nature and impact will depend on the phase in the internationalization process. These are shown diagramatically in Figure 1. At each phase a number of triggers will

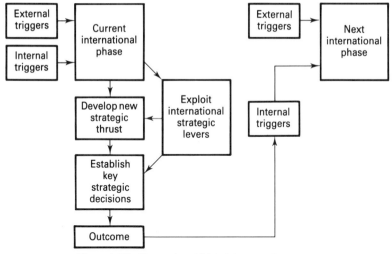

Figure 1. The Dynamics of Global Strategy Development.

prompt movement into a new phase stimulating generation of a new strategic thrust. The direction of this is channelled by the key international levers associated with each phase. Together these will define investment and resource allocation priorities, thus establishing the key strategic decisions and expected outcomes.

The triggers

The triggers which prompt a firm to move from one phase to the next are both external and internal. External triggers, such as environmental factors, or industry trends, or competitive pressures, cause the firm to reassess its current strategy. Internal triggers, on the other hand, are caused by factors such as internal sales and profits or management initiatives. Certain internal triggers, for example, declining sales volume, may be the result of external factors, such as increased competition from foreign firms. Also, firms may respond differently to the same set of external factors. Internal and external triggers may thus combine to generate the development of a new strategic thrust.

The strategic thrust

The strategic thrust determines the direction the firm will pursue and defines the arena in which the firm will compete, as well as its strategic priorities.

In international markets, defining the geographic extent of operations and direction for expansion is of critical importance. As noted above, this varies with the phase of internationalization. In the initial phase, emphasis is placed on geographic expansion, and hence the specific countries to be targeted must be determined. The subsequent phase is one of geographic consolidation, and hence growth within each country centers around expansion of product lines. This leads to rationalization of product lines across country boundaries, and the transfer of product ideas and lines, so that the concept of a domestic market disappears, and planning is formulated on a global basis.

Key international levers

The key strategic levers aid in further redefining the direction of the firm's efforts and determining the decision and investment priorities at each successive stage of internationalization. In the initial phase, lacking experience or familiarity with overseas markets, a firm will seek to lever its domestic position internationally, thus achieving economies of scale. This might, for example, be grounded in superior product quality or technological expertise, cost efficiency, mass-merchandising expertise, or a strong corporate or brand image. As familiarity with the local market environment increases, and a marketing and distribution infrastructure and contacts with local distributors and other organizations are developed, a firm will seek to lever these across a broader range of products and services in order to achieve economies of scope. In the final phase, a firm will try to lever both internal skills and environment-related experience, transferring learning across national boundaries, so as to take maximum advantage from potential synergies in multinational operations.

Strategic decisions

The firm's strategic thrust and the levers to internationalization together determine key strategic decisions at each phase of internationalization. In the initial phase, the key decisions centre on the choice of countries to enter, the mode of operation and the timing and sequencing of entry. Once initial entry has been successfully achieved, decisions at the next phase centre on the development of local market potential through product modification, product line extension, and development of new products tailored to specific local market needs. This typically results in the creation of a patchwork of local operations, and hence leads to the need to improve efficiency, and to establish mechanisms to coordinate and integrate strategy across national markets, allowing for the transfer and exchange of learning and experience, and leading eventually to the establishment of strategy relative to regional and global rather than multi-domestic markets.

Thus, in international markets, the strategic thrust, the key decisions and levers evolve with the degree of experience and stage of involvement in overseas operations. This is analogous to the product life-cycle concept (Day, 1981) where the key strategic imperatives vary with the stage of its evolution. While in practice this evolution is a continuous process, for the purposes of analytical simplicity, three phases may be identified, in addition to a preliminary phase of pre-internationalization: (1) initial foreign market entry; (2) local or national market expansion; and (3) globalization. (See Figure 2 which depicts the relation between the different stages.)

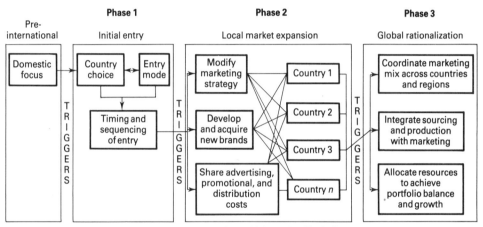

Figure 2. Phases in Global Marketing Evolution.

PHASES OF INTERNATIONAL MARKET DEVELOPMENT

Pre-internationalization

Prior to entry into international markets, the domestic market is the focal point of strategy development and defines the boundaries of operations. Strategy is designed and developed based on information relating to customer needs and interests, industry trends, and economic, sociocultural and technological trends likely to influence demand for the firm's products and services in the domestic market. Similarly, attention is centred on the strategies of domestic competitors viewed as major threats to the firm.

Although in some cases a firm may deliberately decide *not* to enter international markets, and concentrate instead on serving its domestic market, a domestically-oriented firm is likely to be inwardly focused with limited interest or concern for events outside its immediate sphere of operation. Often such a firm will be characterized by a certain lethargy and lack of dynamism, content to supply its traditional customer base with existing technology through established marketing channels. Such an attitude may well be tinged with a certain complacency, satisfaction with present performance and few ambitions to tackle new frontiers.

A domestic orientation may lead to lack of attention to changes taking place in the global marketplace such as new life-styles or target segments, new customer needs, growth of new competition, and the restructuring of market forces worldwide. A firm may thus be vulnerable to the emergence of new technology or the advent of foreign competition armed with a superior product or an aggressive marketing strategy. Such competitors may be quicker to respond to new challenges and opportunities in the marketplace. The failure of the US TV manufacturers to monitor developments in the Japanese TV market in the 1960s and 1970s, and to respond to the entry of low-cost Japanese TV sets into the US market by moving to low-cost off-shore production locations led to their ultimate demise (Rapp, 1973). As a result, Zenith is the sole US manufacturer with a significant share (12% of the US market) in the industry (*Business Week*, May 15, 1989).

Triggers to internationalization

A variety of factors may prompt the domestically-oriented firm to re-examine its position. (See Table 1 for a summary of typical events.) Trends within the industry or product market, in terms of demand and supply conditions, competitive developments or other discrete events may all open up new opportunities in markets abroad. Each of these factors, alone or in concert, may provide impetus for the firm to venture into overseas markets.

Table 1. Triggers to each stage of internationalization

Initial market entry	Local market	Globalization
1. Saturation of domestic market duplication of efforts	1. Local market growth	1. Cost inefficiencies and duplication of efforts between countries
2. Movement overseas of domestic customers	2. Meeting local competition	2. Learning via transfer of ideas and experience
3. Diversification of risk	3. Local management initiative and motivation	3. Emergence of global customers
4. Sourcing opportunities in overseas markets	4. Desire to utilize local assets more effectively	4. Emergence of global competition
5. Entry of foreign competition in home market	5. Natural market boundaries	5. Development of global marketing infrastructure
6. Desire to keep abreast of technological changes		
7. Government incentives to export		
8. Advances in communications technology and marketing infrastructure		

These include:

- *Saturation of the domestic market* resulting from slackening rates of growth or limited potential for expansion.
- *Movement of customers overseas*, stimulating interest in following suit in order to retain the account and supply customers more cost effectively.
- Desire to *diversify risk* across a range of countries and product markets.
- Identification of *advantageous sourcing opportunities*, i.e., lower labour or production costs in other countries.
- Retaliation to the *entry of foreign competition* into the firm's domestic market.
- Concern over keeping abreast of *technological change* in world markets.
- *Government incentives* such as information, credit insurance, tax exemptions.
- *Advances in transportation and communications technology*, such as the growth of international telephone linkages, fax systems, satellite networks, containerization, etc.

Any one or a combination of these factors may stimulate investigation of developments in markets overseas, and of opportunities for sourcing and/or marketing products and services in other countries and trigger initial entry into international markets.

Phase 1. Initial international market entry

The decision to move into international markets constitutes a bold step forward. It opens up new opportunities in a multitude of countries throughout the world and new horizons for expansion and growth. At the same time, lack of experience in and of familiarity with conditions in overseas markets creates a considerable strain on management to acquire the knowledge and skills necessary to operate effectively in these markets. Information relating to differences in environmental conditions, market demand and the degree of competition will therefore be needed in order to select the most attractive country markets, and to develop a strategy to guide the firm's thrust into international markets.

This step is especially crucial, since a false move at this stage may result in withdrawal or retreat from international markets. Mistakes made in initial entry can damage a firm's reputation, and be difficult to surmount. Renault's efforts to penetrate the US compact car market have, for example, been haunted by its early mistakes with the Renault Dauphine. Careful formulation of initial entry strategy is thus crucial in shaping the pattern of international market evolution.

Key strategic thrust

The firm's efforts are therefore directed toward identifying the most attractive market opportunities overseas for its existing (i.e., domestic) products and services. Attention is centred on pinpointing the closest match between the firm's current offerings and market conditions overseas so that minimal adaptation of products or marketing strategies is required. The guiding principle is to extend the geographic base of operations without incurring major incremental marketing or production costs, other than those required to obtain distribution.

International levers

The firm therefore seeks to lever its domestic competitive position and core competency internationally so as to extend economies of scale by establishing a presence in multiple markets (see Figure 3(a)). Given the firm's lack of experience and knowledge in overseas markets, it will focus on product or skill-related assets which can be levered internationally. These might include innovative or high-quality products, a patented process, a brand name, or other proprietary assets (Caves, 1982). In industries such as com-

(a) Scale Economies

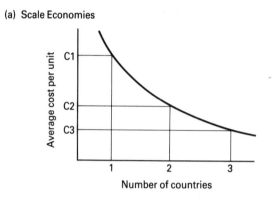

(b) Scope Economies

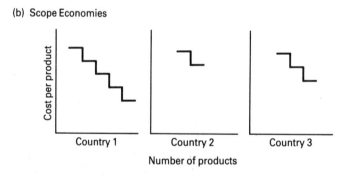

(c) Synergies

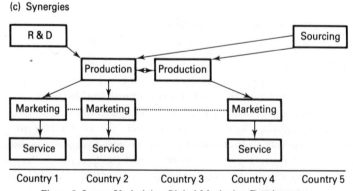

Figure 3. Levers Underlying Global Marketing Development.

puters and medical equipment, the success of many firms has been contingent on the introduction of products new to these markets. High quality price ratios, the outgrowth of superior production skills, have also been a key element in the penetration of world markets for consumer electronics and compact cars by Japanese companies. Patented processes may also be levered internationally as in the expansion of Xerox and Polaroid into world markets in the 1960s. In consumer markets, well-known brand names, such as Coca-Cola, Levis or Kelloggs, are often an important proprietary asset which can be exploited in overseas markets. Process skills such as mastery of mass-merchandising techniques and expertise in managing distribution channels may also be exploited in foreign markets. Such skills have enabled companies such as P&G and Colgate to outpace competitors in markets throughout the world, but are typically more difficult to leverage directly, especially in the initial stages of entry. Furthermore, they may require some degree of adaptation to local market conditions, and hence are less likely to be susceptible to scale economics.

Benetton, the Italian manufacturer of casual clothing, has been highly successful in leveraging its brand image worldwide. In 1978, the company realized $78 million in sales, 98% in Italy. By 1987, the company grossed $830 million with profits of $86.9 million throughout its worldwide network of over 4,000 independently owned retail outlets, in 60 countries, of which, 1,500 are in Italy, and 600 in the US. Not only is the Benetton image projected worldwide through the uniform design format of their clear open-shelved stores, and the use of the bright green Benetton logo, but also through uniform advertising campaigns such as the award-winning 'United Colors of Benetton' campaign.

Key decisions

In the phase of initial entry, the key decisions relate to:

(1) the choice of countries to enter,
(2) the timing of entry, and
(3) how operations are to be conducted in these countries.

While each of these decisions is discussed separately here, they are, nonetheless, highly interrelated. The mode of operation or entry, as well as the timing of entry will depend on perceived opportunities and risks in a given country. Similarly, the timing of entry may affect the choice of mode of entry.

Choice of countries. In choosing which countries to enter, risk and opportunities need to be evaluated relative to both the general business climate of a country and the specific product or service. The stability and rate of economic growth of a country have to be examined as well as the political, financial and legal risks of entry. Similarly, the size and growth of market potential have to be considered relative to the level of competition and costs of market entry. Often a trade-off has to be made between risk and return. Countries with high growth potential frequently also entail high competition or country risks or entry costs.

For the novice in international markets, the degree of familiarity or knowledge about a foreign market and its perceived similarity are often key factors in influencing choice.

Countries which are perceived as similar in terms of language, culture, education, business practices, or industrial development are viewed as lower in risk and likely to offer a more favourable climate for entry than those where the psychic distance is large (Davidson, 1980). On examining foreign investment patterns of US firms, one study found that close to two-thirds chose to enter Canada first and then the UK, though such choices were clearly not warranted by country size and growth potential relative to other countries such as West Germany or France. Similarly, Australia ranked considerably higher in investment priorities than its size would suggest.

Knowledge and familiarity with a country is often an important factor influencing perceived risk and uncertainty of market entry. Both objective information and experiential knowledge affect this uncertainty. Thus, proximity and prior contact or experience in a country will influence market choice. Swedish companies have, for example, been found to enter neighboring countries such as Denmark, Norway and Finland first, and more distant countries such as Brazil, Argentina and Australia last (Johanson and Wiedersheim-Paul, 1975).

Timing of entry. An important issue is whether to enter a number of country markets simultaneously, or alternatively, enter one country first, and then building on this experience, enter other country markets sequentially (Doyle and Gidengil, 1976; Davidson, 1980, 1982). A major consideration in this decision is the level of resource commitment required to enter a given market overseas. Given the lack of familiarity and experience in operating in overseas market environments, financial, managerial and other resource requirements may be significant, especially where an overseas sales organization and/or production facilities are to be established. On the other hand, simultaneous entry will enable the firm to preempt competition by establishing a beachhead in all potential markets, limiting opportunities for imitation. Potential scale economies arising from multiple market entry and interdependence of country markets may also be realized (Ayal and Zif, 1979).

Mode of entry. The decision concerning how to operate in a foreign market is closely interrelated with the evaluation of market potential and country risk (Goodnow and Hanz, 1972). A wide variety of modes of operating in foreign markets may be adopted ranging from exporting, licensing and contract manufacturing, to joint ventures and wholly-owned subsidiaries (Root, 1982). These vary in terms of the level of resource or equity commitment to overseas markets. Companies can thus limit their equity exposure by adopting low-commitment modes such as licensing, contract manufacturing or minority joint ventures in high-risk countries or those which are perceived as socio-culturally different, and, hence, unfamiliar operating environments (Anderson and Gatignon, 1986; Gatignon and Anderson, 1987; Root, 1982).

In the latter case, a company may prefer to enter a country in a joint venture with a local partner, who can provide knowledge and contacts with the local market. This strategy has often been adopted by foreign companies entering the Japanese market. For example, Wella, the German manufacturer of hair care products, initially entered the Japanese market in a joint venture with a manufacturer of beauty salon chairs. Subsequently, as it acquired greater familiarity and understanding of the market, Wella bought out the Japanese company.

Another important element in the choice of mode of operation is the desired degree of control and perceived significance of international operations (Anderson and Gatignon, 1986). Non-equity modes such as licensing or contact manufacturing entail minimal risk and commitment, but at the same time afford little control and limited returns (Contractor, 1985). Joint ventures and wholly-owned subsidiaries provide greater control and potential returns. Thus, companies which desired to retain a high degree of control over operations in entering the Japanese markets, for example, P&G, Scott, Bristol-Myers and Ore-Ida, have typically done so through establishing wholly-owned subsidiaries rather than joint ventures. Companies with limited experience and expectations with regard to overseas markets may also prefer low commitment modes (Bilkey, 1978).

The decision of how to enter a foreign market will also depend on the size of the market and its growth potential, as well as the existence of potential economies of scale and other cost-related factors such as local production costs, shipping costs, and tariff and other barriers. Markets of limited size surrounded by tariff barriers may be supplied most cost effectively via licensing or contract manufacturing. Where there are potential economies of scale, exporting may, however, be preferred. Then, as local market potential builds up and the minimum economic size is reached, a local production and marketing subsidiary may be established.

A firm may also benefit from certain scale economies and other advantages by internalizing or controlling overseas operations rather than contracting them out. These may occur not only in centralization of production, but also in sourcing, R&D, finance and capital asset management, etc. A firm with operations in two or more countries may, for example, be better able to establish large-scale distribution networks and achieve economies in transportation as well as in balancing production scheduling thus diversifying risk (Aliber, 1970).

The decision with regard to the mode of operation is thus often a key factor in determining the rate of international growth. It not only determines the commitment of resources and hence risk exposure in different countries and markets, but also the degree of control exercised over operations and strategy in overseas markets, the flexibility to adjust to changes in market conditions, and the evolution of operations in these markets.

Triggers to overseas market expansion

Once the firm has investigated opportunities overseas and started to establish operations in a number of markets, various factors will trigger a shift in emphasis toward the development of local market potential. The need to develop effective strategies to combat competition in these markets will result in reliance on local market know-how and expertise in local market conditions. The focus thus swings away from foreign opportunity assessment to local market development.

Some of the factors which may underlie this shift are:

- *Concern with increasing market penetration* and hence adapting or developing new products for the local market;
- *Need to meet local competition*, and to respond to local competitive initiatives in pricing and promotion;
- *Desire to foster local management initiative and motivation*;
- *Concern for more effective utilization of local assets*, i.e., the sales organization and distribution infrastructure, or contacts with local organizations;

- *Constraints imposed by natural market boundaries and barriers* such as transportation systems, media networks, distribution systems and financial and other institutions.

Such pressures lead to adoption of a nationally-oriented focus in strategy development. Planning again becomes organized on a domestic or national market basis, though this time in the form of a series of multi-domestic markets or businesses.

Phase 2. Local market expansion

Once the firm has firmly established a beachhead in a number of foreign markets, it will begin to seek new directions for growth and expansion, thus moving into the second phase of internationalization. Here, attention is centred on fueling growth in each overseas market and identifying new opportunities within countries where a base of operations has already been established. The expansion effort is, therefore, often directed by local management overseas in each country rather than from corporate headquarters.

The focus shifts toward penetrating local markets more fully, and building on knowledge, experience and contacts established in the initial phase of entry into overseas markets. Often local management is recruited, and responsibility for strategy development as well as day-to-day operations is shifted to the local subsidiaries, on the grounds that local managers are best qualified to understand the local market environment and to run country operations (Perlmutter, 1969).

Key strategic thrust

The driving force underlying this phase is thus market expansion within countries entered in the initial phase, rather than entering additional markets. Attention is directed to making product and strategy modifications in each country which will broaden the local market base and tap new segments. Product line extensions and new product variants may be considered as well as development of new products and services geared to specific local preferences. The emphasis shifts from 'export' of strategy and its direction from the domestic market base, to development of strategy on a country-by-country basis.

Internationalization lever

The major lever for effective expansion in this phase is to build strategy based on the organizational structure established in each country, in order to achieve economies of scope and to leverage assets and core competencies so as to foster local market growth. Attention centres on identifying opportunities for shared marketing expenditures, joint utilization of production and distribution facilities across product lines and product businesses (Teece, 1980, 1983). Administrative overheads may thus be spread across a higher sales volume, reducing unit operating costs (see Figure 3(b)). These may include not only sharing of physical assets such as production facilities, or a distribution network, but also intangible assets such as R&D knowledge or market familiarity (Wind and Douglas, 1981). The latter may be a particularly critical factor in this phase of operations. Often, the costs associated with initial entry into a country may be substantial, as, for example, in developing familiarity with market conditions and competition, and establishing relations with distributors, agents or regulatory bodies and officials. Consequently, it may be advantageous to amortize such costs across a broad range of products.

In addition to levering the organizational structure in each country, proprietary assets such as brand names, and specific skills such as technological expertise, may also be levered to expand the product line. The benefits accruing from a well-known brand name or company image may, for example, be further exploited by marketing new products or product variants under the same brand or company names. Swatch, the Swiss fashion watch manufacturer, has levered its 'chic' image in marketing a range of other products such as sunglasses, casual sweaters and clothing under the Swatch name. Similarly, a well-known company name and its reputation for producing quality, reliability and service, may be levered in the promotion of new products and product lines, either to end customers or to distributors.

Technological expertise and R&D skills may be applied to the development of new products geared to specific local market needs. P&G has levered its expertise in surfactant technology to develop liquid heavy-duty detergents such as Vizir and liquid Ariel adapted to hard-water conditions in Europe. Similarly, marketing and mass-merchandising skills may be spread over a broader range of product or product lines, or applied to the development of new product businesses. In some cases, brands or product businesses may be acquired from local companies. Thus, the firm may be able to capitalize on the 'goodwill' or customer franchise associated with an established local brand or local company, while at the same time applying its management expertise and marketing skills to operations management.

Key decisions

Concern with local market growth implies that the key decisions centre on the development of products, product lines and product businesses which offer promise of market growth in each country, as well as strategies to market them effectively in each context. This will, therefore, include not only adaptation and modification of products, but also the development and acquisition of new products and brands. Following the strategic thrust and growth levers, the key criteria in making these decisions are the potential for local market development and the realization of economies of scope.

Product modification and adaptation in order to expand the potential market base, for example, may be examined. In developing countries, machine tool manufacturers may consider streamlining and simplifying their products as well as rendering their use and maintenance easier so as to tap less-sophisticated customer segments. Nabisco reduced the salt content of its snack products and increased the sugar content of its cookies to meet local tastes in Japan. Similarly, Kentucky Fried Chicken reduced the sugar content in its coleslaw, and added fish to its menu in Japan.

Opportunities for developing product variants, extending the product line or developing new products specifically adapted to local market preferences may also be considered. Canada Dry has added a range of different flavours such as melon in the Far

East, orange, pineapple and bitter orange in the UK, and strong ginger in Japan. Heinz developed a special line of rice-based baby foods for the Chinese market, and a fruit-based drink for children called Frutsi for Mexico, which was subsequently rolled out in a number of other Latin American markets. Coca-Cola has also developed a number of products specifically for the Japanese market, including 'Georgia', a highly successful canned cold coffee drink, and Real Gold, an isotonic drink. Nabisco has developed 'Parfait', thumb-sized chocolate cupcakes for the Japanese markets, as well as Chipstar, a Pringles-type potato chip packaged in a tall can in two flavours, natural and seaweed.

Based on the economies of scope criterion, additions of new products or product variants within a country are especially attractive if they enable more effective utiliz-ation of the existing operational structure as, for example, administrative capabilities, the distribution network or the salesforce, or if they capitalize on experience acquired in operating in a specific market environment, or contacts and relations established with distributors, advertising agencies and other external organizations. As noted previously, such economies are likely to be particularly marked where there are substantial initial investment or set-up costs in establishing contact with distributors, or developing good-will among the trade in entering a country. In line with the strategic thrust, marketing strategies, including advertising, sales promotion to trade and end users, pricing and distribution channels are geared to local market development. Adaptation of advertising copy and development of new themes should thus be undertaken whenever the costs are outweighed by the potential increase in sales. Similarly, pricing decisions should be designed to stimulate local market penetration. This may, therefore, imply greater attention to pricing based on evaluation of price elasticities in local markets and prices of competing and substitute products rather than on a cost plus basis.

Triggers to global rationalization

The country-by-country orientation associated with this phase, while enabling the consolidation of operations within countries will, however, tend to result in market fragmentation worldwide. Overseas operations functioning as independent profit centres evolve into a patchwork of diverse national businesses. Each national business markets a range of different products and services targeted to different customer segments, utiliz-ing different marketing strategies with little or no coordination of operations between countries. The inefficiencies generated by this system, as well as the external forces integrating markets worldwide, will thus create pressures toward improved coordination across countries.

Some of the factors which may trigger this trend include:

- *Cost inefficiencies and duplication of effort* between country organizations;
- *Opportunities for the transfer of products, brands and other ideas* and of learning from experi-ence in one country to other countries;
- *Emergence of global customers* in both consumer and industrial markets;
- *Emergence of competition* on a global scale;
- *Improved linkages* between national marketing infrastructures leading to the develop-ment of a global marketing infrastructure.

Thus, once again both internal factors and changes in the external environment will trigger a shift in orientation and create pressures toward global nationalization. Attention will thus centre on the elimination of inefficiencies generated by a multiplicity of domestic businesses, and improved coordination and integration of strategy across national boundaries, moving toward the development of strategy on a global rather than a country-by-country basis. (It should, however, be noted that this does not necessarily imply standardization of products, promotion, etc., worldwide, but rather adoption of a global rather than a multidomestic perspective in designing strategy.)

Phase 3. Global rationalization

In the final phase of internationalization, the firm moves toward the adoption of a global orientation in strategy development and implementation. Attention focuses on improving the efficiency of operations worldwide and developing mechanisms for improved transnational coordination of operations and for integrating strategy across countries. Direction shifts toward development of strategy and resource allocation on a global basis. The national orientation thus disappears, and markets are viewed as a set of interrelated, interdependent entities which are becoming increasingly integrated and interlinked worldwide.

Key strategic thrust

In this phase, the firm seeks to capitalize on potential synergies arising from operating on a global scale, and seeks to take maximum advantage of the multinational character of its operations. Attention, therefore, centres on optimal allocation of resources across countries, product markets, target segments and marketing strategies so as to maximize profits on a global basis rather than on a country-by-country basis (Wind and Douglas, 1981).

A dual thrust is thus adopted, combining a drive to improve the efficiency of operations worldwide with a search for opportunities for global expansion and growth. Greater efficiency may be sought through improved coordination and integration of operations across countries. This includes not only marketing activities such as product development, advertising, distribution and pricing, but also production, sourcing and management. Standardization of product lines across countries, for example, may facilitate improved coordination of production, global sourcing, and the establishment of a global production and logistical system, thus resulting in greater cost efficiencies.

At the same time, development on a global scale becomes a key principle guiding strategy formulation. Opportunities for transferring products, brand names, successful marketing ideas or specific skills and expertise acquired or developed in one country to operations in other countries are explored. Global and regional market segments or target customers are also identified, and products and services developed and marketed on a worldwide basis.

Internationalization levers

In this phase, the key levers lie in exploitation of potential synergies arising from operating on a global scale. Skills or assets which are transferable across national boundaries such as production technology, management expertise, and brand or company image, for example, may be levered globally (see Figure 3(c)). While a similar type of leverage occurs in the initial phase from the domestic market to an overseas market, leverage across multiple markets has a synergistic effect.

Improved coordination and integration of marketing strategy across countries may also facilitate realization of potential economies of scale in production and logistics as well as the employment of skills and expertise which would not otherwise be feasible. Leverage may also be achieved through the transfer of experiences, skills and resources from one country or product business to another. Products or promotional campaigns successful in one country may, for example, be transferred to another, just as cash or profits from one business or country may be used to grow a business or compete aggressively in another country (Hamel and Prahalad, 1985).

Key decisions

Following the dual strategic thrust, key decisions focus on (a) improving the efficiency of operations worldwide and (b) developing a global strategy.

Improving efficiency. Efficiency may be increased by improved coordination and rationalization of operations across countries and between different functional areas. This may result in consolidation or centralization of R&D, production, sourcing, or other activities, thus eliminating duplication of effort as well as allowing for realization of potential economies of scale.

For example, in 1982 Black and Decker operated 25 plants in 13 countries on six continents. Overseas operations were organized into three operating groups, below which were individual companies which operated autonomously in more than 50 countries with little or no communication between them (Saporito, 1984). This led to considerable duplication of effort. For example, its eight design centres produced 260 different motor sizes. A global restructuring of operations reduced this number to ten.

Similarly, in preparation for 1992, Suchard, the Swiss packaged goods manufacturer, is rationalizing production operations on a European-wide scale. Production of individual brands is being consolidated in specific factories to gain manufacturing economies of scale. A plant outside Stuttgart and one in Paris were recently closed, and production transferred to plants outside Basel and Strasbourg. Other factories have been modernized and equipped with state-of-the-art automation and flexible manufacturing systems to drive costs down further (Friberg, 1989). Similarly, Electrolux has either closed or focused every factory it has acquired over the past ten years. It now manufactures all front-loading washing machines in Pordenone, Italy, all top-loaders in Revin, France, and all microwave ovens in Luton, England.

Scott Paper has also developed a pan-European approach for 1992 which encompasses not only production and logistics, but also marketing and financial operations. Plants in the UK, France, Spain, Italy and Belgium still supply predominantly local markets, since tissue and paper-towels are high volume/low price items where transportation costs outweigh gains from a high degree of production centralization. Brand names such as Scottex are, however, used throughout Europe (with the exception of the UK) and experience in product launches, brand positioning and advertising in one market are applied in others. Three new plants are being constructed in France, Italy and Spain, and will all use the same technology, thus allowing for the sharing and transfer of experience in plant management. Capital is now being borrowed globally, rather than being raised locally on a country-by-country basis.

In fact, opportunities for rationalization of production, sourcing and logistical systems are enhanced by product standardization across countries. Moves toward greater product standardization thus open up possibilities for increased rationalization upstream (Takeuchi and Porter, 1986). The Stanley Works, for example, decided to effect a compromise between French preferences for handsaws with plastic handles and 'soft' teeth with British preferences for handsaws with wooden handles and 'hard' teeth, by producing a plastic-handled saw with 'hard' teeth. The objective was thus to consolidate production for the two markets and realize substantial economies of scale.

Improved coordination of marketing strategies, such as brand names, advertising themes across countries and standardization of products and product lines, can be facilitated by the establishment of coordinating mechanisms between country management groups. These may take the form of coordinating committees which facilitate transfer of information and ideas across groups and are responsible for coordinating and integrating their activities, or the widely publicized Eurobrand teams developed by P&G, or regional marketing or sales organizations such as that established by Ford of Europe to direct activities within the region.

Global strategy development. In addition to improving the efficiency of existing operations, a global strategy should be established to guide the direction of the firm's efforts, and the allocation of resources across counties, product businesses, target segments and modes of operation worldwide. This should combine global vision and the integration of activities across national boundaries with responsiveness to local market conditions and demand.

A global strategy should determine the customers and segments to be targeted, as well as their specific needs and interest, and the geographic configuration of segments and their needs. As markets for both industrial and consumer products become increasingly international, opportunities for identifying segments which are regional or global rather than national in scope are on the increase. Thus, for example, Bodyshop targets its shampoos and body oils to those concerned with ecology and animal rights, desiring natural-based products not tested on animals, as is generally the case. In the advertising industry, Saatchi and Saatchi targets corporations with multinational operations, supplying services and meeting their needs worldwide.

Marketing programmes to meet the specified needs of these regional and global target segments also must be established. This will require putting into place the organization to implement the programme. In some instances, this requires establishing an organizational infrastructure which matches that of potential customers. Companies servicing the needs of multinational corporations may establish a system of account executives, with an executive specifically responsible for ensuring that the needs of a given client are satisfied worldwide.

Citibank, for example, instituted a Global Account Management System to coordinate world relations with large multinational corporations and develop its international business. Prior to this reorganization, clients were serviced on a geographic basis, i.e., by the country office in which they were located. Each country branch had responsibility for operations within its area, including both local companies and subsidiaries of multinational corporations, and acted as a local profit centre. This led to a number of problems, as local country management often preferred to lend to a local borrower than the subsidiary of a multinational corporation, as 'spreads', and hence profitability, were perceived to be higher and more likely to generate additional business. In addition, internal communications were fraught with difficulties, as client account managers in the US were not in contact or often even aware of their counterparts handling the client's subsidiaries in a foreign country.

Another decision is the appropriate mix of product businesses worldwide. Here, their complementarity in meeting production, resource or cash-flow requirements on an international basis needs to be considered. Thus, for example, Thomson has retained a semi-conductor business in France in order to supply its consumer electronic businesses worldwide. Similarly, BiTicino uses profits from its protected domestic light switch business to finance R&D for the development of its global fibre-optics business.

Effective implementation of a global rationalization strategy thus necessitates establishment of mechanisms to coordinate and control activities and flows of information and resources, both across national boundaries and product businesses (Ghoshal, 1987; Bartlett and Ghoshal, 1986). In addition, coordination with other functional areas such as production, logistics, and finance, will need to be achieved. Thus, in some cases, a radical restructuring of the organizational structure and management system, including lines of responsibility and communication, may be required to achieve globalization.

CONCLUSIONS

Strategy formulation in international markets is thus an evolutionary process, in which the dominant strategic thrust, the international levers and consequently the key decisions vary at each successive phase of involvement in international operations. The major strategic challenges facing the firm: how to transfer strategies and skills developed in response to local market conditions to markets overseas; how to acquire and build on local market knowledge and experience; and how to take advantage of potential synergies of multinational operations, will thus differ in each phase.

The dynamic character of international operations thus implies that strategic priorities should be tailored to the stage of evolution in international markets. Thus, rather than assuming, as is commonly the case, that the basic parameters underlying strategy formulation and specifically the key decisions will be the same for all firms, recognition that these will depend on the nature and evolution of international operations is imperative. Strategy should thus be formulated in the light of the firm's current position overseas, and geared to its vision of growth and future position in markets worldwide. The pattern of strategy evolution in international markets suggests a number of prescriptions for the successful formulation of global strategy.

In the first place, strategy should be tailored to the degree of experience in overseas markets. Thus, in the initial phase of international market entry, the firm's key strength is likely to lie in its existing (domestic) product line and attention should be focused on acquiring experience in marketing that line overseas. As this experience builds up, emphasis should shift to new product development geared to overseas market needs. Only in the final stages, once experience in both marketing and new product development for international markets has been acquired, should the more complex issue of strategy integration and coordination across country markets be addressed.

Secondly, potential economies of scale and scope should be maximized. Economies of scale may be realized through attention to opportunities for marketing existing product lines on a broader geographic scale, while centralizing production and sourcing operations, and extending management and logistical systems. Economies of scope, on the other hand, will be achieved through identification of opportunities for shared production, marketing and distribution facilities, and utilization of the same management and logistical systems by different product lines or product businesses.

Thirdly, marketing strategy, especially relating to product line decisions and product standardization, should be closely coordinated with production and sourcing operations. This establishes guidelines for the design of management, information and logistical systems to direct these operations. Effective coordination of key strategy components becomes especially crucial as the scope and complexity of international operations expand and improved global rationalization of strategy is achieved.

Finally, the ultimate goal of global strategy should be to achieve optimal integration and rationalization of operations and decisions systems on a global scale. Potential synergies arising from coordination and integration of strategy and of decision systems across country and product markets will thus be captured, and maximal efficiency in the allocation of resources worldwide achieved. Focus on the unique advantages provided by the multinational character of operations is thus the key to the formulation of a successful strategy in a global marketplace.

REFERENCES

Abegglen, J. G. and Stalk, Jr., G. (1986) 'The Japanese Corporation as Competition'. *California Management Review*, **28**, 9–27.

'Alain Gomez, France's High Tech Warrior'. (1989) *Business Week*, May 15, 100–106.

Aliber, R. Z. (1970) 'A Theory of Direct Foreign Investment'. In Charles P. Kindelberger (ed.), *The International Corporation: A Symposium*. Cambridge, Mass., 17–34.

Anderson, E. and Gatignon, H. (1986) 'Modes of Foreign Entry: Transaction Cost Analysis and Propositions'. *Journal of International Business Studies*, **11**, 1–26.

Ayal, I. and Zif, J. (1979) 'Market Expansion Strategies in Multinational Marketing'. *Journal of Marketing*, **43**, 84–94.

Bartlett, C. A. and Ghoshal, S. (1986) 'Tap Your Subsidiaries for Global Reach'. *Harvard Business Review*, November–December, 87–94.

Bilkey, W. J. (1978) 'An Attempted Integration of the Literature on the Export Behavior of Firms'. *Journal of International Business Studies*, **9**, Spring–Summer, 33–46.

Caves, R. E. (1982) *Multinational Enterprise and Economic Analysis*. Cambridge: Cambridge University Press.

Cavusgil, S. T. (1980) 'On the Internationalization Process of Firms'. *European Research*, **8**, November, 273–281.

Cavusgil, S. T. and Nevin, J. R. (1981) 'State-of-the-Art in International Marketing: An Assessment'. *Review of Marketing 1981*, Enis B. M. and Roering, K. J. (eds), Chicago: American Marketing Association, 195–216.

Contractor, F. (1985) *Licensing in International Strategy: A Guide for Planning and Negotiation*, Quorum Books, Greenwood Press.

Davidson, W. H. (1983) 'Marketing Similarity and Market Selection: Implications for International Market Strategy'. *Journal of Business Research*, **11**, December, 439–456.

Davidson, W. H. (1982) *Global Strategic Management*, New York: John Wiley and Sons.

Davidson, W. H. (1980) 'The Location of Foreign Direct Investment Activity: Country Characteristics and Experience Effects'. *Journal of International Business Studies*, **3**, Spring, 33–50.

Day, G. (1981) 'The Product Life Cycle: Analysis and Application Issues'. *Journal of Marketing*, **45**, Fall, 60–67.

Douglas, S. P. and Craig C. S. (1986) 'Global Marketing Myopia'. *Journal of Marketing Management*, **2**, Winter, 155–169.

Douglas, S. P. and Wind, Y. (1987) 'The Myth of Globalization'. *Columbia Journal of World Business*, Winter, 19–29.

Doyle, P. and Gidengil, Z. (1976) 'A Strategic Approach for International Market Selection'. *Proceedings European Academy for Advanced Research in Marketing*, Copenhagen, Denmark.

Friberg, E. (1989) '1992: Moves Europeans Are Making'. *Harvard Business Review*, May–June, 85–89.

Gatignon, H. and Anderson, E. (1987) 'The Multinational Corporation's Degree of Control over Foreign Subsidiaries: an Empirical Test of a Transaction Cost Explanation'. MSI Report No. 87–103, October, 1–41.

Ghoshal, S. (1987) 'Global Strategy: an Organizing Framework'. *Strategic Management Journal*, **8**, 425–440.

Goodnow, J. D. and Hanz, J. E. (1972) 'Environment Determinants of Overseas Market Entry Strategies'. *Journal of International Business Studies*, **3**, Spring, 33–50.

Hamel, G. and Prahalad, C. K. (1985) 'Do You Really Have Global Strategy?' *Harvard Business Review*, July/August, 139–144.

Hill, J. S. and Still, R. R. (1984) 'Adapting Products to LDC Tastes'. *Harvard Business Review*, **62**, March/April, 92–101.

Hirsh, S. (1967) *Location of Industry and International Competitiveness*, Oxford: Clarendon Press.

Johanson, J. and Wiedersheim-Paul, F. (1975) 'The Internationalization of the Firm—Four Swedish Cases'. *Journal of Management Studies*, October, 305–322.

Johanson, J. and Vahlue, J-E. (1977) 'The Internationalization Process of the Firm—A Model of Knowledge Development and Increasing Foreign Market Commitments'. *Journal of International Business Studies*, Spring/Summer, 47–58.

Keegan, W. J. (1969) 'Multinational Product Planning: Strategic Alternatives'. *Journal of Marketing*, January, 58–62.

Levitt, T. (1983) 'The Globalization of Markets'. *Harvard Business Review*, May–June, 92–102.

Perlmutter, H. (1969) 'The Torturous Evolution of the Multinational Corporation'. *Columbia Journal of World Business*, January–February.

Prahalad, C. K. and Doz, Y. (1987) *The Multinational Mission*, New York: The Free Press.

Rapp, W. V. (1973) 'Strategy Formulation and International Competition'. *Columbia Journal of World Business*, Summer, 98–112.

Root, F. J. (1982) *Foreign Market Entry Strategies*, New York: AMACON.

Saporito, B. (1984) 'Black and Decker's Gamble on Globalization'. *Fortune*, May 14.

Takeuchi, H. and Porter, M. E. (1986) 'The Strategic Role of International Marketing: Managing the Nature and Extent of Worldwide Coordination'. in Porter, M. E. (ed.), *Competition in Global Industries*, Cambridge, Mass: Harvard Graduate School of Business Administration.

Teece, D. J. (1980) 'Economies of Scope and the Scope of the Enterprise'. *Journal of Economic Behavior and Organization*, **1**, 233–247.

Teece, D. J. (1983) 'Technological and Organizational Factors in the Theory of the Multinational Enterprise'. in Casson, M. (ed.), *The Growth of International Business*, New York: George Allen and Irwin, 51–62.

Vernon, R. (1966) 'International Investment and International Trade in the Product Cycle'. *Quarterly Journal of Economics*, May, 190–207.

Walters, P. G. P. (1986) 'International Marketing Policy: A Discussion of the Standardization Construct and Its Relevance for Corporate Policy'. *Journal of International Business Studies*, Summer, 55–69.

Wells, L. T. (1972) *The Product Life-Cycle and International Trade*, Boston: Division of Research, Graduate School of Business Administration, Harvard University.

Wiedersheim-Paul, F., Olson, H. G. and Welch, L. W. (1978) 'Pre-Export Activity: the First in Internationalization'. *Journal of International Business Studies*, Spring/Summer, 47–58.

Wind, Y. and Douglas, S. (1981) 'International Portfolio Analysis and Strategy: The Challenge of the 1980s'. *Journal of International Business Studies*, Special Issue, Fall.

7

Global Strategy and Multinationals' Entry Mode Choice

W. Chan Kim and Peter Hwang

This paper is concerned with the critical decision of multinationals' foreign entry mode choice. While existing studies have already identified a diversity of variables that influence this decision, in our view these variables can essentially be collapsed into one of two categories: environmental or transaction-specific factors. Common to existing studies identifying these factors is their underlying assumption that each entry decision is made *in isolation* and is driven essentially by efficiency considerations at the level of the individual entrant or subsidiary unit. Recent works by Anderson and Gatignon (1986) and Gatignon and Anderson (1988) provide an excellent review and integration of existing entry mode explanations within a transaction cost framework.

Notwithstanding the central role environmental and transaction-specific factors play in influencing multinationals' institutional mode choice, this paper makes a case directed toward establishing the importance of a third group of factors—global strategic considerations—in determining the foreign entry mode choice. Specifically, it is our contention that beyond the subsidiary unit level considerations already established in the literature, it is also important to consider the role that the global strategic posture of a multinational plays, namely the strategic relationship it envisages *between its operations across borders*, in reaching its entry mode decision.

The theoretical heritage of our contention can be traced in part to the seminal work of Perlmutter (1969) which acknowledged the increasing existence of geocentric approaches to multinational management. The geocentric approach outlined by Perlmutter provided a succinct explanation for the existence of and benefits attached to managing subsidiary units not as a portfolio of independent units but as an interdependent network. The more recent foundation upon which our argument rests, however, is the rich body of literature on global strategy (e.g., Hout, Porter and Rudden, 1982; Hamel and Prahalad, 1985; Kogut, 1985a, b; Kim and Mauborgne, 1988; Yip, 1989) which has either explicitly or implicitly built upon Perlmutter's geocentric conception.

Though the specific global strategic prescriptions advanced throughout the literature vary (Ghoshal, 1987), they are identical in two fundamental respects. The first is that their overriding objective is unwaveringly overall corporate success, not the

Reprinted with permission from *Journal of International Business Studies*, Vol. 23, No. 1, pp. 29–53
© 1992 Journal of International Business Studies

maximization of each individual subsidiary unit's efficiency. The second is that in achieving this objective, interdependencies across subsidiary units must be actively managed. To illustrate, positions in one country market should be continuously leveraged against those in other country markets and hence subsidiary units may well be established and managed for very untraditional reasons such as acting as a competitive scanning outpost in an otherwise unprofitable market or sacrificing subsidiary revenue to check the cashflow of a potential global competitor.

Given that multinationals increasingly compete against one another in multiple markets where the strategic actions taken by a multinational in one market can have repercussions in other markets (e.g., Watson, 1982; Kim and Mauborgne, 1988), as argued herein, we believe that a multinational's global strategic posture has a major impact on its entry mode choice. Thus, as a recent work of Hill, Hwang, and Kim (1990) has argued, an express incorporation of global strategic variables into an analysis of the entry mode decision is an essential research task.

Accordingly, this research incorporates various corporate, global-level strategic variables into what has been termed an eclectic framework of the factors influencing the entry decision (Hill, Hwang and Kim, 1990); this framework consists of not only environmental and transaction-specific factors but also global strategic considerations. Unlike the pure conceptual work of Hill, Hwang and Kim (1990), however, this paper performs the important task of testing the framework at two different levels. First, we test the validity of the overall framework by examining the impact of the identified relevant entry mode variables *operated together* on the final entry mode choice. It is important to recognize that while each of the identified variables influence the entry mode choice, *it is the collective, simultaneous consideration* of all these factors that determines the ultimate decision. Second, we test the importance of each variable in differentiating among distinct entry modes; the aim here is to gain a better understanding of the relative importance of global strategic considerations *vis-à-vis* the other entry mode variables in determining multinationals' entry mode choice. Given the paucity of empirical research conducted at the firm level (e.g., Caves, 1982), such empirical examinations should make a meaningful contribution in advancing our knowledge of this topic beyond its largely conceptual state. Moreover, this study is the first to use firms' direct responses for an empirical investigation of this topic.

INTERNATIONAL ENTRY MODES

Of empirical interest in this paper are the three distinct international entry modes of licensing, joint venturing, and wholly owned subsidiaries. Although something of a simplification, much of the international business literature focuses on these three distinct modes and suggests that each of these entry modes is consistent with a different level of control (e.g., Calvet, 1984; Caves, 1982; Davidson, 1982; Root, 1987) and resource commitment (e.g., Vernon, 1979). Control here means authority over operational and strategic decision making; resource commitment means dedicated assets that cannot be redeployed to alternative uses without loss of value. A review of the literature (e.g., Hill, Hwang and Kim, 1990) suggests that while wholly owned subsidiaries can be characterized by a relatively high level of control and resource commitments, the opposite can be said of licensing agreements. With respect to joint ventures, although the levels of control and resource commitments admittedly vary with the nature of the ownership split, their extent can nevertheless be said to lie between that of wholly owned subsidiaries and licensing agreements.

THE INCORPORATION OF GLOBAL STRATEGIC VARIABLES

In an attempt to expand the existing entry mode analyses beyond the narrow confines of each entry decision in isolation, this paper considers the extent of: (1) global concentration; (2) global synergies; and (3) global strategic motivations exercised by the firm. This broader conception will allow us to expressly consider the strategic relationship a multinational envisages between its operations across borders in reaching its entry mode decision.

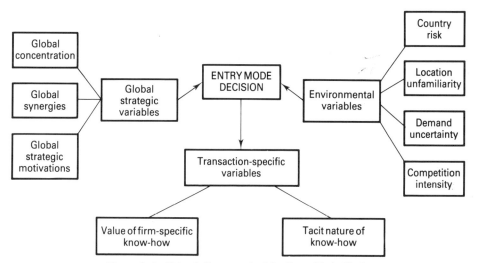

Figure 1. An Eclectic Framework of the Entry Mode Choice.

As shown in Figure 1, three groups of variables are believed to influence the entry mode decision. These are the global strategic variables highlighted herein as well as the already well-established environmental variables (host country risk, location unfamiliarity, demand uncertainty, and competition intensity) and transaction-specific variables (value of firm-specific know-how and tacit nature of know-how). Firm-specific know-how refers to knowledge that is proprietary to a given firm. Tacit know-how involves non-codifiable knowledge not embodied in physical items such as capital goods, equipment, and blueprints. Rather it is the information that must be obtained typically via consulting or advisory services for physical equipment or 'hardware' to be absorbed and utilized effectively by the firm (Teece, 1977). While we believe that it is the collective, simultaneous consideration of all three groups of factors that determines the ultimate entry decision, this paper argues that beyond environmental and transaction-specific factors, global strategic variables would play a critical role in differentiating among distinct entry modes.

In the following, we first discuss the effects of the three global strategic variables on the entry mode decision. We then briefly review the effects of the existing environmental and transaction-specific variables shown in Figure 1 on the institutional mode choice.

Global strategic variables

Global concentration

Increasingly, multinational corporations (MNCs) find themselves in industries that are characterized by a limited number of players who confront each other in many different national markets around the globe. That is, the global industry has become highly concentrated. In such industries, conditions of oligopolistic interdependence spill over national boundaries creating a high level of competitive interdependence among players. When global competitive interdependence exists, the actions taken by an MNC in one market often have repercussions in other national markets (e.g., Watson, 1982; Kim and Mauborgne, 1988). For competitive interdependence implies that organizations can influence one another not only directly but also indirectly in any of the diverse national markets in which they compete.

An example of this is the case of Michelin versus Goodyear. When the North American subsidiary of Michelin decided to expand its share of the North American tyre market it employed the traditional marketing tactic of lowering the price of its tyres. Such a tactic, it surmised, would attract new customers and most likely not be matched by its chief competitor, Goodyear, due to the significance of Goodyear's North American sales and the attendant non-trivial costs such a parallel move would impose on the North American giant. What Michelin did not anticipate, however, was that Goodyear could counter its move not directly but indirectly. Because of the oligopolistic nature of the global tyre industry, Goodyear was able to skilfully parry Michelin's tactic by dropping the price of its tyres in Michelin's profit sanctuary, Europe. This caused a non-trivial negative impact on Michelin's main cash source, causing the firm to retract its North American price drop and in effect rendering its marketing tactic futile and costly.

Given such global industry settings, it follows that MNCs may well be inclined to exercise a high level of control over foreign operations. High control enhances an MNC's ability to ensure that strategic actions taken by a subsidiary in one national market do not produce negative ramifications in other national markets above and beyond the expected gains to be made by a focal subsidiary's strategic move. At the same time, a high level of control enhances a multinational's ability to call on its subsidiary located in one market to assist in a competitive battle being fought in another market for the benefit of the overall organization, as exemplified by the actions of Goodyear. Altogether, this suggests the proposition that: *other things being equal, when the global industry is highly concentrated, MNCs will favour high control entry modes.*

Global synergies

Global synergies arise when the inputs of a multinational 'are shared, or utilized jointly with complete congestion' [Willig, 1978, p. 346]. By inputs we refer to the core factors of a multinational such as R&D, marketing, or manufacturing. Examples of multinationals levering core competencies in an effort to exploit global synergies abound. A good example of this would be Honda who globally levered its advanced engine technology in motorcycles to expand into the automobile, lawn mower, and snow-blower industry segments worldwide. Another example is that of Yves Saint Laurent who levered its prestigious global brand name in high fashion to expand into the perfume, cosmetic and recently cigarette industry domains across the globe.

The implications of global synergies with respect to competitive advantage have become increasingly clear; they produce a positive impact on corporate profitability (e.g., Hamel and Prahalad, 1985; Ghoshal, 1987; Kim, Hwang and Burgers, 1989). This is typically actualized through enhanced innovative capability or some form of cost reduction (Baumol, Panzer and Willig, 1982). For example, Honda's engine technology, once developed for producing motorcycles, was virtually costlessly available for the production of engines in the different capacities in which Honda exploited it across the globe.

Researchers (e.g., Jones and Hill, 1982; Harrigan, 1985a, b; Porter, 1980) have argued that the benefits of synergy, including economies of scope, increase firms' commitment to business units and can best be exploited through hierarchical control. Jones and Hill (1982, p. 161) argue that hierarchy is necessary as market-mediated exchanges aimed at the realization of synergies will typically be beset with hazards. The difficulty is this. To achieve synergies, inputs between transacting parties must be shared or utilized jointly. However, the very fact that inputs must be shared or utilized jointly makes it hard to sort out the unique contribution and performance of each transacting party. This presents a monitoring problem and hence creates room for managerial discretion. Absent internal organization, the very existence of managerial discretion tends to trigger opportunistic behaviour and the shirking of activities between independent transacting parties (Williamson, 1975); hence, the need for hierarchy. Altogether, this suggests the proposition that: *other things being equal, when the extent of potential global synergies between the extrant and other sister business units is great, MNCs will demand a high level of control in the foreign operation.*

Global strategic motivations

When MNCs enter foreign markets, especially their global contenders' home markets, they may have strategic motivations that go beyond the narrow calculus of choosing the most efficient entry mode; that is, they may have global strategic motivations (Edwards, 1971; Watson, 1982; Hout, Porter and Rudden, 1982; Hamel and Prahalad, 1985; Kim and Mauborgne, 1988). Examples of multinationals possessing global strategic motivations, which often go against economic efficiency maximization of a particular business unit, have become a common occurrence in today's reality of global competition. Such motivations for establishing a foreign business unit can range anywhere from setting up a strategic outpost for future global expansion, to developing a global sourcing site, to attacking actual or potential global competitors. Hence, global strategic motivation can be defined as motivation to fulfil strategic aims set at the corporate level for the purpose of overall corporate efficiency maximization.

To effectively achieve global strategic motivations, recent studies have argued the importance of tight coordination across global business units (e.g., Porter, 1986; Bartlett, 1986). Tight coordination is necessary for the effective and efficient execution of global strategic motivations, especially as their implementation often requires business units to 'sacrifice' subsystem gains for the benefit of the overall organization (e.g., Hedlund, 1986). That tight coordination is difficult to accomplish under conditions of coalition formation or licensing has been argued (e.g., Porter and Fuller, 1986); such agreements link a foreign entrant to other independent firm(s) with potentially different strategic motivations. Altogether, this suggests the proposition that: *other things being equal, MNCs exercising global strategic motivations will favour high control entry modes.*

Environmental variables

Country risk

When country risk is high, existing works indicate that an MNC would do well to limit its exposure to such risk by restricting its resource commitments in that particular national domain (Kobrin, 1983; Vernon, 1979; Bradley, 1977). Rephrased, other things being equal, when country risk is high, MNCs will favour entry modes that involve relatively low resource commitments.

Location unfamiliarity

Previous studies argue that the greater the perceived distance between the home and host country in terms of culture, economic systems, and business practices, the more likely it is that MNCs will shy away from direct investment in favour of licensing or joint venture agreements (Anderson and Coughlan, 1987; Davidson, 1982; Green and Cunningham, 1975; Johanson and Vahlne, 1977; Kobrin, 1983; Stopford and Wells, 1972). This is because the latter institutional modes enhance MNCs' flexibility to withdraw from the host market should they be unable to comfortably acclimatize themselves to the unfamiliar setting. Restated, other things being equal, when the perceived distance between the home and host country is great, MNCs will favour entry modes that involve relatively low resource commitments.

Demand uncertainty

When future host country demand for an MNC's product is uncertain, existing works indicate that an MNC may be unwilling to invest substantial resources in the country to effectively adjust to oscillating conditions and to enhance its ability to exit the market without incurring substantial sunk costs should demand fail to reach a significant level (e.g., Harrigan, 1983). Thus, other things being equal, when demand uncertainty is high, MNCs will favour entry modes that involve low resource commitments.

Intensity of competition

When the intensity of competition is high in a host market, existing works (e.g., Harrigan, 1985a, b) assert that firms would do well to avoid internal organization, as such markets tend to be less profitable and therefore do not justify heavy resource commitments. Hence, other things being equal, the greater the intensity of competition in the host market, the more MNCs will favour entry modes that involve low resource commitments.

Transaction-specific variables

Value of firm-specific know-how

Transaction cost theory or internalization theory stresses the importance of the firm-specific advantages MNCs enjoy relative to host country enterprises (Dunning, 1981; Rugman, 1981; Hennart, 1982; Hill and Kim, 1988; Teece, 1977, 1981, 1983; Buckley and Casson, 1976). This theory suggests that when the quasi-rents that can be earned from an MNC's firm-specific know-how are non-trivial, the propensity of licensees (or venture partners) to disseminate that know-how or expropriate it for their own self-interested purposes is likely to be high; quasi-rent being defined as the realizable returns entitled to a firm by way of its differential advantage in know-how. Hence, other things being equal, the greater the quasi-rent stream generated by an MNC's proprietary know-how, the greater the probability that the MNC will favour an entry mode with high control.

Tacit nature of know-how

When the nature of firm-specific know-how transferred by an MNC is tacit, it is by definition difficult to articulate (Nelson and Winter 1982; Teece, 1977). This makes the drafting of a contract to transfer such know-how particularly problematic, resulting in the licensee often lacking the informal routines needed to turn a technological blueprint into a successful product. That internal organization enhances an MNC's ability to utilize its human capital and draw on its organizational memory to transfer tacit know-how is well established. Hence, other things being equal, the greater the tacit component of firm-specific know-how, the more an MNC will favour high control entry modes.

DATA

The data were gathered via a survey methodology. The survey instrument consisted of an extensive mail questionnaire composed of four parts: modes of entry, global strategic factors, environmental factors, and transaction-specific factors. The questionnaire was distributed to a total of 629 US-based multinationals listed in *The International Directory of Corporate Affiliations 1987/1988 (IDCA)*, with the major line of business for each of the selected firms residing in the manufacturing sector. *IDCA* is an extensive directory of multinationals, listing approximately 1,800 US-based MNCs and their foreign subsidiaries; it also includes US family members of foreign ultimate parent corporations. In an effort to focus our attention on the most current entry mode cases, the 1987/1988 version of *IDCA* was carefully compared with the 1982/83 version to select those multinationals that experienced international expansion during the recent five years.

The questionnaires were sent to senior-level management including vice-presidents/ directors of international operations, presidents, and CEOs. In line with the logic of John (1984), who argues for selecting knowledgeable informants, the choice of this respondent group was based on the belief that people in these positions are most knowledgeable on international investment projects and the dynamics of the overall foreign entry decision process. In responding to the questionnaire, managers were asked to reflect back to a recent foreign entry mode decision they were involved in and to answer questions according to the logic employed in reaching that decision. A follow-up letter was sent to those firms that did not respond to the questionnaire two months after its distribution date.

A total of 137 questionnaires were returned, representing a 22% response rate. Of these, 41 were later deemed unusable due to incomplete responses in eight cases, respondents' evaluation of investment projects undertaken prior to 1980 in five cases, and respondents' evaluation of entry modes not classified as licensing, joint venturing, or wholly owned subsidiaries in ten cases. Eighteen cases were further eliminated because management provided a positive response to the question item of whether government regulations imposed restrictions on the mode options available to their firm. Note here that the study examined investment projects undertaken only from 1980 and onwards since it was felt that the investment results of these recent undertakings would most likely not be known at the time of questionnaire completion. The aim here was to minimize respondents' retrospective rationalizations for their entry mode decisions.

Overall, a total of 96 responses were deemed usable for the analyses. A profile of the respondents participating in the study reveals that 89% are senior management, including CEOs, presidents, vice-presidents, and directors. With respect to the location of foreign operations under discussion, no special concentration of country/region exists, rather, the geographic coverage of foreign locations is widely and relatively evenly distributed among major geographic regions: 25 in Pacific Asia, 17 in South America, 25 in Europe, 16 in North America, four in Africa, and nine in the Middle East.

MEASUREMENT

Entry modes

Respondents were asked to identify which of the three distinct entry modes—licensing, joint venturing, or wholly owned subsidiaries—represents the chosen mode of the foreign operation under discussion. In joint venturing cases, respondents were asked to explicitly state the percentage of their equity participation in the foreign operation and the number of partners involved. It is worth noting that a fourth choice was also given to respondents, that of 'other', for those respondents who did not feel that any of the aforementioned categories correctly reflected the form of entry mode characterizing their foreign operation under discussion. The responses showing this category were excluded from the analyses. Of the ten responses classified as such, six were identified by respondents as franchising agreements and two were identified as contract management; the remaining two went unspecified.

Of the 96 foreign entry launches used in the analyses, 32 were wholly owned subsidiaries, 38 were joint ventures, and 26 were licensing agreements. It should be noted that despite US-based multinationals' strong preference for wholly owned subsidiaries, we were able to obtain a sufficient number of joint ventures and licensing agreements for our analyses. This was possible since we asked managers to report the cases of joint venturing or licensing rather than of wholly owned subsidiaries when their firm recently engaged in multiple foreign entry decisions. Moreover, while we checked for the possibility of a nonresponse bias, no clear evidence for its existence was found; there was no systematic nonresponse either from multinationals with any specific industry profile or regarding any specific regional location of foreign ventures. With respect to joint ventures, in most cases (82%) respondents specified the existence of only one equity partner in the foreign venture. Moreover, the equity participation held by respondent firms, in 73% of the cases, showed a majority position.

Key determinants of entry mode

The nine key variables recognized to influence the focal decision of foreign entry mode are latent in that they are linked to the empirical world only through indicators. Moreover, they appear to be wide-ranging, multifaceted constructs. As such, psychometric measurement based on multiple items rather than a single-item proxy seemed a more fitting approach (Peter, 1979; Fornell, 1982; Churchill, 1979), and was used in the analyses.

As no established scales with proven psychometric properties exist to measure the nine constructs, it was necessary to develop indicators that could represent the domain of each construct. Accordingly, a compendium of items thought to be associated with each of the nine constructs was drawn from the relevant literature. Respondents were asked to evaluate the foreign venture under discussion across each of these items on a seven-point Likert-type scale.

After data collection, an iterative procedure was employed to refine the set of indicators for each construct. The item-to-total correlations, i.e., the correlation between the score of each indicator and the total score of those indicators used to capture each construct, was then examined. Following the steps suggested by Nunnally (1978), those indicators with a low correlation with the total score (i.e., $r<0.25$) and those indicators below a sudden drop off in the item total correlation were eliminated. A Cronbach's coefficient *alpha* was then calculated for the remaining set of items.

Drawing on Nunnally (1978), Churchill (1979, p. 68) suggests that in the early stages of basic research, reliabilities of 0.50 or 0.60 suffice. Because this research represents a first attempt at developing multiple-item measures of the identified constructs in the context of market entry, 0.60 was the cut-off point set for coefficient *alpha*. Accordingly, the aforementioned iterative procedure was performed until those items associated with each construct were reduced to a reliable set (i.e., Cronbach's coefficient *alpha* greater than 0.60). The final set of indicators used to measure each construct and Cronbach's coefficient *alpha* for each scale are provided in Table 1.

As shown in Table 1, the coefficient *alphas* for all constructs were above the 0.6 cut-off point established here; in fact, they all either exceeded or came very close to Nunnally's 0.7 criterion for basic research. Hence, the reliabilities of these constructs were judged to

Table 1. Final indicators used to assess the nine key constructs[a]

Constructs	Cronbach's *alpha*

Global concentration
For the industry involved:
  Number of competing players (many/few)
  Global four firm concentration ratio (low/high)
  Proportion of global competitors exercising tight coordination across
    business units (low/high)
	0.8301

Global synergies
  Extent of global scale economies (not at all/great)
  The level of possible sharing between the foreign business unit and the
    organization's other business units with respect to . . . (low/high)
      Manufacturing know-how
      Marketing know-how
      Management expertise
      R&D resources
      R&D personnel
      Production personnel
      Marketing personnel
      Distribution system
	0.7458

Global strategic motivations
Strategic motivations for entering the host market:
  To attack global competitors (low/high)
  To establish a strategic outpost for future market expansion
    (weak/strong)
  To develop a global sourcing site (weak/strong)
	0.6849

Country risk
  Instability of the host political system (low/high)
  Likelihood of host government taking actions to annihilate or limit
    company's ownership of the foreign venture (low/high)
  Likelihood of host government constraining the foreign operation by
    instituting policies with respect to . . . (low/high)
      Price control
      Local content requirements
  Transfer risk of host country with respect to . . . (low/high)
      Currency inconvertibility
      Remittance control
	0.7935

Location unfamiliarity
  Company's prior experience with the host country (great/not at all)
  Perceived differences between the home and host country with respect
    to . . . (not at all/great)
      Culture
      Political systems
      Economic conditions
	0.7102

Demand uncertainty
For the industry involved in the host market:
  Industry growth rate (high/low)
  Stage of industry life cycle (maturity/introduction)
  Frequency of major technological changes (low/high)
	0.8149

Table 1 (continued)

Constructs	Cronbach's *alpha*
Competition intensity	0.6971
Instability of market share (low/high)	
Number of existing and potential competitors (few/many)	
Level of fixed costs relative to value added (low/high)	
Costs facing the buyer of switching from one supplier (competitor) to another (substantial/negligible)	
Value of firm-specific know-how	0.7642
For the product or process involved in the foreign venture:	
The perceived level of reputation with respect to ... (low/high)	
Design	
Quality	
Style	
International recognition of brand name (not at all/great)	
Technological innovativeness (low/high)	
Tacit nature of know-how	0.7531
For the product or process involved in the foreign venture:	
Difficulty to assess the proper price (not at all/great)	
Difficulty to understand the manufacturing/marketing know-how (not at all/great)	
Difficulty to transfer the manufacturing/marketing know-how (not at all/great)	
R&D intensity (low/high)	

[a] All of these indicators were assessed on seven-point Likert-type scales. The anchors are shown in parentheses with the low end of the scale on the left.

be sufficient for our study. It should be noted, however, that while concentrating on the correlated items for each construct shown in Table 1 provides a more 'accurate' evaluation of some aspects of the construct, the iterative procedure used here might have eliminated certain aspects of the construct that were not correlated but were still constitutive of the construct; hence it might have generated a partially incomplete set of indicators for the construct. With this limitation in mind, a score for each construct was derived using a unit weighing scheme. Einhorn and Hogarth (1975) recommended this approach for situations such as ours: a moderate sample size ($50<n<200$) and a vague or nonexistent criterion variable. Unit weighing has strengths in that it uses no degrees of freedom since weights are not estimated from the data, and is estimated without error. The means, standard deviations, and correlations among the nine constructs used in the analyses are reported in Table 2. The fact that most of the constructs are not highly correlated suggests that fairly independent constructs have been tapped.

EMPIRICAL TESTS

The outlined eclectic framework was tested at two different levels. First, we tested the validity of the overall framework using Multivariate Analysis of Variance (MANOVA).

Table 2. Means, standard deviations, and Pearson product-moment correlations

Variables	Means	SD	GC	GS	GSM	CR	LU	DU	CI	VFK	TNK
Global concentration (GC)	14.76	2.44	1.000								
Global synergies (GS)	33.53	11.30	0.067	1.000							
Global strategic motivations (GSM)	12.61	2.84	−0.004	0.223*	1.000						
Country risk (CR)	22.34	14.96	−0.156	−0.188	0.023	1.000					
Location unfamiliarity (LU)	13.62	4.14	0.073	−0.040	−0.035	0.114	1.000				
Demand uncertainty (DU)	9.50	3.43	0.018	−0.200	−0.085	0.016	0.130	1.000			
Competition intensity (CI)	18.40	3.66	−0.009	−0.003	−0.042	0.103	0.186	0.075	1.000		
Value of firm-specific know-how (VFK)	22.24	6.10	0.207*	0.181	0.193	−0.101	−0.009	0.086	−0.060	1.000	
Tacit nature of know-how (TNK)	16.92	4.63	0.094	0.294**	0.084	−0.225*	−0.201*	−0.023	−0.039	0.238*	1.000

* $p<0.05$
** $p<0.005$

Here the analytical interest lay in testing the framework through an examination of the impact of the nine variables operated together on the ultimate entry modes choice. Under MANOVA, distinct entry modes served as the categorized independent variable with the nine constructs as the dependent variables. It is worth noting that MANOVA has a strength in that it takes the inter-relationships among the constructs into account (Pedhazur, 1982; Tatsuoka, 1971).

Second, we assessed the effects of the entry mode variables in discriminating among the distinct modes of entry. Our main aim here was to evaluate the relative importance of global strategic variables *vis-à-vis* the other entry determinants in discriminating among our three entry modes. We first conducted multiple discriminant analysis (MDA) with the entry mode as the grouping variables and the nine constructs as the predictor variables. Here a discriminant territorial map and a two-group breakdown analysis were also developed. Note that MANOVA tested for an overall difference in the profiles of the three distinct entry modes of licensing, joint venturing, and wholly owned subsidiaries whereas MDA provided information on the relative importance of each profile variable in discriminating among the three entry modes.

While MDA provides a macro picture of the importance and effectiveness of the entry variables in discriminating among the three entry modes, it does not provide statistical tests for the significance of the individual coefficients of our predictor variables. Hence, in addition to MDA, we conducted multinomial logit (MNL) analysis to provide such tests.

We specified an MNL model to assess the impact of the independent variables on the probability that each of the three entry modes would be chosen. In our logit model, the dependent variables were the logarithms of the odds that a particular entry mode would be chosen; the independent variables were the nine global strategic, environmental, and transaction specific variables. In particular, given that there are three institutional mode choices, the model was specified as follows (Schmidt and Strauss, 1975):

$$\log_e \left(\frac{P_{ij}}{P_{i1}} \right) = X_i \beta_j$$

where

P_{ij} = the probability that the entry i is of the institutional mode j where $j \in (2,3)$,
P_{i1} = the probability that the entry i is of the institutional mode 1 where 1 is the base of reference mode,
X_i = a vector (1×9) of the independent variables for the ith entry observation,
β_j = a vector (9×1) of parameters of the independent variables for the jth institutional mode.

In the light of the fact that licensing agreements can be characterized by the lowest level of control and resource commitments among our three entry mode choices, we used licensing agreements as the base of reference mode here. Hence, our parameters are interpretable in reference to licensing agreements; note from the above equation that its left-hand side is the logarithm of the ratio of the probabilities with the denominator here being associated with licensing agreements. The model was estimated subject to the condition that the sum of the probability for choosing each of our three entry modes is equal to 1.

Specifically, the estimation of the model was performed by maximization of the likelihood function of the model. This maximization was done by applying the nonlinear maximization program used in Schmidt and Strauss (1975). Given the condition that the sum of the probability for choosing each of our three entry modes is equal to 1, the likelihood function of the model here was specified as:

$$L = \prod_{i \in \theta_1} P_{i1} \cdots \prod_{i \in \theta_j} P_{ij}$$

where $\theta_j = \{i | j\text{th institutional mode is observed; here } j \in (2,3)\}$

$$P_{i1} = \frac{1}{1 + \sum_{j=2}^{3} e^{X_i \beta_j}}$$

$$P_{ij} = \frac{e^{X_i \beta_j}}{1 + \sum_{j=2}^{3} e^{X_i \beta_j}}$$

Furthermore, the unique contribution of global strategic variables as a group in explaining the entry mode choice was examined by Rao's Q-statistic; the aim here was to complement MNL analysis by providing statistical tests for the significance of the variables of our interest as a group rather than individually. A Q-statistic originally proposed by Rao (1952) has been purported by others (e.g., Dillon and Goldstein, 1984) as an appropriate test statistic to deal with the model comparison in the case of categorical dependent variables. The full discriminant model containing all three groups or categories of variables shown in Figure 1 was compared with three restricted discriminant models each containing a different pair of these three groups of variables; the unique contribution of the group left out in each of the restricted models was then analysed.

MANOVA results

MANOVA results indicate that there are significant overall differences in the profiles of the three distinct entry modes with respect to the nine key constructs of the eclectic framework. Wilks' *lambda* was 0.3587 for the overall framework; $F(18,170)=6.3247$ which was significant at $p<0.001$. Thus, the null hypothesis of identical profiles is rejected. The profiles do vary with respect to the nine entry mode determinants of our eclectic framework and hence the central hypothesis is not rejected. To the extent that competitive firms' prevalent practices reflect, in a Darwinian sense, successful strategic behaviour (e.g., Bowman, 1963; Lilien, 1979), one may then conclude that the outlined eclectic framework provides managers with a reasonable way to organize the decision variables for the entry mode choice.

MDA results

The discriminant analysis yielded two canonical discriminant functions. The results are shown in Table 3. The first function explained more variance than the second one (97.04% compared with 2.96%).

Table 3. Discriminant analysis results for the eclectic model

Variables	Structure coefficients	
	Function 1	Function 2
Global concentration	0.3093	−0.7001
Global synergies	0.3746	0.0820
Global strategic motivations	0.2518	0.5047
Country risk	−0.4084	−0.0157
Location unfamiliarity	−0.3016	−0.2814
Demand uncertainty	−0.1250	0.2610
Competition intensity	−0.1155	0.1980
Value of firm-specific know-how	0.2727	−0.1650
Tacit nature of know-how	0.3403	0.2778
Eigenvalue	1.6540	0.0505
Wilks' *lambda*	0.3584	0.9520
% of variance	97.04	2.96
Canonical correlation	0.7894	0.2192
Chi square	91.247	4.382
Degree of freedom	18	8
Significance, $P<$	0.0000	0.8211

As shown in Table 3, while discriminant function 1 was significant ($p<0.000$), function 2 was insignificant ($p<0.821$). As a rule of thumb, it is suggested that structure coefficients >0.30 be treated as significant (Pedhazur, 1982). Inspection of the coefficients of function 1 indicates that the significant coefficients are country risk, global synergies, the tacit nature of know-how, global concentration, and location unfamiliarity. Of these five, except for country risk and location unfamiliarity, all variables showed positive signs. This suggests that function 1 would produce high (low) discriminant scores for the firms with low (high) scores on country risk and location unfamiliarity and high (low) scores on global synergies, the tacit nature of know-how, and global concentration.

It is worth noting here that the constructs of the value of firm-specific know-how and global strategic motivations also approach the meaningful mark. This suggests that these constructs, though not of first and foremost consideration in the entry decision process, may be nonetheless said to influence multinational managers' entry mode choice. Interestingly, however, the results of MDA suggest that demand uncertainty and competition intensity play a minimal role in influencing the ultimate entry decision.

A visual representation of the MDA results is provided by a discriminant territorial map where the abscissa represents the first discriminant variate and the ordinate represents the second (see Figure 2). As can be seen in Figure 2, the centroids of the three distinctive entry modes were mainly separated by function 1 but hardly by function 2; this was so since discriminant function 2 was statistically insignificant.

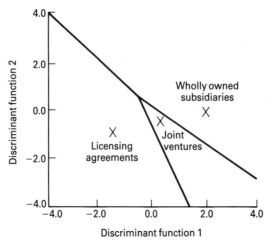

Figure 2. Discriminant Territorial Map.

As shown in Figure 2, wholly owned subsidiaries, joint venturing, and licensing agreements occupied a high, medium, and low centroid or discriminant score position, respectively. Given the results of Table 3, this suggests that firms with wholly owned subsidiaries (licensing) tend to have low (high) scores on country risk and location unfamiliarity and high (low) scores on global synergies, the tacit nature of know-how, and global concentration. While not deterministic, this provides some evidence in support of our hypothesized profiles of the different entry modes.

The classification accuracy of the resulting discriminant functions performed better than would a chance model. Table 4 provides the classification accuracy of the discrimi-

Table 4. Classification accuracy[a]

Actual group	No. of cases	Predicted group membership (%)		
		WO	JV	LA
WO[b]	32	68.8	31.3	00.0
JV	38	10.5	81.6	7.9
LA	26	00.0	23.1	76.9

[a] The overall hit ratio was 76.0%.
[b] Groups defined: WO = wholly owned; JV = joint venturing; LA = licensing agreements.

nant functions for the three distinct entry modes. As shown in Table 4, the overall hit ratio was 76.0%; 68.8% of the wholly owned subsidiary group, 81.6% of the joint venturing group, and 76.9% of the licensing group were correctly classified. All three individual group hit ratios met the criterion that a rough estimate of the acceptable level of predictive accuracy should be at least 25% greater than by chance (i.e., 33.3%, 39.6%, and 27.1%, for wholly owned subsidiaries, joint venturing, and licensing, respectively) (Pedhazur, 1982). The results suggest, therefore, that the discriminant functions performed well in classifying the three distinct entry modes.

Moreover, a two-group breakdown analysis was conducted to examine the performance of the discriminant functions in differentiating the three entry modes (Stevens, 1975). Mahalanobis' D^2 was calculated to examine the distance of each pair of groups on the discrimination map. Mahalanobis' D^2 represents the squared distance between the centroids corresponding to the groups along the discriminant axes. The larger the D^2, the more heterogeneous the groups. In addition, two other multivariate statistics were also reported for each pair of groups: Hotelling's T^2 and Fisher's R^2. These results are reported in Table 5. As shown in Table 5, the discriminant functions proved to be significant ($p<0.001$) across all pairwise comparisons.

Table 5. A two-group breakdown analysis[a]

Groups compared	Mahalanobis' D^2	Hotelling's T^2	Fisher's R^2
WO and JV	1.5405	19.7184	0.2248
JV and LA	1.8577	28.6782	0.3163
WO and LA	3.2745	46.9721	0.4567

[a] All of the statistics were significant at $p<0.001$.

MNL results

Table 6 provides the MNL results. As can be seen in Table 6, all three global strategic variables showed a significant impact on the entry mode choice, but to various degrees. Specifically, while firms showed a greater likehood to choose wholly owned subsidiaries over licensing when they ranked global concentration highly, firms tended to avoid licensing and rather to pursue a higher control mode, either wholly owned subsidiaries or joint venturing, as they scored global strategic motivations or global synergies highly.

As shown in Table 6, while the two environmental variables, demand uncertainty and competition intensity, did not significantly affect firms' entry mode choice, the other two environmental variables, country risk and location unfamiliarity, carried a considerable impact on the entry mode choice. Specifically, firms with high host country risk or location unfamiliarity tended to avoid wholly owned subsidiaries or joint venturing in pursuit of the lower resource commitment mode of licensing.

Lastly, the two transaction-specific variables yielded mixed results. While the value of firm-specific know-how was not found to affect firms' entry mode decision, the tacit nature of know-how did affect the odds of firms' choice of entry mode. Specifically, the higher the tacit component of know-how, the greater the likelihood for firms to choose either wholly owned subsidiaries or joint venturing over licensing agreements.

The fit of the model was tested based on the likelihood ratio shown in Pindyck and Rubinfeld (1981). The fit statistic used was $-2 \log \lambda$. where λ is the likelihood ratio; this statistic follows a *chi*-square distribution. Here λ was defined as L_0/L_{max}, where L_{max} is the likelihood function of the model in question and L_0 is the likelihood function of the null model; the null model is the model where all slope coefficients are zero. Given the results that $\log L_0$ was -105.467 and $\log L_{max}$ was -44.941 as reported in the bottom of Table 6, the fit statistic of $-2 \log \lambda$ was 121.052 and hence significant at $p<0.01$.

Altogether, the MNL results suggest that of the six variables found to influence the

Table 6. Multinomial logit model estimates[a]

	Intercept	Global concentration	Global synergies	Global strategic motivations	Country risk	Location unfamiliarity	Demand uncertainty	Competition intensity	Value of firm-specific know-how	Tacit nature of know-how
log(JV/LA)[b]	-7.022 (-1.502)	0.360 (1.700)	0.119 (2.040)*	0.530 (2.181)*	-0.229 (-2.762)**	-0.720 (-3.318)**	0.122 (0.841)	0.090 (0.671)	0.102 (0.924)	0.211 (1.986)*
log(WO/LA)	-13.907 (-2.187)*	1.031 (3.374)**	0.163 (2.398)*	0.648 (2.382)*	-0.410 (-4.163)**	-0.936 (-3.799)**	-0.026 (-0.154)	-0.072 (-0.419)	0.178 (1.422)	0.311 (2.625)**

[a] Log likelihood = -44.941; asymptotic t-statistics are in parentheses.
[b] Licensing option serves as the base of reference.
* $p<0.05$.
** $p<0.01$.

entry mode choice, three were strategic (global concentration, global synergies, global strategic motivations), two environmental (country risk, location unfamiliarity), and one transaction-specific (tacit nature of know-how). This provides evidence in support of the basic contention of this paper: that researchers would do well to treat the entry mode decision not only as a function of environmental and transaction-specific considerations but also as a function of the strategic relationship an MNC envisages between its operations across borders. This evidence appears to be consistent with that provided by MDA. Considering that these two analyses are applicable to similar research settings, the comparable results are not surprising (see also Anderson and Coughlan, 1987).

Q-Statistic test results

As can be seen in Table 7, the unique influence of global strategic variables as a group was found to be statistically significant ($p<0.05$) only on the choice between wholly owned subsidiaries and licensing agreements. A review of the Q-values suggests, however, that while statistically insignificant the group also carried some unique impact (Q-values>1) on the other two choices: wholly owned subsidiaries versus joint venturing and joint venturing versus licensing agreements. Although not of the focal interest of this test and accordingly, for purposes of brevity, not presented in Table 7, it is worth noting that the groups of environmental and transaction-specific variables played their unique role also in choosing between wholly owned subsidiaries and licensing; they were significant as $p<0.05$ and $p<0.10$, respectively. Overall, the results provide evidence that beyond environmental and transaction-specific factors, the group of global strategic considerations plays an important role in making multinationals' entry mode choice.

Table 7. Unique contribution of the group of global strategic variables

Groups compared	Q-statistic	Degrees of freedom	Significance level
WO and JV	1.494	3,60	n.s.[a]
JV and LA	1.758	3,54	n.s.
WO and LA	3.014	3,48	$p<0.05$

[a] n.s. = not significant.

CONCLUSION

This paper argues that beyond the environmental and transaction-specific factors established in the literature to affect the entry mode decision, we should also consider a multinational's global strategic posture in reaching this decision. Support for this view was found in all levels of our empirical analysis, viz., MANOVA, MDA, MNL and Q-statistic test. The MANOVA results indicate that there are overall differences in the profiles of the three distinct entry modes of licensing, joint venturing, and wholly owned subsidiaries with respect to the nine entry mode determinants of our eclectic framework. This suggests that the eclectic framework presents a reasonable way to explain a multinationals' entry mode decision behaviour.

When assessing the effects of the entry mode determinants in discriminating among the distinct modes of entry, our MDA, MNL and Q-test results consistently suggest that firms' final entry mode choice is significantly influenced by global strategic variables as well as by environmental and transaction-specific factors. These findings further support our assertion that the decision framework for multinationals' entry mode choice should expand beyond the narrow confines of the individual entrant to encompass the strategic relationship a firm envisages between its operations across borders.

This study provides some contribution to management. First, this research helps to reinforce in executives' mindsets the importance of expanding the decision framework beyond the narrow confines of each entry decision in isolation to encompass the global strategy their firm pursues or aims to pursue. Second, managers can be provided with a better understanding of the importance of each variable in influencing the entry mode decision; hence they can better prioritize the relevant variables in evaluating their entry mode alternatives. This appears valuable because it will allow managers, who often confront time and resource constraints, to focus on the variables most relevant to their entry mode decision without going through an exhaustive entry mode analysis.

This work is not without limitations. One limitation stems from the manufacturing emphasis of this study. The investigation of other sectors (e.g., service sectors) remains to be undertaken to test the generalizability of our findings. A further limitation arises from the fact that the entry decisions were studied *post hoc* rather than during the decision process; this might result in the responses being partially based on retrospective rationalizations. However, given that the entry modes evaluated by respondents were recently undertaken and that managers most likely did not know the results of their decisions at the time of questionnaire completion, it appears unlikely that their responses were seriously exposed to such risks.

Notwithstanding these limitations, compared with the existing international entry mode works, this study enjoys a unique advantage in its use of data. Lack of good data on foreign operations especially at the firm level is a notorious problem in international business research. Hence, little empirical research on the choice of international entry modes is known; the topic currently remains largely untested and in a conceptual state. This study is the first to use firms' direct responses rather than secondary data as input in conducting a relatively large-scale empirical investigation of this topic.

ACKNOWLEDGEMENTS

Thanks to Renée A. Mauborgne, C. W. L. Hill, Sumantra Ghoshal, and the participants at the annual conference of the European International Business Association for their comments on an earlier draft of this manuscript. Thanks also to three anonymous reviewers for their helpful comments.

REFERENCES

Anderson, E. and Coughlan, A. T. (1987) 'International Market Entry and Expansion via Independent or Integrated Channels of Distribution'. *Journal of Marketing*, **51**(January): 71–82.

Anderson, E. and Gatignon, H. (1986) 'Modes of Foreign Entry: a Transaction Cost Analysis and Propositions'. *Journal of International Business Studies*, **17**(Fall): 1–26.

Bartlett, C. A. (1986) 'Building and Managing the Transnational: The New Organizational Challenge'. In Michael E. Porter, ed., *Competition in Global Industries*. Boston: Harvard Business School Press.

Baumol, W. J., Panzer, J. C. and Willig, R. D. (1982) *Contestable Markets and the Theory of Industry Structure*. New York: Harcourt, Brace, Jovanovich.

Bowman, E. H. (1963). 'Consistency and Optimality in Managerial Decision Making'. *Management Science*, **9**(January): 310–321.

Bradley, D. G. (1977) 'Managing Against Expropriation'. *Harvard Business Review*, July–August: 75–83.

Buckley, P. J. and Casson, M. C. (1976) *The Future of the Multinational Enterprise*. London: Macmillan.

Calvet, A. L. (1984) 'A Synthesis of Foreign Direct Investment Theories and Theories of the Multinational Enterprise'. *Journal of International Business Studies*, **12**(Spring/Summer): 43–59.

Caves, R. E. (1982) *Multinational Enterprise and Economic Analysis*. New York: Cambridge University Press.

Churchill, G. A., Jr. (1979) 'A Paradigm for Developing Better Measures of Marketing Constructs'. *Journal of Marketing Research*, **16**(February): 64–73.

Davidson, W. H. (1982) *Global Strategic Management*. New York: John Wiley.

Dillon, W. R. & Goldstein, M. (1984) *Multivariate Analysis: Methods and Applications*. New York: John Wiley.

Dunning, J. H. (1981) *International Production and the Multinational Enterprise*. London: George Allen and Unwin.

Edwards, C. D. (1971) 'The Significance of Conglomerate Concentration in Modern Economics'. In H. Arndt, ed., *Die Konzentration in der Wirtschaft*. Berlin: Humboldt.

Einhorn, H. J. and Hogarth, R. M. (1975) 'Unit Weighing Schemes for Decision Making'. *Organizational Behavior and Human Performance*, **13**: 171–192.

Fornell, C. (1982) 'A Second Generation of Multivariate Analysis'. In C. Fornell, ed., *A Second Generation of Multivariate Analysis*. New York: Praeger.

Gatignon, H. & Anderson, E. (1988) 'The Multinational Corporation's Degree of Control over Foreign Subsidiaries: An Empirical Test of a Transaction Cost Explanation'. *Journal of Law, Economics, and Organization*, **4**(2) (Fall): 305–336.

Ghoshal, S. (1987) 'Global Strategy: An Organizing Framework'. *Strategic Management Journal*, **8**: 425–440.

Green, R. T. & Cunningham, W. H. (1975) 'The Determinants of US Foreign Investment: An Empirical Examination'. *Management International Review*, **15**(2/3): 113–120.

Hamel, G. and Prahalad, C. K. (1985) 'Do you really have a Global Strategy'. *Harvard Business Review*, **63**(July–August): 134–148.

Harrigan, K. R. (1985a) 'Vertical Integration and Corporate Strategy'. *Academy of Management Journal*, **28**(2): 397–425.

Harrigan, K. R. (1985b) 'Strategies for Intrafirm Transfers and Outside Sourcing'. *Academy of Management Journal*, **28**(4): 914–925.

Harrigan, K. R. (1983) *Strategies for Vertical Integration*. Lexington, MA: D. C. Heath.

Hayashi, K. (1978) 'Japanese Management of Multinational Operations: Sources and Means of Control'. *Management International Review*, **18**(4): 47–57.

Hedlund, G. (1986) 'A Hypermodern MNC—A Heterarchy?' *Human Resource Management*, Spring: 9–35.

Hennart, J.-F. (1982) *A Theory of Multinational Enterprise*. Ann Arbor: The University of Michigan Press.

Hill, C. W. L. and Kim, W. C. (1988) 'Searching for a Dynamic Theory of the Multinational Enterprise: A Transaction Cost Model'. *Strategic Management Journal*, **9**(Special Issue): 93–104.

Hill, C. W. L., Hwang, P. and Kim W. C. (1990) 'An Eclectic Theory of the Choice of International Entry Mode'. *Strategic Management Journal*, **11**(February): 117–128.

Hout, T., Porter, M. E. and Rudden, E. (1982) 'How Global Companies Win Out'. *Harvard Business Review*, **60**(September–October): 98–108.

Johanson, J. and Vahlne, J.-E. (1977) 'The Internalization Process of the Firm: A Model of Knowledge Development and Increasing Foreign Market Commitments'. *Journal of International Business Studies*, **8**(Spring/Summer): 23–32.

John, G. (1984) 'An Empirical Investigation of Some Antecedents of Opportunism in a Marketing Channel'. *Journal of Marketing Research*, **21**(August): 278–289.

Jones, G. R. and Hill, C. W. L. (1982) 'Transaction Cost Analysis of Strategy-Structure Choice'. *Strategic Management Journal*, **9**: 159–172.

Kim, W. C., Hwang, P. and Burgers, W. P. (1989) 'Global Diversification Strategy and Corporate Profit Performance'. *Strategic Management Journal*, **10**(January–February): 45–57.

Kim, W. C. and Mauborgne, R. E. (1988) 'Becoming an Effective Global Competitor'. *The Journal of Business Strategy*, January–February: 33–37.

Kindleberger, C. P. (1984) *Multinational Excursions*. Cambridge, MA: MIT Press.

Kobrin, S. J. (1983) 'Selective Vulnerability and Corporate Management'. In T. H. Morant, ed., *International Political Risk Assessment: The State of the Art*. Georgetown, DC: Georgetown University Press.

Kogut, B. (1985a) 'Designing Global Strategies: Comparative and Competitive Value Added Chains'. *Sloan Management Review*, Summer: 15–28.

Kogut, B. (1985b) 'Designing Global Strategies: Profiting from Operational Flexibility'. *Sloan Management Review*, Fall: 27–38.

Lilien, G. L. (1977) 'Advisor 2: Modeling the Marketing Mix Decision for Industrial Products'. *Management Science*, **25**(February): 191–204.

Nelson, R. R. and Winter, S. G. (1982) *An Evolutionary Theory of Economic Change*. Cambridge, MA: Harvard University Press.

Nunnally, J. C. (1978) *Psychometric Theory* (second edition). New York: McGraw-Hill.

Pedhazur, E. J. (1982) *Multiple Regression in Behavior Research*. New York: CBS College Publishing.

Perlmutter, H. V. (1969) 'The tortuous Evolution of the Multinational Corporation'. *Columbia Journal of World Business*, January–February: 9–18.

Perreault, W. D., Jr., Behrman, D. N. and Armstrong, G. M. (1979) 'Alternative Approach for Interpretation of Multiple Discriminant Analysis in Marketing Research'. *Journal of Business Research*, **7**: 151–173.

Peter, P. J. (1979) 'Reliability: A Review of Psychometric Basics and Recent Marketing Practices'. *Journal of Marketing Research*, **16**(February): 6–17.

Pindyck, R. S. & Rubinfeld, D. L. (1981) *Econometric Models and Economic Forecasts* (second edition). New York: McGraw-Hill.

Porter, M. E. (1986) 'Competition in Global Industries: A Conceptual Framework'. In M. E. Porter, ed., *Competition in Global Industries*. Boston: Harvard Business School Press.

Porter, M. E. (1980) *Competitive Strategy: Techniques for Analyzing Industries and Competitors*. New York: Free Press.

Porter, M. E. and Fuller, M. B. (1986) 'Coalitions and Global Strategy'. In M. E. Porter, ed., *Competition in Global Industries*. Boston: Harvard Business School Press.

Press, S. J. and Wilson, S. (1978) 'Choosing Between Logistic Regression and Discriminant Analysis'. *Journal of the American Statistical Association*, **73**(December): 699–705.

Rao, C. R. (1952) *Advanced Statistical Methods in Biometric Research*. New York: Wiley.

Root, F. R. (1987) *Entry Strategies for International Markets*. Lexington, MA: D. C. Heath.

Rugman, A. M. (1981) *Inside the Multinationals: The Economics of International Markets*. New York: Columbia University Press.

Schmidt, P. and Strauss, R. P. (1975) 'The Prediction of Occupation Using Multiple Logit Models'. *International Economic Review*, **16**: 471–486.

Stevens, J. P. (1975) *Four Methods of Analyzing Between Variation for the K-Group Manova Problem*. Multivariate Behavior Research.

Stopford, J. M. and Wells, L. T. Jr., (1972) *Managing the Multinational Enterprise*. New York: Basic Books.

Tatsuoka, M. M. (1971) *Multivariate Analysis: Techniques for Educational and Psychological Research*. New York: Wiley.

Teece, D. J. (1983) 'Multinational Enterprise, Internal Governance, and Industrial Organization'. *American Economic Review*, May: 233–238.

Teece, D. J. (1981) 'The Multinational Enterprise: Market Failure and Market Power Considerations'. *Sloan Management Review*, Spring: 3–17.

Teece, D. J. (1977) 'Technology Transfer by Multinational Firms: The Resource Cost of Transferring Technological Know-How'. *Economic Journal*, **87**(June): 242–261.

Vernon, R. (1979) 'The Product Cycle Hypothesis in a New International Environment'. *Oxford Bulletin of Economics and Statistics*, **41**(November): 255–267.

Watson, C. M. (1982) 'Counter-competition Abroad to Protect Home Markets'. *Harvard Business Review*, **65**(January–February): 40–42.

Williamson, O. E. (1975) *Markets and Hierarchies: Analysis and Antitrust Implications*. New York: Free Press.

Willig, R. (1978) 'Technology and Market Structure'. *American Economic Review*, **69**: 346–357.

Yip, G. S. (1989) 'Global Strategy . . . In a World of Nations?' *Sloan Management Review*, Fall: 29–41.

8

Successful Export Marketing Management: Some Empirical Evidence

Tage Koed Madsen

The rationale behind export performance research is that gathering of empirical data about alternative practices and their results is a means for developing guidelines for successful export marketing management. Such a research approach has previously been discussed and advanced in this journal by Bilkey (1985). During the last decade a fairly large body of empirical export performance research has appeared (Madsen, 1987).

The study reported in this article differs from previous studies by having a broader model specification, i.e. including a rich array of explanatory variables relating to export marketing policy as well as to the firm and the market. As a result, specification error problems are reduced and contingency analysis possibilities are increased. The dependent variable is also more broadly specified including measures of export profitability as well as export sales and export growth.

A broad model specification avoids some of the pitfalls of underspecified models. Conceptualization of the export marketing process has typically been much too narrow in previous export performance studies. One result of such underspecification is that findings become unstable between studies. Unstable and in some instances contradictory findings in fact appear in previous studies (Madsen, 1987). The reason may be specification errors in the studies; however, it might be that cross-sectional generalizations about optimal export marketing strategies cannot be made. This latter issue is not yet resolved (Bilkey, 1985).

The contribution of the present study is that it adds to the existing knowledge about successful export marketing management. As the possibility for generalizations is still an open issue, it is necessary to expand on previous efforts. Furthermore, the study elaborates on methodology by having a broader model specification than similar studies. Consequently, more advanced data analysis is possible, e.g. contingency analysis. In that way stability of findings can be examined.

The article does not concentrate much on discussing the conceptualization of the export marketing process. The reason is that both the conceptual variables and indicators (see Appendix 1) included in the study are to a large extent based on the export

Reprinted with permission from *International Marketing Review*, Vol. 6, No. 4, pp. 41–57
© 1989 MCB University Press

marketing literature and on previous studies. The intention of this article is to expand on methodology while building its conceptualization on an integration of previous work. In the findings section, references will be made to previous studies.

RESEARCH METHODOLOGY

This study focuses on the typical Danish exporter, namely a small- to medium-sized manufacturing company which has been established with the purpose of serving the Danish market and from this platform has moved out to the export markets. Danish firms' international activities are nearly entirely devoted to exporting. Licensing, franchising, joint ventures, production in foreign countries, etc., are seldom chosen alternatives.

Out of about 40,000 manufacturing firms in Denmark there are around 9,000 exporters. Direct exports amount to approximately 30% of total sales for the whole manufacturing sector and 40% if one excludes food manufacturing (these figures only include the manufacturers' direct export; if indirect exports are taken into account the figures are much higher). Denmark is a member of the European Common Market. A little more than 50% of all export sales go to other member countries. Denmark has a little more than 5 million inhabitants. It means that the domestic market is rather small. Consequently, many firms are 'forced' to export. Historically, farm products were very important for Danish exports but nowadays they represent only about 20% of total exports.

The *unit of analysis* in the study is the individual export case which is defined as being the marketing of one product in one foreign country (e.g. the sale of cheese from company X to France). For each export case, the participating firm has given information about performance, export marketing policy, firm characteristics and market characteristics.

A total of 82 manufacturing firms have participated in the survey. A random *sample* of 157 relevant firms were contacted. The response rate was about 52%. Each firm was asked to answer two questionnaires, one based on a successful export case and one based on a failure. Thirty firms only answered one questionnaire resulting in 134 usable responses.

Selection of the actual export case was done in cooperation with the firms (by telephone). Each export case was required to be initiated about five years ago for the purpose of ensuring comparability in performance. Another reason for this requirement is the desire to exclude *ad hoc* export activities from the study. As can be seen, this second step in the sampling procedure is not random. Therefore, immediate generalizations of the results are not possible. The statistical tests later in the article should therefore be seen as descriptive.

The participating firms represent a broad cross-section of manufacturing industries. A little less than half of them come from the metal and machinery industries, which are heavy exporting industries in Denmark. Most of the firms in the survey have 20–200 employees (median value about 75 employees). Their median export share is about 50%, but it ranges from 5% to 95%. Export markets are Norway/Sweden (20%), European Common Market member countries (50%), other Western European countries (10%), and countries outside Europe (20%). Most of the export cases have to do with industrial products (60%), the rest with consumer products (40%). When comparing the above distributions with statistical information about Danish exporting manufacturing firms in general, the conclusion is that the sample very well represents the typical Danish exporting manufacturer.

As it appears, the sample is rather heterogeneous; this is deliberate. As mentioned earlier, it is as yet unclear to what extent generalizations are possible concerning relationships investigated in empirical export performance research. From a theoretical point of view, it is preferable first to assess the highest degree of generalizability. This constitutes the first reason for choosing a heterogeneous sample. Another reason is that such a design increases the variation of explanatory variables which is definitely an advantage in data analysis.

The *substance* investigated in the survey has been governed by the theoretical model shown in Figure 1. It shows possible relationships between the four variable groups:

Figure 1. Relationship between the Four Variable Groups.

export marketing policy, firm characteristics, market characteristics, and export performance. The idea behind the model is that the performance of a particular export case is the result of an interaction of the other three variable groups. More simple models would consider only direct effects, e.g. of export marketing policy on performance. Of course, such direct effects are examined in this study, too.

The model of Figure 1 is more comprehensive than models seen in other export performance studies. However, it still represents a strong simplification of the real world export marketing process. Feedback loops from export performance are, of course, present in the real world, as well as relationships between the three groups of explanatory variables.

For each variable group several conceptual variables are investigated. The conceptual variables chosen have a strong foundation in the general export marketing literature but also in previous empirical export performance studies and interviews with Danish exporters. Variables emphasized in these sources as important for performance are included in this study. Each conceptual variable is measured by multiple indicators. The purpose of such a procedure for the development of measures is to improve the validity and reliability of the study (see for example Churchill, 1979; Peter, 1979).

It must be emphasized that there is a trade-off in seeking a minimum of specification errors and at the same time high validity and high reliability. Avoiding specification errors requires a rich array of conceptual variables; increasing validity requires measurement of a rich array of dimensions of each conceptual variable; and increasing reliability calls for multiple measures of each dimension. Clearly a questionnaire will rapidly blow up in size if all three desires should be considered fully. In this study the largest consideration has been given to avoiding specification errors. The reason is that this error source is seen as basic in this kind of study, leading to biased and unstable estimations of relationships (see for example Kmenta, 1971).

Actual conceptual variables and indicators included in the study are shown in Appendix 1. Measurement of dependent and independent variables is discussed below. Values for conceptual variables are calculated as simple means of the respective indicators. It means that all conceptual variables are measured by summated scales. The indicators summed for each conceptual variable are listed in Appendix 1. All summations were prespecified.

All measures tap the perceived value of that variable/indicator; furthermore, indicators of export marketing policy and market characteristics are nearly always measured relative to the same characteristics on the domestic market. One reason for choosing such a measurement design is that a pilot test of the questionnaire showed that many respondents neither could nor would respond to questions about absolute values. Other reasons draw more upon theoretical considerations. First, perceived values might be more relevant than 'objective' ones because management is often seen as guided by their subjective perceptions rather than by perfect, objective knowledge about the world. Theories of bounded rationality lead to such a conclusion, which is reinforced by much of the empirical work on the internalization process of firms. Second, by using relative measures the impact of firms' different general resources (size, product line characteristics, general managerial competence, etc.) is to a large extent removed from the analysis.

All variables are measured on a horizontal seven-point semantic differential scale, Likert scale, or Stapel scale. This number of response alternatives has been suggested by Cox (1980) after a thorough literature review. Alternative scale types were chosen to reduce monotony and resulting response bias. It has been reported elsewhere that the three scaling formats used show no real overall differences (Menezes and Elbert, 1979). One more reason for choosing these scales is that they communicate interval scale properties to the respondent. Research results also indicate that these scale types produce data that can be assumed interval scaled, particularly in connection with cognitive questions as in this study (Schertzer and Kernan, 1985).

Scale mid-points mainly represent the answer 'no difference from domestic market'. Anchoring of scale end points is typically 'much less' and 'much more' of that variable compared with the domestic market. For example the indicator for export sales is measured on a -3 to $+3$ horizontal scale; the zero is given as 'sales volume the same as on the domestic market', the -3 as 'half or less than half the sales volume compared with the domestic market' and $+3$ as 'double or more than double sales volume compared with the domestic market'.

One more measurement issue should be mentioned before addressing data analysis. When analysing variables influencing performance, one can often question the direction of causality: e.g. does top management support lead to higher export performance or *vice versa*? In an attempt to avoid such interpretation problems, time lags are introduced in this study; performance is measured as an average of the past two years; values of explanatory variables relate to the time of export entry or the years thereafter. One can of course question the reliability of data giving information about actions taken five years ago. However, clarity about direction of causality is considered more valuable than the reliability problems created.

In accordance with the reasoning about choice of scales, the data are assumed interval scaled in the *data analysis*. Simple and multiple regression analysis is used for estimating direct effects. Analysis of variance is used for estimating interaction effects. In the latter case, explanatory variables are categorized into three categories.

When performing such multivariate data analysis, *multicollinearity* problems should be addressed. Such problems turn out to be minor in this study. Bivariate correlation coefficients among explanatory conceptual variables are nearly all below 0.30, which does not indicate severe multicollinearity problems (Green, 1978). The variance inflation factor (VIF) suggested by Belsley, Kuh and Welsch (1980) has been calculated but it does not point to severe problems either. The VIF index lies generally about 1.5 with the highest being a little above 2.0. Another method for diagnosing multicollinearity is suggested by Belsley, Kuh and Welsch, namely inspection of the eigensystem of the explanatory variables.

Principal components analysis shows a maximum eigenvalue of 3.57 and a minimum eigenvalue of 0.25 which results in a proportion of maximum eigenvalue/minimum eigenvalue on 14.28. The interpretation of this proportion, too, is that multicollinearity problems are minor. The principal components analysis identifies several significant dimensions in the data. Interestingly, these dimensions are nearly identical with the conceptual variables prespecified in the present study.

The research methodology has now been outlined in quite some detail. The reason is that methodological issues are considered very important for the progress of empirical export performance research. This point of view is advocated in Bilkey (1985) as well.

FINDINGS: VARIABLE GROUP LEVEL

We will first look into the findings regarding the impact on performance of the three variable groups examined (export marketing policy, firm characteristics, and market characteristics). The data analysis undertaken for this purpose is stepwise multiple regression analysis (test procedure in SPSSX). This procedure computes R^2 change and its test significance for the exclusion of a user-specified subset from a complete model.

In the complete model all conceptual variables (see Appendix 1) are included. The three variable groups are then excluded as blocks. All possible inclusion combinations are examined. The results of the data analysis are shown in Table 1. It must be emphasized that interaction effects are not considered in this section.

Table 1. Impact of variable groups on export performance

Inclusion level of variable group	Ability of variable group to explain variation in export sales/growth/profits		
	Export marketing policy	Firm characteristics	Market characteristics
First group	$0.24^a/0.25^a/0.22^b$	$0.22^a/0.07/0.14^b$	$0.20^a/0.04/0.06$
After export policy	—	$0.13^b/0.02/0.08$	$0.11^b/0.01/0.02$
After firm characteristics	$0.14^c/0.20^b/0.16^c$	—	$0.14^a/0.03/0.03$
After market characteristics	$0.15^c/0.22^b/0.17^c$	$0.16^a/0.06/0.11^c$	—
Last group	$0.10/0.19^b/0.14^c$	$0.12^b/0.02/0.08$	$0.10^b/0.01/0.01$

Note: Figures show R^2 change resulting from including that particular variable group in the multiple regression analysis. Level of significance: [a] (0.001 level); [b] (0.01 level); [c] (0.05 level).

Table 1 is read as follows: if the variable group pertaining to export marketing policy is included as the first group then the resultant R^2 is 0.24 when export sales is the dependent variable (significant at 0.001 level). When export growth is the dependent variable R^2 becomes 0.25 (also significant at the 0.001 level). If the same variable group is included as the last group, it produces an additional R^2 of 0.10 (not significant) when export sales is the dependent variable and 0.14 (significant at the 0.05 level) when export profitability is the dependent variable.

The analysis is meant to give a feel for the relative impact of the three variable groups on export performance. It appears from Table 1 that the relative explanatory power of the three variable groups is different for different measures of export performance.

When *export sales* are considered, it is clear that all three variable groups have a strong and independent explanatory power. Inclusion of all three variable groups, i.e. all conceptual variables as explanatory variables, results in an R^2 of 0.47. The ability of the three variable groups to explain variance in export sales is nearly identical. Variance in *export growth*, on the other hand, is almost exclusively explained by export marketing policy. Variance in the last dependent variable, *export profitability*, is primarily explained by the export marketing policy variable group but also to some extent by firm characteristics. The capability of the three variable groups to explain variance in the two last mentioned measures of export performance is smaller (R^2 about 0.30).

How can these differences be explained? Some theoretical reasoning may be useful here: export sales level can be thought of as being a reflection of the export potential of the firm. The 'objective' export potential can be assessed by examining the company's firm-specific advantage (FSA). How easily can its FSA be transferred to the foreign market? Does its FSA lie in a patented product? In its network on the market? A firm's FSA is deeply rooted in the firm itself, and its impact on export sales level is evidence. Therefore, it is not unexpected that firm characteristics have a significant impact on sales performance. An FSA must always be evaluated in connection with market conditions. So it is also natural that market characteristics have a strong impact on sales performance.

Growth and profitability performance, on the other hand, depend more on the firm's ability to carry out the dynamic exchange process effectively, i.e. implement the optimal export marketing strategy and minimize transaction costs. The strong impact of export marketing policy, on these performance measures is therefore logical. Clearly, a firm with a strong FSA as well as high ability to implement transactions effectively should experience a convincing joint effect on overall performance.

Where comparisons with previous research are possible, the findings mentioned above are in accordance with earlier findings. Cooper and Kleinschmidt (1985) report that export growth is closely related to export marketing policy, whereas firm characteristics appear to play a more important role for export sales. Also empirical work on the internationalization process of firms has shown that organizational and management characteristics to a significant extent can explain variance in export intensity/export sales.

The findings of this study therefore reinforce the existing knowledge in the area. They also go further than that by explicitly considering alternative measures of export performance in connection with a broad range of explanatory variables.

FINDINGS: CONCEPTUAL VARIABLE LEVEL

An examination of the impact of conceptual variables on export performance is carried out by means of different methods of data analysis. Ordinary bivariate and multiple regression analyses give evidence of direct effects. In other multiple regression analyses, selected variables have been controlled for with the purpose of disclosing direct effects otherwise suppressed in the data. Interaction effects are examined by means of analysis of variance. In the questionnaire, firms were also asked to indicate their subjective opinion about critical success factors in that particular export case. These opinions were categorized and added to the data base. They are used as supplementary data in this section; they often reveal indirect effects.

Table 2 exhibits bivariate correlation coefficients between dependent and independent variables. The table also reports which explanatory variables are significant at the 0.05 level or better in the multiple regression analyses. The latter results come from stepwise multiple regression analyses. The number of significant explanatory variables of course declines in the multivariate analyses because of the (although not severe) collinearity that exists among these variables. Standardized regression coefficients (BETA coefficients) and R^2 resulting from the three stepwise multiple regression analyses are shown in Table 3.

Table 2. Impact of conceptual variables on export performance

	Export sales	Export growth	Export profitability
Export marketing policy			
A priori market research			
Planning and control intensity	0.35^a	$*0.33^a$	$*0.32^a$
Internalization of marketing functions	i	i	i
Adaptation of marketing policy		0.22^c	
Product strength	$*0.34^a$	$*0.39^a$	$*0.34^a$
Price competitiveness		0.21^c	
Communication intensity	0.29^b	0.24^c	0.25^b
Channel support	0.27^b	0.23^c	
Firm characteristics			
General firm resources	i	i	i
Export experience	$*0.38^a$	0.27^b	$*0.26^b$
Top management support	0.20^c i	i	i
Status of internal export organization	0.25^b i	i	i
Technology and knowledge content of product			
Market characteristics			
Attractiveness of export market	$*0.40^a$		0.23^c
Number of trade barriers	i	i	i
Physical distance to export market	i	i	i
Psychological/cultural distance to market	i	i	i
Attractiveness of domestic market	-0.28^b		

Note: figures show Pearson correlation coefficients. Level of significance: ^{a} (0.001 level); ^{b} (0.01 level); ^{c} (0.05 level). An asterisk indicates that the particular variable is significant at least at the 0.05 level in stepwise multiple regression analyses. An 'i' stands for an important interaction effect or suppressed direct effect.

Table 3. Multiple regression results

	Export sales	Export growth	Export profitability
Planning and control intensity		0.26^b	0.20^c
Product strength	0.25^b	0.31^a	0.27^b
Export experience	0.36^a		0.21^c
Attractiveness of export market	0.31^a		
R^2	0.36	0.25	0.21
Adjusted R^2	0.34	0.23	0.19

Note: figures show the standardised coefficients and R^2 form three stepwise multiple regression analyses.
Level of significance is shown by [a], [b], [c] (see Table 2).

Standard multiple regression analyses have also been carried out. The findings are nearly identical. However, the explanatory power decreases resulting from the fact that the standard method only attributes incremental explanatory power to each variable. Yet all the conceptual variables mentioned above, except two, remain significant at the 0.05 level or better. So the results and their interpretation are not influenced drastically by change of regression method.

Conceptual variables relating to export marketing policy

As it appears from Table 2, export marketing policy again stands out as the most important explanatory variable group. It is clear that the product itself is crucial for successful exports. From a marketing point of view, it is not surprising that product uniqueness and product quality in particular have a strong impact on export performance.

Product strength affects performance directly through better satisfaction of customer needs, but this study also reveals some indirect effects. There is a significant association between product strength and the firm's ability to find good agents/distributors on the export market. The interpretation is that a strong product enables the firm to attract better agents which again has a positive impact on performance. Secondly, a strong product creates larger commitment in the firm itself which among other things leads to better contact with the market and a higher degree of channel support. Also, the latter indirect effect leads to better performance.

There is one further theoretical explanation for the positive impact of product strength on export performance. It is often emphasized in the literature that buyer uncertainty can be a major obstacle for choosing a foreign supplier. Clearly, high product quality can reduce buyer uncertainty by conveying seller credibility and reliability. Therefore product strength might be even more important for export performance than it is for performance on the domestic market.

On opposite grounds one can attempt to explain the weak impact that price competitiveness appears to have on export performance. Low price will tend to increase buyer uncertainty: will the product be satisfactory at that price? Can/will the firm fulfil its obligations at these low prices? The finding in this study is that price competitiveness only marginally affects export performance. This is in accordance with typical findings in previous research (Madsen, 1987).

The two remaining conceptual variables pertaining to the export marketing mix, communication intensity and channel support, both lose explanatory power in the multiple regression analyses. The reason is their positive intercorrelation and association with product strength, planning and control intensity and also export experience.

Analysis at the indicator level, however, shows that good personal contact and joint decision making with the channel members have a positive bearing on performance. The rationale must be sought in the fact that increasing personal contact will lead the firm to better understanding of customer and channel member needs and behaviour. Improved target market selection, adaptation of marketing policy, and better relations to channel members—including qualified joint decision making—is the natural consequence which affects performance positively. Similar findings are reported in a study of manufacturer–distributor relations by Rosson and Ford (1982) and also in other previous empirical export performance studies. The reason for better performance may be attributed to better decision quality and larger commitment from both parties.

Good personal contact with the market and close relationships with channel members furthermore enhance the firm's capability for careful planning and control of the export activity. This study shows a significant relationship between planning and control intensity and export performance. Export growth is mainly affected positively by close monitoring of market changes. This finding reinforces previous findings by Kirpalani and Macintosh (1980). Export profitability, on the other hand, is primarily influenced by the extent of budgeting.

As we have seen, personal contact with and understanding of the market is important for export performance. This finding will be further elaborated below when discussing the impact of firm characteristics on export performance. The importance of such understanding will of course depend on the choice of export entry strategy, i.e. the choice of export channel. Previous research has shown that no single entry strategy can be regarded as universally optimal.

In this study, entry strategy is evaluated through the concept of internalization, i.e. the extent to which the firm chooses to carry out the export marketing functions itself as opposed to buying them on the market (through agents, distributors, etc.). As seen in Table 2, no universal generalizations are possible in this study either. As expected, there is no universal association between degree of internalization and export performance.

However, interaction effects are present. As hypothesized, analysis of variance discloses a significant interaction between internalization, general firm resources and distance to the export market. At the one extreme we find the small firm (up to 50 employees) operating in distant markets (countries outside Europe). In such an export case the optimal internalization strategy appears to be exports through a foreign agent/distributor who is given power over most marketing decisions. At the other extreme we find the larger firm (more than 50 employees) operating in very close markets (other Scandinavian countries). In that case the firm should apparently internalize to the same extent as in the domestic market.

The results make sense because differences in market conditions, compared to the domestic market, are a source of extra transaction costs which the small firm can overcome only with great difficulty if at all. Situations in between the two extremes are more difficult to assess from this study. However, it appears that the small firm should only under special circumstances choose to internalize to the same extent as on the domestic market. Larger firms should apparently only under special circumstances choose to transfer the majority of marketing decision power to foreign agents/distributors. The data show a tendency for small firms to be too 'venturesome', i.e. choose too high a degree of internalization.

The last conceptual variable in the export marketing policy variable group is '*a priori* market research'. Indicators for this variable tap the extent to which the firm has performed formal analysis of market size, market growth, etc., in advance. No significant associations are seen between this variable and export performance. Previous research exhibits similar findings. The reasons for this lack of association need yet to be explored. One explanation might be that such formal market analyses are not able to provide an understanding of the crucial market mechanisms.

Export marketing policy is seen as the most important variable group also by the firms themselves. Looking at their subjective opinions about critical success factors, they primarily stress the product itself and choice of agent/distributor as important for performance. About half of all critical success factors mentioned relate to export marketing policy.

Conceptual variables relating to firm characteristics

Among the conceptual variables relating to firm characteristics it appears from Table 2 that the firm's export experience is by far the most important explanatory variable. The indicators show a strong relationship between a firm's general export share and its performance. Even stronger is the association between performance in a particular country market and the buyer country's share of the firm's total exports (note that these relationships are not tautological since performance is measured relative to performance on the domestic market for only one specific product).

The interpretation is that successful export marketing management is facilitated by export experience in general and to an even larger extent by export experience relating to the buyer country. The study indicates that the causal path is the following: increasing country-specific experience will lead to better understanding of market mechanisms and a network of personal contacts; consequently product decisions, agent/distributor choice, and communication with market participants are improved. This in turn leads to better performance.

As a guideline, therefore, a firm should probably seek to exploit already-covered export markets, rather than spread their efforts over a larger number of countries. Such a concentration strategy can be achieved by extending the product mix exported or by internalizing more export marketing functions, gaining a higher share of the value chain. From a theoretical point of view, market concentration can be justified by considering the extra transaction costs imposed on export marketing: mutual buyer/seller ignorance of and uncertainty towards each other and hence extra transaction costs can be reduced when the selling firm has wide experience with exporting to the buyer country.

However, market concentration is not always a good strategy as has been demonstrated by others (Ayal and Zif, 1979; Piercy, 1981). This study suggests that very small firms will be better off spreading their efforts over several markets. The reason may be that such firms are not in possession of the resources necessary for a concentration strategy to be successful.

Among the other conceptual variables in this variable group, top management support and status of internal export organization exhibit a positive but weak impact on export performance. It is well documented that top management support is very important in the first stages of a firm's internationalization process. This study focuses on experienced exporters. The impact of top management support is then somewhat less prominent. This is a logical consequence of the fact that such experienced exporters typically have a group of employees with high export skills. In that situation, it seems natural to decentralize responsibility and decision power. Is such a guideline justifiable?

This study cannot give a definite answer to the question. However, some interesting (although not statistically significant) interaction effects are revealed in the data:

- When exporting to a very close country (in our case other Scandinavian countries) or to a very distant country (in our case countries outside Europe), top management support shows a higher positive impact on export performance, whereas decentralization of responsibility and decision power tends to be negatively associated with performance. In the former case, the reason may be that top management is a qualified decision-making participant, able to understand market mechanisms through analogy to the domestic market. Decentralization, on the other hand, may be a bad idea because the export manager may want to concentrate efforts on more distant, exciting, and status-giving markets. When exporting to very distant markets it may be that market ignorance and uncertainty is so large in the firm that commitment is needed in the whole organization. If so, top management support is of course of decisive importance.
- When exporting to other countries (in our case other countries in Europe), decentralization shows a fairly strong positive impact on performance, whereas top management support tends to be negatively associated with performance. The reason may be that, in these cases too, top management tries to grasp the market mechanisms by analogy from the domestic market. However, analogies may be misleading because of too large a market differences. In that case top management will be an ignorant decision maker and should rather give decision power to the lower level managers who understand the market.

These interpretations are inspired by the fact that the study has shown a high association between country-specific experience and performance. However, the interaction effects mentioned are not statistically significant and interpretations must be considered tentative. They may also be subjected to biases relating to firm size and cultural aspects.

The last two conceptual variables pertaining to firm characteristics, general firm resources and technology content of product, do not exhibit any direct relationship with performance. As commented earlier, however, 'general firm resources' interacts significantly with other variables. The finding that technological intensity of the product has no bearing on performance is in accordance with typical findings in other empirical export performance studies.

Conceptual variables relating to market characteristics

The last variable group, market characteristics, reveals only a weak immediate impact on export performance. However, export market attractiveness has quite a strong impact on export sales. Export markets with high growth and little local competition, in particular, tend to result in high sales. Such markets will affect sales directly by offering more favourable market conditions. This study also indicates an indirect effect, in that attractive markets create higher commitment in the firm itself; the consequence is better adaptation, closer personal market contact, better planning and control, and hence better performance.

The number of export barriers (represented by the amount of trade barriers, physical distance to export market, and psychological/cultural distance to market) shows no immediate association with export performance. This is contrary to what one would have expected.

However, the data expose a significant (at the 0.05 level or better) relation, in that markets with high export barriers are typically also high growth markets. They are typically penetrated by large, highly committed firms having quite strong products, marketed to a well defined target group. These circumstances affect performance positively and therefore tend to suppress a negative effect from the amount of export barriers. When controlling for the above-mentioned circumstances, evidence of such a negative impact on export performance is seen in the data (level of significance between 0.05 and 0.1). The negative impact of the amount of trade barriers on export sales is particularly significant.

The negative impact is, of course, due to 'hard' barriers such as tariffs and physical distance. The study also indicates, however, that the firm's experience with exporting to such buyer countries is typically low, leading to difficulties in finding a good agent/distributor and problems with understanding the market in general.

Finally, a negative association is seen between domestic market attractiveness and export sales. Also, for these experienced exporters, good sales and profit potential on the domestic market reduce their export efforts. The association must be assumed to be even stronger for firms in their first stages of internationalization. Domestic market attractiveness is clearly much lower in a small country like Denmark than in a huge country like the United States. This fact can probably to a large extent explain why Danish firms have a much higher export intensity than do their American counterparts.

The main findings of the study have now been outlined and implications for export marketing management have been discussed in some detail. In the next section these implications will be summarized.

IMPLICATIONS FOR EXPORT MARKETING MANAGEMENT AND RESEARCH

Analysis at the variable group level revealed export marketing policy as having the largest impact on export performance, especially when the latter concept is measured by indicators for export growth and export profitability. Respondents in this study are experienced exporters. It appears, therefore, that such firms should concentrate their efforts on export marketing policy considerations. This guideline is to some extent contrary to guidelines for firms in their early stages of internationalization where organizational issues are very important.

This study indicates that firms that want to secure stable export activities with high performance should:

- exploit their present export markets fully rather than attack new markets;
- create good personal contact with the export market and obtain insight into how it works;
- offer a strong, high quality product;
- be cautious of selling at low prices;
- adapt export entry strategy/degree of internalization to the situation at hand;
- give decision power to the person(s) who know and understand the market;
- choose close markets rather than distant, exotic markets;
- choose markets with high growth and low local competition.

The background and rationale for these guidelines and their more detailed content has been outlined in the previous sections. A very important question concerns the generalizability of the guidelines. Basically, they can only be claimed valid for the particular sample of export activities included in this study. However, relationships reported in this paper are quite stable in the survey. Furthermore, previous research has reported similar findings in many instances. Although the guidelines can only be regarded as tentative, these facts do give some confidence that they are more than just sample-specific.

Empirical export performance studies have proved to contribute to our understanding of the export manufacturing management process of committed exporters in the medium stages of their internationalization process. The present study also indicates that generalizations about successful export marketing management is possible even for a quite heterogeneous sample. However, the potential of this vein of research is not yet exhausted. Further validation of findings is still needed.

The model specification in this study is very broad. Analysis of suppressed and interaction effects has therefore been possible. Also multicollinearity problems have been explicitly addressed. A disadvantage of having a broad model specification is of course that each concept can only be examined in a rather superficial manner, i.e. a limited set of dimensions measured by a limited set of indicators. Validity and reliability concerns recede somewhat into the background and in-depth analysis of important questions is often not possible. How does a firm, for example, create a strong product? And why is it that export experience with the buying country is so important?

Such questions can only be answered very tentatively on the basis of studies like the present one. Empirical studies with a more narrow model specification are more adequate for providing such complex knowledge. Therefore, in-depth studies of that kind will hopefully be performed in the future. Investigations with a broad model specification help to identify the most important in-depth questions by scanning a more complete set of issues relevant to export marketing management. In conclusion, then, such a mixed research strategy can potentially lead the way to successful export marketing.

ACKNOWLEDGEMENTS

The author thanks L. Peter Jennergren for helpful discussions and comments. The comments of three anonymous *IMR* reviewers have also been very valuable.

REFERENCES

Ayal, I. and Zif, J. (1979) 'Market Expansion Strategies in Multinational Marketing'. *Journal of Marketing*, **43**(Spring): 84–94.

Belsley, D. A., Kuh, E. and Welsch, R. E. (1980) *Regression Diagnostics: Identifying Influential Data and Sources of Collinearity*. John Wiley & Sons, New York.

Bilkey, W. J. (1985) 'Development of Export Marketing Guidelines'. *International Marketing Review*, **2**(1): 31–40.

Churchill, G. A. Jr. (1979) 'A Paradigm for Developing Better Measures of Marketing Constructs'. *Journal of Marketing Research*, **16**(February): 64–73.

Cooper, R. G. and Kleinschmidt, E. (1985) 'The Impact of Export Strategy on Export Sales Performance'. *Journal of International Business Studies*, **16**(1): 37–56.

Cox, E. P., III (1980) 'The Optimal Number of Response Alternatives for a Scale: A Review'. *Journal of Marketing Research*, **17**(November): 407–422.

Green, P. E. (1978) *Analyzing Multivariate Data*. The Dryden Press, Illinois.

Kirpalani, V. H. and Macintosh, N. B. (1980) 'International Marketing Effectiveness of Technology-Oriented Small Firms'. *Journal of International Business Studies*, **11**(Winter): 81–90.

Kmenta, J. (1971) *Elements of Econometrics*, Macmillan Publishing Co., New York.

Madsen, T. K. (1987) 'Empirical Export Performance Studies: A Review of Conceptualizations and Findings', in Cavusgil, S. T. (ed.), *Advances in International Marketing*, Vol. 2, JAI Press Inc., Connecticut: 177–198.

Menezes, D. and Elbert, N. F. (1979) 'Alternative Semantic Scaling Formats for Measuring Store Image: An Evaluation'. *Journal of Marketing Research*, **16**(February): 80–87.

Peter, J. P. (1979) 'Reliability: A Preview of Psychometric Basics and Recent Marketing Practices'. *Journal of Marketing Research*, **16**(February): 6–17.

Piercy, N. (1981) 'Export Strategy: Key Markets vs. Market Spreading'. *Journal of International Marketing*, **1**(1): 56–67.

Rosson, P. J. and Ford, I. D. (1982) 'Manufacturer-Overseas Distributor Relations and Export Performance'. *Journal of International Business Studies*, **13**(Fall): 57–72.

Schertzer, C. B. and Kernan, J. B. (1985) 'More on the Robustness of Response Scales'. *Journal of the Market Research Society*, **27**(4): 261–281.

APPENDIX. CONCEPTUAL VARIABLES AND INDICATORS INCLUDED IN THE STUDY

Conceptual variable export performance	**Indicator**
Export profitability	• Total net income last two years, compared with total net income on domestic market (dom)
Export sales	• Total sales last two years (dom)
Export growth	• Sales growth last two years (dom)

Export marketing policy	
A priori market research	• Number of information sources used
	• Knowledge about market when starting to export
Planning and control intensity	• Extent of budgeting (dom)
	• Degree of monitoring of market changes (dom)
	• Extent of control of results (dom)
Internalization of marketing functions	• Choice of export entry mode
	• Influence on final marketing mix

Adaptation of marketing policy	• Adaptation of target group • Adaptation of product offer • Adaptation of pricing • Adaptation of promotion • Adaptation of distribution channel
Product strength	• User perception of product uniqueness (dom) • User perception of product quality and design (dom) • Strength of augmented product (dom)
Price competitiveness	• Competitiveness of actual price (dom) • Competitiveness of financing conditions (dom)
Communication intensity	• Relative size of promotion campaigns (dom) • Amount of contact with end user (dom) • Magnitude of personal contact with middlemen
Channel support	• Amount of sales support to channel members (dom) • Equality in relationship with channel members (dom) • Stabilities in deliveries (dom) • Size of profits given to channel members (dom)

Firm characteristics

General firm resources	• Total sales volume • Number of employees
Export experience	• Number of countries to whom the firm exports • Export share of the firm • Buyer country's share of the firm's export sales • Manager's experience with exporting to buyer country
Top management support	• General export orientation of top management • Top management support of that particular export case
Status of internal export organization	• Internal prestige of export management • Authority of manager responsible for that particular export case
Technology and knowledge content of product	• R&D costs (per cent) • Technology content of production • Demands knowledge of employees

Market characteristics

Attractiveness of export market	• Intensity of competition (dom) • Market size (dom) • Market growth (dom) • General economic growth in buyer country
Number of trade barriers	• Size of tariffs, quotas, etc. • Size of non-tariff barriers • Support of local competitors
Physical distance to export market	• Aerial distance to export market • Importance for transportation costs
Psychological/cultural distance to market	• Conventions for doing business (dom) • Conventions for personal relationships (dom) • General way of working and living (dom)
Attractiveness of domestic market	• Degree of absence of competition • Sales potential relative to firm goals • Profit potential relative to firm goals

9

Strategic Alliances in the Triad: an Exploratory Study

Vern Terpstra and Bernard L. Simonin

Cooperation between firms, including potential or actual competitors, has attracted growing attention among scholars as well as practitioners (Mowery, 1988; Gomes-Casseres, 1988; Geringer and Hebert, 1991). Perlmutter and Heenan (1986), for instance, stress the necessity to cooperate in order to be globally competitive. Ohmae (1989) goes a step further by stating that globalization mandates alliances, and that these alliances have become a *sine qua non* condition for corporate survival. Thus, firms which used to compete only in national or regional markets must now learn to collaborate with their competitors in the global marketplace. As a result, a complex network of international corporate arrangements has developed, leading to an intricate balance between competition and cooperation.

These 'strategic alliances' represent a variety of cooperative arrangements, frequently between competing firms, which are more than a standard customer-supplier relationship or venture capital investment, but fall short of an outright acquisition (*Business International*, 1987). They correspond to a bilateral relationship characterized by the commitment of two or more partner firms to reach a common goal (Jorde and Teece, 1989). Alliances do not necessarily involve participants from different countries. For example, American Express Co. and Warner Communications Inc. established a joint venture in the US, Warner Amex Cable Communications Inc., based on a potential synergy between cable television and home banking businesses. Nevertheless, the cross-border cooperative agreements have captured most of the attention. In particular, collaborative ventures between firms from Japan, North America, and Western Europe, the Triad regions (Ohmae, 1985), constitute pertinent cases of competitive cooperation that challenge strategists and merit closer examination.

Despite the growing interest demonstrated by researchers in recent years, the study of international cooperation is still at an early stage. More theoretical as well as empirical work is needed to understand the nature and scope of this phenomenon. The purpose of this article is threefold: (1) to present a framework for the analysis of the overall cooperative phenomenon, since many definitional ambiguities still exist in the current literature (Shenkar and Zeira, 1987; Root, 1988); (2) to use this framework to examine

Reprinted with permission from *Journal of International Marketing*, Vol. 1, No. 1, pp. 4–25
© 1993 Journal of International Marketing

the patterns of strategic alliances across the Triad regions; and (3) to compare the motives between partners from different Triad regions.

LITERATURE REVIEW AND STRUCTURAL FRAMEWORK

The importance of inter-firm cooperation is reflected by the increasing attempts by scholars to understand and to explain the cooperative phenomenon in light of established theories. Literature in International Business, in particular, points to the need to integrate inter-organizational cooperation into the Foreign Direct Investment (FDI) research agenda. When reviewing possible extensions of the Eclectic paradigm, Dunning (1988), for instance, points to the relevance of incorporating other forms of transactions, such as arms-length trade, joint ventures, and non-equity contractual agreements. A similar concern is revealed by Buckley (1988), who gives special attention to cooperative ventures in this evaluation of the shortcomings of the internalization theory.

So far, most of the studies looking at cooperation in the context of FDI investigate the relationship between certain given exogenous variables and the choice of international involvement. In this vein, Kogut and Singh (1988) offer a review of some existing studies that contrast the different modes of entry, looking at the determinants of entry choice into foreign markets. The conditions under which a company transfers its technology via an arms-length licensing mode as opposed to direct investment, have been actively researched (e.g., see Contractor, 1984; Adam, Ong, and Pearson, 1988). However, limited attention has been directed to a systematic examination of the big picture: multicountry, multi-industry, multiform, and multipurpose alliances.

As recognized by Kogut (1988), three theoretical approaches are particularly appropriate to explain the choice and motivations of joint venturing. Transaction costs theory (Williamson, 1975, 1979, 1985), which provides a framework for understanding the way firms organize economic activities between market and hierarchy, has been a major building block for analysing inter-firm cooperation (see Hennart, 1987, 1988). The strategic behaviour approach (e.g., see Ohmae, 1989; Bleeke and Ernst, 1991) examines a firm's motivations for entering a collaboration, and the consequences for the competitive positioning of the firm. Lastly, organizational learning focuses on the ability of forms to extract new knowledge or to protect core competencies from competitors (e.g., see Lyles, 1988; Hamel, Doz, and Prahalad, 1989; Hamel, 1991; Parkhe, 1991).

The present analysis is motivated by these three theoretical approaches. First, a comparison is made between the transaction costs approach of Pisano, Russo, and Teece (1988) and the relationship between governance structures and types of activities performed by the ventures. Similarly, from the strategic behaviour perspective, the similarities and differences in the international cooperative ventures formed in each region are identified to determine the distinctive strategies pursued by each member of the Triad. Although Japan, North America, and Western Europe have similar industrial structures, they have somewhat different positions and competitive situations in the world marketplace. Therefore, it is reasonable to assume that while firms from each region will form strategic alliances, they may have different motives and patterns in their cooperative ventures. Finally, the study of these motives and their match between partners allows speculation as to potential learning patterns at the Triad level.

In developing a taxonomy for this study, a framework is proposed based on the following variables: form, mode, market coverage and the alliance, and motives of the partners.

Forms

The variable form refers to the structural organization of the alliance. Two dimensions (equity and number of partners) underline this variable. The equity dimension is composed of two distinct classes: equity purchase from an existing entity and formation/creation of a new and separate legal entity. The following alternatives are distinguished: contractual agreements, equity participation, joint ventures, and consortia. This structural framework parallels that proposed by Pisano, Russo, and Teece (1988), who describe cooperative agreements as being on a non-equity, equity, joint venture, or consortium type.

Contractual agreements

Contractual agreements are a form of cooperation between two participants, for which no legal entity is created. There is neither creation of a separate company, nor purchase of equity by a participant. These agreements tend to be specific and restricted to isolated activities. Traditional arrangements between a producer and a distributor or supplier are not included here. Instead, arrangements between producers which are actual/potential competitors are emphasized. For example, Harris Corp. entered into separate contractual agreements with Matsushita in Japan and Philips N.V. in Europe to distribute PACnet, a data communications product. Similarly, Canon entered into contractual agreements with Burroughs and with Hewlett-Packard for the marketing of microcomputers in Japan.

Equity participation

Equity participation as a form of strategic alliance involves the acquisition of equity in one firm by another firm. This form of partnership is stronger than a contractual agreement. It differs from the traditional joint venture in that no new entity is created. Instead, one firms buys a share of an existing firm, usually because of a desire for greater control than is available in a contractual arrangement. An equity stake alliance is favorable for the development of common projects, as it is a more durable relationship than contractual agreement and less subject to quick termination when problems arise. For example, Mitsubishi Heavy Industries bought a 20% stake of Beloit, in the paper-making equipment industry, gaining a durable foothold in the US market.

Joint ventures

Joint ventures are defined as the formation of new and separate legal entities, resulting from the cooperation between two participants. These cases involve the sharing of an equity stake between two partners in a new venture. For example, GMFanuc Robotics

Corp. (GMF), 50:50 joint venture between Fanuc Ltd. (Japan) and General Motors Corp. (US) aims at developing, manufacturing, and marketing robots. Autolatina is a joint venture between Volkswagen AG. and Ford Motor Co. involving the automotive and credit operations of these companies in Argentina and Brazil. Voluntary joint ventures, as opposed to those required by governments, are often the product of a shared consensus between the participants, and represent an alternative to solo investments.

Consortia

A consortium is a collaborative arrangement among three or more parties, regardless of the equity structure. The distinction between the case of two-partner and multiple-partner cooperations is particularly relevant in light of the increased degree of complexity, a well-established fact in game theory. Consortia are a special form of cooperation for handling extremely large projects where the resources and capabilities of any two firms are inadequate. Consortia often involve government agencies as partners. They tend to be found in industries with very heavy development demands, such as the aircraft and electronics industries. The Microelectronics and Computer Technology Corporation (MCC) is a research consortium focusing on long-term developments in computer and semiconductor technology. In other cases, such as in the aerospace and telecommunication industries, the development of a particularly ambitious and costly project might favour the joint participation of many companies in a consortium. For example, Toshiba (Japan), Siemens A.G. (Germany), and General Electric Co. (United States) agreed to combine their technologies in microchips into a 'cell library'. Each participant researches and develops cells that are added to the common library.

Modes

While the variable *form* refers to the structural component of a strategic alliance, the variable mode focuses on the function of the venture. It underlines the nature of the relationship between the participants. Eight different modes across the three basic activities—R&D, production, and marketing—are discussed. These modes fall into two general categories: joint activities and complementary activities. Joint activities are activities performed by both parties at the same level of the value chain, e.g., both working on product development or R&D. Complementary activities imply that each party cooperates at a different level of the value chain (contributing distinct resources or expertise independently of one another at separate stages of the product development). For example, one party supplies technology and the other manufactures the product; or one party manufactures the product while the other distributes it. Using Porter and Fuller's (1986) terminology, the former category is called a Type Y coalition while the latter is called a Type X coalition.

Joint activities

Joint R&D is a mode of collaboration aimed at the development of a new product or technology. In this case, the eventual production and commercialization stages are conducted independently by the different participants. In contrast, *joint production* involves only the sharing of manufacturing capabilities to achieve economy of scale and production cost efficiencies. *Joint product development* refers to a mode having joint R&D, production, and occasionally some marketing. Marketing can take place within the venture as a natural step in product development, although in many cases the partners conduct the marketing of the venture's output independently.

Complementary activities

Both *licensing* and *cross-licensing* represent an agreement between a firm willing to sell or exchange its know-how, and a firm willing to reciprocate the exchange or to compensate for it. A *manufacturing arrangement* exists when a party uses the production capabilities of a potential competitor to obtain a specific output. This differs from a traditional supplier–customer link because the firm is dealing with a competitor instead of an independent supplier. *Piggybacking* and *cross-distribution* are two types of arrangements by which one company distributes another potential competitor's products in an agreed geographical area. Besides distribution, other marketing activities, such as promotion, advertising, and servicing can be performed by the carrier firm. Cross-licensing and cross-distribution are considered complementary activities (not joint activities), since for a given product or technology the actual cooperation takes place at different levels of the value chain (e.g., for cross-distribution, a product is still manufactured by one party and distributed by the other on a reciprocal basis).

Complementary and joint activities are defined independently of the form of the alliance. Manufacturing arrangements, piggybacking, and even licensing can occur under a joint venture, an equity participation, or a consortium. They do not necessarily have to be contractual agreements. In addition, it is also reasonable to expect a large proportion of technology acquisition (licensing) to take place via contractual agreements.

Market coverage

Market coverage is defined as the initial target market considered for the alliance's output. The Triad markets are the largest markets, but the alliances frequently go beyond the Triad regions, suggesting the global dimensions inherent in these ventures. For example, when AT&T reached an accord with SGS-Ates Componenti Elettronici S.p.A., the Italian semiconductor producer, the deal was a step in AT&T's expansion in Europe. In contrast, when IBM and Microsoft cooperated to integrate software developments with microcomputer technology, the intended market coverage was clearly global.

Motives

For each participant in a given alliance, a set of *motives* can be identified. They represent the benefits sought *ex ante* by the firm when entering the partnership. Frequently, the real objectives of the firms are difficult to observe directly, since hidden agendas and subtle strategies are at the heart of many alliances. For instance, collecting intelligence, blocking competition, or learning new core competencies from a partner are some examples of these less traceable motives. Due to the lack of availability of the data, only six clearly identifiable motives are examined among the many potential rationales for undertaking collaborative ventures: *product, technology, marketing, protectionism* (overcoming of), *production cost,* and *direct payment.*

The first two motives, *product* and *technology,* are similar in that both relate to the goal of assisting entry into new product markets. They differ in the particular means the firms use to get the new product and in the commitment of each partner to the alliance.

Product

The first motive, *product,* captures the fact that one firm obtains a new product from the venture. Two different conditions may motivate a firm to seek a product through a cooperative venture. First, a company may not be in a position to develop the product itself. Second, a company might have the potential to develop a product internally, but it might be obtained more cheaply or quickly by cooperating. SGS-Ates Componenti Elettronici SpA, for instance, received the exclusive European marketing rights to AT&T's bipolar and high-voltage integrated circuits. The products carry the SGS logo.

Technology

Technology means that a company is given access to a technology or process as a direct output of the venture or as an indirect benefit from using the technology. Technology refers to a combination of functional and process knowledge. The functional component builds on human skills in the domains of management, organization, manufacturing, and marketing. Process knowledge deals with the production technique and core product and is often translated in patents or blueprints. The most common use of the new technology is to enter a new product area. In a recent joint venture, Olivetti obtained access to Canon's laser-printing technology.

The next two motives, *marketing* and overcoming of *protectionism,* have the goal of assisting entry into new geographic markets. They differ, however, in the particular entry barrier they address and the strategic need they satisfy.

Marketing

At the core of the marketing function, activities such as distribution, promotion, and service may be performed by several different parties. In this study, *marketing* represents one or more of these activities. In some instances, the distribution activity may involve first time entry into a restricted market. For example, Britain's Glaxo joined with the German company E. Merck in 1982 to sell Zantac, an anti-ulcer drug, in West Germany, thus gaining access to one of the largest drug markets in the world.

Protectionism

The overcoming of *protectionism* represents a motive for companies seeking to overcome tariffs, quotas, or non-tariff barriers in a foreign market. Firms that have adequate product and marketing capabilities may need local help in overcoming protectionist barriers in a market. For example, IBM joined with former state monopoly Nippon Telegraph and Telephone in an attempt to overcome the barriers to foreign participation in the Japanese computer and telecommunications industries.

The last two motives, *production cost* and *direct payment*, are similar in that they are both aspects of enhancing profits in current markets, either through lower costs for a given product or through greater returns on an existing activity or asset.

Production cost

Production costs are a major determinant of competitiveness. Products cannot always be differentiated based on their intrinsic properties or intangible contributions. In this case, production costs play a unique role in determining the viability of a product. Finding a partner with production efficiencies or combining production to achieve the necessary economies of scale can provide a way to reach a competitive cost level. In 1985, US Steel Corp. and South Korea's Pohang Iron & Steel Co. (POSCO) initiated negotiations for a steelmaking venture in California. The US company was seeking low-cost, semi-processed steel from Korea.

Direct payment

Direct payment refers to any direct monetary compensation such as royalties, licensing fees, or payments for service, product, and technology provided. In the case of a manufacturing arrangement, this benefit may be considered as a direct outcome of a venture without a strong strategic motivation. For example, Korea's Samsung entered a deal with Chrysler to manufacture car parts in return for cash payments. Under licensing, direct payment may carry a more subtle message, since the licensor is giving up the option of exploiting its own know-how. In both cases, the real threat concerns the potential surrender of product development expertise in core businesses.

METHOD

Data gathering

As recognized by Doz and Shuen (1987), a number of databases on international partnerships have emerged in recent years. They are based mainly on observations in the business press and are subject to problems of incompleteness, misinterpretation, and bias toward large US firms. The main criticism of these databases concerns the inherent weakness of the data collection procedure for recording information with sufficient detail (Doz, Hamel, and Prahalad, 1986). Nevertheless, this approach is often the only feasible avenue to capture the broad phenomenon of international partnerships. For example, data for Porter's study of international coalitions were gathered in the *Wall Street Journal* for the 1970–1982 period (Porter and Fuller, 1986). Hergert and Morris (1988) used a similar data collection procedure with *The Economist* and the *Financial Times* from 1975 to 1986. When studying US/Japan cooperative ventures, Osborn and Baughn (1987) extracted their data from the *Japanese Economic Journal* and the *Asian Wall Street Journal* from 1984 to 1986. Following a similar approach, this study's database was compiled from observations collected in *The Economist, Wall Street Journal, Business International, Forbes, Business Week,* and *Fortune* magazine, covering the period between 1983 and 1987.

For each press release collected, a decision was made as to whether or not it met the criteria defined earlier. Both uniregional and cross-regional alliances were considered. Information was collected on the form of the alliance, the mode, the year of formation, the industry, the products involved, the market coverage, the participants, their country of origin, and their respective motives. The data were recorded by cross-checking the information in the different business publications. Due to the complexity of the data collection procedure, the variable motive is represented by binary values, indicating whether or not a particular benefit is sought. For a given venture, several motives may be recorded per participant. More detailed information, especially on the motives, could be obtained only from in-depth case studies involving interviews or surveys.

Information on motives was analysed from a dataset involving 658 joint ventures and contractual agreements between firms from different Triad regions. A primary reason for this choice of data lies in the limitations of the data gathering procedure for some of the categories. In particular, most information on consortia can be clearly identified, but distinguishing the individual motives among participants is rarely possible. In fact, one could argue that in consortia, companies behave homogeneously, and that the motives involved are more similar than complementary in nature. In an effort for consistency, the dataset excludes the equity participation forms, since the associated motives were often less traceable in the press.

MODEL TO ANALYSE THE PATTERNS OF MOTIVES IN THE TRIAD

Logit model

Although firms from a particular region have separate agendas and motives, it is important to examine whether there is a similar pattern of motives at the aggregate level between the Triad regions. To identify such a possibility, a logit regression technique is used. Applied to the alliances between two specific Triad regions, the logit model estimates the degree of association between the motives of a firm and the propensity for that firm to be from one region as opposed to another. Logistic analysis was used instead of discriminant function analysis, as the latter technique is based on the assumptions of multivariate normality of the explanatory variables for the tests of significance (see Fienberg, 1987; Goldstein and Dillon, 1978; Klecka, 1988). The logistic model makes no assumption regarding the distribution of the independent variables (Afifi and Clark, 1984) and it also allows the use of categorical independent variables.

The model is run to contrast two regions at a time. For the companies in the sample, the Triad region of origin serves as the dependent variable, and the set of motives as the predetermined variables. The model relates the predictability of the geographical outcome (region A vs. region B) to the motives of firms from region A and B for their specific cross A-B alliances. Conceptually, the model does not imply any causal relationships or influences between partner's origin and motives, but simply captures a degree of association between variables as in multidimensional tables. In fact, since the dependent, as well as the independent, variables are categorical, it can be shown that the results obtained with the logistic regression are identical to those of a general log-linear model (Knoke and Burke, 1986). The relationship is not linear but follows a logistic distribution:

$$P(\text{ORIGIN} = 1) = 1/(1 + \exp(-(B_0 + B_1\text{MARKETING} + B_2\text{PROTECTIONISM} + B_3\text{PRODUCT} + B_4\text{TECHNOLOGY} + B_5\text{PRODUCTION COST} + B_6\text{PAYMENT})))$$

ORIGIN denotes the Triad region of origin for the companies. By convenience and convention, the dependent variable takes the values 0 or 1 to represent one Triad region vs. another (e.g., Europe = 1 vs. Japan = 0). The independent variables correspond to the motives previously discussed. The coefficients B_0 to B_6 are estimated. They determine the direction of the effect, as well as its relative magnitude.

Sharing of motives

The logistic model above serves to differentiate the Triad regions based on the motives of companies entering cross-Triad alliances. Nonetheless, the model that operates on aggregate data does not allow us to capture other collaborative dimensions, such as the true balance of cooperation, or shared motivations *within each* alliance. A better understanding of the phenomenon calls for a complementary and more micro-oriented examination of the role played by common motives. A series of bar charts is used to compare the relative importance of these common motives. This visual support aims at facilitating the analysis of existing patterns, which is difficult with the use of actual numbers. For a given motive, the comparison is made by taking all of the alliances for which the particular motive is observed, and computing the proportion of ventures for which the motive is unique to firms of one region, or of the other, or common to both firms. The information in the charts describes the relative matching of the Triad regions for each motive. The data must be interpreted in light of the prior logistic model, which takes into consideration the relative weight of all the factors as well as their simultaneous effect. Here, all the motives are given a similar importance and are examined separately. This model also draws a picture across all industries, and each case is given a similar weight, so that the results are representative of the overall phenomenon.

RESULTS

The results are reported as follows: (1) the profile of the alliances (including forms, modes, industries, and market coverage); and (2) the patterns of motives in the triad (logit model and the sharing of motives).

1. Profile of the alliances

Forms

The database contains 658 different alliances between two or more companies, of which 586 were clearly identified for their structural form. Table 1 shows that 33% of the alliances are established through contractual agreements. In comparison, equity partici-pations represent 38% and joint ventures 20% of all of the alliances. Only 9% of the observations involved a consortium.

Table 1. Distribution of the structural forms

	Structural forms (%)				
	CA	ER	JV	Consortia	Total (%)
Aggregate data	33	38	20	9	100
Triad regions					
US	32	40	20	8	100
Europe	29	33	25	13	100
Japan	46	20	26	8	100

Note: The figures represent the relative frequencies of the forms contractual agreements (CA), equity participations (EP), joint ventures (JV), and consortia, at the aggregate level and for each Triad region (based on 586 alliances).

Table 1 also presents the breakdown of the structural forms by Triad regions. The frequencies are computed by considering all alliances involving at least one participant of the region under consideration. For example, contractual agreements (CA) represent 29% of the alliances involving a European participant. A relatively similar pattern to the distribution of the aggregate data can be observed for the Triad regions, except for Japan. Differences among the regions exist, and these will be noted when reviewing each region separately.

Modes

Table 2 shows the distribution of modes at the aggregate level. Joint product develop-ment (44% of all cases) modes dominate, and this is followed by manufacturing arrange-ments (20%), piggybacking (11%), and joint R&D (10%).

Table 2. Distribution of modes

Mode Y	Freq. (%)	Mode X	Freq. (%)
Joint R&D	9.5	Licensing	5.0
Joint production	5.7	Cross-licensing	2.0
Joint product devt.	44.1	Mfg. arrangement	20.3
		Piggybacking	11.4
		Cross-distribution	2.0
Total	59.3		40.7

Joint activities

Joint activities (Type Y) represent about 60% of all alliances. The famous saying in architecture is that 'form follows function'. This seems also to apply to the form of alliance preferred by partners. As shown in Table 3 (based on 473 observations), when engaging in joint (or Type Y) activities, partners show an overwhelming preference for joint ventures (81%) or consortia (85%), in the case of very large projects. On the other hand, when partners engage in complementary (or Type X) activities, they show a very strong preference for the looser tie of contractual agreement. Only a little over one-third of the contractual agreements are for joint activities. It can also be noted that equity participations are evenly divided between Type Y (49%) and Type X arrangements.

Table 3. Joint activities (Type Y), distribution of the modes across structural forms

Modes	Structural forms (%)			
	CA	EP	JV	Consortia
No. of obs.	190	114	117	52
Joint R&D	10	7	3	21
Joint production	4	7	3	21
Joint product devt.	23	35	69	60
Type Y	37	49	81	85

Note: The figures represent the frequencies of joint activities modes for the forms contractual agreements (CA), equity participations (EP), joint ventures (JV), and consortia.

Furthermore, Table 3 shows that when collaborative R&D is the only *raison d'être* of the alliance, more companies cooperate via contractual ties than within the limits of a joint venture. On the other hand, when R&D is combined with a production and a possible marketing stage, contractual agreements (23%) have relatively less appeal than joint ventures (69%). If the intensity of an alliance (Klein, 1988) is defined by the number of functions involved, then the following proposition is supported by the observations: the more intensive the collaboration, the more desirable a joint venture over a contractual agreement.

Similar results are obtained by Pisano, Russo, and Teece (1988, p. 62) in their study of collaboration in the telecommunication equipment industry. These authors speculate that joint R&D projects require relatively small transaction-specific investments in comparison to those involved when R&D is coupled with downstream functions such as production and marketing. The findings in Table 3 support their hypothesis: joint R&D projects could be effectively organized through contractual forms, whereas the latter multifunction projects could be better organized through more hierarchical or formal arrangements (equity participation, joint venture, and consortia).

Complementary activities

Complementary activities (Porter's Type X) account for the remaining 40% of the alliances. Manufacturing arrangements account for half of the Type X alliances and piggybacking accounts for another one-fourth. The remainder are accounted for by licensing, cross-licensing and cross-distribution. Manufacturing arrangements and licensing, as well as piggybacking and cross-distribution, occur not only through contractual agreements, but also via equity participation. The equity participation form serves to strengthen a distant operation. In many instances, control over the party involved in the manufacturing or distribution of a product is sought. The equity stake represents an additional guarantee that a negotiated arrangement will not deviate substantially from the initial agreement.

Industries

Strategic alliances take place in a variety of industries. Table 4 shows the breakdown of strategic alliances by industry. Of the 36 industries in the database, 13 account for close

Table 4. Strategic alliances by industry

Industries	Frequencies (%)	Industries	Frequencies (%)
Aircraft	3.3	Food and beverages	3.8
Automotive	16.0	Semiconductors	9.1
Biotechnology	3.5	Software	3.6
Chemicals	2.3	Steel	3.2
Computing equipment	21.3	Telecommunications	14.3
Drug	2.3	Others	13.1
Electronics	2.1		
Energy	2.1	Total	100.0

to 90% of the observed ventures. The concentration becomes even more impressive when industries are grouped by their level of technological intensity. For example, computing equipment, semiconductors, software, and telecommunication industries add up to almost 50% of the observed ventures. These figures are consistent with the conclusions of Hergert and Morris (1988), who found a concentration of collaborative agreements in a few industrial sectors characterized by high entry costs, globalization, scale economies, rapidly changing technologies, and substantial operating risks.

One of the driving forces in these competitive industries is the dependence on large capital investments. R&D activities, as well as production facilities, require large investments, which in turn demand large markets to break even. The semiconductor industry is illustrative of the trend. Combined with a shortening payback time due to fast technology obsolescence, the magnitude of financial commitment has accelerated the internationalization process. Strategic alliance can offer some financial relief by sharing the investment burden. They also provide a means for rapid entry into multiple markets, when broad exposure or the establishment of a standard are needed.

Market coverage

In terms of geographic distribution, Table 5 contrasts the relative importance of each Triad region as a source of partners for the alliances (Partner origin) with the impor-

Table 5. Distribution of strategic alliances by Triad region

Markets	Partner origin O (%)	Market coverage C (%)	International aggressiveness (O−C)/O (%)
US	75.4	36.7	51
Europe	42.3	17.8	58
Japan	29.9	7.7	74
Global	N.A.	37.8	
Total	N.A.	100.0	

Note: The figures show the geographic breakdown of the alliances. Partner origin refers to the proportion of ventures having at least one participant from the given region. Market coverage represents the proportion of ventures whose output is directed to the given market. International aggressiveness is a resulting index, capturing the propensity of each region to serve foreign markets via collaborative arrangements.

tance of the region as a market for the alliances' output (market coverage). In the sample, three-fourths of the alliances had an American partner, whereas less than half (42%, a lower figure than reported by Hergert and Morris) had a European partner and only a third had a Japanese partner. In terms of the target market coverage of the alliances, the American market ranked first, followed by Western Europe and Japan, respectively. There is a difference, however, in the target market for the alliances, in that the largest category is for global market targets, i.e., beyond the Triad regions themselves. This suggests that the alliances are not formed just to defend—or enter—a Triad market, but for global competitiveness as well.

Looking further at the difference between the country of origin of alliance partners and the target markets of the alliances, another insight can be derived. An index of international aggressiveness can be inferred by comparing columns one and two of Table 5 (the computation of the index is mathematically sound since all the proportions apply to the same basis, and all the alliances aiming at a Triad region involve a partner from that region). For example, subtracting the proportion of alliances targeted to the American market (36.7%) from the proportion of alliances with American partners (75.4%) and dividing the difference by the latter figure indicates that for American alliances, one-half (51%) are aimed at markets outside the United States—an equal balance between the US and foreign markets.

In the database, the dominant proportion of alliances involving an American participant (75.4%) reflects some bias, inherent in the data sources. A similar bias is also suspected in the Hergert and Morris (1988) study. In this case, it was biased toward Europe. Hergert and Morris found 73.7% of all alliances involving at least one partner from Europe, vs. 42.3% in this study's database. Similarly, they report 46.8% for the United States vs. 75.4% in this study).

2. Patterns of motives in the Triad

Logit model

Table 6 reports the findings on the logistic model which was run for the three paired comparisons (based on 114 United States/Europe, 152 United States/Japan, and 62

Table 6. Pattern of motives between Triad regions. Logit estimates and T-ratios in parentheses for the three comparisons

Motives	Europe (0) US (1)	Japan (0) US (1)	Japan (0) Europe (1)
Marketing	0.39 (0.91)	−0.48 (−0.96)	−0.31 (−0.41)
Protectionism	27.1 (0.00)	3.27 (2.85)*** US	1.29 (0.94)
Product	0.46 (1.03)	0.76 (1.72)** US	0.03 (0.04)
Technology	−0.52 (−1.22)	−0.19 (−0.45)	−0.04 (−0.05)
Production cost	0.45 (0.46)	1.94 (2.44)*** US	27.0 (0.00)
Direct payment	0.32 (0.58)	−0.81 (−1.57)* Japan	−2.1 (−1.65)* Japan

Note: Significance level: *** $p<0.01$; ** $p<0.05$; * $p<0.10$. The reported Triad regions relate to the sign of a significant coefficient. They represent the region for which the corresponding motive is characteristic.

Europe/Japan observations). The estimates of the regression coefficients are used to evaluate the relative importance of a given motive for one Triad region *vis-à-vis* the other. For the purpose of this study, only the direction of the outcome is of concern. The sign of a statistically significant coefficient (at the $p<0.01$, $p<0.05$, and $p<0.10$ significance levels), as well as the T-ratio, indicates for which Triad region the associated benefit is characteristic. A nonsignificant coefficient, as indicated by the T-ratio, shows that the corresponding motive is either nonrelevant or equally important for both Triad regions. The results will be discussed and contrasted for each Triad region in the next section.

Sharing of motives

Figure 1 reports the regional breakdown by motive (same sample as for the logit analysis). For example, the chart for US/Europe alliances shows that there is an equal number of American and European firms seeking a product while their partner is not. This number is also equivalent to the number of alliances where both American and European firms cooperate to obtain a common product. The findings offer a complementary perspective to those of the logistic model. Although the figure suggests that protectionism strongly characterizes the US region relative to Europe, this motive shows up as insignificant in the logistic regression. This occurs because protectionism is not a frequent motive, and therefore plays a limited role in the regression. The figure is only indicative of the regional breakdown for a particular motive. Attention is directed toward examining the importance of common motives (labelled 'BOTH' on the chart), and detecting the presence of an asymmetric regional pattern for the 'unique' motives (those sought by only one of the two partners).

Figure 1 reveals that direct payment, protectionism, production cost, and marketing are motives generally not shared by two partners. Marketing appears clearly to be a complementary function motivating the existence of the alliance for only one of the participants. Market penetration and access to a new channel of distribution illustrate the point. Production costs play a limited role as a common motive. Technology, marketing and product are the most frequent motives observed. Of these, only technology and product are characterized by a high degree of sharing. These patterns are very consistent across the three regional pairs. More than half of the alliances involving

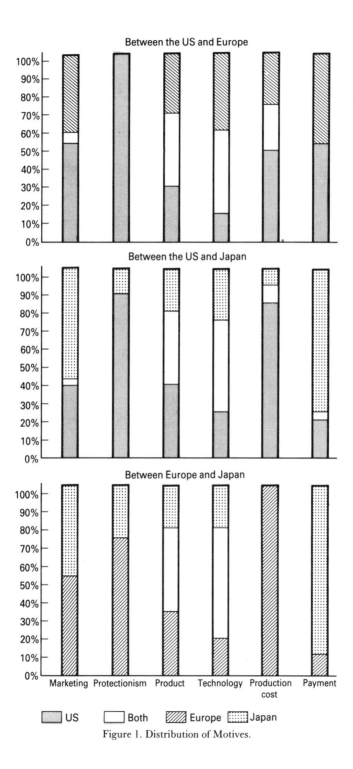

Figure 1. Distribution of Motives.

a technological stake show technology to be a common motive for both partners, regardless of the Triad regions involved. Technology development and transfer of know-how through learning are at the heart of many strategic alliances (Pucik, 1988). The technological race is ferocious, and no one Triad region can claim an absolute superiority, even for a particular industry. The rapid growth of cross-regional ventures centred on technology is also confirmed by the data. The overall picture is one of reciprocal cooperation through which companies, regardless of their Triad of origin, try to strengthen their strategic posture *vis-à-vis* other competitors.

DISCUSSION: CHARACTERISTICS OF THE TRIAD REGIONS

Europe

Looking at the profile of the alliances and at a consumer market of 380 million people, Europe's role should not be discounted. According to Hergert and Morris (1988), European companies are the most active participants in international alliances, with about two-thirds of all ventures involving a European firm. Overshadowed by the focus on US/Japan competitive rivalry, this Triad region definitely deserves more attention. Findings in Table 1 reveal that Europe has balanced distribution of the joint venture, contractual agreement, and equity participation forms. In comparison to companies from the two other Triad regions, European companies are more frequently involved in consortia.

From a market perspective, Europe represents a modest but not insignificant magnet for strategic alliances (about 18%). The potential emergence of the EEC as a huge free trade area after 1992 should trigger a stronger interest in cooperation for a share of this market than was observed in this study. For Europe, the index of international aggressiveness is 58% suggesting that the Europeans have a healthy concern for markets outside of Europe and are not only thinking of 1992 in terms of 'fortress Europe'.

Looking at the logistic regression results in Table 6, striking results are found for alliances involving European companies, For the ventures between American and European firms, no distinctive pattern of motives emerges, indicating a strong similarity between the two Triad regions when their companies form alliances. There is also no trend for the alliances between Japanese and European firms, with the exception of the *direct payment* motive, indicating a significant direction of payments from Europe to Japan. These results for European companies suggest a form of perceived competitive parity between Europe and both the United States and Japan. Except for direct payment, no distinctive trait emerges which indicates a state of dependency or the presence of a differential competitive strategy. That is, when European companies join an alliance, they apparently share the same competitive needs and motivations as their partners from the other Triad regions.

Further examination of Figure 1 reveals that European firms display a *unilateral* interest in lower production costs when collaborating with Japanese companies. However, in the case of US/Europe ventures, a significant number of ventures with production costs as a *common* motive is observed. This observation reflects the similarity of the strategic needs of the two regions for manufacturing and production efficiencies. This trend also underlines a tacit recognition by American and European companies of their manufacturing vulnerability *vis-à-vis* Japan, and the necessity to cooperate to prevent an unhealthy dominance by one partner in this global *ménage à trois*. European companies also show a noticeably more frequent desire than their American counterparts to acquire a specific technology. This asymmetric technological flow to Europe does not hold when the partner is Japanese.

Japan

As the Yen strengthens and Japanese goods become the target of protectionist measures around the world, traditionally export-oriented Japanese firms find new incentives for foreign investment. For the period of this study, however, Japanese alliances were still characterized by a dominance of contractual agreements over joint ventures and equity participations (see Table 1). This reflects the flexibility of Japanese corporations to engage in ventures without a major equity stake. The trend of these findings is consistent with the traditional Japanese value system based on relationships, as opposed to formal arrangements (Ohmae, 1989). According to this value system, the level of commitment in a venture does not have to be materialized into an equity position.

Joint R&D ventures are twice as frequent for American and European as for Japanese companies. The interpretation of such a result is not trivial. Does this mean that Japanese companies have achieved a degree of technological sophistication such that they prefer to conduct their research independently? Does this also imply that US firms have lost their original edge in the technology race to a point where international cooperation becomes a necessity? Or, could this be seen as a manifestation of a strong American vitality, a sign of a healthy scientific and technological environment? In their article, 'Joint Ventures with Japan Give Away our Future', Reich and Mankin (1986) stress the critical issues at stake when technology becomes a strategic commodity.

Japan is represented in less than a third of the alliances (see Table 5). For the Japanese, the index of international aggressiveness is a very high 74%, indicating that most of their international alliances are aimed at markets abroad. Perhaps this last observation should be qualified by noting that the database is biased against Japanese domestic alliances. The Japanese have long had domestic arrangements and alliances to cover their domestic market.

In terms of motives, the picture for Japan is very different from that of Europe. Whereas European parties have similar motives to their counterparts from other regions, Japanese companies have a more differentiated set of motives from their partners. Although Europe–Japan alliances show a similarity of motives for the two parties (save for direct payments), a contrast exists for the US–Japan alliances. *Production cost, protectionism,* and *product* are the dominant motives of American companies. The distinctive Japanese motivation is *direct payments* through licensing or manufacturing arrangements. The pattern of motives reveals the appetite of American companies for competitive products as a distinct motivation to enter a venture with a Japanese partner. These results are consistent with the findings of Reich and Mankin (1986), who observe US companies entering joint ventures with Japanese companies to obtain high quality, low cost products.

Based on a small sample of 21 Japanese joint ventures in the United States, Tyebjee

(1988) suggests that access to technology is a more prevalent motive for US partners. The data, however, do not support the existence of a unilateral transfer of technology from the United States to Japan. In fact, the motive *technology* does not differ between the two regions. However, this result is not incompatible with the conclusions of Reich and Mankin. This article considers technology as an asset actually present in the venture, while Reich and Mankin refer principally to an indirect technological effect, originating from the tendency of Japanese companies to perform the complex and critical functions, and therefore to learn and control the next product generation.

From a strategic point of view, it is commonly accepted that Japanese companies invest in the United States or join with an American partner to protect themselves from the threat of trade barriers and other protectionist forces in the United States. However, this should not mask the reciprocity of protectionist tends, illustrated too often by the complaints of American firms trying desperately to crack Japanese markets. At the aggregate level, the data in this study supports the significance of the latter pheno-menon. *Protectionism* (overcoming) is a more important motive for US alliance partners than for the Japanese during the period of this study.

In comparison to their European and American counterparts, fewer Japanese com-panies seek a product from their alliances, as illustrated in Figure 1. These results agree with the previously observed tendency of Europe and the United States to match each other's strategic posture, facing common, strong competition from Japan. Japanese companies show an interest in technology comparable to their European and American partners. No unilateral trend emerges which would support a transfer of technology or know-how to or from Japan.

United States

The United States is a battleground of fierce commercial competition. The concept of cooperation takes a rather ambiguous meaning in the land of antitrust laws. American firms must learn how to cope with domestic regulations when seeking collaboration. The distribution of structural forms of alliances (Table 1) shows that the United States follows a pattern generally similar to Europe with equity participation playing a some-what larger role.

The market coverage figures reveal the equal importance of the American global markets for the alliance's output when American firms are a partner in an alliance. This reinforces the proposition that strategic alliances aim at combining resources to compete in large markets. Among the Triad regions, the United States also shows the lowest indicator of international aggressiveness (51%). Nevertheless, this figure is still indica-tive of a strong outward orientation for American firms, with half of the alliance aiming at markets outside the United States. The US region also does not show a distinctive pattern of motives when interacting with Europe. On the other hand, American com-panies do seek new products and cost efficiencies from their Japanese partners. On a comparative basis, strategic alliances were observed to serve as a vehicle against protec-tionism more systematically for American than for Japanese companies. This result reflects a general trend, which might seem counterintuitive for specific industries, such as the car industry, for which quota restrictions against Japanese imports are well-publicized.

Figure 1 shows that American firms seek a recourse against protectionism from their European and Japanese partners more often than these partners do. They also more frequently seek lower production costs, not only from Japanese, but also from European companies (much of the data are from the high dollar period of the mid-1980s). Finally, the United States shows an interest in technology similar to that of Japan, but seems to transfer more technology to Europe.

CONCLUSION

From joint ventures to competitive collaborations, a unifying theory is needed. This study has attempted not only to propose a simple structural framework to analyse a phenomenon which lacks definition consensus, but also to expose the patterns of strategic alliances across the Triad regions. Such empirical work based on an extensive database is much needed for this area of research. Too often, strategic alliances are only studied from a theoretical, if not anecdotal, perspective. More empirical research remains to be conducted at an aggregate level, or at a complementary clinical level, to substantiate the validity of the proposed theories. Longitudinal studies are also needed, since the phenomenon is driven by changing external competitive forces, as well as an evolving internal balance of power among the Triad participants. In particular, more attention should be directed towards an understanding of the mechanisms and implications of knowledge transfer between partners from a management as well as a public policy perspective. Likewise, more research should address specifically the marketing side of cooperation since technology seems to have captured the lion's share.

REFERENCES

Adam, Y., Ong, C. and Pearson, A. (1988) 'Licensing as an Alternative to Foreign Direct Investment: An Empirical Investigation'. *Journal of Production Innovation Management*, **5**(1): 32–49.

Afifi, A. and Clark, V. (1984) *Computer Aided Multivariate Analysis*. Belmont, CA: Lifetime Learning Publications.

Bleeke, J. and Ernst, D. 'The Way to Win in Cross-Border Alliances'. *Harvard Business Review*, **69**(6): 127–135.

Buckley, P. (1988) 'The Limits of Explanation: Testing the Internalization Theory of the Multinational Enterprise'. *Journal of International Business Studies*, **19**(2): 181–193.

Business International. (1987) *Competitive Alliances: How to Succeed at Cross-Regional Collaboration*. London: Research Report, Business International Corp.

Contractor, F. (1984) 'Choosing between Direct Investment and Licensing: Theoretical Considerations and Empirical Tests'. *Journal of International Business Studies*, **15**: 167–188.

Doz, Y. and Shuen, A. (1987) *A Process Framework for Analyzing Cooperation between Firms*. Working Paper, September.

Doz, Y., Hamel, G. and Prahalad, C. K. (1986) 'Strategic Partnerships: Success or Surrender? The Challenge of Competitive Collaboration'. Paper presented at the AIB annual meeting in London.

Dunning, J. (1988) 'The Eclectic Paradigm of International Production: A Restatement and Some Possible Extensions'. *Journal of International Business Studies* **19**(1): 1–31.

Fienberg, S. (1987) *The Analysis of Cross-Classified Categorical Data*. Cambridge, Mass: The MIT Press.

Geringer, J. M. and Hebert, L. (1991) 'Measuring Performance of International Joint Ventures'. *Journal of International Business Studies*, **22**(2): 249–263.

Goldstein, M. and Dillon, W. (1978) *Discrete Discrimination Analysis*. New York: John Wiley.

Gomes-Casseres, B. (1988) 'Joint Ventures in Global Competition'. Working Paper No. 89-032, Harvard Business School, December.

Hamel, G. (1991) 'Competition for Competence and Inter-partner Learning within International Strategic Alliances'. *Strategic Management Journal*, **12**(Summer): 83–103.

Hamel, G., Doz, Y. and Prahalad, C. K. (1989) 'Collaborate with Your Competitors—and Win'. *Harvard Business Review*, **67**(1): 133–139.

Hennart, J. F. (1987) 'Can the "New Forms of Investment" Substitute for the "Old Forms"?: A Transaction Costs Perspective'. Paper presented at the 1987 Academy of International Business Annual Meetings, Chicago, November.

Hennart, J. F. (1988) 'A Transaction Costs Theory of Equity Joint Ventures'. *Strategic Management Journal*, **9**(4): 361–74.

Hergert, M. and Morris. D. (1988) 'Trends in International Collaborative Agreements'. In *Cooperative Strategies in International Business*, edited by Contractor, F. and Lorange, P. Lexington, MA: Lexington Books.

Jorde, T. and Teece, D. (1989) 'Competition and Cooperation: Striking the Right Balance', *California Management Review*, **31**(3) (Spring): 25–37.

Klecka, W. (1988) *Discriminant Analysis*. Newbury Park, CA: Sage Publications, no. 19.

Klein, S. (1988) 'Classifying Cooperative Behavior'. Working Paper. Northeastern University, April.

Knoke, D. and Burke, P. (1986) *Log-Linear Models*. Newbury Park, CA: Sage Publications, no. 20.

Kogut, B. (1988) 'Joint Ventures: Theoretical and Empirical Perspectives'. *Strategic Management Journal*, **9**(4): 319–332.

Kogut, B. and Singh, H. (1988) 'Entering the United States by Joint Venture: Competitive Rivalry and Industry Structure'. In *Cooperative Strategies in International Business*, eds. Contractor F. and Lorange, P. Lexington, MA: Lexington Books.

Lyles, M. (1988) 'Learning among Joint Venture-Sophisticated Firms'. In *Cooperative Strategies in International Business*, eds Contractor, F. and Lorange, P. Lexington, MA: Lexington Books.

Mowery, D. (1988) 'Collaborative Ventures between US and Foreign Manufacturing Firms: An Overview'. In *International Collaborative Ventures in US Manufacturing*, ed. Mowery, D. Cambridge, MA: Ballinger Publication.

Ohmae, K. (1985) *Triad Power: The Coming Shape of Global Competition*. New York: The Free Press.

Ohmae, K. (1989) 'The Global Logic of Strategic Alliances'. *Harvard Business Review*, **67**(2): 143–154.

Osborn, R. and Baughn, C. (1987) 'New Patterns in the Formation of US/Japanese Cooperative Ventures: The Role of Technology'. *Columbia Journal of World Business*, **22**(2): 57–69.

Parkhe, A. (1991) 'Interfirm Diversity, Organizational Learning, and Longevity in Strategic Alliances'. *Journal of International Business Studies*, **22**(4): 579–601.

Perlmutter, H. and Heenan, D. (1986) 'Cooperate to Compete Globally'. *Harvard Business Review*, 136–152.

Pisano, G., Russo, R. and Teece, D. (1988) 'Joint Ventures and Collaborative Arrangements in the Telecommunications Equipment Industry'. In *International Collaborative Ventures in US Manufacturing*, ed. Mowery, D. Cambridge, MA: Ballinger Publication.

Porter, M. and Fuller, M. (1986) 'Coalitions and Global Strategy'. In *Competition in Global Industries*, ed. Porter, M. Boston: Harvard Business School Press.

Pucik, V. (1988) 'Strategic Alliances, Organizational Learning, and Competitive Advantage: The HRM Agenda'. *Human Resource Management*, **27**(1): 77–93.

Reich, R. and Mankin, E. (1986) 'Joint Ventures with Japan Give Away Our Future', *Harvard Business Review* **86**(2): 78–86.

Root, F. (1988) 'Some Taxonomies of International Cooperative Arrangements'. In *Cooperative Strategies in International Business*, ed. Contractor, F. and Lorange, P. Lexington, MA: Lexington Books.

Shenkar, O. and Zeira, Y. (1987) 'Human Resources Management in International Joint Ventures: Direction for Research', *Academy of Management Review*, **12**(3): 546–557.

Tyebjee, T. (1988) 'Japan's Joint Ventures in the United States'. In *Cooperative Strategies in International Business*, ed. Contractor, F. and Lorange, P. Lexington, MA: Lexington Books.

Williamson, O. (1975) *Markets and Hierarchies: Analysis and Antitrust Implications*. New York: The Free Press.

Williamson, O. (1979) 'Transaction-Cost Economics: The Governance of Contractual Relations'. *Journal of Law and Economics*, **22**: 233–261.

Williamson, O. (1985) *The Economic Institutions of Capitalism: Firms, Markets, Relational Contracting*. New York: The Free Press.

Part II

The Global Marketing Mix

CONTENTS

10 Identification of global consumer segments: a behavioural framework   135
SALAH S. HASSAN and LEA PREVEL KATSANIS, *Journal of International Consumer Marketing* (1991), **3**(2), 11–28

11 Decentralized R&D for global product development: strategic implications for the multinational corporation   145
ALPHONSO O. OGBUEHI and RALPH A. BELLAS, JR., *International Marketing Review* (1992), **9**(5), 60–70

12 Product development the Japanese way   156
MICHAEL R. CZINKOTA and MASAAKI KOTABE, *Journal of Business Strategy* (1990), **11**(November/December), 31–36

13 Matching product category and country image perceptions: a framework for managing country-of-origin effects   162
MARTIN S. ROTH and JEAN B. ROMEO, *Journal of International Business Studies* (1992), **23**(3), 477–497

14 International counterfeiters: marketing success without the cost and the risk   181
MICHAEL G. HARVEY and ILKKA A. RONKAINEN, *Columbia Journal of World Business* (1985), **20**(Fall), 37–45

15 Product and promotion transfers in consumer goods multinationals   195
JOHN S. HILL and WILLIAM L. JAMES, *International Marketing Review* (1991), **8**(2), 6–17

16 International advertising strategies of multinational corporations   206
ROBERT E. HITE and CYNTHIA FRASER, *Journal of Advertising Research* (1988), **28**(August–September), 9–17

17 Managing the multinational sales force   219
JOHN S. HILL, RICHARD R. STILL and ÜNAL O. BOYA, *International Marketing Review* (1991), **8**(1), 19–31

18 International market entry and expansion via independent or integrated channels of distribution   232
ERIN ANDERSON and ANNE T. COUGHLAN, *Journal of Marketing* (1987), **51**(January), 71–82

19 The developing internationalization of retailing   249
ALAN D. TREADGOLD, *International Journal of Retail & Distribution Management* (1990), **18**(2), 4–11

10

Identification of Global Consumer Segments: a Behavioural Framework

Salah S. Hassan and Lea Prevel Katsanis

INTRODUCTION

This paper provides an alternative to the globalization versus localization framework. Current marketing literature indicates that this dichotomy is not a true reflection of real-life situations (Jain, 1989). It is essential to look from an eclectic perspective at both similarities and differences in evaluating consumer markets on a global scale. Today, consumer marketers are expected to think of global similarities and adapt to local differences as they develop and implement targeted marketing programmes. This perspective helps in determining similarities across national boundaries while assessing domestic (within-country) differences.

The challenge facing today's marketing academics and practitioners alike is to identify and respond to consumers' universal needs, wants, and expectations for products and services. Equally challenging is addressing cultural differences and other unique market conditions which require certain adaptations in any marketing programme. Therefore, the perspective of this paper is based on the analysis of similarities and differences in international consumer markets as basis for identification of global segments that cut across national boundaries.

Within this general framework, the objectives of this paper are: to evaluate recent developments in the global marketing literature, to introduce and define segmentation of global consumer markets, to present examples of emerging global consumer segments, and to illustrate with corporate cases how these profiles are being targeted. Finally, the paper draws conclusions for consumer marketing academics and practitioners.

GLOBAL SEGMENTATION: A REVIEW

The review of the literature will not revisit the debate between the two schools of thought on international marketing strategy: standardization versus adaptation. Others in the

Reprinted from *Journal of International Consumer Marketing*, Vol. 3, No. 2, pp. 11–28

135

field have done an excellent job in analysing the positions of these two groups. This discussion, rather, will take a historical perspective in analysing developments in the body of knowledge since Levitt's (1983) thought-provoking article on the globalization markets. There appears to be a distinct trend in the academic literature when examined on a 'historical' basis, versus a 'school of thought' basis. The pattern is that of segmentation, and it will have significant implications for the development of global marketing.

As the chief proponent of globalization, Levitt (1983) claimed that advancement in technology had affected communications, transportation, and travel; this in turn, led to the convergence of consumer markets worldwide. He described this phenomenon as the 'protelarization' of world consumer markets. What he described, in fact, was the existence of a 'world segment' for whom low-price and high quality would be common buying elements. This increase in market homogeneity on a global scale was caused by what Levitt (1983) refers to as 'segment simultaneity' or the appearance of similar market segments in different countries at the same time. This appears to be the beginning of the concept of global segmentation, on a limited basis.

Porter (1986) echoed some of Levitt's key sentiments in his work on global marketing strategy. He added, however, the consideration of integrating marketing strategy into the overall strategy of the firm. For Porter, the role of marketing is three-dimensional: it involves the geographic concentration of certain marketing activities; the coordination of dispersed marketing activities; and the use of marketing strategy to gain competitive advantage. What is of greater importance in his work, however, is the importance of segmentation. He pointed out that both identification of target segments within countries (country groups and buyers within countries) and physical product configuration, would assist in the determination of global marketing strategy. The segments, however, are not specifically defined.

Sheth (1986) acknowledged that some global activity is occurring with regard to mergers and acquisitions; as well as product safety/quality standards. He also built a model of segmentation, based on the similarity and differences of market needs and market resources. He included as part of this model: specialty segmentation, product segmentation, and market segmentation.

Kotler (1986) challenged the concept of global standardization. He developed a 'customization index' which is based on the identification of countries and the dissimilarities between them on the following factors: products, buyers, and environmental factors. He argued that each element of the marketing mix must be matched against a specific target country. This would ensure that specific differences would be identified in advance, and therefore, built into new product design. At some level, based on Kotler's model, each county represents a specific market segment, which must be addressed individually.

Wind (1986) identified the concept of 'cluster of countries' where specific groups of countries may or may not possess similarities that are reachable through a single strategy. He viewed this clustering approach as an interim point between pure standardization and pure adaptation. This form of segmentation may have merits of its own outside the considerations of the standardization/adaptation debate.

Huszagh, Fox and Day (1986) conducted an empirical study of 21 industrial nations to test for the existence of products with what the authors termed a 'universal' (e.g., global) appeal. The countries were clustered (clustered market does not mean universal or global) into five groups on the basis of economic and demographic data. A product rating scale was developed for 27 different consumer product categories, and the means and coefficients of variation were examined for difference between clusters. They concluded that even within a cluster, significant differences existed in product acceptance; however, the more 'high touch' the product, the more consistent the acceptance rates were within a cluster. It was also concluded that products which have no close substitutes and which are viewed as essential tend to have universal appeal. These findings appear to suggest the existence of segments across countries: country clusters.

Daniels (1987) proposed the concept of regional versus global markets. He argued that cross-national strategies may result in identification of marketing regions. This would not be unlike the country grouping identified in other research. He viewed this grouping as a means of pooling company resources and taking advantage of synergies in regions for improve competitiveness.

Domzal and Unger (1987) argued for the implementation of psychographic segmentation based on global consumer similarities. They presented a 'high-touch/high-tech' continuum to analyse the appropriate global market segment. They identified four themes that appear universal: materialism, heroism, play, and procreation.

Kale and Sudharshan (1987) introduced the concept of a strategically equivalent segment (SES). An SES represents a group of consumers who may cross national boundaries, but respond in the same fashion to a firm's marketing mix. They established a framework for identifying a SES on the basis of a product class (e.g., a frozen dessert).

Douglas and Wind (1987) argued for the existence of global segments as a key condition for the success of any global marketing strategy. They illustrated this point with an example of the emergence of a consumer segment that seeks premium or luxury products on a global scale.

Whitelock (1987) conducted an empirical study of export practices in the British bedlinen industry, and identified a positive relationship between product adaptation and success in export markets. As product age increased and consumption patterns became well-defined, the likelihood of changing this pattern became unlikely. Cultural segmentation appears potentially important to global product success.

Steinberg (1987) conducted an empirical study to show that the psychological meaning of products could not be used as a global segmentation strategy. He demonstrated that this approach suffers from heavy situational biases.

Crawford, Garland and Ganesh (1988) empirically identified the existence of the pro-trade consumer in both developed and developing countries. They define pro-trade as those consumers who show a preference for imported goods. Demographic characteristics, personal characteristics, and experience with imported products were variables used to predict pro-trade tendencies.

Kreutzer (1988) proposed segmentation as a useful concept in the context of marketing globally. He supported the use of a two-stage segmentation approach in evaluating global markets. This approach includes grouping countries, based on environmental indicators, such as technology, culture, ecology, and law. As the second stage in this segmentation model, Kreutzer (1988) recommended a within-country segmentation based on behavioural attributes, such as consumption patterns, information processing, and brand name loyalty.

Verhage, Dahringer and Cundiff (1989) conducted an empirical study to test the similarity of markets on a global scale. They examined the energy conservation behaviour of four countries; and then, used cluster analysis to identify specific categories of behaviour. They concluded that neither a single global strategy nor a strategy across clusters would be justified. However, segmentation across countries within a cluster might be possible. This is the strongest data to date which shows the use of segmentation in identifying global markets.

Jain (1989) presented a framework for the determination of marketing programme standardization. It focuses on the target market, market position, nature of the product, environment and organizational factors. This conceptual framework emphasized the importance of segmentation, with specific mention of intermarket segmentation. Additionally, other aspects such as the consideration of culture, economy and customer perceptions of specific markets were considered in Jain's proposed framework.

There have been several proprietary studies that focus on global segments. Some recent works include Rena Barots' study on female consumers around the world and the life style segmentation studies by several major advertising and media research agencies.

More recently, Goodyear Tire and Rubber (*Marketing News*, 1988) and Ogilvy and Mather (*Marketing News*, 1989) have generated several classifications for global segments.

Goodyear Tire developed six different consumer profiles: the prestige buyer, the comfortable conservative, the value shopper, the pretender, the trusting patron, and the bargain hunter. Different marketing mixes and promotional programmes are utilized for these groups which overlap country boundaries.

Ogilvy and Mather's Futures Division developed 10 segments based on lifestyle characteristics: basic needs, fairer deal, traditional family life, conventional family life, look at me, somebody better, real conservatism, young optimist, visible achiever, and socially aware. As with the Goodyear segments, these can be found in many different countries.

The past literature reveals two consistent patterns: the identification of specific global segments; and the usefulness of segmentation in global marketing. The global segmentation strategies presented in Table 1 shows how these patterns have developed since 1983: the move from one world segment to clusters of countries. The examination of the literature from this perspective shows, in fact, that there is more commonality within the literature than might be apparent by examining dichotomous viewpoints (e.g., standardization vs. adaptation).

There has been an increase in the number of empirical studies to support the existence of global segments. For example, cluster analysis appears to be a useful tool for segment identification. The emerging issue in the global marketing literature at this time seems to be as follows: Global marketers need to identify segments that are both measurable and reachable. In order to attain this objective, a definition of global market segmentation is necessary.

GLOBAL MARKET SEGMENTATION DEFINED

Based on the past literature, it appears that a restatement of global market segmentation is in order. The authors propose that global market segmentation be defined as *the process of identifying specific segments, whether they be country groups or individual consumer groups, of potential customers with homogeneous attributes who are likely to exhibit similar buying behaviour.*

Table 1. Global segmentation strategies

Segment name	Author and date	Segment description
World segment	Levitt (1983)	Low price + high quality part of a world homogenous market
Specialty, product, and market segments	Sheth (1986)	Products adapted to local market, different segments across different markets, product modified from country to country
Country segments	Kotler (1986)	Individual countries represent separate segments
Country groupings or clusters	Porter (1986); Wind (1986); Huszagh, Fox, and Day (1986)	Identification of country groupings with similar demographic, cultural, and buyer behavior similarities
Regional segments	Daniels (1987)	Identification of regions (country groupings) with similar characteristics for economics of scale (similar to clustering)
Psychographic segments	Domzal and Unger (1987)	Segmentation across countries based on lifestyle factors and product benefits
Cultural segments	Whitelock (1987)	Identification of similar cultural values and attributes across country boundaries
'Strategically equivalent' segments	Kale and Sudharshan (1987)	Segmentation tag response to a specific marketing mix
Pro-trade segments	Crawford, Garland, and Ganesh (1988)	Segmentation on the basis of attitudes towards imports in developed and developing countries
Two-stage segments	Kreutzer (1988)	Stage 1: segment by environmental indicators Stage 2: further segment by buyer behavior indicators
Attitude clusters	Verhage, Dahringer, and Cundiff (1989)	Similar consumer attitudes for specific products across countries

The existence of global consumer segments that are measurable and reachable must be considered as a prerequisite for the successful execution of any global marketing strategy.

Traditionally, international marketers segmented work markets based on geopolitical variables (i.e., country segments). This approach presents three potential limitations: (1) it is based on country variables and not consumer behavioural patterns, (2) it assumes total homogeneity of the country segment and (3) it overlooks the existence of homogeneous consumer segments that exist across national boundaries.

As discussed in the literature review, several studies (Kale and Sudharshan, 1987; Kreutzer, 1988) have presented managerial models for segmentation of global markets. Although it is not within the scope of this paper to model the process of segmenting global markets, it is our intention to present profiles of two emerging global consumer segments. These two profiles will be presented with examples of how global firms are responding to current trends in consumption patterns. Additional there will be a discussion of criteria used in the identification of these segments across cultures and/or countries.

CONSUMPTION TRENDS IN GLOBAL MARKETS

It is essential to analyse all elements of commonalities and differences that may exist in today's global consumer markets. On a global scale, trends influencing consumption behaviour can be cited as follows: increases in GNP per capita; steady rises in life expectancy; rapid increase of literacy and education levels; growth in industrialization and urbanization among developing countries; increases in share of manufactured exports by newly industrialized countries; advances in transportation, and, expansion in world travel. These trends are influencing consumption behaviour in a variety of ways. For example, some consumer products are becoming more widely accepted globally, such as consumer electronics, automobiles, fashion, home appliances, food products, and beverages.

Many of these products respond to needs and wants of consumer segments that cut across national boundaries. The challenge facing international marketers is to identify these segments and reach them with marketing programmes that meet the common needs and wants of these consumers. However, uniqueness of certain market characteristics will also require understanding of cultural differences. It may be necessary to introduce certain modifications (i.e., language) to accommodate these differences. Consequently, success in global market segmentation efforts will be based on an eclectic perspective of both similarities and differences in evaluating global markets. Consumer marketers, in particular, should 'think of global similarities and adapt to local differences' (Hassan, 1990). This is, in fact, the essence of segmentation. This perspective helps any manager of consumer markets to determine similarities across national boundaries while assessing domestic (within-country) differences. Several case examples are presented here in order to illustrate how global firms identify and meet the needs of the globally segmented consumer markets.

THE 'GLOBAL ELITE' SEGMENT

A growing market segment on a global scale is composed of consumers aspiring to an 'elite life-style'. The emergence of this global consumer segment has been attributed to increased wealth and widespread travel; this with other influencing factors, has stimulated the desire to own universally recognizable products. Products with prestige images that fit the expectation of being recognizable will be considered as universal in nature. Global marketers may identify commonality in prestige segments and target them accordingly. For example, European retailers such as Harrods, Ferragamo, and Galeries Lafayette reach US consumers with up-scale and unique leading-edge style fashions. These retailers target consumers directly through telemarketing/catalogue retailing without having physical presence, and with relative ease.

Today, global telemarketing is dramatically changing; for example, AT&T International 800 services are now available from 41 countries (Butkus, 1989). Toll-free calls are now available and being accepted from international consumers. In developing such global telemarketing programmes, some adjustment may have to be introduced to the marketing strategy in response to differences such as language and calling-time zones.

Other global marketers targeted the elite consumers with product offerings that fit the image of exclusivity such as:

(1) global durable goods such as Mercedes Benz, an automobile with perceived status;
(2) global nondurable goods such as Perrier, a natural soft drink with a prestige image;
(3) global services such as an American Express Gold Card, which offers financial services with the privileges of status and membership;
(4) global retailers that carry products by Ralph Lauren's Polo franchises.

Such premium products can be targeted internationally to consumer segments that aspire to the images of leadership, exclusivity, high quality, and status, in the same way they are currently targeted in their home market (Quelch, 1987). Elite consumers often differentiate themselves through buying and using products that are distinguishable from that of mainstream consumers (Hassan, 1990). Identification of behavioural factors related to media, selection, information, acquisition, and purchasing decisions can be essential to successful global marketing efforts. For example, the marketing mix should be managed in a way that will target this segment with high quality and high-priced products that are promoted and distributed through selective channels, in order to build and maintain the image of exclusivity.

Table 2 presents these criteria, as well as other variables that are being used in profiling this global segment. It is, however, important to recognize that this profile is rather broad for such a megasegment on a global scale. Other variables such as sex, age, region, and product benefits sought must still be examined to identify elite consumers who are part of certain micro-segments in order to reach them by niche strategies. Further segmentation typically means that consumer needs are being addressed more closely and that brings higher profit margins for the firm (Quelch, 1987).

THE 'GLOBAL TEENAGER' SEGMENT

Teenagers on a global scale, particularly in western and newly industrialized societies, are experiencing intense exposure to television media, international education, and frequent travel. Global teens from New York, Tokyo, Hong Kong, to those from Paris, London, and Seoul are sharing memorable experiences which are reflected in their consumption behaviour. Young consumers whose cultural norms have not become ingrained, and who can share universal needs, wants and fantasies, may be easily influenced by similar marketing programmes (Hassan, 1990).

The 'teenage culture' on a global scale shares a youthful lifestyle that values growth and learning with appreciation for future trends, fashion, and music. Teenagers are very self-conscious about the way they look, and role models play an important influence of their choices (Guber, 1987). For example, MTV Network, the cable company for youth, broadcasts its English-language programming in 25 countries. Music is becoming an effective tool in communicating globally with teenagers and the Coca-Cola Company responded to that by introducing its first global advertising campaign, 'You Can't Beat the Feeling' (Feinberg, 1989). Also, in recognition of the growing similarities among teenagers, regardless of nationality, Benetton introduced colourful Italian knitwear

Table 2. Behavioural aspects related to the identification of global consumer segments

	Name of global segment	
	Global elites	Global teenagers
Shared values	Wealth, success, status	Growth, change, future, learning, play
Key product benefits sought	Universally recognizable products with prestige image high quality products	Novelty, trendy image, fashion statement name brands/ novelty
Demographics	Very high income, social status and class/well travelled/well educated	Age: 12–19, well travelled, high media exposure
Media/communication	Up-scale magazines, social selective channels (i.e. cliques), direct marketing, global telemarketing	Teen magazines, MTV, radio, video, peers, role models
Distribution channels	Selective (i.e. up-scale retailers)	General retailers with name brands
Price range	Premium	Affordable
Targeted by global firms such as	Mercedes Benz Perrier American Express Ralph Lauren's Polo	Coca-Cola Co. Benetton Swatch International Sony PepsiCo, Inc.
Related micro-segments/ clusters	Affluent women Top executives Highly educated professionals Professional athletes	Pre-adolescents Female teens Male teens Adolescents
Factors influencing the emergence of the segment	Increased wealth Widespread travel Advancement of communication Technology	Television media International education Travel Music

based on its global advertising campaign, 'The United Colors of Benetton'. Other examples of global firms that meet the universal needs and wants of the teenage segment include Swatch International, Sony, PepsiCo, and Gillette.

It is projected that in the 1990s, the size of the global teenage market will reach 1.37 billion. According to recent estimates the purchasing power of the young consumers in the US alone increased from $30 to $55 billion in recent years (Hall, 1987; Sellers, 1989). Sony has responded to this booming market segment by introducing the 'My First Sony' line of audio products for children. (Such teenage products are being targeted globally in response to homogeneous teenage consumer desire for novelty, trendier designs and image.) Teenage consumers often with aloof attitudes tend to respond to peer pressure and resist parental control in accepting fads and name brands. Swatch International responded to these behavioural patterns by marketing watches that are trendier in design and which make a fashion statement.

Table 2 illustrates the major product benefits sought by this global segment and show other behavioural variables related to information acquisition, media exposure, and purchasing decisions. Unlike the elite consumers segment, global teenagers are confined by their age range of 12–19. However, further segmentation into clusters by age (i.e., pre-adolescents and adolescents) or by sex can be accomplished. In this context, it is important to recognize that today's teenage consumers may be tomorrow's global-brand loyals.

IMPLICATIONS

There are several fertile areas for research this study has uncovered on the subject of global consumer segmentation. They are: (a) identification of other potential global segments; (b) quantitative research of the elite and teen segments to determine their size, composition and location; (c) profiling the teen and elite segments, as well as other identified segments on variables such as psychographics; (d) development of products needed by these segments; (e) in-depth qualitative research on the buying behaviour of these segments and the identification of commonalities and characteristics of their purchase habits.

Additionally, managers need to consider the ramifications of global consumer segmentation, such as: (a) the 'reach' factor: how marketers actually communicate with regular frequency to these audiences; (b) key tactical decisions; the media and promotional tools which will most effectively influence these segments, (catalogues, radio, video productions, global magazines); (c) the organizational considerations: multinationals in particular will need to harness their subsidiaries for the most efficient use of resources; (d) new product development issues: the type of products and brands that will meet the needs of these global segments; and (e) the potential economies of scale and profit implications which may result from this type of global segmentation.

CONCLUSIONS

It is essential for academics and practitioners of consumer marketing to be on the 'cutting edge' about how the structure of global markets is changing. It is a major challenge for marketers to identify segments that transcend national and cultural boundaries on a global scale. However, this challenge is even greater when it necessitates dealing with the actual implementation of global marketing strategies. This paper is only a start towards the understanding of how the global marketing concept can be moved from corporate offices to the actual marketplace.

REFERENCES

'Attitude Research Assesses Global Market Potential' (1988) *Marketing News*, (August): 10, 11.
Butkus, R. (1989) 'Global Telemarketing'. *Export Today* (December): 5–7.

Crawford, J. C., Garland, B. and Ganesh, G. (1988) 'Identifying the Gobal Pro-Trade Consumer'. *International Marketing Review*, **3**(4): 25–33.

Daniels, J. D. (1987) 'Bridging National and Global Marketing Strategies Through Regional Operations'. *International Marketing Review*, **2**(3): 29–44.

Douglas, S. P. and Wind, Y. (1987) 'The Myth of Globalization'. *Columbia Journal of World Business*, (Winter): 19–30.

Domzal, T. and Unger, L. (1987) 'Emerging Positioning Strategies in Global Marketing'. *Journal of Consumer Marketing*, **4**(4): 23–40.

Feinberg, A. (1989) 'The First Global Generation'. *Adweek*, (February): 18–27.

Guber, S. (1987) 'The Teenage Mind'. *American Demographics* (August): 42–44.

Hall, C. (1987) 'Tween Power: Youth's Middle Tier Comes of Age'. *Marketing & Media Decisions* (October): 56–62.

Hassan, S. (1990) 'Dynamics of Global Consumer Marketing'. (Abstract) In J. Thanopoulos (ed.), *Southwest Review of International Business Research*, Akron, Ohio: Academy of International Business—Southwest Proceedings, 35. Full length in R. Moran *et al.* (eds.), *Global Business Management In the 1990's*. Beachan Publishing Inc. 199–203.

Huszagh, S. M., Fox, R. J., & Day, E. (1986) 'Global Marketing: An Empirical Investigation'. *Columbia Journal of World Business*, (Winger—Twentieth Anniversary Issue), **20**(4): 31–43.

Jain, S. C. (1989) 'Standardization of International Marketing Strategy: Some Research Hypotheses'. *Journal of Marketing*, (January), **53**: 70–79.

Kale, Sudhir H., Sudharshan, D. (1987) 'A Strategic Approach to International Segmentation'. *International Marketing Review*: 60–70.

Kotler, P. (1986) 'Global Standardization—Courting Danger'. *Journal of Consumer Marketing*, **3**(2): 13–15.

Kreutzer, R. T. (1988) 'Marketing Mix Standardization: An Integrated Approach in Global Marketing'. *European Journal of Marketing*, **22**(10): 19–30.

Levitt, Theodore (1983) 'The globalization of markets'. *Harvard Business Review*, (May/June): 92–102.

Porter, M. E. (1986) 'The Strategic Role of International Marketing'. *Journal of Consumer Marketing*, **3**(2): 17–21.

Quelch, J. (1987), 'Marketing the Premium Product'. *Business Horizons*, (May/June): 38–45.

Sellers, P. (1989) 'The ABC's of Marketing to Kids'. *Fortune* (May): 114–120.

Sheth, J. (1986) 'Global Markets or Global Competition?' *Journal of Consumer Marketing*, **3**(2): 9–11.

Steinberg, H. M. (1987) 'Detecting Consumer Attribute Shifts: A Technique for Monitoring International Marketing Strategies'. *Columbia Journal of World Business*: 3–7.

Value Segments Help Define International Market (1989) *Marketing News*: 17.

Verhage, B. J., Dahringer, L. D., & Cundiff, E. W. (1989) 'Will a Global Marketing Strategy Work? An Energy Conservation Perspective'. *Journal of the Academy of Marketing Science*, **17**(2): 129–136.

Whitelock, J. M. (1987) 'Global Marketing and the Case for International Product Standardization'. *European Journal of Marketing* (UK), **21**(9): 32–44.

Wind, Y. (1986) 'The Myth of Globalization'. *The Journal of Consumer Marketing*, **3**(2): 3–26.

11

Decentralized R&D for Global Product Development: Strategic Implications for the Multinational Corporation

Alphonso O. Ogbuehi and Ralph A. Bellas, Jr.

INTRODUCTION

In 1975 Donald Frey, former chief executive of Bell and Howell, decentralized the corporate research and development (R&D) function in his company. The rationale behind this action was that a centralized R&D function was 'too far from the market-place to avoid failures of new products ill-suited for that market, too removed from customer ideas or influence, and too slow to explore new technologies' (Frey, 1989). The Bell and Howell CEO took this action after enduring a decade in which there were no major innovations from the centralized R&D function. As a result of his action, a number of successful major innovations were developed over the next decade.

The timely relationship needed between marketing and technology has received some attention in the literature (Capon and Glazer, 1987; Ford and Ryan, 1981). As posited by Ford and Ryan (1981), understanding the technology life cycle enables the multi-national firm to introduce new products in a timely fashion. In recognizing the strategic coalignment between marketing and technology, Capon and Glaser (1987) argue that corporate success in a rapidly changing world order depends on the ability of firms to integrate technology and marketing strategy. The extent to which such a relationship between marketing and technology are integrated in a centralized or decentralized manner remains an issue to be resolved.

There is an ongoing debate in the strategic management domain over the centralization versus decentralization of activities in the mutlinational corporation (MNC). For most firms, centralization and decentralization differ in *degree* rather than in kind. The dilemma facing the globally-oriented MNC is how to organize authority centrally so that it operates as a vast interlocking system that achieves synergy and, at the same time decentralize authority so that local managers can make the decisions necessary to meet the demands of the local market (Stobaugh and Wells, 1984; Wheelen and Hunger, 1990).

Research and development, historically, has evolved from a geocentric view with development and production intended for local markets. However, a decentralized

Reprinted with permission from *International Marketing Review*, Vol. 9, No. 5, pp. 60–70

process may bring about benefits in such areas as product adaptability and production (Ronkainen, 1983). The successful development and introduction of new products in worldwide markets may require an orientation that significantly deviates from the traditional geocentric viewpoint. A decentralized orientation for R&D may be defined as one in which a multinational corporation seeks to distribute worldwide R&D activities and responsibilities among local subsidiaries. In other words, it is an orientation to withdraw from the historical tendency to concentrate R&D efforts at one particular location. Indeed, there is adequate evidence in the literature to support such a reorientation.

Davidson and Harrigan (1977), in considering problems associated with new product introductions in overseas markets, observed that most innovations by US firms seem keyed to the domestic market. Although products may be adapted to local market requirements little significant product innovation is carried out with foreign markets in mind. They recommend that the next phase of corporate evolution should focus on the product-development *process*. One can make the point that a decentralized R&D will be a logical first step in this process.

Ronstadt and Kramer (1982) argue that firms need to employ overseas-based resources to enhance their ability to compete globally. Their recommendations were based on acquiring international contacts and having R&D investments overseas as ways to add new items to the firm's existing product line. The outcome of this may be R&D decentralization where various units autonomously define their optimal strategies.

In studying how firms adapt products for export, Yorio (1983) observes that firms dependent on international sales are concerned about issues of product adaptation at the design or product-development stage. Findings from this study advocate a 'worldwide' marketing orientation to avoid future adaptation problems. This approach partially implies a de-emphasis of centralized R&D operations, so that new products would be brought on line to serve domestic and overseas markets concurrently.

The purpose of this article is to examine the effect of the strategic dispersion of R&D facilities and product innovation in the MNC. Specifically, the article focuses on the problems associated with a centralized R&D function as they are expressed in Frey's (1989) statement given earlier. Conversely, it also focuses on the advantages for a dispersal R&D function. Furthermore, it outlines how the decentralized R&D function might be organized so it can meet the firm's strategic goals in the most efficient manner. Finally, it discusses various disadvantages to decentralizing the R&D function and offers suggestions for minimizing potential problems.

ADVANTAGES OF DECENTRALIZED R&D

The decentralization of R&D within the MNC has several possible advantages. Some of these include: ease of incorporating local market requirements into the product; reduced product development time; accelerated new product acceptance; and reduced trade frictions. As stated by one executive: 'Our thesis on the international conduct of R&D is simple: new product development is best undertaken closest to the market user' (Ronstadt and Kramer, 1982). By developing a new product in the vicinity of the target markets, it is possible to incorporate local market flavours and uniqueness into the new product. In addition, a company is able to respond more quickly to changing market requirements by developing new prototypes to suit current and future local needs.

Shortening the development time of new products is crucial to beating competitors to the markets and thus establishing brand awareness. Honda Motor Company found that putting designers and factory experts closer to customers gave them an extra edge. Honda executives figure that their new Accord wagon will reach US customers two months sooner than if it had been produced 6,600 miles away (Taylor, 1990).

Customizing the production process and features available on a product allows for quicker introduction of the product. An example of a product which took advantage of customization in the 1988 Toyota Corolla. In this model year, the Corolla was available in 289 basic model variations to reflect different market needs and different use conditions. The car was also produced in 11 different countries. Another illustration of satisfying particular market needs is the Kijang utility vehicle designed for an exclusive market. This vehicle was designed and manufactured exclusively for drivers and driving conditions in Indonesia. Because of this, it has become the best-selling commercial vehicle in that market.

Another advantage of dispersing R&D facilities among strategic global locations is that it reduces trade frictions between the countries involved. Dispersed R&D limits exposure to currency fluctuations and can have the effect of quieting 'Buy home country products' movements. Finally, having R&D facilities located in our international markets can offset the impact the economic downturns that may occur in other countries. If business in one contention becomes economically unfavourable, production can be switched to another. Also, these extra facilities allow a company to spread its R&D costs over a worldwide production.

Multinational companies can also capitalize on economies of scale by expanding their R&D facilities abroad. Companies can achieve these economies mainly through the human resources and equipment components of the R&D department. Additionally, a higher level of research will be achieved by incorporating elements of technical centres of excellence that are globally dispersed. To experience fully the rewards associated with dispersed R&D, several issues must be recognized and understood by the multinational corporation. Some of these issues relate to the various sources of R&D information, the nature and scope of R&D alliances in the global marketplace, the degree and magnitude of corporate commitment required for international R&D, and to the organization of a successful dispersion of corporate R&D programmes. Other pertinent issues include ways of coping with inherent problems of dispersed R&D, as well as considerations in devising a strategy for a dispersed R&D effort. The rest of the article is devoted to addressing each of these relevant issues as they affect MNCs. Whenever appropriate, illustrations are provided to clarify the issue.

SOURCES OF INFORMATION FOR DISPERSED R&D

Multinational companies of all sizes need to be continually informed about the changing technologies around the world. One relatively inexpensive method of staying informed is to monitor and adapt to external factors that affect success or failure of a company. This environmental scanning can include reading R&D journals, perusing patent reports, having face-to-face contact with other R&D personnel, and maintaining contacts with academic researchers. It has been demonstrated that R&D managers stress the value of face-to-face contact with foreign scientists and technical experts through scientific–technical conferences or through in-house seminars (Ronstadt and Kramer, 1982). Multinational companies would do well to increase their involvement in international research by creating advisory panels without outside technical experts. These advisory panels would supply the companies with information regarding any significant emerging technologies. Companies can also include R&D specialists, as well as marketing managers, production personnel, and customer service representatives, on project teams that are assigned the task of seeking new product-related projects in international markets. This will allow companies associated with these markets to take advantage of team members' understanding of the unique characteristics of their respective foreign businesses. Companies could also encourage their R&D experts to undertake overseas assignments so they will be exposed to the different technologies that are available.

IBM has successfully used a strategy of tapping the engineering manpower of less developed nations to carry out competitive research and development (Liu, 1989). What impressed IBM was the pool of talented, eager engineers, the low costs, governmental support, and good credit terms available in less developed countries. They successfully rode the crest of emerging technical development expertise by assigning specific design projects to teams in Taiwan. This benefited local engineers by giving them valuable experience and enabled the country to upgrade its industry. IBM benefited by receiving good, solid products for its peripheral product line. In addition to such benefits, by locating R&D facilities in foreign countries, companies could employ local nationals in the R&D process to provide insight to the local market's unique product and market requirements.

FORMS OF STRATEGIC R&D ALLIANCES

Decentralization of R&D can be carried out through strategic global alliances, which can be achieved in various ways. Some of these include international licensing, co-operative research, mergers and acquisitions, or equity control in R&D firms. Each of these methods offers unique benefits to the MNC and, at the same time, poses different constraints. Each strategic R&D alliance requires varying amounts of commitment, resources, control, risk and flexibility (Jain, 1987; Peet and Hladik, 1989; Rudolph, 1989).

International licensing

Multinational corporations can also obtain external technology through international licensing. The corporation could 'licence-in' the technological innovation it wants from another international company or from a company in the host country. Smith-Kline Beecham, a major international pharmaceutical company, utilizes its R&D resources as a means for attracting licences from other firms to develop and market new products (Liu, 1989). By doing this, Smith-Kline Beecham has been able to enhance its product line.

A corporation might also choose to become involved in cross-licensing, in which firms exchange technological innovations with each other. Some companies are forced to do reciprocal licensing to gain access to the technology they want. As a Hoffman-Laroche executive noted: 'We found that we had to enter negotiations with something to trade rather than just with dollars' (Ronstadt and Kramer, 1982, p. 97). The licensing could be done on a corporate basis and the technology spread to the company's R&D facilities on an as-needed justification.

Co-operative research

Some multinational corporations will enter into cooperative research projects with each other. They do so in order to reduce R&D expenses and to reduce the risk associated with new research projects. Also, by combining their knowledge, multinational corporations can gain access to each other's technology (Perlmutter and Heenan, 1986). For example, Nissan Motor Co. Ltd entered into a research project with Ford Motor Co. to develop a new multipurpose vehicle (Liu, 1989). An R&D unit, Nissan Research and Development Inc., was established to develop the vehicle, as well as other vehicles, from the design stage through manufacturing. This cooperative research project will allow both Nissan and Ford to increase significantly their new product development capabilities.

Mergers and acquisitions

To further improve their R&D capabilities, multinational enterprises may acquire or merge with foreign companies that have extensive innovative capabilities. By adding the newly acquired capabilities to their existing facilities, the mutlinational enterprise can increase its ability to innovate abroad (Hamel *et al.*, 1989). For example, when CPC International acquired Knorr Foods of Switzerland, CPC received new technological capability to help it innovate in the 'processed food' industry.

Equity control

Multinational corporations can also gain access to outside technology by establishing an equity position in a company with innovative technology. By controlling the ownership of an innovative company, the parent company will be able to 'import' the essential technology back to its facilities at little or not cost (Modic, 1988). In the case of Bieri Pumpenbau AG Biral International, which owns a majority share of RCB Electroapparate (RCB), it was able to use RCB's technology of producing efficient electric motors almost exclusively for its own product lines. Biral International was able to expand its product capabilities by making RCB part of its portfolio of businesses.

When and why firms choose a certain mode of strategic R&D alliance rather than another is a function of several factors, including the required level of capital investment and the level of risk. For example, licensing is an acceptable strategy for low risk and minimal commitment that provides an entry point into developing international R&D

exposure for the firm. International licensing may have intuitive appeal for firms that neither possess capital investment not the technological know-how. Thus, it may eliminate the risk of R&D failures and the cost of trying to design around the licensor's patents, or the fear of patent infringement litigation. In addition, most licensing agreements have provisions for continuous cooperation and support, and thereby enabling the licensee to gain from new technological developments.

Overall, however, a significant level of commitment is required if a firm wishes to implement a decentralized R&D structure successfully. The next section of this article addresses some of these commitment issues.

CORPORATE COMMITMENT AS A PREREQUISITE FOR DECENTRALIZED R&D

Although commitment is a nebulous term, often lacking precise definition, its use here is in reference to the level of importance attached to a firm's market presence and the willingness to pledge the necessary resources in support of that presence. Few empirical studies exist in which commitment has been isolated as a causal factor in the performance of MNCs in the global marketplace. The operation of a local subsidiary business in a foreign country is a visible demonstration of commitment to that particular country. It follows, therefore, that the sizeable outlay of cash to develop a productive R&D facility indicates that multinational companies recognize the strategic consequences and importance of their regional image. Japanese automakers provide recent examples of the commitment required to be successful in international markets. Toyota, for example, is spending $400 million on a 12,000-acre test track in Arizona, and on new engineering and design studios in three other United States locations. Honda is building a 7.5 mile test track in California, and doubling the size of its research staff to 500 professionals. Similarly, Nissan is assembling a 500-person R&D staff of its own to supplement the staff at a ten-year-old California design centre (Taylor, 1990). The financial commitment of each of these companies indicates the effort required for success in foreign markets. Perhaps it is also an indication of why these three companies have been so successful in the United States market. In any case, these examples illustrate financial commitment as a function of the large company. Indeed, companies venturing into R&D abroad need to invest sizeable resources into foreign facilities.

A company needs to be fully committed to the advancement and continuity of its R&D facilities abroad to reap the best possible result from the venture. Management must realize that new product development is a precarious venture that requires total commitment of resources and an unrestrained devotion to change. Such commitment is illustrated in the following amusing anecdote:

A chicken and a pig were strolling by a diner one morning and the chicken smiled and said, 'Isn't that nice ... doesn't that make you feel proud, that we are responsible, you and I, for enabling those humans to enjoy their breakfast'. The pig replied, 'That's easy for you to say. For you it's merely a contribution, for me it's total commitment' (Buggie, 1982, p. 27).

Total commitment is required to foster changes and promote new product developments. To ensure that adherence to the R&D commitment is maintained, the company needs to assign the responsibility to someone who will emphasize product development above all else. R&D managers should be selected to oversee their own facilities. This will increase their commitment and responsibility, and encourage efficient new product development activities.

ORGANIZING FOR DISPERSED R&D

To organize effectively for a dispersed R&D, three issues need to be fully addressed:

(1) The need to recognize R&D as a multifunctional activity.
(2) The need for more flexibility in the degree of permanence for R&D units.
(3) The extent to which the firm can harness external resources into the R&D process.

The extent to which the firm can involve representatives from the engineering, marketing and manufacturing departments gives the R&D organization a multifunctional design. Given the market-driven character of most new innovations, it follows then that marketing will play an integral role from the beginning, as would engineering and manufacturing, to achieve timely, competitive, cost and quality advantages (Frey, 1989). Although the findings of a recent study show that virtually all major international product breakthroughs were the result of technological push rather than market pull, co-ordination between all of the operating departments was considered essential (Humble and Jones, 1989). The implication is that firms interested in dispersing R&D pro-grammes should seek a higher degree of collaboration between existing functional units to ensure an effective R&D dispersion.

Flexibility in the degree of permanence is also essential for the effective organizing of dispersed R&D. Committees or teams composed of representatives from engingeering, marketing, and manufacturing need to be created for a specific innovation. If successful, the team will become the core of the new business or product line. However, if unsuc-cessful, the team could be dissolved and its members freed to join new teams. This method of coordinating R&D functions keeps the team members fresh and allows them to get intimately involved with each new innovative team they join. Furthermore, it makes it possible for firms to mobilize an R&D team quickly whenever such a need arises in any part of the globe.

To organize an MNC for overseas R&D properly, the company may also need to incorporate outside resources into the process. Enterprises that desire to be active in overseas R&D may have to pursue projects with foreign academics because they can provide the scientific and technological knowledge important for innovative success. Other MNCs may want to form consulting agreements with foreign faculty members to tap into the local academic stream. Foreign education establishments may also have separate agreements to perform certain tasks for the enterprise. Instead of actually building R&D facilities, some companies have signed contracts with research institutes which conduct paid research and experimental projects for the firms. For example, organizations such as the Battelle Memorial Institute and the Illinois Institute of Technical Research have signed agreements to perform research for various companies. Since the dispersion of R&D can be complex, and sometimes cumbersome, strategic issues of importance to the firm deserve to be considered in the process of implementing a decentralized R&D system. Some of these issues are discussed in the next section.

STRATEGIC CONSIDERATIONS FOR DISPERSED R&D

Careful planning is needed to prevent haphazard acquisition or location of R&D facilities. There is the danger of duplication skills and capabilities when a company has several R&D facilities around the world. Overhead-support functions could also increase and be duplicated across the facilities, thus increasing the overall cost of R&D. In addition, by having R&D facilities spread worldwide, a company may lose control over the activities that the R&D facilities conduct. Consequently, the home office may be unable to maintain senior management's commitment to R&D and strategic objectives in the dispersed facilities.

In some situations, dispersed research and development is neither applicable nor advisable. These occur when the enterprise is such that innovation is not significant, being the first product in a market is not important, and benefits of economies of scale are minimal. When these situations exist dispersed research and development provides little strategic advantage.

However, if dispersed research and development are applicable, then several issues of strategic relevance deserve further consideration. Ronstadt and Kramer (1982) have identified three important areas of consideration in devising an effective strategy that will determine the ultimate success of dispersed R&D activities. These areas include:

(1) Corporate planning.
(2) Corporate control.
(3) Corporate coordination.

Each of these is considered individually.

Corporate planning

Prior to the full implementation of a decentralized R&D system, perhaps the first strategic issue to which a company needs to pay careful attention is the area of corporate planning. The corporate planning process has to include the nature of planned global R&D activities in determining the company's overall strategic plans. Decentralized R&D corporate planning involves defining the strategic objectives of all the proposed R&D facilities, deciding on the overall R&D expense and budgets, according to specific product development and strategic innovation needs, and estimating the proper amount of resources (human, raw material, etc.) to be allotted to each R&D facility. The plans should also include decisions regarding the level of local adaptation for the new products that will be developed. The home office needs to decide on the magnitude of adaptation or standardization of the new product that is necessary to meet local needs. In addition, the corporate strategic plans should include the appropriate time horizon for each foreign R&D laboratory to generate a stipulated number of new product developments.

Corporate control issues

It is important to consider the balance of power and control over decentralized R&D facilities between the home office and the local subsidiary. One corporate R&D manager succinctly described the balancing act as follows: 'The local R&D unit cannot have unbounded discretion over its performance ... We must help them succeed by making certain they do not try to do considerably more than they are capable of doing' (Ronstadt and Kramer, 1982, p. 99). The home office may consider setting restraining limits on the amount and type of R&D activities carried out at the overseas facilities, depending on the available resources. The division of power and control needs to be satisfactory to both sides to minimize unproductive friction between the home office and various R&D units, scattered around the world as a result of the decentralized R&D framework.

Proper reward systems have to be designed according to the needs of the overseas R&D facility's employees. Different nationals working in foreign laboratories have different levels of needs. For example, some nationals may value monetary rewards for excellence in R&D performance, while others may prefer personal recognition. The home office may need to develop and establish an overall standard of performance for each of its foreign R&D laboratories, but allow each subsidiary to design the reward system that it feels is most appropriate for its local R&D personnel.

Corporate coordination

A third area to which the home office needs to pay attention, in implementing a decentralized R&D system, is the coordination of all R&D activities at each overseas R&D laboratory. The home office must have the ability to coordinate the activities of all the facilities to ensure that activities are authorized and conducted properly. This could be accomplished by utilizing modern communications tools such as telephone, FAX machines and computer satellite link-ups. Occasionally, however, it may be necessary to send managers from the home office to various R&D subsidiary locations for observation purposes. The home office could also ensure proper coordination by appointing on-site coordinators for each R&D facility to assure that the activities performed are as specified in the corporate plans. The on-site coordinator should have extensive powers that would allow him or her to carry out the home office's plans effectively. Furthermore, the coordinator should also maintain good contacts and communications with the appropriate home office counterpart and superior.

Attempts by MNCs to coordinate decentralized R&D activities across countries may result in the consolidation of several local R&D activities. This could cause problems with local R&D personnel involved because they may resent losing control over their own R&D activities. Host governments may also express their displeasure in losing access to the available technologies when companies attempt to move their dispersed R&D facilities.

Since the stage of a product life cycle in the home country market does not parallel the life-cycle state in other international markets, increased communication between different R&D facilities is required. This communication will allow company personnel in the international market to learn from and improve on the actions taken in the home country. In this way, different product sophistication levels can be designed to match local requirements. This coordination must be considered in relation to each stage of the product development process, from idea generation all the way to product testing and eventual commercialization. This is crucial because, at any stage of this process, a decision could be made to drop a product concept or to discontinue further product testing. Failure in this downstream coupling mechanism may mean that the product idea would not emerge or, if it did emerge, may not match market needs.

It is apparent from the preceding discussion that the adoption of a dispersed R&D operation requires careful deliberation. Some firms clearly are not in a position to embrace fully a dispersed R&D structure. Others stand to enhance their global competitive position if R&D activities are decentralized. For such firms, it is prudent to consider carefully planning, control and coordination issues associated with a global decentralization of R&D programmes.

SUMMARY AND CONCLUSIONS

Multinational corporations have invested tremendous resources in establishing extensive operations abroad. Foreign operations are important sources of technological innovations for new product developments that improve the chances for global success. The potential increase in new product development capabilities may offset the cost of establishing dispersed R&D facilities, depending on the nature of market opportunities and the level of risk involved.

Companies do not always have to rely on internal R&D facilities. Development capabilities for new products can be obtained in a variety of ways. These include mergers or acquisitions of technologically competent companies, cooperative research projects with other companies, licensing rights to innovate technologies, and partnerships with academia. As yet, there is no evidence in the literature to suggest the presence of any prevailing pattern in the type or size of organizations that are active in dispersed R&D. However, organizations must be large enough to accord the seemingly high, initial cost of implementing a decentralized R&D structure. A company that is capable of employing any of the methods of acquiring technological innovation may benefit from such an alliance. A small company can enter into cooperative arrangements with similar companies to exchange technology. Innovative success in new product development will help to ensure continued competitiveness in the business environment.

Multinational corporations must be aware of the difficulties that might arise from the dispersion of their development facilities. For instance, there are potential problems arising from increases in overall operating costs through duplication of functions and activities in the dispersed laboratories. To avoid any unnecessary problems, careful planning and the appropriate organizational structures have to exist. These will allow for a conducive environment and the successful interrelated existence of all the operating R&D facilities. Suitable coordinating devices have to be utilized to ensure that the R&D activities will benefit the whole organization.

Corporations should also avoid haphazard placement of their research laboratories. Research and development facilities are best located where the corporations intend to market their products. Local, regional and national markets can be served by the products developed at the research laboratories. However, some research facilities can be, and often are, located away from the intended target markets and nearer to scientific and technological pools. Various surveys have shown that corporations prefer to locate their foreign laboratories in industrialized countries, such as Canada, the United States, Japan, the United Kingdom, Germany, Italy and Australia.

There are many uses for foreign R&D facilities. They can be responsible for adapting the home country's technology and products to the local markets. They can generate new products and processes expressly for local uses. They can develop products and technology for commercialization in other countries. Corporations have to determine beforehand how they intend to use their foreign research and development facilities, to avoid any misunderstanding regarding the status of the R&D operations within the organization. As was noted throughout this article, establishing overseas R&D functions is a risky proposition for many companies. However, if a company is totally committed to establishing an international R&D effort, history has shown that the benefits will far outweigh the risks.

REFERENCES

Buggie, F. (1982) 'Strategies for New Product Development'. *Long Range Planning*, **15**(2): 22–31.

Capon, N. and Glazer, R. (1987) 'Marketing and Technology: A Strategic Coalignment'. *Journal of Marketing*, **51**(July): 1–14.

Davidson, W. H. and Harrigan, R. (1977) 'Key Decisions in International Marketing: Introducing New Products Abroad'. *Columbia Journal of World Business*, **12**(Winter): 15–23.

Ford, D. and Ryan, C. (1981) 'Taking Technology to Market'. *Harvard Business Review* (March–April) 117–126.

Frey, D. M. (1989), 'Junk Your Linear R&D!'. *Research Technology Management* (May–June) 7–8.

Hamel, G., Doz, Y. L. and Prahalad, C. K. (1989) 'Collaborate With Your Competitors—And Win'. *Harvard Business Review* (January–February): 133–139.

Humble, J. and Jones, G. (1989) 'Creating a Climate for Innovation'. *Long Range Planning*, **22**(4): 46–51.

Jain, S. C. (1987) 'Perspectives on International Strategic Alliances'. *Advances in International Marketing*, **2**: 103–152.

Liu, P. (1989) 'Big Blue Benefits from Funding R&D in Taiwan'. *Electronic Business*, May: 105–106.

Modic, S. J. (1988) 'Strategic Alliances: A Global Economy Demands Global Partnerships'. *Industry Week*, (October): 46–52.

Peet, J. and Hladik, K. J. (1989) 'Organizing for Global Product Development'. *Electronic Business*, **6**(March): 62–64.

Perlmutter, H. V. and Heenan, D. A. (1986) 'Cooperate to Complete Globally'. *Harvard Business Review*, (March–April): 136–152.

Ronkainen, I. A. (1983) 'Product-Development Process in the Multinational Firm'. *International Marketing Review* (Winter): 57–65.

Ronstadt, R. and Kramer, R. J. (1982) 'Getting the Most Out of Innovation Abroad'. *Harvard Business Review* (March–April): 94–99.

Rudolph, S. (1989) 'Sometimes the Best Solution is in Someone Else's Lab'. *Business Month*, October, 91.

Stobaugh, R. and Wells, R. T. Jr (1984) *Technology Crossing Borders*. Harvard Business School Press, Boston, MA.

Taylor, A. (1990) 'Japan's New US Car Strategy'. *Fortune* (10 September): 65–80.

Wheelen, T. L. and Hunger, J. D. (1990) *Strategic Management*, 3rd edn. Addison-Wesley Publishing Company, New York, NY.

Yorio, V. (1983) *Adopting Products for Export*. The Conference Board, New York, NY.

12

Product Development the Japanese Way

Michael R. Czinkota and Masaaki Kotabe

The decade of the 1980s saw a great surge in the market success of Japan. Increasingly, there has been talk about the beginning of the Japanese century and the emergence of an overpowering Japanese economy.

Policymakers have responded to these visions by expressing concern about the trade competitiveness of the United States and taking actions designed to break down real or perceived trade barriers. Competitiveness, however, is driven and maintained to a large degree by individual firms and their marketing efforts. A quick review of the successes and inroads achieved by Japanese products confirms this perspective.

Japanese firms have been successful in established industries in which US firms were once thought invincible, as well as in newly developed industries. They have been able not only to capture third-country market share from the US competition but also to obtain major footholds in the US domestic market. They supplied almost 20% of US imports in 1989 and achieved their surplus in trade in manufactured goods on the basis of both high technology and non-high-technology products.

As a result, US producers' domestic market share for colour televisions has dropped from 90% in 1970 to less than 10% today, and the domestic share of semiconductor production has declined from 89% to 60%. Even more startling are the developments in the newly emerging high-definition television (HDTV) technology, which harbours the promise of a new electronic age. Several Japanese electronics giants have developed HDTV technology commercially. US producers, which previously balked at the idea of such technology because they did not see a ready market for it, are now seeking shelter behind standard-setting rules by the US Government.

In spite of the expenditure of vast funds on research and development (R&D), a number of US products do not seem to be able to perform sufficiently well in the marketplace. Yankee ingenuity once referred to the ability of US firms to successfully imitate and improve on foreign technology.

For example, the British discovered and developed penicillin, but it was a small US company, Pfizer, which improved on the fermentation process and became the world's foremost manufacturer of penicillin. The Germans developed the first jet engine, but it was two American companies, Boeing and Douglas, that improved on the technology and eventually dominated the jet airplane market.

Reprinted with permission from *The Journal of Business Strategy*, Vol. 11, November/December, pp. 31–36
© 1990 Faulkner & Gray, Inc.

Yankee ingenuity seems to have vanished and reemerged in the form of Japanese marketing techniques, which appear to see what many others do not recognize and often are right on target in identifying market needs. Perhaps it is time that US firms rediscover their former talents in order to compete with renewed vigour in the global market.

INCREMENTALISM VS. THE GIANT LEAP

Technology researchers argue that the natural sequence of industrial development comprises imitation (manufacturing process learning), followed by more innovations. In other words, continual improvements in manufacturing processes enables a firm not only to maintain product innovation-based competitiveness but also to improve its innovative abilities in the future. Failed innovators, in turn, lack the continual improvement of their products subject to a market-oriented focus.

During the postwar period, Japanese firms relied heavily on licensed US and European technology for product development. Product quality was improved through heavy investment in manufacturing processes with the goal of garnering differential advantage over foreign competitors. Continued major investment in R&D earmarked for product innovation heralded the technological maturation within Japanese firms, where the quality and productivity levels began to match or even surpass those of the original licensor.

US-style product innovations has placed major emphasis on pure research, which would allegedly result in 'giant leap' product innovations as the source of competitive advantage. By comparison, incremental improvements in products and manufacturing processes were neglected and relegated to applied research. As Peter Drucker has argued, however, research success may very well require the end of the 19th century demarcation between pure and applied research. Increasingly a minor change in machining may require pure research into the structure of matter, while creating a totally new product may involve only careful reevaluation of a problem so that already well-known concepts can be applied to its solution.

By contrast, the Japanese incrementalist view of product development emphasizes continual technological improvement aimed at making an already successful product even better for customers. Take the case of Japanese very-large-scale integration (VLSI) technology. The origin of VLSI technology was the transistor. Recognizing consumers' unsatisfied need to tune in their favourite music anywhere at any time, Sony introduced small portable transistor radios in 1955. Other Japanese companies quickly followed suit. There was quick market acceptance of the product worldwide.

Mass production made it possible to lower the cost and improve the quality of the product. In a short time, Japan reached a technological level at par with, and soon surpassing, that of the United States in transistor technology. As the age of integrated circuits (ICs) began, compact electronic calculators using this emerging technology boosted the growth of Japan's IC industry. The IC evolved into the large-scale integration (LSI) and now into VLSI.

These emerging technologies are used in consumer products, including personal computers, Japanese-language word processors, video cassette recorders (VCRs), compact disc players, and HDTVs. Many electronic products have sold in extremely large

volumes, a fact which has subsequently made ongoing investment in production possible, as well as further technological development. Incremental improvements in IC
technology have made it possible for Japanese firms to improve continually on a variety
of products. In the end, emerging products such as HDTV are truly different from what
they used to be both in form and concept.

This incremental technological improvement is not limited to high-tech industries.
Steel making is considered a mature or declining industry in most developed countries.
However, Japanese steelmakers are still moving toward higher levels of technological
sophistication, for example by developing a vibration-damping steel sheet (i.e. two steel
sheets sandwiching a very thin plastic film).

It is a small technological improvement that has a wide range of possible applications.
Due to the growing popularity of quiet washing machines in Japan, this steel sheet has
been used successfully as the outer panels of washing machines and is increasingly
finding its way into other noise-reducing applications, such as roofing, flooring, and
automotive parts.

THE MARKETPLACE AS R&D LAB

Due to the incrementalist product-development approach, Japanese firms have also
been able to increase the speed of new product introductions, meet the competitive
demands of a rapidly changing marketplace, and capture market share. Japanese firms
adopt emerging technologies first in existing products to satisfy customer needs better
than their competitors. This affords an opportunity to gain experience, debug technological glitches, reduce costs, boost performance, and adapt designs to customer use.

In other words, the marketplace becomes a virtual R&D laboratory for Japanese firms
to gain production and marketing experience as well as to perfect technology. This
requires close contact with customers, whose inputs help Japanese firms improve their
products on an ongoing basis.

In the process, they introduce newer products one after another. Year after year,
Japanese firms unveil not-entirely-new products that keep getting better, more reliable,
and less expensive. For example, Philips marketed the first practical VCR in 1972, three
years before Japanese competitors did. However, Philips took seven years to replace the
first-generation VCR with the all-new V2000, while late-coming Japanese manufacturers launched an onslaught of no fewer than three generations of improved VCRs in
this five-year period.

The continuous introduction of 'newer' products also brings greater likelihood of
market success. Ideal products often require a giant leap in technology and product
development and are subject to a higher risk of consumer rejection. Not only does the
Japanese approach of incrementalism allow for continual improvement and a stream of
new products, but it also permits quicker consumer adoption. Consumers are likely to
accept improved products more rapidly than they accept very different products, since
the former are more compatible with the existing patterns of product use and life-style.

Japanese firms also display a willingness to take the progress achieved through
incrementalism and develop a new market approach around it. An excellent example is
provided by the strategies used by different Japanese automobile manufacturers. After

decades of honing refinements in their products, these firms, within a short period of time, developed the Infiniti, Lexus, and Acura brands, which were substantially different in the consumer's mind from existing cars.

Each of these new brands was introduced to the market through an entirely new distribution system. Even though pundits had argued that in the automotive sector the time for new brands was over, let alone the likelihood of success for new channels, the approach chosen seems to be crowned by greater success than the more traditional acquisition route taken by Ford (Jaguar) or General Motors (Saab).

Market research is a key ingredient for successful ongoing development of newer products. The goal is to provide customers with more 'value' in the products they purchase. Product value is determined by cost and quality factors. In the United States, cost reduction and quality improvement are too often thought to be contradictory objectives, particularly when quality is perceived to be measured mainly by choice of materials or engineering tolerances.

Japanese firms, by contrast, see cost reduction and quality improvement as parallel objectives that go in tandem. The word *Keihakutansho* epitomizes the efforts of Japanese firms to create value by simultaneously lowering cost and increasing quality. *Keihakutansho* literally means 'lighter, slimmer, shorter, and smaller' and thus implies less expensive and more useful products that are economical in purchase, use, and maintenance.

Furthermore, Japanese perceptions consider quality in a product to be generated as well by the contextual usage of the product. If a product 'fits' better for a given usage or usage condition, it delivers better quality. That is why Japanese firms always try to emphasize both the 'high tech' and the 'high touch' dimensions in their product innovations.

The recent market success of Sony's black-and-white TV sets illustrates this point. Conventional market research failed to show that a market existed for such products in the United States. However, by studying the contextual usage of TV sets, Sony found that in addition to a family's main colour TV set, Americans wanted a small portable TV to use in their backyards or to take away with them on weekends.

HOW DOES JAPANESE MARKET RESEARCH DIFFER?

US market researchers, after developing an insulated staff function of their own, have grown enamoured of hard data. By processing information from many people and applying sophisticated data manipulations, statistical significance is sought and, more often than not, found.

Toru Nishikawa (1989), marketing manager at Hitachi, summarizes the general Japanese attitude toward such so-called scientific market research. He provides five reasons against relying too much on a general survey of consumers for new-product development:

1. *Indifference.* Careless random sampling causes mistaken judgment, since some people are indifferent toward the product in question.
2. *Absence of responsibility.* The consumer is most sincere when spending, but not when talking.

3. *Conservative attitudes.* Ordinary consumers are conservative and tend to react negatively to a new product.
4. *Vanity.* It is human nature to exaggerate and put on a good appearance.
5. *Insufficient information.* The research results depend on the information about product characteristics given to survey participants.

Japanese firms prefer more 'down to earth' methods of information gathering. Johansson and Nonaka (1987) illustrate the benefit of using context-specific market information based on a mix of soft data (e.g., brand and product managers' visits to dealers and to members of the distribution channels) and hard data (e.g., shipments, inventory levels, and retail sales). Such context-specific market information is directly relevant to consumer attitudes about the product or to the manner in which buyers have used or will use specific products.

Several things stand out in Japanese new-product development (or in their continual product improvements). First, Japanese new-product development involves context-specific market research as well as ongoing sales research. Second, some of the widely observed idiosyncrasies of the Japanese distribution system serve as major research input factors. For example, when a manufacturer dispatches his own sales personnel to leading department stores, not only are business relationships strengthened, but a direct mechanism for observation and feedback is developed as well.

Third, significant effort is expended on developing data, be it through point-of-sale computer scanners or the issuance of discount cards to customers, which also carry electronically embedded consumer profiles. Fourth, engineers and product designers carry out much of the context-specific research.

Toyota recently sent a group of its engineers and designers to southern California to nonchalantly 'observe' how women get into and operate their cars. They found that women with long fingernails have trouble opening the door and operating various knobs on the dashboard. Toyota engineers and designers were able to 'understand' the women's plight and redress some of their automobile exterior and interior designs.

City, another highly acclaimed small Honda car, was conceived in a similar manner. Honda dispatched several engineers and designers on the City project team to Europe to 'look around' for a suitable product concept for City. Based on the Mini-Cooper, a small British car developed decades ago, the Honda project team designed a 'short and tall' car, which defied the prevailing idea that a car should be long and low.

Yet, hands-on market research by the very people who design and engineer a prototype model is not necessarily unique to Japanese firms. Successful US companies also have a similar history. For example, the Boeing 737 was introduced about 20 years ago to compete with McDonnell-Douglas's DC-9. However, DC-9s were a somewhat superior plane; they had been introduced three years before the Boeing 737 and were faster.

Witnessing a growing market potential in Third World countries, Boeing sent a group of engineers to those countries to 'observe' the idiosyncrasies of Third World aviation. These engineers found that many runways were too short to accommodate jet planes. Boeing subsequently redesigned the wings, added low-pressure tires to prevent bouncing on shorter landings, and redesigned the engines for quicker takeoff. As a result of these changes, the Boeing 737 has become the best-selling commercial jet in history.

Hands-on market research does not negate the importance of conventional market research, emphasizing quantity of data and statistical significance. In developing the ProMavica professional still video system, which, unlike conventional 35 mm still cameras, records images on a two-inch-square floppy disc, Sony did extensive market research involving a mail survey, personal and telephone interviews, and on-site tests to elicit user response to the product during its development. What was unique was that the ProMavica task force included both engineers and sales/marketing representatives from Sony's medical systems and broadcast units. Sony's engineers gained insights from talking with prospects as much as did their marketing peers, and they incorporated user comments into product modifications.

It is clear that engineers and designers, people who are usually detached from market research, *can* and *should* also engage in context-specific market research side by side with professional market researchers. After all, these engineers and designers are the ones who convert market information into products.

SOME RECOMMENDATIONS

Clearly, US new-product development and market research are sophisticated and successful. Yet, in order to improve competitiveness further, several aspects of Japanese activities could be considered by US firms.

First, the incrementalist approach to product development appears to offer advantages in the areas of costs, speed, learning, and consumer acceptance. Second, such an approach requires a continuous understanding of current and changing customer needs and of the shortcomings of one's own products and those of the competition. In order to achieve such understanding, market research is essential.

In order for such research to be successful, the contextual usage and usage conditions of products need to be investigated and, once found, acted upon. While extremely useful in their own right, hard data alone is not the answer. This type of information often provides only limited insights into these contextual conditions.

It is therefore important to include soft information based on down-to-earth market observations. Since the ability to recognize dimensions of context is not uniquely confined to market researchers, it is important to fully include product managers, designers, and engineers in the research process.

Marketing research should not be a 'staff' function performed only by professional market researchers, but rather a 'line' function executed by all participants in the product development process. Not only will such an approach permit the discovery of more knowledge, but it will also immediately achieve the transformation of gleaned market data into information that is disseminated and applied throughout the entire organization.

REFERENCES

Nishikawa (1987) 'New Product Planning at Hitachi'. *Long Range Planning*, **2**: 20–24.
Johansson, J. K. and Nonaka, I. (1987) 'Marketing Research the Japanese Way'. *Harvard Business Review*, **65**: 16–22.

13

Matching Product Category and Country Image Perceptions: a Framework for Managing Country-of-Origin Effects

Martin S. Roth and Jean B. Romeo

INTRODUCTION

As the manufacture of products and the quest for consumers become increasingly global activities, international marketing research takes on greater importance. One such area, the study of country-of-origin effects (COO), seeks to understand how consumers perceive products emanating from a particular country. The COO phenomenon mirrors the global marketplace's increasing complexity. For example, current research attempts to examine how consumers respond to products exported from another country; designed in one country yet manufactured in another; manufactured in more than one location; and manufactured in one country but branded in another.

Attention has been given in the marketing literature as to why COO influences purchase decisions. Several explanations have been offered including product category involvement, knowledge of a particular country, and patriotism. The purpose of this research is to offer a new perspective on country-of-origin effects. Here, COO is examined in terms of the fit between countries and product categories. By relating country images to product category characteristics, decisionmakers can better understand preference formations for their products. This information provides insight into what underlies consumers' attitudes toward products manufactured in particular countries. Managers can benefit by having a better understanding of when promoting a product's COO is beneficial and when it is not, as well as identifying the dimensions along which country image should be improved.

Research has often contrasted consumer reactions to products originating from countries differing in overall quality. For example, Hong and Wyer (1989) manipulated country favourableness by the extent to which a country was noted for high or low quality products. The concept of country quality is really what makes the COO effect take place. While COO is only one cue consumers may use in evaluating brands (cf. Bilkey and Nes, 1982; Johansson, Douglas and Nonaka, 1985), it typically affects the evaluation of product attributes (e.g., Erickson, Johansson and Chao, 1984; Han, 1989; Johansson, Douglas and Nonaka, 1985).

Reprinted from *Journal of International Business Studies*, Vol. 23, No. 3, pp. 477–497

Past COO research has often treated country quality as a summary construct, rather than as a defined set of dimensions from which quality is inferred (e.g., Crawford and Garland, 1988; Hong and Wyer, 1989; Howard, 1989). In fact, *country image* may be the more appropriate summary construct, of which perceived quality may be just one dimension. The little research conducted to date indicates country image is really a multidimensional construct (Cattin, Jolibert and Lohnes, 1982; Jaffe and Nebenzahl, 1984; Han and Terpstra, 1988; Johansson and Nebenzahl, 1986; Nagashima, 1970, 1977; Narayana, 1981; White, 1979).

However, research on country image has made little attempt to link image dimensions to product categories. While it has been postulated that COO varies by product category (cf. Kaynak and Cavusgil, 1983), only one study (Han and Terpstra, 1988) has investigated product-country relationships. Research has shown that country quality perceptions (measured as a summary construct) may vary across product categories. For instance, in one study Japanese electronic products received high quality evaluations while Japanese food products received low ones (Kaynak and Cavusgil, 1983). Thus, while overall product-country quality stereotypes do occur, managers would be better served to know why such stereotyping exists. A consistent or favourable product-country match would occur when the perceived strengths of the country are important product benefits or features. Are the Japanese perceived to be strong in manufacturing and workmanship, qualities better suited for electronics than food? Whatever the exact explanation, both Japanese managers and their competitors would benefit from knowing what underlies consumers' attitudes toward Japanese electronic and food products.

This research suggests an approach for linking product category perceptions to country image dimensions. Specifically, why certain product categories are preferred from one country and not another is investigated. The purpose is to determine why purchase intentions differ across product categories from a particular country of origin. First, we define and operationalize the country image construct, and identify the underlying dimensions of country image. Second, the country image dimensions are used in a cross-cultural study to determine consumer perceptions of countries and product categories. These perceptions are then related to purchase intention, determining if the dimensions underlying a favourable association between a country and a product can be used to explain product preference. Third, the findings are discussed, with implications offered for both managers and future research.

BACKGROUND

Country image plays a significant role in consumers' perceptions of products. Thus, understanding the dimensions of country image and how it can be operationalized is important for managers whose products and those of their competitors are manufactured around the world. This section reviews how country image has been defined and operationalized in past research.

Country image defined

One of the first studies to look at country image perceptions was Nagashima's (1970) survey of US and Japanese businesspeople. Nagashima defined country image as:

the picture, the reputation, the stereotype that businessmen and consumers attach to products of a specific country. This image is created by such variables as representative products, national characteristics, economic and political background, history, and traditions. (Nagashima, 1970, p. 68)

Narayana's (1981) definition of country image is quite similar—'the aggregate image for any particular country's product refers to the entire connotative field associated with that country's product offerings, as perceived by consumers' (p. 32).

From a marketing perspective, a definition of country image is needed that relates more specifically to product perceptions, as some researchers have attempted to do by defining country image as consumers' general perceptions of quality for products made in a given country (Bilkey and Nes, 1982; Han, 1989). As such, we propose the following definition of country image:

Country image is the overall perception consumers form of products from a particular country, based on their prior perceptions of the country's production and marketing strengths and weaknesses.

This definition brings country image closer to the means consumers use in assessing products. What consumers know (or think they know) about a country's manufacturing ability, flair for style and design, and technological innovativeness, seems much more congruent with product perception formation than do other, less production and marketing-oriented factors. Just what these production and marketing strengths and weaknesses are is examined next.

Country image operationalized

Eight studies were identified that assessed country image. Each study measured the country image construct using scaled items that were either grouped according to mean scores (Nagashima, 1970, 1977), or through factor analytic techniques (Cattin et al., 1982; Han and Terpstra, 1988; Jaffe and Nebenzahl, 1984; Johansson and Nebenzahl, 1986; Narayana, 1981; White, 1979). Thus, means and standard deviations of the scaled items, or the zero-order correlations of the items, would be required to conduct a meta-analysis (Hunter, Schmidt and Jackson, 1982; Hunter and Schmidt, 1990). Only one study reports the item means (Cattin et al., 1982), and only one reports the correlations (White, 1979). Due to a lack of data comparability, a qualitative (rather than quantitative) approach to summarizing previous country image research was used.

Columns one and two of Table 1 show the dimensions found in the eight country image studies. Close examination of the country image research findings revealed certain dimensions consistent across the majority of these studies (i.e., consistent across various national subjects and their perceptions of countries). As shown in the third column of Table 1, four dimensions of country image became apparent—innovativeness, design, prestige, and workmanship. These dimensions met the following criteria: (1) were consistently found in previous research; (2) related to perceptions of country's production and marketing strengths and weaknesses; and (3) with intuitively and/or based on previous research, are applicable to a broad range of product categories. An advantage of identifying country image dimensions is to generate consistency for conceptualizing and operationalizing country images in future studies. This will yield greater

Table 1. Country image dimensions

Study	Country image dimensions	Production and marketing image dimensions
Nagashima (1970, 1977)	Price and value	
	Service and engineering	*Innovation*
	Advertising and reputation	*Prestige*
	Design and style	*Design*
	Consumers' profile	
White (1979)	Expensive	
	Price	
	Technicality	*Innovation*
	Quality	
	Workmanship	*Workmanship*
	Inventiveness	*Innovation*
	Selection	
	Serviceability	
	Advertising	
	Durability	
	Reliability	
	Brand recognition	*Prestige*
Narayana (1981)	Quality	*Workmanship*
	Recognition	
	Prestige	*Prestige*
	Production form	*Innovation*
	Expensiveness	
	Popularity	
	Functionality	*Design*
Cattin, Jolibert and Lohnes (1982)	Pricing	
	Reliability	
	Workmanship	*Workmanship*
	Technicality	*Innovation*
	Performance	
Jaffe and Nebenzahl (1984)	Product-technology	*Innovation*
	Marketing	*Prestige*
	Price	
Johansson and Nebenzhal (1986)	Economy	
	Status	*Prestige*
Han and Terpstra (1988)	Technical advancements	*Innovation*
	Prestige	*Prestige*
	Workmanship	*Workmanship*
	Economy	
	Serviceability	

comparability of research findings, and subsequent generalizability of COO. The country image dimensions are defined as:

Innovativeness: use of new technology and engineering advances.
Design: appearance, style, colours, variety.
Prestige: exclusivity, status, brand name reputation.
Workmanship: reliability, durability, craftsmanship, manufacturing quality.

From this review, two important conclusions can be drawn. First, country image appears to be a multidimensional construct. As such, it is unclear that a single measure of overall quality can be deemed equivalent to country image. Yet, COO studies have frequently used a single measure of product quality rating in order to understand the impact of 'made-in' stereotypes (e.g., Crawford and Garland, 1988; Hong and Wyer, 1989; Howard, 1989).

Second, the dimensions found to underlie country image are all production and marketing oriented. This could be an artifact of the initial 50 adjectives and phrases pretested by Nagashima (1970) in the first country image study. However, the basis for Nagashima's research (Osgood, 1952; Osgood, Suci and Tannenbaum, 1957) was be-havioural rather than applied marketing research. An alternative and more plausible explanation is that consumers' perceptions are formed by relating to a product what they know about a country's ability to produce goods and services. This gives further credence to the country image definition proposed earlier.

Having defined country image and identified four dimensions for operationalizing the construct, we now turn to the relationship of country image perceptions to product categories and subsequent purchase intention.

PRODUCT–COUNTRY MATCHES

Few studies to date have systematically examined what underlies a consistent or favor-able match between products and countries. Figure 1 shows when product and country

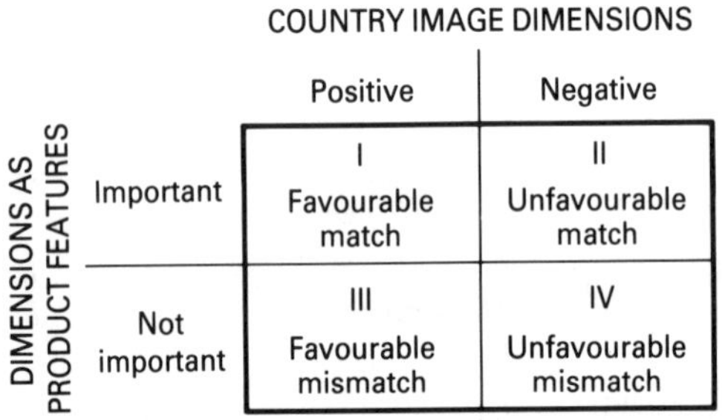

Figure 1. Country and Product Category Dimension Matches and Mismatches.

matches and mismatches should occur. A product–country match should occur when important dimensions for a product category are also associated with a country's image. When there is no such linkage, a mismatch between the product category and country should exist. Consider the following examples of consumer product and country percep-tions regarding the image dimensions design and prestige. First, France may be associ-ated with good design and prestige, while Hungary is perceived as very weak with regard to design and prestige. Further, design and prestige may be important features when consumers consider shoe purchases, but relatively unimportant for the purchase of beer. A product–country match (cell I of Figure 1) would occur when the perceived strengths of a country are important product features or benefits for the particular product category. Hence, a product–country match for French shoes would be evident.

An unfavourable product–country match (cell II) would occur when the important product features are not the perceived strengths of the country. Hungarian shoes would appear to be an unfavourable match. A favourable mismatch (cell III) would occur when the image dimensions for a country are positive, but they are not important for the particular product category. Such would be the case for French beer. Likewise, an unfavourable mismatch (cell IV) would occur when an image dimension is both an unimportant product feature and not a perceived strength of the country. Hungarian beer would likely be an unfavourable mismatch.

Understanding favourable or unfavourable (mis)matches can be very beneficial to managers. Such information can be used, for instance, to select or omit specific product or country information in their marketing communications. A favourable match would indicate to managers the dimensions on which they should promote their product's benefits. In addition, it suggests that a brand that positively correlates with the country-of-origin would be beneficial. Likewise, the presence of an unfavourable match would indicate that country-of-origin information should not be part of the communications strategy. In fact, it may be the case that negative COO effects would occur when the promoted product benefits are not consistent with the country's perceived strengths. In summary, the four cells of Figure 1 illustrate possible relationships between consumer product and country perceptions.

Evidence suggests that country image perceptions may vary across product categories. Nagashima (1970, 1977) asked respondents to recall what products first come to mind when they think of a specific country. However, his study does not give any insight into what underlies a favourable match between a country and a product class. In other words, the dimensions associated with a particular country were not related to specific product categories.

Some studies have made a more specific attempt to determine the quality perceptions of different product categories across various countries. For instance, Kaynak and Cavusgil (1983) had respondents rate the quality of four product classes across 25 different countries. Howard (1989) had respondents rate the quality of six product lines across nine countries. From these studies, product–country match can only be inferred by perceptions of product quality.

Han and Terpstra (1988) assessed the association between five image dimensions (refer to Table 1 for a listing of the dimensions used) and two product categories (automobiles and televisions). They found that country image ratings are not consistent across the five dimensions (e.g., German autos are rated high on prestige, but low on economy). This suggests that country image is specific to the dimensions being measured. They also found that country image ratings tend to be consistent across product categories (e.g., both Japanese autos and televisions have moderate levels of prestige). Since country images on specific product dimensions appear to be generalizable across product categories, Han and Terpstra (1988) concluded that general country images may exist. However, their study was limited to US consumers' perceptions of two products and four countries (Germany, Japan, Korea, US). Further research is needed to investigate whether country image variations across product categories exists for a wider range of both countries and products and whether these perceptions exist for consumers outside the United States.

The cross-national component of COO is important. Research has shown that country image perceptions may vary depending upon the consumer's nationality. Nagashima (1970, 1977) and Narayana (1981) found differences in country image perceptions between Japanese and American consumers. Crawford and Garland (1988) found differences in quality perceptions across West German and American consumers. Cattin, Jolibert and Lohnes (1982) found that stereotyping differed among French and US purchasing managers. Thus, research that investigates country image and COO needs to consider the perceptions of consumers in more than one country.

METHODOLOGY

A study was designed to determine which dimensions are most frequently associated with a country's image and how important these characteristics are to different product categories. Data were collected cross-nationally, as COO may affect consumers from various countries differently (cf. Cattin *et al.*, 1982). Surveys were distributed to graduate students in Ireland, Mexico, and the United States. The questionnaire was administered at the beginning or end of a class. Graduate students were used to ensure a moderate degree of familiarity with the countries and product categories being investigated. Although generalizing from such a homogeneous sample may be limited, it does ensure comparability across the national groups. Furthermore, the use of graduate students, familiar with many product categories and countries, permitted assessing many product–country matches, thus providing more generalizable findings. Response totals were 139 for the US, 130 for Mexico, and 99 for Ireland.

The questionnaire consisted of five sections. The first section measured country image. Country image was measured along the four dimensions discussed earlier (innovativeness, design, prestige, and workmanship). Each dimension was defined for the respondent. For instance, to evaluate countries on innovativeness, the investigator wished to know: 'For the countries listed below, how do you perceive the innovativeness of their products, where innovativeness means use of new technology and engineering advances?' Subjects responded on seven-point scales (1 = not innovative; 7 = very innovative). For each dimension, subjects evaluated ten countries. The countries surveyed were England, Germany, Hungary, Ireland, Japan, Korea, Mexico, Spain, and the United States.

The second section of the survey had subjects use the four image dimensions to evaluate six different product categories. Respondents evaluated (using seven-point importance scales) the extent to which each of the four image dimensions was an important criterion for evaluating each product category. The product categories evaluated were beer, automobiles, leather shoes, crystal, bicycles, and watches. The product categories and countries were selected because (1) the importance of the image dimensions was expected to vary across the products (e.g., innovativeness would be more important to one category than to another); (2) the product categories were expected to associate with one or more, but not all of the countries; (3) no one or set of countries would be perceived as the best fit for all products; and (4) both product categories and countries would be familiar to our informants, thus avoiding familiarity issues which have been shown to affect COO (Johansson *et al.*, 1985; Han, 1989). The data from sections one and two would be used to identify product–country matches.

In the third section, subjects were asked how willing they would be to purchase the product categories from each of the ten countries they evaluated. These willingness to buy measures would be related to the product–country matches to determine how well the matches explain purchase behaviour. The fourth section measured respondents' familiarity with the ten countries and six product categories, and the fifth section surveyed demographic information. A total of 146 items were evaluated (similar to other studies in this area, cf. Nagashima, 1970; Cattin, Jolibert and Lohnes, 1982), requiring on average 15 minutes to complete.

The questionnaire was structured such that respondents rated all stimuli (i.e., the ten countries or the six categories) on the basis of one dimension, then proceeded to the next dimension. This format has been shown to yield high stability over time (Jaffe and Nebenzahl, 1984), and is consistent with the format of previous country image studies. Order of stimuli and dimensions was randomized throughout the questionnaire.

RESULTS

Country image

Prior to investigating the product–country matches, a validity check that the four dimensions were capturing unique information was conducted. Correlations between the four country image dimensions across the ten countries were examined. As shown in Table 2, respondents from each country evaluated the dimensions similarly. Hence,

Table 2. Correlations among four country image dimensions

	Design	Prestige	Workmanship
Irish respondents ($n = 85$)			
Innovativeness	0.6367	0.4656	0.5606
Design		0.3103^a	0.5202
Prestige			0.5552
Mexican respondents ($n = 103$)			
Innovativeness	0.7354	0.6037	0.6018
Design		0.7742	0.7275
Prestige			0.6898
US respondents ($n = 128$)			
Innovativeness	0.6082	0.5262	0.5554
Design		0.4984	0.5701
Prestige			0.5369

Pearson correlations. All correlation coefficients significant at $p < 0.001$ (two-tailed test) except a, $p < 0.01$.

when a country was rated highly on innovativeness, it also tended to be evaluated highly on the other dimensions. This pattern did not vary across the ten countries studied. Such a high degree of correlation was not expected given the multidimensional nature of country image found in past research.

To address the dimensionality issue, factor analysis was used. First, factor analysis using the principal components method (to account for as much variance in the data as possible) was conducted (Kim and Mueller, 1978). Table 3 shows the factor analysis results across all three country respondents (results did not vary cross-nationally). All four dimensions load very highly on one factor, explaining 76% of the variance (because only one factor was extracted, the solution was not rotated). This one-factor solution indicates a potential lack of discriminant validity among the four dimensions, and suggests a unidimensional country image construct.

Table 3. Factor loadings of country image

	All respondents (n=319) Factor
Design	0.88912
Workmanship	0.88288
Prestige	0.86244
Innovativeness	0.85776

Variance explained = 76%.

Confirmatory factor analysis using LISREL was then conducted to gain further insight into the fit of the unidimensional model for each group of respondents. Compared to competing two-dimensional models, the one factor model best captured the country image construct for the US ($chi^2_{(df=2)}$ = 1.85, adjusted goodness of fit = 0.964) and Mexican ($chi^2_{(df=2)}$ = 3.41, adjusted goodness of fit = 0.914) respondents. For the Irish respondents, a two-factor model ($chi^2_{(df=1)}$ = 0.20, adjusted goodness of fit = 0.987) consisting of (1) innovativeness and design and (2) prestige and workmanship significantly improved fit (chi^2 reduction from the one-factor model was significant at p < 0.005). However, these two factors were extremely highly correlated (0.933), making the discriminant validity of the two constructs questionable. The one-factor solution exemplified good fit ($chi^2_{(df=2)}$ = 4.50, adjusted goodness of fit = 0.854), and was determined the most applicable for the Irish respondents. An investigation of the reliabilities of the four dimensions across the three sets of respondents further supports the use of the unidimensional solution (Cronbach's *alpha* Irish = 0.815, Mexican = 0.898, US = 0.835).

Correlation and factor analyses also revealed that the measures of image importance for the six product categories were highly related. Within each product category, there was little variation in the dimension importance evaluations.

The finding that the country image construct was only unidimensional runs counter to past research. It is difficult to determine whether this occurrence is due to (i) subjects' perceptions of the countries investigated, (ii) dimension definitions that were too similar, or (iii) the use of single-item image dimension measures. A pretest of the instrument on US respondents did not reveal significant correlations among the four dimensions, and debriefings indicated the dimensions were perceived clearly and uniquely. This study used four items to capture country image, while past research used 20 (Narayana, 1981), 14 (Han and Terpstra, 1988), and 13 (Jaffe and Nebenzahl, 1984; Johansson and Nebenzahl, 1986) items. The greater number of items makes obtaining multiple factors more likely. In fact, the more items used, the more factors were found (20 items yielded five factors, 14 items yielded four factors, and 13 items yielded two factors). Although the four dimensions used here comprised the items used in past research, by definition they all relate to the production and marketing perceptions of countries, and as such appear to capture a single country image construct.

Product–country match and mismatches

Having identified one dimension for country image, the relationship of the dimension between product category and country evaluations was investigated. A product–country match occurs when the perceived strengths of a country are related to product characteristics. A strong positive match would exist when the country is perceived as being very strong in an area that was also an important feature for a product category.

Country and product images were operationalized by computing an average evaluation across the four dimensions. The importance of the image dimensions for the product category was determined by averaging the importance of the four dimensions across each product category (for example, the importance of the image variables for autos is the average of importance of innovativeness, design, prestige, and workmanship for autos). As can be seen from Table 4, there was a favourable product–country match

Table 4. Perceptions of country image and product categories, Irish, Mexican, and US respondents

	Irish respondents ($n = 85$)	Mexican respondents ($n = 103$)	US respondents ($n = 128$)
Country image			
Germany	6.071	6.087	6.234
Japan	6.062	6.425	6.206
US	5.639	5.965	5.600
France	5.131	5.191	4.593
England	4.791	5.289	4.408
Korea	3.997	4.913	4.245
Ireland	4.422	3.968	3.498
Spain	3.601	4.340	3.632
Mexico	2.410	3.930	2.445
Hungary	2.266	3.514	2.381
Image importance for products			
Auto	6.503	6.506	6.601
Watch	6.066	6.178	6.009
Bicycle	5.214	5.379	5.502
Leather shoe	4.952	5.267	5.041
Crystal	5.344	4.975	4.941
Beer	3.717	4.242	3.400

Mean scores are averages of the four dimension evaluations. All items measured using seven-point Likert-type scales.

between Germany, Japan, and the US for automobiles and watches. These countries had high image perceptions, while the image dimension was an important characteristic for autos and watches. An unfavourable match is evident between Mexico and Hungary for autos and watches. These image perceptions were important product characteristics, and respondents had low image perceptions of these countries.

A product–country mismatch would exist when the benefits being investigated are not important for the product category and these benefits are either associated with a country (favourable mismatch) or not associated with a country (unfavourable mismatch). An example of a favourable mismatch is Japanese beer. The image dimension was not important for the beer product category, yet Japan received high country image ratings. An unfavourable mismatch would exist for Hungarian beer, since Hungary's country image was relatively low.

The degree of match or mismatch was not as evident for the remaining countries (Korea, England, Ireland, France, and Spain) and product categories (bicycles, leather shoes, crystal). These countries received average evaluations, while the image dimensions were of moderate to average importance for the product categories.

The product–country matches have implications for mangers who may want to improve the use of COO information in advertising strategies. The presence of a favourable product–country match would indicate that the product's COO could enhance product evaluations. A favourable mismatch, however, would indicate that the COO would not enhance evaluations. In fact, promoting COO when a favourable mismatch exists may be detrimental to evaluations. Where the degree of match or mismatch is not as evident, it may be possible for country image to be improved by communicating to consumers that the country's products have high delivery on features related to country image. While German car manufacturers often promote their cars' 'German engineering', our results indicate that Irish, Mexican, and US consumers would also react favourably to claims about German styling and craftsmanship. Simply put, these consumers feel Germans have manufacturing and market competencies that relate well to the benefits derived from automobiles and watches. Mexican car manufacturers, or US cars being manufactured in Mexico, would not be well served by promoting Mexican engineering, styling, or craftsmanship, as these are important product features on which Mexico is perceived to be relatively weak. Consumers would likely perceive such claims to be false, and thus dismiss the credibility of the communication. Finally, French car manufacturers may not benefit from promoting their cars' French qualities, as the country's effect may have little positive (or negative) effect. Communication time and money would be better spent focusing on the product benefits themselves, rather than their COO.

Prediction of willingness to buy

Finally, the product–country matches were related to consumers' willingness to buy the foreign products. The identification of product–country matches should help predict a consumer's purchase intention. When a strong, favourable match exists, a COO effect is likely to occur, positively affecting product evaluation. When a mismatch is evident, COO should have little impact on willingness to buy. The relationship between willingness of respondents to buy the six products from the ten countries (see Table 5 for willingness to buy results) and the product–country matches was explored to see if such predictions can be made. Given the product–country match results, we anticipated the following: (1) autos and watches from Germany, Japan, and the US would be moder-

Table 5. Willingness to buy products: US, Mexican, and Irish respondents

	Auto	Watch	Bicycle	Leather shoe	Crystal	Beer
US respondents ($n = 128$)						
Japan	6.41	5.66	5.54	3.68	3.70	4.20
Germany	6.54	5.88	5.78	4.86	5.40	6.38
US	4.88	5.65	5.99	5.77	4.90	6.11
France	3.68	4.86	5.55	5.66	5.67	4.15
England	4.37	4.57	4.80	4.91	5.48	5.49
Korea	3.72	3.77	4.25	3.48	3.01	3.03
Ireland	2.60	3.51	3.91	4.08	4.98	5.49
Spain	2.36	3.30	3.44	5.13	4.08	3.92
Mexico	1.93	2.53	2.91	3.58	2.78	4.78
Hungary	1.70	2.48	2.76	3.03	3.40	3.42
Mexican respondents ($n = 103$)						
Japan	6.14	6.06	5.89	3.91	4.71	3.43
Germany	6.36	6.16	6.13	4.85	5.75	6.66
US	6.16	5.85	6.38	4.52	4.95	5.45
France	5.03	5.27	5.63	5.34	5.37	3.98
England	4.83	5.16	5.31	4.76	4.96	4.79
Korea	3.91	4.54	4.77	3.82	3.85	2.58
Ireland	3.91	4.06	4.14	3.89	4.43	4.38
Spain	3.39	3.95	3.88	5.27	3.69	3.70
Mexico	4.98	3.93	4.73	6.46	6.03	6.36
Hungary	3.02	3.37	3.49	3.64	3.73	3.42
Irish respondents ($n = 85$)						
Japan	6.06	5.48	5.57	3.20	2.93	2.51
Germany	6.70	5.96	6.15	5.07	4.50	6.30
US	5.00	5.30	5.54	4.65	3.35	5.27
France	5.31	5.42	5.94	5.99	4.89	4.37
England	4.71	4.81	5.35	5.18	4.35	4.70
Korea	2.94	3.14	3.82	2.82	1.94	1.97
Ireland	3.90	4.61	4.99	5.40	6.76	6.27
Spain	3.41	3.67	3.76	5.46	3.23	3.52
Mexico	1.90	2.35	2.57	3.65	2.11	3.14
Hungary	1.82	2.19	2.49	2.73	2.57	2.88

ately preferred over those from France, England, Korea, Ireland, and Spain, and strongly preferred over those from Mexico and Hungary; and (2) preference for bicycles, leather shoes, crystal, and beer would not be related to the ordering of countries by image, since the image dimension(s) were not very important for these products. Correlation analysis (see Table 6) was used to investigate these predictions (the country image column from Table 4 was correlated with each column representing willingness to buy a particular product category in Table 5).

As expected, for all respondents, the correlation between country image and the willingness to buy an automobile and a watch from that country was positive and highly significant. Thus, willingness to buy autos and watches from Japan, Germany, and the US appears related to these countries' high overall image, and the components of this image, workmanship, design, prestige, and innovativeness are important to these product categories. Likewise, respondents' unwillingness to buy these products from

Table 6. Correlations between country image and willingness to buy foreign products

	US	Mexican	Irish
Auto	0.9712*	0.8811*	0.9495*
Watch	0.9792*	0.9861*	0.9298*
Bicycle	0.9388*	−0.0987	0.9297*
Leather shoe	0.4678	0.9274*	0.313
Crystal	0.4822	0.39	0.296
Beer	0.4446	0.1986	0.3624

Pearson correlations.
* Denotes correlation coefficient significant at $p <$ 0.001 (two-tailed test).

Mexico and Hungary appears due to the poor overall image of these countries. Thus, while COO information might enhance attitudes towards Japanese, German, and US autos and watches, it would probably be detrimental to these products manufactured in Mexico or Hungary. These findings support the favourable match and unfavourable match cells in Figure 1 (cells I and II, respectively.) These results are similar to other studies that found that automobiles manufactured in Japan, West Germany and the US were preferred over those from England, France, Brazil, Mexico, Taiwan, and South Korea (cf. Howard, 1989).

The results also indicate that for beer, where the image dimension was not important, the correlation between country image and willingness to buy these products was not significant for all respondents. For example, Japan was rated as having a high country image, yet this positive image appears unrelated to willingness to buy beer from Japan (favourable mismatch). While an unfavourable mismatch exists for Hungarian beer, there is really no difference in purchase intentions between Japanese and Hungarian beer. Although the mismatch is favourable, COO information will have no effect on the evaluation of Japanese beer. It should be noted that the data here indicate a favourable mismatch for German beer which received a high willingness to buy rating from all respondents. Thus, features that are important for beer (features other than those measured by this study) are probably also associated with Germany (but not with Japan).

Some differences in the product–country matches to predict willingness to buy did exist among the groups of respondents. Mexican respondents' willingness to buy leather shoes was related to country image. This was not the case for Irish and US respondents. This result likely occurred since Mexican respondents perceive the image dimensions investigated in this study to be more important for leather shoes than did the other groups. Irish and US respondents' purchase intentions for bicycles were related to country image while Mexican respondents' were not. A possible explanation may be an ethnocentrism effect, since unlike Mexico, bicycles are manufactured both in the US and Ireland.

Other studies have investigated consumers' willingness to buy products from certain countries. For instance, Johansson et al. (1985) suggest that previous experience with a particular country and/or product category may influence the COO effect. Garland and Rhea (1988) and Han (1988) looked at the influence of patriotism on willingness to buy.

The contribution of this study is that it offers an additional explanation as to when COO information is used by consumers. In summary, strong product–country matches along the image dimension(s) do seem to predict willingness to buy foreign products.

Country and product familiarity

Research has indicated that consumer familiarity with countries and products may affect COO (e.g., Han, 1989; Johansson, Douglas and Nonaka, 1985). The effects of country and product familiarity on the product–country matches and prediction of willingness to buy were investigated. Generally, consumers in this study exhibited moderate to high country familiarity (mean scores for familiarity were all 3.5 or higher as measured on seven-point scales). The only exception was Hungary, for which all three groups of respondents were much less familiar (overall mean across the three groups was 1.8). Analysis of variance indicated that for nine of the ten countries evaluated (all except Hungary), US, Mexican and Irish respondents differed in country familiarity. Newman–Keuls tests indicated the following patterns: (1) Irish respondents were more familiar with EC countries than US and Mexican respondents; and (2) Irish respondents were less familiar with East Asian and North American countries than were US and Mexican respondents.

The impact of these country familiarity differences was explored by splitting the country samples into high and low country familiarity groups and using first-order partial correlations (controlling for country familiarity) to reassess the product–country match and willingness to buy relationships. Controlling for country familiarity did not affect the relationship; the patterns of statistical significance for both the high and low familiarity countries were almost identical to those found in Table 6. As such, country familiarity differences did not appear to affect consumers' use of image dimension(s) when assessing willingness to buy.

Analysis was also performed to see whether product category familiarity differences existed, and if so, the extent to which they affected the product–country matches and prediction of willingness to buy. Familiarity of all subjects across the six product categories was above average (greater than 4 on a seven-point rating scale), indicating prior knowledge of the categories. Analysis of variance indicated no differences in familiarity with beer and bicycles across the US, Mexican, and Irish respondents. Significant differences were found for the other four product categories. Newman–Keuls tests indicated that Irish respondents were more familiar with crystal and less familiar with autos than were US and Mexican respondents. Within-group differences revealed no clear patterns of product familiarity. These familiarity differences do not appear to affect the product image assessments nor the image-willingness to buy correlations (Tables 4 and 6). In addition, analyses on demographic differences between groups revealed very homogeneous samples, and resulted in no changes in the prediction of willingness to buy.

These findings indicate that product–country match may be an indicator of willingness to buy foreign products. If a country is perceived as having a positive image, and this image is important to a product category, consumers will be more willing to buy the product from that country. In this study, US, Irish, and Mexican consumers were willing to buy a car or watch from Japan, Germany, and the US since these countries were evaluated highly on dimensions that were also important to these product categories. Likewise, an unfavourable product–country match may explain why consumers are unwilling to buy certain products from certain countries. Respondents were less likely to buy Mexican and Hungarian autos and watches as these countries had poor evaluations on dimensions that were important car and watch characteristics.

DISCUSSION

While consumers may prefer automobiles from Japan and Germany, they would rather buy crystal from Ireland and leather shoes from Italy. Thus, the interesting question for marketers is, What underlies consumers' attitudes toward products from a particular country?

Although previous research has shown that perceptions of countries may vary across different product categories, there is little insight into why these perceptions vary. In other words, what constitutes a favourable match between a country and a product? This study found that willingness to buy a product from a particular country will be high when the country image is also an important characteristic for the product category. Thus, perceptions vary depending on how well the country's perceived production and marketing strengths are related to the product category.

In addition, this paper introduced a definition of country image in order to bring this construct closer to production and marketing-oriented factors consumers use in assessing products. Four measures were developed to operationalize country image— innovativeness, design, prestige, and workmanship. In contrast to previous research, this study found these four measures to be highly correlated. Across three national samples, country image was unidimensional. Thus, it is possible that perceptions of a country's production (e.g., workmanship) and marketing (e.g., prestige) strengths and weaknesses are considered together when evaluating a country's products. The possible formation of general country images has been noted in other recent country image research (Han and Terpstra, 1988), and provides greater validity to past studies using summary measures of country quality (e.g., Crawford and Garland, 1988; Hong and Wyer, 1989; Howard, 1989).

The unidimensionality finding differs from past country image studies. A possible explanation for our unexpected result is that the use of single-item measures for each dimension may not tease out subtle differences in consumer perceptions of foreign countries. Studies employing multiple measures found anywhere from five (Nagashima, 1970, 1977; Narayana, 1981; Cattin, Jolibert and Lohnes, 1982) to two (Johansson and Nebenzahl, 1986) country image dimensions. Multiple measures may enable consumers' to make finer distinctions about country characteristics. The issue for researchers and managers is, what really affects consumer evaluations of countries and their products— separate constructs determined by multiple item measures, or an overall evaluation of the country's image? In other words, while consumers may delineate country differences from multiple measure surveys, do they in fact use such detail in product evaluations?

The only prior research relating country dimensions to product evaluations (Han and Terpstra (1988), who used multidimensional measures of country image) found mixed results. Similar to this study, dimensions rated highly for one country's product tended to be rated highly for other products manufactured in the same country. However, unlike this research, they also found that countries were not ranked consistently across image dimensions. Clearly, more research needs to be done to determine the impact of unidimensional versus multidimensional country images on product evaluations.

Consistent with past research on COO, the results of this study indicate that it is important for managers to recognize that cross-national differences should be taken into account. Specifically, some differences in product–country matches and willingness to buy predictions were found across the three groups of respondents.

As expected, country and product familiarity did not affect image perceptions. Except for evaluations of Hungary, all respondents were moderately to highly familiar with the countries and product categories surveyed. The sampling procedure used was designed to control familiarity. Perhaps greater variance along the familiarity dimensions would affect product–country matches and prediction of willingness to buy. Further, measurement of actual country experience and product usage may provide better evaluations of familiarity than the self-assessments used here.

The findings reported in this study have managerial implications that are summarized in Figure 2. When favourable matches exist, consumers' willingness to buy products can

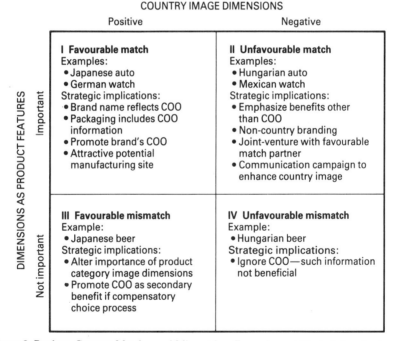

Figure 2. Product–Country Matches and Mismatches: Examples and Strategic Implications.

be enhanced by promoting COO (cell I, Figure 2). For instance, the product would benefit from having a brand reflect its COO (e.g., German-sounding brand name for a car, Japaneses-sounding brand name for a watch). Placing the brand's COO on the packaging, or on the product itself, would also have a positive effect on attitudes.

Favourable matches also indicate potentially attractive manufacturing sites for multi-national companies.

If an unfavourable match exists (cell II, Figure 2), COO information would be detrimental to product evaluations. In this case, advertising should emphasize import-ant product benefits other than the brand's country of manufacture. One possible strategy when an unfavourable mismatch exists is to consider a joint venture within a favourable match country. For instance, a Hungarian car manufacturer may benefit from manufacturing and/or marketing its cars with a German partner. Another, long-term strategy, is for the company whose image is unfavourable to initiate a campaign to alter perceptions of country image. The focus of the campaign would be on improving consumers' image along dimensions that are viewed negatively for that country. For instance, a Mexican manufacturer may want to show consumers that Mexican products have good design and workmanship qualities.

The mismatch cells also offer interesting implications for marketing managers. Although COO information is positive in the favourable mismatch condition, it may not be beneficial for promoting the particular product category (Japanese beer did not receive a high willingness to buy rating). One option if a favourable mismatch exists (cell III, Figure 2) is to alter the importance of the image perceptions. For instance, a Japanese beer company could promote that its innovativeness allows it to brew a superior tasting beer. Consumers who would not normally associate innovativeness with beer may be influenced to view it as a positive dimension for the beer product category. Furthermore, when consumer decisionmaking is compensatory (cf. Wright 1975), including favourable (mismatch), COO information may improve overall brand evalu-ations. For unfavourable mismatches (cell IV, Figure 2), COO will likely not be ben-eficial and should probably be ignored.

Future research is needed to provide more evidence as to whether country image is a multidimensional or unidimensional construct. Perhaps the dimensions in this study could be redefined. A check should be made to see if the unidimensional image construct found here is applicable to a more geographically dispersed group of consumers. In addition, research is needed to further investigate potential product familiarity effects on product–country matches and predictions of purchase intent. If respondents with little product familiarity (as compared to the average to above-average levels reported here) evaluate matches differently, marketers will need to adapt their strategies accordingly.

The generalizability of the framework presented here should also be examined for other consumer groups. While comparable cross-national graduate student samples were used here, research on other socioeconomic groups should be conducted as well. The product–country match framework introduced here should be incorporated into a multi-attribute choice model (Erickson, Johansson and Chao, 1984; Johansson, Douglas and Nonaka, 1985). The relative importance of the match to other product attributes with respect to overall brand evaluation is an important area of future research.

ACKNOWLEDGEMENTS

The authors thank Timothy Heath and the anonymous *JIBS* reviewers for their con-structive comments, and A. C. Cunningham (University College, Dublin), Juan

Antonio Meejia (Monterey Institute of Technology), and Michael Peters (Boston College) for their valuable data collection assistance.

REFERENCES

Bilkey, W. J. and Nes, E. (1982) 'Country-of-Origin Effects on Product Evaluations'. *Journal of International Business Studies*, **13**(Spring/Summer): 89–99.

Cattin, P., Jolibert, A. and Lohnes, C., (1982) 'A Cross-Cultural Study of "Made-In" Concepts'. *Journal of International Business Studies*, **13**(Winter): 131–141.

Crawford, J. C. and Garland, B. C. (1988) 'German and American Perceptions of Product Quality'. *Journal of International Consumer Marketing*, **1**(1): 63–78.

Erickson, G. M., Johansson, J. K. and Chao, P. (1984) 'Image Variables in Multi-Attribute Product Evaluations: Country-of-Origin Effects'. *Journal of Consumer Research*, **11**(September): 694–699.

Garland, B. C. and Rhea, M. J. (1988) 'American Consumers: Profile of an Import Preference Segment'. *Akron Business and Economic Review*, **19**(Summer): 20–29.

Han, C. M. (1989) 'Country Image: Halo or Summary Construct?' *Journal of Marketing Research*, **26**(May): 222–229.

Han, C. M. and Terpstra, V. (1988) 'Country-of-Origin Effects for Uni-National and Bi-National Products'. *Journal of International Business Studies*, **19**(Summer): 235–255.

Hong, S-T. and Wyer, R. S. Jr. (1989) 'Effects of Country-of-Origin and Product-Attribute Information on Product Evaluation: An Information Processing Perspective. *Journal of Consumer Research*, **16**(September): 175–187.

Howard, D. G. (1989) 'Understanding how American Consumers Formulate their Attitudes about Foreign Products'. *Journal of International Consumer Marketing*, **2**(2): 7–24.

Hunter, J. E. and Schmidt, F. L. (1990) *Methods of Meta-Analysis*. Newbury Park, CA: Sage Publications.

Hunter, J. E., Schmidt, F. L. and Jackson, G. B. (1982) 'Meta-Analysis: Cumulating Research Findings Across Studies'. *Sage Series on Studying Organizations: Innovations in Methodology*, **4**. Beverly Hills, CA: Sage Publications.

Jaffe, E. D. and Nebenzahl, I. D. (1984) 'Alternative Questionnaire Formats for Country Image Studies'. *Journal of Marketing Research*, **21**(November): 463–471.

Johansson, J. K., Douglas, S. P. and Nonaka I. (1985) 'Assessing the Impact of Country-of-Origin on Product Evaluations: A New Methodological Perspective'. *Journal of Marketing Research*. **22**(November): 388–396.

Johansson, J. K. and Nebenzahl, I. D. (1986) 'Multinational Production: Effect on Brand Value'. *Journal of International Business Studies*. Fall: 101–126.

Kaynak, E. and Cavusgil, S. T. (1983) 'Consumer Attitudes Towards Products of Foreign Origin: Do They Vary Across Product Classes?' *International Journal of Advertising*, **2**: 147–157.

Kim, J-O. and Mueller, C. W. (1978) *Factor Analysis*. Sage University Paper series on quantitative applications in the social sciences, series no. 07–014. Beverly Hills and London: Sage Publications.

Nagashima, A. (1970) 'A Comparison of Japanese and US Attitudes toward Foreign Products'. *Journal of Marketing*, **34**(January): 68–74.

Nagashima, A. (1977) 'A Comparative "Made in" Product Image Survey among Japanese Businessmen'. *Journal of Marketing*, **41**(July): 95–100.

Narayana, C. L. (1981) 'Aggregate Images of American and Japanese Products: Implications on International Marketing'. *Columbia Journal of World Business*, **16**(Summer): 31–35.

Osgood, C. E. (1952) 'The Nature and Measurement of Meaning'. *Psychological Bulletin*, **49**(May): 197–262.

Osgood, C. E., Suci, G. J. and Tannenbaum, P. H. (1957) *The Measurement of Meaning*. Urbana, IL: University of Illinois Press.

White, P. D. (1979) 'Attitudes of US Purchasing Managers toward Industrial Products

Manufactured in Selected Western European Nations'. *Journal of International Business Studies*, **10**(Spring/Summer): 81–90.

Wright, P. L. (1975) 'Consumer Choice Strategies: Simplifying versus Optimizing'. *Journal of Marketing Research*. **11**(February): 60–67.

14

International Counterfeiters: Marketing Success Without the Cost and the Risk

Michael G. Harvey and Ilkka A. Ronkainen

The United States trade deficit reached a record $130 billion in 1984. Contributing to this imbalance was an estimated $20 billion of domestic and export sales lost by United States industry because of foreign product counterfeiting and trademark patent infringement of consumer and industrial products.

The United States is the largest single market for foreign counterfeits. At the same time, United States export markets are affected by foreign counterfeiting and span the globe. The Far East contains the most affected foreign markets. Hong Kong, Taiwan, Korea, Singapore, Thailand, Malaysia, Indonesia, the Philippines, Mexico, Brazil, and India have been cited by the US Department of Commerce for their varying lack of protection in all areas of product and patent infringements.

The practice of product counterfeiting has spread from the traditionally counterfeited products—high-visibility, strong brand-name consumer goods—to a wide variety of consumer and industrial goods, and even services. The European Economic Community estimates that trade in counterfeit goods now accounts for about two percent of total world trade, while the International Chamber of Commerce estimates the figure at close to 5% of world sales.

Counterfeiting has been a problem for a long time. It mushroomed in the 1970s; then it seemed the only victims were manufacturers of overpriced consumer goods, such as apparel and luggage, and for the most part, the economic effects of counterfeit operations went unnoticed. However, the damage done by counterfeiters is not only economic; some consumers have been killed or injured because of substandard counterfeit products. The American Medical Association recently drew attention to the growing problem of bogus, look-alike amphetamines and tranquillizers which are believed to have caused 12 deaths in 1983. The counterfeiters have even duplicated heart pacemakers and sold them to unsuspecting hospitals to be implanted in heart patients. In November 1984, 1.26 million bogus Ovulen-21 birth control pills entered the market and caused internal bleeding among unsuspecting users before a successful recall by the manufacturer, G. D. Searle.

Since the onslaught of the counterfeiting boom, businessmen have bemoaned the

Reprinted from *Columbia Journal of World Business*, Vol. 20, Fall, pp. 37–45
© 1985 Columbia Journal of World Business. Reprinted with permission

weakness of the only United States federal law that addresses the problem: the Lanham Act, the 1946 Federal Trademark Law. The Lanham Act is a civil law that permits a court to order one company to stop using another's trademark/logo, or to pay damages. However, counterfeiters have hidden their assets or disappeared and routinely violated court orders banning them from the use of identifying trademarks or outright product forgeries. If an importer is caught, he simply forfeits his goods. New legislation, the Trademark Counterfeiting Act of 1984, was passed after two years of Congressional deliberations, and imposes heavy criminal penalties for marketing counterfeit goods: fines up to $1 million and 15 years imprisonment for individuals. State legislatures, for example California and New York, are also starting to take the problem seriously by passing tougher criminal laws and allowing trademark owners to prosecute those who violate court orders. But the environment for counterfeiting still appears to be attractive to those who want to sell copies on the world market.

This paper examines: (1) four common counterfeiting strategies; (2) the economic impact of counterfeiting on United States based MNCs; (3) the non-economic influence of counterfeit products; (4) legislation passed in the United States to deal with counterfeiters; and (5) corporate strategies to reduce counterfeiting.

ILLUSTRATIONS OF TYPICAL COUNTERFEITING STRATEGIES

While there are a multiple of counterfeiting strategies, four basic approaches help to illustrate the variety of schemes employed by international counterfeiters. The four types of counterfeiting strategies will help to clarify the role of each party in the counterfeiters' strategies. The basic typologies discussed are divided into direct and indirect counterfeiting strategies.

I. Direct counterfeiting strategies

Direct counterfeiting strategies are characterized by explicit involvement of the counterfeiter in the theft or duplication of the product. The two direct counterfeiting strategies are briefly discussed below.

The first type of direct counterfeiting scheme involves the foreign firm/individual that wishes to counterfeit products (Figure 1(a)). The counterfeiter (C) illegally acquires a product or in some cases purchases a product to have counterfeited. The counterfeiter obtains the product of the originating company (O) and has the product manufactured in a third country (M). The product is then sold in the counterfeiter's home market. The reason for manufacturing in the third country may be to reduce the probability of detection and/or to decrease legal remedies if the counterfeiter is legally prosecuted for selling counterfeit products.

The second direct method of counterfeiting—theft by employees of a company—has become commonplace in the computer industry (Figure 1(b)). Although accounts of such thefts are sometimes mentioned in the mass media, most are not reported. Such thefts are not reported because the company is unaware of how the counterfeiters have obtained the necessary data to duplicate their products, and secondly, the company does

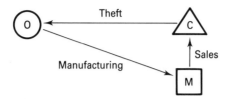

(a) Direct theft; manufacture in third country; sales in counterfeiter's market

Key: O = originating country/company   M = foreign markets
          of product and/or trademark   ⟶ = indicates direction of specified
      C = counterfeiting organization   activity
      A = agent/intermediary   3rd = third market where the product is sold

(b) Theft in originator's company; manufacture in counterfeiter's market; sales
     in originator's market

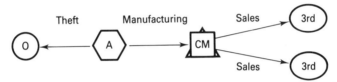

(c) Intermediate theft; manufacturing in counterfeiter's sales in third markets

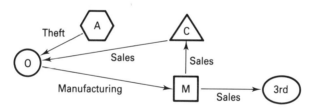

(d) Intermediate theft; manufacture in third market; sales in all markets

Figure 1. Four Typical Counterfeiting Strategies.

not want the publicity surrounding the theft because they may target themselves for future counterfeiters.

The employee confiscates inside information and sells this information to foreign competitors. The foreign competitor then uses the information to manufacture the product to be sold in the originator's home market. Approximately 75% of counterfeit goods are manufactured outside the United States, while 25% are either made in the United States or made elsewhere and labelled in the United States.

II. Indirect counterfeiting strategies

Indirect counterfeiter strategies typically employ an agent and/or an intermediary to steal product information or specifications to be used by the counterfeiter. The agent becomes an intermediary working on behalf of the foreign firm that wants to manufacture/market the counterfeit products. The two most common strategies are outlined below.

The counterfeiting firm (C) contracts with an intermediary (A) to obtain the product and/or information necessary to counterfeit the product of the originating company (O) (Figure 1(c)). Once the agent has obtained the product/information, the bogus products are manufactured in the counterfeiter's home market and then sold in other foreign markets (3rd). The use of an agent reduces the potential legal consequence of the theft of the original product/information for the foreign MNC. When Pfizer Inc. introduced Feldene, an antiarthritic drug, to Argentina in 1980, the company found that five Argentine firms already had generic copies of the pharmaceutical on the market.

A more complex form of indirect counterfeiting involves the use of an agent (A) and the manufacturing of the counterfeit product in a foreign market (M) other than that of the counterfeiter (Figure 1(d)). The counterfeit product is then sold in the counterfeiter's home market (C), other foreign markets (3rd) as well as the originator's home market (O). This type of counterfeiting strategy is used by MNCs located in developed economies. Manufacturing the bogus product in less developed countries, the counterfeiter thus takes advantage of lower labour rates and weaker legal manufacturing restraints. At the same time, the counterfeiters are able to shelter themselves from legal inquiries from the United States based MNC. For example, more often than not a buyer from outside Taiwan brings a sample of a famous brand to a local manufacturer and asks him to copy it. Taiwan's copies are often superb. One Western maker of running shoes went there to see a suspected copier and rather than prosecuting him decided to enlist the company as a supplier.

These four counterfeiting strategies are not exhaustive but rather demonstrate the various orientations to obtaining, manufacturing and marketing counterfeit products.

ATTRACTIVENESS OF UNITED STATES PRODUCTS TO COUNTERFEITERS

Counterfeiting is a significant problem for organizations throughout the world. However, MNCs based in the United States appear to be the primary targets of many counterfeiters. The reason behind this focus on United States based MNCs may be attributed to a combinations of factors which are listed below.

- Typically, US consumer/industry products are heavily advertised. Because of heightened competition in the domestic market, many producers have used advertising to help differentiate their products in the marketplace. Therefore, many United States produced products are known throughout the world.
- US consumer and industry products are widely distributed not only in the United States but also in world markets. This extensive distribution increases the awareness of United States produced products among customers in foreign markets.
- Established branding strategies are employed by US MNCs. Branding as a means to establish customer loyalty has been practiced extensively by customer goods producers; thus, strong customer brand affiliation has accrued over the years.

- US produced products are generally considered prestigious throughout the world. While consumers in the United States do not attribute a great deal of status to domestically produced products, many foreign consumers hold them in high regard, if for no other reason than they are made in the United States.
- US MNCs typically employ the latest technology in their products, and US produced products represent technologically advanced products to most of the world's consumers.
- Shortages of products exist in many foreign markets. Because of the limited supply of well-established products in less developed economies, copies of products produced in the United States have strong customer appeal.
- There is a lack of adequate legislation in the United States and foreign countries to prevent counterfeiting of United States produced products. A vast majority of laws pertaining to counterfeiting appear to be outdated or ineffectual in combating counterfeiters.
- The US Freedom of Information Act of 1966 is often mentioned as a source of problems, aiding and abetting the piracy of products and technologies. Pfizer Inc., for example, estimated that more than four-fifths of the 34,000 FOIA requests for the release of information received in 1982 by the Food and Drug Administration were commercially motivated.
- The United States market is an easy one for counterfeiters to enter. Importers often conceal fake goods in legitimate shipments, and some products are routed through other countries. In 1984, US Customs seized $13.5 million worth of contraband, but to stop the flow entirely, each shipment would have to be inspected, for which the Service does not have the manpower.

The attention of counterfeiters on United States based manufacturers has not centered only on consumer goods. The impetus to counterfeit products can be traced to the needs of various end markets. Both consumer goods and services as well as industrial goods and services are being counterfeited. Table 1 illustrates the current level of interest in US produced products to the worldwide counterfeiters. One of the fastest growing areas of interest is in high technology and services because of less developed countries' need to produce goods than can be sold on the world market to gain hard currency.

Table 1. Attractiveness of product/service to counterfeiters by end-market

	Consumer goods/services		Industrial goods/services	
Product/service counterfeited	3rd World*[a]	Industrialized	3rd World*	Industrialized
Nationally branded product	High[b]	High	High	High
Unbranded/generic product	High	Low	Moderate	High
Original technology/innovation	Moderate	High	High	High
Service	High	Low	High	Low

[a] End-market for counterfeited products/services.
[b] Level of attractiveness to counterfeiters to sell bogus products in end-markets (high ... moderate ... low).

THE ECONOMIC MAGNITUDE OF COUNTERFEITING

In Mexico City's Calle Amberes in the Zona Rosa shopping district, one might notice that there is a brand new Cartier boutique with its windows filled with gold jewellery, fashionable watches and lustrous leather goods. But only eight doors away, another Cartier boutique exists. Its windows are also filled with gold jewellery, fashionable watches, and lustrous leather goods. The second shop with merchandise that appears to be identical to the first is a counterfeit Cartier boutique.

The genuine Cartier shop was opened in November of 1983 to battle the imposters. The fake boutique is a creation of Fernando Pelletier, a Mexican who has 14 'Cartier' boutiques, half of them in the capital, and others in places like Acapulco, Guadalajara, and Puerto Vallarta. Pelletier once offered to sell his stores to the Paris firm for $4.5 million, but irate Cartier officials decided to pay lawyers instead. Cartier has won 25 suits against Pelletier, but the bogus Cartier retailer remains in business and still costs the Paris original up to four million dollars a year in lost profits.

Cartier is not alone. Counterfeit merchandise of all types has flooded the United States market, duping the brand-conscious consumer and costing firms millions of dollars in detective work, lawsuits, and lost sales. This counterfeit merchandise ranges from fake Rolex, Cartier, and Omega watches, to La Coste sweaters, Levi jeans, and Michael Jackson albums. It extends into the industrial market as well: Ford and Chrysler auto parts and bogus Apple computers, to industrial nuts and bolts. A Bell Helicopter crash, in which one person died, was reportedly caused by a fake replacement part. Puritan Fashions, makers of Calvin Klein jeans, lost an estimated 15 to 20 million dollars in wholesale revenue to 'rip-off artists' last year alone. Christian Dior estimates that it loses around 500 million dollars in annual revenues to counterfeiters. Posh Courreges says that it has only 40% of its 'own' market, worth $15 million a year. And according to Thomas F. Kelleher, vice-president for security at MasterCard International, total losses from counterfeit MasterCards in 1981 amounted to nearly $26 million, a 36% increase over the previous year. And by 1982, dollar losses escalated to $45 million, an increase of 77% over 1981 alone.

According to Congressman John Dingell, the chairman of the House Commerce, Oversight and Investigations Subcommittee, the counterfeiting problem is more costly than the explicit dollars lost to the foreign counterfeiters show. It is estimated that $3 billion in sales and 210,000 jobs are lost every year to fake auto parts alone. Furthermore, an International Trade Commission study estimated that at least $400 million in US record and tape sales were lost in 1982, along with another $258 million in export sales. Manufacturers of machinery, electrical goods, and metal products lost another $40 to $60 million.

In addition, millions of dollars are being spent yearly on undercover work and lawsuits against counterfeiters. Christian Dior spends $380,000 a year policing its 313 trademarks and employs a staff of three to work solely on counterfeiting problems. Cartier spends more than $1 million a year tracking down and suing counterfeiters. Gucci Shops, Inc., spends similar sums fighting fraud, as do Levi Strauss and the makers of Spalding sporting goods. Ford Motor Company won $3.6 million in damages and costs last year from a distributor accused of stamping the Ford trademark on cheap auto parts.

It can only be concluded that counterfeiting is a significant problem facing US companies and respected foreign competitors as well. How this happened is a question that needs attention. It appears that the more successful a marketing campaign, seemingly the more attractive it becomes for competitors to skirt copyright and trademark laws or to make outright illegal copies of an originator's line.

THE NON-ECONOMIC IMPACT OF COUNTERFEIT PRODUCTS

Counterfeiting may also have a devastating impact on a company because it invariably results in low-cost, inferior products which can damage a firm's or its products' image. Counterfeiters take advantage of and tread upon the good name, reputation and goodwill the firm has established for its brand over an extended period of time. Robert R. Miller, group vice-president of the Automotive Aftermarket Group of the Parker Hannifan Corp., explains that 'in some cases foreign producers have copied parts so closely that they include government certification marks and manufacturing date codes. If that exact copy were tested at random and found to be inferior or unsafe, it would have disastrous effects on the company's business and reputation before it was learned that the defective part was a counterfeit.' Watch manufacturers like Rene Dentan, president of Rolex USA, and Gedalio Gringberg, president of North American Watch Company (Piaget), also insist that counterfeiters are debasing the reputation, style and exclusivity of their expensive, highly profitable timepieces. According to Dentan, 'they are bloodsuckers and parasites'. Many other companies affected by counterfeiting indicate the loss of brand loyalty and the 'good' name of the company has greater implications than the explicit economic losses.

The flood of pirated Apple personal computers into markets throughout the world illustrates what counterfeiters can do to a company or even a market for a product. According to the House Oversight and Investigation Subcommittee, 'Apple II has had the dubious distinction of being the pirates' personal computer of choice by virtue of its popularity and the very large number of software programs, more than 15,000, written for the machine'. The counterfeit Apple computers began appearing in the Far East in early 1982 and reached the United States market shortly thereafter. Despite Apple's registering its trademarks and copyrights with US Customs, filing an enormous number of lawsuits, and bringing an action before the International Trade Commission, the House Commerce Subcommittee said that the volume of counterfeit Apple computers has steadily increased each year. In retail outlets in Taiwan and Hong Kong, 'knock-offs' of the best selling Apple II Plus model are available for prices as low as $300, as compared to $1,530 for the genuine article in the United States. An Apple executive advised the subcommittee that in one instance it was found that another $10 would even buy a copy of the distinctive trademark, a multicoloured apple with a bite missing. Most of these duplicated computers have copied the Apple II Plus in virtually every detail, including an identically copied electronic printed circuit board, pirated Apple software, and a look-alike case. A group of the imported bogus computers was displayed to the House Subcommittee alongside the genuine Apples to demonstrate their confusingly similar configuration and features. These Asian manufacturers have so successfully duplicated the silicon microchips in the core of the Apple machines that the imitations can use a broad range of software, from Visicalc, the top selling business budgeting and planning program, to video games like 'Snack Attack' and 'Rocket Intercept'. In addition, they were advertised as being 'Apple compatible'.

Apple's new counterfeit competitors have already captured more than half of the firm's East Asian market, and they are now exporting their computers to South Africa and South America. Counterfeiting is especially pervasive with personal computer programs, which are easy to copy with a blank diskette and a computer with two disk drives.

A security firm specializing in the computer and semiconductor industries conducted an undercover investigation into the theft and subsequent illegal movement of electronic components. It is understood from intelligence sources that there are several electronics companies in northern California that are generally considered to be fronts for Eastern bloc countries or the People's Republic of China. During a 'sting-type' operation conducted in 1983, a wide spectrum of organizations and individuals—from sophisticated international counterfeiting networks to simple opportunists—were identified, and their methods of trafficking in counterfeit goods was tracked.

Because it provides access to the marketplace, the distribution network is considered the key element in the marketing of counterfeit products. Without this link, thieves would find it very difficult to dispose of stolen goods and buyers would be very hesitant to deal directly with suppliers. The middleman provides a colour of legitimacy to the end-users.

During the 'sting' operation, Barry Ching-bor Poon was identified as a Hong Kong-born resident alien who owned a firm called Microwave Exceltek. When he was arrested, police found the Poon residence crammed with 75,000 integrated circuits valued at between $200,000 and $300,000. Many of the circuits were said to have been sold to Mr. Poon as part of the undercover operation. The investigators had negotiated with Mr. Poon and his brother for importation from Hong Kong of large quantities of the counterfeit Apple computers. In exchange for a preferential price and the promise of a steady supply of chips in the future, the Poons offered counterfeit Apple IIs for $300 per unit delivered. The undercover agents requested a sample of the counterfeit computers. Mr. Poon attempted to import 15 units, but they were seized by US Customs agents. However, he did manage to get at least one sample into the country, which was purchased by the agents. The facts suggested that Mr. Poon was part of a network that purchased stolen chips in California, shipped them to Asia for use by counterfeiters of Apple and other computers, and assisted the sales and distribution of the counterfeit merchandise back in the United States.

The impetus for Apple, Inc. to sue was more than purely economic, given the fact that the brand image of Apple's products was being damaged. The undercover operation and ensuing litigation exemplifies the problems Apple and other major manufacturers face. In 1983, Apple filed two lawsuits in Taiwan against Sunrise Computer Services, Inc. and Golden Formosa Co., Ltd. Apple charged the two companies with violating the copyrights of its ROM software. The other lawsuits filed in Taiwan and Hong Kong were for patent and copyright infringement. As Apple has learned, prosecution against counterfeiters is rare and the laws themselves are weak or lightly enforced where they do exist. For example, Taiwan's high court had to overturn a 1931 statute, clearing the way for Apple to prosecute the alleged computer counterfeiters. And under Taiwan's copyright laws, convicted counterfeiters can receive prison terms of up to 3 years and an equivalent fine of $225. If sentenced to 6 months or less, convicted counterfeiters can usually trade the prison term for a fine at the rate of about 23 cents a day. Some courts are also testing a novel self-enforcement tool by appointing the companies' own lawyers as special prosecutors to bring criminal contempt charges. In one case involving lug-gage-maker Louis Vuitton, the court even allowed Vuitton's lawyer to set up a complete 'sting' operation to prove that a counterfeiter was still in operation.

In the US, federal anticounterfeiting laws do not represent much of a deterrent to sophisticated counterfeiters. For copyrighted properties such as films and tapes, federal statutes carry maximum first-offence penalties of one year in jail and $25,000 in fines. Under the federal laws dealing with credit cards (the Truth in Lending Act and the Electronic Funds Transfer Act), it is currently not a federal crime to counterfeit a credit card, to knowingly possess a bogus card or counterfeiting equipment, or to knowingly deal and traffic in account numbers taken off of credit card sales slips. Victims must prove that counterfeiters have broken mail-fraud statutes or some other federal law, or they must prosecute under state laws that mostly treat counterfeiting as a misdemeanour.

ANTICOUNTERFEITING LEGISLATION

The 98th Congress focused a great deal of attention on intellectual property rights. In October 1984, President Reagan pushed to pass the Omnibus Tariff and Trade Act of 1984. The Act requires the Office of the US Trade Representative to report to Congress by October 1985 on intellectual property-related barriers and determine the extent to which a country provides 'adequate and effective means under its laws for foreign nationals to secure, exercise and enforce exclusive rights in intellectual property, includ-ing patents, trademarks, and copyrights'. It also amends Section 301 of the Trade Act of 1974 to clarify that the violation of intellectual property rights is an unreasonable practice within the terms of the statute. This is especially important in protecting the high-technology sector where new products require significant research and develop-ment expenditures which must be recognized over a relatively short term. Without adequate protection, the ability to reap adequate returns can be undermined as pirated products are sold at cut-rate prices—there being no need to cover development costs.

The Omnibus Tariff and Trade Act also introduces a major 'carrot and stick' policy. The President is directed to complete a review of the Generalized System of Preferences eligibility of certain countries. The adequacy of protection of intellectual property rights of United States manufacturers is a factor that will be considered in the designation of beneficiary countries.

The Trademark Counterfeiting Act of 1984 made trading in goods and services using a counterfeit trademark a criminal rather than a civil offense, and established stiff penalties for such practices.

The Semiconductor Chip Protection Act of 1984 clarified the status and protection to be afforded to semiconductor masks, i.e., the intricate designs which determine the capabilities of a chip. Reflecting the inadequate state of international protection for chip designs, the Act provides that this new form of protection will be available to foreign-designed masks only if the home country of the manufacturer also maintains a viable system of mask protection. Japan is the country most affected by this legislation and is currently considering legislation along similar lines.

The patent terms for pharmaceuticals and other products were extended up to five years to compensate delays due to federal premarketing clearance procedures. Still another new provision closes a loophole allowing competitors of the owner of the patent to make the product in the US but avoid infringement by completing the assembly abroad.

The Freedom of Information Act must still be redefined in order to exempt trade secrets and confidential business information from FOIA disclosure. The Act should also be amended to require firms be notified when information they have filed has been requested. Legislation has also been introduced to protect computer software which calls for strict reciprocity. Under the bill proposed by Senator Frank Lautenberg, if a country denied or limited protection of US software, the United States would not protect software first published in that country.

INTERNATIONAL ACTION BY US GOVERNMENT FOR PROTECTION OF INTELLECTUAL PROPERTY

The US government is also seeking to limit counterfeiting practices through bilateral and multilateral negotiations and education.

The International Trade Administration and the Patent and Trademark Office have joined forces to identify the major problem areas in terms of violations. Ten countries have been targeted for bilateral consultation: Taiwan, Korea, Singapore, Indonesia, Malaysia, the Philippines, Thailand, India, Brazil and Mexico. Many positive developments have taken place, especially in the Far East, where the countries planning for vigorous expansion see counterfeiting as detrimental in the long-run. For example, Malaysia, which is not a signatory to international multilateral copyright treaties, decided that all foreign works published in Malaysia within 30 days of first publication overseas will enjoy protection under the country's Copyright Act of 1969. Tightening of anticounterfeiting measures have been evident in Taiwan and Singapore. In 1983, Taiwan toughened its trademark laws, increasing fines for violations to $3,750 and jail terms to up to five years.

The United States government has held copyright seminars for both private and public sector experts in Malaysia, Indonesia and Thailand in order to address the problems of intellectual property protection. This effort is especially important in countries which are undergoing major legislative revision.

Since 1979, the United States and the EEC have been trying to get the countries of the General Agreement on Tariffs and Trade to adopt an anticounterfeiting code. Canada, Japan and Switzerland also support this code, but opposition from the developing countries within GATT has stalled its adoption. Many of these countries believe an anticounterfeiting code would hinder their domestic industries. The EEC is moving on its own to combat imports of counterfeit goods from non-member countries. A newly proposed framework would empower memberstate customs officials to seize suspected counterfeit goods upon receipt of written complaints from trademark holders.

The US government is intensifying its efforts toward gaining commitment from foreign nations, particularly developing countries, for stronger measures to deter counterfeiting and trade in counterfeit goods.

PRIVATE SECTOR ACTION

A number of private sector efforts have emerged in the battle against counterfeit goods. Private sector activities focus on incorporating and defending the interests of manufacturers, retailers and consumers legislatively on a worldwide and industry-wide scale.

In 1978, the International Anticounterfeiting Coalition was founded to lobby for stronger legal sanctions worldwide. It consists of 375 corporate members and has as its mission both educating the consumers and lobbying for changes in inadequate remedies for counterfeiting.

The International Chamber of Commerce has given preliminary approval to the establishment of a Counterfeiting Intelligence and Investigation Bureau (CIIB) which will act as an information clearinghouse capable of synthesizing global data on counterfeiting. The bureau would be based in London and would distribute information to members on a regular basis. In addition, seminars on practical methods of prevention and detection would be conducted.

For the publishing, recording, and film and software industries, the International Intellectual Property Alliance coordinates the members' activities.

PROACTIVE ACTIONS OF MNCs AGAINST COUNTERFEITERS

In the past decade four basic strategies have been identified for dealing with counterfeiters by MNCs: (1) the hands-off strategy—some MNCs are hesitant to prosecute because they fear customers switching to other brands to avoid false products; (2) the prosecuting strategy—to illustrate the integrity of the products' brand and to gain goodwill with distributors and customers; (3) the withdrawal strategy—reducing the flow of goods to the market, thereby increasing their status appeal. Products are registered, numbered and only added at a limited number of company-owned retail outlets, e.g., strategy of Vuitton, a French luggage manufacturer; and (4) the warning strategy—warning the public of imitation and how to tell the genuine product.

In today's environment, companies are taking more aggressive steps to protect themselves. The measures are both proactive and reactive. On the proactive side, companies are: (1) registering trademarks immediately, which in some cases calls for exhaustive paperwork (such as in the case of 'non-use' of a registered trademark); (2) recording the copyright with US Customs (which enables Customs to seize pirated copies upon entry into the country); and (3) building a strong network of communication in the marketing of the product. The network calls for a responsible person or entity within the company in charge of anti-counterfeiting efforts, and a vigilant attitude by employees and distributors. Larger companies employ outside investigators for their monitoring efforts. Company communications should extend to direct or association lobbying efforts and the education of enforcement officials, especially if the product is a highly technical one.

Swift legal action is the only appropriate reactive measure, especially with the new legislative call for stiffer penalties. Previously, counterfeiters would risk only the seizure of inventory, but the new jail terms have become a major deterrent. Counterfeiters have been found to be 'folks who, as a general rule, find the thought of going to jail abhorrent'.

Other methods have also been developed to help reduce the attractiveness of counterfeiting. In one instance, a system has been devised for using a computer generated beam of light to read the patterns in a predetermined quarter-inch-square portion of a label, translating the patterns into a code and printing the code number on the label. In effect, the label would be a fingerprint. It would be very difficult for a counterfeiter to reproduce the random patterns in the label itself. Only the system can reread the label and determine whether it is the original. Goldman, Inc. patented this technology and licensed it to Light Signatures, Inc. (LSI). Signa One, a prototype able to process 3,000 units an hour, was developed, and LSI began doing tests for Levi Strauss & Co. and Chrysalis Records. The tests were so successful that both companies have expanded their use of the system. Other companies like Anheuser-Busch, Puritan Fashions, Arista Records, and Nike, Inc. have started using the system.

In July, 1984, LSI introduced Signa Two, a second generation system being built at a cost of nearly $1 million by Recognition Equipment, Inc., in Dallas. Signa Two will be able to process 100,000 units an hour at an average cost to the client of 2½ cents per unit. It will also be able to handle a wider range of documents and do magnetic printing. An added advantage of the system is that it provides an opportunity for a company to gather market data. An additional possibility exists for protecting stock certificates and other securities by using paper keys instead of plastic. And in the developmental stage is a six pound remote terminal that can verify documents on the spot and is expected to sell for under $1,000.

The Polaroid Corp. has developed a new technology called Polaproof. According to Polaroid marketing officials, Polaproof is an authentication material which consists of a transparent polyester film incorporating special optical effects virtually impossible to duplicate. Being only .003 inches thick and about the size of a postage stamp, Polaproof can be adapted for use as adhesive labels, stickers, or hang tags. It is now being used by US and foreign manufacturers of record albums, tapes, videocassettes and videogame cartridges. It can also be used to prevent 'knock-offs' of designer jeans, cosmetics, jewellery, fashion accessories, entertainment and sporting events tickets and other trademark goods often counterfeited.

Polaproof functions similar to Signa One. When viewed in normal light, it produces a rapidly changing array of visual effects encompassing both form and colour. According to Polaroid, trademarks or designer and manufacturer logos can be incorporated into the material, customizing labels or tags to individual client requirements. Viewed from different angles, a label made with Polaproof appears to change colour, while design elements appear and reappear. Tampering destroys the optical effects, which are created by 1,500 cylindrical lenses per square inch. The label can be examined both in normal light and by high-speed verification machines. Depending on production volume, Polaproof labels have about a 2 cent per-unit cost, providing security that can be maintained on a relatively easy basis at minimum cost.

The present legal and corporate remedies to counterfeiting varies by the type of counterfeiter and the avenues open to go after the offenders (see Table 2). With counterfeiting being an escalating problem and costing firms millions of dollars, new legislation designed to deal with it has been enacted. The Customs Service has also been given more authority in dealing with counterfeit products. And companies themselves can get together and fight back by helping to get legislation passed as well as by using some of the new technology that has been developed to deter counterfeiting of brand-name products. In addition, some substantial effort by the Federal Government must also be

Table 2. Classification of counterfeiters and present remedies

Originator vs. counterfeiter	Present remedies available			
	Current legislation	Civil/ criminal	Gov't intervention	Increase company security
US MNC vs. foreign MNC	✕	✕	√	√
US MNC vs. individual (foreign)	✕	✕	✕	√
US MNC vs. agent	✕	✕	✕	√
US MNC vs. domestic employee	✕	√	✕	√
US MNC vs. foreign government	✕	✕	√	√

√ = appropriate avenue to confront counterfeiters.
✕ = lack of current means to seek resolution.

developed to exert pressure on foreign governments to address the counterfeiting issues. All of the recommended strategies will have to be used in concert to reduce the onslaught of counterfeiting that is taking place today. Reports have already surfaced that there is growing participation of organized crime, particularly in the developing countries, in the counterfeit goods markets, a fact that calls for more decisive action. Without a coordinated effort between governments and MNCs, counterfeiters will continue to carve out a larger and larger share of the world market for United States based MNC's products.

REFERENCES

§154. Copyright and Literary Property. *American Jurisprudence*, 1984.
§154. Willful Infringement, Copyright and Literary Property. *American Jurisprudence*, 1984.
§1127 Trademarks (Lanham Act). *United States Code Services Title*, 1984.
'$2,000 Apple-Type CPUs to be released by Customs'. *Electronic News*, February 27, 1984: 14.
'Anticounterfeiting Bill Endorsed'. *Automative News*, November 21, 1983: 22.
'Apple Counterattacks the Counterfeiters'. *Business Week*, August 16, 1982: 82.
'Apple Seeks Legislative Action'. *Electronic News*, August 15, 1983: Supp. C.
'Apple Sues to Stem Counterfeiters'. *Electronic News*, October 1983: 18.
'Asian Orchards'. *Industry Week*, November 28, 1983: 69.
Bikoff, J. (1985) 'Imitation is the Most Dangerous Flattery, Counterfeit Products Can Kill You'. *People*, May 25: 110–116.
'Bogus Blues'. *Time*, November 24, 1983: 92.
'Call for Tougher Int'l Stand on Product Counterfeiting'. *Electronic News*, September 19, 1984: Supp. K.
'Congress Told of Far East Ring'. *Electronic News*, August 8, 1983: 58.
'Counterfeiting Curb Stirs Debate'. *Automotive News*, October 3, 1983: 41.
'Credit Card Fraud'. *The Banker*, December 1983: 66.
'Fake Resolution'. *The Economist*, April 2, 1983: 79.
'Fakes'. *Life*, September 1984: 45–48.
'Fighting Fakes From Taiwan'. *Fortune*, May 30, 1983: 114–116.
'Genuine Phonies'. *Forbes*, January 21, 1982: 32.
Hill, E. 'Commerce Department Program Seeks Greater Protection for US Intellectual Property Rights'. *Business America*, March 8, 1985: 3–9.
'House to Push Anticounterfeiting Legislation'. *Marketing News*, November 26, 1983: 18.

Kailhati, J. and LaGrace, R. (1980) 'Beware of International Brand Piracy'. *Harvard Business Review*, March–April: 52–60.

Masson, T. (1985) 'How High Tech Foils the Counterfeiters'. *Business Week*, May 20.

McClenahan, J. S. (1985) 'They'll Steal You Blind'. *Industry Week*, May 27: 78–80.

Miller, M. (1985) 'US Software Firms Try to Curb Foreign Pirates to Protect Big Share of World Markets'. *The Wall Street Journal*, April 18: 34.

'New Technology to Foil Counterfeiters'. *National Business*, June 1984: 77.

'Putting Teeth into the Trademark Wars'. *Business Week*, October 8, 1984: 75–76.

'Piracy Relief Advocated'. *Electronic News*, March 26, 1984: Supp. F.

'Polaproof Labeling Technology Deters Counterfeiting of Brand-Name Products'. *The Economist*, March 8, 1983: 38.

'Retailer's Bogus Products Could Be Seized'. *Merchandizing*, May 1984: 184.

'Those Prestige Goods'. *U.S. News & World Reports*, September 7, 1983: 57.

'Trademark Counterfeiting Act'. *Stores*, November 1983: 68.

15

Product and Promotion Transfers in Consumer Goods Multinationals

John S. Hill and William L. James

Product and promotion transfers between country-markets are the essence of multi-national marketing. Americans travelling abroad notice the presence of Coca-Cola, Hilton Hotels, McDonalds and Kodak cameras and film in overseas markets. They hear about Coca-Cola and Pepsi being sold in over 150 countries and being promoted in similar fashions in many of them. They see perhaps a European Madge soaking her cuticles in Palmolive liquid on British or French television.

Given such experiences, it is tempting to believe that most products and promotions, with or without modifications, are easily transferable into overseas markets. Indeed, such transfers have been documented in the product sector by Davidson and Harrigan (1977) and Hill and Still (1984) and in the promotions arena by Peebles, Ryans and Vernon (1978) and Killough (1978).

Limited empirical attention however, has been paid to the transfer abroad of market-ing mix components. The topic is important for two reasons. First, the transfer of marketing mix elements among subsidiaries highlights MNC efforts to gain multi-national marketing synergies. Second, it showcases attempts to take advantage of cus-tomer similarities across country-markets. The transfer issue also has strong connections with globalism, as product movements among markets demonstrate that there are basic similarities among world markets. The alternative to transfers—developing new pro-ducts—would be used only when MNCs find unique, profitable segments for which they have no suitable products elsewhere. Product transfers also impact promotional strat-egy, since the intermarket transfer of products opens up opportunities to standardize brand images through promotions.

The objective of this article is to present evidence of the extent to which MNC producers of consumer non-durables globalize their product lines and attempt to influ-ence brand images through the transfer of promotion materials. The research reported is based on a study of the product and promotion practices of 120 subsidiaries of 15 large consumer goods multinationals.

Reprinted with permission from *International Marketing Review*, Vol. 8, No. 2, pp. 6–17

A CONCEPTUALIZATION OF THE PRODUCT AND PROMOTION TRANSFER AND ADAPTATION PROCESS

Prior international marketing studies have only touched on selected aspects of the process by which MNCs transfer marketing mix elements among subsidiaries. Figure 1 is a conceptualization of how MNCs might strategically manage their intra-company flows of products and promotions. There are three components to the process.

The first concerns market screening and decisions about filling subsidiary product lines. The second component pertains to how product mix composition might be affected by corporate and environmental factors. The third component involves promotion transfers, their frequency, what gets transferred, and general usefulness.

Market screening and transfer process

The market screening and transfer process begins with market need diagnosis. This might be done locally, using research and/or managerial inputs, or with head office advice and guidance. Do home offices 'force' products onto subsidiaries? Or does local wisdom prevail in product line-filling decisions? Once market needs are identified, decisions can be made about how those needs might best be filled. Where needs are similar to the US or other markets, product transfers can be initiated. Where there are no suitable candidates for transfer, MNCs may custom-build goods if such ventures look worthwhile.

There has been little research on MNC product lines abroad (Terpstra, 1981). Davidson and Harrigan (1977) looked at product transfers from a home market perspective. They found that over 70% of MNC product innovations in the US were eventually transferred abroad. Leroy's (1976) study found that it was six times more expensive for companies to custom-build products than to transfer and adapt them. He also showed that much new product development work was done in overseas subsidiaries. Indeed, Leroy cited one MNC where only five out of 21 new products originated from the US market.

There is some anecdotal evidence about product transfers. Gillette begins its Third World marketing campaigns with its traditional double-edge blades. If they are successful, its US-based pens, deodorants, shampoos and toothpastes are added. Sometimes, custom-made products are necessary. Gillette created Prestobarba, a tub-packaged shaving cream for the Guadalajaran Mexican market when it perceived its US product, the aerosol version, to be too expensive. After initial successes, the company transferred the product into Colombia and Brazil. Similarly, its Black Silk hair relaxer product— developed for the South African market, was also introduced into Kenya (Wessell, 1986). However, how often MNCs transfer goods rather than create new ones is unclear, and as such, is an objective of this research.

Influences on subsidiary product mixes

Subsidiary product mixes are likely to change depending on the company's situation and the type of market it is in. Terpstra (1987) posited that subsidiary age and level of market development would affect what products are offered. Both are examined in this

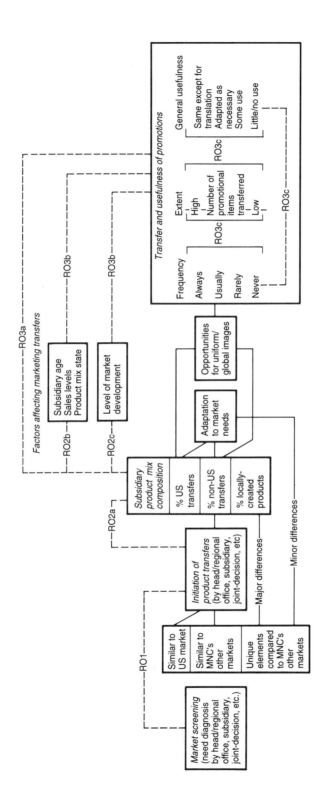

Figure 1. Conceptualization of the Multinational Product and Promotion Transfer Process.

study. We also investigated sales levels and product mix size to evaluate scale economy effects on subsidiary product policies.

Once MNCs have determined strategically which product transfers best suit corporate and market needs, there remains the question as to whether a group of products exist whose brand identities can be kept intact. For these 'international' products (Keegan, 1985; Hill and Still, 1984), there are opportunities to develop uniform brand images. However, for products to fulfil their global potential, promotions carrying these uniform images must be transferred. Hence, we examined promotional transfer activities, how frequently they occurred, how much was transferred, and how useful they were. Logically, we felt that these activities should be related. Finally, once promotional ideas and materials have been imported there is the question of how well they fit into individual campaigns. Of interest to this article was Killough's (1978) conclusion that the more a product appealed to personal values, the less likely accompanying promotions would be useful. If so, consumer non-durable MNCs are not likely to be extensive transferrers of promotions, and those transferred are probably going to have only limited usefulness. Also, since level of market development (i.e. developed, developing countries) has been featured in previous works on product and promotion transferability (Michel, 1979; Hill and Still, 1984), we incorporated it into these analyses.

RESEARCH OBJECTIVES

The conceptualization presented in Figure 1 highlights some of the missing links in the product and promotion transfer process and our efforts to measure them. Our first research objective (RO1) was to evaluate the relative influences of headquarters and subsidiaries in diagnosing market needs and initiating product transfers.

The second objective was to examine subsidiary product mix compositions to see whether MNCs mainly transferred or built products for their subsidiaries. Additional focuses were on influences on product mix compositions, specifically: (a) whether head office or local influences on product transfers affected how localized lines became (RO2a); (b) if product mixes altered over time, or with changing company conditions (sales levels, product mix size, etc.) (RO2b); and (c) whether level of market development affects transfer or build decisions for products (RO2c).

The final objective was to assess whether promotional transfer variables, such as frequency of transfers, extent of transfer, and usefulness of promotional materials transferred are: interrelated (RO3c); related to subsidiary product strategy (RO3a); associated with specific corporate conditions or market development factors (RO3b).

RESEARCH METHODOLOGY

Sample frame

Fifty firms with 556 subsidiaries overseas constituted the sample frame of consumer non-durable MNCs. Selections were taken from *Directory of American Companies Operating in Foreign Countries*. The major qualification for inclusion in the sample frame was that the company's main business was in consumer non-durable products such as food/drink, pharmaceutical, cosmetic and general consumer goods. Thirty-three of the better-known MNCs (i.e. those with widely-recognized offerings) were selected and their head-offices in the US were contacted by telephone to ascertain their interest in being part of the survey. Fifteen agreed to participate and allowed us to send mail questionnaires either to their international divisions in the US or directly to marketing executives in their overseas subsidiaries. The 15 cooperating MNCs were: Shulton International, Kellogg's Warner-Lambert, Johnson and Johnson, Quaker Oats, Kraft, General Foods, Procter and Gamble, Pillsbury, Chesebrough-Pond's, Nabisco-Brands, Beatrice, Libby's, General Mills, and Bristol-Myers.

Responses were received from 135 countries. Nine responses could not be coded by country. Three came from MNC international divisions in the US. Five were generalized by continent (e.g. South America, Western Europe etc.); and one came from a company's international division headquartered outside of the US. Because a number of MNCs sent out and collected responses through company channels, 120 questionnaires were returned out of 220 sent out, giving an average response rate of 55%.

RESEARCH FINDINGS

Product transfers: need diagnosis and transfer initiation (RO1)

Before product transfers can occur, MNC personnel evaluated individual market needs against their global product portfolios. After this, transfers from US or other subsidiaries can be initiated. Tables 1(a), (b) and (c) show the joint effects of product-need diagnosis and initiation of transfers with separate analyses of need diagnosis and transfer initiation by market-type.

Most noticeable is the lack of headquarters' direction in the initiation of product transfers. In most cases subsidiaries both diagnose needs and, perhaps using the worldwide product portfolios mentioned by Hill and Still (1984), select appropriate products for testing and possible commercialization. In only about one fifth of the sample were head or regional offices primary instigators of product transfers. This suggests considerable power at the subsidiary level over product strategy.

Equally significant is the role played by subsidiary marketing managers in the transfer process. Alone, or with inputs from market research, they are instrumental in the majority of market diagnoses for transferred products. This is particularly noticeable in Tables 1(b) and 1(c) which show that local inputs both in the need-diagnosis and the product transfer processes are more likely in the case of developing markets. Clearly, head and regional offices are more confident in dealing with advanced market transfers than those to developing countries. Equally interesting is the finding that in 42 out of 115 subsidiaries (37%), diagnosis of market needs is done just by marketing managers (see Table 1(b)). This suggests that managerial judgement is an acceptable substitute for research-based decision-making in both developed and developing markets.

Subsidiary product line origins (RO2a)

Results obtained from 117 subsidiaries show consumer non-durable product lines to be predominantly American in origin, with an average 57% ex-US products. This suggests

Table 1(a). Diagnosis of market needs by initiation of product transfer

	Initiation of product transfer			
Market need diagnosis	Unilaterally US/regional	Initiated subsidiary	Joint decision	Total number subsidiaries
Headquarters involvement	5	5	0	10
Local involvement				
Market research alone	5	25	1	31
Marketing manager alone	11	31	1	43
Joint local decision*	1	23	5	29
Total number of subsidiaries	22	84	7	113

* Combinations of market research, marketing manager and/or competition.

Table 1(b). Diagnosis of market need by market development

	Level of market development		
Market need diagnosis	Developing country	Developed country	Number of subsidiaries
Headquarters involvement	1	9	10
Market research	15	16	31
Marketing manager	18	24	42
Joint local decision	18	14	32
Totals	52	63	115

Chi-square (3df) = 6.80, $p < 0.10$

Table 1(c). Initiation of product transfer by market development level

	Level of market development		
Initiation of product transfer	Developing country	Developed country	Totals
Unilaterally initiated by:			
US/regional			
head office	5	17	22
subsidiary	46	38	84
Joint decision	2	5	7
Number of subsidiaries	53	60	113

Chi-square (2df) = 7.23, $p < 0.05$

that American products are as acceptable in other parts of the world as Levitt (1983) thought they should be. Our results also show that MNCs respect market idiosyncracies enough to custom-build 26% of their lines for individual markets.

Increasing interdependencies among international markets is shown by the average 17% of subsidiary product lines transferred from non-US markets. This supports Hill and Still's (1984) contention that when market opportunities arise, local managers first scan MNC portfolios to determine whether other subsidiaries have products that might be useful, and if so, to ship samples for testing.

With regard to product transfer initiation and subsidiary product mix orientation (RO2a), we found no evidence that either strong head office or subsidiary influences impacted affiliate product mixes. That is, when head offices or subsidiaries were primary initiators of transfers, neither US-dominated nor local-dominated mixes resulted. This suggests that products are not 'pushed' onto subsidiaries, and that US products are truly acceptable in many markets.

Factors influencing subsidiary product mixes (RO2b, RO2c)

Subsidiary product mixes do not evolve without corporate or marketplace influences. In this study, preliminary analyses were undertaken with selected variables (see Table 2).

Table 2. Subsidiary product line origins: analysis by subsidiary sales levels, length of establishment, product line size and level of market development

	Subsidiary product line origins		
	US-originated products (%)	Non-US products (%)	Locally conceived (%)
Subsidiary sales level			
Less than $25m	70^a	18	12^a
Over $25m	40^a	19	41^a
Length of establishment			
Less than 10 years	77^d	8	14
10–20 years	56^d	24	20
Over 20 years	53^d	16	30
Less than 20 years	62	20	18^c
Over 20 years	54	16	30^c
Product line size			
1–49 products	62^c	16	23
Over 50 products	47^c	21	32
Level of market development			
Developing market	67^b	13	20^c
Developed market	47^b	21	32^c

Significant differences: ^{a} at $p < 0.001$ level; ^{b} at $p < 0.01$ level; ^{c} at $p < 0.05$ level; ^{d} at $p < 0.10$ level.

What these analyses show is that as subsidiaries became more experienced, their product lines became more localized. This conclusion is based on findings with regard to sales levels, length of establishment and product line size (see Table 2). Subsidiary sales levels under $25 million have higher percentages of US originated products (70%) and lower percentages of locally-created products (12.1%) than those with over $25 million in sales (where ex-US products constitute 40 and locally created products 41%).

Similar conclusions can be derived from examining product mix development over time. Results show that, depending on the time frame chosen, the proportions of American and locally built products used vary with subsidiary age (see Table 2). Percentages of US-originated products decrease from an average of 77 for subsidiaries less than ten years old to 53 for those established over 20 years. Similarly, proportions of locally created products increased from 18% for affiliates less than 20 years old to 30% for those over 20 years old. Finally, if product line size increases over time, then subsidiaries with smaller product lines (in this case, less than 49 products) should have significantly more ex-US products than those with 50 or more products. Table 2 shows this to be the case, since subsidiaries with less than 49 products average 61.9% US goods against 46.7% for those subsidiaries with 50 or more products. Clearly, older subsidiaries have the experience, the facilities, and perhaps the autonomy to convince head offices that custom-building products is a better strategy than accepting 'hand-me-downs' from other affiliates.

Level of market development also impacts subsidiary product strategies. Developed market subsidiaries averaged 47% ex-US products and 32% local goods while those in developing countries had 67% ex-US products and 20% local lines. This suggests that developed market affluence and potential is critical when MNCs determine whether product additions should be transferred in or custom-built. Country-markets like those in Western Europe can perhaps support new product research and development costs more comfortably than can developing markets.

PROMOTIONAL MATERIALS TRANSFERS

Promotion plays a key role in determining the success (or otherwise) of consumer non-durable products. Hence, when products are transferred, it is logical that successful promotions also be transferred. It further indicates that MNCs are looking for consistent brand images which can only occur with the sharing of promotional ideas.

Frequency of transfer (RO3a, RO3b)

Our findings show that less than half the subsidiaries surveyed (48 out of 116 responses or 41.3%) are frequent recipients of promotional transfers. A further 58 affiliates rarely received promotional materials with products. This suggests that most MNCs in our sample either are not habitual sharers of promotional ideas or that they are selective in what brands they choose for global notoriety.

What factors might account for variations in promotional transfer frequency? Perhaps surprisingly, there were no significant differences between developed and developing markets. A weak association was found with extent of transfer (RO3b), (at the 0.09 level), with subsidiaries that 'always' and 'usually' received materials averaging 4.4 types of promotions against 3.5 types for the rarely/never categories. This confirms, though not strongly, that habitual transferers of promotions also send more materials.

However, product mix composition was a significant influence on promotion transfer frequency (RO3a). Subsidiaries that always or usually received promotional back-ups had more US transfers in their lines than the infrequent receivers of materials (66.4% against 52.2%); and less custom-made products (18.4% against 29.9%). Our conclusion is that as product mixes localize, so affiliates become more proficient at producing promotions to the extent that MNCs assume, (rightly or wrongly) that promotional support for product transfers is less necessary.

Extent of promotional materials transfer (RO3a)

Given that most subsidiaries receive some form of promotional help, what sorts of materials are transferred? Survey results show that television, the key medium in the US market, is also the most transferred type of promotion. Advisory materials are also an important transfer with 73% of subsidiaries receiving sample advertising campaigns. This shows that Peebles, Ryans and Vernon's (1978) pattern standardization approach, or something similar, is widely used in consumer goods MNCs. Such advisory materials indicate strongly that MNCs are wary of forcing ideas onto subsidiaries. This probably relates to the culturally sensitive nature of non-durable products (Ward, 1973) and the risk of involving themselves in promotional fiascos of the sort Ricks (1983) describes.

However, MNCs do not adopt a *laissez-faire* attitude to all product and promotion transfers. When arrays of synchronized promotions are transferred internationally, these are probably signals that MNCs are seeking to unify the global images of particular products. The transfer of complete promotional campaigns then, is a means through which standardized brand images can be achieved over a number of markets. If such is the case, then almost a third of subsidiaries (34 out of 108, or 31%) experience pressure to standardize selected brand images. This type of prototype standardization would be logical for flagship products such as Coca-Cola, Pepsi, and Canada Dry mixers that provide global visibility to company marketing efforts. It also suggests that standardization can occur because companies wish it to (Peebles, 1989).

What other types of promotional materials should managers transfer with products? Our results show both sales promotions (52 out of 108 subsidiaries, or 48%) and magazine layouts (41%) to be popular, since both are important in consumer goods promotions. Other media such as dealer sales promotions (39 affiliates out of 108, or 36%) and press releases (29 out of 108 subsidiaries, or 27%), are probably oriented to specific types of consumer goods, with dealer promotions being popular in the cosmetics industry (display stands etc.), and press releases for pharmaceuticals. Newspaper layouts (18%) and radio advertisements (17%) are less transferable since they can be easily produced locally where formats can be tailored to individual media vehicles.

Regarding the number of promotions subsidiaries receive, our sample averaged 3.8 types. While we found that there were no significant differences between the numbers transferred to developed and developing markets (RO3b), nor between the relative usefulness of materials (RO3c), there were significant correlations again with the proportions of US-made and local products in subsidiary lines (RO3a). Using correlation analysis, we found that promotion transfer was positively correlated to US product transfers $(0.2112, p = 0.014)$; and negatively related to the creation of localized lines $(-0.1691, p = 0.041)$. While these are not strong relationships, they confirm that as subsidiaries become more localized (as they appear to over time), then fewer promotion transfers occur.

Usefulness of transferred promotional materials (RO3c)

Transferring promotional materials only makes sense when such materials are useful in recipient markets. Hence, we asked how useful promotional materials transfers were. Only two of 103 subsidiaries reported that materials could be used 'as is' except for translation. This suggests that strict advertising standardization among markets (of the sort Coca-Cola and Pepsi do) is a comparative rarity. A further 34 subsidiaries reported 'some use', but only six said that little or no use was made of promotional transfers, suggesting that accompanying materials are rarely wasted.

The majority (61 out of 103) adapt materials as necessary and use them. This was interesting as the majority of our sample—66 out of 116 subsidiaries either rarely (58) or never (8) received transferred promotional materials. A cross-tabulation of these two variables showed that about a quarter of our sample, (26 subsidiaries), rarely receive promotional materials but make good use of them when they are received. This indicates that either these subsidiaries should receive more promotional transfers or that materials are only requested when they are likely to be useful.

It was also interesting to find that promotional material usefulness varied by market-type (RO3b). As shown in Table 3, 73% of developing country affiliates (35 of 48) found promotion transfers to be at least useful. This may relate to a lack of advertising skills or technical knowhow in the production of advertising materials. Such shortfalls in advertising expertise are more likely in developing country circumstances.

Table 3. Usefulness of promotion transfers: analysis by level of market development

Promotion transfer usefulness	Developing market	Developed market	Number of subsidiaries
Little/no use and some use	13	27	40
Adapted as necessary and used and same except for translation	35	27	62
Number of subsidiaries	48	54	102

Chi-squares (after Yates' correction) significant at 0.03 level.

CONCLUSIONS

The intention of this research was to contribute to the important but relatively neglected area of product and promotion transfers in MNCs. This article has a number of implications for managers. First, our findings indicate that an average 60% of affiliate lines are US-originated, suggesting that with or without adaptations, managers can build overseas lines around home-country goods. Further, American MNCs in particular can be more aggressive in their overseas uses of US products, never forgetting though, that products should be thoroughly screened before launch. They should however, expect affiliate product mixes to become more locally oriented over time.

Second, US MNCs should focus more attention on transfers from non-home-market subsidiaries. Our findings suggest that foreign affiliates are good sources of new product ideas. This may involve increased circulations of global product portfolios around subsidiaries, and encouraging communications among traditionally autonomous affiliates.

Third, it is our general contention that consumer non-durable MNCs should habitually circulate promotions to subsidiaries, especially those in developing markets. Over 60% of our sample found promotion transfers to be useful, yet only about 40% received promotions regularly. The costs of promotion transfers are small but the payoff is significant if materials are useful. We would urge MNCs to err on the side of transferring too many, rather than too few, promotions.

From an academic viewpoint, this study provides support for Levitt's global thesis that transfers dominate MNC product line selections for subsidiaries, and that basic similarities among countries are a primary force in international product strategies. We would suggest that researchers focus their efforts more on customer and country similarities in the future.

There are numerous potential areas for follow-up studies. A more in-depth analysis is needed about the mechanics of product transfers, especially from non-parent locations. Promotional transfers also need more attention. In this article we concentrated on the simultaneous transfer of both products and promotions. Additional work is necessary in industries that try to standardize their promotions from year to year in multiple markets. Do they do so for all products? If not, which ones? What promotional materials does the head office prepare? What aspects of individual promotions are changed?

Clearly the study of multinational transfers is still in its infancy. This article should serve as a building block for future conceptualizations, and encourage further research efforts in this area.

REFERENCES

Davidson, W. H. and Harrigan, R. (1977) 'Key Decisions in International Marketing: Introducing New Products Abroad'. *Columbia Journal of World Business*, **12**(Winter): 15–23.

Hill, J. S. and Still, R. (1984) 'Adapting Products to LDC Tastes'. *Harvard Business Review*, **62**(March): 92–102.

Keegan, W. J. (1985) *Multinational Marketing Management*. Prentice-Hall, New Jersey, 3rd edition.

Killough, J. (1978) 'Improved Payoffs from Transnational Advertising'. *Harvard Business Review*, **56**(July): 102–114.

Leroy, G. P. (1976) *Multinational Product Strategies: A Typology For Analysing of Worldwide Product Innovation Diffusion*. Praeger Publishers, Inc., New York.

Levitt, T. (1983) 'The Globalization of Markets'. *Harvard Business Review*, **61**(May): 92–102.

Michel, P. (1979) 'Infrastructures and International Marketing Effectiveness'. *Columbia Journal of World Business*, **14**(Spring): 91–98.

Peebles, D. M. (1989) 'Don't Write Off Global Advertising'. *International Marketing Review*, **6**(1): 73–78.

Peebles, D. M., Ryans, J. K. Jr. and Vernon, I. R. (1978) 'Co-ordinating International Advertising'. *Journal of Marketing*, **42**(January): 28–34.

Ricks, D. A. (1983) *Big Business Blunders: Mistakes in Multinational Marketing*. Dow-Jones-Irwin, Illinois.

Terpstra, V. (1981) 'On Marketing Appropriate Products in Developing Countries'. *Journal of International Marketing*, **1**(Spring): 3–15.

Terpstra, V. (1987) *International Marketing*. Dryden Press, New York, 4th Edition.

US Department of Commerce: Bureau of Economic Analysis (1985) *Survey of Current Business*, **65**(August): 35–38.

Ward, J. J. (1973) *The European Approach to US Markets: Product and Promotion Adaptations by European Multinationals*. Praeger Publishers, Inc., New York.

Wessell, D. (1986) 'Gillette Keys Sales to Third World Tastes'. *Wall Street Journal*, January 23: 35.

World Trade Academy Press (1979) *Directory of American Companies Operating in Foreign Countries*. Simon and Schuster, New York.

16

International Advertising Strategies of Multinational Corporations

Robert E. Hite and Cynthia Fraser

International advertisers are often faced with the problem of whether, to what extent, and in which manner advertising should be adapted or changed prior to deployment in diverse foreign markets. That is, under what circumstances should advertising campaigns be standardized or localized, and to what extent?

In this article, the international advertising strategies of a sample of successful US multinational corporations (MNCs) are examined to determine levels of standardization being utilized, to identify those factors which are important determinants of the transferability of advertising, and to identify demographic variables which are systematically related to attitudes and behaviours regarding international advertising standardization. First, a review of prior work related to international advertising strategies is presented; then the results of an international advertising study will be presented and discussed.

PREVIOUS RESEARCH

Prior research concerning international advertising transferability has largely been based upon arguments derived from business experiences or surveys of small convenience samples of multinational managers. That research has focused upon the merits of standardization versus localization/adaptation of advertising, ways in which alternative strategies might be managed, descriptive reports of degrees of standardization being utilized, and factors affecting the suitability of standardization.

Arguments in favour of standardization

Dunn (1966), Elinder (1964), Fatt (1967), and Lorimer and Dunn (1968–69) were early proponents of standardization of international advertising. They argued that firms had successfully transferred advertising and that standardized themes provided consistent corporate and brand images worldwide. Buzzell (1968) argued further that standardiz-

Reprinted with permission from *Journal of Advertising Research*, Vol. 28, August/September, pp. 9–17

ation allows realization of economies from scale in the production of advertising materials, reducing advertising costs and enhancing profitability.

Arguments in favour of localization

Other authors have stressed the importance of adaptation to local differences in foreign markets. Ricks, Arpan, and Fu (1974) analysed actual blunders in international advertising and suggested that most of those blunders occurred because executives failed to understand the foreign culture and its social norms. Green, Cunningham, and Cunningham (1975) and Green and Langeard (1975) found that groups of consumers from three foreign countries rated the importance (in the purchase of two convenience products) of product attributes differently from each other and from consumers in the United States, suggesting the inadvisability of standardized global advertising.

Killough (1978) studied the transfer of advertising resources (including the content and the form of the advertising message) from one country to another in a survey of senior executives who had been involved in more than 120 multinational campaigns. Those executives felt that the 'idea content' can be transferred intact, but the 'strategic content and executional form' face barriers, including cultural, communication, legislation, competition, and execution problems.

Popularity of standardization

Using small convenience samples, several researchers have surveyed international managers to determine whether or not advertising was, in fact, standardized worldwide. Sorenson and Wiechmann (1975) reported high standardization of advertising messages and creative expressions by 71% of 27 US and European multinationals doing business in packaged goods; only 20% utilized localized advertising. A decade later Boddewyn, Soehl, and Picard (1986) reported that only 20% of 70 executives substantially standardized international advertising in Western Europe, while 39% used localized international advertising. Despite the small convenience samples employed in these two studies, together they provide some indication that international advertising had been highly standardized in the 1970s but has become less standardized and more localized since.

Factors influencing transferability

A final stream of research has attempted to identify those factors which encourage or discourage international advertising standardization. Hornik (1980) performed a study to compare American advertising campaigns with locally tailored advertisements for the same American products distributed in Israel. Some ads were transferred intact, some prepared by a local agency, and some ads were neutral, non-identified ads. Localized advertising themes were preferred except when advertising strategy was geared toward international appeal, worldwide corporate image, or a common international connotation. In those instances, standardization may be employed.

Dunn (1976) surveyed 90 executives of US-based multinational corporations and found that eight factors influence the perceived transferability of advertising across global regions. They were, in order of decreasing importance: (1) levels of education; (2) attitudes toward work and monetary gain; (3) competence of personnel in foreign agencies or branches; (4) degrees of nationalism in countries and attitudes toward the United States; (5) rate of economic growth and acceptance of trademark; (6) eating patterns; (7) attitudes toward authority and transferability of slogans; and (8) independence of media from governmental control.

The studies cited above suggest that international advertising ought to be standardized whenever cultural, demographic, governmental, competitive, and infrastructural barriers are surmountable. In particular, evidence indicates that advertising messages ought to be similar across global regions, even in cases in which executions or media differ. Unresolved are clear indications of the importance of the various factors which discourage standardization and the universal popularity of standardization versus localization.

In order to address these issues, a survey of successful US multinational corporations was conducted. Specific research objectives were:

(1) To determine the extent of standardized versus localized advertising campaigns by successful United States multinational corporations in foreign markets and presence or absence of trends.
(2) To determine the importance of environmental factors regarding the transfer of advertising strategy and presence or absence of trends in those importances.
(3) To determine the importance for transferability of changes in the components of advertising executions.
(4) To determine if the attitudes, behaviours, or demographics of an MNC relate to the advertising strategy used in foreign markets.

METHODOLOGY

The sample utilized for this study consisted of all of the 418 Fortune 500 business firms conducting international trade. A self-administered questionnaire was mailed to each firm and 150 useable responses were generated (response rate = 36%). A description of the sample is shown in Table 1. Respondents were fairly evenly distributed across business types. Most (60%) were experienced in the international marketplace, reporting more than 20 years of involvement. The greatest number (36%) owned subsidiaries in fewer than six countries, while the median number of countries in which subsidiaries are located was 11–25. Forty percent report that foreign sales accounted for less than 11% of worldwide sales, and the median foreign sales percentage category was 11–25. Median firm sales category was $500–999 million, while modal sales category level was $1–25 billion.

The sample of firms was asked to respond to items concerning advertising strategy (i.e., degree of standardization, site of responsibility for preparation of campaigns, and importance of adapting advertising components). Eleven items were utilized to measure the importance of environmental barriers to transfer of promotional strategies isolated by Dunn (1976). Demographic variables measuring type of business, years of experience

Table 1. Description of the sample ($n = 150$)

	Number		Number
Type of business		**Number of countries—**	
Industrial materials	27	**subsidiaries or branch offices**	
Consumer goods (not food or		5 or less	51
automotive)	22	6–10	19
Food and beverages	12	11–25	36
Business services	11	26–50	13
Capital goods (except automotive)	10	Over 50	23
Automotive	7		
Conglomerate	6	**Percent of sales—foreign**	
Natural resources	5	**markets**	
Other	50	10% or less	56
Total	150	11–25%	43
		26–50%	28
Years involved in international		51–75%	13
marketing		Over 75%	1
5 or less	30		
6–10	17	**Total sales**	
11–15	6	Less than $100 million	42
16–20	4	$100 million–$499 million	7
21–25	5	$500 million–$999 million	26
Over 25	79	$1 billion–$25 billion	65
		$26 billion–$50 billion	2
		Over $50 billion	2

in international marketing, geographic dispersion, foreign sales share, and total world-wide sales were included to identify associations between firm types and international advertising strategies.

RESULTS

International advertising strategies of MNCs

The majority of firms in this study (66%) advertise internationally and (54%) use a combination strategy of standardizing some portions of advertising or localizing advertising for some foreign markets (see Table 2). Only 9% report use of totally standardized advertising for all foreign markets, strikingly lower than those reported in the previous case studies cited above and indicating a trend toward less standardization. A total of 37% reported using all localized advertising. Comparison of the popularities of standardization and localization observed in this and prior studies is illustrated in Figure 1.

Site of responsibility for advertising preparation

About half (50%) report use of foreign advertising agencies for preparation of advertising campaigns for foreign markets; 27% use a US agency, 20% use an in-house agency,

Table 2. Summary of international advertising strategies

	Percent	Number
Firms which advertise internationally	66%	(99)
(1) using all standardized advertising	8%	(8)
(2) using all localized advertising	36%	(36)
(3) using a combination strategy	56%	(55)
Preparation of advertising campaigns		
(1) Foreign advertising agency	50%	
(2) US advertising agency	27%	
(3) International agency/network	21%	
(4) Corporate in-house agency	20%	
(5) Foreign affiliates in-house agency	18%	

Importance of changing items to blend with culture	SA	A	NO	D	SD
(1) Language	77%	18%	1%	4%	0%
(2) Product attributes	23%	36%	13%	19%	10%
(3) Models	15%	54%	12%	12%	7%
(4) Scenic background	10%	48%	22%	13%	7%
(5) Colours of ad	8%	25%	42%	17%	9%

Importance of environmental factors regarding transfer	Very	Fairly	Somewhat	Not	Average[a]
(1) Acceptance of trademark or brand name	66%	24%	7%	3%	2.5
(2) Transferability of slogan	52%	24%	16%	8%	2.2
(3) Level of consumer education	28%	54%	11%	7%	2.0
(4) Attitudes toward US	39%	26%	23%	11%	1.9
(5) Degree of nationalism in country	28%	44%	20%	7%	1.9
(6) Competence of personnel in foreign office	27%	38%	18%	16%	1.8
(7) Rate of economic growth	21%	38%	26%	14%	1.7
(8) Independence of media from government control	22%	18%	38%	21%	1.4
(9) Attitude toward work and monetary gain	14%	19%	49%	18%	1.3
(10) Eating patterns of market	13%	28%	8%	50%	1.0
(11) Attitudes toward authority	7%	12%	27%	54%	0.7

[a] Very = 3, fairly = 2, somewhat = 1, not = 0.

21% use an international agency or network, and 18% use an in-house agency within a foreign affiliate.

Attitudes regarding standardization of advertising components

Most (77%) strongly agree that it is important to change the language to blend with the cultures of foreign markets. Firms tend to agree that it is also important to change models, scenic backgrounds, and product attributes. Most have no opinion regarding the change of colours in ads.

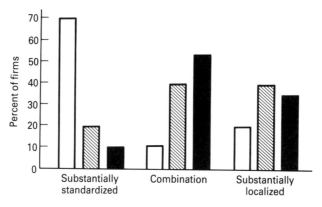

Figure 1. Shifts in Popularity of Standardization and Localization of International Advertising. □: Sorenson and Weichman (1976); ▨: Boddewyn, Soehl, and Picard (1986); ■: this study.

Importance of factors influencing transferability

The majority rate acceptance of trademarks/brand names as very important in assessing transferability of promotional campaigns. Transferability of slogans, levels of education of consumers, attitudes toward the United States, the degree of nationalism in foreign markets, and competence of personnel in foreign offices are rated important (in that order). The rate of economic growth in a country, independence of media from government control and attitudes toward work and monetary gain are rated 'somewhat' important (in that order). Only eating patterns of markets and attitudes toward authority are considered unimportant by the majority, perhaps in the former case because the majority of businesses surveyed do not compete in food-related industries.

The perceived levels of importance of factors influencing transferability of international advertising are consistent with those reported by Dunn (1976) 10 years ago; however, differences in relative importance levels are apparent. In Dunn's study, factors related to consumers' levels of education, attitudes toward work and monetary gain, eating patterns, and attitudes toward authority were perceived as relatively more important than in this study, suggesting that consumer-related barriers to standardization are thought to have declined in importance. The relative importance of rates of economic growth has diminished, as has the relative importance of competence of personnel in foreign offices. Perhaps the overall competence of personnel in foreign offices has improved over the years, thereby causing the importance of such competence to diminish as a barrier to advertising transferability. Shifts in the relative importance of the 11 potential barriers to transfer to promotional strategies are shown in Figure 2.

Differences between firms based on international advertising strategy

To assess the power of attitudinal and behavioural differences in distinguishing between firms which use substantially standardized, substantially localized, or partially standardized/localized advertising, a discriminant analysis was conducted. A single significant discriminant function emerged and is dominated by perceptions concerning the

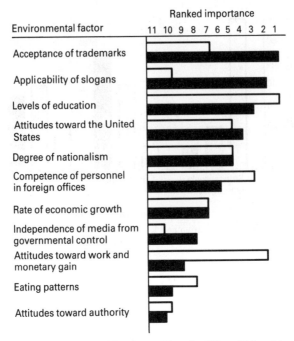

Figure 2. Shifts in the Relative Importance of Barriers to Transferability of Advertising Strategies. □: Dunn (1976); ■: this study.

importance of barriers to transferability of advertising strategies, the choice of advertising agency, agreement that advertising components must be modified prior to transfer, and type of main business, as shown in Table 3.

Attitudinal differences. 'Eating patterns of markets' is perceived by marketers as the most important determinant of whether or not advertising strategies will transfer from one foreign market to another. Firms which standardize international advertising rate the eating patterns of consumers in foreign markets significantly lower in importance than firms which localize some or all international advertising decisions. This dimension is the single most powerful discriminating variable, with standardized discriminant coefficient equal to -0.69. Concern over unique behavioural patterns or attitudes in foreign markets appears to encourage localized decision-making.

Advertising strategy groups also differ significantly in agreement on the importance of changing components of advertising prior to transfer in order to blend with foreign cultures, although those dimensions are only weak discriminators, with standardized discriminant coefficients ranging in absolute size from 0.08 to 0.20. Agreement that it is important to change scenic backgrounds, language, models, and colours of ads prior to transfer increases with the level of localization, too. On the average, firms which standardize international advertising report uncertainty or weak disagreement that scenic backgrounds, models, and colours of ads must be altered prior to transfer. Firms which localize some or all portions of advertising report uncertainty or weak agreement that those components, scenic backgrounds, models, and colours must be altered prior to transfer. Firms which standardize agree that the language in advertisements ought to be altered prior to transfer, while firms which localize some or all advertising agree strongly that language must be localized. Firms which standardize international advertising apparently perceive that identical executions may be transferred successfully with only modification in language.

Behavioural differences. The reported uses of a foreign advertising agency or a US advertising agency are powerful discriminators of advertising standardization, with standardized discriminant coefficients equal to -0.60 and 0.49 respectively. The use of foreign advertising agencies is positively associated with localization, while the use of US agencies is positively associated with standardization. None of the firms using totally standardized international advertising uses a foreign advertising agency, while 44% of firms which localize some advertising functions and 69% of firms which localize all advertising functions rely upon foreign advertising agencies. Conversely, half of the firms which standardize international advertising use a US advertising agency, while only a third of those which localize some functions and 11% of those which localize all functions use a US agency.

Demographic differences. A single demographic dimension, involvement in capital goods industries, significantly distinguishes firms using different advertising strategies, and that dimension is only weakly discriminating (with standardized discriminant coefficient equal to 0.27). Standardization of international advertising functions is positively associated with involvement in capital goods business, where buyers are presumably more sophisticated and homogeneous. Thirty-eight percent of the firms using standardized advertising report capital goods as their primary business; while only 7% of the firms which localize some advertising functions and only 3% of the firms which localize all advertising functions report primary business in capital goods.

Demographic differences in worldwide sales level, experience with international marketing, geographic dispersion, and proportion of sales from foreign markets are neither powerful discriminators of advertising strategies (with standardized discriminant coefficients ranging in absolute size from 0.02 to 0.30), nor significantly different between firms employing varying levels of standardization.

To assess the predictive capability of attitudes and behaviours as indications of international advertising strategies, two subsamples of equivalent size were randomly selected; each contained equal proportions of firms reporting the use of (1) substantially standardized, (2) substantially localized, and (3) partially standardized/localized international advertising. A second discriminant analysis was conducted on the first calibration subsample, utilizing the 11 measures which had been most influential in the full sample analysis; firms in the remaining hold-out sample were then classified. With only 11 measures, 88% of the hold-out sample firms were correctly classified, suggesting that distinct differences—primarily related to attitudes and agency choice—do, indeed, distinguish firms using different international advertising strategies.

DISCUSSION

The majority of firms (66%) who advertise internationally utilize the following strategies: a combination of localized and standardized advertising (56%) all localized

Table 3. Discriminant analysis of firms using standardized, localized, and combination international advertising

	Standardized discriminant coefficient	F	p	Standardized	Mean combination	Localized
1. Importance in determining whether advertising strategy will transfer to foreign markets[a]						
Eating patterns of market	−0.69	4.1	0.02	0.5	0.9	1.4
Competence of foreign personnel	0.60	2.1	ns	1.8	1.9	1.5
Acceptance of brand name	0.52	1.3	ns	2.4	2.6	2.4
Attitudes toward US	−0.26	1.1	ns	1.8	1.8	2.1
Independence of media from government	−0.16	1.8	ns	0.9	1.6	1.3
Attitudes toward work	0.11	0.1	ns	1.1	1.3	1.3
Levels of education	−0.08	0.4	ns	1.9	2.1	2.0
Degree of nationalism in country	−0.06	2.9	0.05	1.3	2.0	1.9
Transferability of slogan	0.06	0.1	ns	2.1	2.2	2.1
Attitudes toward authority	0.05	1.2	ns	0.3	0.7	0.8
Rate of economic growth	0.01	0.0	ns	1.8	1.7	1.7
2. Extent of agreement that to blend with foreign cultures it is important to change[b]						
Scenic backgrounds	0.20	5.7	0.005	−0.6	0.4	0.6
Language	−0.18	6.5	0.002	0.9	1.7	1.8
Models	−0.13	6.4	0.003	−0.4	0.5	1.0
Colours of ads	−0.08	3.4	0.04	−0.8	0.1	0.3
Product's attributes	−0.02	2.5	ns	−0.5	0.5	0.6

3. Percent of firms which use						
Foreign ad agency	-0.60	8.1	0.0006	0	44	69
US ad agency	0.49	4.2	0.02	50	33	11
Foreign affiliates in-house agency	-0.37	3.0	ns	13	11	31
Headquarters in-house agency	-0.07	0.5	ns	13	24	17
4. Percent with main business in						
Industrial materials	-0.33	1.7	ns	0	18	28
Capital goods	0.27	5.8	0.004	38	7	3
Natural resources	-0.26	2.8	ns	0	0	8
Business services	-0.25	2.1	ns	0	4	14
Conglomerate	0.17	0.7	ns	0	7	3
Food and beverages	0.07	0.5	ns	0	9	11
Consumer goods	0.07	0.1	ns	25	18	17
Automotive	-0.02	1.0	ns	0	9	3
5. Number of countries with subsidiaries	0.30	0.4	ns	14	21	19
6. Worldwide sales in billions of dollars	-0.22	0.4	ns	15	18	20
7. Years experience in international marketing	-0.10	0.3	ns	20	23	23
8. Percent sales in foreign markets	0.02	0.9	ns	33	24	23
Discriminant index		1.8	0.003	2.0	0.6	-1.4
Number of sample firms				9	54	37
Percent of holdout sample correctly classified		88				

[a] 3 = Very, 2 = somewhat, 0 = not important.

[b] -2 = Strongly disagree, -1 = disagree, 0 = no opinion, 1 = agree, 2 = strongly agree.

advertising (36%), and all standardized advertising (8%). Two key benefits of standardization are cost savings and the maintenance of a consistent image, while a major risk is a lack of communication (or miscommunication) due to cultural differences. The majority of firms reported using a blend or combination of the two strategies, thereby realizing the advantages of each to some extent while minimizing the disadvantages.

The respondent firms reported that trademark/brand name acceptance, transferability of slogans, levels of consumer education, attitudes toward the United States, degrees of nationalism, competence of personnel in foreign offices, and rate of economic growth are very important in determining the transferability of advertising campaigns. A corporation with a well-known and accepted brand name is more likely to be successful using greater levels of standardization than a firm without such acceptance and name recognition.

Firms which utilize a totally standardized advertising strategy are more likely to be involved in capital goods industries and are more likely (than firms who localize) to select a single US advertising agency. Firms using localized advertising are more likely to agree on the need to change advertising elements (i.e., language, models, and scenic backgrounds) in order to accommodate foreign cultures. As expected, firms using an all localized strategy were most likely to use foreign advertising agencies.

Somewhat surprising is the lack of significant demographic differences between firms which standardize, those which localize, and those which partially standardize/partially localize advertising functions. All three groups report similar worldwide sales levels, similar years of experience in the international arena, similar levels of geographic dispersion, and similar foreign sales shares.

In conclusion, about two thirds of the Fortune 500 firms who responded to this study engage in international advertising and slightly over half do so using a combination strategy. The majority of firms reported that it is important to adapt advertising components (language, models, scenic backgrounds, and product attributes) to blend with the culture. The acceptance of trademarks/brand names was the most important factor regarding transfer.

Since World War II the volume of world trade has expanded to approximately $2 trillion a year. The United States is the single largest international trader with exports of $218 billion in 1984 (United States Department of Commerce, 1984). In recent years direct foreign investment by multinational corporations has grown at even a faster rate than international trade. The US share of direct foreign investment has grown from $11.8 billion in 1950 to $192.6 billion in 1979. Direct foreign investment for all nations tripled from 1967 to 1976 (Hodgson and Herander, 1983).

These statistics are an indication of the increasing amount of contact that MNCs have with other countries and cultures. Behind these dollar values of trade and investments are individual products and services. In order to sell these products and services in foreign markets, promotional strategies are needed, as are advertising campaigns to help execute these strategies.

Due to the current federal trade deficit in the United States, the degree of intense competition, and relative saturation levels of many internal markets, it has become increasingly important for American corporations to adopt a multinational advertising strategy. The degree to which advertising may be standardized, should be localized, or is adapted using a combination strategy is pivotal in the design and implementation of international advertising. This strategic issue may be viewed in terms of a continuum, with total standardization and total localization being the extremes and a pure combination strategy being the midpoint. While the results of this study indicate that the majority of MNCs are in the midrange of the continuum, many other firms can be successful operating toward one extreme or the other. Adjustments in advertising strategy should be made regularly, as the various cultural, legal, and economic environments are changing and product offerings interact differently with external variables as they move through the product life cycle.

SUGGESTIONS FOR FUTURE RESEARCH

It is suggested that future research examine the advertising effectiveness of standardization, localization, and combination strategies in order to determine where a firm should be positioned on the continuum presented above. It would be fruitful to identify the effectiveness of various advertising adaptation strategies for various products across differing cultural environments. Strategy adjustments (continuum movement) over time would be interesting to document, for example, as a US trademark/brand name becomes more recognizable in a foreign culture over time. Such movement (we theorize) is likely to enable a firm to be effective using additional degrees of advertising standardization in such a culture where higher levels of brand-name recognition have been established. Variables which inhibit advertising transferability for specific product groupings across specific cultural boundaries should also be identified.

REFERENCES

Boddewyn, J. J., Soehl, R. and Picard, J. 'Standardization in International Marketing: Is Ted Levitt in Fact Right?' *Business Horizons* (1986): 69–75.

Buzzell, R. D. 'Can You Standardize Multinational Marketing?' *Harvard Business Review* (1968): 102–113.

Dunn, S. W. 'The Case Study Approach in Cross-Cultural Research'. *Journal of Marketing Research,* **3**(1) (1966): 26–31.

Dunn, S. W. 'Effects of National Identity on Multinational Promotional Strategy in Europe'. *Journal of Marketing,* **40**(4) (1976): 50–57.

Elinder, E. 'How International Can Advertising Be?' In *International Handbook of Advertising,* Dunn, S. W., ed. New York: McGraw-Hill, 1964.

Fatt, A. C. 'The Danger of "Local" International Advertising'. *Journal of Marketing,* **31**(1) (1967): 60–62.

Green, R. T., Cunningham, W. H. and Cunningham, I. C. M. 'The Effectiveness of Standardized Advertising'. *Journal of Advertising* (1975): 25–30.

Green, R. T. and Langeard, E. 'A Cross-National Comparison of Consumer Habits and Innovator Characteristics'. *Journal of Marketing,* **39**(3) (1975): 34–41.

Hodgson, J. S. and Herander, M. G. *International Economic Relations.* Englewood Cliffs: Prentice-Hall, Inc. 1983.

Hornik, J. 'Comparative Evaluation of International vs. National Advertising Strategies'. *Columbia Journal of World Business,* **15** (1980): 36–45.

Levitt, T. 'The Globalization of Markets'. *Harvard Business Review* (1983): 102.

Killough, J. 'Improved Payoffs from Transnational Advertising'. *Harvard Business Review,* **56** (1978).

Ricks, D. A., Arpan, J. S. and Fu, M. Y. 'Pitfalls in Advertising Overseas'. *Journal of Advertising Research*, **14**(6) (1974): 47–50.

Sorenson, R. I. and Wiechmann, U. E. 'How Multinationals View Marketing Standardization'. *Harvard Business Review*, (1975): 48.

US Department of Commerce, International Trade Commission. *United States Trade Performance in 1984 and Outlook*. Washington DC: US Government Printing Office, 1985.

17

Managing the Multinational Sales Force

John S. Hill, Richard R. Still and Ünal O. Boya

As multinational corporations (MNCs) expand internationally they are faced with the task of establishing and managing sales forces in foreign markets. Once in place, they must then decide how much home office influence to exert on subsidiary sales policies. When faced with the diversity of the international marketplace, top marketing management is often uncertain about how much it should influence its overseas sales forces. Clearly, management benefits from knowing which sales decisions are amenable to home-office input and, just as important, which are not.

To help executives determine their involvement in subsidiary sales strategies and policies, subsidiaries of 14 MNCs across four industry categories were surveyed. The purpose was to learn how these organizations manage multinational sales force decision making. In particular we focused on whether head office influence varies:

- with type of decision;
- by industry-type.

Cavusgil and Nevin (1981) summed up the state-of-knowledge in the international sales management area when they noted: 'The entire area of research in international sales management has been virtually neglected in the marketing literature ... research on a variety of sales management issues would be extremely useful for companies establishing and maintaining their own sales force in countries with different cultural values'. Except for Gestetner's (1974) piece on international sales management, the lack of interest in this topic prevailed through the 1980s. *Business International*'s (1986) survey of sales management practices in Europe and Still's (1981) essay on cross-cultural aspects of sales management are two major notable contributions. However, most of what is known about international sales has been published in anecdotal or case-history formats (e.g., *Business International*, 1985a, b, c, 1986; Terpstra, 1987; Kirpalani, 1985). A review of available literature showed that most anecdotes and examples were concentrated in relatively few industries—general consumer goods, pharmaceutical, industrial and electronic data processing (EDP) industries.

Recognizing this void in the international marketing literature, a study was conducted on sales policies and practices in multinational corporations. MNCs in the general

Reprinted with permission from *International Marketing Review*, Vol. 8, No. 1, pp. 19–31
© 1991 MCB University Press

consumer, pharmaceutical, industrial and EDP industries were approached to participate in the research. Fourteen co-operated and responses were obtained from 135 of
their subsidiaries in 45 different countries (see Appendix for details).

STUDY RESULTS

MNC head offices are selective in the subsidiary sales policies they influence. The
analysis of subsidiary perceptions of head office influence by all industries reveals that
international sales planning and sales training receive the most attention, with much less
influence being exerted on country-level sales planning, administration and control (see
Table 1).

At the international level, decisions are strategic and affect the entire MNC. Type of
sales organization (sales force, distributors, or both), for example, is a resource commitment affecting sales returns from markets over long periods. Large markets or those with
high potentials warrant not only their own sales forces but also independent sales
organizations. Small markets, or troubled countries (like Iran), usually draw small
commitments—perhaps just a minimal sales organization.

The second strategic decision, subsidiary sales goals, is also an ongoing concern for
top management. Today's multinationals commonly integrate with their manufacturing
systems worldwide, with individual subsidiaries having global responsibility for components, or sub-assemblies (Davidson, 1982). In some industries, including autos, computers, industrial goods and electronics, sales goals are key inputs into global plans that
co-ordinate group manufacturing efforts and markets. Accordingly, head office influence
on sales goals usually has high visibility.

Table 1 also shows that local management of most MNCs have significant inputs in
planning, training, administration and control decisions. This reflects beliefs that local
designing of selling operations is important to success. When subsidiaries are first set up,
for example, they feature many home market products in their offerings. Amway's Asian
ventures were started with US products, but once established quickly went local, establishing local production in both New Zealand and Japan (*Business International*, 1985c). It
is apparent, though, that if subsidiary product offerings feature high proportions of ex-
US products, opportunities exist for utilizing American techniques to sell them.

When sales policies and guidelines are formally expressed in written form, they are
likely to have an impact. Items like training manuals, job descriptions and administrative reports, appropriately translated, facilitate the transfer of sales ideas from market to
market.

Many companies are wary of using American sales methods abroad, but in some
countries they work well. Two companies with heavy reliance on personal selling,
Amway and Electrolux, found this out when they took their 'hooplah' management
methods into Hong Kong and Malaysia. Despite the fact that hooplah methods do not
work well with Europeans and Japanese, both companies found them to work well in
Hong Kong and Malaysia (*Business International*, 1985b, c).

Table 1. Perception of GHQ influence by subsidiaries: total sample and industry analyses

Perceived influence on subsidiary sales functions[a]

	All industries				Food/drink				Pharmaceutical				Industrial products				EDP			
	1	2	3	4	1	2	3	4	1	2	3	4	1	2	3	4	1	2	3	4
Sales organization	17	20	16	47	23	39	23	15	20	15	10	55	13	19	26	42	14	7	0	79
Subsidiary sales goals	16	20	28	36	44	28	24	4	8	18	32	42	14	21	27	38	7	7	22	64
Sales force structure	48	30	14	9	69	19	4	8	56	31	10	3	33	47	7	3	7	7	46	40
Sales force compensation	28	40	16	16	50	34	8	8	22	51	22	5	30	44	13	13	7	0	13	80
Sales training	30	36	26	8	50	38	8	4	28	33	27	12	30	37	33	0	7	40	40	13
Sales content	20	33	27	20	39	42	15	4	13	28	25	34	24	33	33	10	7	33	40	20
Sales presentations	36	37	18	9	57	31	8	4	31	33	23	13	43	47	3	7	7	46	40	7
Job descriptions	42	29	17	12	54	31	11	4	49	28	15	8	36	29	19	16	0	28	36	36
Sales tasks	53	28	12	7	58	27	11	4	60	23	10	7	45	32	16	7	29	43	14	14
Recruitment/selection criteria	54	31	12	3	69	31	0	0	65	28	7	0	37	40	23	0	20	20	33	27
Individual sales person target	67	20	7	6	73	27	0	0	78	13	7	2	62	24	4	10	13	29	29	29
Salesperson evaluation criteria	49	33	10	8	61	27	8	4	56	34	10	0	43	37	10	10	13	27	13	47
Sales administration	40	33	20	7	42	35	19	4	45	35	18	3	40	33	17	10	13	27	40	20

[a] Values are percentage subsidiaries reporting: no influence (1); slight influence (2); noticeable influence (3); strong influence (4).

BARRIERS TO HEAD OFFICE INFLUENCE OF SALES STRATEGIES: ENVIRONMENTAL IMPEDIMENTS OF SALES TRANSFERS

It is apparent from the all industries analysis (Table 1) that there are a number of obstacles to transferring American sales practices overseas. But just what deters MNCs from taking US-style personal selling and sales management techniques abroad? A review of the available literature shows that there are five types of impediments: (1) geographic and physical dimensions of individual countries; (2) level of market development; (3) country-level political and legal systems; (4) human relations aspects of sales practices; and (5) local market conditions.

Geographic and physical dimensions

These dimensions of countries affect MNCs as they structure their sales forces market by market, and along with restructuring, changes occur in representative's sales tasks. The large size and vast sales potential of the US market allows for greater specialization of sales responsibilities and encourages divisions of sales tasks by territory, product and customer. The considerably smaller overseas markets often rule out sales specialists (especially product and customer specialists) as non-economical. In the EDP industry, for example, Burroughs compresses its product structures in smaller markets into geographic designs and directs its representatives to sell broad ranges of products. With such realignments come changes in responsibilities. In Sweden, for example, Electrolux sales representatives service refrigeration units as well as sell them (Terpstra, 1987).

Degree of market development

This has marked and diverse effects on multinational selling, since under-developed educational, economic and social infrastructures complicate the recruiting, training and deploying of salespersons in developing markets.

This research shows recruiting suitable sellers is always problematic in developing countries. University-educated applicants in particular are difficult to attract into sales because of competition from high-paying, prestigious jobs in government and the professions. Most MNCs, given limited people or applicants, make the best of available sources. In Central and Southern Africa, the military is known to be a good source of sales recruits (Griggs and Copeland, 1985). Even when there are large pools of available recruits, selection is difficult when MNCs go after top-calibre candidates. Electrolux interviewed 400 applicants to fill just ten sales positions in Hong Kong (Terpstra, 1987). Other MNCs, including Procter and Gamble and Johnson and Johnson, do some foreign national recruiting in US business schools.

MNCs entering developing markets for the first time, soon learn that well-developed infrastructures and distribution structures are inadequate in certain foreign countries. This in some cases results in readjustments in selling operations. In its European markets, for example, Electrolux sells 85% of its vacuum cleaners through retail dealers. In developing markets, such as those in Southeast Asia, the company found a dearth of suitable outlets, especially in rural areas, so it reverted to its traditional door-to-door sales approach (*Business International*, 1985b).

Low labour costs are an attractive feature of developing markets. In Peru, Sunbeam found it economical to hire an additional sales force to sell its private brands alongside its manufacturer's brands. This greater sales effort proved to be effective in expanding market penetration (Terpstra, 1987).

Differing political and legal environments

These make it difficult to standardize compensation packages. National political orientations to a large extent dictate the fringe benefits that subsidiaries offer employees. Europe's mixed economies legislate rather generous benefits (by US standards), including profit sharing, year-end bonuses, coverage of medical and dental expenses, high severance pay, and bountiful maternity and vacation allowances. Fringe benefits, which average about 35% of wages in the USA rise to 45% in Germany, 55% in Belgium, 70% in France and 92% in Italy (Ball and McCulloch, 1985).

While these benefits programmes are financed jointly by governments and companies, the costs place additional burdens on public finances, and European personal taxation levels are high, often ranging from 60% to over 90% for high earners. This limits the effectiveness of sales commissions as incentives. Consequently, many companies, as in Germany and Switzerland, level down the incentive side of compensation systems from 70/30 salary-to-commission splits to 90/10 divisions (*Business International*, 1986).

Government-sponsored benefit programmes do fall short in some countries, causing many MNCs to step in to supplement benefits. Swedish Match's Southeast Asian sales forces receive clothing allowances to bolster moral and foster pride in being part of the company 'family' (Kirpalani, 1985).

Human relations aspects of personal selling and sales management

It is in this area that MNCs make their greatest adjustments. Country differences in social class systems, ethnic divisions and business practices make deviations from US practices necessary and desirable.

Social class is a factor in US society, but its importance is dwarfed compared to elsewhere. The United States is an advanced economic society, fast paced and change oriented, and social rankings are strongly influenced by objective economic criteria such as income, wealth and education. Indeed, 'time is money, money is power' speaks volumes about the US social class system. More traditional societies, including some in Europe and most of the developing world, regard historical criteria such as family background and seniority as prime determinants of social position. In the sales setting, MNCs adjust compensation systems, recruitment practices, training programmes and evaluation methods to reduce difficulties arising from social differences.

In Thailand, a traditional society, family background determines social position. Because money confers only limited status, straight salaries are more 'respectable' and desirable than larger incomes with substantial but variable commission components (Still, 1981).

Tradition is also an important determinant of Japanese compensation plans. Because their social system is based on hereditary and seniority criteria, salary raises, even for sales forces, are based on longevity with the company. Similarly, commission systems are tied to the combined efforts of the entire sales forces, fostering the Japanese team ethic and downplaying the economic aspirations of individuals.

Occupational hierarchies in Europe and developing countries traditionally attach little prestige to selling as a profession, making selling relatively unattractive to university graduates. NCR has worked the Japanese market for over 70 years, but has succeeded in recruiting university graduates only in the past 20 (Terpstra, 1987).

MNCs face special recruitment and selection problems in culturally diverse markets. In developing markets where over 80% of them are culturally heterogeneous, most MNCs do what Swedish Match does in India. Faced with between 300 and 1,000 dialects, including more than 50 with a million or more speakers, the company completely decentralizes its recruitment activities to ensure not only that recruits speak the correct dialect(s) for the area but that they are respected members of their communities and can capitalize on personal contacts (Kirpalani, 1985).

Local business practices, especially in traditional Eastern cultures, require total indigenization of sales practices. Written job descriptions, a key feature in American sales management, are scarcely used in Japan. Salespersons are oriented through on-the-job practice rather than through job descriptions. Even sales training sessions between instructors and trainees, featuring appraisals, feedback and coaching, are conducted with ritualistic decorum so that even the most constructive of criticism does not result in 'loss of face' for trainees.

Relationships between salespersons and clients are the most critical in the area of selling. In the USA and parts of Western Europe, nurturing client relationships generally takes a back seat to emphasizing product features and competitive pricing. Elsewhere, notably in Latin America and Southeast Asia, the non-economic side of business is the major part of transactions, and client–salesperson relationships are cultivated to establish trust and respect. Often, out-of-hours socializing is the key to cementing relationships with clients. The effects of such 'client entertaining' are so marked that in Germany big-ticket salespersons are said to be able to sustain only 12 years of peak sales before experiencing social burnout.

Local market circumstances

These often impede MNC transfers of US sales techniques. In some markets for example, import restrictions or boycotts (e.g. South African, Israel) cause product shortages, especially in industrial and high-tech items. This causes MNC salespersons to be order takers rather than order getters, and results in little use of US-style competitive selling techniques.

Special market conditions provide opportunities to capitalize on customer preferences in sales presentations. In Southeast Asia, Muslim and Indian pride-in-ownership of fine carpets enables Electrolux salespersons to give extra attention to the merits of their vacuum cleaners in maintaining carpets in peak condition. In China, the sales emphasis is on floor polishers to cater to Chinese preferences for stone floors (*Business International*, 1985).

In spite of numerous environmental impediments, respondents reported varying patterns of headquarters' influence on sales activities. Because industry habits are important determinants of sales behaviour, an inter-industry comparison was undertaken.

INDUSTRY INFLUENCES ON SALES POLICIES AND PRACTICES

Table 2 shows the mean scores of the four industries on a four-point scale (no, little, noticeable and strong influence). The marked effect of industry on subsidiary sales strategies shows nine of thirteen F-tests having significance levels less than 0.05. Differences among individual industry means were evaluated using Student–Newman–Keuls and Scheffe tests. Of the 30 significant differences found, 26 involved one or both of general consumer goods (GCG) and electronic data processing (EDP) industries, suggesting that these two sectors have definite and distinguishable influence patterns on subsidiary sales practices. These patterns are illustrated in Figure 1. Over all 13 variables, general consumer goods affiliates have the lowest mean scores of all four sectors, suggesting uniformly little GHQ interference in sales activities, described by Gestetner (1974) as a 'non-centrist' approach. Additionally, except for the sales training variables (method, content and presentations), EDP head offices exercise the most influence on sales activities (a 'centrist' approach to overseas sales). Because of these trends, industry practices are individually profiled in Figure 1.

GENERAL CONSUMER GOODS INDUSTRY

Why do MNC home offices pay little attention to sales policies and practices in general consumer goods subsidiaries? Many relate to industry needs for locally formulated marketing strategies. For example many general consumer subsidiaries transfer and adapt goods or create their own products, producing in-market. Similarly, in mass media promotions, while head offices transfer promotional suggestions, ultimately local managers determine how to promote products, the amount of advertising, the copy and the media.

Promotional mixes of general consumer goods companies usually emphasize mass media rather than personal selling, but the primitive or undeveloped state of key mass media in some countries causes MNCs to rethink promotional strategies. The relative inexpensiveness of personal selling prompted Philip Morris to hire 200 assistants to work with its regular 100 person sales force in Venezuela. The assistants acted as missionary salespersons, delivered products and helped with local promotions, thus allowing the regular sales force to concentrate on selling (Terpstra, 1987).

Presenting consumer goods to buyers, especially in direct selling, would normally not be thought of as an area where head office help would be useful. But Avon found that its door-to-door and party-plan selling methods work overseas, although sometimes requiring modifications. Sales presentations were toned down in the British market, because Avon representatives disliked pressuring friends to buy. In the Far East and Southeast Asia, Avon and other direct selling representatives rely mainly on extended family kinship patterns and go-betweens for contacts.

Controlling consumer goods salespersons is important anywhere. Electrolux controls

Table 2. By-industry analysis of headquarter influence on subsidiary sales practices and policies

Subsidiary sales function influenced	Mean industry scores[a]				F-test significance	Significant differences among industry means[b]
	GCG[c]	PH	IND	EDP		
Sales organization decision (own sales force, sales organization)	1.91	2.00	2.19	2.50	0.0150	At 0.05 level: EDP with GCG and PH
Subsidiary sales goals	1.76	2.04	2.22	2.61	0.0013	At 0.01: GCG with EDP
Within-market sales force structure	1.90	2.28	2.94	3.00	0.0000	At 0.05 level: EDP with PH and IND At 0.01 level: GCG with IND and EDP At 0.05 level: GCG with PH; PH with IND, EDP
Sales compensation package	1.94	2.08	2.29	3.24	0.0000	At 0.01 level: EDP with GCG, PH, and IND
Sales training method	1.95	2.28	2.59	2.30	0.0256	At 0.01 level: GCG with EDP
Sales training content	1.96	2.21	2.51	2.30	0.1245	No significant differences
Sales presentations	2.00	2.41	2.48	2.25	0.0836	No significant differences
Job descriptions	1.95	2.24	2.57	2.88	0.0005	At 0.01 level; GCG with EDP. At 0.05 level: GCG with IND; PH with EDP
Sales tasks performed	2.10	2.41	2.37	2.55	0.2267	No significant differences
Salesperson recruitment selection criteria	1.99	2.25	3.06	4.00	0.0000	At 0.01 level: GCG with IND and EDP; PH with IND and EDP At 0.05 level: IND with EDP
(Perceived) influence on individual sales targets	2.03	2.31	3.00	3.38	0.0000	At 0.01 level: GCG with EDP. At 0.05 level: GCG with IND; PH with IND; PH with EDP
Salesperson evaluation criteria	2.02	2.28	2.38	3.45	0.0000	At 0.01 level: GCG and PH with EDP At 0.05 level: IND with EDP
Administration reports	2.10	2.21	2.44	2.89	0.0622	No significant differences

[a] Scores based on four-point scale: No, Little, Noticeable or Strong influence.
[b] Using Student–Newman–Keuls tests (0.05). Scheffe tests (0.01).
[c] GCG = general consumer goods; PH = pharmaceuticals; IND = industrial goods; EDP = electronic data processing.

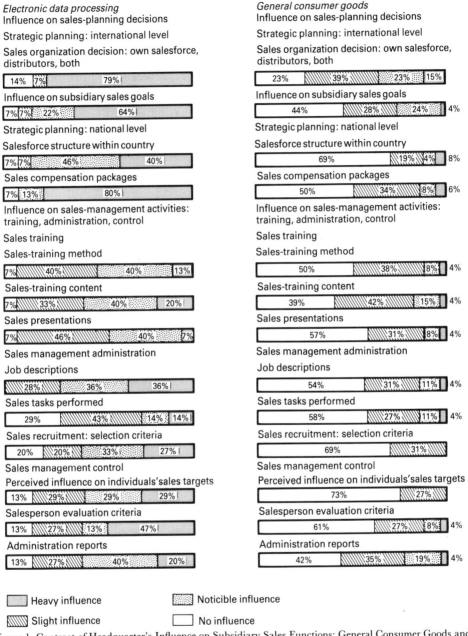

Figure 1. Contrast of Headquarter's Influence on Subsidiary Sales Functions: General Consumer Goods and EDP Industries.

its Latin American direct selling operation by an elaborate matching up of six sales receipts in four separate departments (*Business International*, 1985b). Other companies use more orthodox controls—Swedish Match, for instance, uses daily reports, total sales, sales to quota, sales expenses, appearance and improvements in distributor relations as yardsticks to assess its Southeast Asia sales forces (Kirpalani, 1985).

PHARMACEUTICAL INDUSTRY

The importance of personal selling in pharmaceutical promotional mixes guarantees considerable home office interest in sales practices abroad. From sources such as the World Health Organization, head offices collect and collate country statistics on doctors, hospitals, pharmacies and diseases. From these data they assess and draw comparisons on market size growth and potential among countries, enabling them to influence subsidiary decisions on sales organization and sales goals. Target audiences for pharmaceutical presentations—doctors, hospital administrators, pharmacists—world-wide share similarities in education and social backgrounds, thereby facilitating standardization in sales presentations. Pfizer's New York office produces and translates material for worldwide use on sales techniques and sales management, which are used (with appropriate amendments) in subsidiary training programmes.

Organizational structures for pharmaceutical sales forces abroad reflect country market conditions, especially the extent of socialization of the health industry. Pfizer's Swiss representatives vary their sales tasks according to how the doctor prescribes the product. Two-thirds of Swiss physicians issue prescriptions. For these doctors, traditional product detailing is the main assignment. The remaining one-third of physicians are 'self-dispensing'—they provide the product directly to the patient. For these doctors, Pfizer salespersons do both detailing and selling.

Pharmaceutical MNCs pay special attention to the training of overseas sales forces. The possibility of product misuse or abuse (and consequent legal actions) makes MNCs wary of undertrained or under-informed salesforces. E. R. Squibb's sales education in Latin American, Middle Eastern and Far Eastern countries includes special training in anatomy, diseases, and pharmacology to ensure that sales forces have the appropriate technical backgrounds for their markets (Terpstra, 1987).

INDUSTRIAL PRODUCTS INDUSTRY

Industrial marketing greatly resembles pharmaceutical marketing. Target markets—companies, institutions, and hospitals—are easily identifiable, giving head offices needed statistical overviews, which are used as inputs in sales-organization and sales-target decisions. It also allows top management to adjust the subsidiaries' competitive postures. During the late 1970s and early 1980s Rank-Xerox (a joint venture of UK's Rank Organization and Xerox) met intense competitive pressure in Europe and Canon and other copier makers. To recoup its position Rank-Xerox made strategic adjustments in sales goals, increased its European sales force to more than 8,000 and upgraded sales training to get more decision-making power at grassroots sales level. These actions helped to halt the company's deteriorating European market share (*Business International*, 1986). Head offices also influence three other sales elements: sales compensation, sales training content, and job descriptions.

The *modus operandi* that industrial companies use overseas explains why these three sales elements receive attention. Many industrial MNCs service foreign markets through exports. This focuses home office attention both on overall total sales targets and on sales of individual product lines. It also presents opportunities to push certain lines through adjustments to compensation plans. Consequently industrial firms often use variable commissions, separate quotas for individual lines, and commissions based on profit contributions to focus attention on certain products. Through this, salesperson compensation packages become susceptible to head office input. They also provide the home office with discretion to deal with unusual situations. Babcock and Willcox, a British engineering firm, was forbidden by government ordinances to pay its Eastern European representatives cash bonuses. The company responded by offering outstanding performers training trips to England. These proved to be effective incentives (Terpstra, 1987).

The export method of supplying overseas markets also heightens home office interest in sales training content and job descriptions. When Eastman Kodak brought out its Ektapoint line of copiers, its US sales force was recruited internally, but its European sales personnel were recruited externally. To ensure continuity of sales activities, the company gave its European sales managers and trainers intensive 'instructional' courses in New York and translated all US training materials into appropriate languages. On their return to Europe, managers and sales trainers were able to set up their own training programmes (Lawton, 1984).

ELECTRONIC DATA PROCESSING INDUSTRY

A prominent characteristic of the EDP industry is strong head office influence on overseas selling (see Table 1 and Figure 1). This can be traced to high-tech market needs first to achieve technological breakthroughs and then to diffuse those innovations to customers worldwide.

A product-type global structure facilitates the flows of products and technologies between the US and foreign markets. Most high-tech MNCs adopted product-type global structures during the 1970s, because they needed to move new products abroad rapidly (Davidson and Haspeslagh, 1982). Many high-tech subsidiaries model their structures on those of their parent companies to safeguard the orderly flows of products and technologies, hence the noticeable influence of parent companies on local sales structures.

Market considerations sometimes make sales structure modifications necessary. Hewlett-Packard combined its dozen or so product groups into three: (1) information systems and networks (formerly five product groups); (2) components, measurement. and design systems (from four groups); and (3) manufacturing, medical, and analytic systems (from three groups), enabling the company's salespersons to take a total systems approach to customer problems (*Business International*, 1985a).

Similarities in country product mixes, target markets and salesperson backgrounds make compensation packages and fringe benefits easy to standardize among country markets. This standardization occasionally transcends cultural barriers. Commissioned sales, the staple EDP compensation plan, was even introduced successfully into Japan by NCR—which until that time had been the deathbed of commission-driven compensation systems (Terpstra, 1987). As with industrial products, head office influence over commission systems enables high-tech companies to highlight certain lines by manipulating fiscal incentives.

However, the usually strong head office influence on EDP sales management does not surface in training activities. This may result from dividing product lines into software and hardware. Hardware mainframes are mainly US-made and exported to overseas marketing divisions. Sales forces know the hardware's features and capabilities, but have to learn the software that makes the systems effective. Because software is often locally developed in overseas markets, training takes on a more local flavour.

With constant updating of products and systems, it is important to review salesperson activities continuously. Clearly, the long lead times associated with complex systems, and negotiation processes covering multiple management layers in client organizations make most traditional ratios, like calls per day or sales per call, meaningless or at least misleading. In this environment, managerial control focuses mostly on sales expense ratios and on new customers and lost accounts.

EDP managers are front runners in computerizing elements of sales procedures and administration. For example, computerized prospecting systems and telephone sales are adopted rather than face-to-face solicitations not only by high-tech firms like Digital Equipment but by less technical outfits like Otis and Johnson and Johnson. The result is not just an increase in effective selling time but a constant stream of sales information for use in monitoring. Sales ratios, such as customers gained and lost, calls per day, and sales per call, are there at the push of a button (*Business International*, 1986).

CONCLUSIONS

Subsidiary managers can expect some headquarters influence on most of their sales policies and strategies but this influence varies by type of decision and industry. The extent of influence that MNCs should exert over their affiliates will be contingent on several factors. MNCs should not interfere with subsidiary sales administration and personal selling practices when:

- personal selling is not the major element in industry promotion mixes;
- distribution is intensive, sales channels are long, or markets have tradition-oriented distribution, such as in the case of developing countries or in less open markets like Japan;
- relatively low percentages of subsidiary product lines (less than 50–60%) originate in the USA as obtainable synergies fall below acceptable levels.

MNCs should unify sales practices worldwide most appropriate when:

- subsidiary product lines contain high proportions of items originating in the USA (in excess of 90%); this is most evident in industries like EDP which centralize manufacturing and compete overseas through export-led strategies;
- personal selling is the primary thrust of company promotional efforts;
- companies are organized primarily by product on a global basis, facilitating the worldwide flows of products and marketing technologies.

REFERENCES

Ball, D. A. and McCulloch, W. H. Jr. (1985) *International Business: Introduction and Essentials*, 2nd edn. Business Publications, Plano, Texas.

Business International (1985a) 'The Marketing Challenge: How One MNC Reorganized to Meet Customer Needs'. 22 February: 57, 63.

Business International (1985b) 'Selling to Asian Consumers Mixes Hooplah with Tight Controls'. 28 June: 204–205.

Business International (1985c) 'Amway Translates its US-style Hoopla into Asian Consumer Sales'. 1 November: 346–347.

Business International (1986) 'Sales Force Management in Europe'. Geneva, Switzerland.

Cavusgil, S. T. and Nevin, J. R. (1981) 'The State of the Art in International Marketing: an Assessment'. In Enis, B. and Roering, K. (eds), *Review of Marketing*. American Marketing Association, Chicago.

Davidson, W. H. (1982) *Global Strategic Management*. John Wiley and Sons, New York.

Davidson, W. H. and Haspeslagh, P. (1982) 'Shaping a Global Product Organization'. *Harvard Business Review*, **60**(4): 125–132.

Gestetner, D. (1974) 'Strategy in Managing International Sales'. *Harvard Business Review*, **52**(4): 103–108.

Griggs, L. and Copeland, L. (1985) *Going International*, Random House, New York.

Kirpalani, V. H. (1985) *International Marketing*, Random House, New York.

Lawton, J. A. (1986) 'Kodak Penetrates the European Copier Market with Customized Marketing Strategy and Product Changes'. *Marketing News*, 3 August, 1, 6.

Levitt, T. (1985) 'The Globalization of Markets'. *Harvard Business Review*, **63**(2): 92–102.

Still, R. R. (1981) 'Cross-cultural Aspects of Sales Force Management'. *Journal of Personal Selling and Sales Force Management*, **1**(2): 6–9.

Terpstra, V. (1987) *International Marketing*, 4th edn. Dryden Press, Chicago.

APPENDIX. SURVEY DETAILS

For the initial sample we chose companies listed in the *Directory of American Companies Operating in Foreign Countries*. The primary criterion for inclusion was a world-wide company involvement in either general consumer goods, pharmaceutical, industrial or high-tech industries.

Twenty-seven companies were telephoned, and 14 granted permission to mail questionnaires either to their world headquarters or directly to subsidiaries. With few exceptions (12 out of 135 responses) subsidiaries responded directly. Persons completing questionnaires included international marketing managers, international marketing VPs, country managers and subsidiary sales and marketing managers.

The 14 MNCs providing information were: *Consumer Goods*: S. C. Johnson-Wax; Kimberly-Clark; and Avon. *Pharmaceutical*: Sterling Inc.; Pfizer; Merck; Sharp and Dohme. *Industrial Goods*: American Hospital Supply; Ingersoll-Rand; and Hoover. *Electronic Data Processing*: NCR; IBM; Burroughs; Honeywell; and Hewlett-Packard.

Questionnaire returns came from subsidiaries in 45 countries: Argentina, Australia, Austria, Bangladesh, Belgium, Brazil, Canada, Colombia, Costa Rica, Denmark, Egypt, El Salvador, Finland, France, West Germany, Greece, Hong Kong, India, Indonesia, Italy, Jamaica, Japan, Malaysia, Mexico, Netherlands, New Zealand, Nigeria, Norway, Peru, Philippines, Portugal, Puerto Rico, Singapore, South Africa, Spain, Sri Lanka, Sweden, Switzerland, Taiwan, Thailand, Turkey, United Kingdom, Venezuela, Zambia and Zimbabwe.

The information collected related to the extent of perceived parent company influence on subsidiary sales management decisions and practices and was part of a broader study of multi-national sales management.

18

International Market Entry and Expansion via Independent or Integrated Channels of Distribution

Erin Anderson and Anne T. Coughlan

Once a domestic manufacturer decides to introduce an industrial product to a foreign market, a difficult question must be resolved. Should the new product be distributed via a company-owned distribution channel, or is it more efficient to contract distribution to an independent organization? To an economist, this is a question of vertical integration, in which the choice is between primarily captive agents (company salesforce and company distribution division) or primarily independent intermediaries (outside sales agents and distributors). The former option is an integrated channel, which generally affords the manufacturer more control than the latter, which is a non-integrated channel.

To a manager, this is the 'make or buy' issue, the company system being the 'make' option and the independent channel the 'buy' alternative. Robinson (1978) calls these make-or-buy issues 'one of the most debated and critical areas in international business' (p. 357). The reason is that ownership gives the entrant control over its international distribution channel, its link to the industrial customer. However, ownership also brings responsibility, commitment, and attendant risks (Ahmed, 1977). Channel choices, once made, are often difficult to change. Hence, the question of whether to integrate foreign distribution can have a large and lasting impact on the success of a firm's international operations.

We explore the intertwined issues of ownership and control through an empirical investigation of distribution in foreign markets by US companies in the semiconductor industry. The products we study first were commercialized in the US between 1955 and 1975 and were immediately or subsequently sold in major overseas market areas. We use the marketing, international management, and economics literatures to generate a list of factors affecting the organizational forms (integrated or independent) chosen by these firms in various foreign markets. Specifically, we model this choice as a function of both production and transaction cost considerations.

In our data analysis we use detailed proprietary information gathered by field interviews about distribution decisions for 94 product introductions in foreign markets. From this information we develop scales to measure critical variables. We then employ the

Reprinted with permission from *Journal of Marketing*, Vol. 51, January, pp. 71–82
© 1987 American Marketing Association

scales to estimate, by logistic regression, the probability that a new product will be introduced via an integrated (rather than independent) channel of distribution.

Our approach is a significant departure from most of the empirical international management literature, which tends toward intensive case studies (e.g., Schellberg, 1976) or, alternatively, analyses of single-proxy indicators gleaned from published sources (Caves, 1982).[1] Further, we explicitly model the impact of a number of factors taken together. In contrast, empirical research to date generally has considered only one or two factors per study, ignoring or holding constant a broad variety of influences on organizational form (e.g., Coughlan, 1985). In most of the international marketing and management literature the researchers do not even ask why the channel assumes a particular form. Instead, the form is taken as given and other issues are examined, such as conflict within the independent channel (Rossen and Ford, 1982).

In the next section we use analytical and empirical literature to postulate a model of distribution channel choice. We then describe the data base and how psychometric procedures were used to build scales measuring the variables of interest. Next the model estimation results are reported and discussed. We conclude with discussion and managerial implications.

A MODEL OF INTEGRATING DISTRIBUTION IN FOREIGN MARKETS

The choice between an integrated or independent distribution channel to serve a foreign market is complex and poorly understood. We cannot capture all the factors that contribute to a particular integration decision, but attempt to describe major, generalizable forces influencing channel selection.

We begin by framing the problem according to transaction cost analysis (Williamson, 1981), which posits that *a priori* the entrant is better off choosing an independent channel. This choice enables the entrant to tap the benefits of a distribution specialist in the foreign market. These benefits include the economies of scale and scope that the independent obtains by pooling the demand for distribution services of several manufacturers. Further, by avoiding integration, the entrant avoids some of the disabilities of bureaucratic governance structures (Williamson, 1979), in particular, organizational politics. Market contracting is thought to work well when the market for distribution services is competitive, because a distributor who fails to perform can be replaced. Indeed, it is argued that the threat of replacement alone is sufficient to keep an independent distribution system running well.[2]

---

[1] Coughlan and Flaherty (1983) combine the case study/single-proxy approaches to examine the productivity of marketing channel resources, using a subset of the data used here. However, they consider primarily dichotomous predictors of channel choice rather than scales (as used here), and do not focus on analysing the predictive ability of the range of theories we consider. Coughlan's (1985) model is concerned only with the impact of differentiation on channel choice, and uses only single-proxy indicators; it also uses just a subset of the data used here.

[2] The transaction cost presumption of the superiority of market contracting is in marked contrast to other approaches to the issue of vertical integration of distribution. For example, Stern and El-Ansary (1982) stress the benefits of integration much more than the benefits of independence. Similarly, Coughlan (1985) notes that her analysis 'ignores the transactions costs of dealing with marketing middlemen or the specific benefits and services arising out of the use of marketing middlemen' (p. 128). In contrast, our proposition is that middlemen's advantages are so large as to make them the default option, unless the transactions costs of dealing with the independents rise to a high level.

The presumption of the superiority of market contracting is based on the manufacturer's ability to replace nonperforming distributors. When this ability is diminished, for whatever reason, the impetus to integrate is increased. A proposition derived from transaction cost analysis is that integrated channels are more likely to be used when substantial 'transaction-specific assets' accumulate. These assets are specialized knowledge and working relationships built up over time by the agents (either employees or independents) distributing the brand in question (Williamson, 1979). These experience-based assets are specialized to the task of distributing the brand. Hence, the manufacturer will face difficulty in replacing the current agent, because any replacement agent must duplicate the experience needed to acquire the assets. In short, the current agent, by virtue of experience, can become highly valuable to the firm. Hence, the firm will be reluctant to terminate the agent, even if the agent is abusing his/her agreement with the firm ('opportunism').

Williams (1981) and Klein, Crawford, and Alchian (1978) propose that firms can better monitor and motivate their difficult-to-replace distribution agents (i.e., dampen opportunism) if the agents are employees rather than outsiders. Hence, where task-specialized knowledge and relationships are important, we expect firms to select integrated distribution channels. In support of this proposition, Anderson (1985) finds the selling function tends to be integrated when two transaction-specific kinds of knowledge are important: brand knowledge and confidential inside information. However, she finds no influence due to several other forms of asset specificity.

The product category's age also influences channel selection.[3] It is reasonable to expect that older product categories are more likely than newer product categories to be distributed through independent channels, because the older categories are more established and well known. Manufacturers therefore should be able to find a large number of qualified (knowledgeable) independent distribution agents to replace nonperforming agents. This fact in turn tends to encourage good performance on the part of any agent. In accordance with this reasoning, Lilien (1979) studied the channel choice decision by *Fortune* 500 firms in the US and found a tendency to use independent channels for mature product categories.

Davidson (1982) adds another reason to use independent agents for mature products in foreign markets. In many countries, governments pressure multinational firms to use local agents whenever they are available. Where they are plentiful, as for a well-diffused product, a foreign firm may have difficulty persuading the host government that it needs to set up its own distribution branch.

Service requirements can affect channel selection. Where the firm's marketing strategy calls for a high level of service (before or after sale), integrating the channel helps ensure that service will be performed (Etgar, 1978; Keegan, 1984; Terpstra, 1983). Though performing service can be specified in contracts with independent entities, ascertaining whether the independent adheres to the contract can be difficult and costly (Jensen and Meckling, 1976) because there are few readily available indicators of service performance unless the firm integrates the channel. Giving the distributor employee status grants the firm the legitimate authority needed to monitor an agent's behaviour and adjust rewards subjectively.

---

[3] The point is more generally posited by Stigler (1951). He argues that as a market grows in size, parts of the production and marketing processes (e.g., distribution) can be spun off to independent firms simply because of their scale.

Hence, we would expect integrated channels to be used more commonly than independent channels for products with high service requirements. Some limited empirical support is provided by Anderson (1985), who found that employee salespeople are used more commonly than contract independent salespeople for service-intensive products. Though the selling function is only one part of distribution and the sample was confined to US sales, Anderson's findings may generalize to international distribution activities.

Product differentiation also may influence channel choice. McGuire and Staelin (1983) develop an analytical model of retail channel choice in a duopoly wherein retailers carry only one manufacturer's product. They conclude that integration (company store) is more profitable for the manufacturer than non-integration (independent retail store) when consumers perceive the two manufacturers' products to be highly differentiated (not substitutable). In their analytical model, the reason is that such products do not compete directly. In contrast, nondifferentiated products do compete directly, creating price wars that drain the manufacturers' profits in integrated channels. If such products are sold through middlemen, however, the manufacturers' ability to respond to price changes (wage price wars) is inhibited, thereby protecting the manufacturers' profits. Coughlan (1985) tested this theory using 62 industrial (not retail) distribution choices by 26 electronics firms.[4] The findings support the proposition that highly differentiated products are more likely to be sold through integrated channels.

Legal restrictions on foreign direct investment can have a major impact on whether the channel selected to carry a product in a foreign market is integrated or independent (Robinson, 1978). Another important influence is the presence of established distribution arrangements (Coughlan and Flaherty, 1983; Davidson and McFetridge, 1985). If the firm has an integrated channel in place, the new product may be added to the line carried by this channel to utilize fixed assets (e.g., salaried personnel) more fully. Conversely, if an independent channel is already in place, adding the new product may be less costly than installing an integrated channel. In short, firms are likely to introduce a new product through their existing channel.

Integrating distribution is especially likely if the new product is closely (rather than peripherally) related to the firm's principal business. For such 'core' products, the entrant may be more willing to commit resources to distribution to ensure direct contact with customers and greater control over decision making. For peripheral products, however, management may not view the product as important enough or synergistic enough to merit a major resource commitment (Davidson, 1982; Davidson and McFetridge, 1985).

The strength of the firm's patent may have an impact on channel choice, though the direction is difficulty to specify. A firm with a strong patent is protected and may not worry about information leaking via independent channels to actual or potential competitors (Root, 1982). However, patent protection is never ironclad (Davidson, 1982). A product sufficiently innovative to warrant an inclusive patent may need further protection in the form of closely guarding *all* information about the product, as well as access to it (so-called 'trade secret' protection). This protection is accomplished best in an integrated channel, where the manufacturer can control distribution activities (including information dissemination) relatively closely.

---

[4] Coughlan considers only *de novo* entry in a market with established competitors. This restriction eliminates the pressure, mentioned before, to add a product to the portfolio of whatever channel is already in place.

Competitive behaviour may influence an entrant as well. If firms already established in the market have integrated channels, the entrant may wish to have one also. In this way, entrants signal to customers that they, too, are committed to serving that market and are willing to dedicate resources (e.g., personnel) to do so. A game theoretic interpretation of this behaviour is that oligopolistic competitors 'exchange threats' by imitating the establishment of subsidiaries in each other's markets (Calvet, 1981).

The choice of an integrated or independent channel may be influenced by the country being entered (Keegan, 1984; Terpstra, 1983; Thorelli, 1980). In particular, managing an integrated channel may be more difficult in countries culturally dissimilar to the US because US management techniques may not transfer readily to the foreign environment (Davidson, 1982).

In sum, the literature suggests a model of overseas distribution channel choice depending on many factors. In this model, integration of the distribution channel function is more likely

- the greater the level of transaction-specific assets in the salesforce,
- the less mature the product category,
- the higher the service level associated with the product,
- the more differentiated the products in the product class,
- the less prevalent the legal restrictions constraining direct foreign investment,
- when an integrated distribution channel is already in place (the converse is true for the case of a non-integrated channel),
- the more closely related the product to the company's core business,
- the more important the trade secrets relative to patents in protecting the technology,
- the more competitors have integrated distribution channels in the foreign market, and
- the more similar to the US the culture of the country being entered.

We next discuss the operationalization of the model's hypotheses.[5]

DATA BASE DESCRIPTION AND SCALE DEVELOPMENT

The setting of our study is the international semiconductor industry. A National Science Foundation study undertaken in 1978–1980 yielded extensive original interview information on 94 overseas distribution operations that were started between 1955 and 1975. These operations were carried out by 36 US-based firms.

Each structured interview, consisting of both scaled response and open-ended questions, was conducted with a senior executive knowledgeable about the market entry in question. For more complex technology transfers, more than one executive was interviewed (up to six per entry) and their responses were cross-checked until a consistent picture of the transfer was obtained. This consistent picture was treated as one observation. Interviews lasted approximately three hours each and covered a given market

---

[5] Of course, this model is not a complete representation of all factors that may affect the integration decisions. For a complete discussion, including factors that depend on transient circumstances, see Root (1983).

entry in considerable detail. This approach enabled the interviewer to probe certain responses and to follow up on questions perceived as ambiguous by the respondent.

On the basis of interview notes, the interviewer coded some of the open-ended responses into semantic differential scales.[6] Compared to asking the respondent to complete a set of scales, this interview method has the drawback that subjectivity is introduced by the coding step. However, the advantage is consistency across respondents; the interview process attenuates response styles (e.g., yea-saying), thereby standardizing responses. Further, the coding is based on all the relevant questions and probes posed throughout the interview. This rich background reduces subjectivity as well as the possibility that the respondent's answer is influenced by the wording of a particular question and by order effects.

Ideally, several raters would code independently and their inter-rater reliability would be used to assess their degree of agreement. Unfortunately, respondents refused to permit taping or transcription of interviews because of the sensitive and proprietary nature of the information. The interviewer's notes were, of necessity, brief and in the interviewer's 'shorthand'. Hence, the interviewer coded by the following procedure. Each scale point (rather than just the end points) was marked with a verbal description as well as a number. The number of scale points was kept small to avoid making fine distinctions subjectively. The interviewer filled out an information sheet for each respondent for each question detailing why the interviewer assigned each code. Then a second coder reviewed these sheets and discussed any ambiguities or disagreements with the first coder. When the first and second coder reached agreement, their consensus became the response used in later analysis.

Overview of scale development

From these data we derived some single-question measures, as well as several multi-item scales. Scale development was carried out in accord with standard psychometric techniques, as detailed by Nunnally (1978). Each scale served as an indicator of one construct in the model. Each indicator then was treated as an independent variable in a logistic regression, which predicted the probability of using an integrated channel (rather than an independent channel) to distribute a given product upon entering a given foreign market.

A multi-item scale is the sum of two or more variables. Each variable is designed to capture one facet of the construct; taken together as a scale, they form a composite indicator of the construct. The procedure recommended by Nunnally (1978) is to standardize all variables (removing differences in response scale) and compute Cronbach's alpha to assess measurement reliability. Nunnally (1967) indicates that an alpha value of at least 0.5 is adequate for basic research, but in apparent reconsideration (1978) suggests 0.7 is more appropriate. In the empirical literature published in well-recognized marketing journals, 85% of scales meet the 0.5 criterion and 69% meet the 0.7 criterion (Churchill and Peter, 1984).

We next describe each indicator.

[6] There were two interviewers; however, most interviews were conducted by one person, who was also the coder.

Transaction-specific assets

Table 1 is a list of the five questions proxying the extent to which transaction-specific assets are involved in distributing the product in question. Cronbach's alpha is 0.69, indicating a reasonable level of reliability for exploratory research.

Table 1. Asset specificity: distribution

---

1. How much training at the sales office do you provide to salespeople who handle your product? (0 to 5 scale anchored 'no training' and 'very high level of training')

(Questions 2 and 3 refer to the type and duration of training you supply to employees of the firms that purchase your product.)

2. How much training do you give employees of purchasers at their installation? (0 to 5 scale anchored 'very little training' and 'very high level of training')

3. How much training do you give employees of purchasers in your US facilities? (0 to 5 scale anchored 'very little training' and 'very high level of training')

4. How many years of education do you require for sales employees to be qualified to handle this product? (example: bachelor's degree coded as 16 years of education)

5. How much sales experience do you require for salespeople to handle this product? (coded as the number of months of experience required)

Cronbach alpha = 0.69.

Of interest here is how much the salesperson needs to learn about the product to sell it effectively. It is this learning that is transaction-specific (tailored to the product). Question 1 taps product learning directly by asking how much formal training the firm gives sales representatives. Products with a high learning content tend to be complex and sophisticated; further, such products require considerable education and training on the part of both salespeople and customers (Anderson, 1985). Questions 2–5 indirectly tap the degree of learning the product demands by assessing the training and background the product demands. Questions 2 and 3 elicit the customers' training requirements. Questions 4 and 5 tap the background (education and experience) required of salespeople who handle the product.

By itself, no one of these variables covers the domain of transaction-specific product learning. By combining them into a scale with reasonable internal consistency (as evidenced by an alpha of 0.69), we derive a more accurate measure of the asset specificity that arises in distributing the product in question.

Product age

The age of the product is measured as the number of years between the date of commercialization (not development) of the product in the US and the date of entry into the foreign market in question. By using commercialization as the starting point, we focus on how long the product has been available in the marketplace. This definition is consistent with our interest in the product's commercial maturity rather than how long it has physically existed.

Service requirements

We measure a product's service requirements by summing responses to the following questions.

- Describe the service and maintenance usually required by users of your product in this geographic area. (0 to 6 scale anchored 'no service and maintenance' and 'extremely high level of service and maintenance'.)
- How much of the required service and maintenance do you contract to supply in your typical sales agreements? (0 to 5 scale anchored 'no service and maintenance provided' and 'virtually 100% provided'.)

These two questions, one reflecting the user's needs, the other reflecting factory support provided,[7] combine to indicate how service-intensive the product is. Cronbach's alpha is a modest 0.53. The principal way to increase alpha is to add more questions. Though 0.53 is good for a two-item scale, more questions relating to service intensity would considerably improve the scale's reliability (Nunnally, 1978).

Product differentiation

Our measure of product differentiation is a dummy variable coded 1 for components and materials (high differentiation) and 0 for equipment (low differentiation). In the semiconductor industry, equipment (which is used to manufacture electronic components) is relatively interchangeable; product differentiation is low. In contrast, manufacturers differentiate their brands of components and materials sufficiently that buyers do not consider them interchangeable; product differentiation is high.

This measure is crude but captures an important gross difference in this industry. Coughlan and Flaherty (1983) and Coughlan (1985) also used this equipment/other distinction as a proxy for differentiation and found that, as expected, more differentiated products were more likely to be sold through integrated channels in foreign markets.

Legal restrictions

To examine the impact of legal restrictions on channel choice, respondents were asked to 'describe the impact of US antitrust law on the form of this transfer'. Their open-ended responses were coded 1 for 'little or no impact on taking equity positions' and 0 for 'discouraged you from taking equity positions'. Similarly, respondents were asked to 'describe the impact of the recipient country's tariff laws on the form of this transfer'. Encouragement to take equity was coded as 1, discouragement was coded as −1, and no impact was coded as 0.

Respondents uniformly indicated that US antitrust law had no impact (1). Further, virtually all respondents indicated that the host country had little impact (0); several responded that the foreign country encouraged taking equity (1) and none indicated they were discouraged from taking equity (−1). Because of this lack of variation, legal

[7] Typically, service-intensive products demand considerable backup from the factory, regardless of the channel used to distribute them.

restrictions were not considered in later analysis. It is likely that firms chose not to enter restricted markets. Under these conditions, the problem is considerably simplified.

Existing distribution arrangements

Given any existing distribution channel, a firm makes a marginal cost–benefit calculation when choosing a channel through which to sell a new product: will the added return of using an integrated channel for the new product justify the marginal cost? Because establishing an integrated channel involves significant fixed setup costs, use of an integrated channel is much more likely when one is already in place (so that the fixed setup costs are sunk) than in the case of either *de novo* market entry or a previously established non-integrated channel (when the fixed costs have yet to be incurred and are thus not yet sunk). Similarly, when a non-integrated channel is already in place in the foreign market, the incremental cost of selling a new product through the existing channel is lower than that of selling through an integrated channel.

The 'distribution channel' was treated as the set of all units involved in transferring the product from the manufacturer to the customer (see Lilien, 1979). Some of these units perform only the selling function (title does not change hands), whereas others take title (thereby assuming pricing authority), as well as warehouse, transport, and extended credit.

Dummy variables were used to indicate what, if any, distribution channel firms had in a market when they entered with the product in question. If no channel was in place, the observation is an *entry*, the *de novo* case considered by Coughlan and Flaherty (1983) and Coughlan (1985). If a channel was in place, the observation is a case of *expansion* (rather than new entry) by the firm, and respondents indicated what percentage equity they held in the distributing organization(s). Consistent with Lilien (1979), equity up to 50% was categorized as an independent channel, whereas majority ownership (greater than 50%) was treated as an integrated channel. In this data set, virtually all observations constituting expansion (i.e., involving an established facility) are either 0 or 100% owned by the entering firm. The low frequency of intermediate degrees of ownership is consistent with the overall pattern for American firms abroad (Robinson, 1978).

Relatedness to principal business

Respondents indicated whether the product was better classified as 'relevant to your firm's traditional and desired production activities' (coded 1) or as 'spinoff technology' (coded 0). This item serves as a measure of relatedness to the firm's principal business.

Strength of patent

The strength of the entrant's patent on the introduced product was assessed by three questions.

- For each country for which you have received a patent for this product, please scale the patent according to whether you consider it to be strong or weak. Score 1–5 with 5 representing an ironclad patent and 1 representing a very weak patent. (The variable used is the average score across countries.)

- Estimate the cost, in thousands of dollars, required to 'invent around' the patent protection you established beginning at the time of your commercialization.
- Estimate the time, in number of months, that a competitor would require to 'invent around' the patent protection you established beginning at the time of your commercialization.

Cronbach's alpha for this scale is a relatively modest 0.59.

Competitive behaviour

The interviews constituted a virtually complete census of one sector of the semiconductor industry. The companies interviewed for each technology produced at least 95% of the market share for that technology. Therefore, it was possible to infer from the pool of interviews the number of an entrant's competitors that, when the manufacturer entered the market, were already established in the geographic area of entry (e.g., Western Europe) and had an integrated distribution channel there. Hence, our measure of competitive behaviour is the number of competitors with integrated channels facing the entrant.[8]

Country of entry

Dummy variables were created to represent the region (Western Europe, Japan, or Southeast Asia) where the entry occurred. Of the 94 entries represented here, 36 were in Western European countries, 33 in Japan, and 24 in Southeast Asia. The one remaining entry, to Australia, was classified with Western Europe because of cultural similarity. These three regions were selected because there are substantial differences between them and a reasonable degree of similarity within them (Ronen and Shenkar, 1985).

ESTIMATION RESULTS

Our hypotheses about the factors leading to integrated (rather than independent) channels were tested via logistic regression, estimated by the method of maximum likelihood. In logistic regression the dependent variable is binary (0, 1; in our case independent or integrated, respectively). Once the model has been estimated, the predicted values are probabilities (of integrating, in our case). The predicted proportion of integrated product introductions follows the logistic model $\exp(U)/(1 + \exp(U))$, where U is a linear function of our independent variables.

Problems of this nature are frequently handled via discriminant analysis, a well-accepted and useful procedure. Logistic regression, however, has two advantages: (1) it

---

[8] An alternative operationalization is the percentage, rather than the absolute number, of competitors facing the entrant who were integrated. Operationalizing competitive behaviour in this way did not change the results.

is more robust to violations of underlying assumptions (Press and Wilson, 1978) and (2) the coefficient divided by its standard error is asymptotically interpretable as a t-statistic (Domencich and McFadden, 1975). In contrast, the confidence intervals of discriminant coefficients are uninterpretable (Crask and Perreault, 1977). Results are reported and compared for both logistic regression and discriminant analysis.

Table 2 is the correlation matrix of independent variables, which gives no indication of major multicollinearity problems. Further evidence of lack of multicollinearity is given by the stability of the coefficients in the stepwise estimation logistic regression procedure. Beginning with a full model (all independent variables included), we deleted terms if they failed to improve the fit of the data to the model at a confidence level of 0.15. The coefficients of the remaining terms were not greatly affected by the stepwise deletion process.

Table 2. Correlation matrix of independent variables

	A	B	C	D	E	F	G	H	I	J	K
A	1.00										
B	0.05	1.00									
C	0.15	0.11	1.00								
D	0.16	0.28	−0.35	1.00							
E	−0.13	−0.04	−0.25	0.06	1.00						
F	−0.18	−0.14	−0.06	0.00	0.05	1.00					
G	−0.57	0.28	−0.21	0.34	−0.07	0.26	1.00				
H	0.03	0.00	−0.05	0.04	−0.34	−0.02	0.23	1.00			
I	−0.15	−0.19	0.07	−0.15	−0.29	−0.04	0.03	−0.17	1.00		
J	0.13	0.00	0.00	0.08	0.04	0.03	0.00	−0.13	0.01	1.00	
K	−0.15	0.00	−0.05	−0.06	0.14	−0.12	0.08	0.00	−0.06	−0.46	1.00

A = transaction specificity of assets.
B = product's degree of relatedness to principal business of entrant.
C = service requirements.
D = strength of patent protection.
E = age of product (number of years since commercialization).
F = number of competitors using integrated channels facing entrant.
G = product differentiation.
H = existing distribution arrangement is integrated (dummy).
I = existing distribution arrangement is independent (dummy).
J = Japan dummy.
K = Southeast Asia dummy.
N = 94.

Table 3 shows the estimated logistic regression coefficients at the final step. Of 11 terms in the initial model, five were deleted. The deleted terms were the strength of the firm's patent protection, the age of the product (time since commercialization), the number of competitors using integrated channels that the entrant faces when introducing the product, the product's service requirements, and how related the product is to the firm's principal business.

The remaining six terms form a model that fits a logistic curve reasonably well, as indicated by the C. C. Brown goodness-of-fit chi-square statistic. Small chi-square values and large p-values indicate a good fit, contrary to the usual interpretation of p-values. The fact that our model achieves a p-value of 0.205 indicates a reasonable fit (albeit room for improvement).

Table 3. Logistic regression estimation results

	Coefficient	Coefficient/standard error
Transaction specificity of assets	0.90	2.25
Age of product	—[a]	
Service requirements	—[a]	
Product differentiation	1.21	3.06
Existing distribution arrangement		
Integrated	1.13	2.03
Independent	−0.59	−1.58
Product's degree of relatedness to principal business		
of entrant	—[a]	
Strength of patent protection	—[a]	
Number of competitors using integrated channels		
facing entrant	—[a]	
Region of entry		
Japan	−0.59	−1.67
Southeast Asia	−0.72	−1.92
Constant	0.56	0.83

C. C. Brown goodness-of-fit chi-square = 3.174, 2 d.f., $p = 0.205$.
Correction classification rate 82%.
[a] Deleted.

Further evidence of fit is given by the model's classification rate ('hit rate') of 82% overall (94% of the integrated channels, 82% of the independents). This rate should be compared with the rate expected by chance, which, by the proportional chance criterion (Morrison, 1969), is 54%. However, this difference must be interpreted with caution, as the same data that were classified were also used to estimate the model, creating an upward bias in the model's hit rate.

The remaining terms all have the hypothesized sign. Transaction specificity of assets is associated positively with integration (coefficient of 0.90). This finding indicates that products requiring the development of specialized skills and working relationships in order to be distributed tend to be handled by company channels rather than independent organizations.

Products that are more differentiated (less substitutable) also tend to go through integrated channels (coefficient of 1.21). This finding replicates and extends the results of Coughlan and Flaherty (1983) and Coughlan (1985). Their conclusion, that product differentiation is associated with channel integration, proves to be robust in the presence of other variables (i.e. survives the stepping procedure and retains a positive direction in the final model). Further, the finding holds outside the context of *de novo* entries (when the entrant has no experience in the market).[9]

An important issue is whether the foreign commercialization of the product constitutes a new market entry for the firm or a market expansion, that is, whether there was not or was a distribution facility in place. This distinction—entry versus expansion—has a powerful impact on channel choice, as shown by two dummy variables. The coefficient of the first dummy variable (1.13) shows that if a firm already has an

---

[9] We estimated our model with only *de novo* entries and the results were substantially similar to those obtained with the full sample of market entries, reported in Table 3.

integrated channel, it tends to add a new product to its integrated distribution channel The coefficient of the second dummy (−0.59) indicates that if a firm has an independent channel in place, it adds the new product to it.[10] In short, where entry is not *de novo* (market expansion rather than market entry), firms tend to add products to whatever channel (integrated or independent) is already in place, if any. In other words, once a firm has a distribution structure in place, it tends to expand by pyramiding new products onto the structure.

Finally, the region does seem to have an effect. In comparison with entries into Western European markets,[11] product introductions are less likely to be via integrated channels in Japan (−0.59) and Southeast Asia (−0.72). This finding is consistent with the argument that firms are less likely to exert operating control and more likely to delegate to local firms in countries whose cultures are very different and unfamiliar to the foreign firm.

To assess the robustness of these result, the model was estimated via stepwise discriminant analysis. That the results are substantially similar suggests the findings are not highly sensitive to the logistic specification and maximum likelihood estimation of the logistic regression model. The discriminant model does differ in one respect, however. The country dummies, which are marginally significant in the logistic regression model, fail to enter the discriminant analysis model. Nonetheless, the discriminant model correctly predicts 73% of the sample (80% of the integrated cases and 61% of the independent cases).

An advantage of discriminant analysis is that the jackknifed classification rate can be estimated readily by the U method. The U method affords an analytical estimate of the classification rate that would be obtained via the jackknife procedure.[12] In a jackknife procedure, observations are classified by a discriminant function computed from all data except the observation being classified. This procedure reduces the aforementioned upward bias when one is classifying the same data used to estimate the model. Hence, the jackknifed rate comes closer to the classification rate of a new sample. Here, the jackknifed classification rate of 70% compares favourably with the 54% expected by chance, which suggests that the model successfully discriminates between integrated and independent channels.

INTEGRATING DISTRIBUTION: DISCUSSION AND MANAGERIAL IMPLICATIONS

The results lend support to several complementary approaches to the choice of distribution channels for products introduced in foreign markets. The neoclassical economic approach emphasizes achieving scale economies and fully utilizing lumpy indivisible inputs. Consistent with this rationale, in instances of market expansion we find manufacturers tending to add their new products to their established channels (if any), thereby more fully utilizing the relationships they have developed with independent organizations or the distribution branches they have installed in the host country.

---

[10] In both cases, *de novo* entry is contained in the intercept term.
[11] Western European markets are contained in the intercept term.
[12] The U method estimate is an option in the BMDP analysis package.

Interestingly, these scale effects override whether the product is related to the firm's principal business or to its periphery.

Our results indicate that entrants tend to pyramid their products within a channel, thereby cementing their current arrangements and raising exit barriers (Caves and Porter, 1977). The 'inertia' entrants display in adding to existing arrangements underscores the importance of selecting the appropriate channel in the first place. Should this choice prove inferior, the entrant becomes vulnerable to new competition, which can elect the more appropriate channel for the product class without incurring switching costs. Interestingly, extensive research on how managers actually make these critical strategic decisions (Kobrin et al., 1980; Robinson, 1978) indicates that the decision-making process is often nonsystematic and based on little information. One of the primary reasons is that managers operating outside the familiar domestic settings have few guidelines to use.

Consistent with transaction costs analysis is the finding that entrants use integrated channels for products whose distribution entails asset specificity. These products have a common profile: they require the distribution agent to undergo considerable training to learn about the product. This finding is consonant with Lilien's (1979) that complex technical products tend to be distributed through integrated channels.

Though we did not measure the importance of relationships, we speculate that complex products also require the development, deepening, and specialization of working relationships in order to be distributed effectively. The specialized learning and these relationships constitute transaction-specific assets, which figure prominently in Williamson's explanation of why organizations choose to perform a function internally (make) rather than contract with outsiders (buy).

Our results indicate that where these assets arise in international distribution, entrants elect to use the distribution agent rather than write a contract with an independent party. Presumably, they do so because employee status facilitates the monitoring of these difficult-to-replace agents. Further, entrants then can use legitimate authority and a broad range of subtle incentives to influence their agents' behaviour.

The results also support the widespread belief that firms are somewhat hesitant to manage integrated operations in cultures that are very foreign to the managers of the multinational firm. Such caution appears warranted. The successful efficient operation of an integrated distribution channel demands significant managerial and financial resources and capabilities even in the domestic setting that management knows. In settings unknown to management, successfully managing an integrated distribution channel is even more demanding.

What do the findings mean for managers? One important managerial implication is that there are high costs to making an incorrect initial channel decision when entering a foreign market. Our evidence indicates that once such a decision is made (whether right or wrong), it tends to be reinforced over time as new products are sold through established channels. If the 'wrong' channel form is set up upon initial market entry, high costs of changing the channel face the firm. This possibility emphasizes the importance of taking a long-run, dynamic view of marketing channel choice rather than settling on an alternative that meets transient criteria (such as convenience or availability). The empirical evidence only reinforces the long-held institutional view that marketing channel choice is a significant investment that should not be made lightly (Becker and Thorelli, 1980). We also find support of McGuire and Staelin's (1983) proposition that differentiated products are more likely to be integrated. Their model is developed under a variety of restrictions, leading the authors to caution that 'to confront our models to empirical data would be premature' (p. 190). Our results suggest otherwise.

CONCLUSIONS AND IMPLICATIONS

The lack of impact of several other factors on channel choice is striking, notably the unimportance of service requirements. This finding is in contradiction to prior empirical work in the domestic (US) setting (Anderson, 1985). However, we caution that these nonsignificant findings have at least three explanations. First, the insignificant variables were the ones with the weakest measures (low reliability or single-item measures). Because measurement error attenuates correlations (Nunnally, 1978), it is not surprising that these factors are correlated only weakly with channel choice. Second, our sample size (94) is not large, particularly for maximum likelihood estimation. Thus statistical power, the ability to detect a variable's influence on another variable, is reduced. Third, the fact that we restrict our analysis to industrial products and one industry undoubtedly reduces the amount of variation in our data.

The fit of the model, though good for basic research, indicates need for improvement. Future research may find improvement not only by developing better measures, but also by including variables not covered here. One such variable is the company's overall level of international experience (our measure, the existence of a distribution arrangement is crude and specific to one market and one function). Much of the international management literature indicates that experienced firms are more willing than inexperienced firms to make international resource commitment (Stopford and Wells, 1972).

An interesting variable we did not consider is the size of the market being entered. These data are extremely difficult to obtain (Kobrin et al. (1980) note that many firms do not try to estimate market sizes because it is such an arbitrary exercise). Davidson and McFetridge (1985), studying the overseas transfer of innovative technologies, find the effect of characteristics of the country being entered to be minor (indeed, largely insignificant). In their study, as in ours, product features and the firm's existing arrangements are the more prominent influences. Nonetheless, market size may influence integration decisions.

Further research is needed to develop knowledge of what drives a firm's methods of introducing its products to foreign markets. One approach would be to include other explanations for international channel choice, such as the firm's expectations and level of risk aversion and the availability of qualified distribution agents. Another would be to study joint ventures as an alternative to either integrated or independent channels.

Clearly, our work is exploratory and subject to limitations. Nonetheless, Curhan, Davidson, and Suri (1977) note the extreme difficulty of obtaining *any* data about a firm's international operations, particularly at the division or product level. Our data, though somewhat crude, do afford some insight about launching a product in a foreign market—an important strategic issue in international management. In particular, we find indications that entrants tend to

- reinforce channel choices by adding new products to their current channels,

- erect a protective, restrictive governance structure around the distribution of complex, sophisticated products that require an investment in learning,
- integrate the distribution of products whose differentiation protects them from price competition,
- distribute substitutable products through independent middlemen, who bear the brunt of the price competition common to such products, and
- use middlemen when introducing products to non-Western markets.

Lilien (1979) argues that modelling the decisions of recognized, established firms (as we do here) can provide a useful benchmark for future decision making. If so, our findings may be of considerable value to managers faced with the complex task of selecting an international channel of distribution for a new product.

REFERENCES

Ahmed, A. A. (1977) 'Channel Control in International Markets'. *European Journal of Marketing*, **11**(4): 327–336.

Anderson, E. (1985), 'The Salesperson as Outside Agent or Employee: A Transaction Cost Analysis'. *Marketing Science*, **4**(Summer): 234–254.

Becker, H. and Thorelli, H. (1980) 'Strategic Planning in International Marketing', in *International Marketing Strategy*, rev. ed, H. Thorelli and H. Becker, eds. New York: The Pergamon Press, pp. 367–378.

Calvet, A. L. (1981) 'A Synthesis of Foreign Direct Investment Theories and Theories of the Multinational Firm'. *Journal of International Business Studies*, **12**(Spring–Summer): 43–59.

Caves, R. E. (1982), *Multinational Enterprise and Economic Analysis*. Cambridge: Cambridge University Press.

Caves, R. E. and Porter, M. E. (1977), 'From Entry Barriers to Mobility Barriers: Conjectural Decisions and Contrived Deterrence to New Competition'. *Quarterly Journal of Economics*, **91**(May): 241–261.

Churchill, G. A., Jr. and Peter, J. P. (1984), 'Research Design Effects on the Reliability of Rating Scales: A Meta-Analysis'. *Journal of Marketing Research*, **21**(November): 360–375.

Coughlan, A. T. (1985) 'Competition and Cooperation in Marketing Channel Choice: Theory and Application'. *Marketing Science*, **4**(2): 110–129.

Coughlan, A. T. and Flaherty, M. T. (1983) 'Measuring the International Marketing Productivity of U.S. Semiconductor Companies'. In *Productivity in Distribution*, David Gautschi, ed. Amsterdam: Elsevier Science Publishing Company.

Crask, M. R. and Perreault, W. D. Jr. (1977) 'Validation of Discriminant Analysis in Marketing'. *Journal of Marketing Research*, **16**(February): 60–68.

Curhan, J. P., Davidson, W. H. and Suri, R. (1977) *Tracing the Multinationals*. Cambridge, MA: Ballinger Publishing Company.

Davidson, W. H. (1982) *Global Strategic Management*. New York: John Wiley & Sons, Inc.

Davidson, W. H. and McFetridge, D. G. (1985) 'Key Characteristics in the Choice of International Technology Transfer Mode'. *Journal of International Business Studies*, **11**(Summer): 5–21.

Domencich, T. A. and McFadden, D. (1975) *Urban Travel Demand: A Behavioral Analysis*. Amsterdam: North-Holland Publishing Company.

Etgar, M. (1978) 'The Effects of Forward Vertical Integration on Service Performance of a Distributive Industry'. *Journal of Industrial Economics*, **26**(March): 249–255.

Jensen, M. C. and Meckling, W. N. (1976) 'Theory of the Firm: Managerial Behavior, Agency Costs and Ownership Structure'. *Journal of Financial Economics*, **3**: 305–360.

Keegan, W. J. (1984) *Multinational Marketing Management*. Englewood Cliffs, NJ: Prentice-Hall, Inc.

Klein, B, Crawford, R. G. and Alchian, A. A. (1978) 'Vertical Integration, Appropriable Quasi-Rents, and the Competitive Contracting Process'. *Journal of Law and Economics*, **21**(October): 297–325.

Kobrin, S. J., Basek, J., Blank, S. and La Palombara, J. (1980) 'The Assessment and Evaluation of Noneconomic Environments by American Firms: A Preliminary Report'. *Journal of International Business Studies*, **11**(Spring–Summer): 32–46.

Lilien, G. L. (1979) 'Advisor 2: Modeling the Marketing Mix Decision for Industrial Products'. *Management Science*, **25**(February): 191–204.

McGuire, T. W. and Staelin, R. (1983) 'An Industry Equilibrium Analysis of Downstream Vertical Integration'. *Marketing Science*, **2**(2): 161–192.

Morrison, D. G. (1969) 'On the Interpretation of Discriminant Analysis'. *Journal of Marketing Research*, **6**(May): 156–163.

Nunnally, J. C. (1967) *Psychometric Theory*, 1st edn. New York: McGraw-Hill Book Company.

Nunnally, J. C. (1978) *Psychometric Theory*, 2nd edn. New York: McGraw-Hill Book Company.

Press, S. J. and Wilson, S. (1978) 'Choosing Between Logistic Regression and Discriminant Analysis'. *Journal of the American Statistical Association*, **73**(December): 699–705.

Robinson, R. C. (1978) *International Business Management: A Guide to Decision Making*, 2nd edn. Hinsdale, IL: The Dryden Press.

Ronen, S. and Shenkar, O. (1985) 'Clustering Countries on Attitudinal Dimensions: A Review and Synthesis'. *Academy of Management Journal*, **10**(3): 435–454.

Root, F. J. (1982) *Foreign Market Entry Strategies*. New York: AMACON.

Rossen, P. J. and Ford, I. D. (1982) 'Manufacturer—Overseas Distributor Relations and Export Performance'. *Journal of International Business Studies*, **13**(Fall): 57–72.

Schellberg, R. E. (1976) 'Kodak: A Case Study of International Distribution'. *Columbia Journal of World Business*, **11**(Spring): 32–38.

Stern, L. W. and El-Ansary, A. (1982) *Marketing Channels*. Englewood Cliffs, NJ: Prentice-Hall Inc.

Stigler, G. J. (1951) 'The Division of Labor is Limited by the Extent of the Market'. *Journal of Political Economy*, **59**(June): 185–193.

Stopford, J. M. and Wells, L. T. Jr. (1972) *Managing the Multinational Enterprise*. New York: Basic Books.

Terpstra, V. (1983) *International Marketing*, 3rd edn. New York: The Dryden Press.

Thorelli, H. (1980) 'International Marketing: An Ecologic View', in *International Marketing Strategy*, rev. edn., Hans Thorelli and Helmut Becker, eds. New York: The Pergamon Press, 5–20.

Williamson, O. E. (1975) *Markets and Hierarchies: Analysis and Antitrust Implications*. New York: The Free Press.

Williamson, O. E. (1979) 'Transaction Cost Economics: The Governance of Contractual Relations'. *Journal of Law and Economics*, **22**(October): 233–262.

Williamson, O. E. (1981) 'The Modern Corporation: Origins, Evolution, Attributes'. *Journal of Economic Literature*, **19**(December): 1537–1568.

19

The Developing Internationalization of Retailing

Alan D. Treadgold

INTRODUCTION

At the junction of the old decade and the new, it is clear that one of the most important forces of change shaping retailing in the 1990s will be the continuing internalization of what has been historically only a domestic activity. The orthodox view that retail companies should confine their activities to their local, home market is increasingly difficult to reconcile with a period when political and perceptual 'barriers' between countries are throughout the world being lowered, if not removed completely. Nowhere is this more apparent than in Western Europe where a retailer who confines his trading presence to just one Member State of the European Community is confined also to the status of a regional operator as the EC proceeds, however falteringly, towards becoming a Single European Market. In North America also, how appropriate is it to regard Canada and the USA as separate markets following the 1986 Free Trade Agreement between these two countries? In the Pacific basin, Australia and New Zealand are proceeding through a highly ambitious programme of economic integration, with the aim of establishing closer economic relations (CER) by the middle of this year. Most recently of all, the extraordinary events in Eastern Europe are opening up new trading opportunities which a number of continental European, particularly West German, retailers have been quick to exploit.

While in some respects the world is being divided into a set of internally cohesive but discrete trading blocks—the EC, European Free Trade Association (EFTA), Association of South East Asian Nations (ASEAN) and so on—a trading presence in one block does not preclude the possibility of exploiting opportunities elsewhere. Were this the case, it would be more appropriate to talk, not of international retailing, but rather of domestic retailing being played out on a different sized arena. It is the truly global perspective of a growing number of retail companies which characterize the developing internationalization of retailing.

The internationalization of retailing has its expression in a number of ways. Consumers in Europe, North America and the Far East are all familiar with department

Reprinted with permission from *International Journal of Retail & Distribution Management*, Vol. 18, No. 2, pp. 4–11 store formats, limited-line convenience stores, hypermarkets and shopping mall develop-ments, for example. Many of these stores will also be trading everywhere under the same names, such as Benetton, 7-Eleven, Toys R Us and McDonalds. These, and other retailers trading in developed markets are facing similar sets of problems and employing common solutions to these problems including, for example, the effective application of information technology to enhance business efficiency and increase sophistication in market segmentation and consumer targeting strategies. Indeed, the transfer between retailers in different countries of trading formats, ideas and practices is at least as significant in the internationalization of retailing as the physical presence of the same retailer in a number of countries. As such, those retail companies which continue to trade in their home markets only are nevertheless participants, however passive, in the internationalization process.

The aim of this article is confined to presenting an overview of the ways in which retail companies themselves are developing a trading presence outside their home markets. Firstly, consideration is given to identifying the forces which are encouraging a growing number of retailers to trade internationally. This is followed by an attempt to gauge the scale of international activity by retailers and the strategies being employed to develop an international presence. Finally, some thoughts are offered on the ways in which the internationalization of retailing is likely to develop further in the 1990s.

FORCES DRIVING THE INTERNATIONALIZATION OF RETAILING

Almost all of the retailers leading the internationalization movement have their origins in mature and highly developed retail markets, particularly Western Europe and Japan. Indeed, it is the perception of a relative absence of growth opportunities at home matched by the perception of identifiable growth opportunities overseas which is the principal motivating factor for retailers seeking to develop a trading presence outside their home markets.

At the risk of over-simplification, a retailer faced with constrained opportunities to sustain corporate growth in his/her core retail offer at home has two main options. On the one hand, he/she may seek diversification in the home market. For example, the actions of leading grocery retailers in the UK in developing into new market sectors, creating new store formats and moving vigorously into property development (for retail and non-retail uses) may all be interpreted in this light. A second route is to develop the core (and, in some instances, non-core) retail business outside of the home market and there can be no doubt that, in a range of guises, this is emerging as a preferred growth strategy for a growing number of retail companies. Of course, this should not be taken to imply that these routes to sustain corporate growth are exclusive in the sense that the pursuit of one strategy precludes adoption of the other. Indeed, the truly successful retailers are invariably those whose strategic thinking is constrained by neither sectoral nor geographic boundaries.

During the 1980s, the path towards achieving a meaningful and successful inter-national presence has been made smoother by what may be termed 'facilitating factors' including, for example, enhanced data communication technologies, new forms of inter-national financing and the progressive lowering of barriers to international development. Viewed in this light, the 1992 programme of integration in Europe is more properly seen as facilitating the continuing internationalization of retail companies rather than the main driving force which a number of commentators have erroneously interpreted it to be. Other key facilitating factors are identified in Table 1.

Table 1. Key facilitating factors in the internationalization of retail companies

- Enhanced data communication technologies
- The growing processionalization of senior management
- The international mobility of senior retail management
- Accumulation of in-company experience of trading internationally
- The presence of other international retailers as role models
- The growth of support service providers and advisers, market researchers, consultants, etc.
- 'Bandwagon' effects and imitative activity
- New forms of international financing
- Lower barriers (actual and perceived) to growth internationally
- The growing scale and internationalization of supplier companies

Source: Treadgold and Gibson (1989).

This table deliberately makes no mention of the proposition that increasing homogeneity of consumers is a facilitator in the transfer internationally of retail companies, formats and concepts. Considerable attention is now being paid to the search for 'Euro-consumers' (see, e.g., Gibson and Barnard, 1989; MacLachlan, 1988) and it is certainly the case that a number of themes driving consumer behaviour, perhaps most notably a heightened concern for environmental issues, have a pan-European expression. However, this should not be allowed to deflect attention from the fact that it is the differences between countries in the aspirations and expectations of the bulk of their consumers which remain far more compelling than any identifiable similarities (see, e.g., Schouten, 1989; Croft, 1989).

THE SCALE OF INTERNATIONAL RETAILING

Identifying the scale of activity by retail companies in overseas markets is made problematic by a paucity of reliable and current data which are comparable between countries. However, time series data from the US Department of Commerce's annual Survey of Current Business provide a reliable guide to the scale of foreign direct investment by retail companies into the USA—still the preferred destination for many European retailers.

For the period 1980 to 1987, the total (unadjusted) level of foreign direct investment by retail companies into the USA increased by over 260% from $3,650 million to $9,546 million. It is significant that, in 1987, 75% of foreign direct investment into the retail trades in the USA was made by European-based retailers, most notably from the UK

Table 2. Origin of foreign direct retail investment into the USA, 1987

Country of origin	Value ($m)	Percentage of total
Canada	1,181	12.4
Europe	7,215	75.6
EC12	7,194	75.4
Belgium	145	1.5
France	311	3.3
West Germany	1,071	11.2
Italy	−4	—
Luxembourg	n/a	—
The Netherlands	1,803	18.9
UK	3,879	40.6
Other EC	n/a	—
Other European	21	0.2
Japan	320	3.6
Australia, New Zealand and South Africa	70	0.7
Latin America	664	7.0
Middle East	4	0.0
Other African Asian and Pacific countries	92	1.0
Total	9,546	100.0

Note: Percentages may not add up to 100 due to rounding off.
Source: US Department of Commerce, Survey of Current Business, various years.

and The Netherlands (see Table 2). Some of the best known names in American retailing are now owned by foreign companies. Some of the most important US retail businesses in foreign ownership are listed in the Appendix. Nowhere is this buying-up of American retailing more apparent than in the department store sector where, for example, BAT of the UK owns Saks Fifth Avenue and Marshall Field, Hooker Corporation of Australia operates three regional department store groups and Campeau Corporation of Canada owns Allied and Federated Department Stores, including Bloomingdales. While each of these parent companies are, either for reasons of corporate strategy or indebtedness, anxious to divest of their interests in US retailing, many of these department store groups are expected to be sold to other foreign companies. In the first round of bidding for Bloomingdales, for example, a number of the strongest bidders were Japanese companies attracted by the potential for exporting a highly regarded and well known trading name into the Japanese retail environment.

By comparison with the activities of Europeans, US retailers have been relatively slow to develop interests outside their domestic market. Speciality store formats such as Toys R Us, The Gap (clothing), The Limited (clothing), 7-Eleven (convenience stores) and, of course, the ubiquitous fast food chains like McDonalds and Kentucky Fried Chicken are prominent exceptions. Amongst the US mass merchandisers, however, the trend has been quite different. Some of the most important US retailers have eschewed the trend towards internationalization and sold many of their overseas interests. For example, in the 1980s, both Sears Roebuck and J.C. Penney divested their interests in European retailing—in Belgium and Spain respectively—after a number of years of poor performance. By 1989, just ten of the 50 largest US retailers had a trading presence outside the USA (Treadgold and Gibson, 1989), confined for the most part to the adjacent

Canadian and central American markets. Given that even the largest US retailers have yet to develop a truly national coverage in their home market, it seems unlikely that the 1990s will witness any heightening international ambition amongst the US mass merchandisers.

Despite reassurances from the European Commission, there remains concern in business communities outside the EC over the prospect of a so-called 'Fortress Europe' where the removal of non-tariff barriers to trade within the EC proceeds in tandem with the erection of common barriers around the Community to restrict the free entry of non-EC capital. In this scenario, the imperative is for non-EC retailers to move quickly to develop a presence within the Community. In this respect, one might look in particular to the Far East where the leading Japanese retailers, constrained by limited and very expensive opportunities to develop new stores at home, are taking an increasingly international perspective on their opportunities to sustain corporate growth.

Japanese retailers are already prominent in Hong Kong, Singapore, Thailand and other countries in the Pacific rim and over the next two years the department store groups Seibu and Daimaru will both open stores in Australia. The arrival into Australia of these two groups is being interpreted by a number of commentators as part of a learning exercise before these and other Japanese retailers make substantial moves into the United States and Western Europe. In this respect, the acquisition in 1988 by the Japanese supermarket company, Jusco, of the US womenswear and mail order retailer, Talbots, is significant as the first major acquisition by a Japanese company of a US retailer.

Within the European Community itself, a growing number of EC-based retailers are establishing a trading presence in other EC markets. In particular, retailers from the congested north European countries are paying increased attention to establishing in the relatively under developed markets of the southern states, and Spain and Italy in particular. Indeed, Spanish retailing is coming increasingly under the ownership of foreign companies (see Table 3), and French hypermarket operators in particular.

While most attention is being focused on development opportunities for retailers in the southern states, this should not be taken to imply an absence of opportunity in the northern states. Leading retailers in Germany, Belgium and The Netherlands have for many years traded in each others' countries, for example, and recent research from the Oxford Institute of Retail Management (1989a) identified 96 European speciality retailers with a presence in more than one of the EC Member States, in many cases adjacent to their home markets.

Further impetus to the internationalization process has been given most recently by the opening-up of Eastern Europe. A number of retailers, particularly from West Germany, have moved quickly to exploit these emerging opportunities. For example, Europe's largest mail order company, Quelle of West Germany, established a joint venture, called Intermoda, with two Russian companies in 1989. Starting in February 1990, Intermoda has printed and distributed a fashion catalogue in Russian. Towards the end of 1989, the West German grocery retailer, Asko made its first moves into Eastern Europe when it signed joint venture agreements with two Bulgarian department store operators. IKEA, the flat-pack furniture retailer of Swedish origin with 83 stores in 20 countries, also plans major expansion into the Soviet Union in the next few years. By 1991, Ikea plans to have six stores trading in the USSR in addition to stores in Budapest (scheduled to be open from March 1990) and Prague.

Table 3. Foreign Retailers in Spain: some leading examples

Ashley Industrial Trust (UK). Owner of the 'Digsa' chain of around 130 food supermarkets, 450 franchised and 1,500 affiliated outlets. Digsa was acquired by Ashley Industrial Trust from the Dee Corporation (now Gateway) in June 1988 for £30m.

Carrefour (France). Holds an 80% stake in the 'Pryca' chain of 25 hypermarkets (1988 sales of over Fr10bn). Further store openings are planned.

Docks de France (France). Owner of the 'Sabeco' chain of 28 supermarkets. Sabeco also trades from 74 franchised 'Aro Rojo' grocery outlets.

European Home Products (UK). Acquired the 'Ivarte' electrical goods chain in Spain for £3.3m in 1987. EHP also runs electrical and photographic departments in Galerias Preciados department stores.

GIB Group (Belgium). Operates three 'Bricobi Aki' DIY stores in Spain as a joint venture with Alba (39%), a subsidiary of March, the Spanish investment group, and Pryca (11%). GIB holds a 50% stake in Bricobi.

Marks & Spencer (UK). In August 1989, M&S successfully negotiated the purchase for £7m of the Celso Garcia department store in Madrid from Corefiel. This will be the company's first joint venture development. M&S already has two shop-within-shop units trading in Galerias Preciados department stores in Madrid and Barcelona.

Mountleigh (UK). Owner, since early 1988, of Galerias Preciados, Spain's second largest chain of department stores (30 stores, 12 of which contain supermarkets). Mountleigh announced in 1989 its intention to float Galerias Preciados in either 1990 or 1992, following the group's return to profitability under Mountleigh.

Promodes (France). Owner of 'Continente' chain of 13 hypermarkets (1986 turnover £480m) and the Dia chain of supermarkets. In 1988, 15% of group turnover came from Promodes' businesses in Spain.

Samu (France). 100% ownership of Alcampo chain of 11 hypermarkets (1986 turnover £400m).

Source: Treadgold and Gibson (1989).

STRATEGIES FOR DEVELOPING AN INTERNATIONAL PRESENCE

Just as the increasingly global search by a growing number of retailers is making it difficult, not to say misleading, to identify dominant flows in the movement of retailers' investments across political borders, it is also the case that retailers are employing an increasingly wide range of strategies to develop an international presence.

It is well-known that the exceptionally rapid international growth of specialist retailers such as Benetton and McDonalds has been achieved through the use of franchising which has made it the preferred means for many speciality retailers to develop an international presence. These include the relatively low capital commitment required of the franchisor, the opportunity to employ local management with their attendant familiarity with local trading practices, and the chance for the parent company to spread the risk of the venture with a second party (the local franchisee). However, franchising is only appropriate for rolling out substantially the same concept in a number of countries as the franchise agreement required to maintain control over the quality of each store usually leaves the franchisee with little scope to tailor his/her offer to local trading circumstances.

While it is the speciality retailers such as Laura Ashley, Body Shop, Tie Rack and

Sock Shop which are the most visible and recognizable internationally through their use of a common fascia and trading format wherever they trade, this is not to say that they are the most important. A further identifiable group of international retailers are those which are building a presence outside their domestic market through alliances with or takeovers of established companies.

At the risk of over-generalization, those retailers who do not have a unique selling proposition, differentiated from well-established local competitors in a new geographic market and capable of being transferred into a different trading environment, have shown a strong preference for international expansion by takeover of established retail companies. This was illustrated towards the end of 1989 in UK grocery retailing when the West German retailer, Tengelmann, attempted (ultimately unsuccessfully) to develop a presence in the UK by acquiring Gateway, through its US subsidiary A&P. At around the same time another West German grocery retailer, Aldi, began to grow its business organically in the UK with stores trading under the Aldi banner. Aldi's trading format—limited-line packaged groceries sold from a price platform in warehouse-style units—is quite different from any of the trading formats of established food retailers in the UK.

CROSS-BORDER RETAILER ALLIANCES ARE EMERGING WITH SPECIAL PROMINENCE

A growing number of retailers are now showing great flexibility in their strategies for entering new geographic markets. An important trend amongst many speciality retailers, for example, has been towards developing initially outside their home markets with company-owned stores and only later to attempt growth by franchising. Consider also the case of Marks & Spencer. During the 1980s especially, M&S has built up extensive interests in retailing outside the UK through acquisitions in the USA (Kings Supermarkets and Brooks Brothers), organic growth in France, Belgium and Hong Kong and, most recently, by joint venture in Spain.

One of the most important but least understood mechanisms by which retailers are developing internationally is through the formation of alliances with retailers in other countries. Cross-border retailer alliances are emerging with special prominence between West European retailers and can, in many cases, be interpreted as explicit responses to the perceived threats posed and opportunities created by the 1992 programme.

It is possible to identify perhaps four main types of alliance between retailers on the basis of the principle reason for establishing the alliance.

Development-led

First are those alliances *development-led* in the sense that the main aim of the alliance is for the participants to exploit joint development opportunities. In Europe, these alliances are most typically between a prospective entrant into a new country and a local retailer already well established in that country as, for example, between the Belgian grocery retailer Delhaize 'Le Lion' and the Portuguese supermarket group, Pingo Doce; the French hypermarket group Euromarché and the Portuguese company, Espirito Santo;

between the French DIY retailer, Castorama, and the Italian DIY retailer, Euromercato; and the joint venture agreement between Marks & Spencer and Cortefiel of Spain to acquire and develop the Celso Garcia department store in Madrid. Such alliances afford a foreign retailer the opportunity to utilize local management and expertise as a means to shorten considerably the learning curve associated with developing a new retail business in an unfamiliar trading environment.

Purchasing-led

A second type of cross-border retailer alliance is that which may be characterized as *purchasing-led* in that the aim is to enhance the purchasing power of the participants through joint buying, or to develop jointly new product-sourcing opportunities. It is this type of alliance which is developing particularly strongly between European retailers in the run-up to 1992, partly in response to the activities of some leading supplier companies in restructuring on a pan-European basis.

One such alliance is 'Eurogroupe', established in 1989 between the diversified Belgian retailer, the GIB Group, Vendex International of The Netherlands and Rewe Zentrale of West Germany. The initial function of Eurogroupe is the joint purchasing of fresh fruit and vegetables by its members. A second purchasing alliance, again involving GIB, but with the French retailer, Paridoc, is SODEI (Société de Développement International), which engages the two participating retailers in joint purchasing of groceries, textiles, clothing and certain household goods.

Skills-based

A third type of cross-border alliance is *skills-based*, in the sense that here the relationship is being driven by an exchange of knowledge or expertise between the participating retailers. One such alliance involves GIB which holds a 25% stake in Sainsbury's Homebase DIY business. GIB's established expertise in DIY retailing has helped Sainsbury to develop into what was an unfamiliar market for the company.

Multifunction

The most significant type of cross-border alliance between retailers in different countries are those open-ended, or *multifunction* alliances which embrace wide-ranging co-operation in development, purchasing and skills. The most important such group to emerge in Europe so far is the European Retail Alliance (ERA), established in May 1989 by three leading food retailers—Argyll from the UK, Ahold of The Netherlands and Casino of France. While the ERA participants themselves are still unclear how the group will ultimately evolve, the original motivation for the alliance was a perceived need by the participating companies to maintain their buying strength. Possible future areas of co-operation include marketing, distribution, production and exchange of expertise on information technology. It is worth noting that ERA holds a 60% stake in an associated organization, Associated Marketing Services (AMS), through which the ERA's participants can explore co-operation in the areas of marketing and buying with other retailers in the EC and EFTA, who can each take a share of up to 5% in AMS. Associated companies already include Migros of Switzerland, Dansk Supermarked of Denmark and ICA of Sweden.

CONCLUSIONS

In 1988, Treadgold attempted a relatively crude classification of retailers trading internationally, assigning companies into clusters defined by the extent of their geographical trading presence and by their preferred mode of entry into overseas markets (see Figure 1). Re-examining this summary diagram in the light of developments in the last 18 months suggests a number of trends in the developing internationalization of retailing into the 1990s.

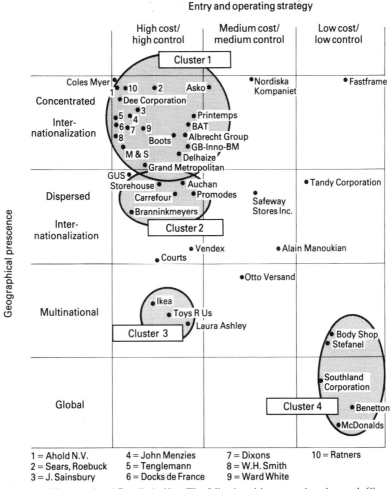

Figure 1. A Typology of Transnational Retailers. *Note:* The following titles are assigned to each Cluster: 1—Cautious Internationalists; 2—Emboldened Internationalists; 3—Aggressive Internationalists; 4—World Powers.

Despite the difficulties presently being faced by many retailers in Europe and else-where, perhaps the only certain feature of the diagram is that it will be populated by a larger number of companies as the forces working to promote retail internationalization continue to strengthen. The origins of many of the new international retailers will be predominantly in the mature retail markets of northern Europe and Japan while the North American mass merchandisers remain above all national operators. For the most part, new entrants are likely to be cautious in their early moves, implying border-hopping moves into nearby countries with fundamental similarities to the home market. One such new entrant is the multisector Australian company, Coles Myer—one of the largest retailers in the world outside the USA. Coles Myer's international expansion has begun with the acquisition of one of New Zealand's leading retailers, a move widely interpreted as a precursor to a substantial acquisition in either Western Europe or North America.

Amongst those retailers already featuring in the international arena, we might antici-pate movement down the diagram as the scale of their geographic presence continues to increase. The members of Cluster Three in Figure 1 are all extending their presence into new markets, for example. However, it will become increasingly inappropriate to identify 'dominant' flows of cross-border investment by retailers as the search for growth opportunities becomes increasingly a global one.

While these trends may be predicted with reasonable certainty, the detailed picture will become increasingly unclear and complicated. The boundaries of the diagram are becoming more fluid in the sense that a growing number of retailers are employing innovative ways of developing interests outside their home markets. Particularly note-worthy in this respect are cross-border retail alliances which extend into new countries, the influence of the participating retailers but not necessarily their trading presence. It will also be the case that retailers will not be easy to position according to their entry strategies as more than one mode of entry is employed according to prevailing circum-stances.

REFERENCES

Croft, M. (1989) 'Getting the Goods on the Continental Shelf'. *Marketing Week*, 12 May: 40–47.

Gibson, G. and Barnard, P. (1989) 'Consumer Trends in the EC—How can Retailers Respond?'. Section 4 in OXIRM and Coopers and Lybrand, *Responding to 1992: Key Factors for Retailers*. Longman, Harlow.

MacLachlan, M. (1988) 'Retailing', in Phillips and Drew, *Europe 1992: Breaking Down the Barriers*. Phillips and Drew, London.

Oxford Institute of Retail Management (1989a) *Europe's International Retailers*, OXIRM Fact Sheet.

Oxford Institute of Retail Management (1989b) *Foreign Retailers in the USA*, OXIRM Fact Sheet.

Schouten, A. (1989) 'Internationalising Retail Chains', paper presented at The Economist Confer-ence, *Retail Chains: Creating the Winners of the 90s*, London, 9–10 November.

Treadgold A. and Gibson, G. (1989) 'Retailing in Continental Europe: The Opportunities and the Costs'. *Europe 2000*, **1**(6): 93–96.

APPENDIX. FOREIGN OWNERSHIP OF US RETAIL COMPANIES: SOME LEADING EXAMPLES

Company	Country of origin	Main US interests
Ahold	The Netherlands	Owner of three grocery retailers with combined sales in 1988 of over $6bn.
Asko	West Germany	Owner of Furr's supermarkets of Texas. 181 stores and sales in 1987 of $1.1bn.
BAT Industries	UK	Owner of Saks Fifth Avenue and Marshall Field department store groups, Imasco's Peoples Drug stores and Hardees fast food chain.
Campeau Corp.	Canada	Owner of Allied and Federated Department Stores (including Bloomingdales).
Delhaize 'Le Lion'	Belgium	44.3% stake in the Food Lion supermarket business with 567 stores and sales in 1988 of $3.8bn.
Dixons	UK	Owner of Silo, the second largest consumer electronics retailer in the US (202 stores and sales in 1987/88 of £398.3m).
Grand Metropolitan	UK	Owner of Pearle Health Services with over 1,000 opticians stores in the US and the Burger King fast food restaurant business.
Hooker Corp.	Australia	Operates 22 department stores, including Bonwitt Teller (13), B. Altman (6) and Sakowitz (4).
Jusco	Japan	Owner, since 1988, of Talbots women's wear and mail order business (126 stores and sales in 1987/88 of $340m). The first major acquisition by a Japanese company into US retailing.
Marks & Spencer	UK	Owner of Brooks Brothers menswear business, one of the oldest and best known retail companies in the US and the Kings Supermarket business.
Panfida	Australia	Owner of two convenience store chains, Majik Markets and TOC, trading from a total of more than 900 stores with combined sales close to $500m.
Peoples Jewellers	Canada	Owner of Zales, the largest jewellery chain in the USA.
J. Sainsbury	UK	Owner of Shaws Supermarkets of New Jersey (70 stores and 1987/88 sales of $1.4bn).
Tengelmann	West Germany	53% stake in A&P food stores, the third largest grocery retailer in the USA (1987/88 sales of $10bn).
Vendex International	The Netherlands	Extensive US interests, including a 50% stake in the B. Dalton Company, the largest bookstore chain in the US.

Source: Oxford Institute of Retail Management (1989b).

Part III

Global Marketing Performance and Implementation

CONTENTS

20 The influence of global marketing standardization on performance 263

SAEED SAMIEE and KENDALL ROTH, *Journal of Marketing* (1992), **56**(April), 1–17

21 Innovation orientation, environment and performance: a comparison of US and European Markets 288

FRANKLYN A. MANU, *Journal of International Business Studies* (1992), **23**(2), 333–359

22 A performance comparison of continental and national businesses in Europe 312

GEORGE S. YIP, *International Marketing Review* (1991), **8**(2), 31–39

23 Bridging national and global marketing strategies through regional operations 322

JOHN D. DANIELS, *International Marketing Review* (1987), **4**(Autumn), 29–44

24 Implementing a pan-European marketing strategy 340

GIANLUIGI GUIDO, *Long Range Planning* (1991), **24**(5), 23–33

25 Competition in global markets: a case study of American and Japanese competition in the British market 356

PETER DOYLE, JOHN SAUNDERS and VERONICA WONG, *Journal of International Business Studies* (1992), **23**(3), 419–442

26 Creating European organizations that work 376

NORMAN BLACKWELL, JEAN-PIERRE BIZET, PETER CHILD and DAVID HENSLEY, *McKinsey Quarterly* (1991), **24**(2), 31–43

27 The new country managers 386

JOHN A. QUELCH, *McKinsey Quarterly* (1992), **25**(4), 155–165

20

The Influence of Global Marketing Standardization on Performance

Saeed Samiee and Kendall Roth

McDonald Corporation markets its services through 12,000 outlets in 59 countries. The firm maintains standardized specifications for its equipment technology, product offerings, customer service, cleanliness, value, and operational systems. Though its menus vary somewhat from country to country, its core product offering is consistent on a global basis. McDonald's global marketing also includes standardized positioning and distribution strategies. Likewise, some Coca-Cola and Colgate-Palmolive products are marketed in more than 160 countries. The Coca-Cola Company uses relatively standard brands, formulations, packaging, positioning, and distribution in its global markets. IBM and the manufacturers of many industrial products also design, manufacture, and market their products on a global basis.

It is not surprising, then, that global standardization of marketing activities has emerged as an increasingly important topic of discussion among academicians and practitioners. As multinational corporations (MNCs) have matured through accumulation of experience and knowledge from operating worldwide (Douglas and Wind, 1987), aided by more efficient and less costly international communications, travel, transportation, and distribution infrastructure (Buzzell, 1968; Levitt, 1983), observers have argued that world markets are becoming increasingly similar and, hence, a standardized approach toward sourcing, production, marketing, and other functions is both feasible and desirable.

The pursuit of global standardization is generally considered to be appropriate only to the extent to which it has a positive influence on financial performance. Buzzell (1968), in his pioneering piece on marketing standardization, expressed the importance of profitability in assessing the suitability of standardization. Other authors also have stressed the importance of economic payoff in decisions about standardizing global marketing practice (Jain, 1989; Keegan, 1969; Wind, 1986). Hence, long-term *economic payoff* is considered to be a critical element on which the decision to standardize should be based. Inasmuch as lower costs *may* lead to increased profitability, several authors have also emphasized the scale effects associated with standardization (Henzler and Rall, 1986; Hout, Porter, and Rudden, 1982; Jain, 1989; Levitt, 1983; Rutenberg, 1982;

Reprinted with permission from *Journal of Marketing*, Vol. 56, April, pp. 1–17
© 1992 American Marketing Association

Sorenson and Wiechmann, 1975; Terpstra, 1987). However, to date no attempt has been made to validate the financial payoff associated with standardization.

The primary purpose of our study is to examine empirically the relationship between global standardization and financial performance of business units (BUs) within the global industry context. Because of the lack of prior research on this topic, an exploratory approach is taken to develop a more comprehensive understanding and explanation of the role and impact of global standardization. That is, inasmuch as marketing strategy is implemented and driven by environmental and key corporate and marketing dimensions, we also investigate the relationship between global standardization and (1) the technological environment, (2) stage of the product life cycle (PLC) for BUs, and (3) the importance of key corporate policies and the components of the marketing plan.

THEORETICAL CONSIDERATIONS

From a theoretical perspective, the central consideration in pursuing global standardization involves market definition and market segmentation. In particular, market segmentation is a *necessary* and *critical* component of the marketing plan. Adapted from the microeconomic theory of price discrimination, market segmentation accomplishes one thing. Using the relevant criteria, segmentation groups customers into homogeneous subsets that enable the firm to cultivate particular market niches in which fewer or no competitors are present. The theoretical model is normative, with the goal of profit maximization.

The competitive advantage resulting from market segmentation can be significant. First, a firm may remain a quasimonopolist in its selected market segment(s), which enables it to price its products with relative freedom from its competitors. All things being equal, price freedom should lead to higher margins and, therefore, better BU performance. Second, by focusing on individual target markets, the firm can anticipate and react to market changes more effectively and efficiently, which leads to a higher level of customer loyalty. However, the implementation of an effective segmentation programme requires the presence of several *a priori* conditions, including potential profits from a selected segment(s).

From a conceptual point of view, validation of global standardization requires a reexamination of the marketing management process (Onkvisit and Shaw, 1987). A critical consideration in this process is the development of separate marketing plans for various segments a firm chooses to service. Consequently, for standardization of international marketing activities to be successful, the firm must show the presence of *intermarket segments* in countries earmarked for standardization. The concept of intermarket segments is defined as the presence of well-defined and similar clusters of customers across national boundaries that have the same characteristics and are identified by similar criteria. This concept is central to Levitt's (1983) position on globalization which other authors have supported (Douglas and Wind, 1987; Jain, 1989; Kale and Sudharshan, 1987; Onkvisit and Shaw, 1987; Sheth, 1986; Simmonds, 1985). If this position is valid and practical, applying the segmentation concept internationally should enable the firm to standardize its programmes and offering(s) and, by definition, achieve a higher level of *economic performance*.

HYPOTHESES

The subject of standardizing international marketing has been studied and debated for nearly three decades. Their research worthiness notwithstanding, the majority of the studies on international marketing standardization are conceptual (Jain, 1989). Furthermore, most empirical studies have addressed relatively narrow aspects of international marketing such as product adaptation to local tastes in less developed countries (e.g., Hill and Still, 1984) or the advertising function (e.g., Green, Cunningham, and Cunningham, 1975; Peebles, Ryans, and Vernon, 1977, 1978). Recognizing these trends, we extend the literature through an examination of the relationship between global standardization and industry and technology, components of the marketing plan, key corporate policies and strategies, and performance.

The influence of industry and technology

Jain (1989, p. 74) has proposed that industrial and high technology products are more likely candidates for standardization than consumer products. Industrial products typically fill specific needs that do not vary greatly from one country to another. They are also more likely to involve significant capital investment and, hence, the rationale for maintaining fewer manufacturing facilities, each of which is capable of producing much larger quantities than smaller plants throughout the firm's global network. This pattern provides opportunities for increased standardization. Naturally, some modifications may be necessary as these products must meet different specifications and safety standards, but in most cases such changes are not thought to inhibit the offering of a standardized product. Furthermore, purchasing of industrial products is typically rationalized to meet organizational objectives and needs and is conducted in accordance with established policies and procedures. In contrast, consumer markets are more likely to be context sensitive. Consumer preferences across national boundaries are more likely to be idiosyncratic to local cultures, value structures, tastes, economies, and other factors. Hence, global standardization may be more suitable for industrial products.

H_1:   Firms producing industrial products are more likely to emphasize global standardization than consumer goods companies.

The relationship between global standardization and the pace of technology change has not been examined. The global standardization decision is internal to the firm whereas technological changes are typically external forces. In a macro, comparative sense, the rate of intra-industry technological change and the response of competitors to that change influence the pursuit of standardization. Boddewyn, Soehl, and Picard (1986) reported that competition is perceived as the most important obstacle in standardizing the marketing mix for industrial products. We therefore examine three scenarios involving technology and standardization.

First, we consider industries marked by rapid technological change (e.g., electronic storage devices), in which the life cycle might be less than 12 months. At least from manufacturing and communications perspectives, firms in such industries have less time to plan adequately and implement a standardized global strategy in numerous affiliates.

Hence, global standardization is possible if manufacturing processes are globally concentrated to one or a very few facilities (Porter, 1986b). Even when technology changes are small and incremental, their implementation in multiple plants can be a nightmare.[1] When technological shifts are radical, significant financial outlays are needed to retool the manufacturing plants and retrain employees as well as customers. Likewise, the price of technologically short-lived components drops relatively rapidly as newer products are introduced, leading to sourcing and pricing pressures at various manufacturing sites around the world. Firms in such volatile environments are therefore more likely to rely on one or very few manufacturing facilities and operate globally by exporting a standardized product.

In the second scenario, we consider firms operating in technologically stable industries. Despite the many advantages of standardization for such firms, when the MNC supplies its markets from numerous plants around the world, it has the ability to focus on the particular characteristics of local markets. In addition, when the technology is stable, the likelihood of major product differences among competitors is lessened and there is an added incentive for customizing the product for local markets. Therefore, the relative stability of technology in the industry may allow competitors to become more responsive to the needs of local markets through a higher level of customization to meet local needs and preferences.

Finally, a related development that enhances the feasibility of adaptation to local needs in some industries is technological advancements in design and manufacturing. New technologies offer a cost-efficient basis for customizing products for various market segments that warrant cultivation from multiple plants. This strategy is analogous to *pattern standardization* as suggested by Peebles, Ryans, and Vernon (1978) and Colvin, Heeler, and Thorpe (1980) as a compromise between standardization and customization of advertising programmes. Though this approach facilitates marketing planning for multiple markets, it stops short of realizing the full benefits of standardization advocated in the literature.

The introduction of technology to markets is also likely to vary according to their needs; state-of-the-art products may be marketed in some countries while the older generation products based on older technologies are marketed in others.[2] Thus, several products based on several technologies are offered to various markets, depending on their needs and ability to utilize them. This situation is consistent with the international product life cycle theory (Vernon and Wells, 1968). In the strictest sense, production

---

[1] An anonymous reviewer suggests that a distinction must be made between incremental and radical technology change. The underlying argument is presumably that incremental changes in technology do not present major obstacles to standardization, whereas radical changes involve significant investment, retooling, and retraining, as well as switch-over time. This observation is congruent with the position that when technology is short lived and each new cycle represents a major change, firms concentrate their global manufacturing to one or a few facilities because with every change the factory(ies) must be redesigned from the ground up.

Furthermore, it is easy to misinterpret the extent of technological change, particularly when functions performed by the final product remain largely the same. Consider, for example, surface-mount technology in the electronics industry, which required a complete retooling of equipment as well as systems and procedures for manufacturing and also forced both suppliers and customers to retool. For example, the manufacturers of IC ceramic casings (e.g., Kyocera) had to make significant investments in the design and manufacture of equipment capable of complying with the specifications of the new technology. Concurrently, they must continue to supply replacement parts for the older generation for an extended period.

[2] We are grateful to an anonymous reviewer who pointed out the possibility of marketing older products to some markets and state-of-the-art products to others.

and marketing of several products and lines based on different technologies to various markets constitute a form of regional, not global, standardization.

H_2: Firms emphasizing global standardization are more likely to face a rapid rate of technology change than a low rate of technology change.

Another consideration that can motivate firms to adopt a standardization strategy is the frequency of product obsolescence. Technological change does *not* necessarily lead to product obsolescence and products based on several technologies with different life spans may be marketed in the same industry. For example, technological change may lead to more advanced versions of a product without replacing the older versions (e.g., black and white versus colour television). By the rationale offered previously, shorter technological life cycles, as measured by the number of years it would take a technology to become obsolete, are expected to be more conducive to global standardization.

H_3: Firms operating in industry segments that have fast technology obsolescence are more likely to emphasize global standardization than firms confronting relatively slow technology obsolescence.

The intensity of competition has been cited as an obstacle to global standardization (Boddewyn, Soehl, and Picard, 1986). One form of competitive activity is the frequency with which firms make major changes in their products, thus encouraging the competition to follow suit. It follows that global standardization is more feasible when competitors modify their products frequently.

H_4: Firms emphasizing global standardization are likely to compete in industry segments where major changes in all or parts of the products offered are initiated frequently by major competitors.

The stage of a product in its life cycle also may influence the firm's decision to pursue global standardization. BUs with products in the introductory and growth stages of their life cycles face more frequent changes and refinement of their products than those offering products in the maturity or decline stages. It follows that during the early stages of the PLC firms seek to rationalize their global production and sourcing. In addition, firms might choose third-party supply sources for their finished products. Hence, uniformity in policies, processes, and programmes is more likely when products are in the early stages of the PLC. For example, since the early 1980s IBM personal computers have been produced and marketed with nearly identical designs for the North American market in Boca Raton, FL (now in Raleigh, NC) and for the Europe–Middle East–Africa division in Scotland. The Americas–Far East supplies are outsourced through a manufacturing agreement with Matsushita in Osaka.

During the maturity stage of the PLC, product awareness and purchase rate are high and market size has peaked. The number of competitors is high in relation to the other stages. In addition, technology changes are fewer, leading to a greater focus on market segmentation and product differentiation (Kotler, 1986). Indeed, during this stage firms seek to reach a wider market by developing new uses for their products. Thus, newer versions of the product are offered to narrower customer groups. As market segmentation intensifies and differentiation proliferates, the possibility of identifying intermarket segments is significantly reduced. It is also likely that during the latter stages of the PLC, global firms must compete with an increasing number of domestic and multidomestic firms which, by definition, emphasize customization. Furthermore, because the product is widely known and adopted during this stage, global firms can customize their products on a regional or even local basis without much change in their cost structure.

H_5: Firms that produce and market products in the early stages of the PLC (i.e., introduction and growth) are more likely candidates for global standardization than firms that produce and market products in the maturity and decline stages.

The components of the marketing plan

The first studies of standardization examined the advertising component of the marketing plan (e.g., Elinder, 1961; Fatt, 1964; Roostal, 1963) and set the stage for a more comprehensive treatment of the marketing programme. Earliest conceptual contributions in this area were made by Bartels (1968) and Buzzell (1968). Whereas the former focused on the similarities of international and domestic marketing, the latter examined marketing programming aspects of standardization. The question raised by Buzzell is as pertinent today as it was more than two decades ago: 'Which *elements* of the marketing strategy should be standardized, and to what degree?' This sentiment is echoed by Sorenson and Wiechmann (1975), Killough (1982), and Jain (1989), who have suggested that *total* standardization is unlikely.

For the most part, the literature gives recognition to differences between markets and consumers as obstacles to the effective use of standardization in marketing activities. If the concept of *intermarket segments* can be applied on a global basis, market and customer differences in various markets become immaterial. Standardization therefore appears likely where the environments and marketing infrastructures are most alike (Britt, 1974; Hill and Still, 1984; Huszagh, Fox, and Day, 1985; Jain, 1989; Ohmae, 1985; Sorenson and Wiechmann, 1975). However, the concept is yet to be tested.

Such market differences as income, taste, media habit, and education provide support for an adaptation strategy, or at most a very limited standardization (Boddewyn, 1981; Buzzell, 1968; Jain, 1989). There are a great many differences among markets even in industrial nations. Adequate means of transportation, availability of refrigeration and storage facilities, preference for fresh products, and differences in product usage[3] frequently require changes in product design, packaging, price, and distribution. Even in addressing the needs of markets that are economically alike, as with less developed countries, standardization presents problems (Hill and Still, 1984). Availability and cost of communications media, as well as media habits, further undermine the suitability of a

---

[3] This is a particularly important consideration for consumer goods, which must be redesigned to address local preferences and usage patterns. Procter & Gamble provides a good illustration. Their disposable diapers had to be designed differently in Japan because Japanese mothers prefer to change their babies more frequently. Likewise, larger containers of fabric softener (marketed under the Lenor brand, not Downy) had to be used for the German market because of the popularity and excessive use of this product following its introduction in the 1970s. In addition, Liquid Tide was conceived and developed in Japan for the cold-water washing habits of the Japanese market and later extended to the US.

standardized programme. In addition, differences in the length of distribution channels, functions performed by channel intermediaries, and their financial resources and management know-how are deterrents to global standardization. Given these circumstances, one might argue that standardization may lead to suboptimization and, hence, reduced profitability.

In a longitudinal study of the European Community (EC) countries, Boddewyn, Soehl, and Picard (1986) found that though the globalization trend is on the increase, the proportion of firms adopting such a policy for matters other than branding and advertising of consumer nondurable goods is still small. Likewise, Aylmer (1970) reported local affiliates command a high degree of autonomy in such areas as advertising, pricing, and distribution. Sorenson and Wiechmann (1975), in contrast, reported a relatively high proclivity among 27 major MNCs to standardize their marketing programme.

Though these studies shed light on the status of standardization, the degree of emphasis (i.e., direction) on various components of the marketing programme by firms using standardization in comparison with other firms has not been examined. Also, given the contradictory findings in the standardization literature, it is apparent that commitment to and emphasis on global standardization vary across firms. Hence, it is reasonable to expect the roles of the components of the marketing plan to vary, depending on the extent to which firms pursue global standardization.

H_6: Firms emphasizing global standardization view the importance of the components of the marketing plan differently than firms that do not stress standardization.

Importance of key policies and strategies

The relationship between key corporate policies and strategies and global standardization has largely been ignored in the literature. Environmental constraints to standardization such as governmental standards (e.g., what is or is not allowed as a constituent of a product) and trade regulations (e.g., local content requirements), differences in availability and costs of resources (Buzzell, 1968), and differences in competitive climate of markets influence key policies pursued by firms. No less important are firm-level obstacles to standardization. Even within global industries, firms that have maintained a traditional multidomestic[4] structure (e.g., Campbell Soup, Procter & Gamble, and Sara Lee) are less likely to adopt a standardized programme. Accordingly, when MNC subsidiaries are given a high level of local autonomy, implementation of standardized programmes via subsidiary managers and personnel is likely to be more challenging and require a longer time span. The presence of numerous products and brands for local markets, which is typical of multidomestic firms, further complicates the matter. On the one hand, these local products may be cash cows or rising stars. On the other hand, the introductions of new global brands may well cannibalize current brands (Douglas and Wind, 1987).

The decision to adopt a global standardization strategy affects some key policy areas. Marketing activities are not independent of other developments in the firm (e.g.,

---

[4] Strictly speaking, a multidomestic firm maintains a polycentric method of managing global operations, whereby foreign affiliates are relatively autonomous in their decision making.

manufacturing), which are often controlled elsewhere in the organization.[5] Certain firm-level policies and activities have important implications for global standardization. Specific policy and strategy factors suggested in the literature include co-operative arrangements and alignments, worldwide vertical and horizontal integration of operations, more control over manufacturing stages, long-term contracts with suppliers and distributors, international marketing agreements, developing external international information networks, formal international R&D agreements, and seeking US government assistance in penetrating foreign markets (Morrison and Roth, 1989). These key policy factors require closer scrutiny. Emphasis on these elements might be different for firms stressing standardization. However, the degree of emphasis (i.e., direction) on various policies and strategies by BUs is not known.

H$_7$: Firms emphasizing global standardization view the importance of key policies and strategies differently than do firms that do not stress standardization.

Financial influence of global standardization

The primary element that encourages standardization of marketing across markets is the associated cost savings. These savings include economies of scale in research and development (Buzzell, 1968; Keegan, 1969; Terpstra, 1987), purchasing (Douglas and Wind, 1987), production (Douglas and Wind, 1987; Keegan, 1969), and marketing (Buzzell, 1968; Green, Cunningham, and Cunningham, 1975; Keegan, 1969; Onkvisit and Shaw, 1987; Terpstra, 1987), the possibility of rationalizing international production (Carapellotti and Samiee, 1984), and operating via exports (Terpstra, 1987). Also, implicit in many economies and advantages favouring a standardized programme is easier implementation and management of a single (or a group of related) programme(s). In addition, standardization affords more control over marketing programmes (Green, Cunningham, and Cunningham, 1975; Walters, 1986).

Despite repeated calls to investigate the financial impact of global standardization, the marketing literature is void of such studies. Conceptual and case studies have made frequent mention of cost savings associated with standardization. Hout, Porter, and Rudden (1982), for example, point to 'superior effectiveness', 'cost savings', 'timing', and 'financial' (i.e., cash flow due to higher volume or lower costs) dimensions as benefits associated with standardization strategies. Though a strong case can be made for placing emphasis on reduced costs and competitive prices due to standardization (Levitt, 1983), lower costs are not the primary objective of firms; their primary objective is increased *profitability*. Lower costs result in higher profits only under the assumption of *relatively* fixed global, industrywide prices. Economic theory, market segmentation, and

---

[5] The supply-chain management concept, for example, requires a high level of coordination among the buying units, components manufacturing division (who are in essence internal suppliers, i.e., marketers, to the core manufacturing unit), external suppliers, and manufacturing. On the other hand, some global firms have adopted a zero outbound inventory policy. IBM Data Entry Systems Division, for example, has achieved a high level of coordination among its many functional units and external suppliers. They have an inbound inventory turnover of two hours and no outbound inventory, i.e., the products are shipped to customers as they come off the assembly line. Thus, marketing within these firms, as a matter of necessity, is highly coordinated and likely to be related to key policies on strategic and contractual linkages as well as horizontal and vertical integration.

the conceptualizations offered previously point to the necessity for firms to achieve freedom in pricing in global markets through identification and cultivation of *intermarket segments*.

Thus, the theoretical arguments and the realities of the marketplace significantly weaken the appropriateness and applicability of global standardization. There is no empirical evidence in the literature that firms actually seek and identify intermarket segments, a task that provides the necessary condition for global standardization as prescribed by the theoretical basis for marketing and segmentation. Concurrently, widespread use of market segmentation within the national markets, in particular in the US, is not a reassuring sign that firms are seeking to identify intermarket segments. Though the many economies associated with global standardization are intuitively sound, they are aimed at lowering costs, which is *not* the same as increasing profitability. Because of the overwhelming number of environmental, organizational, planning, implementation, and other obstacles that firms must overcome in their pursuit of global strategy, that alternative would be difficult to make financially sound. Accordingly, the main proposition of our study is that *global standardization does not lead to greater profitability*.

H_8: Financial performance of firms that emphasize global standardization is not different from that of firms that do not stress standardization.

RESEARCH METHOD

Sample and industry selection

To investigate the extent of standardization practice among firms, we conducted a field survey of BUs competing in global industries. The basic premise of our study is that firms operating in global industries are better *positioned* to pursue global standardization. Within global industries, industry structure forces transcend national boundaries, thereby creating similar markets across countries. If firms are to remain competitive and cost effective in this context, we would expect that one or more economies offered by standardization would be adopted. In turn, standardization should lead to a *relative* positive influence on the performance of BUs.

However, not all firms competing in such industries perceive their industries as being global or use a standardized approach. That is, as a part of their overall corporate strategy, *some* firms seek and identify areas in which they can improve their global competitive position in their respective industries through standardization, whereas others may maintain a multidomestic structure and, hence, a polycentric management and marketing posture, or may adopt limited standardization.

Firms in global industries therefore can be classified as those with policies emphasizing standardization and others that place less emphasis on standardization. Given this dichotomy, we would expect the former group to have adopted a series of marketing policies and strategies conducive to global standardization. Marketing policies and strategies of firms that are less standardized, in contrast, would be expected to be less uniform and generally adapted to local market conditions. If differences cannot be shown between the two groups, adopting a standardization strategy may be more a function of management orientation and preference than of environmental and corporate conditions.

A multiple-industry sampling was considered appropriate because such a procedure would enhance the external validity of the findings. With the exception of a distinction between consumer and industrial products, generalizations made in the standardization literature are not industry-specific. Hence, a multiple-industry database would be in congruence with the literature. In addition, focusing on a single industry would have severely limited the size of the sample containing the appropriate number of BUs with extensive international involvement.

Global industries were identified through a three-stage process. The first stage, a review of the literature previously identifying global industries (Bartlett and Ghoshal, 1987; Cvar, 1984; Hout, Porter, and Rudden, 1982; Porter, 1980, 1986b; Prahalad and Doz, 1987), resulted in the initial identification of 16 global industries. In the second stage, the trade ratio of each global industry was examined. A high level of intra-industry trade is considered a necessary (though not sufficient) condition for an industry to be global (Porter, 1980, 1986b).[6] Trade flows were measured in terms of imports plus exports as a percentage of US consumption. Consistent with the research of both Prescott (1983) and Cvar (1984), a 50% trade-flow level was used as a minimum limit to control for the global nature of industries. Actual trade-flow levels were obtained through both industry sources and the United States International Trade Commission (ITC) *Summary of Trade and Tariff Information*. Consequently, 12 manufacturing industries were identified as meeting or exceeding the 50% ratio.[7]

Finally, beyond the use of trade-flow levels as a necessary indicator of industry globalization, several researchers have suggested that at least one competitor in the industry must be competing globally in order for the industry to actually become global (Hamel and Prahalad, 1985; Hout, Porter, and Rudden, 1982; Porter, 1986b). As noted by Bartlett (1985, p. 7), 'environmental conditions . . . only create a *latent* potential for an industry to develop a global structure'. Hence, it takes the actions of individual businesses to create global-scale economies and the resulting structural changes to the industry itself. The final stage in the selection of global industries therefore involved ascertaining whether a key competitor in each industry competed globally. An extensive review of secondary data sources, including industry reports, published case studies, and annual reports, confirmed the presence of at least one global company in each of the industries.

BUs competing within each industry were subsequently identified through Dun and Bradstreet's *America's Corporate Families* and *The Directory of Corporate Affiliations*. A mail questionnaire was sent to the CEO or president of the 322 identified BUs and two followup letters were sent to nonrespondents. Executives of 147 of those BUs responded, for a response rate of 46%.

Nonresponse bias was examined in two ways. First, total sales and the number of employees of 30 randomly selected BUs that did not respond to the questionnaire were compared with those of the responding firms. The results indicated no statistically

---

[6] Porter (1986b, p. 29) states that, '. . . intra-industry trade is a good sign of the presence of global competition, and its growth is one indication that the incidence of global industries has increased'.

[7] The industries include balances, watches and watch parts, textile machinery, mining machinery, oil field machinery, certain consumer and electronic products, semiconductors, sewing machines, electromedical and X-ray apparatus, synthetic insecticides and fungicides, civil aircraft and parts, and typesetting machinery.

significant difference between the two groups. Second, average sales, average return on sales, and average growth rate of responding firms were compared with their respective industry averages. These results also indicated no significant difference between responding firms and the industry averages. The relatively high response rate and the test results suggest that the responding BUs are representative of the original sample as well as their industries.

Questionnaire Design and Pretest

The questionnaire design involved two separate stages. During the first stage, six interviews were conducted with general managers of BUs competing in global industries. These interviews were intended to uncover and validate dimensions of global standardization policy and strategy as well as functional components identified in the literature search. During the second stage, the hypotheses guided a search of the strategic planning and marketing literature, which led to the development of a series of items relating to (1) marketing policy and strategy and (2) tactical marketing measures.

The questionnaire was pretested in three steps. First, the initial questionnaire was reviewed by six academicians to assess its content validity. Second, interviews were held with six executives who further assessed its content as well its clarity and comprehensiveness. For the final step of the pretest, the instrument was administered to 17 executives in six BUs so that the consensus among multiple respondents could be examined. Dunn (1976) and Onkvisit and Shaw (1987) have cautioned against blind acceptance of the executive viewpoint. As Dunn points out, 'Some marketing executives do not really know what is and what is not being transferred across boundaries'. It is therefore likely that the practice of global standardization is to some extent a matter of respondent perception. Hence, this step was considered critical to the study as it helped ensure that responses represent the international perspectives and operations of the BUs and not the idiosyncratic perspective of one respondent. The responses within each business were found to be consistent by the coefficient of concordance (Kendall's tau).

Measures of constructs

Global standardization was operationalized by using an index comprising five items. The measure was designed to infer the firm's orientation toward global standardization through structural analysis of the firm's position in the industry. Essentially, this analysis maps the industry into strategic groups, each of which consists of firms following similar strategies (McGee and Thomas, 1986; Porter, 1980). This measurement method was selected for three reasons. First, the pretest indicated that global standardization is a popularized notion and often considered desirable. Thus acquiescence bias toward reporting a globalized approach might occur if respondents were queried directly about their firms' level of standardization. Second, the measure is consistent with the need to identify the intermarket segment in which the firm competes rather than attempting to identify or measure alternate approaches taken by firms in their global standardization efforts. Third, the use of this approach has empirical support (see, e.g., Cool and Schendel, 1988; Fombrun and Zajac, 1987; Mascarenhas, 1989).

Global standardization items are shown in Table 1. These items are necessary prerequisites for standardization within global industries. Delineating intermarket segments that are the starting point for standardized marketing plans, for example, is not possible in the absence of standardized customer needs. Standardized technology and sourcing must also be present to manufacture and market a standardized product. In addition, for global standardization strategy to be viable, global product awareness and information flows must be present. Finally, competitive forces within an industry can determine the degree to which standardization can be pursued (Copeland and Griggs, 1985; Henzler and Rall, 1986; Porter, 1986a; Quelch and Hoff, 1986). Industrywide modes of competition are a function of the collective actions of the participants that are reflected in their strategies.

Table 1. Measures of global standardization

Global standardization measure	Mean high standard[a]	Mean low standard[a]
Customer needs are standardized worldwide	3.24	1.79
Product awareness and information exists worldwide	3.95	3.00
Standardized product technology exists worldwide	3.78	2.28
Competitors market a standardized product worldwide	3.55	1.98
Standardized purchasing practices exists worldwide	2.55	1.43

[a] Measured on five-point scales where 1 = not at all characteristic and 5 = highly characteristic.

Coefficient alpha was used to test the reliability of the global standardization index. The resultant coefficient (p. 73) was considered satisfactory.[8] The index of standardization then was used to divide the responding firms into two groups. Given that the measure ranges between 5 and 25, a mean score of 15 $[(5 + 25)/2]$ was selected as the dividing point for the two groups. All firms scoring above that value were classified as seeking 'high standardization' and others as pursuing 'low standardization'. This classification scheme is robust and, as anticipated, produces individual and group mean scores that are significantly different.

The validity of this classification scheme was examined independently with a subsample of 20 MNCs. At least two pertinent information clues about the global standardization approach of BUs were gathered from business publications and annual reports. Four coders were asked independently to classify the firms into high standardization or low standardization groups. The number of firms correctly classified by coders averaged 19 and the intercoder reliability measure was 0.90 and satisfactory.

As a final measure of classification validity, the basic characteristics of the two groups were compared. High standardization firms in the sample do not differ significantly from low standardization firms on such factors as their number of foreign affiliates, number of employees, total sales, international sales, international operating profit as a percentage of total profits, international assets as a percentage of total assets, and industry concentration (i.e., the combined market shares of the four largest competitors).

Performance evaluation is a complex issue as it is a multifaceted construct (Bourgeois, 1980; Morsicato and Radebaugh, 1979). In an attempt to be as comprehensive as

[8] Nunnally (1967) has suggested that in the early stages of research, reliability levels of 0.50 to 0.60 are indicative of measurement reliability.

possible, we used multiple performance indicators and measurement scales. Three indicators of financial performance were selected: return on investment (ROI), return on assets (ROA), and sales growth. Because the performance of BUs may be subject to short-term (one-year) fluctuations and not representative of their long-term results, respondents were asked to report the average performance of their BUs over the previous three-year period. This approach is thought to lessen the influence of short-term fluctuations.

Self-reported objective and relative intra-industry performance measures were used. The objective performance data were reported by CEOs, who were asked to rate the after-tax ROI and ROA of their BUs, as well as their sales growth, on seven-point scales. Each scale point reflected a five-percentage-point range in performance (e.g., 15 to 20%). However, such 'accounting-based' measures of performance are potentially biased because of the limited time horizon of such measures, variance in the level of data aggregation across organizations, and departures from the actual purpose of such measures (McGuire, Schneeweis, and Hill, 1986). In addition, as previously stated, the fundamental benefit or intent of global standardization is *relative competitive positioning*. Relative intra-industry measures therefore were also considered critical indicators of BU performance. Relative performance indicators of ROI, ROA, and sales growth were measured on five-point scales adapted from Dess and Davis (1984) and Robinson and Pearce (1988). Each scale point for the intra-industry measure reflects performance by BUs within 20-percentage-point intervals (e.g., in the upper 20% of the industry).

There is evidence supporting the general reliability of self-reported performance measures (Dess and Robinson, 1984; Venkatraman and Ramanujam, 1986, 1987). This evidence is consistent with our own pretest results, but there is a potential reporting bias. As the unit of analysis in our study was the BU instead of the corporation, responding executives can be expected to have the benefit of detailed knowledge about their performance. Therefore, in relative terms, both validity and reliability of responses are higher than those in studies that simply seek responses from headquarters.

Three additional performance measures were used in our study. Unlike previous measures, they were actual ratio data for the responding BUs for the latest fiscal year: (1) total sales, (2) total international sales, and (3) international operating profit as a percentage of total profits.

Performance is often found to vary by industry. Consequently, prior to aggregating the BUs irrespective of the classification, we compared the performance among the industries represented in the sample. No significant performance differences were found ($p > 0.05$) among the industries.

The business strategy–marketing policy components are variables previously identified as being critical dimensions to the strategy of internationally oriented businesses (Morrison and Roth, 1989). The marketing plan measures were taken from previous studies examining business strategy (Dess and Davis, 1984; Galbraith and Schendel, 1983; Robinson and Pearce, 1988).

To assess the influence of the PLC, we developed working definitions for its various stages. To avoid arbitrary assessment of the stages of the PLC, ensure consistency across respondents, and be consistent with prior research, we adapted the definitions used for the PIMS database for each of the four stages of the PLC. Several tests were performed to make certain we did not have a concentration of large BUs with products in the latter stages of the PLC. Successively, the sample was divided into two groups based on the mean and median figures for total sales, international sales, and employment and tested against the PLC measure. None of the tests were significant, indicating that within the context of global industries, firm size and the PLC are not related. Measures for technological change, product changes, technological obsolescence, and product type also were adapted from the PIMS programme.

RESULTS

Characteristics of responding firms

Characteristics of responding BUs are shown in Table 2. The average total sales of the responding BUs was $721 million with an average international sales figure of $285

Table 2. Characteristics of responding business units

Characteristic	
Sales	
Total	$721 million
International	$285 million
Employees	4311
Foreign assets as a percentage of total assets	15.7%
Importance of penetrating international market[a]	5.16
Product type	
Consumer	15%
Industrial	85%

[a] Measured on seven-point scale where 1 = not important at all and 7 = extremely important.

million, and typically the BUs employed more than 4300 individuals. Foreign assets as a percentage of total assets was 15.7%. However, the average foreign operating profit as percentage of total profit was nearly twice as large (28%). It is therefore understandable that penetrating international markets is relatively important to these firms. Only a handful of responding firms (15%) classified themselves as manufacturers of consumer products and, because their markets and marketing processes are likely to be different from those of the manufacturers of industrial products, they were excluded from further analysis except in the case of the first hypothesis.

The nature of products

H_1 asserts that industrial products are more suitable for global standardization than consumer products. It is partly supported by virtue of the fact that 85% of respondents are manufacturers of industrial products. However, mere presence in a global industry is not an indication that responding firms view the industry as a global one or are pursuing a strategy of global standardization. In fact, a higher proportion of consumer firms

(60%) than industrial firms (45%) in the sample focus on standardization. Nevertheless, this difference is not statistically significant ($p < 0.217$).

Technological environment and competitive response

Data for H_2–H_4 (i.e., technological environment and corporate response issues) are reported in Table 3. The relationship between global standardization and the rate of

Table 3. Technological environment and competitive response

	Mean high standard	Mean low standard	$p <$
Rate of technology change within the industry[a]			0.02
Product and production technology obsolescence rate[b]	1.89	1.90	0.98
Rate of product modification instigated by competitors[c]	3.52	3.90	0.06

[a] Measured on a three-point scale. Chi-square = 7.40.
[b] Measured on a five-point scale where 1 = greater than 10 years, 2 = between 5 and 10 years, 3 = between 2.5 and 5 years, 4 = between 1 and 2.5 years, 5 = less than 1 year.
[c] Measured on a five-point scale where 1 = seasonally, 2 = periodically (but at intervals less than 1 year), 3 = annually (e.g., annual model changes), 4 = periodically (but at intervals longer than 1 year), 5 = no regular periodic patterns of change. The last category was set aside for the computation of mean figures.

intra-industry technological change (H_2) is significant ($p < 0.026$). The data support our stipulation that firms facing a high rate of technological change stress global standardization. Sixty-four percent of BUs competing in an environment of rapid technological change have adopted global standardization and consolidated their global operations.[9] A relatively slow pace of technology change enables firms to address local needs and preferences; as anticipated, the majority (67%) of BUs facing a slow technology change are in the low standardization group. In addition, the majority of BUs (56%) that attempted to match technologies with markets do not emphasize standardization. These results are in line with the rationalization offered in the Hypotheses section and support the second hypothesis that technology change and global standardization are related.

H_3 explores the technological obsolescence rate for both groups of firms. As the mean values for this variable are almost identical for both groups, the hypothesis is not supported. However, instigation of major changes in products manufactured by competitors (H_4) varies across the two groups. Eighty-six percent of firms that face changes in their products in periods of less than one year focus on global standardization. This finding is also consistent with H_2 and provides further support for the notion that firms facing rapid technological change stress standardization. In contrast, about 53% of firms whose competitors change their products in intervals longer than one year and 59% of firms facing irregular product change periods do not emphasize global standardization. Thus, global standardization appears to be a more likely pattern in industries where competitors more frequently make changes in their products. Both the means and the distributions for the instigation of product change by competitors are significantly

[9] As expected, there is a significant relationship between technological change and the number of foreign affiliates whereby rapid rate of technology change leads to fewer but larger plants.

different between the two groups ($p < 0.064$ and $p < 0.072$, respectively). Hence, H_4 is supported.

The influence of the PLC

H_5 posits that products offered by firms using global standardization are generally in the early stages of the PLC. For the sample as a whole, most products (68%) are in the maturity and decline stages. It is noteworthy that 40% of BUs in the maturity stage face a relatively slow pace of technology change and customize products to local needs and another 40% match technology to markets where they operate. Only 20% of the BUs in the maturity stage face rapid technological change and standardize products for global markets. However, the relationship between the PLC and technology is weak ($p < 0.14$).

As expected, the proportion of BUs using global standardization in the introductory and growth stages is less than the proportion of the low standardization group (46 vs. 54%). Also, more firms with emphasis on standardization are in the decline stage (60%). However, fewer BUs emphasizing global standardization (47%) are in the maturity stage. Though the trend in the data in three stages of the PLC is supportive of our previous rationalization, the means and the distribution of responses are not significantly different from one another ($p < 0.81$ and $p < 0.94$, respectively); hence, the fifth hypothesis is not supported.

Components of the marketing plan

H_6 examines the relationship between marketing planning variables and global standardization. Importance levels of various components are reported in Table 4. To retain their competitive edge, firms using global standardization were expected to view the importance levels of marketing components differently than other firms. The underlying assumption is that BUs stressing global standardization *do not* necessarily seek to identify intermarket segments as prescribed in the literature. Rather, they are likely to pursue mass markets globally or at least subjectively defined (but not operationalized) intermarket segments. Hence, their focus on the elements of their marketing plans should differ from that of the group that does not stress standardization. Successful market segmentation, even on a national or regional basis, has certain requirements that cannot always be met (i.e., clearly defined segments that are mutually exclusive and exhaustive are not present). Cross-nationally, meeting these requirements is considerably more complex and difficult. Indeed, as noted previously, there is no evidence of operationalization of the intermarket segment concept in the literature.

Only three variables are significantly different for the two groups of firms. Firms using standardization place a greater emphasis on capacity utilization ($p < 0.01$) and coverage of a wide range of geographic markets ($p < 0.05$). The development of a highly skilled salesforce, though important for the members of both groups, is significantly more important for firms that do not stress standardization ($p < 0.10$). In addition, the direction of the means of two variables contradicts the common sense view. Firms using standardization have a greater tendency to pursue specialty products ($p < 0.20$) and emphasize the production of high priced products for market niches ($p < 0.13$), whereas the opposite would typically be expected.

Table 4. Marketing plan measures

Marketing plan variable	Mean high standard[a]	Mean low standard[a]	$p <$
Product-related components			
Emphasize new product development	5.37	5.48	0.69
Emphasize product quality	6.43	6.41	0.90
Offer a broad number of products	3.97	4.05	0.78
Develop unique product features	5.30	5.33	0.91
Emphasize specialty products	4.90	4.50	0.20
Promotion-related components			
Emphasize advertising and promotion	3.31	3.19	0.63
Build brand awareness	4.91	4.90	0.96
Build reputation in the industry	6.05	5.93	0.58
Develop a highly skilled salesforce	5.37	5.76	0.10
Pricing-related components			
Produce high priced products for market niches	5.28	4.84	0.13
Price at or below competitive price levels	4.31	4.30	0.97
Price leadership in the industry	4.28	4.18	0.70
Customer service and distribution-related components			
Emphasize customer service and service quality	6.13	6.24	0.56
Influence and/or control channels of distribution	3.82	3.79	0.93
Serve a wide variety of customers	4.36	4.35	0.97
Operate in a wide range of geographic markets	5.40	4.79	0.05
Sourcing and production-related components			
Emphasize low cost per unit	5.11	4.96	0.62
Emphasize high capacity utilization	4.82	4.02	0.01
Market intelligence and tactical planning			
Monitor market opportunities on an ongoing basis	5.25	5.19	0.80
Develop innovative marketing techniques	4.90	4.97	0.80

[a] Measured on seven-point scales where 1 = not at all important and 7 = extremely important.

Though it is apparent that firms stressing global standardization are different on some critical elements of their marketing plans whereby they are likely to be benefiting from significant economies, for the great majority of marketing measures examined, they are not significantly different from firms that view their strategy in a different light. Hence, H_6 is generally not supported.

Global marketing policies and BU strategies

H_7 addresses *marketing policy and strategy* that influence the international competitive position of firms. Importance levels of marketing policy and strategy components are reported in Table 5. Because the global marketing philosophy of BUs that stress standardization is different from that of others that place less emphasis on standardization, we expected the former to stress different policies than other respondents to retain a competitive edge. For example, because the BUs that place less emphasis on standardization serve markets and customers that tend to be unique, they would have a higher propensity to develop external global information networks and secure governmental assistance for penetrating foreign markets. We do not suggest that the more standardized firms do not need market information; rather, the standardized nature of their operations reduces the frequency and the need for the types of detailed data demanded by firms that view the industry as fragmented and nonstandardized (i.e., a low level of standardization requires closer monitoring of more segments and products). Vertical and horizontal integration and long-term contractual agreements with suppliers and distributors are expected to be more characteristic of firms emphasizing global standardization.

As shown in Table 5, differences between the means of the eight policy and strategy measures are not very large. The two groups of BUs do not differ significantly on any of the components of marketing policy and strategy; therefore, H_7 also is not supported.

Table 5. Business strategy–marketing policy components

Marketing policy and strategy areas	Mean high standard[a]	Mean low standard[a]	$p <$
Secure US government assistance for penetrating foreign markets	3.18	3.37	0.60
Develop external international information networks	3.90	4.15	0.44
Formalize international marketing agreements with outside firms	3.84	3.79	0.90
Secure long-term contractual agreements with international distributors and suppliers	4.22	4.44	0.52
International control of the manufacturing cycle from raw materials to distribution of finished products	2.94	3.13	0.58
Formal international R&D/technology agreements with outside firms	2.99	3.33	0.28
Horizontal integration of operations worldwide	3.28	2.93	0.23
Vertical integration of operations worldwide	3.25	3.23	0.96

[a] Measured on seven-point scales where 1 = not at all important and 7 = extremely important.

The influence of standardization on performance

H_8 pertains to the performance issue and is the central consideration in supporting or refuting the adoption of global standardization. Information on the nine performance measures for the two groups of firms is reported in Table 6. When averages for three-year performance levels are considered, firms stressing global standardization have a higher sales growth rate but the low standardization group has higher ROA. The cyclicity of many businesses and/or competitive conditions may lead to a weak performance, yet such a showing may be respectable in comparison with the industry level. When *comparative* intra-industry performance measures are considered, BUs using standardization have lower ROI, ROA, and sales growth than the low standardization group.

The third group of performance variables consists of actual latest-year total sales, international sales, and the percentage of operating profit derived from international

Table 6. Standardization strategy and business unit performance

Performance measure	Mean high standard	Mean low standard	$p <$
Business unit performance[a]			
Return on investment	4.26	4.27	0.98
Return on assets	4.53	4.35	0.59
Sales growth	4.58	5.03	0.15
Relative intra-industry performance[b]			
Return on investment	3.88	3.91	0.90
Return on assets	3.84	3.96	0.62
Sales growth	3.54	3.59	0.84
Actual latest-year performance			
Total sales (in millions of $)	806.31	507.67	0.42
International sales (in millions of $)	422.86	140.88	0.20
International operating profit (percent)	32	22	0.15

[a] Measured on seven-point scales where 1 = greater than 25%, 2 = 20% to 25%; 3 = 15% to 20%, 4 = 10% to 15%, 5 = 5% to 10%, 6 = 0% to 5%, 7 = negative return or drop in sales.
[b] Measured on five-point scales where 1 = lowest 20%, 2 = lower middle 20%, 3 = middle 20%, 4 = upper middle 20%, 5 = top 20%.

operations. The mean figures for all three variables are higher in the case of firms stressing standardization.

It is evident from this information that in global industries where more opportunities and higher likelihood for global standardization are anticipated, performance is not affected by standardization. When three-year BU performance and actual latest-year performance figures are considered, firms emphasizing standardization show a better performance. In contrast, when relative intra-industry figures are considered, the low standardization group has a superior performance.

To ensure that the findings on the financial impact of global standardization are not affected by the way in which BUs were classified into high and low standardization groups, an additional analysis was conducted. The data for firms with the 10 highest and the 10 lowest global standardization scores were examined along the nine performance measures. The results of this analysis were consistent with previous findings. Hence, the classification criterion used in our study apparently has not influenced the results.

The respondents in our study were manufacturers of industrial products and the majority offered products in the maturity stage of the PLC. Therefore we examined firm-level and industry-level performance without regard to the PLC stage or product type. However, a separate analysis of performance data for the maturity stage of the PLC for the two groups of firms resulted in similar findings. Hence, our main proposition (H_8)— *that global standardization does not lead to greater profitability*—is supported.

LIMITATIONS

As in any research, our findings are influenced by the definitions and measurement methods used for various strategy and marketing variables. Furthermore, the elaborate sampling technique employed was aimed at isolating and selecting only BUs that operate in global markets.

The global standardization construct reflects executive opinions and perceptions and was tested for intrafirm consistency. We therefore expect that because of the executives' key positions, their responses reflect the strategic choice of their respective BUs and, hence, are reliable and valid. However, what the firms actually do globally cannot typically be observed by a researcher without utilizing considerable resources to take multiple measures of the same BU across several markets.

We used a multiple-industry sample to enhance the external validity of the findings. An industry-level analysis is also desirable but, depending on how global industry is defined, it may yield a sample that is too small for meaningful analysis.

Operational definition of the standardization construct remains a challenge to researchers. The issue is likely to become the subject of debate if measurements are to be based on firm activities as opposed to executive opinion. There is no consensus among scholars about what constitutes a 'standardized process or programme'. To demonstrate the complexity of this issue, consider that only a handful of products (e.g., watches) and brands (e.g., Coca-Cola) are commonly associated with global standardization. Is the marketing programme of Mercedes Benz globally standardized? Though its cars look the same everywhere, there are significant differences in their structure and components for certain markets, they are perceived differently in various markets (i.e., a major positioning consideration), and a variety of distribution strategies are used in different markets (e.g., company-owned sales offices in some markets, independent dealers in some others, and joint ventures in a third group). Future research might focus on developing a range of testable definitions for studying global standardization.

The policy and marketing measurements used in our study are *all* critical competitive tools. The relatively high mean scores across the numerous variables used may reflect this point. These variables represent important policy and functional factors pertinent to competing in global markets, but they are relatively weak discriminators between the two groups of firms.

CONCLUSIONS AND IMPLICATIONS

We examined the influence of global standardization on technology, the PLC, marketing and strategy measures, and, in particular, BU performance. Our findings do not support certain views about global standardization expressed in many conceptual studies. In the areas of marketing policy and strategy, we found few differences between firms stressing standardization and others. In particular, the critical issue of superior performance through global standardization, which follows the theoretical underpinning of market segmentation, is not supported. The absence of significant differences between the performance levels of the two groups is likely to be an indication that intermarket segments have not been properly defined and identified by firms using standardization. If this is true, our findings do not necessarily reflect the inappropriateness of global standardization, but rather its fragmentary or incomplete implementation.

Common views about standardization have rarely been supported empirically. It may well be that such views are based on a few casual observations. The fact that Coca-Cola and Colgate-Palmolive sell some of their products in more than 160 countries does not signify that they have adopted a high degree of standardization for all of their products globally. Only three Coca-Cola brands are standardized and one of them, Sprite, has a different formulation in Japan. Some Colgate-Palmolive products are marketed in just a few countries. Axion paste dishwashing detergent, for example, was formulated for developing countries and La Croix Plus detergent was custom-made for the French market. Colgate toothpaste is marketed the same way globally, though its advanced Gum Protection Formula is used in only 27 nations. Perhaps brand names have the highest likelihood of becoming global, but the presence of a global brand implies a global position (i.e., the same position in every intermarket segment). Achieving a global position for the brand, however, may not be easy or beneficial. Johnson & Johnson, for example, changed its Affinity shampoo brand name to Radiance in the Spanish market because it learned that the position of the former (i.e., women over 40) was unacceptable there (Rutigliano, 1986). Even when brands achieve a global status, however, better performance might result from positioning them differently in various markets. Kashani (1989), for example, noted that Unilever's Domestos household cleaner succeeded only after the management abandoned its uniform positioning strategy.

Thus, though global standardization does take place, it is not necessarily an optimal approach in all markets, nor is it evident that it is taking place for all of the products of the firm, nor necessarily to the same extent across all of the elements of the marketing mix. Respondents in our study operate in global industries and span the range of standardization. Therefore, at least a limited standardization policy may be pursued by the BUs identified as having a lesser focus on global standardization. In fact, Buzzell (1968), Sorenson and Wiechmann (1975), and Boddewyn, Soehl, and Picard (1986) have suggested that standardization is a matter of degree. The rationale for supporting global standardization in the literature appears to be intuitively sound and, when appropriate, such a strategy can offer many *cost* advantages to the firm. Nevertheless, the ultimate decision criterion for a firm considering global standardization is long-term performance, which is not supported in our study.

The need for and the usage patterns for industrial products are likely to be cross-culturally similar. In addition, purchase processes for such products are likely to be rationalized and policy-driven. However, only 47% of responding BUs in our study stress standardization. For this class of products, many technical, cosmetic, service, and other adaptations may be necessary and may play a greater role in national markets. Differences in the rationalization process and policies may also require that marketing plans be adapted to match local market conditions for industrial products.

An important finding of our study is the positive relationship between rapid changes in technology and global standardization. It is also apparent from the findings for H_4 that firms emphasizing standardization are more likely to be affected by competitor-led product changes. These findings are congruent with greater focus by these firms on capacity utilization. Rapid changes in technology appear to necessitate significant retooling and retraining expenses and hence a focus on more concentrated manufacturing for the global market, leading to larger facilities, emphasis on high capacity utilization, and the pursuit of a wider range of geographic markets. When technology shifts are relatively slow, however, firms tend to stress customization. It is also evident that firms that place less emphasis on standardization put greater emphasis on the development of a highly skilled salesforce, possibly because of the diversity of products and markets served.

Greater emphasis on capacity utilization by firms stressing global standardization implies that standardization may be of greater importance in sourcing and production functions. It is also likely that the greatest benefits of standardization are realized at the functional levels. Nevertheless, these benefits are not reflected in the performance of the BUs.

Our data indicate that regardless of the level of emphasis on global standardization, the technology used is matched with the needs of the national markets served. The largest proportion of firms in the study (37%) attempted to follow this strategy, leading to multiple products from various classes of markets at any given point in time. Such a strategy stops short of reaping the full benefits of standardization. A nearly equal group (36%) indicated that even in the face of slow technological change, they must remain highly responsive on a country-by-country basis and customize products to the needs and preferences of local markets. Nevertheless, 75% of firms that pursue a strategy of standardization face rapid technological changes (leading to concentrated production and standardized products) or varied market conditions (necessitating matching technologies to markets).

Both groups of firms appear to favour the production of high priced products for market niches over price leadership in the industry. Global standardization appears to depend on high capacity utilization, but competitive response in global markets is likely to lead to a downward pressure on prices and margins. Thus, the propensity to seek market niches, particularly on the part of firms stressing standardization, is understandable. Eastman Chemical International division of Kodak, for example, sells generic as well as proprietary chemicals worldwide. Despite the fact that those products or their equivalents are available through local and global competitors, the firm has been able to carve out a sufficient market share to remain profitable. Their intermarket segment is thus broadly defined as firms that favour service over price. In fact, quality service is central to the marketing strategy of Eastman Chemical. The firm does not typically engage in price competition; when competitors lower their prices, Eastman reacts with a measured response, but generally does not attempt to match competitors' prices. This pattern may also be an indication that intermarket segments, as defined and prescribed by the theoretical underpinnings of marketing, are difficult to operationalize.

For the marketing programme as a whole, the issue of control associated with global standardization (Green, Cunningham, and Cunningham, 1975; Walters, 1986) is not supported by the findings. Nor did the firms feel that this was an area of critical importance. As noted in Table 5, control received the lowest mean ratings among the considerations. Control may be less important in a comprehensive global sense, but more important for administering specific functions such as advertising or sales.

The ability of firms to pursue global standardization may hinge on their international business philosophies and organizational structures. A firm that is organized in a multi-domestic fashion is less likely to plan for and implement a standardized strategy. In contrast, global firms as well as those with a market extension[10] philosophy are better

[10] Global and market extension strategies differ in both philosophy and organization. Firms following the former view the world as their market, i.e., foreign markets are as important as their home country market, whereas those using the latter view the world as being of secondary importance and an extension of their domestic operations. Global firms have a very high degree of coordination with limited control of their activities, i.e., regiocentric distribution of authority. Market extension orientation, in contrast, typifies centrally controlled and coordinated organizations, and international marketing activities are primarily separate from their domestic marketing functions.

positioned to use global standardization because the former can concurrently implement planning or product modifications laterally in their global operations through various divisions, whereas the latter can centrally coordinate and implement the necessary modifications. In fact, everything else being equal, market extension firms can implement global standardization and implement modifications more quickly than others. This position is supported by Jain (1989), who suggests that centralization of authority in firms is related to the effective implementation of standardization. Central control of global operations has been noted as a necessary requirement for achieving a high level of standardization (Rutigliano, 1986). A distinction must be made, however, between central control and rigid implementation of standardization. Successful firms seek input and ideas from throughout their network of operations and typically do not dictate strategies in a top-down fashion (Kashani, 1989, 1990).

Definitional problems hinder the use of corporate strategic orientation in international marketing studies. Nevertheless, its inclusion in future studies may assist in uncovering an important dimension of global standardization. In addition, global standardization, aside from depending on firm philosophy and organization, is likely to be more dependent on the *process* than on the *programme* (Jain, 1989; Sorenson and Wiechmann, 1975). Our study focuses on major components of the latter without regard to organizational formats. Hence, multidomestic firms or a subset of them may exercise *process* standardization to a greater degree whereas global and market extension firms may be more likely to pursue *programme* standardization. At least in highly competitive markets, corporate response may be in the form of process standardization. Little is known about these issues and future research might address these aspects of global standardization.

REFERENCES

Aylmer, R. J. (1970) 'Who Makes Marketing Decisions in Multinational Firms?' *Journal of Marketing*, **34**(October): 25–30.

Bartels, R. (1968) 'Are Domestic and International Marketing Dissimilar?' *Journal of Marketing*, **32**(July): 56–61.

Bartlett, C. A. (1985) 'Global Competition and MNC Managers'. ICCH Note No. 0-385-287, Harvard Business School.

Bartlett, C. A. and Ghoshal, S. (1987) 'Managing Across Borders: New Strategic Requirements'. *Sloan Management Review* (Summer): 7–17.

Boddewyn, J. J. (1981) 'Comparative Marketing: The First Twenty-Five Years'. *Journal of International Business Studies*, **12**(Spring–Summer): 61–79.

Boddewyn, J. J., Soehl, R. and Picard, J. (1986) 'Standardization in International Marketing: Is Ted Levitt in Fact Right?' *Business Horizons*, **29**(November–December): 69–75.

Bourgeois, L. J. (1980) 'Performance Consensus'. *Strategic Management Journal*, **1**(3): 227–248.

Britt, S. H. (1974) Standardizing Marketing for the International Market'. *Columbia Journal of World Business*, **9**(Winter): 39–45.

Buzzell, R. (1968) 'Can You Standardize Multinational Marketing?' *Harvard Business Review*, **46**(November–December): 102–113.

Carapellotti, L. and Samiee, S. (1984) 'The Use of Portfolio Models for Production Rationalization in Multinational Firms'. *International Marketing Review*, **3**: 5–13.

Colvin, M., Heeler, R. and Thorpe, J. (1980) 'Developing International Advertising Strategy'. *Journal of Marketing*, **44**(Fall): 73–79.

Cool, K. and Schendel, D. (1988) 'Performance Differences Among Strategic Groups'. *Strategic Management Journal*, **9**(3): 207–23

Copeland, L. and Griggs, L. (1985) *Going International*. New York: Random House, Inc.

Cvar, M. (1984) 'Competitive Strategies in Global Industries'. Unpublished PhD dissertation, Harvard Business School.

Dess, G. G. and Davis, P. (1984) 'Porter's Generic Strategies as Determinants of Strategic Group Membership and Organizational Performance'. *Academy of Management Journal*, **27**(3): 467–488.

Dess, G. G. and Robinson, R. B. (1984) 'Measuring Organizational Performance in the Absence of Objective Measures: The Case of Privately-Held Firm and the Conglomerate Business Unit'. *Strategic Management Journal*, **5**(3): 265–273.

Douglas, S. P. and Wind, Y. (1987) 'The Myth of Globalization'. *Columbia Journal of World Business*, **22**(Winter): 19–29.

Dunn, S. W. (1976) 'Effect of National Identity on Multinational Promotional Strategy in Europe'. *Journal of Marketing*, **40**(October): 50–57.

Dunn, S. W. and Ryans, J. K. Jr. (1969) 'Standardized Global Advertising, a Call as Yet Unanswered'. *Journal of Marketing*, **33**(April): 57–60.

Elinder, E. (1961) 'How International Can Advertising Be?' *International Advertiser* (December): 12–16.

Fatt, A. C. (1964) 'A Multinational Approach to International Advertising'. *International Advertiser* (September): 17–20.

Fombrun, C. J. and Zajac, E. J. (1987) 'Structural and Perceptual Influences on Intra-Industry Stratification'. *Academy of Management Journal*, **30**(1): 33–50.

Galbraith, C. and Schendel, D. (1983) 'An Empirical Analysis of Strategy Types'. *Strategic Management Journal*, **4**(2): 153–173.

Green, R. T., Cunningham, W. H. and Cunningham, I. C. (1975) 'The Effectiveness of Standardized Global Advertising'. *Journal of Advertising*, **4**(Summer): 25–30.

Green, R. T. and Langeard, E. (1975) 'A Cross-National Comparison of Consumer Habits and Innovator Characteristics'. *Journal of Marketing*, **39**(July): 34–41.

Hamel, G. and Prahalad, C. K. (1985) 'Do You Really Have a Global Strategy?' *Harvard Business Review*, **63**(July–August): 139–148.

Henzler, H. and Rall, W. (1986) 'Facing Up to the Globalization Challenge'. *McKinsey Quarterly* (Winter): 52–68.

Hill, J. S. and Still, R. R. (1984) 'Adapting Products to LDC Tastes'. *Harvard Business Review*, **62**(March–April): 92–101.

Hout, T., Porter, M. E. and Rudden, E. (1982) 'How Global Companies Win Out'. *Harvard Business Review*, **60**(September–October): 98–105.

Huszagh, S., Fox, R. J. and Day, E. (1986) 'Global Marketing: An Empirical Investigation'. *Columbia Journal of World Business*, **21**(Twentieth Anniversary Issue): 31–44.

Jain, S. (1989) 'Standardization of International Marketing Strategy: Some Research Hypotheses'. *Journal of Marketing*, **53**(January): 70–79.

Kale, S. H. and Sudharshan, D. (1987) 'A Strategic Approach to International Segmentation'. *International Marketing Review*, **4**(Summer): 60–71.

Kashani, K. (1989) 'Beware the Global Pitfalls of Global Marketing'. *Harvard Business Review*, **67**(September–October): 91–98.

Kashani, K. (1990) 'Why Does Global Marketing Work—Or Not Work'. *European Management Journal*, **8**(June): 150–155.

Keegan, W. J. (1969) 'Multinational Product Planning: Strategic Alternatives'. *Journal of Marketing*, **33**(January): 58–62.

Killough, J. (1982) 'Improved Payoffs From Transnational Advertising'. *Harvard Business Review*, **60**(July–August): 102–110.

Kotler, P. (1986) 'Global Standardization: Courting Danger'. *Journal of Consumer Marketing*, **3**(Spring): 13–15.

Kotler, P. (1988) *Marketing Management: Analysis, Planning, Implementation, and Control*, 6th ed. Englewood Cliffs, NJ: Prentice-Hall, Inc.

Levitt, T. (1983) 'The Globalization of Markets'. *Harvard Business Review*, **61**(May–June): 92–102.

Mascarenhas, B. (1989) 'Strategic Group Dynamics'. *Academy of Management Journal*, **32**(2): 333–352.

McGee, J. and Thomas, H. (1986) 'Strategic Groups: Theory, Research and Taxonomy'. *Strategic Management Journal*, **7**(2): 141–160.

McGuire, J., Schneeweis, T. and Hill, J. (1986) 'An Analysis of Alternative Measures of Strategic Performance'. *Advances in Strategic Management*, **4**: 127–154.

Morrison, A. and Roth, K. (1989) 'International Business-Level Strategy: The Development of a Holistic Model'. In *International Strategic Management*, A. R. Neghandi and A. Savara, eds. Lexington, MA: Lexington Books, pp. 29–51.

Morsicato, H. G. and Radebaugh, L. H. (1979) 'Internal Performance Evaluation of Multinational Enterprise Operations'. *International Journal of Accounting Education and Research*, **15**(1): 77–94.

Nunnally, J. C. (1967) *Psychometric Theory*. New York: McGraw-Hill Book Company.

Ohmae, K. (1985) *Triad Power: The Coming Shape of Global Competition*. New York: The Free Press.

Onkvisit, S. and Shaw, J. J. (1987) 'Standardized International Advertising: A Review and Critical Evaluation of the Theoretical and Empirical Evidence'. *Columbia Journal of World Business*, **22**(Fall): 43–55.

Peebles, D. M. Jr., Ryans, J. K. and Vernon, I. R. (1977) 'A New Perspective on Advertising Standardization'. *European Journal of Marketing*, **11**(8): 569–576.

Peebles, D. M. Jr., Ryans, J. K. and Vernon, I. R. (1978) 'Coordinating International Advertising'. *Journal of Marketing*, **42**(January): 28–34.

Porter, M. E. (1980) *Competitive Strategy*. New York: The Free Press.

Porter, M. E. (1986a) 'The Strategic Role of International Marketing'. *Journal of Consumer Marketing*, **3**(Spring): 17–21.

Porter, M. E. ed. (1986b) *Competition in Global Industries*. Boston: Harvard Business School Press.

Prahalad, C. K. and Doz, Y. L. (1987) *The Multinational Mission: Balancing Local Demands and Global Vision*. New York: The Free Press.

Prescott, J. E. (1983) 'Competitive Environments, Strategic Types and Business Performance: An Empirical Analysis', unpublished PhD dissertation, The Pennsylvania State University.

Quelch, J. A. and Hoff, E. J. (1986) 'Customizing Global Marketing'. *Harvard Business Review*, **64**(May–June): 59–68.

Robinson, R. B. and Pearce, J. A. (1988) 'Planned Patterns of Strategic Behavior and Their Relationship to Business-Unit Performance'. *Strategic Management Journal*, **9**: 43–60.

Roostal, I. (1963) 'Standardization of Advertising for Western Europe'. *Journal of Marketing*, **27**(October): 15–20.

Rutenberg, D. P. (1982) *Multinational Management*. Boston: Little, Brown & Company.

Rutigliano, A. J. (1986) 'Global Versus Local Advertising'. *Management Review*, **80**(June): 27–31.

Sheth, J. N. (1986) 'Global Markets or Global Competition?' *Journal of Consumer Marketing*, **3**(Spring): 9–11.

Simmonds, K. (1985) 'Global Strategy: Achieving the Geocentric Ideal'. *International Marketing Review*, **2**(Spring): 8–17.

Sorenson, R. Z. and Wiechmann, U. E. (1975) 'How Multinationals View Marketing Standardization'. *Harvard Business Review*, **53**(May–June): 38.

Terpstra, V. (1987) *International Marketing*. Chicago: The Dryden Press.

Venkatraman, N. and Ramanujam, V. (1986) 'Measurement of Business Performance in Strategy Research'. *Academy of Management Review*, **11**(October): 801–814.

Venkatraman, N. and Ramanujam, V. (1987) 'Measurement of Business Economic Performance: An Examination of Method Convergence'. *Journal of Management*, **13**(1): 109–122.

Vernon, R. and Wells, L. Jr. (1968) 'A Product Life Cycle for International Trade'. *Journal of Marketing*, **32**(July): 1–6.

Walters, P. G. (1986) 'International Marketing Policy: A Discussion of the Standardization Construct and Its Relevance for Corporate Policy'. *Journal of International Business Studies*, **17**(Summer): 55–69.

Wind, Y. (1986) 'The Myth of Globalization'. *Journal of Consumer Marketing*, **3**(Spring): 23–26.

21

Innovation Orientation, Environment and Performance: a Comparison of US and European Markets

Franklyn A. Manu

One of the most significant trends in business today is the growth in the internationaliz-ation of business and markets. This trend has led to a greater need for analysis of the role and effectiveness of strategies in different geographic markets. Such an analysis requires an assessment of whether particular strategies are associated with particular market characteristics, as well as with particular kinds and levels of performance. An important issue that arises for US businesses in this regard is the extent to which relationships identified in US markets are generalizable to non-US markets. Some empirical and other evidence suggest that differences in the market environments of different countries may influence types of strategies developed by companies, as well as the impacts of those strategies (Douglas and Craig, 1983; Douglas and Rhee, 1989; Freeman, 1974; Schneeweis, 1983). This has implications for the ability of US businesses to lever successful strategies for US markets to non-US markets.

The particular aspect of strategy chosen for investigation has to do with innovation, specifically the innovation orientation of a business. Innovation orientation, as used in this context, is a multiple construct having to do with innovative output (new products and processes), innovative effort (R&D) and timing of market entry. As an orientation it encompasses the total innovation programmes of companies and is strategic in nature because it provides direction in dealing with markets. It is therefore a very important strategic issue. In fact Miller (1986) described innovation as a major dimension of strategic content on the basis of a review of literature dealing with strategy. A com-parison of this major dimension of strategy across US and non-US markets can provide insights on the applicability of strategies developed for the US. Given suggestions of differences in national market conditions it is not so clear that identified relationships in US markets on innovation will necessarily hold in other markets. If they do not hold then guidelines have to be provided for competing in those markets because managers cannot rely on their received knowledge and experience of US markets. For example, the popular notion that innovation is vital to company growth and survival may not apply in markets that do not reward such behaviour. Additionally it is important to specify what

Reprinted with permission from *Journal of International Business Studies*, Vol. 23, No. 2, pp. 333–359 kind of innovation the strategy deals with since different national markets may require a focus on different aspects of innovativeness.

The basic premise of this article then is that differences in the characteristics of different national market environments suggest that innovation orientation is unlikely to have similar impacts or influences. Given the importance of innovation it is important to understand how it relates to markets and environments outside the US. This will provide guidelines for appropriate strategies in those markets.

The previous discussion and proposed investigation suggest the following research questions:

1. Can similar types of innovation orientation be developed for businesses in US and non-US markets?
2. Are there similarities in the environments and performance levels associated with the innovation orientation types across US and non-US markets?

In the next section of the paper previous research relating to innovation orientation is reviewed to provide a basis for this study. The conceptual framework and research methodology are then described, followed by a discussion of the results of the study and its implications. In the final section conclusions are stated and suggestions made for future research.

PREVIOUS RESEARCH ON INNOVATION ORIENTATION

One main objective of strategy is to enable an organization adapt to its environment (Miles and Snow, 1978). This includes such business-level objectives as the development of specific products and services, entry into new markets, and the establishment of major R&D projects (Cohen and Cyert, 1973). Innovation is thus a means of an organization's adaptation to its environment, and is generally considered vital to survival and growth (Cooper, 1984; Kamm, 1987). Differences in the outlook or orientation of different companies towards innovation have resulted in the development of strategic archetypes based on classifications of those differences.

Ansoff and Stewart (1967) developed a typology of strategies based on the timing of entry of a technologically intensive firm into an emerging industry. This timing of entry represents an aspect of innovativeness, with earlier entry indicating a greater degree of innovativeness. In this typology 'First to Market' strategy is the most innovative, followed by 'Follow the Leader', 'Application Engineering', and 'Me-Too' strategies in that order. The underlying implications of this timing of market entry for R&D, marketing, and manufacturing form the basis of this typology. The typology indicates the role played by timing of market entry in influencing strategy and as such it is a major component of innovation orientation.

Freeman (1974) also developed a classification of strategic options available for firms faced with changes in their technological environments. This typology relates to the innovative efforts of firms and their focus, primarily in terms of R&D expenditures. Based on posture towards R&D expenditures, 'Offensive', 'Defensive', 'Imitative', 'Dependent', 'Traditional' and 'Opportunist' firms were identified.

Miles and Snow (1978), Snow and Hrebiniak (1980) and McDaniel and Kolari (1987) based their notion of innovation orientation on the key dimension of the rate at which organizations changed their products and markets in response to changes in the environment. They focused on the self-perceptions of top managers in the industries they studied to identify the archetypes of the typology, and their associated characteristics. Viewing this as subjective, Hambrick (1983a), offered an operationalization based on actions relative to the competition. His classifying variable was relative percent of new products which is the difference between a business's percent of new products and that of its three largest competitors. Contrary to some of his arguments, however (1983a, p. 8), he used an absolute percent of new products variable in parts of his analysis. Based on these operationalizations four types of organization were identified. Prospectors have a strong concern for product and market innovation and attempt to pioneer in those areas. Defenders have narrow product-market domains, conduct little or no new product/market development and pay a great deal of attention to improving efficiency of operations. Reactors are unable to respond effectively to their environments and only make adjustments when forced to do so by environmental pressures. Analysers are a hybrid of the first two types, Prospectors and Defenders.

Cooper (1984) focused on the new product programs of successful and unsuccessful firms. Each firm's product innovation programme was characterized by a number of dimensions describing the programme orientation, types of products, types of markets, technology type, and programme commitment. Five strategy types were identified as follows: Technologically Driven; Balanced; Technologically Deficient; Low-Budget Conservative; and High-Budget Diverse. The general conclusion of the study was that, while both the strategy adopted and the type of industry had an influence on programme performance, a firm's characteristics did not.

With the exception of the Cooper (1984) study, the above studies focused on innovativeness as a single variable construct. They were based on such factors as timing of market entry, rate of new product introductions, or responses to the innovation efforts of competitors. The Cooper study itself ignored the issue of timing of market entry which may have major implications for the competitive and cost effects of innovativeness. These operationalizations did not take into account possible interactions between different aspects of innovativeness, and also did not consider the broad scope of what constitutes innovativeness. This scope relates to products, markets, processes, technology and market entry as well as the effort behind them. In order to fully understand the ramifications of innovative orientation it is important to include as many of these dimensions as possible. A focus on a single dimension of innovativeness may ignore other potentially important dimensions.

Only the Cooper (1984) study, which was based on a sample of Canadian companies, dealt with innovation in non-US markets. Most of the research relating to innovation orientation has been conducted either in the US or on US-based companies. Since innovation orientation is a form of adaptation to an environment the issue for a company operating in non-US markets is to what extent findings in the US market are generalizable to those markets. To assume the universal validity of such strategic archetypes without explicit investigation is similar to assuming the universal validity of concepts and measures developed in the US (Douglas and Rhee, 1989). The available evidence on innovation internationally suggests a conditioning influence for market environments. Franko (1976), for example, found European innovations to be biased toward material-saving processes, ersatz material substitutes, and goods oriented toward low-income consumers. American innovations, on the other hand, were typically focused towards goods and processes that had an appeal to the unique high-income, labour-short American market. He attributed these patterns of innovations to differences in incomes and relative factor costs. Pavitt (1969) also found the demand for new technology to be lower in the European than in the US market.

In addition comparative marketing studies have demonstrated that marketing environments are associated with differences in marketing strategy (Bartels, 1968; Boddewyn, 1981). This view forms the basis of the argument for local adaptation in developing international marketing strategy (Buzzell, 1968; Keegan, 1969). Douglas and Craig (1983) also suggested that differences in market structure, market size, the degree of market fragmentation and differences in the character and degree of competition imply that relations that hold in the US do not necessarily hold in countries outside the US.

Related to the issue of the conditioning role played by market environments is the point that companies of different national origin often pursue different strategies (Brandt and Hulbert, 1977; Franko, 1976; Mazzolini, 1975; Pavitt, 1969). These so-called national strategies may be developed in part as a response to national market conditions, with the companies involved subsequently attempting to lever those strategies internationally. In this instance, too, the market environment plays a conditioning role in the development of strategies. To the extent that companies of different national origin pursue different strategies, because of their adaptation to national market conditions, it can be expected that different market conditions will play a conditioning role in the development of innovation orientations. This conditioning role of the environment probably explains the finding of Schneeweis (1983) that R&D and introduction of new products are not very important in explaining ROI levels in Europe as in the US.

Given this evidence is it likely that companies operating in different parts of the world will exhibit similar kinds of innovation orientation? If similar orientations are indicated then an important issue that arises is what kinds of environments they are associated with and to what extent they have similar impacts in terms of performance.

CONCEPTUAL FRAMEWORK

The study follows the environment–strategy–performance paradigm. This paradigm suggests that a company's performance is a function of differences in market conditions and the strategy pursued (Lenz, 1981). In a sense there must be an appropriate alignment between strategy-making behaviour and the nature of an environment to ensure effective selection of strategies (Miller and Friesen, 1983). Empirical evidence for this viewpoint is provided by Jauch, Osborn and Glueck (1980), Cooper and Schendel (1976), and Paine and Anderson (1977). Miles and Snow (1978), on the other hand, suggested that in any industry the various innovative types in their typology would exist, and with the exception of Reactors, be equally effective. Extrapolating to non-US markets the inference is that businesses need not worry about the particular characteristics of those foreign markets because they would be successful so long as they exhibited the respective competencies. This can only be partially correct because whether or not a particular competence is appropriate depends on the requirements of the environment.

Differences in income, consumption patterns, tastes, attitudes toward innovation, and lifestyles, all affect the size and growth of markets for new products. They determine a market's acceptance of innovation as well as its rate, and thus, its strategy and performance impacts. Lower levels of income in Europe, for example, restrict the ability of innovators to charge higher prices to cover their product development and introduction costs. This effect may be worsened by the generally smaller and more fragmented markets of Europe which reduces the ability of a firm to amortize its costs over a wider base. These two effects are likely to result in a much worse impact on the financial performance of innovators in Europe than in the US. Thus, it is very unlikely that different innovative types would be equally effective even though they may all exist within the foreign market environment. This viewpoint is consistent with the environment–strategy–performance paradigm of industrial organization and provides the framework for this study.

Specific variables relating to each of the three components—strategy, environment and performance—were chosen on the basis of a literature review of previous research and the objectives of this study described in preceding pages. The literature is not described in detail here but chosen variables are indicated and fully described in the Appendix.

As indicated earlier, innovation orientation as a strategy consists of a number of intertwined elements that have to do with outputs, inputs and timing. In output terms innovation has been measured primarily with statistics on new products, new processes and patents while in input terms the key statistics have been R&D expenditures and numbers of scientists and engineers as a proportion of the work force (Freeman, 1974; Nelson and Winter, 1977; Pavitt, 1982). New products and R&D expenditures are the measures chosen for this study. They facilitate comparability across industries, especially when they are measured as a proportion of sales. The new products measure reflects the results aspect of innovative effort as indicated by R&D expenditures.

The third component of innovation orientation has to do with timing of entry. There are usually three categories of timing involved in descriptions of innovation: pioneer or first to market; quick second or early follower; and late follower (Ansoff and Stewart, 1967; Kamm, 1987). The particular aspect of timing used in this study has to do with the position of a business with respect to these dimensions at the time of its initial entry into a particular product market. To the extent that a firm is one of the first to develop a particular product or service it can be classified as being more innovative.

A number of variables relating to the environment have been used in innovation strategy research. Industry and market concentration have been found to influence both profitability and behaviour of firms. In terms of innovation, high levels of concentration may make it easier for firms to appropriate the returns from new product development effort. On the other hand, they may feel less compelled to engage in innovation because concentration acts as a barrier to entry. Since there are very few absolute barriers to entry the former effect is likely to prevail. Other factors that have similar effects are product development times and patient protection which may be viewed as measures of innovative opportunity (Angelmar, 1985; Ravenscraft, 1983). Other environmental variables relating to innovation strategy have to do with competitive pressure in the form of frequency of product changes, market share instability and competitors' new product intensities (Hambrick, 1983a; Miller, 1988). Businesses may choose to be either product or process innovative in the face of intense competition.

Another set of variables relating to innovation strategy have to do with industry and market growth. Key factors here have been growth rates, stage in product life cycle and stability of growth rates (Hambrick, 1983a; Moore and Tushman, 1982; Thietart and Vivas, 1984). Growth rate is one indicator of the attractiveness of a market or industry, and the stability associated with this rate reflects environmental uncertainty.

The last component of the framework is performance. It has been measured in a number of ways including success rates, contribution to corporate sales and profits, and the extent to which profits from new products exceeded their costs of development (Collier, 1977; Cooper, 1984; Hopkins, 1980). For the purposes of this study two broad categories of measures relating to marketing (market share; relative market share; market share growth; return on sales) and financial (ROI; Cashflow on Investment—CFOI; gross margin; cash flow from operations) performance are used. Both categories of measures have been studied extensively in previous research on strategy and performance in both domestic and international markets (Buzzell and Gale, 1987; Douglas and Craig, 1983). Multiple measures are used because innovation has differing impacts in the short and long term, and on different measures of performance.

The review of literature and conceptual framework provide a basis for addressing the research questions posed in the introduction. They suggest a conditioning impact for national market factors and thus we would not expect innovation orientation to have the same features or be associated with similar environments or levels of performance.

These issues are examined, within the context of the PIMS database, through the development of a taxonomy of innovation orientation using consumer businesses operating in the US and in European markets. The environments and performance levels associated with the different groups in the two geographic areas are also compared.

METHODOLOGY

Database

The paper examines the above issues using a sample of businesses drawn from the PIMS (Profit Impact of Market Strategy) database. Instructions for responding to the Strategic Planning Institute survey define a product business as one that:

- sells a distinct set of products or services
- to an identifiable group of customers
- in competition with a well-defined set of competitors.

This database results from an ongoing survey of the environments, competitive characteristics, strategy and performance of businesses in a number of countries undertaken by the Strategic Planning Institute. The particular component of the database used in this study is the SPI4 which provides data averaged over four-year periods for the different variables.

The international portion of the database indicates the national or regional locations of the headquarters and served markets of businesses. These locations are in the categories US, the UK, Europe and Other Countries. It should be noted that served markets are not necessarily international. Served markets, as defined by reporting managers of the businesses, may cover a region in a country, all of a country, or several countries. However, there are no served markets that cover the US and countries in Europe together. It is only in the case of Europe that there exists an international served market in a real sense because served markets there may go across national boundaries.

Two subsamples were chosen since a basic objective was to compare innovation in US and European markets. The first subsample was made up of 350 businesses serving the US market with corporate headquarters in the US. A second subsample consisted of 123 businesses operating in European markets, of which 44 had their corporate headquarters in the US, and 79 in Europe. The businesses operated in consumer durable and non-durable markets.

Data analysis

Data analysis was conducted in two phases with each related to one of the research questions posed earlier on. Phase 1 dealt with the issue of identifying similar innovation orientation types in US and non-US markets. Phase 2 compared the environments and performance of the types across the two markets.

For each subsample variables relating to innovation orientation, environment and performance were chosen on the basis of the previously discussed literature review and conceptual framework. These variables and their definitions in the PIMS database are described in the Appendix.

All observations in the subsamples were standardized to have mean zero and unit standard deviation. This was done to alleviate the problem of different measurement units for the various variables. With standardization comparison of variable scores for different groups is facilitated because they are all transformed into the same unit of measurement.

Phase 1

As indicated earlier, Phase 1 of the data analysis aimed at identifying similar innovation orientation types in US and European markets. The approach to doing this was through taxonomy development, specifically, a taxonomy of innovative orientation. Cluster analysis was performed separately for each subsample (i.e., US and European markets) of observations based on variables identified as relating to innovation orientation in order to come up with this taxonomy.

The goal of the cluster analysis, then, was to identify a taxonomy of innovation orientation based on the derived clusters. The cluster method used comes from the Analysis of Quantitative Data (AQD) package provided by the Strategic Planning Institute. The particular method involved a hierarchical algorithm using the minimum squared error method (Schlaifer, 1981) which has been indicated as producing better results when euclidean measures of similarity are used, as is the case in this approach (Punj and Stewart, 1983). Schlaifer (1974) also indicated the minimum square error approach as a good method for forming homogeneous groups.

Due to limitations in the software package available on the AQD system provided by SPI, the clustering routine could not be applied to the total number of observations in the US market sample. The routine was thus applied to a random sample of 350 observations in the US market. For the European market all observations were used.

Criteria used in choosing an appropriate number of clusters to serve as a basis for identifying different innovation orientation types were as follows:

1. The interpretability and practicality of the derived clusters in terms of the concept of innovation orientation discussed earlier;
2. The drop in the overall root-mean-square prediction error at different merger levels.

This approach follows Galbraith and Schendel (1983) and Douglas and Rhee (1989).

The first criterion was based on an examination of the mean scores on the cluster variables for the various cluster solutions. The second criterion was applied by examining the dendrograms (a chart indicating the cluster process) and levels of the overall root-mean-square prediction error as computed after the merger of observations into a cluster. On the basis of these two criteria the four cluster solutions were chosen. The scores on the cluster variables for the two markets and comparisons of the groups are shown in Tables 1 and 2.

Table 1. Profiles of innovation orientation types (mean scores on cluster variables)

Cluster variable	Product Innovators US (44)	Eur. (16)	Process Innovators US (24)	Eur. (9)	Late Entrant Non-Innovators US (123)	Eur. (24)	Original Pioneers US (159)	Eur. (74)
Order of market entry	−0.1891	−0.4641	−0.0911	−0.3429	−0.8849	−1.4335	0.7506	0.6070
Relative % new products	1.7104	1.9725	0.6239	−0.3409	−0.2888	−0.5061	−0.3441	−0.2209
Percent new products	1.9491	1.6840	0.2968	0.4046	−0.4063	−0.4031	−0.2699	−0.2826
Product R&D	0.0085	0.6042	1.2635	0.3807	−0.468	−0.2147	0.1689	−0.1073
Process R&D	−0.1713	−0.0140	2.6879	2.8144	−0.3979	−0.1678	−0.0505	−0.2849

It must be borne in mind when following the discussion, and also in reading the figures in the tables, that the numbers represent the mean scores of the different cluster groups relative to the average for the sample as a whole. Thus the cluster comparisons are made in terms of their relative differences from that average. It should be noted that a negative score indicates that a particular group is below the average while a positive score shows that it is above the average for all the businesses in that particular market (the subsample). With respect to the order of market entry variable though, a negative score indicates relative late entry while a positive score describes relatively early entry.

Phase 2

In order to examine the effects of the geographic location of the served market on the different innovative orientations, each type in the US was compared to its counterpart in

Table 2. Comparison of innovation orientation types on cluster variables in US and European Markets (mean scores)

	US	Europe	Significance (*t*-test)
(a) *Product Innovators*			
Cluster variable			
Order of market entry	−0.1891	−0.4641	NS
Relative % new products	1.7104	1.9725	NS
Percent new products	1.9491	1.6840	NS
Product R&D	0.0085	0.6042	0.10
Process R&D	−0.1713	−0.0140	NS
(b) *Process Innovators*			
Cluster variable			
Order of market entry	−0.0911	−0.3429	NS
Relative % new products	0.6239	−0.3409	0.01
Percent new products	0.2968	0.4046	NS
Product R&D	1.2635	0.3807	0.10
Process R&D	2.6879	2.8144	NS
(c) *Late Entrant Non-Innovators*			
Cluster variable			
Order of market entry	−0.8849	−1.4335	0.001
Relative % new products	−0.2888	−0.5061	0.10
Percent new products	−0.4063	−0.4031	NS
Product R&D	−0.4680	−0.2147	0.01
Process R&D	−0.3979	−0.1678	0.05
(d) *Original Pioneers*			
Cluster variable			
Order of market entry	0.7506	0.6070	0.05
Relative % new products	−0.3441	−0.2209	NS
Percent new products	−0.2699	−0.2826	NS
Product R&D	0.1689	−0.1073	0.10
Process R&D	−0.0505	−0.2849	0.05

the European market. The statistical approach used was a series of *t*-tests comparing the mean scores of each group across a number of environmental and performance variables. It should be noted in these comparisons that the focus is on relative positions within geographic served markets. For example, the relative position of Product Innovators in the European market is compared with the relative position of Product Innovators in the US market. The comparisons basically reflect the magnitude of the differences in relative positions. The profiles of the environments and performance of the clusters are shown in Tables 3–6.

RESULTS

The innovation orientation clusters (types)

A key finding was the high degree of similarity in results for the two geographic markets, especially in terms of the innovation profiles of the identified innovative types. There were differences though in the market characteristics associated with the types across the two geographic areas.

Similarities and differences in the composition of the two sets of clusters were ascertained through an examination of their scores on the cluster variables. At the four-cluster solution chosen for each of the two subsamples two types of innovative groups emerged. The first group typically rated high on new product introductions and product R&D expenditures but much less so on process R&D. This first group is fairly similar to the Prospectors identified by Miles and Snow (1978) and the Offensive type of Freeman (1974) in that they are both research intensive and have relatively high rates of new product introduction. They are labelled Product Innovators.

The second innovative group typically scored high on process R&D expenditures, slightly lower on product R&D, and much lower on new product introductions. This second group appears fairly similar to the Defenders identified by Miles and Snow (1978) and the Imitators of Freeman (1974) in that their high process R&D expenditures may indicate a focus on the engineering task and production efficiency. They are labelled Process Innovators.

A third group was identified across the two subsamples. The major characteristics of this group were their relatively late entries into their markets and their extreme non-innovativeness. This suggests that they are closest to the Reactors of Miles and Snow (1978), the Dependents of Freeman (1974) and the Me-Toos of Ansoff and Stewart (1967). They are labelled Late Entrant Non-Innovators.

The fourth group was characterized by the fact that those businesses had typically pioneered in their markets at the time of their initial entry. They most closely relate to the Applications Engineers of Ansoff and Stewart (1967) and the Traditionalists of Freeman (1974). As such they are labelled Original Pioneers.

Comparisons of the innovative types

US market product innovators and European market product innovators (Table 3)

Innovative orientation. Contrary to expectation there exists a significant (0.10 level) difference in the relative positions of the two groups with respect to product R&D expenditures. The European market Product Innovator group ranks first in terms of these expenditures whereas the US market group ranks third in its sample. This may indicate the ability of the US market group to introduce many new products without necessarily engaging in a high level of product R&D. It may also imply the introduction of new products by the US group that are essentially minor modifications of existing ones and thus do not require a high product R&D effort.

Environment. Significant differences exist in the market growth associated with these two groups of Product Innovators even though they both experience the highest rates in their markets. These differences are in terms of real market growth (0.05 level) and served market size (0.05 level). Not surprisingly, a similar situation occurs with respect to their respective product life cycles. While both groups operate in the earlier stages the difference between them and the other groups in their markets is greater for the European market group, and significant at the 0.1 level.

Table 3. Comparison of environments and performance levels of innovation orientation types in US and European markets (mean scores): Product Innovators

	US	Europe	Significance (*t*-test)
1. Environment			
1a. Market growth/product life cycle stage			
Industry long-term growth	0.6482	0.0223	NS
Real market growth	0.0932	0.8123	0.05
Served market size	0.0547	0.6294	0.05
Life cycle stage	−0.3105	−0.8791	0.10
1b. Competition			
Industry concentration	−0.3319	−0.0344	NS
Served market concentration	−0.1021	0.1952	NS
Industry instability	−0.0713	0.6519	0.10
Served market instability	−0.1859	0.0310	NS
Total market share instability	0.1559	0.0780	NS
Competitors' % new products	1.1476	0.1592	0.05
1c. Innovative opportunity			
Product patent protection	0.3394	−0.0391	NS
Process patent protection	0.4480	−0.1405	NS
Frequency of product changes	−0.2659	0.3474	0.05
Development time for new products	−0.4102	0.0506	0.10
2. Performance			
2a. Financial measures			
Gross margin	0.0123	0.7395	0.05
Return on investment	−0.4756	−0.2934	NS
Cash flow on investment	−0.5704	−0.6436	NS
Cash flow from operations	−0.6021	−0.6506	NS
2b. Marketing measures			
Market share	−0.3972	−0.4711	NS
Relative market share	−0.3269	−0.4861	NS
Market share growth	0.3946	0.5017	NS

For the competitive situations in their environments key differences exist in industry instability and competitors' rate of new product introductions. Both groups face relatively lower levels of industry instability, but this is more marked for the European market group, and is significant at the 0.1 level. The US market group has about the same level of industry instability as the Late Entrant Non-Innovators in their market. The opposite situation holds for competitors' new product introductions. The US market group has by far the highest rate of competitor's new product introductions (more than one standard deviation from the mean) whereas the European market group is second in its market. In the European market Process Innovators face the greatest pressure from competitors' new product introductions. This difference is significant at the 0.05 level, and suggests product innovativeness as a response to competitive pressure in the form of a high rate of new product introductions for the US market. In the European market, on the other hand, it gives rise to process innovativeness presumably aimed at achieving efficiency in operations to counter competitive pressure. If product innovativeness is considered a higher level form of innovation than process innovativeness then the US market Product Innovators may be said to respond to competitive pressure by being more innovative. The presumed objective of operational efficiency for the European market Product Innovators is supported to an extent by their comparatively higher relative process R&D expenditures in relation to the US market group.

Differences exist in terms of the innovative opportunity in their environments with respect to frequency of product changes and development time for new products, at the 0.05 and 0.1 levels respectively. Whereas European market Product Innovators have fairly infrequent product changes their counterparts in the US market face much more frequent changes. The US market group also faces much shorter product development times in their markets than does the European market group. In fact, the latter group is just around the average in its market. Product Innovators in the US market therefore face greater product dynamism in the form of frequent product changes and shorter product development times. The longer product development times may be a contributing factor to the observation that a high rate of new product introductions by competitors in the European market is associated with process innovativeness. Since it takes a long time to develop new products businesses may opt for operational efficiencies in the short run in the face of competitive pressure. Another contributing factor may be the fact that US market Product Innovators typically have greater product and process patent protection than their European market counterparts, even though this difference is not statistically significant.

Performance. The only performance variable that provides a significant difference is gross margin at the 0.05 level. The European market group has a substantially larger margin than the other groups in its markets compared to the US market group. In fact, Product Innovators in the US outperform only Late Entrant Non-Innovators in terms of gross margin. Thus, there is a high degree of similarity in the performance levels associated with product innovativeness in both US and European markets.

These findings indicate that although a similar strategic innovation orientation type (Product Innovator) may be identified in both US and European markets, key differences exist in some of the environments and performance levels associated with them. These differences may be either in terms of their positions relative to other groups in their markets, or in terms of the type of association. The key differences have to do with product R&D expenditures, market growth rates, competitors' new product introductions, product dynamism and gross margins.

US market Process Innovators and European market Process Innovators (Table 4)

Innovative orientation. Key significant differences exist with respect to relative percent new products (0.01 level) and product R&D (0.1 level). Whereas Process Innovators in the US market have a high rate of new product introductions relative to their leading competitors (second only to Product Innovators), their European market counterparts are substantially below the average for those markets. The European market group has a rate higher than only that for Late Entrant Non-Innovators.

Process Innovators in the US have the highest expenditures for product R&D by a substantial margin over other groups whereas their counterparts in the European market rank second. This suggests that Process Innovators in the US market are innovative in general, given their relatively high rates of new product introductions and high process and product R&D expenditures.

Table 4. Comparison of environments and performance levels of innovation orientation types in US and European markets (mean scores): Process Innovators

	US	Europe	Significance (*t*-test)
1. Environment			
1a. Market growth/product life cycle stage			
Industry long-term growth	−0.0388	0.2862	NS
Real market growth	−0.1141	0.4240	NS
Served market size	0.2491	0.2882	NS
Life cycle stage	−0.1430	0.0562	NS
1b. Competition			
Industry concentration	0.0754	0.0494	NS
Served market concentration	0.2175	0.0433	NS
Industry instability	0.3039	0.2819	NS
Served market instability	−0.0711	0.0436	NS
Total market share instability	0.1724	0.1419	NS
Competitors' % new products	−0.0199	0.7994	NS
1c. Innovative opportunity			
Product patent protection	−0.1491	0.5994	0.10
Process patent protection	0.0769	0.6930	NS
Frequency of product changes	−0.2782	−0.5334	NS
Development time for new products	0.1948	0.4050	NS
2. Performance			
2a. Financial measures			
Gross margin	0.2831	−0.7398	0.01
Return on investment	−0.0924	−0.2878	NS
Cash flow on investment	−0.0730	−0.0226	NS
Cash flow from operations	0.0134	−0.0172	NS
2b. Marketing measures			
Market share	0.3657	−0.0801	NS
Relative market share	0.2530	0.0269	NS
Market share growth	−0.0838	−0.3352	NS

Environment. The only significant difference is product patents protection at the 0.1 level. European market Process Innovators have the highest such protection in their markets whereas the US market group has one of the lowest. The European market group has either been unable to take advantage of this protection, or their competitors have such strong protection that the group would not benefit from a focus on many new products.

There are other differences that are not statistically significant. For example, the European market group typically operates in higher growth markets and industries in its markets relative to the other groups than the US market Process Innovators. Also European market Process Innovators face the highest pressure from competitors' new product introductions by a substantial margin whereas their US market counterparts face about average pressure from that source.

Performance. The only statistically significant difference at the 0.01 level is gross margin for which the US market Process Innovators have the highest performance in their markets, whereas the European market group has the lowest in their markets by a substantial margin. Although not statistically significant the US market group also has comparatively higher performance in terms of both market share, relative market share, and ROI in their markets than the European market groups.

A similar conclusion to that reached in the comparison of Product Innovators may be made in this instance. Although a similar strategic innovation type may be identified in both US and European markets some differences exist in their associated environments and performance levels. The results indicate differences in terms of both their positions relative to other innovative types and the type of association in relation to relative new product introductions, product R&D, product patent protection and gross margins.

US market Late Entrant Non-Innovators and European market Late Entrant Non-Innovators (Table 5)

Innovative orientation. Significant differences exist between the two groups in terms of the components of innovative orientation except in the case of absolute new product introduction. Although significant differences exist in terms of standardized scores (reflecting differences in magnitude), there is consistency in terms of their positions relative to other groups in their markets.

Environment. The only significant differences in their environments relate to rate of competitors' new product introductions (0.05 level) and development time for new products (0.1 level). In terms of the latter, whereas the US market group has the least frequent changes in its markets the European market group has a frequency second only to Process Innovators. The US market group also faces the least pressure from competitors' new product introductions by a large margin whereas the European market group has just about average pressure from that source in their markets. The European market group thus appears to face more dynamic and competitive environments.

Although not statistically significant, the US market group also has the lowest growth rates in its markets, whereas the European market group has a comparatively higher level of growth in relation to other groups in their markets. For the competitive situation, differences exist in concentration and served market instability. The European market group has substantially higher relative served market instability than the US market group which is just around the average in its market. The European market group also has the highest served market concentration and lowest industry concentration in relation to other groups while the US market group is at average levels in terms of both those elements.

Performance. The results indicate significant differences with respect to ROI (0.05 level), CFOI (0.05 level), cash flow (0.01 level), market share (0.05 level), and relative market share (0.05 level). The US market group has the second lowest level of performance with respect to ROI, market share and relative market share; an average level of cash flow and about average CFOI. The European market group has the lowest level of ROI, market share and relative market share, and the second lowest level of CFOI and cash

Table 5. Comparison of environments and performance levels of innovation orientation types in US and European markets (mean scores): Late Entrant Non-Innovators

	US	Europe	Significance (t-test)
1 Environment			
1a. Market growth/product life cycle stage			
Industry long-term growth	−0.0818	−0.0887	NS
Real market growth	−0.1107	0.0986	NS
Served market size	−0.0851	−0.0523	NS
Life cycle stage	0.1204	0.0274	NS
1b. Competition			
Industry concentration	−0.0276	−0.2405	NS
Served market concentration	0.0914	0.3532	NS
Industry instability	−0.0863	0.0075	NS
Served market instability	0.0270	0.1559	NS
Total market share instability	−0.1511	−0.1824	NS
Competitors' % new products	−0.3176	−0.0453	0.05
1c. Innovative opportunity			
Product patent protection	−0.1554	−0.2980	NS
Process patent protection	−0.2395	−0.2493	NS
Frequency of product changes	0.2360	0.1082	NS
Development time for new products	0.2450	0.0000	0.10
2. Performance			
2a. Financial measures			
Gross margin	−0.2380	−0.2502	NS
Return on investment	−0.1047	−0.4928	0.05
Cash flow on investment	−0.0474	−0.5272	0.05
Cash flow from operations	0.0016	−0.6285	0.01
2b. Marketing measures			
Market share	−0.3254	−0.7010	0.05
Relative market share	−0.2843	−0.5936	0.05
Market share growth	0.0661	0.2201	NS

flow. In sum, the European market group exhibits relatively poorer performance in its markets.

US market Original Pioneers and European market Original Pioneers (Table 6)

Innovative orientation. There are statistically significant differences with respect to order of market entry (0.05 level), product R&D (0.1 level) and process R&D (0.05 level). In terms of order of market entry though, relative positions remain the same. For product R&D, although the US market group has the second highest such expenditures, the European market group has the second lowest. The latter group also has the lowest process R&D expenditures, while the US market group has a level close to the average for their market. These differences suggest the notion of the US market group engaging in some form of product modification as evidenced by relatively high product R&D expenditures. In terms of relative percent of new product introductions, although not statistically significant, we find the US market group with the lowest such rate in their markets whereas the European market group has the second highest rate in theirs.

Table 6. Comparison of environments and performance levels of innovation orientation types in US and European markets (mean scores): Original Pioneers

	US	Europe	Significance (*t*-test)
1. Environment			
1a. Market growth/product life cycle stage			
Industry long-term growth	−0.1102	−0.0012	NS
Real market growth	0.0771	−0.2592	0.05
Served market size	0.0883	−0.1542	0.10
Life cycle stage	0.0144	0.1744	NS
1b. Competition			
Industry concentration	0.1018	0.0794	NS
Served market concentration	−0.0752	−0.1620	NS
Industry instability	0.0406	0.1043	NS
Served market instability	0.0413	−0.0626	NS
Total market share instability	0.0477	0.0251	NS
Competitors' % new product	−0.0689	−0.1169	NS
1c. Innovative opportunity			
Product patent protection	0.0489	0.0322	NS
Process patent protection	0.0497	0.0269	NS
Frequency of product changes	−0.0670	0.0248	NS
Development time for new products	−0.1054	−0.0602	NS
2. Performance			
2a. Financial measures			
Gross margin	0.1379	0.0112	NS
Return on investment	0.2265	0.2583	NS
Cash flow on investment	0.2056	0.3129	NS
Cash flow from operations	0.1633	0.3466	NS
2b. Marketing measures			
Market share	0.3064	0.3390	NS
Relative market share	0.2722	0.2943	NS
Market share growth	−0.2030	−0.1391	NS

Environment. A number of statistically significant differences exist in the environments associated with these two groups. Whereas the US market group has about average rates of market growth, the European market group has the lowest rates of growth in its markets by a fairly large margin. The levels of significance are 0.05 for real market growth, short and long term, and 0.10 for served market size.

In terms of competitive situations and innovative opportunity no statistically significant differences exist. The only notable differences in comparative positions has to do with pressure from competitors' new product introductions. The European market group faces the lowest such pressure while the US market group is only slightly below the average for their markets. This, and the comparatively higher market growth, may be the rationale for the product modification engaged in by the US market group.

Performance. No statistically significant differences are observed but some differences in comparative positions are indicated. While the European market group has the highest market share, the US market group is second to the Process Innovators in their markets.

The US market group also has the lowest increases in market share while their European market counterparts have the second lowest such increase.

DISCUSSION

A taxonomy of innovation orientation was developed that held across the US and European markets. This is a contribution for two reasons. In the first place, even though this study uses a multidimensional conceptualization of innovation, types similar to single variable conceptualizations are generated. This type of conceptualization however does indicate the linkages between various aspects of innovativeness. The similarity of the innovative types developed in this study to existing typologies provides an indication of their relevance for strategic analysis.

The second contribution lies in the implications of this existence of similar innovative orientation types across US and European markets. A major implication is similar to a key postulate of the Miles and Snow (1978) typology: in any given geographic market or environment these different innovative types may be present. In terms of international strategy this suggests a firm moving from one geographic location to another (at least between the US and European markets) will encounter similar strategic types with respect to innovative orientation. This implies a lack of a conditioning influence by environmental factors and provides further confirmation of the universality of the types.

In addition, differences in terms of market characteristics indicate the lack of a one-to-one correspondence in the environments associated with a particular innovative type across the two geographic locations. Thus, for aspects of an environment such as concentration and stability, businesses pursuing a similar innovation orientation are likely to be faced with different associations in the two geographic locations. This makes it difficult to predict some of the market characteristics competitors are going to be associated with. For other aspects of environments, such as growth and competitive pressure in the form of new product introductions, greater similarity exists across US and European markets for similar innovative types. This makes it easier for businesses to predict what market characteristics their competitors are going to be associated with. The problem in all of this is that environments are multidimensional in nature, thus the lack of a one-to-one correspondence on all the features of environments used in this study makes the provision of guidelines that would be relevant for both geographic locations very difficult.

In terms of the performance levels associated with the different innovative types, some relationships are consistent across the board. Product Innovators typically exhibit the poorest financial performance but the greatest increases in market share growth. The poor financial performance may be attributed to the high costs of developing and introducing new products (Blois, 1985; Farris and Buzzell, 1979; Haas, 1987; Moore and Tushman, 1982). The high market share growth associated with this strategy may be due to the newness of products which enables them compete effectively against established brands (Porter, 1980). Both findings are consistent with Hambrick's (1983a) results for Prospectors.

For Late Entrant Non-Innovators performance is generally poor in both markets. Businesses pursuing this strategy, having entered their markets late, lack enduring advantages or the resources to compete against the strengths of established businesses. Surprisingly though, in the European market case, this group shows the second highest increase in market share, a finding for which there is no obvious explanation.

Original Pioneers experience the best performance in both geographic locations, reflecting the long term advantages of pioneering brands. The strong relationship between the Pioneer groups and superior marketing performance confirms the findings of Robinson (1988), Robinson and Fornell (1985), and Urban et al. (1986). These studies indicated the superior market share associated with pioneering in a market.

For Process Innovators there is no consistency in performance results between the US and European markets. For example, in the US, they have superior absolute and relative market shares, whereas in the European market they have around average market shares. These inconsistencies do not lend themselves to ready interpretation. In the US Process Innovators also have a high rate of product introductions and product R&D expenditures which should lead to poor financial and marketing performance based on results for Product Innovators. A potential explanation is that their production efficiencies more than offset the projected negative consequences of product innovativeness. This is reflected in the superior gross margins of the US market group. The relatively lower margins and poorer performance of the European market group may be attributable to intense competitive pressure from high rates of competitors' new product introductions. Although not explicitly tested for, these observations suggest the conditioning impact of the environment as indicated by Douglas and Rhee (1989). The general conclusion reached is that emphasis on process innovation leads to generally positive, if not spectacular, marketing performance. This particular group does not exhibit any consistently greater financial performance contrary to what is suggested by Miles and Snow (1978) and Hambrick (1983a).

The major implication of these findings is that, *in general*, certain performance levels are associated with each innovative orientation type which vary only in terms of magnitude across geographic location. Some relationships too do not show any consistency across the two markets as in the case of Process Innovators. For the former, while the strength of the relationship may vary, the direction is typically the same. This variation in the strength of the relationship leads to differences in relative positions of the innovative orientation types. It may create, in fact, situations similar to those caused by differences in the direction of the relationship, which may also lead to differences in relative position. Results from the study clearly indicate that different types of innovation orientation are associated with different kinds and levels of performance. This suggests a difference from the Miles and Snow (1978) contention that different orientations would be equally effective with the exception of their Reactor type.

Relating these findings back to the conceptual framework, the main implication is that the environment–strategy–performance paradigm is borne out in both geographic locations. The differences in performance indicate a need for an appropriate alignment of these strategies with market conditions for effective performance.

For US businesses interested in European markets the results of this study indicate the potential complexities associated with trying to extend their domestic strategies abroad. Even though companies may be pursuing similar generic strategies abroad great care must be taken to understand their implications. Further consideration must also be given to the requirements of the market environments in which they operate. The consistent relationships indicated above can only be used as a starting point because there is not a one-to-one correlation across geographic location. Selection of an innovation strategy should be a function of the characteristics of the market environment as well as the type of performance desired.

CONCLUSION

This study examines and extends findings on the environments and performance levels associated with innovation orientation to European markets. Similar innovation orientation types were identified for both US and European markets which suggests that geographic market location is not an influencing factor in the adoption of these orientations. However, the existence of some differences in environments associated with the types suggests a need for closer examination of these links. Specifically, the issue of whether particular kinds of environments give rise to particular types of innovation orientation should be further investigated. The role of an environment as a contingency factor influencing effectiveness of different innovation orientations should also be examined. This could be done, for example, by first developing a typology or classification of environments and then examining the performance associated with different innovation strategies. This is necessary because this study only deals with association between innovation orientation, environment and performance. It does not specify cause–effect relationships.

While the environment–strategy–performance framework is borne out, the paradigm would be enriched for comparative analysis if further work were done on establishing the equivalence of environmental and other variables across geographic locations. For example, studies should be conducted to identify the relative importance of different environmental variables in determining the effectiveness of different innovation strategies.

The different innovation orientations are clearly associated with different kinds and levels of performance. Product innovativeness results in high market share increases but at the expense of very poor financial performance, especially in terms of cash flow. This reflects the lag between expenditures and income generation associated with high rates of new product development and introduction. Businesses following this strategy in both US and European markets must have the financial resources to bridge this lag. Relatedly the findings indicate that the effectiveness of this strategy is restricted to enabling businesses to gain market share rapidly.

Findings for Original Pioneers and Late Entrant Non-Innovators indicate the benefits of entering markets early. Thus, timing of market entry is a key influence on level and type of performance in both geographic locations, the exception being market share growth for Process Innovators which has a differential impact across markets. This suggests a conditioning influence for market characteristics. Findings for Process Innovators also reflect this conditioning influence. These findings clearly indicate that the innovative types are not equally effective within and across geographic locations. They also give a clear indication of the appropriateness of each type.

A concern with this study derives from software limitations of the AQD package. For instance, MANOVA or multiple group discriminant analysis could not be used to test for differences across blocks of variables describing components of the framework. Thus, differences were tested across one variable at a time, a procedure that may not capture the intricacies of such components as environment and performance. There is therefore a need to examine these issues with multivariate analysis which may shed further light on the linkages between various items comprising the components of the framework.

The study is based on the SPI4 version of the database which has data in four-year blocks. It is virtually impossible to link the various four-year blocks of data for individual business units. Thus, the study is cross-sectional in nature. Given the potential longer term ramifications of some innovations it may be useful to investigate these issues with longitudinal analysis to capture the time dimension of innovation strategy.

Finally, businesses from the database are mostly larger, more successful and operating in growing or mature industries. The European sample is also much smaller. These businesses then may not be representative of the full range of businesses operating in US and European markets. Caution must therefore be exercised in extrapolating these results to other types of businesses. More extensive investigation with a wider variety of businesses would be most useful. In particular further research on organizational contingencies associated with the effectiveness of innovative types is needed.

ACKNOWLEDGEMENTS

I am deeply indebted to Dr. Susan Douglas of New York University who made invaluable suggestions during the conduct of this study. Financial support was provided by the Marketing Science Institute, Cambridge, Massachusetts. My thanks also go to the Strategic Planning Institute, Cambridge, Massachusetts for providing access to the PIMS database.

REFERENCES

Angelmar, R. (1985) 'Market Structure and Research Intensity in High Technological Opportunity Industries'. *Journal of Industrial Economics*, **34**: 69–79.

Ansoff, H. I. and Stewart, J. M. (1967) 'Strategies for a Technology-Based Business'. *Harvard Business Review* (November–December): 71–83.

Bartels, R. (1968) 'Are Domestic and International Marketing Dissimilar?' *Journal of Marketing*, **32**: 56–61.

Blois, K. J. (1985) 'Matching New Manufacturing Technologies to Industrial Markets and Strategies'. *Industrial Marketing Management*, **14**: 43–47.

Boddewyn, J. J. (1981) 'Comparative Marketing: the First 25 Years'. *Journal of International Business Studies*, **12**: 61–79.

Brandt, W. K. and Hulbert, J. M. (1977) 'Headquarters Guidance in Marketing Strategy in the Multinational Subsidiary'. *Columbia Journal of World Business*, Winter: 6–12.

Buzzell, R. D. (1968) 'Can You Standardize Multinational Marketing?' *Harvard Business Review*, **46**: 102–113.

Buzzell, R. D. and Gale, B. T. (1987) *The PIMS Principles*. New York: The Free Press.

Buzzell, R. D. and Sultan, R. (1975) 'Market Share—A Key to Profitability'. *Harvard Business Review*, January–February: 135–144.

Cohen, K. J. and Cyert, R. M. (1973) 'Strategy Formulation, Implementation, and Monitoring'. *Journal of Business*, **46**: 349–367.

Collier, D. W. (1977) 'Measuring the Performance of R&D Departments'. *Research Management* (March): 30–34.

Cooper, A. C. & Schendel, D. (1976) 'Strategic Responses to Technological Threats'. *Business Horizons*, **19**: 61–69.

Cooper, R. G. (1984) 'The Performance Impact of Product Innovation Strategies'. *European Journal of Marketing*, **18**(5): 5–54.

Craig, S. C. and Douglas, S. P. (1982) 'Strategic Factors Associated with Market and Financial Performance'. *Quarterly Review of Economics and Business*, **22**(2): 101–112.

Douglas, S. P. and Craig, C. S. (1983) 'Examining Performance of US Multinationals in Foreign Markets'. *Journal of International Business Studies* (Winter): 51–62.

Douglas, S. P. and Rhee, D. K. (1989) 'Examining Generic Competitive Strategy Types in US and European Markets'. *Journal of International Business Studies* (Fall): 437–463.

Farris, P. W. and Buzzell, R. D. (1979) 'Why Advertising and Promotional Costs Vary: Some Cross-Sectional Analyses'. *Journal of Marketing* (Fall): 112–122.

Franko, L. G. (1976) *The European Multinationals*. Stamford, CT: Greylock.

Freeman, C. (1974) *The Economics of Innovation*. Manchester, UK: Penguin.

Galbraith, C. and Schendel, D. (1983) 'An Empirical Analysis of Strategy Types'. *Strategic Management Journal*, **4**: 153–173.

Haas, E. A. (1987) 'Breakthrough Manufacturing'. *Harvard Business Review* (March–April): 75–81.

Hambrick, D. C. (1983a) 'Some Tests of the Effectiveness and Functional Attributes of Miles and Snow's Strategic Types'. *Academy of Management Journal*, **26**(1): 5–26.

Hambrick, D. C. (1983b) 'An Empirical Typology of Mature Industrial-Product Environments'. *Academy of Management Journal*, **26**(2): 213–230.

Hofer, C. W. (1975) 'Toward a Contingency Theory of Business Strategy'. *Academy of Management Journal*, **18**: 784–810.

Hopkins, D. S. (1980) 'New Product Winners and Losers'. Conference Board Report No. 773.

Jauch, L. R., Osborn R. N. and Glueck, W. F. (1980) 'Short Term Financial Success in Large Business Organizations'. *Strategic Management Journal*, **1**: 49–63.

Kamm, J. K. (1987) *An Integrative Approach to Managing Innovation*. Lexington, MA: D.C. Heath.

Keegan, W. J. (1969) 'Multinational Product Planning: Strategic Alternatives'. *Journal of Marketing*, **33**: 58–62.

Lenz, R. T. (1981) 'Determinants of Organizational Performance: An Interdisciplinary Review'. *Strategic Management Journal*, **2**: 131–154.

Mazzolini, R. (1975) 'European Corporate Strategies'. *Columbia Journal of World Business*, (Spring): 98–108.

McDaniel, S. W. and Kolari, J. W. (1987) 'Marketing Strategy Implications of the Miles and Snow Strategic Typology'. *Journal of Marketing*, **51**: 19–39.

Miles, R. E. and Snow, C. C. (1978) *Organizational Strategy, Structure and Process*. New York: McGraw-Hill.

Miller, A. (1988) 'A Taxonomy of Technological Settings, with Related Strategies and Performance Levels'. *Strategic Management Journal*, **9**: 239–254.

Miller, D. (1986) 'Configurations of Strategy and Structure: Towards a Synthesis'. *Strategic Management Journal*, **7**: 233–249.

Miller, D. and Friesen, P. H. (1983) 'Strategy-Making and Environment: The Third Link'. *Strategic Management Journal*, **4**: 221–235.

Moore, W. L. and Tushman, M. L. (1982) 'Managing Innovation Over the Product Life Cycle'. In M. L. Tushman and W. L. Moore, editors, *Readings in the Management of Innovations*. Boston, MA: Pitman.

Nelson, R. and Winter, S. (1977) 'In search of a Useful Theory of Innovation'. *Research Policy*, **6**: 36–76.

Paine, F. T. and Anderson, C. R. (1977) 'Contingencies Affecting Strategy Formulation and Effectiveness: An Empirical Study'. *Journal of Management Studies*, **14**: 147–158.

Pavitt, K. (1969) 'Technological Innovation in European Industry: The Need for a World Perspective'. *Long Range Planning*, December: 8–13.

Pavitt, K. (1982) 'R&D, Patenting and Innovative Activities'. *Research Policy*, **11**: 33–51.

Porter, M. E. (1980) *Competitive Strategy*. New York: Free Press.

Punj, G. and Stewart, D. W. (1983) 'Cluster Analysis in Marketing Research: Review and Suggestions for Application'. *Journal of Marketing Research*, **20**(5): 134–148.

Ravenscraft, D. J. (1983) 'Structure-Profit Relationships at the Line of Business and Industry Level'. *Review of Economics and Statistics*, **65**: 22–31.

Robinson, W. T. and Fornell, C. (1985) 'Sources of Market Pioneer Advantages in Consumer Goods Industries'. *Journal of Marketing Research*, **22**(8): 305–317.

Robinson, W. T. (1988) 'Sources of Market Pioneer Advantages: The Case of Industrial Goods Industries'. *Journal of Marketing Research*, **25**(2): 87–94.

Schlaifer, R. (1974) *AQD Manual for Statistical Programs*. Cambridge, MA: Harvard University.

Schlaifer, R. (1981) *User's Guide to the AQD Collection*. Cambridge, MA: Harvard University.

Schneeweis, T. (1983) 'Determinants of Profitability: An International Perspective'. *Management International Review*, **23**(2): 15–21.

Thietart, R. A. and Vivas, R. (1984) 'An Empirical Investigation of Success Strategies for Businesses Along the Product Life Cycle'. *Management Science*, **32**: 645–659.

Urban, G. L., Carter, T., Gaskin, S. and Mucha, Z. (1983) 'Market Share Rewards to Pioneering Brands: An Empirical Analysis and Strategic Implications'. *Management Science*, **32**(6): 645–659.

Venkatraman, N. and Ramanujam, V. (1986) 'Measurement of Business Performance in Strategy Research: A Comparison of Approaches'. *Academy of Management Review*, **11**: 801–814.

APPENDIX. DEFINITIONS OF SELECTED PIMS DATABASE VARIABLES DESCRIBING COMPONENTS OF CONCEPTUAL FRAMEWORK

Innovation orientation

Order of market entry

At the time the business first entered the market whether it was:

(i) one of the pioneers in first developing such products or services (=3);
(ii) an early follower of the pioneer(s) in a still growing, dynamic market (=2); or
(iii) a later entrant into a more established market situation (=1).

New products

A new product is described as follows in the PIMS database: '... may either replace existing products or be added to the product line within the served market. They differ from improvements and product-line extensions in that they are characterized by one of the following: relatively long gestation periods, major changes to the manufacturing facilities, separate promotional budgets, or separate product management' (*PIMS Data Manual*, January 1978, pp. 3–8). Two variables exist in the database describing new products:

(i) *Relative new products*: percent of total sales accounted for by products introduced by a business during the three previous years minus percent of total sales accounted for by products introduced during the three previous years averaged for the three largest competitors.
(ii) *Percent new products*: percent of total sales accounted for by products introduced by a business during the three previous years.

R&D expenditures

All expenses incurred to

(i) improve the existing products or services of a business or to develop new products or services, including improvements in packaging as well as product design, features and functions; or
(ii) improve the efficiency of manufacturing and distribution processes.

Environment

Market growth/product life cycle stage

(i) *Served market size/growth*: A number of variables indicating short-run, and inflation-adjusted growth rate of total sales in the served market and industry: (a) served market size (SR); (b) industry long-term growth; (c) real market growth.

(ii) *Product life cycle stage*: introductory stage—primary demand for product just starting to grow; products or services still unfamiliar to many potential users (=1); growth stage—demand growing at 10% or more annually in real terms; technology or competitive structure still changing (=2); maturity stage—products or services familiar to vast majority of prospective users; technology and competitive structure reasonably stable (=3); decline stage—products viewed as commodities; weaker competitors beginning to exit (=4).

Competition

(i) *Industry concentration*: the percentage of sales in the industry accounted for by the four largest competitors.

(ii) *Served market concentration*: the percentage of sales in the served market accounted for by the four largest businesses competing in the served market.

(iii) *Industry instability*: the average percentage difference in the growth rate of the industry from an exponential trend.

(iv) *Served market instability*: the average percentage difference in the growth rate of the served market from an exponential trend.

(v) *Total market share instability*: the sum of the market share changes for the focal business and the three largest competitors.

(vi) *Competitors' percent new products*: the simple average of the percentage of total sales accounted for by products introduced during the three preceding years for the three largest competitors.

Innovative opportunity

(i) *Patents and trade secrets*: Whether a business benefits to a significant degree from patents, trade secrets, or other proprietary methods of production or operation pertaining to products or services (Yes = 1; No = 0).

(ii) *Development time for new products/services*: for a business and its major competitors what the typical time lag is between the beginning of development effort for a new product and market introduction. Less than 1 year = (1); 1–2 years (=2); 2–5 years (=3); more than 5 years (=4); little or no new-product development (=5).

(iii) *Frequency of product changes*: whether it is the typical practice for the business to change all or part of the line of products or services offered 'Annually' (=1), 'Seasonally' (=2), 'Periodically, but at intervals longer than one year' (=3) or with 'No regular, periodic pattern of change' (=4).

Performance

Financial measures

(i) *Gross margin*: value added less manufacturing and distribution expense and depreciation as a proportion of net sales.

(ii) *Return on investment*: net income over the book value of average investment (ROI).

(iii) *Cash flow on investment*: cash flow from ongoing operations over the book value of average investment (CFOI).

(iv) *Cash flow from operations*: cash flow from ongoing operations as a proportion of revenue.

Marketing measures

(i) *Market share*: sales of a business as a percentage of the served market (MS).
(ii) *Relative market share*: sales of a business over the sales of the three largest competitors in the served market (RMS).
(iii) *Market share growth*: growth rate of market for a business over relevant time period (MSC).

22

A Performance Comparison of Continental and National Businesses in Europe

George S. Yip

The creation of the single European market ('Europe 1992') is widely expected to enhance the performance of European businesses as they expand from a national to a continental scope. Sources of benefit include a combination of economies of scale, the elimination of trade barriers and the free movement of people, products and currency. At the macroeconomic level, Cecchini (1988) and others have made quantified estimates of the potential benefits to the European Community (EC) as a whole. At the business level many writers (e.g., McGee, 1989; Quelch and Buzzell, 1989; Vandermerwe 1989; and Yip, 1989) have proposed ways for companies to take advantage of the coming changes.

The US continental market is often cited as the forerunner of the benefits to come, as the EC moves towards a 'United States of Europe'. We might, therefore, look to the US experience of a continental market as a guide, while recognizing that Europe will not be as homogeneous as the United States in the foreseeable future. In the United States, businesses are usually eager to expand to a continental market scope in order to enjoy economies of scale. In Europe today, however, the benefits of a continental market scope may be more than offset by the drawbacks. These drawbacks stem from co-ordination costs, the cost of crossing national frontiers and the loss of customer focus. Therefore, based on these barriers, it is hypothesized that, today, continental businesses in the *United States* should be *more* profitable than regional (i.e., sub-national) businesses, while continental businesses in *Europe* should be *less* profitable than regional or national businesses.

THEORY

The expected performance difference concerns single businesses with a continental scope (a 'continental business'), and not a collection of national businesses within a single multinational company (a 'multinational business'). The difference can be subtle, but is crucial for this study. A European *continental* business operates across national boun-

Reprinted with permission from *International Marketing Review*, Vol. 8, No. 2, pp. 31–39

daries, including some transfer of raw materials and final products. An example is Mercedes's automotive business. Mercedes sells primarily standardized products, designs the products in Germany, does most of its manufacturing in Stuttgart, and uses a common market positioning. A European *multinational* business operates primarily within national frontiers and is more a collection of businesses than one single business. An example is Unilever's frozen food business. Unilever sells different products in each country (British steak and kidney pie is not a big hit elsewhere), manufactures locally, and uses different brand names (e.g., Birds Eye in Britain and Iglo in Germany) and advertising approaches. Many European businesses have been shifting from the multinational mode to the continental mode. For example, both Ford of Europe and Nestlé, in some of their businesses, have been increasing the level of sharing and integration across their country units. They key distinction is that a continental business faces more opportunities, than does a multinational business, to enjoy the scale benefits of broad geographic scope. At the same time continental businesses face the disadvantages of operating across national boundaries as described below.

BENEFITS OF BROADER GEOGRAPHIC SCOPE

A broader geographic scope helps to achieve a minimum efficient scale and reduce overhead costs. In many industries, the minimum efficient scale may be achievable only with a very large share of one country-market or a smaller share of many country-markets. Furthermore, *unit* overhead costs, such as research and marketing, can decrease indefinitely as sales expand. Offsetting these potential declines are potential increases in co-ordination costs (the classic argument in economic theory for a U-shaped cost curve). Cecchini (1988) and others expect economies of scale to be a major source of gain in EC 1992, although this view is questioned by Geroski (1989).

DRAWBACKS OF MULTICOUNTRY GEOGRAPHIC SCOPE

There are several potential drawbacks to a multicountry geographic scope.

Co-ordination costs

Expansion in geographic scope across national boundaries is particularly likely to increase co-ordination costs. The simple need to set up separate legal entities is one example of a major source of complexity. Furthermore the legal entity usually requires some management structure to be responsible for it. Thus a multicountry business will typically require more layers of management than a national business covering the same geographic size of territory. Other sources of increased co-ordination cost include inter-country differences in technical standards, language, culture and operating practices.

Crossing national frontiers

A business that operates across national frontiers incurs trade barrier costs, transportation costs, and inventory costs. Tariff and non-tariff trade barriers hurt performance by reducing sales and/or increasing costs. Transportation is slower and more costly because of border checks. Also, the combination of trade barriers and transportation difficulties may require a multicountry business to maintain a higher level of inventory relative to sales than would a single-country business.

Losing customer focus

Multicountry businesses are also less likely to be able to customize for buyer needs than single-country businesses. Comparing Western Europe with the United States, differences in customer tastes are probably greater among European regions than among US regions. For example, many US food companies are now struggling to cope with the diversity of the distinctive European national eating habits (*Wall Street Journal*, 1990). A multicountry business in Europe will, therefore, have to offer many more product versions or else provide lesser customer satisfaction than single-country competitors. Offering additional product lines incurs most cost, while providing less customer satisfaction can only hurt sales.

EFFECTS OF EUROPE 1992

The creation of the single European market will reduce each of the above drawbacks for multicountry businesses operating in the European Community. Europe 1992 will reduce some of the co-ordination drawbacks, particularly in the area of differences in technical standards. Europe 1992 will also greatly reduce frontier-related drawbacks. Tariff and non-tariff barriers will eventually be totally eliminated. Similarly, there will be no frontier controls slowing transportation, nor will there any longer be the need to maintain national, as opposed to continental, inventory locations.

METHODOLOGY

Based on the preceding literature, the hypotheses in this study are that, today, continental businesses in the United States should be more profitable than regional (i.e., subnational) businesses, while continental businesses in *Europe* should be less profitable than regional or national businesses.

Database

Testing these hypotheses requires data on the performance of both continental and regional/national businesses in both Europe and the United States. The PIMS Program database of the Strategic Planning Institute provides this type of information (Buzzell and Gale, 1987). Although this database has been criticized by a number of researchers (e.g., Anderson and Paine, 1978), strong rejoinders have been provided in Phillips, Chang and Buzzell (1983), and Marshall and Buzzell (1990). In the latter study, the authors conducted a validation test against the US Federal Trade Commission's Line of

Business database. Their study found that strategic relationships held true across the FTC and PIMS databases, even though these two data sets were collected with very different methods, i.e., any weaknesses in data collection were not serious enough to affect the quality of the data. In addition, Douglas and Craig (1983) found comparable results, using PIMS data, in explaining the performance of US and European national businesses.

Sample

The PIMS SP14 database contains over 2,000 manufacturing businesses, of which 342 are European. Data are reported for four-year periods, with all time-dependent data provided as four-year averages. Yearly data are also available, but sacrificing the stability of four-year data would have been worthwhile only if there were a measure of change in the market scope of a business, but analysis of the data indicated otherwise. Therefore, this study used businesses in four-year average periods ranging from 1972–1975 to 1984–1987.

Measure of performance

Strategy researchers often use return-on-investment (ROI) as the measure of performance. Finance researchers increasingly criticize profitability, particularly ROI, as a measure of strategic performance, preferring increases in shareholder value (Fisher and McGowan, 1983). Jacobson (1987) reviewed these criticisms but argued that the high level of correlation between stock prices and ROI mitigates many of the problems. Also, business unit managers can affect ROI much more easily than they can affect the stock price of their company.

PERFORMANCE COMPARISONS

By scope of served market

Table 1 compares the ROI of the businesses serving the different types of markets defined by PIMS. The *Common Market* businesses have a much lower four-year average ROI than businesses with other market scopes. Interestingly, the next lowest group of businesses is those with *Regional within US and/or Canada* as their market scope. So not only do the Common Market businesses perform worse than national businesses in Europe, but they perform worse than regional businesses in North America.

Test of hypotheses

The hypotheses were tested by setting up two pairs of comparisons: continental versus national/regional in Europe and in North America. Figure 1 groups the *United Kingdom* and *Regional within Europe* markets into one category of *National/Regional within Europe* businesses. As hypothesized, the *Common Market* businesses have a much lower average

Table 1. Profitability by market scope 1972–1987

Market	Four-year averages ROI%	n
Common Market	13.4	89
Regional within Europe	21.9	109
United Kingdom	24.5	144
Entire United States	23.1	869
All of Canada	23.2	65
US and Canada	25.6	312
Regional within US and/or Canada	18.5	272
Other	22.4	187

ROI (13.4%) than do the *National/Regional within Europe* businesses (23.4%). The proportionate difference is 75%, which is statistically significant at the 0.01 level. In contrast, in the North American pair, the difference is reversed, again as hypothesized. The businesses serving the *United States and Canada* have a much higher average ROI than those serving *Regional within US and/or Canada* markets (statistically significant at the 0.01 level). The results are similar when either *Entire United States* or *All of Canada* is substituted for *US and Canada*.

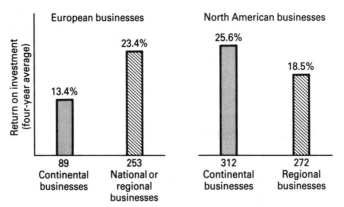

Figure 1. Profitability of European and North American Businesses. *Note*: differences between each pair are statistically significant at the 0.01 level.

The findings are consistent with some studies of individual industries. For example, Baden, Nicolaides and Stopford (1987) found that national businesses in the European major appliance industry were more profitable than continental businesses. The performance gap is particularly important as more companies shift toward a continental rather than national definition of their markets. Even the food industry, a bastion of national differences, is moving in that direction (Segal-Horn and McGee, 1989).

Also interesting is that the national/regional businesses in Europe performed better than the regional businesses in North America (23.4% versus 18%) (see Figure 1). This implies that inter-region differences are greater in Europe than in North America, i.e., regional businesses can more successfully exploit these differences in Europe.

Furthermore, the US and Canada businesses have slightly
Entire United States or *All of Canada* businesses, rather than l(
suggesting that scale economies are more important than na
America (with interesting implications for the recent US–Cana

The above results confirm that market scope affects profitai
Europe and North America. It seems that in Europe the multin
tal market scope causes negative effects that are often not oi
geographic scale. The explanation of this difference lies in the e. ... current
barriers. Removal of the co-ordination and cross-border costs is ...ιy to increase the
profitability of continental businesses in Europe. Furthermore, the performance difference between Europe and North America suggests the possible size of gain from Europe
1992. Because there are greater differences among regions in Europe than in North
America, the North American example should be viewed as the maximum potential
gain.

Time and age effects

The performance differences were about the same in different time periods. Nor did the
differences in the ages of the businesses account for the performance differences. The
entire sample of businesses averaged about 25 years from the first year of commercial
sales. The Europe-wide sample was only about three years younger on average than the
national/regional sample. Indeed, none of these businesses, were startups, which are not
part of this database. We do not know, however, how long the Europe-wide businesses
have defined their market continentally. The poor performance may, therefore, be
attributable in part to the expansion of their market definition. Nevertheless, even that
conclusion would be significant in itself.

By type of business

An obvious question is whether the difference between European continental and
national served markets might be primarily due to differences in the type of business in
each group. Table 2 shows the mix of business types for each of the two main pairs of
served markets, and provides ANOVA results for the percentage of variance accounted
for by business mix (row) and market definition (column) effects. There are some
apparent business mix effects—in some cases there are differences in both the average
ROI and the number of observations between national and continental served markets
for a type of business. The ANOVA results overstate the importance of the business mix
effects (which account for about two-thirds of the variance in the European analysis (see
Table 2), because there are a larger number of categories of business types than there are
market types. The effect of business type is much less in the North American sample,
accounting for only 25% of the variance in ROI. That the effect of business type is
limited is evidenced by making comparison *within* business types. ROI is *lower* for
Common Market for five of the six business types (recognizing the very small sample sizes
in some cases). In contrast, ROI is *higher* for *US and Canada* for five of the six business
types, and fractionally lower in the sixth.

Table 2. Profitability by type of business and type of served market

| | Europe | | | | | North America | | | | |
Type of business	(1) National/Regional within Europe (incl. UK) ROI	n	(2) Common Market ROI	n	Significance of difference between (1) and (2)	(3) Regional within US and/or Canada ROI	n	(4) All of US and Canada ROI	n	Significance of difference between (3) and (4)
Consumer durable products	20.0%	15	(0.2%)	6	n.s.	21.7%	31	25.1%	50	n.s.
Consumer non-durable products	27.3%	96	26.9%	10	n.s.	13.4%	49	19.5%	18	n.s.
Capital goods	10.0%	13	15.9%	5	n.s.	16.9%	14	23.1%	89	n.s.
Raw or semi-finished materials	15.3%	27	8.6%	28	n.s.	23.9%	72	23.4%	27	n.s.
Components for incorporation into finished products	22.5%	56	17.4%	31	n.s.	17.8%	64	26.3%	97	**
Supplies or other consumable products	26.0%	46	7.3%	9	**	14.5%	42	35.5%	31	***
		253		89			272		312	

ANOVA—Europe	% of variance	ANOVA—North America	% of variance
Row effects	67.1% F—1.84**	Row effects	25.4% F—2.98***
Column effects	38.3% X^2—6.60 n.s.	Column effects	44.0% X^2—18.43***
Interaction effects	(5.4%)	Interaction effects	30.6%
	100.0%		100.0%

*, ** and *** indicate significance at 0.10, 0.05 and 0.01 levels.

LIMITATIONS

The results need to be tempered by recognizing possible limitations of the data:

- Businesses are characterized as continental on one dimension only—their market scope. PIMS does not record whether these businesses are continental along other dimensions. Performance differences may be influenced by these other unobserved characteristics.
- Of the three possible reasons for the poorer performance of European continental businesses, only one, the cost of crossing national frontiers, is directly supported by PIMS data. The European continental businesses did, indeed, incur higher inventory costs than the regional businesses (but there are no measures of trade barrier or transportation costs). The other reasons, higher co-ordination costs and loss of customer focus, were not supported. The continental businesses' costs relative to competitors were no higher than those of the regional businesses; nor did they have a broader range of customer types relative to competitors than did the regional businesses.
- For the national businesses in Europe, the identity of the specific countries is not known. But even businesses in the United Kingdom, one of the least profitable European countries in this period (OECD, 1988, Table 7.2, p. 74), were more profitable than the European continental businesses.
- Accounting differences may affect the findings, although the data are reported as ratios, and the PIMS staff work with companies to fit the PIMS definitions.

FUTURE RESEARCH

Future research might include pairwise case studies of truly continental versus multinational companies to understand how their market scope affects their strategy, costs and performance. In addition, theories of globalization stress the importance of the management dimension in terms of cross-country co-ordination and integration for multicountry businesses (Barlett and Ghoshal, 1987). We can only infer that inadequate management processes contributed to the poor performance of the continental businesses. Future research should attempt to measure both the strategy and management dimension.

IMPLICATIONS FOR MANAGERS

The advent of the single European market should offer opportunities for significant performance improvement for businesses that are already continental in market scope. Many national businesses are planning to become continental, and many multinational businesses are planning to integrate their independent subsidiaries. But these currently national and multinational businesses are likely to incur performance problems, as they expand their market scope. The legislative changes creating the single market will make it easier to serve a Europewide market, but probably not fast enough to prevent serious difficulties. This study should alert managers to some of the potential problems and opportunities.

The findings of this article argue against the quixotic assumption that continental expansion will bring immediate financial reward; instead this market should be treated as an investment with a longer-term payback. Furthermore, the findings here should warn managers to expect continental expansion to bring short-term deterioration in financial performance, and not to be discouraged in their strategy. Managers may choose to wait for the single market effects to become stronger before expanding to a continental market scope, and hope to minimize the performance losses indicated by this study. On the other hand, managers need to be beware of pre-emptive action by competitors who may move faster or who may seek to consolidate an already continental market scope.

Finally, managers should remember that, even after 1992, there will continue to be far greater cultural, linguistic and economic differences among European regions than among North American regions. The possible affiliation of Eastern European countries would add to this diversity. Fully integrated continental strategies will continue to be elusive.

ACKNOWLEDGEMENTS

The author thanks the Strategic Planning Institute for making available the data used in this study, and Paul Chussil of the Strategic Planning Institute for his assistance in conducting the computer-related work. The author also thanks Robert D. Buzzell of the Harvard Business School, Keith J. Roberts of the Strategic Planning Institute, and Johny K. Johansson and Alan Roshwalb of Georgetown University, and four anonymous referees for their comments.

REFERENCES

Anderson, C. R. and Paine, F. T. (1978) 'PIMS: A Reexamination'. *Academy of Management Review*, July: 602–612.

Baden, F. C., Nicolaides, P. and Stopford, J. (1987) 'National or Global? The Study of Company Strategies and the European Market for Major Appliances'. Working Paper, *Centre for Business Strategy*, London Business School.

Bartlett, C. A. and Ghoshal, S. (1987) 'Managing Across Borders: New Strategic Requirements'. *Sloan Management Review* (Summer): 7–17.

Buzzell, R. D. and Gale, B. T. (1987) *The PIMS Principles: Linking Strategy to Performance*. Free Press, New York.

Cecchini, P. (1988) *The European Challenge: 1992, The Benefits of a Single Market*. Wildwood House, England.

Douglas, S. P. and Craig, C. S. (1983) 'Examining Performance of US Multinationals in Foreign Markets'. *Journal of International Business Studies* (Winter): 51–57.

Fisher, F. M. and McGowan, J. J. (1983) 'On the Issue of Accounting Rates of Return to Infer Monopoly Profits'. *American Economic Review* (March): 82–97.

Geroski, P. (1989) 'On Diversity and Scale—Extant Firms and Extinct Goods?'. *Sloan Management Review* (Fall): 75–83.

Jacobson, R. (1987) 'The Validity of ROI as a Measure of Business Performance'. *American Economic Review* (June): 470–478.

Marshall, C. T. and Buzzell, R. D. (1990) 'PIMS and the FTC Line of Business Data: A Comparison'. *Strategic Management Journal*, **11**: 269–282.

McGee, J. F. (1989) '1992: Moves Americans Must Make'. *Harvard Business Review* (May–June): 78–84.

OECD (1988) 'Historical Statistics 1960–1986'. *OECD Economic Outlook*. Paris, France.

Phillips, L. W., Chang, D. and Buzzell, R. D. (1983) 'Product Quality, Cost Position and Business Performance: A Test of Some Key Hypotheses'. *Journal of Marketing*, **47**(Spring): 26–43.

Quelch, J. A. and Buzzell, R. D. (1989) 'Marketing Moves through EC Crossroads', *Sloan Management Review* (Fall): 63–74.

Segal-Horn, S. and McGee, J. (1989) 'Strategies to Cope with Retailer Buying Power'. In Pellegrini and Reddy (eds), *Retail and Marketing Channels*, Routledge, London.

Vandermerve, S. (1989) 'From Fragmentation to Integration: A Conceptual Pan-European Marketing Formula', *European Management Journal*, **7**(3): 267–272.

Wall Street Journal (1990) 'Slim Pickings: US Firms Find Protectionism, Divergent National Tastes Impede Sales in Europe'. May 15, p.A2.

Yip, G. S. (1989) 'Global Strategy . . . In a World of Nations?'. *Sloan Management Review*, **31**(1): 29–41.

23

Bridging National and Global Marketing Strategies Through Regional Operations

John D. Daniels

INTRODUCTION

International standardization versus differentiation has long been a major issue in international marketing. Greater standardization of such things as products and promotion will usually result in some global cost savings which, in turn, enable a company to gain competitive price advantages.

However, these savings must be weighed against any losses in effectiveness of country level operations, such as lost sales by avoiding local adaptations. Standardization versus differentiation is related to the issue of centralization versus decentralization of marketing management. This is because global standardization is much more likely to occur when decisions are made at some level above the heads of the country level operations.

Both standardization versus differentiation and centralization versus decentralization may be thought of as continuums, with companies' operations lying somewhere between the extremes. Many international companies have traditionally handled their worldwide operations as a loose confederation of highly autonomous country units, thus their operations lay closer to the differentiated and decentralization ends of the continuums.

An indication that a more standardized and centralized operation will be increasingly appropriate comes from the possible levelling of cultures as improvements in transportation, communications, and incomes bring people from different countries in closer contact with each other, thus resulting in a greater acceptance of a global standard (Child, 1981).

A second indication is the reduction of trade barriers through various arrangements, thus allowing for more centralized production of standardized products to minimize costs.

A third indication is increased international competition brought about by more rapidly maturing products and greater openness of economies. This necessitates greater global means of fighting the competition.

Finally, centralized control of foreign operations is increasingly feasible as headquarters managers gain more international experience and confidence, as standardization reduces the complexities for which they are responsible, and as innovations in

Reprinted with permission from *International Marketing Review*, Vol. 4, Autumn, pp. 29–44 transportation and communications allow them to evaluate and correct foreign performance more easily.

But how can firms move along the two continuums? One possibility is to move regionally before moving globally.

In fact many of the factors discussed above, such as the increasing contact among people from different countries, may occur more on a regional than on a worldwide basis. Although there is substantial evidence that more companies have been establishing regional headquarters, the recent studies of them have been limited primarily to their reasons for choosing specific locations for their offices (Dunning and Norman, 1979; Heenan, 1979; Van Den Bulcke and Van Pachterbeke, 1984) and to their organizational structures (Daniels, 1986). Some earlier studies described the functions of regional offices; however, these addressed neither the question of standardization versus differentiation nor centralization versus decentralization of marketing programmes through regionalization (Williams, 1967; *Business International*, 1974).

The objectives of this study are to describe the numerous purposes for regional coordination and integration of business, to characterize the problems brought about by organizing on a regional basis, and to depict some successful methods which firms have used to help achieve the purposes for which they were established.

Overall the aim of this study has been to uncover a variety of approaches so that practitioners can consider alternatives which might otherwise not be apparent to them. As such, there is no attempt to build a model in terms of which practices will likely work for which types of companies; nevertheless, key company characteristics are described when they appear to influence the results of the practices that have been undertaken.

METHOD

The study was conducted in Europe because of that region's significance in world business, the large number of countries in relation to the region's size, the movements to remove regional restrictions on trade and factor mobility, and the area's high development of transportation and communications. These latter factors are important in that they should foster a trend toward greater homogeneity of consumer demands and business methods.

Information was collected directly from 16 companies (all from among the 75 largest US industrial firms) or 42% of the 75 which indicated in their annual reports the existence of some type of office responsible for a group of countries in Europe. Representatives of each were interviewed at European regional offices in Belgium, France, Switzerland, the United Kingdom, or West Germany. Because of being promised anonymity, respondents were quite candid in expressing their opinions and assessments of situations. Each firm also completed a questionnaire to indicate the location of line and/or staff responsibility, including where activities are undertaken as well as where approval lies for their conduct.

The companies vary substantially by product lines, and they fall into 14 different *Forbes* product classifications.[1] They also vary in terms of product diversity. Eight of

[1] The *Forbes* lists of January 3 1983 place 13 firms uniquely into only one product group and three into more than one. The categories and number of participants are as follows: aerospace and defence, 1; auto suppliers, 1; autos and trucks, 3; branded foods, 1; computers, 2; construction equipment, 1; electrical equipment, 1; energy, 3; household goods, 1; multicompany, 1; nonferrous metals, 1; soft drinks, 1; steel, 1; and tobacco, 1.

them have a dominant product group, segmenting only this one within their annual reports. In each case this product group accounts for nearly all the worldwide sales, ranging from 74 to 91%. All the other extreme are four diversified participants for which no segmented product group comprises more than 30% of total sales. Between these two extremes are another four participants which have been formed by fairly recent mergers of two large firms that now comprise relatively autonomous divisions.

The participants' foreign revenues range from 12 to 74% of their total sales, with an average of 31%. Half depend on their European region for more than 50% of their foreign sales, but the overall range is from less than five to more than 90% of foreign sales.

The typical respondent, although beginning European sales by exporting from the US, is now most dependent on local manufacturing as a means of tapping the European market. This typical respondent exports and licences to Europe as well. There are a few exceptions: two companies whose US exports to Europe exceed the output from their European facilities, one that depends almost entirely on franchise, and another that relies on a combination of exports to and co-production in Europe.

Most of the participants (13 of 16) had well established European operations prior to the inception of the EEC. Three of these operations go back as far as the nineteenth century; and another nine were established before World War II.

In spite of their early development of European operations, all the participants have only recently moved toward regional integration or co-ordination of their various European activities. None established European regional offices prior to the end of World War II. Only four did so before the creation of the EEC; and two did not organize theirs until the 1980s.

PURPOSES OF A REGIONAL APPROACH

Although the following discussion focuses on marketing, interviews elicited a much broader array of reasons for taking a regional operating approach. Although many of these have symbiotic relationships to marketing, such as regional financial management efficiencies which may free resources for marketing activities, I have used my own discretion in not discussing those activities that I think are peripheral to the major marketing questions.

Table 1 summarizes the regional activities within four main categories, along with the marketing purposes of each and the conditions under which the activities may be best undertaken. In examining this exhibit or the discussion that follows, the reader should bear in mind that no respondent mentioned all of these activities, simply because each faces somewhat different internal and external constraints on their operations.

POOLING OF RESOURCES

Resources from a group of company operations, especially if these operations are small, may often be combined to increase efficiency or to provide services which might otherwise not be available to those country level operations.

Table 1. Marketing use of regional operations

Means	Positive effects on marketing	Best used when
1. Pooling of resources	• Better sales and regulatory forecasting • Lower product development cost • Increase the variety of products available	• High interdependence within region • Product development costs high • History of dividing sales territory by country
2. Gaining synergy among operations	• Better external relations with government customers • Marketing concessions in one country to help sales elsewhere • Gain easier access to corporate clients • Retarding growth of large competitors • Preventing costly internal competition	• Government sales are high portion of total sales • Sales to same customers in more than one country • One product group has success with client; another group wishes to make sales • Competition is from regional or global firms • Nearly homogeneous products
3. Standardization	• Faster transference of successful campaigns • Lower priced products	• County characteristics are similar • Sales are not to government buyers • Scale of production will reduce prices substantially • Price is most important competitive weapon
4. Control of the strategic product thrust	• Balance between national and global product needs	• Product life cycles vary among countries • Company's strategy depends on introduction of new products

Forecasting

An area which elicited considerable response in terms of consolidation is in the monitoring of region-wide economic conditions.

Interdependence has made it difficult for country marketing managers to forecast sales without knowing what is happening within the region as a whole; consequently, the regional office prepares and disseminates information and projections in order to prevent costly duplication among the subsidiaries within the various countries. Another area is in monitoring region-wide regulatory developments, particularly those affecting product standards and advertising restrictions. This monitoring is at two levels, EC directives which affect marketing programmes in member countries and country regulations which may harbinger changes elsewhere.

The pooling of resources for the improvement of sales and regulatory forecasting has a greater advantage for Europe than for other regions of the world. Most of the countries' major trading partners are also within the region; thus there is high economic inter-dependence. Furthermore, the possibility of facing region-wide regulations is much more likely where there is a strong and successful trading group, such as the European Community.

Product development costs

Although some of the participants have subsidiaries with a long history of product development autonomy, they have found it advantageous to use a regional operation to pool product development activities.

Although such a pooling might bring cost savings for almost any type of product, the need to effect savings is much greater when it is both difficult to re-coup the development costs and when the failure to do so would cause a substantial financial hardship to the firm. This can occur when the firm depends on few products or product models, when there is a long lead time before a new product is introduced, and when the cost of a specific product development is high relative to the firm's revenues.

Product variety

Related to the above discussion is the expansion of sales territory in order to justify the expenditures necessary to introduce certain products.

For example, the branded foods participant uses regional operations as a means of broadening the product lines available for country units to sell. Branded foods are still produced and sold much more on a country-by-country basis than many of the other products represented in this study. This is because of such factors as the greater need to adapt products to meet local requirements, the availability of capital equipment which optimizes on a smaller scale, and the higher transportation expense as a percentage of production costs.

This participant found that when country units made product decisions based only on what they could sell within their own country markets, many new product opportunities which required larger scale process technology production were rejected. The regional group assesses regional demand so that, if large enough, it will push for co-operative arrangements among national units.

GAINING SYNERGY

Government sales

A regional operation may enhance common or leveraged associations with various external publics.

The consolidation of public relations is especially important when government pur-chases are a high potential portion of sales. This is because government purchasers may consider a firm's economic impact on the country when deciding whether or not to purchase from it. Since companies may operate various subsidiaries within and among the European countries and since the names and products of these subsidiaries may not be readily associated with each other, governmental authorities may not be aware of the important total impact the company is making in the area. A unified external relations approach can result in a more complete message than if each subsidiary, each product group, or each country group were to take on the duties separately.

International customers

Frequently a supplier sells to subsidiaries of the same multinational firm in more than one country.

By combining efforts, the supplier may be able to deal with regional or global decision makers, rather than those within each country, and determine what types of concessions will be needed to gain region-wide sales. Such regional control also helps assure that one group does not make concessions, such as price decreases or product modifications, which are inconsistent with other corporate entities within the area.

Take auto supplies for example. Some of the same customers are in both the UK and West Germany. The supplier may be willing to make certain concessions only if it is assumed of getting business in both countries. Similarly what the supplier's subsidiary does in the UK may have considerable effect on what the supplier's subsidiary is expected to do in West Germany. Only through some type of cross national control can the firm achieve the necessary synergy.

Product group synergy

Another approach is to gain leverage among customers when two or more product groups are operating in the area, particularly if the product groups have strong bases in different countries.

One company, for example, has two product divisions operating independently of each other in Europe. The separation was brought about by the technical differences in production, the fact that one of the divisions came about as the result of an acquisition, and the need to market the products to different purchasers. The company discovered that, although the major sales were generally to different customers, there was some effort by each of the product divisions to make direct sales to the same corporate clients.

One of the divisions might have long-standing relationships with top corporate officials in the client firm; whereas, the other division might be trying unsuccessfully to sell and communicate ideas or directives elsewhere. For instance, the head of the regional group for a consumer products firm said. 'The advertisement programmes which are successful for us in the UK will usually work in Ireland or vice versa. By watching a group of countries over time, we get a feel for these types of similarities. When a new advertisement programme works in the UK, we can immediately let the people in Ireland know about the campaign. It would be impractical for each country to communicate directly with every other country in order to exchange experiences.'

Lower-priced products

In addition to the growing standardization of certain activities within the region because of resource pooling and the sharing of information, the regional group has sometimes helped to bring about greater product standardization. The cost-saving possibilities and pursuant competitive price advantages for regional or global products have received considerable attention in recent years (e.g., Levitt, 1983).

Surprisingly, though, only two firms indicated that they have established a regional structure to bring about greater product similarity among the countries. This should not imply a lack of product uniformity by other participants. Rather, some have a long-standing practice of selling the same variations of products in all the countries, although selling more of one variation in some countries than in others—such as a higher percentage of large sized tyres in West Germany and a higher percentage of small sized tyres in Italy.

This situation has generally not been altered through the regional management of the operations; however, there has been a slight decrease in the need to make small adaptations to fit the needs of different countries' markets.

Some other participants have always conducted their product R&D in the US, allowing foreign subsidiaries to make only those adaptations which are both relatively inexpensive and necessary. They have reported no change to this approach.

That not all firms have moved substantially toward regional product standardization is due in great part to national legal and quasi-legal variations. These affect some products differently than others. The differences have come about partly because of varying opinions on how best to protect consumers. Food products, particularly, face different regulations concerning purity, testing, additives, labelling of contents, and use of preservatives. High external costs are another cause. Automobiles face quasi-legal barriers, such as the high cost to move traffic to the right in Britain or to the left on the Continent, which necessitate steering wheel modification.

Still another cause is the desire by governments to protect their own employment. If sales are to governments, it is more difficult to gain cost savings from long production runs even when the product can be highly standardized. In this respect participants which make such diverse products as office equipment, pipes, and defence equipment all indicated strong pressures to produce locally and sell through a highly independent domestic marketing operation, a situation which seems little changed from that reported some years ago (Doz, 1980). Companies are trying to overcome these pressures through various off-set trade arrangements, but complications persist. At the other extreme from the various products mentioned above are commercial aircraft, which face little in the way of national differences in regulations.

Marketing programmes may need to be altered substantially even though the product can be standardized. This is a particular at a much lower level of the organization. By establishing a regional group, the company can now determine where high level contacts exist so that introductions can be made for representatives of the other product group, thereby bypassing the bottlenecks which had previously existed at a lower tier in the client organization.

International competitors

Although much has been written about the possibility of attacking a competitor's strong market as a means of thwarting that competitor elsewhere (Hout, Porter, and Rudden, 1982), only one respondent indicated that this was a reason for moving toward a regional management approach.

Previously the firm's control span between multiple European operations and head-quarters in the US was so broad that too much autonomy was given at times to the subsidiaries within the region. Subsidiaries concentrated on strengthening their pos-itions in relation to local competitors, leading them occasionally into new but related products. The resources to attack local competitors could have been better spent by concentrating on efforts to attack global competitors, even though this would not have served the immediate best interests of some of the countries or even the region as a whole.

With the smaller control span brought about by a European regional structure, there is better co-ordination of objectives and strategies between headquarters and the region. The regional group, in turn, can better assure that the country activities are compatible with the global efforts.

Preventing internal competition

At one extreme, a firm may be able to centralize production in order to reduce costs.

At the other extreme, a firm may have products, such as soft drinks, where transpor-tation costs are too high to justify taking advantage of the scale of economy in produc-tion. In between these two extremes are products for which multiple production locations are necessary, but for which there is product arbitrage potential when costs move differently among the countries, due to such factors as inflation rates or an exchange rate re-alignment. There is also the potential for price competition among these subsidiaries when there is excess capacity.

Several firms have instituted regional control in order to prevent sales shifts which could be disruptive to their production facilities. In one case, an auto supplier has simply centralized control so that adjustments in the profit margins compensate for cost changes among countries. In as much as this form has rather compelling reasons to maintain multiple production locations for similar products, this price centralization policy is apt to serve as a rather long-term solution to its product arbitrage problem.

For another firm (construction equipment), the product arbitrage problem is shorter term since it is in process of a shift over several years toward having different countries produce different parts of its product line. The company has taken a regional policy to span its transition and long-term needs by establishing a sales headquarters in a 'neutral' country. This headquarters is independent of the manufacturing operations and is responsible for all marketing duties in the region.

STANDARDIZATION

Transference of information

Because of the growing market homogeneity within the region, most respondents report a growing ability to predict success or failure for a group of countries on the basis of their experience in one of them.

Regional management can quickly monitor the results from all the countries in the area problem for companies which must incur high promotion and distribution costs relative to manufacturing costs. The soft drink manufacturer, for example, has low product development costs because of product uniformity and few new products; however, it has little opportunity to cut costs through standardization of other marketing functions which constitute the bulk of expenses. The promotion and distribution needs are so different among some of the countries that marketing programmes must be customized for each.

For instance, the company could find no satisfactory bottler and distributor in Belgium so it manufactures and distributes on its own. In France, a national distributor is large enough to develop most of its own marketing campaigns, but its low distribution intensity means that the soft drink firm must develop marketing programmes to increase the number of places carrying its products. In Norway, the company concentrates on national marketing campaigns and the management of marketing uniformity because it must use many small bottlers and distributors who lack experience in widescale marketing and in co-operative campaigns. In the UK, one bottler with intensive national coverage has low sales per outlet; therefore, the soft drink firm must concentrate on increased through-put by developing advertising and point of purchase promotion.

STRATEGIC PRODUCT THRUST

Balance national and global needs

There is a need sometimes to re-allocate among product lines within countries as part of a firm's strategic product thrust.

Yet, for various reasons, a company may have different product portfolios within each country. The idea for making investments to expand the product portfolio will often originate at the country level; however, divestment possibilities seldom do (Boddewyn, 1983). After all, the evaluation and employment of managers at the sudsidiary depend on growth; thus, these subsidiary managers have little compulsion to propose divestments. One participant has recognized this by putting its regional headquarters in charge of deciding what new efforts will replace old ones, a practice which the company calls 'pediatrics' and 'geriatrics'. They can effectively balance the global need to develop a mixture of growth and mature products with differences in shapes or stages among local product cycles.

SOME PROBLEMS AND APPROACHES

Autonomy—the problem

Peter Drucker recently gave a hypothetical example of a US multinational's German subsidiary which had been producing most of the company's brands for 70 years in the German market (Flanigan, 1985).

If the parents were to try to get that subsidiary to move to a cross-national production strategy, he said 'the union will fight you, the state government will fight you and you will be attacked by the German newspapers'. Although this prognosis is perhaps a bit exaggerated, this study confirmed that autonomy, once given, is difficult to take away.

Acquisitions

Acquisitions, especially those that retained the existing local management, were particularly singled out in discussions.

This was not surprising in as much as many researchers have reported control problems for this type of expansion strategy (e.g., Mazzolini, 1974). One participant, for example, has been able to use its regional office only to give staff support, and it attributes this inability of moving more aggressively toward a regional strategy to the fact that its European expansion has been primarily by acquiring small firms in which the former owners have stayed on as managers.

A way to avoid the problem of acquisitions is, of course, to avoid acquisitions themselves. There is some evidence that this is taking place. Other research has noted both a decline by US firms in the use of acquisitions as an international expansion strategy (Daniels and Patil, 1980) and US firms' higher failure rate through acquisitions than through other forms of foreign penetration (Kitching, 1974). The difficulty of controlling acquisitions within a unified cross-national strategy may, thus, be an additional explanation of those earlier findings. Yet foreign expansion into the US continues largely by means of acquisition. This anomaly may be due in part to the more positive experience of non-US firms because of their acquisition of subsidiaries with better performance records than those acquired by US firms (Kitching). It may also be due, because of the largeness of the US market, to the operation of foreign subsidiaries in the US as entities independent from an integrated global strategy (Drake and Caudill, 1981).

Joint ventures

Joint ventures were also singled out, especially those with government partners.

The need to satisfy more than one partner's interests may necessitate considerable compromise and decentralization (Holton, 1981), demands not easily compatible with the needs of a cross-nationally integrated strategy. Government partners may additionally seek macro-political or economic objectives from the ventures, such as attainment of full employment which might run counter to such cost efficiency measures as production rationalization.

Private partners pose less of a problem since objectives are generally more compatible. Furthermore, there is more of a tendency to allow one partner to control the operation rather than to attempt to share the control. This has been shown to increase the likelihood of joint venture success (Killing, 1982). This may also allow one partner to pursue cross national strategies while the other attains a narrower range of objectives from the venture.

Whereas US firms may be avoiding the control problem of acquisitions by decreasing their propensity to acquire, they have been increasing their shared ownership arrangements, particularly with governments, in spite of the control problems (e.g., 'Global Report', 1986). The findings of this study, therefore, lead to some intriguing questions. Will an increase in ownership sharing make global marketing strategies more difficult to attain? Will firms which insist on wholly owned operations have a long term advantage over those which have embraced shared ownership as a quicker means of accessing some foreign markets?

Rival and dominant operations

Rival operations have been most difficult to bring into a regional strategy when two conditions have existed.

The first is when large operations existed in more than one European country prior to the realization that European trade barriers would come down. The second is a history of product development autonomy at the country level. For instance, where these conditions existed, it has been very difficult to pool resources or standardize end products.

Where these conditions did not exist, such as within firms whose country level managers have depended on US corporate headquarters to decide which innovations would be transferred to them almost intact, it has been relatively easy to move toward a regional thrust. The evidence from this study, though admittedly from a small sample, is indicative that it is easier for an ethnocentric firm to move to a cross-national strategy than for a polycentric firm.

Although late European entrants have had to struggle less with the problem of assimilating rival and autonomous country units, they have had to contend with a different potential problem—the dominance by one country. In six of the cases studied, the regional offices and the companies' largest European facilities are almost one and the same in as much as they are attached to each other. They are sometimes legally separate, but not observably separate as personnel from the largest country operation take over some duties for the entire region.

This attachment of the regional office to the largest facility was observed in a study of regional offices in Belgium as well (Van Den Bulcke and Van Pachterbeke, 1984). There are obvious cost saving efficiencies in this type of attachment; however, the influence by management in one country sometimes retards the ability to develop and market products for the region as a whole because national interests are put ahead of regional ones.

It may be inevitable that operations in one country are much larger than elsewhere simply because of production advantages or market location. It may also be advantageous to follow a concentration strategy in international expansion, i.e., develop a very strong involvement and competitive position in one country before going on to another (Ayal and Zif, 1979). These situations will lead to a short or long term presence which is much higher in one country than in others. In order to offset the potential of excess influence by one country, some firms have located their regional offices away from the largest facilities and have staffed them with personnel from various locations. This approach may increase the regional office's operating costs; however it may enhance the development and implementation of a region-wide strategy.

One participant used a 'carrot' approach to fuse two very independent country units, offering them funds to develop a product aimed at a target segment that neither had been servicing. The stipulation was that these funds would be available only if the two groups would work together under the auspice of a regional headquarters in which they would share responsibility. After this initial effort, the regional group gradually gained authority over joint efforts to develop new models which were more similar between the countries than in the past. Greater similarity followed for other aspects of the marketing programme.

Autonomy is particularly difficult to break down when country managers do not understand or are not committed to practices which do not have visible payoffs to their own operations. One way to deal with this is to rotate managers among countries (Eldstrom and Galbraith, 1977; Pazy and Zeira, 1983).

The regional office facilitates this in two ways. The first is through planned rotation of managers into regional offices. Managers from the European subsidiaries are rotated in so that they gain line or staff experience with a cross-national perspective in the process of being promoted within their own country operations. American managers are transferred into the regional offices so that they can gain similar experiences in route to greater responsibilities at the corporate headquarters, an especially important concern among those firms which are reluctant to transfer American managers to the country units because of policies to staff as nearly as possible with host country nationals.

LACK OF CLEAR CUT RESPONSIBILITY

Diversity among respondents

If one is looking for a pattern among these 16 participants in order to conclude whether their European regional offices should have line versus staff responsibilities or both, whether they should have duties for all or just a part of their firms' products, whether they should have single or multifunctional responsibilities, and what countries should be in the region, the study offers little guidance.

The respondents' approaches simply vary too widely, yet a few patterns did emerge. The variation in approaches is a finding consistent with earlier studies (Gross, 1981; Dunning and Norman, 1979).

There is a slightly greater tendency among the dominant product firms to give duties to the regional office which are related to all the companies' products (five out of eight) than in merged firms (one out of four) or multiproduct firms (one out of four). The major conditions which induce firms to consolidate their product groups are a belief that smaller businesses would otherwise not be able to support the types of services offered by the regional office and that the product groups are sufficiently related in some manner to attain some synergy. Without these conditions, firms have either established separate regional offices for each product group or have refrained from taking a regional approach for one or more of their businesses. Other contributing factors for these firms were (1) a fear that the growth of smaller product groups would suffer because of their subservience to major businesses and (2) that there has been little history of co-operation among the product divisions domestically.

The geographic coverage is particularly diverse. Nine of the participants include an area larger than Europe within their regional offices' domain, primarily the addition of Africa and/or the Middle East. This additional inclusion is due in part to Middle Eastern or African operations which are too small to support their own regional operations or to report directly back to headquarters. It is also due to the carry-over of business relationships which existed in the colonial era, such as the development of African subsidiaries by the firms' subsidiaries in the UK and France as well as to special trading arrangements which have developed because of historical ties. At the other extreme are two firms which include only part of Europe within the regional office which was studied. In one case Iberia is included within the Latin American region instead, because of cultural and language affinity. In another case Europe is divided into four regions in order to give more representation at high levels of headquarters.

Changes of time

The above discussion highlights differences among the participants at one point in time.

There have also been differences for each of the participants over time. They have sometimes taken on additional obligations. They have also sometimes handed over duties to managers in the subsidiaries or at headquarters. These changes may come about for several reasons.

For instance, one firm's regional office has no responsibility for licensing arrangements but does oversee production and sales of company owned facilities; therefore, a change in operating form (e.g., from licensing to equity) alters the coverage of the office. Another regional office lost jurisdiction over two European countries when the operations in those countries became large enough to support their own staff personnel. In another case, a regional group moved from staff to line supervision in response to a growth in area-wide production integration. Finally, one participant's move to global component sourcing has shifted production control away from the region and to US headquarters.

The variability in regional office responsibilities creates organizational stress. Autonomy may have to be relinquished. New reporting relationships bring uncertainty and power shifts. One of the biggest challenges to the success of cross-national marketing strategies is, therefore, the development of an environment which will allow for changes in what is controlled where.

Ambiguities

Most respondents, whether with line or staff obligations, indicated that the intervention of a unit between corporate headquarters and the country operations creates ambiguities on the location of decision authority. This is true regardless of what is stated explicitly in corporate directives. Subsidiary managers resent what they perceive as delays when decision making passes through an additional organizational tier before reaching headquarters.

As a regional office attempts to impose an area viewpoint on an organization which has been structured to give another emphasis, for example a history of strong marketing autonomy by country level matters, there are bound to be problems for regional managers. They must reorient the thinking of both their superiors and their subordinates. Regional managers feel they must rely more on the force of personality than they had previously been accustomed in order to influence either country level or headquarters level decisions. They are unsure of how to achieve the right balance between control on one hand and too much bureaucracy on the other.

Since most of the regional offices are relatively new, it is not surprising that there are concerns about regional managers' lack of experience. This has sometimes resulted in a hesitancy to seize authority from managers who have traditionally had it and for mergers to cede responsibility to individuals who lack a long 'track record'. Different means of staffing the regional office offers no panacea. This is a problem, however, which will be healed with time.

In fact there was fairly general agreement that the existence of a regional office is facilitating the development of managers who will work well within the dynamic environment as firms move to a more global type of strategy. This is due in part to the previously discussed organizational development brought about by planned rotation of personnel. In addition it is felt that the creation of some higher level and higher paying positions than exist within the country subsidiaries creates a positive enticement for very highly qualified Europeans to join and stay with the companies. Because of various personal and corporate barriers to their entry into high level headquarters positions in the US, they might otherwise gravitate to European competitors where their upward mobility is less stymied.

REGIONAL VERSUS GLOBAL CONTROL

The advantages and problems which have been discussed for operating a regional office would generally apply for global control as well. Therefore, if control is to be vested above the country management level, why not bypass a regional office and have corporate headquarters handle the functions instead?

Since this study relied on the responses of managers only in firms with regional operations and, therein, only the managers within the regional offices, it is understandable that respondents all thought positively of the regional concept. Had we interviewed firms without regional offices, we might have found nevertheless that some were following regional strategies. How? There has been recent evidence that firms are stopping short of making complete structural changes, choosing instead to adopt a variety of mechanisms to bring functional, area, and product perspectives together (Bartlett, 1983; Pitts and Daniels, 1984).

Number and size of units

A recurring response was that there are simply 'too many' subsidiaries in the European region or that they are 'too small' to report directly to headquarters in the United States.

One of the companies, for example, has investments in 120 countries; therefore, it is necessary to divide responsibilities somehow so that there are not 120 different subsidiaries reporting to the same manager at headquarters. A regional separation for reporting purposes is as logical as any other that could be used.

In some companies there is also a philosophy of trying to maintain profit or sales centres of similar size at the same level in the corporate hierarchy. One of the companies, for instance, has investments in 14 European countries; however, the amount of business done in each is small compared with units in the US or some other areas of the world. By consolidating the region, the country units are pushed down one tier in the corporate structure, thus better approximating the importance to the overall corporation.

Closeness

As part of their overall control process, companies use corporate visits and frequent verbal communications as means to determine what is happening at the operating level and to decide with rapid two-way communications what practices should be undertaken.

This can be done entirely with personnel from the US headquarters; however, most respondents feel that it would be more costly and cumbersome than with personnel from a regional office. The location of a cross-national management group within Europe saves the time necessary to make connections across the Atlantic, prevents efficiency losses due to 'jet lag', and overcomes some of the problems of telephoning through different time zones.

Respondents feel that the regional headquarters is especially important for trouble-shooting. Not only can managers be on the spot quickly (and alert when they get there), they are more prone to get on the spot than if they had to come all the way from the US. The alternative, of course, is to give more autonomy to the country units; however, this would be contrary to the objectives for which cross-national control is sought.

There was also some feeling that since the European regional offices are usually staffed in large part with personnel who have come from the subsidiaries within Europe, there is a better commitment from the subsidiaries to comply with the regional offices' dictates and suggestions. This is because they are perceived as knowing the local needs and constraints.

In terms of size, European operations are large enough to justify additional staff and important enough so that corporate headquarters wants to assure that operations are watched closely by a higher tier of managers. In addition the respondents tend to sell a large variety of their total corporate products within Europe. Furthermore, they produce most of them there rather than exporting them to Europe. These factors create a need for the infusion of different production and marketing technology into the European region, thus there is a justification and need for close supervision at higher than the country level of operations.

Integration

The above factors make the European area more suitable for regional control than some other areas where US firms have international business operations.

In addition the vast transportation system that connects the European countries, the density of multiple operations which the participants have there, and the relative freedom of trade restrictions in the area all make this a natural area for regional control. This is not the case for most of the companies' other operations elsewhere in the world.

These other operations tend to fall into one of three types and are less suitable to the regional control which is used in Europe.

The first situation is when foreign operations are small and highly dispersed, too much so to justify the expense of a regional office presence. In these situations, there is a tendency for operations to have almost total autonomy because they are too small and too distant from corporate headquarters for anyone to be greatly concerned.

The second situation is where the foreign operations are used to source supplies for the US, especially in the Far East. There is a need to control these from headquarters, rather than on a regional basis, because of the integration with domestic operations.

The third type is when there is little trade within the region, such as within Latin America, because of trade restrictions and transportation problems. Here the regional efforts are apt to be handled from a base in the US which has little in the way of integrative responsibility.

Relationship to global

One of the enigmas of regional operations is what effect they will have on global strategies.

Here there was considerable disagreement. As discussed earlier, some of the respondents have global control over some functions but regional over others, most commonly global production and regional marketing. In this type of situation there is compatibility between the regional and global strategic thrusts, albeit control problems of bringing the two types of responsibilities together. Some other firms see no need to move to a global strategy because of the types of scale economies, customers, competitors, etc. which are a part of their operating environment. If their assessment is correct, then the regional concept poses no particular problem to a global strategy.

For some respondents, however, the regional headquarters is viewed as a transitory step in route to global strategy and control. The question here is whether regionalism will speed up or retard the globalism.

For two of the companies, regional production rationalization is already a part of a global rationalization by product. For example, one of the participants manufactures small tractors in four European countries, with each country producing different models. One third of these are exported to the US which, in turn, supplies larger tractors to Europe.

For some other companies, the future is not nearly so clear-cut. The personnel within their European centres have come largely from the European subsidiary offices. Although there is some rotation of personnel between the regional office and corporate headquarters, none of the participants has a planned interchange between the European and other regions of the world. There was some concern, therefore, that it may be difficult to wrest control in the future from a fairly autonomous region, the same way that it has been difficult to move away from country operating independence.

CONCLUSIONS

Advantages of internationally standardized versus differentiated marketing programmes have been explicitly delineated by various researchers.

So have the advantages of controlling international marketing programmes at the corporate versus subsidiary level. Most would agree that firms are moving more toward standardization and toward centralization, the major advantage of the former being cost savings and the latter, the unlikely occurrence of standardization without centralization. Little emphasis has been given to the thorny problem of how to move along the continuums from one extreme to another.

This study found that the move toward centralization on a regional basis has been premised on broader objectives than standardization, for example, to facilitate sales and regulatory forecasting, to increase the likelihood of gaining government sales, to facilitate marketing synergy among different countries and product lines, to share marketing experiences, to divide markets, to increase the number of products sold in the area, and to manage the strategic product portfolio on a country-by-country basis.

This study also found that, even when standardization was an overwhelmingly important objective, there are formidable barriers to bringing this about. At the forefront are national differences and managerial autonomy. These barriers have not been, nor are they likely to be, overcome easily. Until they are, we will see companies operating with hybrid degrees of standardization and centralization, varying these by product, by area of the world and over time. We shall also see different pragmatic attempts to move faster and more smoothly toward implementation of global marketing strategies. The regional approach, through its varied permutations, is one such pragmatic effort which should endure.

Although the regional approach should endure, its degree of importance will depend in great degree on what happens to trade barriers on both a global and a regional basis. The strongest scenario for European regional office growth would be a continued reduction of trade barriers within the area while simultaneously facing more restrictions in trade with the rest of the world.

REFERENCES

Ayal, I. and Zif, J. (1979) 'Marketing Expansion Strategies in Multinational Marketing'. *Journal of Marketing*, **43**(22): 84–94.

Bartlett, C. A. (1983) 'MNCs: Get Off the Reorganization Merry-Go-Round'. *Harvard Business Review*, **61**(2): 138–146.

Boddewyn, J. J. (1983) 'Foreign and Domestic Divestment and Investment Decisions: Like or Unlike?' *Journal of International Business Studies*, **14**(3): 23–35.

Business International (1974), *European Regional Headquarters Study*. Geneva: Business International Research Report.

Child, J. D. (1981) 'Culture, Contingency and Capitalism in the Cross National Study of Organizations'. In *Research in Organizational Behavior*, L. L. Cummings and B. M. Staw, eds. Greenwich, Conn.: JAI Publishers.

Daniels, J. D. (1986) 'European Regional Management by Large U.S. Multinational Firms'. *Management International Review*, **26**(2): 27–42.

Daniels, J. D. and Patil, S. (1980) 'US Foreign Acquisitions: An Endangered Species?' *Management International Review*, **20**(2): 25–34.

Doz, Y. L. (1980), 'Strategic Management in Multinational Companies'. *Sloan Management Review*, **21**(2): 27–46.

Drake, R. L. and Caudill, L. M. (1981) 'Management of the Large Multinational: Trends and Future Challenges'. *Business Horizons*, **20**(3): 83–91.

Dunning, J. and Norman, G. (1979) *Factors Influencing the Location of Offices of Multinational Enterprises in the UK*. London: Economists Advisory Group Limited.

Edstrom, A. and Galbraith, J. R. (1977) 'Alternative Policies for International Transfers of Managers'. *Administrative Science Quarterly*, **22**(2): 248–261.

Flanigan, J. (1985) ' "Multinational", As We Know It, Is Obsolete', *Forbes*, **136**(5): 30–32.

'Global Report: International Joint Ventures Are On the Increase'. (1986) *Advanced Materials & Processes*, **3**(86): 7–11.

Gross, R. (1981) 'Regional Offices in Multinational Enterprise: The Latin American Case'. *Management International Review*, **22**(2): 48–56.

Heenan, D. A. (1979) 'The Regional Headquarters Decision: A Comparative Analysis'. *Academy of Management Journal*, **22**(2): 410–415.

Holton, R. H. (1981) 'Making International Joint Ventures Work', in *The Management of Headquarters-Subsidiary Relationships in Multinational Corporations*, Otterbeck, L. ed. London: Cower, Aldershot, 255–267.

Hout, T., Porter, M. E. and Rudden, E. (1982) 'How Global Companies Win Out'. *Harvard Business Review*, **60**(5): 98–108.

Killing, J. P. (1982) 'How to Make a Global Joint Venture Work'. *Harvard Business Review*, **60**(3): 120–127.

Kitching, J. (1974) 'Winning and Losing With European Acquisitions'. *Harvard Business Review*, **52**(2): 124–136.

Levitt, T. (1983) 'The Globalization of Markets'. *Harvard Business Review*, **61**(3): 92–102.

Mazzolini, R. (1974) 'European Transnational Concentration'. *California Management Review*, **16**(3): 43–51.

Pazy, A. and Zeira, Y. (1983) 'Training Parent-Country Professionals in Host Country Organizations'. *Academy of Management Review*, **8**(2): 262–272.

Van Den Bulcke, Van Pachterbeke, D. and M-A. (1984) *European Headquarters of American Multinational Enterprises in Brussels and Belgium*, Brussels: ICHEC.

Williams, C. R. (1967) 'Regional Management Overseas'. *Harvard Business Review*, **45**(1): 87–91.

24

Implementing a Pan-European Marketing Strategy

Gianluigi Guido

By the end of 1992, the European Community's plan for the completion of the Internal Market is intended to remove the physical, fiscal, and technical barriers to trade among the 12 EC nations and this should create a single European market of more than 320 million consumers, in which goods, services, labour, and capital can move freely across borders.

If the goal of the Single Market is achieved, it will have important consequences for international marketing. The fragmentation of the European marketing, which arises from the existence of national regulations and non-tariff barriers, has discouraged companies from operating in more than one country. Now, each firm will be challenged to examine its own individual opportunities for its products or services.

Firms cannot opt out of Europe: even if their managements decide not to trade with the new EC, they will still face increased competition in their home markets. Questions about the most appropriate set of product, pricing, promotion, and distribution policies across Europe and the desirability or competence to execute a common market programme will no longer be limited to a few multinationals but must be considered by small- and medium-sized firms as well.

A MARKETING BACKGROUND

1. The Euro-market

Opportunities and competition

To be successful in a changing Europe, firms will need to take an active approach. Two elements are necessary to understand the nature of this integration process.[1]

(1) The eventual gain is supply led: the improvements in economic performances (e.g.,

Reprinted with permission from *Long Range Planning*, Vol. 24, No. 5, pp. 23–33 growth, increased demand, etc.) are contingent on the company's ability to decrease prices as a result of lower costs and increased competition.

(2) Not all the benefits will be immediate or direct (such as those coming from the elimination of frontier controls), but most of them will require the company's action or reorganization (such as those which will be derived from enlarged competition, economies of scale, reallocation of resources, and increased innovation and dynamism).

The threat of a more competitive market has driven companies towards a wave of consolidation, both via mergers and acquisitions (for gaining control of distribution channels, spreading administrative overhead costs on larger bases, etc.), and through strategic alliances (for exchanging technologies, participating in joint ventures, and so on). This process of concentration could be very harmful, especially for those firms in which large scale economies exist but which have been impeded by national regulations (such as banks, telecommunications, publishing, transportation, construction, etc.) which now could be acquired or forced out of business.

Exporting vs marketing

The greatest changes will probably take place in exporting rather than in marketing.[2] When the barriers come down, small companies previously not organized for complex export trade will be able to move across borders with the same ease as multinationals. Previously unknown competitors will suddenly be contending with established market leaders.

The 1992 plan will enable every EC company to sell in one Community country what it can legally sell in another. The acceptability of another country's goods is subject only to two principles: they must not be considered injurious to health or safety anywhere in the Community and they must not be offered for sale in a manner that could mislead. An imported product cannot be banned merely because it has been manufactured to different standards.[3]

Exporting will become simpler and easier, but marketing will still face difficulties. The main problem will be how to serve 320 million different people, each with their own individual needs and desires: most with increasing wealth, autonomy, and sophistication.

2. The euro-consumer

The myth of euro-consumers

The problem is that governments cannot make markets. If they could, there would be no need for marketing and 320 million consumers would be suddenly transformed into 320 million euro-clones, 'drinking euro-beer, eating euro-wurst and watching euro-soaps on euro-satellite television'.[4]

The 1992 plan focuses on supply rather than demand: its reforms will make the single national markets more accessible, not more identical. The forces pushing toward a pan-European market are very powerful: the increasing wealth and mobility of European consumers (favoured by the relaxed immigration controls), the accelerating flow of information across borders, the introduction of new products to children or where local preferences are not well-established, and the publicity surrounding 1992 itself all promote globalization: *but,* the persistence of local tastes and preferences (and regulations) still prevents most companies from marketing their products on a genuine pan-European basis even after the elimination of formal trade barriers.

With the increase in competition, the marketers' responsibilities will increase. They will not decrease in spite of fewer and simpler rules. Even if the EC's plan allows businesses to sell their home-market products abroad or to sell standardized merchandise throughout the Community, this does not mean that customers will want to buy it.

A possible scenario

Treating Europe as one market, with marketing standardization and homegenization of products, is an over-simplification, not applicable to every kind of product.[5] Nevertheless, marketers must plan a strategy to take advantage of the possible scale economies. Those who wait and do not search for the opportunities of a pan-European approach, might easily fall prey to competitors.

Three connected studies spanning 25 years [6–8] suggest that standardization of marketing varies in relation to the kinds of products. In the case of industrial goods and consumer durables (such as cameras, toasters, watches, portable radios) standardization is fairly advanced. For consumer non-durables, such as foods, standardization is difficult to achieve, primarily because of differences in national tastes and habits.

According to a research developed in Geneva by S. Vandermerwe and M. L'Huillier,[9] the European market is reasonably homogeneous in its needs and purchasing behaviour if divided in six major 'clusters'. These clusters have similar demographic and economic characteristics cutting across cultural and national boundaries (see Figure 1). Managers working in those markets should be able to reach larger cross-cultural euro-consumers' groups without marketing separately. The clusters indicate important changes in market configuration, but within each there are segments that share life-style and specific psychographic needs.

Three distinct segments, or social groups, have been identified by a recent study conducted by Eurisko, an Italian research company, as being ready for the pan-European approach (as reported by Martin[10] and Kossoff[11]). First, young people who have unified tastes, across Europe, in music, sports, and cultural activities. Second, the trend-setters and social climbers who are the wealthier and more educated Europeans, who tend to value independence, refuse consumer stereotypes, and appreciate exclusive products.[12] Third, Europe's business people who are a rich target audience of 6 million. They are about 40 years old, regularly travel abroad and have a taste for luxury goods: they are almost exclusively male.

In conclusion, a standardization of marketing is possible in a pan-European approach, restricted by the type of product, in relation to market clusters and (above all) to common market segmentation. This will require suppliers with the necessary capabilities to conduct marketing research studies in different countries simultaneously and make adjustments in the companies' marketing and operating strategies. For each of the

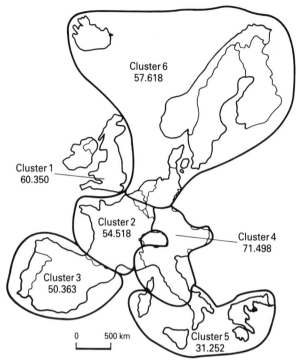

Figure 1. The Six Clusters and Their Population (1990, in 000s of People). (*Source*: World Bank and CartaGen DemoGraphics.)

specific areas of the marketing mix (the four Ps: product, pricing, promotion, and place), marketers should be aware of the changes brought about by the EC programme, the threats which could affect their planning, and the possible strategic options within their reach (see Table 1).

Table 1. 1992: the implications of pan-European marketing

	Effects of the EC plan	Does say	Does not say
Consumers	The 1992 reforms focus on supply rather than demand	Firms should act to exploit market economies	Consumers will change considerably their preferences
Market	Exporting will become easier, not marketing	National markets will become more accessible	National markets will become more identical
Marketing strategies	Standardization of marketing is possible depending on: • Type of products • Geographic clusters • Market segmentation	Marketers should be aware of: • Changes • Threats • Strategic options in each area of marketing mix	Marketers are able to wait before exploiting the opportunities of the EC plan

MARKETING MIX STRATEGIES

1. Product strategies (Table 2)

National product standards

Different product standards, testing and certification procedures are of crucial importance in linking technological development and competitiveness in the marketplace.
Their harmonization in 1992 should be beneficial to producers by avoiding costly
product modifications and lengthy delays due to varying country-specific requirements.
To comply with them, a product would need to be built in different versions, thus
creating all kinds of inefficiencies and a lack of economies of scale. The results are: more
complex manufacturing processes (assemblers have to be trained to make the product in
different ways with increasing possibilities for errors), loss of purchasing power, and
bigger storage facilities.

Table 2. Product strategies in Europe of 1992

Changes affecting strategies	Threats to marketers' planning	Management's strategic options
Harmonization in product standards, testing, and certification procedures	Untimeliness of directives	Consolidate production
	Rules of origin	Obtain marketing economies
	Local content rules	Shift from brand to benefit segmentation
Common patenting and branding	Differences in marketing research	Shift from brand to market management
Consumer protection regulations		Extend strong national brand names in the EC
Harmonization in packaging, labelling and processing requirements		Standardize packaging and labelling where possible

Some European standards organizations (namely CEN, CENELEC, and ETSI, for
non-electrical, electrotechnical, and telecommunications products, respectively) are
working to satisfy the guidelines listed in the EC directives. Originally the European
Commission tried to do all the standardization work in Brussels, a lengthy and difficult
process that could be overcome only with the approach of 'mutual recognition' and
'minimal harmonization'. Now, the EC directives only call for groups of products to
meet 'essential requirements', relating to possible risks to health, safety, and the environment.[13]

Part of these directives, still in their pre-ratification phase, are creating some concern
in companies both for their untimeliness, given the fact that marketers have to plan in
advance their product strategies,[14] and for their eventual protectionist effect. Especially
for non-EC manufacturers, insurmountable obstacles could be raised by issues such as
'rules of origin' and 'local content'. The former require that the major production
process be made within the EC: the latter calls for a minimum European content, for
avoiding stiff tariffs or for bidding in government procurement. The EC might also

engage in restrictive tactics by refusing to recognize product tests administered abroad, forcing foreign producers to ship goods to the EC at a high expense for testing and sale without the assurance of certification.

Strategic options

Once the market inconsistencies relating to national standards are eliminated, firms should focus on the development of product strategies in order to gain production and marketing economies. Changes in product policies should occur especially among small- and medium-sized companies and in R&D. As a whole, EC countries spend as much on product research as Japan, but because research is carried out on a national basis, much of it is duplicated. This compartmentalization becomes disruptive, particularly for some industries like electronics where technological innovation is very quick and the revenues of the market share should be earned to invest in the next round of innovation.

Two directional changes will influence product strategies.[15] The first one is a shift from brand to benefit segmentation. This means that, in the future, products will be sold putting more emphasis on their benefits rather than their attributes.[16] The second subsequent shift will be from brand management to market management. People do not have a need for brands. They have a need for products that solve problems. Organizing marketing by consumer use rather than brands should also avoid internal competition among brands.[17]

Euro-products and euro-brands

As more uniform technical requirements and standards are introduced, firms are likely to try to develop pan-European products and brands. The result will most probably be a smaller total number of new products introduced in the 12 nations, but each with more potentiality because they are targeted at a wider population. Newly identified pan-European consumer segments, and the acquisitions of strong national brand names able to be extended throughout Europe, should allow common positioning and package design to become more widespread in the Community. In spite of the difficulty of an acceptable common name in different languages, more basic goods should be introduced as euro-brands across the Community.

Handling new products could present difficult exercises, at least during the run up to 1993. The difficulties of assessing profitable areas to enter and the potential response of customers could be increased by marketing research, traditionally less developed in Europe, which would not provide homogeneous information about products. For example, lemon-flavoured Perrier could be classified as mineral water in France, but a soft-drink in Italy.

Patenting and branding of the products will also become more significant, because a successful product will potentially have a larger market than before. The Community is currently seeking a 'single patent system', which could lower registering and reviewing patent costs in Europe (presently very high), and unifying the law on protection of trademarks and copyrights which is particularly significant in combating piracy in computer software.

Packaging

New technologies could also affect the packaging and distribution process and improve production. The 'aseptic packaging system', for example, should increase shelf-life and allow products to be shipped over greater distances. This development, in combination with the principle of 'mutual recognition' should permit consolidated production. For instance, a large yogurt supplier with plants in France, where its product is not pasteurized today, and in other EC countries, where it is pasteurized, could centralize its production in one place to serve all markets.

Reduced barriers will push towards standardized packaging and labelling, providing considerable savings, but marketers will still face the problem of capturing the imagination of 12 different nations. This issue is particularly important for US marketers approaching the European market.[18] The aesthetic standards are higher in Europe, so that if US products use the blatant approach which sells in their domestic market, they will be perceived as low-quality in Europe. For example, flagging on packaging is considered cheap.

In addition, while in the US the brand name is one of the most important elements in packaging because of faith in well-known brands, in Europe the brand name is not emphasized. Europeans are interested in products with natural purity, and packaging should address these needs. Finally, packaging has to look as if it is aimed at the individual. This can be found in the European private label products, which are often packaged in a more attractive, imaginative, and appealing way than the generic, low-priced look of US private label products.

2. Pricing strategies (Table 3)

Price competition

According to global marketers, consumers are becoming more similar in their tastes and accept globally standardized products—even if they are not exactly what they want—provided that the price is low enough and the quality good. There is no research amongst EC consumers to check this assumption (of course, people everywhere desire the most value for the least expenditure, but this does not imply global marketing). From a study conducted by Boddewyn, Soehl, and Picard[19] among US international firms who had business in the EC, the majority answered that price was not a competitive tool: the crucial discriminant was quality. The same researchers noticed, nevertheless, that price competition in the EC had increased since 1973.

This trend should be intensified after 1992. According to Quelch and Buzzell,[20] price will be pushed downward for the following reasons:

(1) decreased costs;
(2) the opening up of public procurement contracts to broader competition;
(3) foreign investment that increases production capacity;
(4) more rigorous enforcement of competition policy; and
(5) the general intensified competition generated by the 1992 reforms. Increases in primary demand flowing from the reforms will only partly offset this trend.

Table 3. Pricing strategies in Europe of 1992

Changes affecting strategies	Threats to marketers' planning	Management's strategic options
More competitive environment Withdrawal of restrictions to foreign products Antimonopoly measures Widening up of the public procurement market	Parallel importing Different taxation of goods Less freedom in setting transfer prices	Exploit different excise and value-added taxes Understand price elasticity of consumer demand Launch new higher-margin products Introduce visible low-cost brand names Promote efficiency

The European Commission has estimated that the prices of goods and services through-out the EC could decrease as much as 8.3%. In industries as ubiquitous as chemicals, consumer goods, and financial services, there are enormous price differentials for the same product among countries that cannot be justified by the costs of raw materials, labour or transportation, and these differences will be unsustainable in a more competi-tive environment. The withdrawal of existing restrictions on foreign producers—par-ticularly important in the case of automakers—and the tendency of the European Commission to strongly enforce anti-monopoly measures, should further heighten com-petition.

In the short term, price cutting (in the form of temporary trade or consumer pro-motions rather than reductions in list prices) could be used by firms before realizing cost savings on suppliers in order to build market share. In the long run, although the average price should be lower than before integration, the role of pricing in the market-ing mix could depend on effective competition coming from non-EC countries, especially those based in Asia.

Different price structures

In a Europe without barriers, manufacturers are concerned that products sold in differ-ent countries at lower prices could more easily find their way into countries where the pricing structure for the same products is higher. 'Parallel importing', which is not illegal in Europe, but which is inhibited by complex customs and shipping procedures, could prosper in an unified Europe thanks to strong retail chains.

Price differences among countries can reflect diverse positioning based on the stage of product life-cycle in each market, exchange rate fluctuations, different distributors' margins, national social costs, delivery clauses, and so on. Principally, however, the differences are caused by excise and value-added taxes.

Taxation of goods, which is not harmonious in Europe, nor is it likely to be in the foreseeable future (because of the different position of member states on the subject), will greatly influence the pricing policies of companies. 'At present, consumption taxes vary enormously among the EC nations. A bottle of whisky is taxed 36 times as heavily in Denmark as in Greece. Books, food, and baby clothes are not taxed at all in Britain. In France, consumers pay a twenty-eight per cent 'luxury tax' on new automobiles (. . .).

The Commission argues that, once frontier barriers are abolished, widely differing rates will cause economic chaos'.[21]

Pricing decisions

To survive and remain profitable with lower margins, manufacturers, especially small companies, will have to improve efficiency. The European market of the future will be typified by surplus production and, wherever there is surplus, price is always the dominant form of competition.

To complicate pricing decisions, other factors will influence the manufacturers' choices: less freedom in setting transfer prices: pressures on manufacturers' margins from the consolidated distributors' side: savings in distribution and warehousing costs: and economies from lower cost locations.

Quelch and Buzzell[20] suggest that to face these trends manufacturers should:

(1) understand the price elasticity of consumer demand for each product in every single EC nation, and identify the product substitution effect at different price points:[22]
(2) launch new higher-margin products before 1992 in the low-priced markets, to convince consumers to buy them:
(3) introduce visible low-cost brand names to discourage parallel importing:
(4) try to increase control of distribution channels in high-priced markets to cross-subsidize aggressive pricing in other markets.

3. Promotion strategies (Table 4)

A pan-European campaign

In the issue of global vs local marketing, the essential question seems to be is it possible to run a truly pan-European promotional campaign? While in Europe, major players, like the world's largest advertising conglomerate Saatchi & Saatchi, strongly believe that the people are growing more alike in lifestyle and attitudes (a trend which it calls 'cultural or consumer convergence'), in the USA, the world's biggest mass-market, companies are moving to regional and local sales and marketing. It could be seen as a signal for European marketers that US companies, such as Colgate-Palmolive, Procter & Gamble, Pepsi-Cola, Campbell Soup, and others have been reorganized to focus more closely on small geographic targets.

A pan-European (or 'global') campaign could have appropriate results when 'the same product specification is sold in each country to the same target consumers, for the same end use, against competition that offers the same mix of advantages and disadvantages, and with a similar market maturity'.[23] But even if this happens, despite efforts to communicate the same message with the same promotional tools, only one thing remains certain: consumers will respond to any marketing strategy as individuals. The customer does not differentiate in terms of segmented communications: advertising, sales promotion, and public relations. He simply takes information from magazines, dealers by and word-of-mouth. Therefore, it is vital for a company to speak with one voice through integrated communication which requires the co-ordination of the compo-

Table 4. Promotion strategies in Europe of 1992

Changes affecting strategies	Threats to marketers' planning	Management's strategic options
Common guidelines on television broadcasting	Restrictions on alcohol and tobacco advertising	Co-ordinate components of promotional mix
Deregulation of national broadcasting monopolies	Limits on foreign TV production	Exploit where possible advantage of pan-European media (ad space, standardized ads, etc.)
Uniform standards for TV commercials	Differences in permitted promotional techniques	Position the product according to local markets
		Provides promotional programs with 'residual market value'
		Encourage brand loyalty

nents of promotional mix, including advertising, sales promotion, direct marketing, publicity and point-of-purchase material.

Communications in the common market

The necessity to regulate the media sector has encouraged the Council of Europe to advance a draft convention on common guidelines on television broadcasting, specifying the minutes of advertising permitted per hour, the placement of advertisements during and between programmes, etc. In addition, the European Commission has proposed common restrictions on alcohol and tobacco advertising and limits on foreign TV productions to encourage European programming by setting a minimum air time of 30%. (The 60 networks in Europe require 125,000 hours of programming, of which only 25,000 hours have to come from within Europe. That gives a considerable quota which could be exploited by non-EC competitors.)

Ever since it was developed, European television has largely remained under strict government control and has been financed by the viewers through annual fees. Advertising is severely restricted not only in time (which resulted in artificially maintained high prices), but also by the different national broadcast regulations governing advertising. For example, a thirty-second Kellogg cereal commercial, if introduced in three different European countries, should actually require the following adaptation to comply with different laws: in the Netherlands, deletion of references to iron and vitamins; in France, deletion of child actors; in Germany, deletion of the claim that 'Kellogg make their corn flakes the best they've ever been'.[24] If the 1992 programme achieves uniform standards for TV commercials, the savings in production costs would be substantial by using the same spot across Europe, only differing in voice-overs.

These promotional strategies will become significant when viewed in conjunction with the deregulation of Europe's national broadcasting monopolies, because competition from commercial pan-European satellite networks will force European governments to allow new advertisement time. European television, for example, has been shaken by the arrival of satellite channels, like Sky Channel and Super Channel, conceived from the beginning as advertising media, whose penetration level is expected to reach 21%, capturing 8% of EC television advertising by 1992.

Advertising in Europe

Deregulation of markets is almost always accompanied by increased spending, and Europe's advertising expenses are expected to increase by at least 30%. Higher spending on advertising should be justified in the transitional phase for supporting entries into new markets, and in the long run by the larger gross margins and increased availability of media. Presently, European advertisement business is half the size as that of the USA, but it is growing at 12% a year, twice the US rate. The growth is expected to be greater in France, Italy and Spain.[25]

This media trend cannot be totally exploited by the agencies in developing standardized advertising, because different languages, cultures, needs and attitudes do not create the conditions for the ultimate advertisement: i.e. one selling message directed to 320 million people. However, limited attempts at pan-European advertising have already been made, where the product and market have shown connotations of homogeneity prevailing over different elements.

From the perspective of global marketing, advertisers promoting products on a pan-European basis should avoid 'slice of life' advertising and adopt, less referential, more symbolic advertising. In such cases, opportunities exists for advertising that emphasizes a common graphic language.

From the area of local marketing, it should be noted that advertisements often exhibit national features that are unintelligible beyond their frontiers. British advertising, with its tradition of creativity, is often too subtle and indirect for continental Europeans. France, with its more relaxed attitudes to nudity, creates advertising that would be banned as pornography in puritan England. West German advertising uses unemotionally factual headlines. Spaniards use melodrama: Italians, songs and shouts; and so on.

Positioning

There is a temptation for many consumer-goods marketers to imitate the 'one sight, one sound, one sell' dictum governing the sales of a few global products like Coca Cola. Pepsi, and Marlboro cigarettes. But even Coca Cola, the arch-exponent of globalism, tailors the advertising of its other drinks, like Fanta, to appeal to different markets.

The fact is that dissimilarities exist in the way products are viewed within countries in the European Community. The Renault 11, for example, may be a good economy car in the UK, but in Spain it is still perceived as a luxury item. These ways of thinking, desires, needs, and consumer habits are not going to change considerably, and this cannot be ignored in positioning a product. Toothpaste and oral care are another example of products which cannot be marketed in the same way across Europe. In Spain and Greece, toothpaste is regarded as cosmetic, so their commercials look glamorous, like soft drink ads. In the UK and in Holland toothpaste is seen as a therapeutic product and its consumption is three times as high as in Spain and Greece.

European businesses with a mass-market product should concentrate on micro-marketing too, because different positioning will be required by many other products, from beer to household appliances, computers, and so on. The motto of the new Europe should be: 'Plan globally, act locally'.

Sales promotion and public relations

No company should assume that it is easily well-recognized across Europe notwithstanding its size or potential. Companies like ICI, Hanson, BAT Industry, are difficult to identify even if they are among the 100 largest public corporations in the world. Size alone does not give presence. It takes solid, consistent communications to do that.

Promotional programmes in the 1990s have to provide 'residual market value' and 'relationship value'.[15] The fist is defined as the image of the product or service which remains after the promotion is over. Consumers should not simply take advantage of the promotion (e.g., a discount of 15%), and then forget and move on. The second, 'relationship value', refers to the bond created between the customers, the company and the brand. Since people buy from companies they like, loyal customers should be encouraged.

Public relations cannot create the image of a company. Image is, by definition, the reflection of something that already exists. However, they can improve it. Also the use of non-traditional agency services, such as event marketing, package design, or direct marketing, can help in a competitive environment like the European Community. For the moment, a maze of national regulations hinder the growth of pan-European promotion and EC directives have not been proposed other than to regulate promotion for specific industries, like toys or drugs.

4. Distribution strategies (Table 5)

Transportation in Europe

The unified Europe will have a larger population than the USA or Japan, yet most of the manufacturers and consumers live and work within a radius of 800 km. They are located in an area which is only 12% of the land mass of the US. In spite of this concentration, transportation in the EC has been overburdened with regulations and the associated administrative paperwork, resulting in great inefficiency. For example, 'a truck travelling from Glasgow to Athens, a distance of 2368 miles, and crossing five national boundaries, including a sea crossing, will travel at an average speed of eight miles per hour'.[26] The Commission has estimated that, on average, truck drivers spend 30% of their time at border crossing just waiting or filling out as many as 200 forms. Border delays have increased overall prices by 2% and cut EC firms' profits by 25%.

The Community transportation policy should reduce formalities and harmonize regulations, so that goods can quickly cross national boundaries more quickly. Since January 1988, one 13-page EC customs document, the Single Administrative Document (SAD), has already replaced two pounds of forms previously required by the national regulations. Other improvements and harmonization are expected to be in the following areas:

(1) cabotage, the prohibition against a driver picking up or delivering loads outside his country of origin;[27]

Table 5. Distribution strategies in Europe of 1992

Changes affecting strategies	Threats to marketers' planning	Management's strategic options
Simplification of national transit documents and procedures Elimination of customs formalities	Increase in distributors' margins Lack of direct marketing infrastructures Restrictions in the use of computer databases	Consolidate manufacturing facilities Centralize warehouses and distribution centres Implement JIT production and EDI technology Develop non-traditional distribution channels (direct marketing, telemarketing, etc.)

(2) restrictions on backhauls—the freight motor carriers haul on their return trip (fully 40% of the commercial vehicles crossing internal borders are empty, according to the EC report);

(3) fiscal, technical, and social barriers (highway user fees and fuel taxes; truck size and weight limits; working conditions and duty hours).[28]

Distribution strategies

Transportation deregulation is expected to cause significant changes for the European transportation industry, which will become smaller and more competitive, and for European firms in global competition. Both will be encouraged by lower freight and fewer trade barriers. The challenge is to rationalize manufacturing and distribution to cope with the growing number of customers, increased competition, and uniform standards. It will no longer be necessary for a plant in almost any country to conform to national product and transportation standards. Companies will be able to justify consolidated manufacturing facilities, allowing economies of scale and the replacement of small warehouses with centralized, highly mechanized distribution centres—while maintaining, or even improving, customer service.

Pan-European franchising is likely to increase following the removal of trade barriers, while inventory holding costs should decrease, since fewer safety stocks will be necessary to protect against road haulage delays. In the area of inventory reduction, European manufacturers will increasingly implement Just-In-Time (JIT) production, which requires frequent deliveries and no delays.

Finally, the growing use of electronic links will enable transportation companies to provide new services to their clients. These might include a database of routes and prices, access to information on market trends, reports on new packaging, loading and distribution techniques, and possibly even distribution of performance statistics. Companies with the technology in place to support EDI (Electronic Data Interchange) may have a great advantage with European customers. EDI allows the sending of invoices, orders, customs documents, and design drawings between trading partners via computer rather than on paper, without the delays and the errors typical of the printing process.

Retailers and supermarkets

Major companies, especially American ones, are presently moving towards mergers and acquisitions to build strong product lines across Europe, as are retailers, distributors, and brokers in order to consolidate their buying power. 'All this activity springs largely from the same phenomenon that consolidated America's food industry in the 1970s; the growing power of supermarkets. Big European chains like to stock only top brands backed by strong consumer advertising'.[29]

As a direct consequence, brands which are not in the top three positions in terms of market share will find difficulties in securing market shelf space at retail level. This should allow distributors' the power to increase their margins as manufacturers' margins decrease. Part of the benefits of larger buying-programmes should also be passed on to consumers by means of lower prices.

A proposal by the European Commission is likely to block acquisitions and mergers. Distribution arrangements which affect trade or restrict competition are already prohibited by the Treaty of Rome. Article 85(3) of the Treaty, however, provides an exemption for those exclusive sales agreements that contribute to the production or distribution of goods or to the promotion of technical and economic progress. This allowed the EC Commission to grant automatic exemption to certain types of exclusive licensing arrangements which met certain criteria. Nevertheless, the Community does not want an irreversible market situation where the supply comes from a few big companies. This is what appears to be happening as Europe's giant chains rush to attain control of the market.

Direct marketing

Much of the sales strategy of consumer goods makers is now addressed to tailoring products to even more specialist and, thus, narrow markets. The latest trends in distribution strategies—direct mail and allied powerful, consumer databases – are instruments to develop and exploit, rather than blur, national and regional peculiarities.

Europe will remain, for the immediate future, a challenging environment for direct marketers. Still the hope exists for developing a more mature receptive environment for direct selling, telemarketing, and other non-traditional distribution channels (one medium expected to introduce broad opportunities is satellite TV). On the other hand, European direct marketers face several difficulties:

(1) Europeans are not as used to buying direct as Americans and, in some quarters, perceive direct marketing as intrusive:
(2) they speak different languages and a universal message will find difficulty in 'travelling';
(3) inclusion of direct-response telephone numbers in TV spots is forbidden by the privacy laws of member states, e.g., West Germany;
(4) information about potential clients is fragmented and almost unobtainable;
(5) supported infrastructure for direct marketing is weak because credit cards, toll-free numbers, and computer databases (which could provide larger and better documented lists) are in their infancy in Europe.

Nevertheless, the European Community remains a main target because it is large and rich, and it is the logical alternative for expanding beyond the saturated US market.

CONCLUSIONS

As regulatory barriers within the EC break down, marketers (both inside and outside Europe) should define strategies to grasp new opportunities from what will become one of the largest, most stable, and wealthiest markets in the world. Although some multi-nationals have occasionally regarded Europe as one market, most corporations have had to deal with a number of small segments regulated by individual laws.

For 1992, corporations must determine to what extent they can treat the enlarged market as one entity and how they can structure their organizations. By adapting their marketing strategies to the new realities, firms can take advantage of a unified Europe.

Dallmer,[30] chief executive officer of an important European corporation, once told a story which symbolizes the European situation: 'Two people were walking through the Black Forest where it was rumoured a very dangerous lion lurked. They took a break and were sitting in the sun when one of them changed from his big hiking boots to jogging shoes. The other one smiled and laughed and asked, "You don't think you can run away from the lion with those jogging shoes?" "No," he replied, "I just need to be faster than you." '

The integration of Europe is a complicated process and the implications for marketing are not immediately apparent. What we do know, though, is that the companies that will lose will be those who wait. It is not necessary to be first, but what is needed is to be faster than the others.

NOTES

1. Quelch, J. A., Buzzell, R. D. and Salama, E. R. (1990) *The Marketing Challenge of 1992*. Addison-Wesley.
2. Van Mesdag, M, (1988) '1992: The Cant Dispelled'. *Industrial Marketing Digest,* **13**(4): 49–55.
3. This principle of 'mutual recognition' has been used by the European Court to abolish numerous national restrictions, such as the most publicized beer and sausage purity laws in Germany and the pasta purity law in Italy.
4. 'The Myth of the Euro-Consumer'. (1989) *The Economist,* (4 November): 79.
5. The debate generated by Levitt ('The Globalization of Markets', *Harvard Business Review,* **61**(3): 92–102, 1983) supported the possible availability of standardized market strategies in the unified Europe, the reason being that the EC has been developing a common market since 1958 and, therefore, should be in theory a fertile ground for globalization. International experience has shown, however, that extreme globalization cannot be imposed by the top, but should be justified by consumers' behaviour.
6. Terpstra, V. (1963) *American Marketing in the Common Market*. Praeger, New York.
7. Boddewyn, J. J. and Hansen, D. M., (1977) 'American Marketing in the European Common Market'. *European Journal of Marketing* (11): 548–563.
8. Soehl, R. (1985) 'US Marketing in the European Common Market 1963–1983: A Longitudinal Study'. MBA Thesis. Baruch College, City University of New York.
9. Vandermerwe, S. and L'Huillier, M. (1989) 'Euro-consumers in 1992'. *Business Horizons,* January/February: 34–40.
10. Martin, J. (1988) 'Beyond 1992: Lifestyle is Key'. *Advertising Age*. 11 July: 57.

11. Kossoff, J. (1988) 'Europe: Up for Sale'. *New Statesman & Society* **1**(8): 43–44.
12. Heineken, Coca Cola and Marlboro are typical brands that position themselves towards this group.
13. The integration of Europe will imply an era of expanded product liability. Every company will have to do a better job in the areas of the marketing mix:
    - product: testing new products in accordance with common EC standards;
    - promotion: avoiding deceptive or illegal advertising (in the case of alcohol or tobacco);
    - distribution: reinforcing customer service in supermarkets, an area whose importance is become crucial in US.
14. Until final ratification by individual countries, nobody knows how much time it will take to pass some directives and how they will affect marketers and advertisers. Even if some regulations can severely affect competitiveness in the market, companies must move ahead for the single market, so as not to remain unprepared. For instance, still subject to approval are restrictions for ads using tobacco-product brand names for non-tobacco products; 'fresh' and nutrient labelling for food; band of duty-free sales at airports; and so on.
15. Schultz, D. E. (1989) 'New Directions for 1992'. *Marketing Communications*, (March): 28–30.
16. From the four-P approach, Schultz[15] suggests to move to the four-C approach: Channels (how to get the product in distribution; Competition (how to work with distributors, retailers, and competitors); Costs (how suppliers affects the costs, etc.): and Customers (Moving from mass-media to personalized database knowledge).
17. 'Handling so many brands can be confusing and costly'. It's what occurred to Unilever in Fall 1989. Having bought several cosmetic firms, controlled brands, 'Calvin Klein, Passion, and Elizabeth Arden each launched a men's fragrance, which competed against each other' (W. Konrad, (1989) 'The New Improved Unilever Aims to Clean Up in the US'. *Business Week*, (27 November): 102–106. Another example is given by Richardson-Vicks, which sells 'Oil of Ulay' in the UK, but 'Oil of Olaz' in Spain and Italy. Such approach, is against an efficient pan-European branding.
18. Goldman, T. (1989) 'Packaging for a Unified Europe'. *Marketing Communications*, (March): 26–27.
19. Boddewyn, J. J., Soehl, R. and Picard, J. (1986) 'Standardization in International Marketing: is Ted Levitt in Fact Right?' *Business Horizons*, (November/December): 69–75.
20. Quelch, J. A. and Buzzell, R. D. (1989) 'Marketing Moves Through EC Crossroads'. *Sloan Management Review*, **31**(1): 63–74.
21. Sullivan, S. (1988) 'Who's Afraid of 1992'. *Newsweek*, (31 October): 8–15.
22. 'For example, excise rate harmonization would dramatically reduce liquor prices in Ireland, Denmark, and the UK and dramatically increase them in Italy; assuming the tax break was passed to the consumers, additional production capacity would be needed to meet incremental demand.' (Ref. 20, p. 68).
23. Roberts, J. (1989) 'Advertising the European Way'. *Europe*, (November): 30–32.
24. Kotler, P. (1986) 'Global Standardization—Courting Danger'. *Journal of Consumer Marketing*, **3**(2): 13–15.
25. Ryans, J. K. Jr. and Rau, P. A., (1990) *Marketing Strategies for the New Europe*. American Marketing Association.
26. Abell, J. N. (1990) 'Europe 1992: Promises and Prognostications'. *Financial Executive*, **6**(1): 37–41.
27. Today, truck freight hauled within a single country can only be carried by a motor carrier who is a citizen of that country, but the EC Court of Justice has already ruled these restrictions as not allowed under the Single Market Act's liberalization of services.
28. Harmonization, however, should be required also in the way rules are enforced (which involves the independence of police forces and judges). In a 1-year period for example, West Germany registered over 42,000 commercial driver violations while Belgium only 35 infractions. Trunick, P. A. (1990) 'Transportation is No Simple Matter'. *Transportation & Distribution*, (February) 24–26.
29. Toy, S., Melcher, R. A. and Therrien, L. (1989) 'The Race to Stock Europe's Common Supermarket'. *Business Week* (26 June): 80–82.
30. 'Fortress Europe'. *Target Marketing*, **12**(6): 12–14 June, 1989.

25

Competition in Global Markets: a Case Study of American and Japanese Competition in the British Market

Peter Doyle, John Saunders and Veronica Wong

This article presents the results of a detailed three-year study into a sample of 90 major American, Japanese and British companies that competed against each other in the UK market. The primary objectives of the study were to identify the strategic goals of each of the sample companies and to describe the strategies they employed to achieve these goals. The second objective was to test some common hypotheses about the differences between Western and Japanese businesses. Finally, the results are used to speculate on the roots of successful marketing performance and to identify those strategic and organizational features most associated with success in international markets.

The study is unusual in two respects. First, it compares the *overseas* practices of American and Japanese companies rather than the characteristics of their home operations. By contrast, most studies of the international competitiveness of American and Japanese industry have looked at the features and practices of management in their home bases. But the success of American companies in overseas markets, depends more on how they organize themselves overseas, than on how they behave in Chicago or Detroit. Most major US and Japanese companies have production or assembly operations abroad serving these markets and all have managers located in the key markets responsible for sales and marketing. Our study explores how these subsidiaries relate to their headquarters at home, how they perceive their objectives and marketing strategies, and how they organize local management to implement these plans and achieve results.

A second feature of the study is its effort to hold constant differences in objectives or strategy which are due to the idiosyncrasies of particular markets or industries. It does this by limiting analysis to one overseas market, the UK. In addition, each US company in the sample was matched with a Japanese and British company with which it was in direct competition. The result was a sample of 90 companies, consisting of 30 triads of American, Japanese and British firms competing for customers in the same UK market.

Reprinted with permission from *Journal of International Business Studies*, Vol. 23, No. 3, pp. 419–442
© 1992 Journal of International Business Studies

BACKGROUND

The rise of Japanese industry, the decline of America's share of both world exports and overseas investment, and its enormous trade deficit have all spurred the debate on America's international competitiveness. There is now vast literature and many, inter-related explanations for the comparative decline of America's industrial and inter-national performance. Much of the comment has compared US industry unfavourably with Japan's. Researchers have focused on the sociocultural features of Japanese society that support a stronger competitive drive (Prestowitz, 1988; Hamel and Prahalad, 1989), the government's interventionist industrial policies (Johnson, 1982). Its greater manufacturing skills (Wheelwright and Sasser, 1988), the high levels of industrial ef-ficiency (Hayes and Abernathy, 1980) and the supportive financial system in Japan that permits the longer term profit orientation that appears so inimical to US financial markets (e.g., van Wolferen, 1989). Several commentators have referred to America as catching the 'British disease'—a spiral of declining competitiveness caused by an in-ability to change and match the performance of international rivals.

Two areas of research have received less attention. First, as noted above, the studies have concentrated overwhelmingly on how businesses are organized in the home country—in the USA or Japan. The characteristics of US and Japanese manufacturing, sales and distribution subsidiaries overseas have attracted much less interest. Second, there have been no direct detailed empirical comparisons of US and Japanese marketing strategies.

This lack of comparative research into international marketing is partly explained by the difficulty of making generalizations. While Japanese production efficiency is a common factor, marketing policies normally have to be heterogeneous—tailored to the idiosyncrasies of customers, competition and distribution systems in the different coun-tries. A video camera or CNC machine is marketed quite differently in Britain, Taiwan, and Canada. In each country, there may well be differences in product specifications, advertising, promotion, distribution channels and price positioning. A consequence of this need to match local conditions is that, unlike decisions about finance or production, marketing decisions tend to be decentralized with the local subsidiaries having con-siderable autonomy. In our sample, 80% of US and all 30 managements of Japanese subsidiaries claimed to have complete, or near complete, discretion in determining marketing decisions.

If marketing is of importance, studying the relative capabilities of American and Japanese subsidiaries is interesting because these features are likely to be more open to emulation. After all, both US and Japanese subsidiaries are overwhelmingly run and managed by local personnel who, as we show, do not differ in age, experience or background from each other, or indeed, from those in local British firms with which they compete.

Certainly there is much incidental evidence from case studies and business comment that marketing has been a significant factor in the success of the Japanese overseas (e.g., Kotler, Fahey and Jatusripitak, 1985; Ohmae, 1989). A comprehensive survey of these sources together with a pilot study of Japanese competition (Doyle, Saunders and Wong, 1986) suggest a number of hypotheses that can be tested. These hypotheses form the basis for the design of our study. The main hypotheses are:

1. Japanese subsidiaries are more orientated to long-term market share objectives than their Western rivals (e.g., Prestowitz, 1988; Fallows, 1989; Tsurumi, 1984).
2. Managers in American and British subsidiaries are encouraged to give greater priority to short-term profit performance than those in Japanese subsidiaries (Johnson, 1982; Thurow, 1985).
3. Japanese companies are more market orientated; they have clearer market objectives, strategies and plans than their Western counterparts (Kotler and Fahey, 1982; Lazer, Murata and Kosaka, 1985).
4. Japanese subsidiaries are more adept at tailoring their strategies to local market conditions than American companies (Bartlett and Ghoshal, 1989; Prahalad and Doz, 1987).
5. The greater commitment of Japanese companies to long-term success in the local market creates greater support and confidence among personnel in the local subsidiary (Doyle, Saunders and Wong, 1986).
6. Successful companies will employ market focused rather than functional organizational structures (Pascale and Athos, 1982; Ohmae, 1988).
7. Reporting relationships, control procedures and job boundaries will be more rigid and bureaucratic in Western companies (Beresford, 1982; Morishima, 1982).
8. Headquarters information systems and controls will emphasize financial measures in Western companies and market performance measures in Japanese (Pascale and Athos, 1982; Wright and Pauli, 1987).
9. Japanese subsidiaries will show a greater commitment to training, especially on-the-job development (Johnson, 1982; Ohmae, 1982).
10. Successful competitors in the UK market will exhibit common features which transcend national characteristics.

METHODOLOGY

The focus of this study is on competition between American, Japanese and local British companies in the UK market. The UK is, with Germany, the most important market for US and Japanese companies in Europe. In 1988 Japanese exports to the UK amounted to $10 billion and US exports were $16 billion. In terms of investment in the UK, the US has again been much more important, although Japanese investment is also now rising at a far higher rate. In 1988 American companies employed 530,000 workers in the UK and accounted for 12% of the country's manufacturing output. Japanese companies still employ only 40,000 workers and accounted for only 1% of manufacturing output in the UK. However, there are many major Japanese projects in the pipeline, and it is predicted that the Japanese will overtake US companies as employers in the UK by the mid-1990s.

The basic data for the study were obtained from interviews with senior management in 90 companies drawn from defined product groups. The sectors were chosen on the bases of: (1) being significant nationally in terms of size or growth, (2) being within the top 30 UK imports from Japan and the US, and (3) having some British competitors with which to form comparisons.

The product sectors selected for the study are listed in Table 1. Companies within the sectors were chosen by purposive sampling in view of the small population of companies available in each sector, the need to find triads that were reasonably matched in terms of product-markets, and the importance of having the limited sample reflect the attitudes and the approaches of the firms constituting the most significant proportion of the industry. The data were collected in three stages:

Table 1. Product sectors covered by the study

Consumer goods	Audio/hi-fi, microwave ovens, automobiles
Industrial goods	Machine tools, photocopiers, ball-bearings, materials-handling equipment, scientific instruments, telecommunications
Services	Financial capital markets

1. *Interviews with marketing directors/managing directors.* All the companies were approached via letter and telephone follow-up. Confidentiality of individual responses was emphasized as an inducement to participate. Only ten of the 90 firms originally approached declined to be interviewed. The final list of participating firms is given in Table 2.

Table 2. Companies participating in the study

American	Barden, Brown and Sharpe, Cincinnati-Millicron, DeVlieg, Ex-Cello, Geo. Kingsbury, Gidding and Lewis-Frazer, Hewlett-Packard, IBM, ITT, Jones and Shipman, Kodak, Litton, Textron, Torrington, Ford, GM/Vauxhall Motors, Hyster, Caterpillar, J.I. Case/International Harvester, Computer Peripherals Bristol, Gould Scientific Instruments, GE Medical Systems, Diasonics, AT&T, Northern Telecom, Salomon Brothers, Goldman Sachs, Morgan Stanley, Citicorp Investment Bank
Japanese	Akai, Canon, Hitachi-Seiki, Nakamura Tome, Niigata, National Panasonic, NSK Bearings, Pioneer, Ricoh, Sansui, Sharp, Sony, Takisawa, Toshiba, Yamazaki, Subaru, Nissan, Toyota, Marubeni-Komatsu, Kubota, Rikadenki Mitsui, Hitachi Scientific Instruments, Toshiba Medical, Shimadzu, Fujitsu, NEC, Nikko Securities, Daiwa Securities, Yamaichi Securities, Long Term Credit Bank of Japan
British	Alba, Amstrad, Binatone, Ferguson, Fidelity Radio, Beaver Machine Tools, Colchester Lathe, Gestetner, Kearney and Trecker Marwin, Rank-Xerox, RHP Industrial Bearings, TI Creda, TI Matrix and Hebert Churchill, Tricity, Wadkin, Rover Group, Jaguar, Lansing Bagnall, Lancer Boss, JCB, Advance Bryans, Lloyd Instruments, Picker International, Vickers Medical, GEC Telecommunications, STC Telecommunications, Samuel Montagu, SG Warburg, Lloyds Investment Bank, County NatWest

2. *Multilevel interviews.* One in three of the companies were chosen for more detailed interviewing. This involved interviewing, in addition to the marketing director, the functional heads of finance, production and R&D. The objectives were to explore the marketing interfaces within the firm and to examine the barriers to adopting a market orientation.

3. *Headquarter interviews.* Interviews were organized within 13 of the Japanese and 14 of the American companies headquarters in Japan and the USA. The objectives were to

determine parent company attitudes, strategies and control procedures for their overseas subsidiaries

All three sets of interviews were semi-structured to obtain a wide scope of information to check for bias and misunderstandings of the responses, and to obtain valuable qualitative judgements, while, at the same time, obtaining data that would be broadly consistent and comparable across companies.

THE FINDINGS

Strategic objectives

There were striking contrasts in the goals of the sample companies. As hypothesized, managers of the Japanese subsidiaries were remarkably more ambitious and clear about their marketing objectives than their American and British counterparts. As Table 3

Table 3. What was your market share/sales strategy?[a]

	Prevent decline	Defensive	Maintain position	Steady growth	Aggressive growth	Dominate market
US (%)	7	3	17	23	33	17
Japanese (%)	3	0	0	17	57	23
British (%)	27	17	23	13	13	7

All tables are tested using chi-squared tests. Yates' correction is used to adjust for small sample cell size where appropriate.
[a] Statistical significance is at the 5% level.

illustrates, four out of five Japanese companies gave aggressive growth or market domination as their objective, against only half the American companies and only one in five of the British. The managers of the Japanese subsidiaries were exceptionally ambitious in their strategic intent. Equally striking are the differences in attitudes towards short-term profit performance (Table 4). Virtually all the American and British companies

Table 4. How well does 'good short-term profits are the objective' describe your company?[a]

Japanese (%) 27	US (%) 80	British (%) 87

[a] Statistical significance is at the 5% level.

placed the highest priority on maintaining short-term profitability, while the Japanese managements rated short-term profit performances as an important objective in only one out of four cases. In remarkable contrast to Western companies, Japanese management reported that the headquarters were not unduly unsettled by low profits provided that long-term market performance showed steady improvement. American and British companies, on the other hand, looked for quick action if profits were under pressure.

Generally they would expect to be forced to cut costs, and if necessary, allow market shares to erode. If the attitudes reflected in Tables 3 and 4 are typical, the disappointing performance of American and British manufacturing industry becomes more comprehensible.

Figure 1 interprets these differences in terms of our discussions with subsidiary and headquarter managements. All the sample companies recognized *both* market share (left-hand) and financial (right-hand) objectives, but the emphasis on each of these objectives differed markedly. The Japanese placed much more emphasis on the left-hand or market objectives and most of the American and British companies gave overwhelming emphasis to right-hand or profit performance.

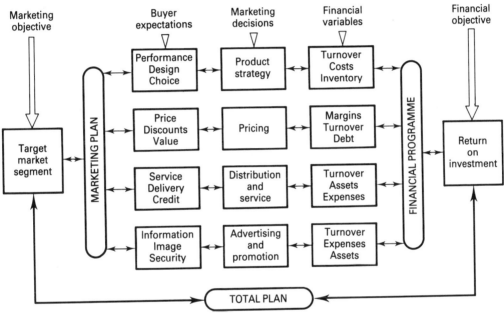

Figure 1. Integrating Marketing and Financial Strategies.

In the left-hand-orientated companies, business decisions were clearly market orientated. Managers started with ambitious share objectives negotiated with headquarters. Target market segments in the UK were then selected and the expectations of these customers were the basis for market plans. These plans often took many years before they were fulfilled because of the necessity to invest in product development, brand building and distribution systems that would satisfy more effectively than competitors the aspirations of customers. In the long run the strategies were clearly working and giving these companies both market and financial success.

By contrast, the majority of Western companies in our sample were right-handed. Profitability or return on investment targets were dictated by headquarters. Budgets rather than marketing plans provided the focus for top management. In the recession of the early 1980s, American and British companies had generally sought to restore profitability by retrenchment: costs were cut, product development was held back and investments were postponed. By the late 1980s this had produced a predictable, but in fact unappreciated paradox. Productivity and profitability were indeed restored to record levels by the rationalizations which had taken place. But this right-hand focus had (with the predictable lag), left market shares eroding and competitiveness declining. Western companies had traded short-term improvements in efficiency for long-term enhancement of market effectiveness.

  This paradox also appeared to explain much of the takeover boom that occurred in the late 1980s. By then American and British companies were finding it difficult to boost profits further by continued retrenchment policies, yet they were ill equipped, after a decade of rationalization, to boost growth via new product or market development. With strong cash positions and low internal growth potential, acquisitions were the obvious alternative. Hence, another paradox appeared to be explained by our study. American and British manufacturing industry, while exhibiting the worst performances of all the OECD countries in the late 1980s, outstripped them all in terms of acquisitions. While Japanese and German companies invested in their own businesses, American and British companies seemed to prefer to invest in others' businesses.

Strategic focus

This difference in focus appeared due to differences in attitudes to profitability. This is illustrated in Figure 2. The Japanese executives said that they saw profit performance in

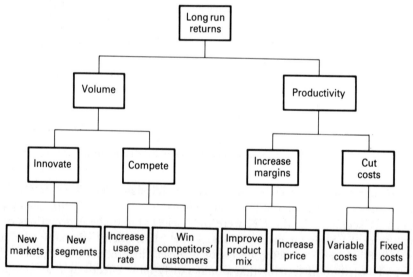

Figure 2. Strategic Focus.

the long run being more assured by a focus on volume—expanding into new market segments or aggressive market penetration (Table 5). They believed a focus on increased volume now would enable them to build competitive cost structures, to generate the resources to sustain product development and to control their distribution channels in the future. The American and British companies, however, saw inadequate profits to be solved by an immediate right-hand focus on cost reduction and improved productivity.

Table 5. How well do these statements describe your strategic focus?

	US (%)	Japanese (%)	British (%)
'Enter newly emerging market segments'[a]	50	77	40
'Winning share by beating competition'[b]	73	83	53
'Focus on cost reduction and improved productivity'[b]	70	43	83

Statistical significance: [a] 20% level; [b] 5% level.

The advantage of the Western focus on productivity is that it leads to quick profit enhancement—operating expenses can be cut and return on investment can be rapidly boosted when profits are under pressure. The problem with this approach is that it can often lead to a longer run erosion of market position. Cost reduction means a reduced investment in new product development, brand building and market support. Maintained for more than a year or two, such policies inevitably lead to declining market share, weaker distribution and further pressure on profits as the Western brands become increasingly marginal to the trade and to the consumer. In a number of the markets we studied, this trend was clearly in evidence.

Customer targets

The successful competitors—Western or Japanese—had a dynamic view of markets. In general, the Japanese approach to attacking markets has been to enter at the low price end and then move upwards to the mass market and higher value added segments. In the early 1970s when the Japanese invasion of the UK market began, Japanese products were invariably seen as cheap and inferior to American and local products. By the late 1980s, however, this had all changed and positions were increasingly reversed. It was the local products that were more often perceived by customers as the cheap, down market merchandise and it was the Japanese who were increasingly perceived as offering the superior quality, prestige brands, often at significant price premiums, to the local competitors.

This reverse positioning was most marked in consumer electronics and machine tools, where brands such as Sony, Canon, National Panasonic and Toshiba were clearly seen as quality leaders. But the trend was becoming noticeable in cars, material handling equipment and scientific instruments.

This is reflected in Table 6 where a fifth of British companies admitted they had cheap 'down market' products. None of the Japanese and few American companies would accept this definition of their offers. The Japanese products squarely fit the mass market and stretched upwards to the higher value segments. American products were generally seen as expensive and sophisticated. However, this had left many of them too costly and over engineered for the mass consumer and industrial markets in the UK.

A buyer's perception of a brand is normally a lagged function of reality. As Japanese competitors caught up to and often surpassed Western standards of quality, and accelerated their rate of new product introductions, customers perceptions of them changed. Their image for offering value improved and often that of their Western competitors declined. A second characteristic of Japanese customer targeting appeared to be their search for new or emerging market segments. Photocopiers, 35mm cameras, CNC

Table 6. Characteristics of customer targets[a]

	Down-market			Up-market	
	1	2	3	4	5
US (%)	0	3	27	60	10
Japanese (%)	0	0	43	33	20
British (%)	3	17	43	27	10

[a] Statistical significance is at the 5% level.

machine tools and lap top computers are classic examples of this strategy. Coming into the market behind the Western innovators, the Japanese strategy has not been to attack the market leaders head on, but rather to spot emerging segments not yet prioritized by the leaders. For example, the 35mm camera market was dominated by the German companies Rollei and Leica. When the Japanese entered they focused not on the professional market but, by simplifying the product and lowering the price, they took the rapidly growing amateur market. After this market was won, the Japanese simply rolled back into the professional segment, using the newly won scale and experience advantages to sweep aside the German manufacturers.

Competitive targets

The British and American suppliers not only appeared to have frequently misunderstood the customer dynamics but also the evolution of competition. American companies and some of the mores sophisticated UK competitors frequently withdrew too rapidly from mass markets when they were attacked by Japanese competitors. The American companies, in particular, defended their withdrawal by arguing that they were pursuing 'niche strategies'—focusing on specialized, high value segments. Unfortunately, by withdrawing from the volume markets they gave the Japanese a foothold in the market upon which to build experience, cash flow and distribution capabilities, which were subsequently used as the base to move up into the 'niches' held by their Western competitors.

As American companies such as Hewlett-Packard, Hyster and Gould, and UK companies such as Jaguar, Tube Investments and GEC have found, reliance on relatively small volume, high margin segments tends not to be sustainable long term. Skilful competitors with substantial resources and scale economies built upon mass market dominance, can move into the niches using their advantages to lower costs, accelerate the rate of product introductions and match the quality and features of their smaller competitors. The launch of the Lexus, Infiniti and Acura model ranges in the executive sector of the car market, by Toyota, Nissan and Honda respectively, are typical examples of this type of attack on niche markets.

Competitive advantages

Market success and profit performance depend upon an ability to match the needs of the customers more effectively than competitors. Again the Japanese appeared more often to have the clearer and stronger positioning strategies. The focus of many of the Japanese companies contained the classic components of strategic success. Numerous studies (e.g., Buzzell and Gale, 1987; Clifford and Cavanagh, 1985; Jacobson and Aaker, 1987) have shown the primary importance of quality in determining both market share and profit performance. After quality, service, product differentiation and innovation appear to be the most significant drivers of performance.

Table 7 demonstrates some remarkable differences in these key determinants of market performance. Only in product range do American managements score themselves highly. In terms of service support, quality, reliability, and innovation the Americans saw themselves as significantly weaker than the Japanese. The local British companies rated themselves poorly on all the key performance drivers.

Table 7. In which dimensions do you have competitive superiority?

	US	Japanese	British
Quality and reliability[c]	77	93	47
Service and support[a]	50	70	44
Range[a]	63	60	43
Product innovation[b]	63	68	33
Traditional brand name[c]	20	10	64
Low prices[a]	40	60	60

Statistical significance: [a] 20% level; [b] 10% level; [c] 5% level.

The most frequently mentioned competitive advantages the British saw themselves as possessing were: low prices, 'a traditional brand name' and 'being British'. Too often these managers appeared to look backwards, at distant periods of market leadership, not appreciating how much competition had changed in the 1980s. Unfortunately, when one looks at what has happened to so many traditional British manufacturing companies relying on long established brand names, it is not easy to be sanguine about the future of many of them. Less than half the British companies saw themselves as having any advantages in terms of quality, service, product range or product innovation. Given the views reflected in Table 7 it is not difficult to see why American and British companies have so frequently lost ground to their Japanese competitors.

ORGANIZATION

Besides examining the marketing strategies of the competitors, the study also sought to understand how successful companies manage to motivate their local employees to perform. We looked at where there were real organizational differences between American and Japanese subsidiaries operating overseas. Finally we sought lessons that could be learned from the practices of the more successful organizations.

A pilot study (Doyle, Saunders and Wong, 1986) suggested three hypotheses:

1. Did successful companies have objectives that were distinctly more ambitious than their rivals?

2. Were successful companies more market orientated and consequently more responsive to the needs of the domestic customers?
3. Did successful businesses have organizations that were more flexible and responsive to environmental change?

Headquarter–Subsidiary Relations

The characteristics of the subsidiaries were examined and the extent to which local managers had discretion in determining local policies. In the three sets of companies, the majority of managers were British. They differed little in age, education or experience. At the chief executive level, 80% of American subsidiaries had an American, as against 70% of Japanese with an expatriate head. The American subsidiaries had significantly more expatriates running other line management positions. Seventeen of the US subsidiaries had an American marketing director as against only two Japanese companies with a Japanese marketing director. Thus the Japanese relied significantly more on local personnel at the higher levels.

Both the American and the Japanese companies tended to follow the usual practice of delegating marketing decisions to the local subsidiary. However, as Table 8 shows, the Japanese subsidiaries considered themselves more autonomous in their marketing. Autonomy covered the selection of products to sell, pricing, promotion and distribution policies.

Table 8. US and Japanese subsidiaries: have you responsibility for marketing and distribution decisions?

	Not responsible		Sole responsibility		
	1	2	3	4	5
US (%)	0	0	13	40	47
Japanese (%)	0	0	0	41	59

A majority of American companies exhibited a classic home country orientation. Few appeared to be really committed to the UK market. One US marketing director admitted, 'The parent company lacks an understanding of the need to be aggressive in Europe. They don't understand the UK at all.' Another US headquarters manager justified it as follows: 'The USA is the largest market. Competitors, including the Japanese, will have to succeed in the US if they are to achieve dominance. That is why our emphasis is on developing products for the US—we anticipate that they will serve the UK market as well.'

While many US respondents stressed the importance of the American home market and American technological leadership, the Japanese in contrast stressed the importance of the UK. Many saw the UK as a springboard into the European Community markets. They also saw the need to consolidate and expand their UK operations as a safety measure to overcome potential trade hostilities and restrictive quotas. Japanese headquarters also tended to put more emphasis on being close to their European customers.

To summarize, while the American companies had typically operated in the British market significantly longer than their Japanese competitors (a sample average of 37 years vs 15 years), the Americans appeared to have adapted less. In terms of their home country orientation, their relative reliance on US managers and their centralized control systems, they retain an ethnocentricity more typical of companies at the early stage of internationalization (Perlmutter, 1969).

Ambitions, Goals and Shared Values

Several recent researchers (e.g., Prahalad and Doz, 1987; Bartlett and Ghosal, 1989) have noted how Japanese companies achieve scale economies via global products but local adaptation through finely tuned marketing policies. This pattern is seen in the sample companies here. Table 9 suggests that American companies on average are more

Table 9. Adaptation of marketing strategies to the UK market

	US (%)	Japanese (%)
Marketing strategies are modified to a great extent to suit the UK[b]	47	73
Products modified to a great extent to suit the UK	47	40
Promotions modified to a great extent to suit the UK[b]	57	80
Distribution approaches adapted to a great extent to suit the UK[c]	66	93
Pricing policies are adapted to suit the UK[a]	33	53

Statistical significance: [a] 20% level; [b] 10% level; [c] 5% level.

likely to incur the substantial costs of tailoring their products to the UK market than the Japanese counterparts. But in promotion, pricing, distribution and overall strategy the Japanese adapted more effectively. This pattern of global product efficiency and local adaptation may account for the superior financial and marketing results of the Japanese sample. For despite the emphasis Western companies placed on profitability, Japanese companies were twice as likely as American companies to be reporting satisfactory profit and sales performance. For example, 71% of Japanese headquarters reported that their UK subsidiaries' profits had been satisfactory or very satisfactory in the last five years, compared to only 38% of American headquarters.

Even in terms of labour relations, American companies appear to have had greater problems. All 100% of Japanese headquarters reported satisfactory UK management/ worker relations, against only 46% of American companies. American managers recognized that the streamlining and rationalization that had occurred in their UK operations had not helped labour relations. By contrast, most Japanese subsidiaries had seen continual growth and enhanced opportunities for their workforces. Not only had the past performance of many American companies been disappointing, but the disparity between them and their Japanese rivals was expected to continue. As Table 10 shows, virtually all Japanese headquarters expected to see improved market share and stronger profitability in their UK subsidiaries in the future, as against under one quarter of American companies. As shown earlier, Japanese subsidiaries usually had extremely ambitious goals in the UK and they were optimistic about achieving them. The Americans appeared more defensive in their objectives and pessimistic in their expectations.

Table 10. Medium term expectations of UK
subsidiary's performance[a]

	US (%)	Japanese (%)
Greater market share	23	92
Stronger profitability	23	92

[a] Statistical significance is at the 5% level.

The Japanese were more committed than the Americans to the British market. Their employees felt more secure as they had been unaffected by the rationalizations which the majority of their American and British competitors had been through. Managers in the Japanese companies were much clearer about their objectives and these appeared to be effectively communicated throughout the workforce. While many of the American and British companies appeared confused about their long-term goals in the UK, 70% of the Japanese stated that they were pursuing 'part of a planned global expansion' or were attracted by 'the high potential of the UK market'.

Marketing-orientated organizations

There were significant organizational differences between the three sets of companies. The American organizations were generally the most complex, employing elaborate matrix structures. Many of the US subsidiaries reported through European or international divisions. Strategies were developed at this level and sometimes different countries were responsible for different parts of the programme. For example, one US company had the French in charge of market segmentation, the British, promotional planning, and the Germans looked after product development. A problem with this type of approach appeared to be that often overall responsibility for performance of the UK market was obscured. Subsidiary managers blamed headquarters for dictating inappropriate policies, and headquarters blamed local managers for inadequate cooperation. By contrast, none of the Japanese employed these types of complex international structures; all gave their UK subsidiaries clear responsibility. The major rationale for this simplicity was that 'the parent company in Japan is set up this way—every business is a profit centre'.

Two-thirds of the Japanese also segmented their UK organizations into often very small business units, focused around an individual market or product line. Seventy percent of American and British companies, on the other hand, employed traditional functional structures supervising a wide portfolio of different products and markets (e.g., hi-fi, TVs, computers, video, etc.). This often resulted in two predictable problems. First, the functional structure meant that managers refused to accept responsibility for overall performance. Second, competitive weaknesses in individual products were often disguised by movements in the whole portfolio. The American managers, in particular, seemed to lack detailed knowledge and were disinclined to respond rapidly to emerging problems or opportunities.

Information systems also appeared to be much weaker in many of the Western companies. As a consequence of their smaller focused business units, managers in Japanese subsidiaries invariably possessed detailed up-to-date information on movements of their and competitive brands in each individual market. By contrast, many of the American companies did not have information systems showing performance at the market or product line level. Systems were frequently designed to show factory rather than market performance.

Headquarter control appeared to amplify this dichotomy between the Japanese and Western competitors. The American companies placed much greater stress on financial performance, while the Japanese headquarters monitored much more closely sales performance in the market. These divergencies are strikingly evident in Table 11.

Table 11. Which budget and performance criteria are most scrutinized by top management?

	US (%)	Japanese (%)	British (%)
Profitability[b]	87	7	60
Cash flow[a]	33	7	40
Sales[a]	33	53	47

Statistical significance: [a] 20% level; [b] 5% level.

In summary the American (and British) organizations were much less market focused. Information systems were more geared to monitoring financial and production measures than market results. The result was that the level of individual management commitment and professional responsibility for overall results in the market that characterized the Japanese firms, was often missing in the Western ones.

Organizational flexibility

Besides being more complex, American companies appeared less flexible in responding to outside events. As Table 12 shows, work in American subsidiaries tended to be seen as

Table 12. How well do these statements describe your company's management style?

	US (%)	Japanese (%)	British (%)
Group responsibility and teamwork[a]	63	73	50
Strong hierarchical distinctions in management[c]	57	35	83
Variable and ad hoc job specifications[b]	30	73	33
Both top-down and bottom-up communications[c]	30	62	27

Statistical significance: [a] 20% level; [b] 10% level; [c] 5% level.

organized hierarchically with quite precise job boundaries. Managers saw themselves primarily as functional specialists and tension and conflict between marketing, manufacturing and finance was marked. Task forces and cross-functional teamwork to attack problems did not occur easily in these businesses. By contrast, 73% of senior managers in Japanese subsidiaries regarded their style as creating group responsibility and teamwork. Functional boundaries were weak with only one-third of their Japanese firms regarding hierarchical distinctions as important.

The management style of the Japanese subsidiaries appeared to have two effects on their largely British managers. The latter acknowledged that the informal teamwork and group responsibility for the development of the marketing strategy gave them all a greater sense of commitment to it than was apparent among their US and British competitors. Second, their strategies develop a visibility and clarity by a process that might be termed *sequential decisionmaking*. Marketing plans in the characteristic Japanese subsidiary appear first to be developed by the British managers alone. This 'collective decision' is then conveyed to the Japanese managing director, normally by the senior British manager. Clarity and simplicity are necessary in part because of the substantial barriers of language and culture that still usually separate the British and Japanese managers. Once accepted, the Japanese then act to report and defend this plan in the continual dialogue with headquarters.

The results are clarity, commitment and shared values. Too often the American companies' organizations appeared to produce complexity, dissent and conflict between the different parts of the business.

DISCRIMINATORS OF SUCCESS

The previous analysis focused on the strategic and organizational factors that discriminated between American and Japanese subsidiaries. These factors may be termed the independent variables. This section looks at an alternative approach to exploring the data by introducing a dependent variable—relative 'success'. The focus is on identifying the characteristics of successful companies, whatever their national origin, rather than on comparing Western and Japanese competitors. The approach was first to identify those of the ninety companies that could be regarded as successful. Second, discriminant functions were developed to identify those strategic and organizational variables most associated with success or failure. Third, since the potential bias in discriminant analysis applied to small samples is well known, it was important to validate the initial results. Finally, we sought to interpret the conclusions.

To identify the successful businesses, information was obtained on their marketing and financial performance. Being business units rather than autonomous companies, it was impossible generally to obtain the required data from published sources. Instead, senior management were asked to rate in confidence the performance of their own company and their triad competitors. As others have found (e.g., Burke, 1984; Buckley, Pass and Prescott, 1988; Kotabe, 1990), three of the most common measures of performance used by managers are profitability (return on investment), relative sales growth and change in market share. Following this approach five-point scales were used to elicit responses along these performance measures, judged over the previous five years.

Clearly, the threat of bias from this type of self-assessment has to be recognized. Nevertheless, validation studies have suggested that self-assessment measures of performance are consistent with measures based upon internal or published information (Dess and Robinson, 1984; Venkatraman and Rumanujam, 1986). In addition, the data used in the analysis comprise an average of the self-assessment plus the two outside assessments.

Table 13 shows the results of these performance assessments. The Japanese are seen to be consistently strongest on average, followed by the American subsidiaries. The market share growth measure is the only one strongly significant statistically. To measure overall success the average score on all three performance variables was computed and companies classed as 'successful' if their score exceeded 3.5. This resulted in a split of 40 successful and 50 unsuccessful businesses. Of the successful ones 23 were Japanese, 10 were American and seven were British.

Table 13. Measures of company performance

	US	Japanese	British
Relative profitability	3.40	3.67	3.27
Relative sales growth	3.33	3.73	3.33
Market share growth[a]	3.47	3.80	3.20
Successful[b]	33%	77%	23%

[a] Significant at 5% level using one-way analysis of variance.
[b] Significant at 5% level using chi-squared test.

Two sets of discriminant analyses were then undertaken. The first used those variables that described the *strategies* of the participating companies as discriminators. The second employed the *organizational* descriptors as independent variables. Both sets of variables were good discriminators, although the strategic variables were more effective.

Because of the potential bias both the U-method (Lachenbruch and Mickey, 1968) and Jack-knife analysis (Tukey, 1958) were used to validate the results. The former seeks to avoid the bias that occurs when the same observations are used to estimate and validate the model. With a limited number of observations, the problem is to provide a validation sample that minimizes the loss of observations. The U-method does this by estimating N discriminant functions (where N equals the number of observations) from $N-1$ observations, with a different observation being held out for each estimation. The N held-out observations are then used to form a confusion matrix that yields a virtually unbiased estimate of the misclassification probabilities (Dillon, 1979). Jack-knife analysis provides alternative estimators based upon drawing a series of samples from the observations available (Diaconis and Efron, 1983). The Jack-knife statistics are less biased than the full sample estimators and t-tests can be applied to the confidence intervals of the estimates (Mosteller and Tukey, 1968).

Table 14 shows the discriminant matrix calculated from the entire sample and Table 15 shows the validation matrix derived from the U-method. The strategic and organizational variables explain 94% and 72%, respectively, in the original sample, and 76% and 70% in the validation test. All the matrices are highly significant and both sets of variables can be accounted as reasonable discriminators between successful and unsuccessful companies.

The discriminant functions and Jack-knife statistics permit some comment on the most significant predictors. For the strategic variables, three primary sets of variables discriminated the successful companies. First, successful companies placed a lower priority on short-term profitability and a much higher priority on market share. Companies, both American and Japanese, which placed the highest priority on short-term profits and cost reductions, paradoxically had weaker performance in both profit and market criteria. Poor market performance generally triggers pressure to focus on short-run profits and often a vicious circle of market and financial decline. The second most

Table 14. Confusion matrices of successful companies: strategic and organizational variables

	Predicted membership			
	Strategic model		Organizational model	
	Successful (%)	Unsuccessful (%)	Successful (%)	Unsuccessful (%)
Successful	95.3	4.7	67.1	32.1
Unsuccessful	6.2	93.8	23.8	76.2

Table 15. Confusion matrices based upon validation observations

	Predicted membership			
	Strategic model		Organizational model	
	Successful (%)	Unsuccessful (%)	Successful (%)	Unsuccessful (%)
Successful	67.5	32.5	62.5	37.5
Unsuccessful	16.0	84.0	23.4	76.6

important discriminator was the emphasis given to innovation. Successful companies gave a higher priority to new product development and on pioneering new market segments. The third major characteristic of successful companies was in their careful market segmentation and positioning strategies. They emphasized quality rather than price as the major competitive weapon. Unsuccessful companies, by contrast, were less innovative and were positioned in the 'down-market' price-orientated sectors of the market and tended to be late entrants into these markets.

The second discriminant analysis explored the organizational variables. Again the variables discriminated fairly well. Three sets of characteristics stood out. First was the clear sense of mission amongst successful companies. They had clearly communicated and had achieved enthusiastic endorsement for their long-term goals, notably about market dominance or market share. Their organizations were markedly more informal with loose job specifications, absence of hierarchy and a strong emphasis on teamwork across functional boundaries. Successful companies also invested more heavily in training, with most of it being in-company. By contrast, less successful companies lacked clear goals, were characterized by rigid organizational structures, and their managers and workers tended to have clearly defined specialized job boundaries.

While the discriminant analysis focused on successful companies, whether American, British or Japanese, it did exhibit a profile broadly similar to the Japanese companies discussed earlier. The explanation is that the majority (58%) of successful companies were Japanese and almost all (86%) of relatively unsuccessful ones were Western. Consequently, the successful Western companies analysed had marketing strategies and profiles similar to the Japanese. Being Japanese is not synonymous with success; instead the results are explained by there being more Japanese companies in the set of successful businesses identified.

CONCLUSIONS

In the 1990s companies will face markets that are globally competitive. International business is no longer about domestic manufacture and exports. Today's companies have to be global with integrated systems of sourcing and manufacturing on an international basis. Central to success in this type of environment is the management of overseas subsidiaries. Major country-based subsidiaries are likely to have sourcing and manufacturing, and certainly sales and marketing operations. Such units will be predominantly staffed by local personnel and it is their abilities, teamwork and commitment that will be substantial determinants of the global companies' competitive performance.

Much writing on American and Japanese competitiveness has implied an older form of international competition. The studies have focused on home country rather than host country operations. They have implied an ethnocentric export-based model of trade, rather than the geocentric global competitiveness of today. Japanese companies, in particular, as a result of the rapid appreciation in the value of the yen in the 1980s, shifted from reliance on exports to overseas manufacture and distribution. Their ability to manage the manufacturing and marketing operations of these subsidiaries has been another of the newly acquired strengths of Japanese management. Their operations in the UK seem to have avoided some of the weaknesses and handicaps that characterize many of their longer established American and British competitors.

Three organizational features characterized the successful (mostly Japanese) subsidiaries in our sample. First, they had created highly committed businesses. While Japanese companies did not extend lifetime employment to their British employees, in fact, the virtuous circle of growth and employment they created acted to provide much greater perceived security and confidence among employees. Second, the organizations were highly flexible. Bureaucracy, hierarchies and job boundaries were much weaker than in traditional Western organizations. This provided the framework for innovation, teamwork and mutual problem solving. Third, most of these subsidiaries had a clear sense of mission to be a leader in the market. This appeared to be consciously created by top management's participative style of leadership and the emphasis given to extensive top down and bottom up communications.

In contrast, two-thirds of the American subsidiaries were uncertain or pessimistic about their company's long-term commitment to the UK. In half of them, morale had been scarred by redundancies caused by the retrenchment policies of the 1980s. Even more than British companies, American subsidiaries were characterized by strong hierarchical distinctions in management, and tight job specifications and rules that discouraged teamwork and innovation.

The differences in strategy were even more marked than the organizational disparities. The major Japanese subsidiaries were clearly market orientated. They did not see profit as the central objective, but rather the result of satisfying the aspirations of customers. As one Japanese managing director put it, 'the best guarantee of profits tomorrow are satisfied customers today'. The Japanese also appreciated that it took time, even a decade, to build strong brand names and customer franchise. They talked of the requirements for steady investment, continuous incremental improvements and, in particular, a persistence when market conditions temporarily turn against the business.

The Japanese subsidiaries were also significantly more ambitious in their market share objectives than their Western competitors. With the emphasis in the later 1980s on shareholder value and cash flow, few Western companies any longer gave market share top priority, but to the Japanese subsidiaries market share appeared to be the name of the game. Market dominance was characteristically their central objective. Hardly surprising, therefore, that American companies tended to be losing share over this period.

Besides extremely ambitious market share objectives, the Japanese usually had clear market segmentation and positioning strategies. In terms of segments, they tended to enter at the low end of the market and, over the years, push up into the mass market and eventually penetrate the high value-added end. The elements of strategic groupings could be intimated with the British firms being clustered in the low value-added segments, the Americans in the high technology premium niches, and the Japanese straddling the mass market with increasing penetration of the higher value-added areas. In terms of positioning, the Japanese had a clear focus on quality, service and innovation. The US firms emphasized product range and technology, and the British, traditional brand names.

American companies tended to be short-term, financially orientated. Their ambitions in and commitment to the UK market were limited and the UK tended to be lumped into their overall European strategy. Their subsidiaries were constrained by this lack of commitment and by the financial controls imposed upon them. Like the British companies, they had a different view of productivity from the Japanese. The Western companies saw cost cutting as the route to productivity improvement. The Japanese, by contrast, saw growth and market share as the way to reduce costs and boost productivity. The result was that when market conditions were unfavourable, the Americans tended to retrench and rapidly loose market share to the more aggressive Japanese approach.

These organizational and strategic differences appear to explain fairly clearly the success of the Japanese subsidiaries in the UK. There are few surprises in the findings. Indeed as a number of leading Japanese executives have explained (e.g., Ohmae, 1989), the Japanese success is based on the business principles that have been extolled in American texts for decades. The major difference is that the Japanese were more effective at applying these principles.

ACKNOWLEDGEMENT

This study was financed by a grant from the Economic and Social Research Council.

REFERENCES

Bartlett, C. A. and Ghosal, S. (1989) *Managing Across Borders*. London: Heinemann.
Beresford, M. (1982) 'Why the Japanese Excel at Personnel Management'. *International Management* (March): 203–206.
Buckley, P. J., Pass., C. L. and Prescott, K. (1988) 'Measures of International Competitiveness: a Critical Survey'. *Journal of Marketing Management*, **2**(Winter): 175–200.

Burke, M. (1984) 'Strategic Choice and Marketing Managers: an Examination of Business Level Marketing Objectives'. *Journal of Marketing Research* (November): 345–359.

Buzzell, R. D. and Gale, B. T. (1987) *The PIMS Principles*. Free Press: New York.

Clifford, D. K. and Cavanagh, R. E. (1985) *The Winning Performance*. New York: Bantam Books.

Dess, G. G. and Robinson, R. B. (1984) 'Measuring Organizational Performance in the Absence of Objective Measures'. *Strategic Management Journal*, **5**: 265–273.

Diaconis, P. and Efron, B. (1983) 'Computer Interview Methods in Statistics'. *Scientific America*, **5**: 96–108.

Dillon, W. R. (1979) 'The Performance of the Linear Discriminant Function in Nonoptimal Situations and the Estimation of Classification Error Rates: A Review of Recent Findings'. *Journal of Marketing Research*, (August): 370–381.

Doyle, P., Saunders, J. and Wong. V. (1986) 'A Comparative Investigation of Japanese Marketing Strategies in the British Market'. *Journal of International Business Studies*, **1**:(Spring): 27–46.

Fallows, J. (1989) 'Containing Japan'. *The Atlantic* (May): 17–25.

Hamel, G. & Prahalad, C. K. (1989) 'Strategic Intent'. *Harvard Business Review* (May–June): 16–28.

Hayes, R. H. & Abernathy, W. J. (1980) 'Managing Our Way to Economic Decline'. *Harvard Business Review* (July–August): 67–77.

Jacobson, R. & Aaker, D. A. (1987) 'The Strategic Role of Product Quality'. *Journal of Marketing* (Fall): 31–44.

Johnson, C. (1982) *MITI and the Japanese Miracles: The Growth of Industrial Policy, 1925–1975*, Stanford, Calif.: Stanford University Press.

Kotabe, M. (1990) 'Corporate Product Policy and Innovative Behaviour of European and Japanese Multinationals: An Empirical Investigation'. *Journal of Marketing* (April): 19–33.

Kotler, P. & Fahey, L. (1982) 'The World's Champion Marketers: The Japanese'. *Journal of Business Strategy* (Summer): 3–13.

Kotler, P. & Jatusripitak, S. (1985) *The New Competition*. Englewood Cliffs, N.J.: Prentice-Hall.

Lachenbruch, P. A. & Mickey, M. R. (1968) 'Estimation of Error Rates in Discriminant Analysis'. *Technometrics* (February): 1–11.

Lazer, W., Murata, S. & Kosaka, H. (1985) 'Japanese Marketing: Towards a Better Understanding'. *Journal of Marketing* (Spring): 69–81.

Morishima, M. (1982) *Why has Japan Succeeded?* Cambridge, Mass.: Cambridge University Press.

Mosteller, F. & Tukey, J. W. (1968) 'Data Analysis, Including Statistics'. In Lindzey, G. & Aronson, E. eds, *The Handbook of Social Psychology*, **2**, 80–203. Reading, Mass.: Addison-Wesley.

Ohmae, K. (1982) *The Mind of the Strategist*. New York: McGraw-Hill.

Ohmae, K. (1988) 'Getting Back to Strategy'. *Harvard Business Review* (November–December): 242–252.

Ohmae, K. (1989) 'Planting for a Global Harvest'. *Harvard Business Review* (July–August): 136–145.

Pascale, R. T. & Athos, A. G. (1982) *The Art of Japanese Management*. London: Allen Lane.

Perlmutter, H. V. (1969) 'The Tortuous Evolution of the Multinational Corporation'. *Columbia Journal of World Business* (January–February): 9–18.

Prahalad, C. K. & Doz, Y. L. (1987) *The Multinational Mission*. New York: Free Press.

Prestowitz, C. V. (1988) *Trading Places*. New York: Free Press.

Thurow, L. C. (1985) *The Management Challenge*. Cambridge, Mass.: MIT Press.

Tsurumi, Y. (1984) *Multinational Management: Business Strategy and Government Policy*. Cambridge, Mass.: Ballinger.

Tukey, J. W. (1958) 'Abstract, Bias and Confidence in Not-quite Large Samples'. *Annals of Mathematical Statistics* (June): 614.

Van Wolferen, K. (1989) *The Enigma of Japanese Power*. Cambridge, Mass.: MIT Press.

Venkatraman, N. & Vasudevan, R. (1986) 'Measurement of Business Performance in Strategic Research: A Comparison of Approaches'. *Academy of Management Review*, **4**: 801–814.

Wheelwright, S. C. & Sasser W. E. Jr. (1988) *Dynamic Manufacturing*. New York: Free Press.

Wright, R. W. & Gunter, A. P. (1987) *The Second Wave*. London: Waterlow Publishers.

26

Creating European Organizations that Work

Norman Blackwell, Jean-Pierre Bizet, Peter Child and David Hensley

Building the right kind of organization for Europe is a most difficult and demanding task. One common example: a pharmaceuticals manufacturer, intent on rationalizing its production facilities across Europe, needed a strong central function to plan and control its operations network, but also great local autonomy in designing and delivering customer service. In this, as in so many other cases, as we argued in a previous *Quarterly* article,[1] finding the proper balance between responsiveness to local needs and central control, let alone the proper coordinating mechanisms, can be a headache-inducing challenge (*see* Tables 1–3).

Table 1. Levels of international coordination

Level	Description
5. Central control	No national structures
4. Central direction	Central functional heads have line authority over national functions
3. Central coordination	Central staff functions in coordinating role
2. Coordinating mechanisms	Formal committees and systems
1. Informal cooperation	Functional meetings: exchange of information
0. National autonomy	No coordination between decentralized units, which may even compete in export markets

Level 5 = highest; Level 0 = lowest. Most commonly found levels are 1–4.

But this is only the beginning. Once the most suitable form of organization has been identified, the problems really start. There are, of course, all the usual stresses and complications associated with organizational restructuring, but they are magnified many times by the tensions and complexities of managing across national borders. In a pan-European context, strong emotional resistance often appears to the idea of surrendering 'sovereignty' to foreign managers. One British company, which had been wholly owned by a German parent for more than a decade, still fought to preserve its British identity by holding its own formal board meetings and publishing its own separate glossy annual report.

[1] Norman Blackwell, Jean-Pierre Bizet, Peter Child, and David Hensley, 'Shaping a pan-European organization', *The McKinsey Quarterly*, 1991 No. 2, pp. 94–111.

Reprinted with permission from *The McKinsey Quarterly*, Vol. 24, No. 2, pp. 31–43

Table 2. Levels of international coordination: business unit

	Research	Product development	Sourcing	Manufacturing	Logistics	Product management	Sales
5. Central control	Independent centralized research	New products created and decided at centre	Fully-centralized sourcing	Centrally managed, may have dispersed locations	Fully centrally-managed logistics	Centralized product management	Centrally-managed sales
4. Central direction	Central responding to local needs, financed by local companies	Common development but local launch decisions	Centrally negotiated procurement contracts, local companies have option of using or not	Significant specialization between some countries	Central management of all but fully national product logistics	International brands, central campaigns, where local managers want them	Major accounts handled on international central basis
3. Central coordination	Lead countries for specific areas of research	Some shared development in lead countries	Lead countries, e.g., negotiating with suppliers in that country for all	Some division of responsibilities for specific parts and/or products	Logistics services for others when crossing the country	International brands, local campaigns	Coordinated approach to international customers
2. Coordinating mechanisms	Conferences and sharing detailed technical know-how	Local development with some product swapping	Regular sourcing meetings, sharing details of prices, etc.	Regular meetings, plant visits and review of technical developments and best practice	Coordination of international logistics, e.g., shipping	Some international brands and sharing of market research	International standards for sales performance
1. Informal cooperation	Top-level discussions on direction	Local development with some development meetings	Sourcing managers meet annually, informal network	Infrequent meetings and discussions of new developments	Meetings and comparison of best practice	Some meetings, sharing of research	International sales meetings
0. National autonomy	Research spend and direction entirely local decision and management	Entirely local initiatives and products	All local sourcing	Manufacturing in and for each country	Entirely locally-managed logistics	National brands only	Local salesforce and channel management

Table 3. Levels of international coordination: corporate headquarters functions

	Finance	Planning	Government public relations	Personnel	IT/Systems
5. Central control	All finance raised, allocated, and monitored centrally	Central planning	PR and government relations managed on European/global basis	International recruitment and appointment of all executive grade staff	Standard systems, managed centrally
4. Central direction	Centralized treasury function	Common planning assumptions and objectives set by centre	Some PR and relations with European global institutions handled centrally, national government, locally	International staff managed centrally but with national 'parentage'	Standard systems, managed locally
3. Central coordination	Regular funds flow in and out of centre and across countries	Plans consolidated and challenged as a whole	Lead PR roles with lead companies	Explicit rotation of staff to give international experience	Some common systems managed by lead companies
2. Coordinating mechanisms	Common financial policies, central fund-raising	Common planning assumptions agreed between companies	Some common PR policies	Coordinated personnel policies to facilitate transfers and avoid trade union read-across	Systems designed for compatibility
1. Informal cooperation	Some lending across companies	Discussions of major strategic opportunities and threats	PR meetings and informal network	Personnel managers meet to discuss major issues	Occasional IT staff meetings
0. National autonomy	Full local finance department raising own loans and remitting annual dividends	Strategic business decisions at national level	PR and government relations managed locally	Independent and different personnel functions	Systems responsibility of each local company

Beyond this kind of emotional response, however, lurk a number of more systemic difficulties. Among them:

- *A lack of widespread commitment* to the logic of dismantling traditional national structures, driven in many cases by an inadequate understanding of the broader forces at work. One packaged goods manufacturer, for example, found it difficult to convince its subsidiaries to support the proposed new regional organization. The reason: lack of agreement that changes in channel power and in the general business environment made it necessary for them to join more closely together to reach critical mass in R&D and strategic planning.

  Even where such agreements exists, however, loyalties to traditional domestic markets can be hard to break. Numerous efforts to rationalize production facilities across Europe have come to grief because plant managers, having no effective way to set priorities among competing demands from multiple national sales organizations, fall back on their established relationships with those at home.

- *Power barriers* resulting from perceived threats to the personal roles of national managers and staff. Simply making the logic of pan-Europeanism clear is not enough. A concern that national autonomy will be lost and that key responsibilities will shift to new centres of power within the overall European structure can easily lead to low energy for change and even to outright resistance. This is often the case with national units that see another nationality as the likely focus of power in the new European structure. The fear of being marginalized—influence limited, prospects for promotion curtailed—puts an effective damper on managerial enthusiasm.

- *Inadequate skills (including language skills)* to operate successfully in the new organization. The operational talents of country-level managers do not always translate into an ability to think strategically on a region-wide basis. Or, at a more mundane level, to be comfortable enough in various languages to discuss issues in a pan-European forum or maintain informal contacts through telephone calls and memos.

- *Inadequate supporting infrastructure* to allow managers to operate effectively across borders. There is often, for example, no easy way to match different accounting procedures so that central managers can accurately compare the costs or the performance of different national units. Moreover, differences in personnel policies mean that it is often hard to get managers to move from one national location to another because of inconsistencies in remuneration packages and employment terms.

Virtually every organization that tries to become genuinely—and generally—European will face one or more of these generic difficulties. What follows are some practical, no-nonsense lessons, about what works and what does not.

BUILDING COMMITMENT

Our experience underscores the commonsense wisdom that, without widespread understanding of—and commitment to—the need for greater regional integration, no leadership group can mandate successful cooperation. Restructuring that relies entirely and exclusively on goodwill and communication among individual managers in separate national structures can easily go wrong.

As noted above, a Europe-wide rationalization of production can lead to dramatically poorer service for many national sales organizations. Much the same is true with other central support functions. When a manufacturing company moved to integrate local engineering activities into a stronger, pan-European function, major customers were promised a higher, uniform level of technical support. In reality, however, local managers were often reluctant to allow a central team to 'interfere' in this way with their traditional customers. The pattern is disturbingly familiar: good intentions to cooperate in manufacturing, engineering, product development, marketing, and pricing are legion, but managers often just go through the motions of attending coordinating meetings while exploiting every opportunity to carry on as before.

A starting point

The essential foundation for building a strong commitment to the development of a true pan-European business has to be a clear and powerful vision for the future, shared by the CEO and key members of the leadership team. To be effective, such a vision depends not only on a compelling business logic, supported by a clear, fact-based justification of the benefits of integration. It also requires a well-developed communication programme to ensure that a consistent message reaches all European managers.

But this, by itself, is not enough. Other mechanisms are needed to enable an organization to internalize and own its vision. *Ad hoc* pan-European taskforces, for example, can help build recognition of the need for change.

When Procter & Gamble set out to increase brand coordination across Europe, it introduced a 'Eurobrand' concept to bring national product managers together in a taskforce to thrash out common brand requirements. In another food company, which had local operations spread across Europe, the key lever was a manufacturing taskforce. This group was able to get national production managers to agree on a radical, comprehensive rationalization of facilities into a single European manufacturing structure. Similarly, under intense pressure from international buying groups, a freight company set up a pricing taskforce. Its charter: get front-line managers to recommend the appropriate level of coordination for optimizing European pricing policy.

By itself, of course, a new piece of organization is not the answer. Many companies have established high-level taskforces or strategy boards or working groups to review overall European development. It is only when these groups get down to nuts-and-bolts practicalities that commitment really starts to develop.

Indeed, experience shows that most successful efforts focus initially on only a few lead functions, where the urgency of need is most apparent and where good early results can start a ripple effect, creating champions for change within the rest of the organization. In addition to its main task, the pricing taskforce just mentioned also uncovered a need for better coordination among functions on such issues as sales management, product labelling and packaging, and distribution.

REALIGNING THE POWER STRUCTURE

A compelling vision is an essential starting point, but no more than that. Many attempts to build European organizations have come to grief not because a vision was lacking but because established national power structures opposed it. One recent example: a US-based firm was able to form a European organization only by agreeing to let its powerful UK operation opt out and remain a separate, autonomous unit.

Shortcuts do not work. Trying to create alignment simply by imposing a functional 'head of Europe' frequently proves ineffective because these leaders often do not have power over—or respect from—the various national operations. When a German company appointed a European operations manager, it left the product managers in Germany with control of production. As a result, sales and marketing companies elsewhere in Europe soon discovered that they were better off ignoring the new operations manager and dealing directly with the German product managers. The problem is even more acute with staff responsibilities. When a US company sent over a senior staff manager to collect information and make recommendations for Europe, no one paid serious attention. He had no real authority.

A question of balance

In some cases, of course, the opposition of local managers to the real or perceived erosion of their power is so intense and intractable that removing them becomes unavoidable. But because such changes in management always involve major risks, there is a premium on finding ways to accommodate them to a gradual shift in the power structure.

One approach is to give the individual managers most threatened by prospective changes part of the responsibility for planning them. Some consumer goods companies, for example, have expanded the roles of national marketing managers to include responsibility for developing certain brands across Europe. Procter & Gamble has done this with its category managers. In another firm, the three top country managers are now, respectively, also the European directors of sales and marketing, operations, and control and administration.

This even works with line/staff issues. When the creation of a Europe-wide corporate staff threatened the role of national managers, giving some of them more say over franchises in smaller neighbouring markets, it restored their sense of proper balance.

An acceptable new balance of power can also be facilitated by changes in systems—in particular, the development of centralized systems for production control, order scheduling, or customer order handlng. When Avis wanted to encourage offices in one country to sell the services of other country subsidiaries, the introduction of its 'Wizard' computerized reservation system—which automatically provided an integrated service across Europe—provided a powerful boost.

DEVELOPING PEOPLE

Truly European organizations cannot function if key positions are not held by people who have international capabilities. Past success, by itself, is no guarantee. It is not unusual to find that a company that has done well developing products for separate local markets turns out to be short of the marketing and development skills essential to the 'next generation' pan-European product line needed to compete with its more integrated

US and Japanese rivals. True, some of these skill-critical positions can be rapidly filled through external recruitment. Even so, the overall pace of change will be dictated by the widespread development of individual skills at many organizational levels, which is inevitably a slow process.

Because of this time delay, it is important to address skill-related issues as early as possible. This means careful attention to such appointment policies as:

- *Finding individuals in the current organization with high potential for broader international careers.* For example, a consumer company found that the multi-cultural taskforces used to develop a common European perspective on organizational needs did more than broaden the team members' international perspectives. They also provided a screen to help top management identify prospective Euromanagers.
- *Reassigning staff internationally to best utilize their potential*—and to create precedents for international careers. An English company, which had recently acquired a German engineering firm, initially decided to leave the operations separate but to have them swap a number of key executives. In the same vein, wanting to build a strong pan-European business, an insurance company that lacked staff with international experience established a formal system for circulating key individuals around its European subsidiaries.
- *Recruiting staff in countries where the organization is weak and training them in countries where it is strong.* When ICL declared in 1987 that 'the homebase we will have to protect will be Europe, not the United Kingdom', under 10% of its British graduate recruits spoke a second language. In response, ICL actively stepped up its recruiting in France, Spain, and Germany to fill European, not local country, roles.

Starting early also means training managers already in place. Electrolux, which has adopted English as its corporate language to help build a common European culture, launched a major language programme for the managers of Zanussi after their acquisition of the Italian company. Similarly, British Aerospace has for several years been sending key managers to a specially-designed programme at INSEAD to help increase company cohesion and nurture a stronger international focus.

DEVELOPING SUPPORTING PROCESSES

Building an effective European organization also requires identifying and correcting problems in its multitude of supporting systems and processes. More than once, for example, we have seen a company, facing severe overcapacity in Europe and needing a new mechanism for allocating production among national plants, discover that incompatible cost accounting systems meant it could not accurately compare plant economies across geographical borders. We have also seen incompatibilities among nationally-developed computer systems make it nightmarishly impossible to track a consignment of goods through different stock control systems.

When the European MD of one US company tried to push continent-wide integration, the country managers disputed the benefits, claiming that comparisons across countries were not appropriate because of accounting difficulties and varying quality requirements. Careful one-off analyses overcame these protests, but not the general questions they raise. In many companies, new processes have to be developed for such activities as:

- order processing (since each country is not producing all the products it needs for its own markets);
- quality testing (since there is need for standardized tests for adherence to the quality specifications required for each market); and
- setting transfer prices (since the current procedure of adding a percentage to costs is a disincentive to internal sourcing).

As with people skills, the usual timescale for effective changes in systems and procedures is long. That means important changes in accounting, management information, and personnel systems need to be tackled early on so they do not become major impediments to later progress. An example: one of the first steps taken by an insurance company to support the development of its European division was to develop a pan-European computer network, which linked all its European offices with electronic mail, allowed them to share insurance data, and gave them the capability to provide responsive pricing and coverage of pan-European risks.

CREATING AN INTEGRATED PROGRAMME

The smoothest examples we have seen of companies moving to a pan-European organization are those where purpose, power, people, and process issues have been resolved in a synchronized way. The leader of one such company, recognizing the need for personal, top-level commitment to change, charged a senior group of executives with the task of setting the direction for change. They then articulated a shared vision, including elements of strategy, skills, and values—all of which helped provide clarity of purpose.

Next, they appointed carefully-selected members of the top management team with great personal credibility to critical new positions with pan-European influence. These appointments—as well as the clear and explicit mission attached to them—helped modify the balance of power within the company. Several initiatives, most notably the development of new performance measurement systems, were given top priority and sufficient resources to guarantee success. So was an innovative effort to stimulate intensified communication about results throughout the organization.

In our experience, these are all essential elements of good practice. But lessons can also be learned from other, less fortunate, attempts. One large MNC received a mandate to Europeanize all its business units from its chairman, who really had little personal commitment to making it happen. Thus, as the new organization became a hot political topic, conflicts over power arose between newly-appointed business unit heads and the well-established country managers. Survival of the fittest was the only clear rule of the game. Needless to say, the process stalled, the old organizational formulas remained in place, and business performance continued to deteriorate—to everyone's frustration.

Time and sequence

The phasing of an effective change programme is dependent on the nature and magnitude of potential barriers. The first step is normally to build commitment to a common understanding of both the purpose and the benefits of the proposed change. The clearer the sense of purpose, the easier it is to resolve subsequent power conflicts or people reassignments—particularly when the process engages a wide range of people across the organization.

Intelligent phasing also addresses the relative urgency of structural changes as opposed to capability building, whether of people or systems. When an organization with an urgent need to change and most of the required capability is obstructed by power issues, the early resolution of these issues is clearly needed to unlock the change process. In most situations, however, ample time must be spent building skills, capabilities, and supporting systems *before* any changes in the power structure can really have effect. In such cases, there may be value in going through an iterative series of changes in capability building, power structure, further building of capabilities, and further adjustment of the power structure.

For example, one organization that has successfully moved to greater pan-European coordination focused first on creating a European management style with shared vision and values. The European MD visited all the subsidiaries to understand their needs and explain his vision. He also established his multinational team in a small European headquarters in a neutral city. This helped to reinforce the common purpose and to gain broader acceptance for the company's 'European' aspirations.

The challenge of building capability led to a two-phased approach, which allowed the power structure to be adjusted in stages, each lasting about one year. The initial change in the power structure gave the central European staff limited responsibility for establishing coordination mechanisms and information systems. At the same time, the major national managers took on additional responsibility for franchising operations in neighbouring countries, which gave them an opportunity to demonstrate their international capabilities.

In the second phase, those who were successful moved into Europe-wide functional roles with enhanced operational responsibilities. Simultaneously, the former national organizations were restricted to sales and distribution activities. In both phases, various aspects of the organization were adjusted at different times, with the formal structure always being the last thing to be changed.

CONCLUSION

Creating European organizations that work is so demanding a managerial task because the interests of the whole are not perceived identically by each of the affected constituencies or individuals. In strict economic terms, of course, if a business is genuinely a pan-European business, it should be in the interest of all national units to participate in a Europe-wide organization, rather than to seek to retain local independence. In the real world, however, cultural traditions and human nature get in the way. The challenge for management, therefore, is to make the concrete benefits of Europe clear to everyone—

and to provide opportunities and incentives that satisfy individual aspirations. Only when all these interests are aligned, can the promise of Europe be realized in workable organizational terms.

ACKNOWLEDGEMENT

This article is drawn from a major research project on 'European Organization', which was jointly carried out by the European Organization Performance practice and McKinsey's EuroCenter.

27

The New Country Managers

John A. Quelch

Generations of MNC executives have aspired to be appointed as country managers (CMs). With profit and loss responsibility, oversight of multiple functions, and the benefit of distance from headquarters, the CM has traditionally enjoyed considerable decision-making autonomy, as well as the opportunity for entrepreneurial initiative, while retaining the option of calling on headquarters for support if necessary. For many CMs, authority matches responsibility for the first time in their careers—so long as promised profits are delivered on time.

Today, however, the scope of the CM's job is being reduced by the forces of global and regional integration. As one put it, 'I used to run the business in my country from A to Z. Now I run it from F to Z.' According to another, 'I was once a big fish in a small pond. Now I'm a small fish in a big regional pond.' In their efforts to become more global, MNCs must be careful not to demotivate or even lose CMs like these, whose local market knowledge is a precious but often underestimated resource.

What follows is a brief report, based on the findings of the first phase of a two-phase research project to investigate the changing role and task mix of country general managers in multinational corporations. Phase 1 involved 50 in-depth personal interviews with country general managers in 12 Asian, European, and North American MNCs operating in the consumer goods, industrial goods, and service industries. Interviewees were selected on the basis of size of country market, type of industry, and location of corporate headquarters. In some cases, other senior executives in the co-operating organization—such as regional managers—were interviewed to obtain background information.

Phase 2 will involve the development of a survey instrument to be administered to a broad sample of 200 country managers. The purpose will be to test the hypotheses offered here and, in particular, to establish the relative importance of different variables in determining the role and task mix of country general managers.

GLOBAL TRENDS

During the 1990s, the CM's role, task mix, and required skills will be in a state of flux. Five key factors are responsible:

Reprinted from *The McKinsey Quarterly*, Vol. 25, No. 4, pp. 155–165

- *Global competition.* A decade of mergers and acquisitions has led many industries previously characterized by competition at the national level to a situation of dominance by a few global competitors. Small national companies continue to be absorbed as MNCs reach for global coverage, and a grab for market share by a competitor in one country market may require retaliation against that competitor in another. As a result, a CM may find that maximizing the subsidiary's local profitability has to be subordinated to the global chess game. To combat global competitors, MNCs have increasingly come to emphasize the product dimension of the product-geography matrix: power and profit responsibility in many cases have shifted—or are in the process of shifting—from CMs and regional managers to worldwide strategic business unit and product-line managers.
- *Global customers.* Many MNCs now have to provide excellent service simultaneously to national customers in individual country markets and to other MNCs seeking discounted prices on a worldwide or regional basis. That means CMs are often called on to give important MNC customers priority over local customers, despite the fact that sales to MNC customers are often credited to another subsidiary. Even grocery product manufacturers, for whom adapting to national tastes remains essential, now have to negotiate with retailers who invest in multiple country markets and belong to cross-border procurement alliances.
- *Global integration.* Both consumer goods and industrial MNCs have now discovered the efficiencies of organizing manufacturing on a global or regional, rather than country-specific, basis. Rarer and rarer is the CM who oversees a single plant making the full line of products sold in that country. Today, plants are much more likely to specialize in long runs of a narrow range of products, most of which are exported to subsidiaries in other countries. Similarly R&D activities are increasingly concentrated in 'centres of excellence' located in countries where essential research skills are well developed. Even financial accounting and control systems are becoming standardized; an invoice to a customer in one country may well be processed through a regional accounts-receivable office located elsewhere.
- *Regional trading blocs.* The emergence of regional trading blocs, notably the European Community and North American Free Trade Area, is enabling MNCs to integrate their manufacturing operations and to substitute a few high-efficiency plants for separate plants in each country. An unintended conseqence is that each national government is paying more attention, not less, to the contribution (in terms of investment and employment) that a foreign MNC makes to its national economy. So CM's have to negotiate with government officials more, not less, than they did in the past. In addition, lower tariffs, along with computer-assisted grey marketing, restrict CMs' freedom of action by preventing individual country subsidiaries from charging widely-varying prices to their customers.
- *Strategic alliances.* MNCs are entering a growing number of strategic alliances, often with their own competitors, to cross-market products and services in those countries where each partner has a stronger sales and distribution capability than the other. To extend their global reach, MNCs are also subcontracting manufacturing and operations to other MNCs and local companies. These developments inevitably place CMs in the position of having to deal with suppliers, licensees, and joint venture partners outside their own organizations.

Collectively, these trends threaten to diminish the CM's traditional decision-making autonomy and to transform the CM's role from that of a general manager into that of a local sales and distribution manager, who is merely implementing strategies created by worldwide business managers at headquarters. Hence the concern of CMs and their parent corporations alike. Too swift a change in emphasis from the geographic to the product dimension of the organizational matrix will likely jeopardize headquarters–subsidiary relations, blur lines of authority, discourage good ideas from being volunteered from the field, and demotivate the most successful, entrepreneurial, and knowledgeable CMs. If these CMs were lost, their replacements might obediently implement headquarters-defined policies but lack the entrepreneurial drive needed to penetrate local markets further.

In those MNCs so hard pressed by financial crisis or competitive threat that they cannot afford to offer their country managers the luxury of a gradual change in role, some CMs have already left (and will inevitably continue to leave), unable to accept the shift in perceived status, role, or task mix. By contrast, others, many of whom rose to their current positions through sales or marketing, may be secretly happy with a narrower range of responsibilities so long as they retain their CM titles.

CHANGING TASK MIX

All the CMs interviewed for this study recognized that their managerial roles and task mixes were changing. As one said, 'I am at the fulcrum of the tension between local adaptation and global standardization. My boss tells me to think global and act local. That's easier said than done.' Table 1 shows how those 50 CMs spent their time, on average, in the 12 months prior to being interviewed. It also shows how they expect their successors will spend their time in the same countries in the year 2000. The main conclusions are as follows:

Table 1. How CMs spend their time

	Actual[a]	Expected[b]
Marketing, sales, customer meetings	29.8%	30.0%
Planning, forecasting, budgeting	13.4	12.3
Financial management, accounting and control	13.4	10.0
Research and development	3.9	4.5
Manufacturing/operations	11.6	8.7
Human resource management/labour relations	13.0	14.9
Government/community relations	8.0	10.2
Industry/trade association relations	5.3	7.2
Other	1.7	2.3
	100%	100%

Source: Interviews with 50 CMs.
[a] In the year prior to interview.
[b] In the year 2000.

- In the future, CMs will spend less time on backroom functions like manufacturing and more time in the front office dealing with customers and with government, community, trade, and industry relations. This is especially true of CMs running large subsidiaries of consumer goods MNCs. Those heading smaller subsidiaries in the same companies, as well as those in industrial companies, have already seen their backroom responsibilities reduced.
- Human resource management and labour relations will take more of the CM's time. In the short term, this is because of manufacturing restructuring, plant shutdowns, and the need to integrate acquisitions. In the long term, the work of coaching and developing managers will expand as MNC structures become less hierarchical, job mobility increases, and CMs more frequently lose their most promising local managers to tours of duty at regional or world headquarters or to other subsidiaries.

The averages in Table 1 mask a wide variance among responses. All CMs define their task mix differently, for good reasons. (In fact, the long-standing use of the CM position in MNCs reflects the opportunity inherent in the job for flexibility, self-definition, and personal growth.) As Figure 1 indicates, interviews with the CMs in our sample suggest that there are four sets of variables determining how CMs spend their time:

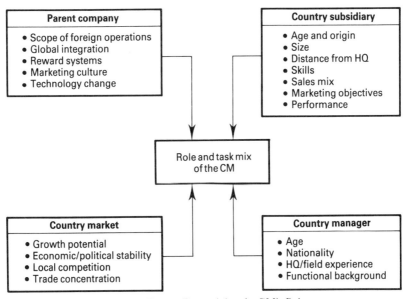

Figure 1. Factors Determining the CM's Role.

- *Parent company.* Not surprisingly, CMs tend to emphasize tasks stressed in the corporate culture: a production or marketing orientation at headquarters will be reflected in the field. Thus, the greater the global strategic integration within a company, the more time a CM can allocate to front-office versus backroom functions.
- *Country market.* A CM will spend more time on financial planning in an unstable economic environment with high inflation. In practice, CMs running Latin American

subsidiaries have often risen through finance rather than marketing. In high-growth country markets with strong local competitors, a CM is likely to pay special concern to customer relationships and adapting marketing programmes to local needs.

- *Country subsidiary.* CMs are more likely to retain broad functional responsibilities if they work in large subsidiaries that are long established, distant from headquarters, well endowed with quality local managers, and performing well. CMs usually focus on those functions that are central to the strategic role of their subsidiaries. Sometimes, however, they have to spend more time on functions that are staffed by weaker managers, regardless of whether these are critical to the business. CMs in subsidiaries where the sales mix emphasizes local over global brands are likely to spend more time on marketing.
- *Country manager.* The functional background of CMs often biases them toward spending more time on what they enjoy or know best. Nationality is also important: a 'local' CM—particularly one with grey hair and some years on the job—will, for example, probably spend more time on government, industry, and trade association relations.

A TYPOLOGY OF COUNTRY MANAGERS

Given the many variables that determine how they spend their time, it is hardly surprising that all CMs are not 'created equal'. Nor should they be. An MNC faces different challenges in different countries, which require CMs with different sets of skills, different orientations, and different priorities. But these variations are not endless; there is a clear pattern to them. All the CMs interviewed for this study can be grouped into the four categories listed in Table 2 and profiled in more detail in Table 3. Each type of CM supplies the skills a company needs at a separate stage of its development from an international to a fully global organization.

Table 2. Company evolution and CM's roles

	Company evolution	Role played by CM
Stage 1	International	Trader
Stage 2	Multinational	Potentate
Stage 3	Transnational	Cabinet member
Stage 4	Global	Ambassador

International: the trader

In these companies, domestically-conceived products are exported through independent local distributors in foreign markets, and an international division usually handles all overseas sales. In the larger, more promising markets, there may be wholly-owned country subsidiaries, some of which may have acquired local distributors. The CMs

Table 3. Features of CM roles

	Trader	Potentate	Cabinet member	Ambassador
Management skills	Young entrepreneur: good implementer with general management potential	Entrepreneurial general manager	Team-oriented strategist/ coordinator	Elder statesman/ proven administrator
Personality	Maverick	Rebel	Adapter	Good soldier
Functional background	Sales	Marketing	Marketing/ operations	Legal/financial
Marketing focus	Sales, service, distribution	Entire marketing mix	Entire mix	Service, distribution
Nationality	Local national *or* missionary from HQ country	Usually local national or from same region	Usually from same region	Usually local national
Performance measurement	Country sales/ market share	Country profitability	Country/region/ line-of-business sales, profits, ROA *plus* qualitative measures	Country ROA, costs *plus* business-development and account service objectives
Next assignment	Manager of larger country *or* HQ assignment	Country manager in same region *or* term position	Region or mini-region manager *or* HQ assignment	Term position
Where found	Asia	Americas	Western Europe	Western Europe

needed for these young subsidiaries are entrepreneurial traders with strong implementation skills who focus primarily on sales and distribution.

Multinational: the potentate

To achieve greater local market penetration, companies usually devolve more functional responsibilities to their CMs. They, in turn, capitalize on economies of scope and scale by developing and manufacturing an ever-broader line of locally-adapted products. International sales are no longer an afterthought. As these companies become genuine MNCs, CMs, evaluated on the profits they deliver, become potentates.

Transnational: the cabinet member

To achieve the benefits of transnational integration, MNCs then reduce the CM's decision-making authority on R&D, sourcing, and manufacturing, consolidating these functions in centres of excellence. Financial controls and management information systems are also standardized. Decision-making power shifts from the CM to the region manager, and regional taskforces, sometimes managed by CMs, become central to marketing decision making. No new products can be introduced unilaterally. The CM has to become a team player, a cabinet member.

Global: the ambassador

In genuinely global firms, worldwide line-of-business units dominate the geography-product matrix. Line-of-business directors in each country usually oversee marketing and sales, reporting directly to regional or global functional bosses, rather than through a CM. Now an ambassador and administrator, the CM is invariably a local national with good government contacts—and often an elder statesman in the company. In some cases, the senior line-of-business director in a country (by length of time in the country) doubles as the CM.

Today, many MNCs are trying to decide whether they are international, multi-national, transnational, or global. But most are at varying stages of development in different regions of the world, or even in different countries. Such circumstances call for a variety of organizational approaches and, therefore, for a portfolio of CMs with different sets of skills. For example, a typical Western European consumer goods company might appoint cabinet members as CMs in an increasingly integrated Europe, but hire traders in Asia, where markets are growing faster and socioeconomic differences among countries are much greater. Meanwhile, the potentates who run the company's subsidiaries in Latin America, where tariff barriers still limit cross-border commerce, might remain in place.

As many MNCs transform themselves into transnational or global companies, the CM as potentate is fading in favour of the CM as cabinet member. Traders are still required to open up and develop new country markets. In addition, the integration of manufacturing, as well as of backroom functions, means that more and more CMs are likely to remain traders, focusing on marketing, sales, and distribution, and not evolve into potentates as they did in the past.

Some CMs both desire and are able to make the transition from one role to another. It should, for example, be possible for trader CMs to evolve into cabinet member CMs as they develop their general management skills. Even so, some CMs are excellent as traders building beachheads in new country subsidiaries, but poor as cabinet members in large, mature subsidiaries where the CM's role is less hands-on and requires more teamwork. The concept of the CM portfolio enables top management to match CMs with the assignments that require and/or will develop their particular management skills.

NEW SKILLS

We asked the CMs in our sample to describe the skills or attitudes they thought they and their successors would need in the future. Reflecting the trend toward transnational integration, they consistently mentioned five themes:

- *External focus.* As regional or worldwide functional managers assume greater responsibility for overseeing manufacturing, R&D, financial controls, and information systems, the CM will have more time to focus on the front office. That means listening to local customers, staying alert to new marketing initiatives by local and global competitors, and cultivating relations with the trade, industry associations, and government. This increased external focus calls for MNCs to appoint more local nationals as CMs.

- *Government relations.* CMs must be able to articulate to public policy makers the financial contributions that their enterprises make to the economies of the host countries. In particular, CMs who sell products and services to departments or agencies of host governments will need better advance training in government and community relations than they currently receive.
- *Corporate perspective.* CMs will increasingly be called on to compromise performance in their own country markets in the interests of their MNCs' overall regional or global success. They must not merely identify the differences that make their local markets special, but also be able to see the similarities across national markets, encourage the export and import of good ideas among subsidiaries, and gather intelligence useful to others in the organization.
- *Entrepreneurial team player.* Global integration calls for managers with a seemingly contradictory combination of talents: an ability to work through persuasion rather than fiat and an ability to use taskforces to speed up rather than slow down decision making. Ideal CMs now have multifunctional backgrounds, which add to their persuasive credibility. They derive satisfaction not only from enhancing the financial performance and capabilities of their subsidiaries, but also from influencing results beyond the boundaries of their own markets.
- *Ability to wear many hats.* To save on management overhead, minimize the bureaucratic obstacles to quick decision making, and promote a team perspective, CMs will increasingly be asked to wear many hats. A CM for Spain or Sweden might also oversee a sub-region like Iberia or Scandinavia, be the strategic director for a product line throughout southern or northern Europe, and oversee a function such as manufacturing on a pan-regional basis.

As one CM told us, 'Globalization is turning the traditional CM into a dinosaur'. It is true that the country manager as potentate is a dying breed and that many MNCs now have their small subsidiaries run not by CMs, but by sales managers reporting to CMs in larger neighbouring countries. CMs, however, are still needed in transnational and global companies, particularly to stay close to local customers, competitors, and policy makers in host governments. As another CM said, 'The country manager will not disappear. Governments still need one man to go after to put in jail.'

ACKNOWLEDGEMENTS

I gratefully acknowledge the support of Alexander Biel, Stephen King, and the WPP Center for Research in facilitating this study.

Index

A & P 255, 259
Acquisitions *see* mergers and acquisitions
Adaptation 196–8
Advertising strategies 69, 206–18, 348–50
  attitudinal differences 212–13
  behavioural 213
  demographic 213, 216
  differences between firms 211–13
  localization of 207, 211, 212–15, 216
  segmentation 140–2
  site of responsibility for 209–12
  transferability 207–8, 211, 212, 216
  see also standardization of advertising
Africa 184, 196, 252, 267
  African, Caribbean and Pacific (ACP)
    colonies 17
  regional operations 333–4
  sales force 222, 224
  trading blocs 2, 15, 16–17, 21
AFTA (ASEAN Free Trade Area) 16, 18
Age of product and distribution channels 234,
  238
Agriculture 51
Ahold 256, 259
Aims *see* objectives
Aircraft firms 122, 156
Aldi 255
Alliances
  retailing 255–7
  see also strategic alliances
Allied and Federated Department Stores 252,
  259
Altman (B.) 259
Ambassador typology of country manager 391,
  392
Ambiguities and regional operations 334–5
Ambitions and organization 367–8
American Express 111, 141, 142
American Marketing Association 4, 12–13
American Medical Association 181
AMS (Associated Marketing Services) 256
Amway 220
Analysis of Quantitative Data *see* AQD

ANCOM (Andean Common Market) 16
Andean Common Market 16
Anheuser-Busch 192
ANOVA (Analysis of Variance) 317
  see also MANOVA
APEC (Asia Pacific Economic Cooperation)
  16, 18
Apple computers 186, 187–8
Appliances firms 140, 158
AQD (Analysis of Quantitative Data) 294–6,
  306
Argentina 62, 114, 184
Argyll 256
Arista Records 192
ASEAN (Association of Southeast Asian
  Nations) 16, 18, 22, 249
Ashley Industrial Trust 254
Ashley (Laura) 254
Asia 10, 175, 244, 267, 337
  counterfeiting 181, 184, 187–8, 190
  decentralized R & D 147–8
  evolution of strategy 65
  retailing 249, 252, 253, 258
  sales force 220, 222, 223–4, 225, 227, 228
  trading blocs 16, 17–18, 22, 23, 27
  see also in particular NICs; Japan
Asia Pacific Economic Cooperation 16, 18
Asko 253, 259
Associated Marketing Services 256
Association of Southeast Asian Nations 16, 18,
  22, 249
AT & T 115–16, 140, 359
Attitudinal differences and advertising
  strategies 211–13
Australia 154
  evolution of strategy 62
  retailing 249, 252, 253, 258, 259
  trading blocs 16, 18
Autolatina 114
Automobile firms
  competition, Japanese and American in
    Britain 359, 364
  counterfeiting 186

country image and product category 167, 168, 173–4, 177, 178
creating European organizations 380, 381
decentralized R & D 147, 149, 150
evolution of strategy 59, 69
Japanese product development 158–9, 160
MNC entry mode choice 76–7
pan-European strategy 350
performance comparison 313
segmentation 140, 142
standardization 282
strategic alliances in Triad 114, 117, 122
tyres 76, 138
see also advertising strategies; transport
Autonomy problem and regional operations 327, 330–1
Avis 380
Avon 225

Babcock and Willcox 229
Banks 69
Barriers to head office influence over sales force 222–5, 226–7
degree of market development 222–3
geographic and physical 222
human relations 223–4
local market 224–5
political and legal environments, differing 223
BAT Industries 252, 259, 351
Beatrice 199
Beecham see SmithKline
Beer and country image and product category 168, 173–4, 177, 178
Behaviour/behavioural
advertising strategies 213
competitive, distribution channels and 236, 241
see also segmentation
Belgium 223
regional operations 323, 332
retailing 252, 253, 254, 255, 256, 259
see also EC
Bell Helicopter 186
Bell and Howell 14
Beloit 113
Benetton 61, 141, 142, 250, 254
Beverage firms 6, 61, 66, 122
pan-European strategy 345, 347, 348, 350
product and promotion transfers 195, 203, 204
segmentation 140, 141–2
standardization 263, 282–3
see also advertising strategies
Bicycles and country image and product category 168, 173–4, 177

Bieri Pumpenbau 149
Bilateral arrangements see strategic alliances
Biotechnology 122
Biral International 149
BiTicino 70
Black and Decker 68
Bloomingdales 252, 259
Body Shop 69, 254
Boeing 156, 160
Bonwitt Teller 259
Brazil 62, 114, 174, 196
counterfeiting 181, 190
Bristol-Myers 63, 199
Britain 46, 154, 156, 191, 195, 267, 293
country image and product category 18, 171, 173–4
creating European organizations 376, 381, 382
evolution of strategy 62, 65, 68–9
pan-European strategy 347, 350
performance comparison in Europe 313, 315–16
regional operations 323, 327, 334
retailing 250, 251, 252, 254–5, 256, 259
sales force 225, 229
segmentation 137, 140, 141
strategic alliances in Triad 116
see also competition, Japanese and American in Britain; EC
Brooks Brothers 255, 259
Brunei 18
Bulgaria 253
Burger King 259
Burroughs 113
Business practices, different 223, 224

Cabinet member typology of country manager 391–2
Cabotage 351
CACM see Central American Common Market
Campbell Soup 269, 348
Campeau 25, 252
Canada 154, 190, 290, 357
evolution of strategy 62
export assistance policy 46, 49–50
performance comparison in Europe 316, 317
retailing 249, 252, 253, 259
trading blocs 16, 17, 18
Canada Dry 65, 203
Canon 113, 228, 359, 363
Caribbean
Basin Initiative 14, 16, 17
Common Market (CARICOM) 16, 17
see also Central America and Caribbean
Carrefour 254

Cartier 186
Castorama 256
CBI (Caribbean Basin Initiative) 14, 16, 17
Celso Garcia 256
Central America and Caribbean
  counterfeiting 181, 186, 190
  country image and product category 168–78
  evolution of strategy 65–6
  product and promotion transfers 196
  retailing 252, 253
  sales force 225, 227
  trading blocs 14, 15, 16–17, 20
Central American Common Market 15, 16,
  17
Central Europe *see* Eastern and Central
  Europe
CER (closer economic relations) 249
Channels *see* distribution channels
Chemicals industry 122
Chesebrough-Pond's 199
Children *see* 'teenage' culture
China 10, 65, 224
Chrysalis Records 192
Chrysler 117, 186
CIIB (Counterfeiting Intelligence and
  Investigation Bureau) 191
Citibank 69
Class 223, 224
Clothing and textiles 137, 181, 252
  see also fashion firms
Cluster analysis 136–8, 139, 294–7
CMs *see* country managers
Coca-Cola 6
  evolution of strategy 61, 66
  pan-European strategy 350
  product and promotion transfers 195, 203,
  204
  segmentation 141, 142
  standardization 263, 282–3
Coles Myer 258
Colgate-Palmolive 61, 263, 282–3, 348
Colombia 196
COMECON 31
Commitment, building 379–80
Communications 349–50
  firms and strategic alliances in Triad 111,
  117, 122
  telemarketing 140, 141–2
  see also information
Competition
  advantage changes in Europe 29–33
  corporate conditions 31–2
  demand 30–1
  government 32–3
  local factors 29–30
  related and supporting industries 31

behaviour and distribution channels 236,
  241
country managers 387
innovation orientation 298–304
intensity and MNC entry mode choice 78–
  9, 83, 84, 87, 90
Japanese and American in Britain 356–75
  discriminators of success 370–2
  organization 365–70
  research methods and results 358–65
national export assistance 44–5
price 346–7
regional operations 328–9
standardization 277–8
US-Japan relations 40–1
Complementary activities and strategic
  alliances 114, 115, 121–2
Computers *see* electronics and computers
Concentration, global, and MNC entry mode
  choice 76, 82, 84, 87, 90
Conservation of energy 137
Consortia 114, 120
Consumer *see* global marketing; segmentation
Continental and national businesses in
  Europe, performance comparison of
  312–21
  definitions 312–13
  drawbacks to multicountry scope 313–14
  research methodology and results 314–19
  Single European market 312, 314
Contractual agreements and strategic alliances
  113, 120
Control and decentralized R & D 152–3
COO (country-of-origin) effects *see* country
  image
Cooperation and collaboration
  decentralized R & D 149, 153–4
  profit and export assistance 51
  in US-Japan relations 40–1
  see also strategic alliances
'Co-Prosperity Sphere' 17
Corporations
  competitive advantage changes in Europe
  31–2
  and decentralized R & D 150–1, 152–4
  trading blocs 22–3
  see also firms
Cortefiel 256
Costs *see* finance
Counterfeiting 181–94
  attractiveness of US products 184–5
  economic magnitude of 186–7
  international action by US government
  190–1
  legislation 182, 189–90, 193
  non-economic impact of 187–9

private sector action 191
proactive action by MNCs 191–3
strategies 182–4
Counterfeiting Intelligence and Investigation
    Bureau 191
Country
    approach to segmentation 136–7, 139
    image and product category 162–80
        definition 163–4
        familiarity with product and country
            175–6
        operationalization of 164–6
        product-country matches 166–8, 171–2
        research methods and results 168–76
        willingness to buy prediction 172–5
    managers, new 386–93
        changing task mix 388–90
        global trends 386–8
        new skills 392–3
        typology of 390–2
    risk and MNC entry mode choice 78, 82, 84,
        87, 90
Courreges 186
CPC International 149
Creating European organizations that work
    376–85
    commitment, building 379–80
    integrated programme creation 383–4
    people development 381–2
    power structure alignment 380–1
    supporting processes, developing 382–3
Credit cards 111
    counterfeiting 189
    segmentation 141, 142
Cross-distribution and strategic alliances 115,
    122
Cross-licensing and strategic alliances 115,
    122
Crystal firms and country image and product
    category 168, 173–4, 177
Cultural segmentation 139
Customer service see service
'Customization index' 136
Customizing, lack of 314
Cyprus 15
Czechoslovakia 2, 27, 28, 32, 253

Daimaru 253
Dalton (B.) 259
Dansk Supermarket 257
Decentralized R & D see under multinationals
Decisions
    in evolution of strategy 56–7, 65–6, 68–70
    pricing 348
Delhaize 'Le Lion' 255, 259
Demand

competitive advantage changes in Europe
    30–1
uncertainty and MNC entry mode choice
    78, 82, 84, 87, 90
Demographic advertising strategies 213, 216
Denmark 15, 62, 347
    see also EC; successful export
Department stores 252, 256, 259
Design 165, 168–70, 176–8, 266
Detergent and toiletries firms 199, 222
    creating European organizations 380, 381
    evolution of strategy 61, 63, 65, 69
    pan-European strategy 348, 350
    standardization 263, 268n, 269, 282–3
Development-led retailing alliances 255–6
Differentiation, product 235, 239
Digital Equipment 230
Dior (Christian) 186
Direct counterfeiting strategies 182–3
Direct investment 10–11, 112, 216
Direct marketing 353–4
Direct payment and strategic alliances 117,
    124
Discriminant analysis 85, 87–9, 91–2
Discriminators of success 370–2
Dispersed R & D see multinationals
    decentralized
Distribution
    channels, integration of 232–48
        managerial implications 244–6
        model 233–6
        research methods 236–44
        research results 241–4
    pan-European strategy 351–4
Dixons 259
Docks de France 254
Douglas 156
Drinks see beverage firms
Drugs see pharmaceutical firms

EAEG (East Asian Economic Group) 16, 18
EAI (Enterprise for Americas Initiative) 16,
    17, 20
East Asian Economic Group 16, 18
East Germany 27, 28, 39
Eastern and Central Europe 3, 8–9, 229, 253
    country image and product category 166–7,
        168, 171, 173
    EC and 25–9, 34–5
    see also competition advantage
    global marketing study in 4, 12–13
    impact on integration in Europe 33–4
    trading blocs 15, 17
    US-Japan relations 36, 39–41
    see also Czechoslovakia; East Germany;
        Hungary; Poland; Romania

Eastman Kodak 195, 229, 284, 359
EC (European Community) 15–16, 97, 175,
    269, 312, 325, 366
  constructive role 19–20
  counterfeiting 181, 190
  destructive role 21
  retailing 249, 252, 253, 256
  see also Europe; integration in Europe; pan-
    European strategy
ECMT (European Conference of Ministers of
    Transport) 27
EDI (Electronic Data Interchange) 352
EDP see electronic data processing
Education see training and education
EEA (European Economic Area) 15–16
EFTA (European Free Trade Association) 15–
    16, 249
Electrolux 68, 220, 222, 224, 225–6
Electronic data processing and sales force
    management 219–21, 222–3, 229–,30
  headquarters influence 225, 226–7
  see also electronics and computers
Electronic Funds Transfer Act (US) 189
Electronics and computers
  competition, Japanese and American in
    Britain 359, 363–4
  counterfeiting 186, 187–8
  creating European organizations 378, 381
  evolution of strategy 58, 61, 70
  Japanese product development 156, 157–9
  segmentation 140, 141–2
  standardization 263, 265, 267, 270n
  strategic alliances in Triad 113, 114, 115–
    16, 117, 122
  see also distribution channels; electronic data
    processing; technology
Elite lifestyle and segmentation 137, 138, 140–
    1, 142, 342
Employment see human capital
Endaka 39
Energy 11, 122, 137
Enterprise for Americas Initiative 16, 17, 20
Entry
  barriers and integration in Europe 27–9
    government-imposed 26, 27–8
    natural 26, 28–9
  country and distribution channels 236, 241
  market and evolution of strategy 59–64
  modes and evolution of strategy 62–3
  see also under multinationals
Environment 5
  multinationals entry mode choice 78–9
  segmentation 137, 139
  see also innovation orientation
Equity
  control and decentralized R & D 149–50

participation and strategic alliances 113,
    120, 122
ERA (European Retail Alliance) 256
Ericsson (L.M.) 22
Espirito Santo 255
Ethnicity 223
Euro-products and euro-brands 345
'Eurogroupe' 256
Euromarché 255
Euromercato 256
Europe 3, 76, 195, 244
  advertising strategies 207
  counterfeiting 181, 190, 191
  country image and product category 166–76
  decentralized R & D 148, 149, 154
  evolution of strategy 61–2, 65, 68–70
  export assistance policy 46
  foreign direct investment 10–11
  global marketing study in 4, 6, 12–13
  human capital 8
  Japanese product development 156, 160
  retailing 249, 251–6, 258–9
  sales force 219, 222, 223, 224, 228–9
  segmentation 140–2
  standardization 267, 268n, 283
  trading blocs 15–17, 20, 21, 22, 23
    see also EC
  US–Japan relations 36, 39–41
  see also Eastern and Central Europe; EC;
    innovation orientation; integration in
    Europe; regional operations; strategic
    alliances in Triad
European Conference of Ministers of
    Transport 27
European Economic Area 15–16, 20
European Free Trade Association 15–16, 249
European Retail Alliance 256
Evolution of strategy in international markets
    53–72
  formulation 54–7
  phases of development 57–70
    initial market entry 59–64
    local market expansion (phase 2) 64–7
    global rationalization (phase 3) 67–70
Exports 341
  see also national export assistance; successful
    export
External focus skill 392–3

Fanuc Ltd. 114
Far East see Asia
Fashion firms 77
  counterfeiting 186, 192
  segmentation 140, 141, 142
  see also clothing and textiles
FDI (foreign direct investment) 10–11, 112, 216

Federal Trademark Law (US, 1946) 182
Ferragamo 140
Finance 10–11, 359, 378
  financial institutions 69
  innovation orientation 298–304
  standardization 270–1, 275
  see also credit cards
Finland 62
Firms
  characteristics and successful export
    marketing 100, 102, 105–6, 110
  major categories *see* automobile; beverage;
    detergent; electronics and computers;
    fashion; food; general consumer;
    pharmaceutical
  major names *see* Benetton; Coca Cola;
    Colgate-Palmolive; Electrolux; Ford;
    Honda; IBM; Johnson and Johnson;
    McDonald's; PepsiCo; Procter and
    Gamble; Sony
  —specific advantage 101
  —specific know-how and MNC entry mode
    choice 79, 83, 84, 87, 90
  see also corporations; global marketing;
    multinationals
Flexibility and organization 369–70
Focus 362–3, 392–3
FOIA (Freedom of Information Act) 185, 190
Food industry 122, 140, 380
  pan-European strategy 348, 349
  performance comparison in Europe 313, 314
  product and promotion transfers 195, 199
  retailing 250, 252, 253, 254, 255, 256–7,
    259, 353
  standardization 263, 269
  see also advertising strategies; beverage firms
Ford 69, 149, 159, 186, 359
Forecasting and prediction
  and regional operations 325–6
  trading blocs 15–18
  willingness to buy 172–5
Foreign direct investment 10–11, 112, 216
France 191, 195, 223, 283, 368, 382
  country image and product category 166–8,
    171, 173–4
  evolution of strategy 62, 68–9, 70
  pan-European strategy 345, 347, 349, 350
  regional operations 323, 334
  retailing 252, 254, 255–6
  segmentation 140, 141
  see also EC
Free Trade and Investment Area, OECD 19
Freedom of Information Act (US, 1966) 185,
  190
Fringe benefits 223
FSA (firm-specific advantage) 101

Fujitsu 22, 359
Furr's 259
Future *see* forecasting and prediction

Galeries Lafayette 140
Gap, The 252
Gateway 255
GATT (General Agreement on Tariffs and
    Trade) 11, 36, 190
  trading blocs 14, 18–20, 21, 22, 23
  Uruguay Round 12, 19, 21, 23
GCG (general consumer goods) 219–21, 225,
  226–7
GEC 359, 364
General Agreement on Tariffs and Trade *see*
  GATT
General consumer goods 219–21, 225, 226–7
General Electric 114
General Foods 199
General Mills 199
General Motors 114, 159, 359
Generalized System of Preferences 189
Geographic barrier to head office influence 222
Germany 34, 114, 154, 156, 268n, 313
  competition, Japanese and American in
    Britain 358, 360, 364, 368
  country image and product category 167–8,
    171, 173–4, 176, 177, 178
  creating European organizations 376, 381,
    382
  evolution of strategy 62
  export assistance policy 46
  pan-European strategy 349, 350, 353
  regional operations 323, 327
  retailing 252, 253, 255, 256, 259
  reunification 27, 28
  sales force 223, 224
  segmentation 140, 142
  strategic alliances in Triad 116
  US-Japan relations 39
  see also EC
Giant leap versus incrementalism 157–8
GIB Group 254, 256
Gillette 141, 142, 196
Glaxo 116
Global Account Management System 69
Global marketing
  global village debate 12–13
  globalization 5–6
  see also implementation; issues, strategic;
    marketing mix; performance
GMFanuc Robotics 113–14
Goals *see* objectives
Golden Formosa Company 188
Goldman 192
Goodyear Tire and Rubber 76, 138

Gould 359, 364
Government 378, 393
    competitive advantage changes in Europe
        32–3
    counterfeiting 182, 189–91, 193
    entry barriers in Europe 26, 27–8
    sales 326–7
Grand Metropolitan 259
Greece 15, 34, 347, 350
    see also EC
Grocery see retailing under food
GSP (Generalized System of Preferences) 189
Gucci 186

Hanson 351
Harris 113
Harrods 140
HDTV (high-definition television) 156, 157–8
Headquarters 222, 366–7, 369
Heinz 65
Hewlett-Packard 113, 229, 359, 364
'High touch' product 137
High-definition television 156, 157–8
Hilton Hotels 195
Hitachi 159, 359
Hoffman-Laroche 149
Honda 77, 147, 150, 160, 364
Hong Kong 9, 141
    counterfeiting 181, 187, 188
    retailing 253, 255
    sales force 220, 222
    trading blocs 16, 18
Hooker Corporation 252, 259
Hooplah methods 220
Hotels 195
Human capital 8, 378
    barrier to head office influence 223–4
    development 381–2
    see also sales force
Hungary 8, 17, 253
    country image and product category 166–8,
        171, 173–4, 175, 176, 177, 178
    EC and 27, 30, 31, 323
Hyster 359, 364

IBM 22–3, 359
    decentralized R & D 148
    standardization 263, 267, 270n
    strategic alliances 115, 117
ICA 257
ICI 351
ICL 382
IKEA 253
Implementation
    support and US-Japan relations 42
    see also competition, Japanese and

American; country managers; creating
        European organizations; pan-European
        strategy; performance; regional operations
Imports see trade
Incrementalism versus giant leap 157–8
India 181, 190, 224
Indirect counterfeiting strategies 183–4
Indonesia 9, 18, 147, 181, 190
Information 7
    assistance and US-Japan relations 41–2
    gathering and Japanese product
        development 159–61
    sources and decentralized R & D 147–8
    technology (IT) see electronics and
        computers
    transfer and regional operations 329–30
    see also communications
Infrastructure 351–2
    inadequate 379
Innovation
    country image and product category 165,
        168–70, 176–8
    orientation and performance 288–311
        conceptual framework 291–3
        non-innovators 296, 301–2
        original pioneers 296, 302–4
        previous research 289–91
        process innovators 296, 299–301
        product innovators 296, 297–9
        research methodology and results 293–
            304
    see also counterfeiting; product development;
        technology
Integration
    country managers 387
    in Europe 25–35
        emergence of 25–6
        continued change 26–7
        competitive changes see competition
            advantage
        Eastern Europe's impact on EC 33–4
        see also entry barriers
    programme creation 383–4
    and regional operations 336–7
    see also distribution channels
Intermoda 253
Internal competition prevented 329
International Anticounterfeiting Coalition 191
International Chamber of Commerce 181, 191
International Intellectual Property Alliance
    191
International market development see
    evolution of strategy
International marketing see global marketing
International trade see trade
International Trade Administration 190

International Trade Commission (USA) 187, 272
Investment, foreign direct 10–11, 112, 216
Ireland, Republic of 327
  country image and product category 168–76
  see also EC
Israel 207, 224
Issues, strategic *see* evolution of strategy; integration in Europe; multinationals entry mode; national export assistance; strategic alliances in Triad; successful export marketing; trading blocs; United States-Japan relations
Italy 115, 154, 223
  evolution of strategy 61, 68
  pan-European strategy 345, 350
  retailing 252, 253, 256
  segmentation 140, 142
  see also EC
ITC (International Trade Commission) 187, 272
ITT 359

Jaguar 159, 359, 364
Japan 3, 244, 382
  counterfeiting 190
  country image and product category 163–4, 167–8, 171, 173–4, 176, 178
  decentralized R & D 149, 150, 154
  evolution of strategy 58, 61, 62, 63, 65–6
  export assistance policy 46, 49–50
  global marketing study in 4, 12–13
  human capital 8
  as leader of Pacific Rim 9
  product development 156–61
    incrementalism versus giant leap 157–8
    market research 159–61
    marketplace as R & D laboratory 158–9
  retailing 252, 253, 258, 259
  sales force 220, 223–4, 229
  segmentation 141, 142
  standardization 267, 268n
  trading blocs 15–19 *passim*, 22, 23
  see also competition Japanese and American; strategic alliances in Triad; United States—Japan relations
JIT (Just-in-Time) 352
Johnson and Johnson 199, 222, 230, 283
Joint
  activities and strategic alliances 114–15, 120
  product development 120
  ventures 331–2
    and retailing 253, 255–6
    and strategic alliances 111, 113–14, 120
Jusco 253, 259
Just-in-Time 352

Keihakutansho 159
Keiretsu 38
Kelloggs 61, 199, 349
Kentucky Fried Chicken 65, 252
Kenya 196
Kings Supermarkets 255, 259
Knorr Foods 149
Know-how and MNC entry mode choice 79, 83, 84, 87, 90
Kodak *see* Eastman Kodak
Korea *see* South Korea
Kraft 199

La Coste 186
Labour *see* human capital
Language problems 382
Lanham Act *see* Federal Trademark Law
Large-scale integration 157
Lauren (Ralph) 141, 142
Legislation/legal affairs
  counterfeiting 182, 189–90, 193
  distribution channels 235, 239–40
  sales force 223
Leica 364
Levers in internationalization of strategy 56, 60–3, 64–5, 67–8
Levi Strauss 61, 186, 192
Libby's 199
Licensing
  decentralized R & D 148–9
  and strategic alliances 115, 122
Lifestyle *see* elite; 'teenage' culture
Light Signatures 192
Limited, The 252
Linkages, profit and export assistance 48–9
Local factors
  competitive advantage changes in Europe 29–30
  local market barrier to head office influence 224–5
  local market expansion phase 64–7
Localization of advertising strategies 207, 211, 212–15, 216
Location unfamiliarity and MNC entry mode choice 78, 82, 84, 87, 90
Logit model and strategic alliances 118–19, 123–4
Lome Convention 16, 17, 20
LSI (large-scale integration) 157
Luxembourg 252
  see also EC
Luxury products *see* elite

Maastricht Treaty 15
McDonald's 195, 250, 252, 254, 263
McDonnell-Douglas 160

Mail order 253
Majik Markets 259
Malaysia 9, 220
  counterfeiting 181, 190
  trading blocs 18, 22
Malta 15
MANOVA (Multivariate Analysis of
    Variance) 83, 85, 86, 306
Manufacturing arrangement and strategic
    alliances 115, 120, 122
Market
  barrier to head office influence over sales
    force 224–5
  characteristics and successful export
    marketing 100, 102, 106–7, 110
  coverage and strategic alliances 115, 122–3
  R & D laboratory as marketplace 158–9
  research 159–61, 279
  screening and transfer process 196
  see also marketing
Marketing, global see implementation;
    marketing mix; performance; issues,
    strategic
Marketing mix see advertising; counterfeiting;
    distribution; product; promotion;
    retailing; sales force; segmentation
Marks and Spencer 254, 255, 256, 259
Marlboro 350
Marshall Field 252, 259
MasterCard International 186
Matsushita 113, 267
MCC (Microelectronics and Computer
    Technology Corporation) 114
MDA (multiple discriminant analysis) 85, 87–
    9, 91–2
Media 349–50
Mercedes Benz 140, 142, 282, 313
Merck (E.) 116
MERCOSUR (Southern Common Market)
    16, 17
Mergers and acquisitions
  decentralized R & D 149
  pan-European strategy 353
  regional operations 331
  segmentation 136
Mexico
  counterfeiting 181, 186, 190
  country image and product category 168–78
  evolution of strategy 65
  product and promotion transfers 196
  trading blocs 16, 17, 20
Michelin 76
Microelectronics and Computer Technology
    Corporation 114
Microsoft 115
Microwave Exceltek 188

Middle East 207, 224, 228, 252, 267, 333
Migros 257
Mitsubishi Heavy Industries 113
MNCs see multinationals
MNL (multinomial logit analysis) 85, 86, 89–
    92
Modes of entry see under entry; multinationals
Morocco 17
Morris (Philip) 225
Motivation
  global strategic, and MNC entry mode
    choice 77–8, 82, 84, 87, 90
  see also under strategic alliances in Triad
Motor vehicles see automobile firms
Mountleigh 254
MTV Network 141
Multifunction retailing alliances 256–7
Multinationals
  decentralized R & D 145–55
    advantages 146–7
    corporate commitment 150–1
    information sources 147–8
    organizing for 151
    strategic alliances and 148–50
    strategies 152–4
  entry mode choice 73–95
    data 79–80
    measurement 83
    tests and results 83–91
    variables 75–9
  see also counterfeiting; creating European
    organizations; product transfers;
    promotion materials transfers;
    standardization and performance
Multinomial logit analysis 85, 86, 89–92
Multiple discriminant analysis 85, 87–9, 91–2
Multiple regression analysis 100, 102–3
Multivariate Analysis of Variance
  see also MANOVA
Music 141–2, 157, 186, 192
Myth of euro-consumer 341–2

Nabisco 65–6, 199
NAFTA see North American Free Trade
    Agreement
National businesses compared with
    continental see continental and national
National export assistance policy for new and
    growing businesses 44–52
  competitiveness 44–5
  coping with obstacles 45–6
  policy implications and issues 50–2
  promotion 46–50
National Panasonic 359, 363
National product standards 344–5
NCR 229

NEDs (newly-emerging democracies) *see*
  Eastern and Central Europe
Needs 199, 330
Netherlands
  pan-European strategy 349, 350
  retailing 252, 253, 256, 259
  see also EC
New businesses *see* national export assistance
New Zealand 220
  retailing 249, 252, 258
  trading blocs 16, 18
Newly-emerging democracies *see* Eastern and
  Central Europe
Newly industrialized countries *see* NICs
NICs (newly industrialized countries in Asia)
  9, 141, 357
  counterfeiting 181, 184, 187, 188, 189, 190
  country image and product category 167,
    168, 171, 174
  decentralized R & D 147, 148
  retailing 253, 255
  sales force 220, 222, 223
  strategic alliances in Triad 117
  trading blocs 16, 18, 22
  see also Hong Kong; Indonesia; Malaysia;
    Singapore; South Korea; Taiwan;
    Thailand
Nike 192
Nintendo 36
Nippon Telegraph and Telephone 117
Nissan 149, 150, 359, 364
Non-innovators 296, 301–2
North America 6
  trading blocs 14–17, 18, 20, 27, 36
  see also Canada; United States
North American Free Trade Agreement 15,
  16, 17, 20, 36
North American Watch Company 187
Norway 62, 97

OAU *see* Organization of African Unity
Objectives
  organization 367–8
  strategic 360–2
OECD (Organization for Economic
  Cooperation and Development) 18–19,
  319, 362
Omega 186
Omnibus Tariff and Trade Act (US, 1984)
  189
Opportunities
  innovation orientation 298–304
  pan-European strategy 340–1
Options and product strategies 345
Ore-Ida 63
Organization

competition, Japanese and American in
  Britain 365–70
  see also creating European organizations
Organization of African Unity 17
Organization for Economic Cooperation and
  Development *see* OECD
Original pioneers and innovation 296, 302–4
Otis 230

P & G *see* Procter and Gamble
Pacific Rim 3, 9
  see also Asia; Australia; Japan; New
    Zealand; NICs
Packaging 346
Palmolive 195
Pan-European strategy 340–55
  euro-consumer 341–3
  Euro-market 340–1
  marketing mix 343, 344–54
    distribution 351–4
    pricing 346–8
    product 344–6
    promotion 348–51
Panfida 259
Paper industry 68, 113
Paridoc 256
Parker Hannifan 187
Patents 345
  strength and distribution channels 235,
    240–1
Pearle Health Service 259
Penney (J.C.) 252
People *see* human capital
Peoples Jewellers 259
PepsiCo
  pan-European strategy 348, 350
  product and promotion transfers 195, 203,
    204
  segmentation 141, 142
Performance *see* continental and national
  businesses; implementation; innovation
  orientation; standardization and
  performance
Perrier 140, 142, 345
Personnel 8, 378
Peru 223
Pfizer 184, 185, 228
Pharmaceutical firms 122, 148, 156, 376
  counterfeiting 181, 184, 185
  sales force management 219–21, 222, 226,
    228
Philippines 18, 181, 190
Philips 113, 158
Photographic firms 192, 195, 229, 284, 363–4
Physical barrier to head office influence over
  sales force 222

Piggybacking and strategic alliances 115, 120, 122
Pillsbury 199
PIMS (Profit Impact of Market Strategy) 276, 293–4, 314–15, 319
Pingo Doce 255
Pioneers and innovation 296, 302–4
Planning 152, 378
  and standardization 268–9, 278–9
  see also strategies
PLC (product life cycle) 264, 267–8, 278, 281
Pohang Iron & Steel 117
Poland 8, 27, 28, 29
Polaroid 61, 192
Policies see national export assistance; strategies
Political environments, different 223
Pooling of resources and regional operations 324–6
Portugal 15, 34, 255
  see also EC
POSCO (Pohang Iron & Steel) 117
Positioning and pan-European strategy 350–1
Potentate typology of country manager 391
Power structure 379, 380–1
Prediction see forecasting
Preferences for imported goods 137
  see also segmentation
Premium products see elite
Prestige and country image and product category 165, 168–70, 176–8
Pricing
  pan-European strategy 346–8
  regional operations 327–8
  standardization 279
Private sector action against counterfeiting 191
Process innovators 296, 299–301
Procter and Gamble 199, 222, 348
  creating European organizations 380, 381
  evolution of strategy 61, 63, 65, 69
  standardization 268n, 269
Product
  age and distribution channels 234, 238
  category see country image
  development 377
    costs 326
    joint 120
    strategic alliances 115, 116, 120–1, 124, 125 •
  see also innovation; Japan, product development; multinationals, decentralized R & D
  ⌐⌐⌐ ⁿⁿ and distribution channels

  327
  ⌐, 297–9

life cycle 264, 267–8, 278, 281
management 377
mixes 196, 198, 201–2
pan-European strategy 344–6
regional operations 326, 327–8
segmentation 136–7, 139, 140–1
standardization 264, 267–8, 278, 279, 281
standards, national 344–5
thrust, strategic 325, 330
transfers in consumer goods multinationals 195–202
  research and findings 198–202
  transfer and adaptation process 196–8
variety 326
see also counterfeiting
Production cost and strategic alliances 117, 120, 124, 125
Profit
  Profit Impact of Market Strategy see PIMS
  risk and export assistance 47–8
  successful exports 101, 109
'Proletarianization' of consumer markets 136
Promodes 254
Promotion
  export 46–50
  materials transfers 202–4
  pan-European strategy 348–51
  standardization 279
Protectionism and strategic alliances 116–17, 124, 125
Pro-trade segmentation 137, 139
Psychographic segmentation 137, 139
Public relations 351
  see also promotion
Purchasing-led retailing alliances 256
Puritan fashions 186, 192

Q-Statistic 91–2
Quaker Oats 199
Quelle 253

R & D (research and development) 6–7, 77, 270, 328, 345, 377
  decentralized see under multinationals
  evolution of strategy 63, 64–5, 68, 70
  laboratory, marketplace as 158–9
  strategic alliances 114–15, 120–1, 122, 127
  see also counterfeiting; innovation orientation; product development; technology
Rank-Xerox and Xerox 61, 228, 359
Rationalization phase in strategy evolution 67–70
RCB Electroapparate 149
Recognition Equipment 192
Regional operations and strategies 322–39
  method 323–4

pooling of resources 324–6
problems and approaches 330–3
responsibility, lack of 333–5
segmentation 137, 139
standardization 325, 329–30
strategic product thrust 325, 330
synergy, gaining 325, 326–9
versus global control 335–7
see also trading blocs
Regression analysis 100, 102–3, 241–4
Renault 59, 350
Research and development *see* R & D
Resource pooling and regional operations 324–6
Responsibility
regional operations and lack of 333–5
for transferability of advertising strategies 209–12
Retailing 249–59
alliances 255–7
counterfeiting 186
distribution 353
forces driving 250–1
foreign ownership of US outlets 259
scale of 254–5
segmentation 140, 141
strategies 254–5
Risk, profit and export assistance 47–8
Road transport 351–2
ROI and ROA (return on investment and return on assets) 275, 315–16, 317
Rolex 186, 187
Rollei 364
Romania 27
Russia *see* Soviet Union, former

Saab 159
Saatchi and Saatchi 69, 348
SAD (Single Administrative Document) 351
Sainsbury (J.) 256, 259
Saint Laurent (Yves) 77
Sakowitz 259
Saks Fifth Avenue 252, 259
Sales 377
force management 219–31
industrial products 219–21, 226, 228–9
pharmaceutical 219–21, 222, 226, 228
see also barriers to head office influence; electronic data processing; general consumer goods
promotion *see* promotion
Samsung 117
Samu 254
Sara Lee 269
Scandinavia 15, 62, 97, 104, 347
retailing 253, 257

sales force 222, 223
see also successful export marketing
Scotland 267
Scott 63, 68
Searle (G.D.) 181
Sears Roebuck 252
'Segment simultaneity' 136
Segmentation, consumer 135–44, 342
consumption trends 139–40
defined 138–9
'teenage' culture 141–3
see also elite
Seibu 253
Selling *see* sales force
Semiconductor Chip Protection Act (US, 1984) 189–90
Service
requirements and distribution channels 234–5, 239
standardization 279
Service industries 8
see also advertising strategies
7-Eleven 250, 252
SGS-Ates Componenti Elettronici S.p.A. 115, 116
Shared values and organization 367–8
Shaws Supermarkets 259
Shoe firms 168, 173–4, 177, 192
Shulton International 199
Silo 259
Singapore 9, 253
counterfeiting 181, 190
trading blocs 18, 22
Single European market 312, 314
see also pan-European strategy
Skills
-based retailing alliances 256
country managers, new 392–3
inadequate 379
see also training
SmithKline Beecham 22, 148
Social class 223, 224
Socialising with clients 224
Société de Développement International 256
Sock Shop 255
SODEI (Société de Développement International) 256
Sony
competition in Britain 359, 363
product development 157, 159, 161
segmentation 141, 142
Sourcing 279, 377
South Africa 184, 196, 224, 252
Customs Union 15
South America 114, 174, 252, 334
counterfeiting 181, 184, 188, 190

South America—*cont.*
  evolution of strategy 62, 66
  product and promotion transfers 196
  sales force 223, 224, 225, 227, 228
  trading blocs 16, 20
South Korea 9, 141
  counterfeiting 181, 190
  country image and product category 167,
    168, 171, 174
  strategic alliances in Triad 117
  trading blocs 16, 18
Southern Common Market 16, 17
Soviet Union, former 8, 10, 17, 253
  EC and 26, 28, 29, 30, 34
  trading blocs 16
  US—Japan relations 36, 39–41
Spain 15, 34, 68, 283, 350, 382
  country image and product category 168,
    171, 173
  retailing 252, 253, 254, 255, 256
  see also EC
Spalding 186
Speciality products
  see also segmentation
Squibb (E.R.) 228
Standardization
  of advertising strategies 212–16
    arguments for 206–7
    attitudes to 210–11
    popularity 207
  pan-European strategy 342–3
  and performance 263–87
    financial influence of 270–1
    hypotheses 265–71
    limitation 281–2
    research method and results 271–81
    strategies 269–70, 279–80
    technology 265–8, 277–8
    theory 264
  regional operations 325, 329–30
  segmentation 138
Stanley 69
Steel companies 117, 122, 158
Stepwise multiple regression analysis 100,
  102–3
Strategic alliances 387
  multinationals and decentralized R & D
    148–50
  in Triad 111–31
    forms 113–14, 119–20
    market coverage 115, 122–3
    methods of research 117–18
    ⌐15, 120
    ⌐17, 123–6
    ⌐18–19
    ⌐earch 119–26

  see also alliances; strategies
Strategic Planning Institute *see* AQD; PIMS
Strategies (strategic)
  alliances *see* strategic alliances
  counterfeiting 182–4
  Impediments Initiative 37
  issues *see* issues
  multinationals and decentralized R & D
    152–4
  retailing 254–5
  standardization 269–70, 279–80
  strategically equivalent segment (SES) 137,
    139
  see also advertising strategies; innovation
    orientation; pan-European strategy;
    regional operations
'Structural Convergence Talks' 37
Subsidiary product
  line origins 199–201
  mixes 196, 198, 201–2
Success, discriminators of 370–2
Successful export marketing management 96–
  110
  conceptual variance level findings 102–7,
    109–10
  implications and research 107–8
  research methodology 97–100
  variable group level findings 100–1
Sunbeam 223
Sunrise Computer Services 188
Supporting processes, developing 382–3
Survival guide 3–13
  finance 10–11
  international interconnections 11–13
  major areas 8–10
  major issues 4–5
  technology 6–8
Swatch International 141, 142
Sweden 62, 97
  retailing 253, 257
  sales force 222, 223–4, 227
  Swedish Match 223, 224, 227
Switzerland 68, 149, 190, 257
  sales force 223, 228
Synergies
  gained in regional operations 325, 326–9
  MNC entry mode choice 76–7, 82, 84, 87,
    90

Tacit nature of know-how and MNC entry
  mode choice 79, 83, 84, 87, 90
Taiwan 9, 148, 174, 357
  counterfeiting 181, 184, 187, 188, 190
  trading blocs 16, 18
Takeovers *see* mergers and acquisitions
Talbots 253, 259

Tariffs *see* GATT; protectionism
Taxation 223, 347
Team player skill 393
Technology 6–8, 122
  segmentation 136
  standardization 265–8, 277–8
  strategic alliances 116, 124, 125
  see also counterfeiting; electronic data;
    electronics and computers; innovation;
    product development; R & D
'Teenage' culture 141–3, 342
Telecommunications *see* communications
Telemarketing 140, 141–2
Television
  promotion 349–50, 353
  and video firms 58, 167
  Japanese product development 156, 157–8,
    159, 160
Tengelmann 255, 259
Textiles *see* clothing and textiles; fashion
Thailand 9, 18, 181, 223, 253
Theft of intellectual property *see* counterfeiting
Third World 3, 9–10, 196, 200
  see also Africa; Asia; Central America; South
    America
Thomson 70
Tie Rack 254
Time/timing
  changes and regional operations 334
  of entry and evolution of strategy 62
  and sequence 384
TOC 259
Toiletries firms *see* detergent and toiletries
  firms
Toshiba 114, 359, 364
Toyota 147, 150, 160, 359, 364
Toys R Us 250, 252
Trade Act (US, 1984) 189
Trade, international 11
  see also national export assistance; successful
    export; trading blocs
Trademark Counterfeiting Act (US, 1984)
  182, 189
Trading blocs 6, 14–24, 249, 387
  constructive role of 19–20
  corporate role and response 22–3
  defined 14–15
  destructive role of 20–2
  GATT 18–19
  now and in future 15–18
  versus stumbling blocks 19
  see also in particular EC
Training and education 8, 38, 229
Transactions costs 112–13
  transaction-specific assets and distribution
    channels 234–5, 238

transaction-specific variables and
    multinationals entry mode choice 79
Transfers
  promotion materials 202–4
  transferability of advertising strategies 207–
    8, 211, 212, 216
  see also product transfers
Transport 351–2, 380
  see also automobile firms; distribution
    channels
Triad *see* Europe; Japan; strategic alliances in
    Triad; United States
Truth in Lending Act (USA) 189
Tube Investments 364
Turkey 15
Tyres 76, 138

Unilever 283, 313
United States 3, 107, 348
  creating European organizations 382–3
  decentralized R & D 147, 150, 154
  evolution of strategy 58, 59, 61–2, 65, 70
  export assistance policy 44–5, 46, 49–50,
    51
  foreign direct investment 11
  global marketing study in 4, 12–13
  human capital 8
  —Japan relations 36–43
    alternatives 38–9
    bilateral focus 37–8
    collaboration and competition 40–1
    implementation support 42
    information assistance 41–2
    Soviet Union and Eastern Europe 36, 39–
      41
  Japanese product development 156, 157,
    159, 160, 161
  Pacific Rim 9
  performance comparison in Europe 312,
    314–18
  product and promotion transfers 195–6,
    198–9, 201–2, 204
  retailing 249, 251–2, 255, 258–9
  segmentation 140, 141–2
  standardization 267, 270–2
  trading blocs 14–17, 18, 19, 20, 21, 22
  see also advertising strategies; competition,
    Japanese and American; counterfeiting;
    distribution; innovation orientation;
    multinationals entry mode; regional
    operations; sales force; strategic alliances
    in Triad
'Universal' appeal 136–7
Uruguay Round of GATT 12, 19, 21, 23
US Steel 117
USSR *see* Soviet Union, former

Variance inflation factor 100
Vendex International 256, 259
Venezuela 225
Very-large-scale integration 157
Videos *see* television and video
VIF (variance inflation factor) 100
VLSI (very-large-scale integration) 157
Volkswagen AG. 114
Vuitton (Louis) 189, 191

Warner Communications 111
Warner Lambert 199
Watches
    counterfeiting 186, 187
    country image and product category 168,
        173–4, 177

segmentation 141, 142
Wella 62
Western Europe *see* Europe
Willingness to buy prediction 172–5
Women customers 138
Wood trade 49–50
Workmanship and country image and product
    category 165–6, 168–70, 176–8

Xerox *see* Rank-Xerox

Yen revaluation (*endaka*) 39

Zales 259
Zenith 58